BOCCACCIO IN ENGLAND
from Chaucer to Tennyson

BOCCACCIO IN ENGLAND

from Chaucer to Tennyson

HERBERT G. WRIGHT

Professor Emeritus of the University of Wales,
now of the University of Basle

UNIVERSITY OF LONDON

THE ATHLONE PRESS

1957

Published by
THE ATHLONE PRESS
UNIVERSITY OF LONDON
at 2 Gower Street, London, W.C.1
Distributed by Constable & Co. Ltd
12 Orange Street, London, W.C.2

Canada
University of Toronto Press
Toronto, 5
U.S.A.
Essential Books Inc.
Fair Lawn, New Jersey

Printed in Great Britain by
WESTERN PRINTING SERVICES LTD
BRISTOL

*To my Dear Wife
but for whom this book
would never have been
completed*

PREFACE

THIS study was completed in 1954 but owing to various causes its appearance has been postponed. It was begun some twenty-five years ago in the over-sanguine expectation that it would be completed in two. The richness and complexity of the material and the need for detailed preliminary investigations account for the long delay. My object throughout was to see Boccaccio, so far as was possible, in relation to the personality of the writers to whom he appealed and simultaneously to observe the changing taste of successive ages as it was revealed by their choice among Boccaccio's writings. It also appeared desirable to bear in mind that Boccaccio was a European literary phenomenon, and I attempted, within the limits of my capacity, to consider his fortunes on the Continent.

I have profited by the labours of older writers such as Attilio Hortis, A. C. Lee, Mary A. Scott, Arturo Farinelli, Henri Hauvette and Emil Koeppel, not to speak of a large number of scholars of the present day. I have not thought it necessary to record every single book or article on literary indebtedness to Boccaccio, sometimes real, sometimes imaginary, but have restricted myself to what seemed to me the most relevant to my purpose.

Chaucer offered a special problem because so much important work had been done on him in recent years, particularly in America. While taking all this into account, I have examined Chaucer's poems afresh in the hope that here and there I may have added a point or two. In this connexion I have studied the Italian original closely in order to ascertain the precise nature of the English adaptation or transformation. Inevitably this has led to a certain fullness of treatment which is perhaps justified in a monograph of this kind. For the same reason various minor figures in the history of English literature are dealt with at some length because in the survey of Boccaccio's influence their importance is greater than their intrinsic merit.

The organization of the somewhat recalcitrant material was difficult. In the end I thought it best to investigate the fortune of Boccaccio's writings one by one. I was especially reluctant to apply this method to Chaucer, for it is obvious that in this way justice is hardly done to his work as a living whole. Truly, one may say 'We murder to dissect'. Moreover, the stimulus of Boccaccio's example as an artist is not sufficiently emphasized. However, while these disadvantages are recognized, the plan adopted does, I trust, conduce to lucidity in the treatment of the whole subject.

I wish to thank the Early English Text Society for permission to use material in two volumes which I prepared for their series of publications, and Professor H. B. Charlton and the Manchester University Press for leave to draw on the text and introduction to *Ghismonda*. I am under a similar obligation to Professor Charles J. Sisson, editor of the *Modern Language Review*, and to the Cambridge University Press, Professor James Sutherland and Professor John Butt, former editors of the *Review of English Studies*, and the Oxford University Press, and to the editor of *The Times Literary Supplement*.

I owe much to the Lord Chamberlain for his courtesy in giving me access to his archives at St. James's Palace; to the Duke of Devonshire for placing at my disposal rare books at Chatsworth and the manuscript containing a translation of part of *De claris mulieribus* which Lord Morley presented to Henry VIII; to the Earl of Crawford for lending me a unique incunabulum, and to the authorities of the Henry E. Huntington Library for the privilege of quoting from the manuscript of William Percy's play, *A Forrest Tragaedye in Vacunium*.

I should also like to express my indebtedness to the Trustees of the Leverhulme Research Awards for the Fellowship that I held in 1935–6 and to the Council of the University College of North Wales for a grant from the Mary Rathbone Fund in the autumn term of 1951. These two periods were invaluable for my research.

This has also been facilitated by a succession of Superintendents of the Reading Room at the British Museum—Mr. A. I. Ellis, Dr. F. G. Rendall, Mr. R. A. Wilson, Mr. N. F. Sharp—and of Bodley's Librarians from Dr. H. H. E. Craster to Mr. J. N. L. Myres. Again Sir C. T. Hagberg Wright, Mr. C. J. Purnell and Mr. S. Nowell-Smith of the London Library, Dr. H. Guppy and Dr. E. Robertson of the John Rylands Library, Dr. M. Tyson of the Manchester University Library, Mr. H. L. Pink of the University Library, Cambridge, Mr. Francis Thompson, librarian to the Duke of Devonshire at Chatsworth, Mr. H. M. Adams of Trinity College, Cambridge, and Mr. J. A. Wilkes of University College, London, have all helped me to make progress in my long task. In the Department of Manuscripts at the British Museum I have been aided by Mr. E. G. Millar, Dr. Robin Flower, Sir H. Idris Bell, Mr. A. J. Collins and their staff. To Mr. C. J. Hindle of the Bodleian Library and Mr. O. G. W. Stallybrass of the London Library I am grateful for their patience in replying to numerous inquiries.

I have had the good fortune to possess friends and colleagues who, despite their own duties, have found time to advise me about various details or to check references. I would mention Professor W. F. Schirmer, Professor A. Chiari, Professor V. Branca, Professor Giuliano Pellegrini, Professor A. Obertello, Professor René Fréchet, Professor E. Purdie, Professor G. Bullough, Professor G. Tillotson, Professor R. Weiss, Professor R. J. McClean, Professor D. J. Gordon, Professor A. W. Reed, Professor H. J. Thomson, Professor Sir John Neale, Dr. N. Denholm-Young, and my old pupil, Mr. R. E. Morton. I should also like to say how much I owe to the practical encouragement of Professor S. B. Liljegren.

Dr. R. J. Carnie rendered special service in the final stages of preparation of the manuscript, and I am glad to express my indebtedness to him. I must also thank Professor H. Lüdeke for kindly reading my proofs.

Finally, I wish to record with gratitude the financial support that my book has received from the University of Wales Press Board and the Freiwillige Akademische Gesellschaft der Stadt Basel.

Bangor, North Wales   H. G. W.
4 September 1956

CONTENTS

Cue-titles and Abbreviations   *page* xiii

Introduction   1

Chapter I. The Latin Works   3
    1. *De casibus virorum illustrium*   5
    2. *De claris mulieribus*   28
    3. *De genealogia deorum*   36

Chapter II. The Minor Italian Works   44
    1. The *Corbaccio*, *Ameto*, and *Amorosa Visione*   44
    2. The *Teseida*   44
    3. The *Filostrato*   59
    4. The *Filocolo*   101
    5. *Fiammetta*   105
    6. The *Ninfale Fiesolano*   108

Chapter III. The *Decameron* in the Fourteenth, Fifteenth, and Sixteenth Centuries   113
    1. Tales in Verse derived through French and Latin   116
    2. Tales in Verse derived from the Italian Text   142
    3. Tales in Prose based on the French or Italian   156
    4. Collections of Tales and Romances in Prose, derived from an unknown Source   161
    5. The Ballad   170
    6. The Drama   173

Chapter IV. The *Decameron* in the Seventeenth Century   189
    1. Collections of Tales in Prose and Verse   191
    2. Individual Tales in Prose and Verse   193
    3. The Drama   196
        (a) *Tragedy*   196
        (b) *Comedy*   207

Chapter V. The *Decameron* in the Eighteenth Century   *page* 261
    1. Tales in Verse   265
    2. Tales in Prose   308
    3. The Drama   318

Chapter VI. The *Decameron* in the Nineteenth Century   331
    1. Comments on Boccaccio, more particularly on the *Decameron* 336
    2. Tales in Verse   366
    3. The Drama   455

Conclusion   479

Index   483

CUE-TITLES AND ABBREVIATIONS

Add. MS.	Additional Manuscript, British Museum.
Archiv	*Archiv für das Studium der neueren Sprachen und Literaturen*, 1846–.
Bergen	Lydgate's *Fall of Princes*, ed. H. Bergen, Carnegie Institution of Washington, No. 262, 1923; E.E.T.S., 1924–7.
B.M.	British Museum.
Campbell	*Mirror for Magistrates*, ed. L. B. Campbell, Cambridge, 1938 (Add. parts ed. 1946).
C.B.E.L.	*Cambridge Bibliography of English Literature*, Cambridge, 1940. 4 vols.
Chambers	E. K. Chambers, *The Elizabethan Stage*, Oxford, 1923. 4 vols.
Cummings	H. M. Cummings, *The Indebtedness of Chaucer's Works to the Italian Works of Boccaccio*, Cincinnati, 1916.
Dibdin	T. F. Dibdin. *The Bibliographical Decameron; or Ten Days Pleasant Discourse upon Illuminated Manuscripts and Subjects connected with early Engraving, Typography and Bibliography*, London, 1817. 3 vols.
D.N.B.	*Dictionary of National Biography*, ed. Leslie Stephen and Sidney Lee, London, 1885–1901.
E.E.T.S.	Early English Text Society, 1864–.
F.Q.	E. Spenser, *The Faerie Queene*, Baltimore, 1932–8. Variorum Edition ed. E. Greenlaw, C. G. Osgood, F. M. Padelford.
Farinelli	A. Farinelli, *Italia e Spagna*, Turin, 1929. 2 vols.
Gesamtkatalog	*Gesamtkatalog der Wiegendrucke*, Leipzig, 1925–.
Griggs	*Unpublished Letters of Samuel Taylor Coleridge*, ed. E. L. Griggs. London, 1932. 2 vols.
Grosart	*The Life and Complete Works in Prose and Verse of Robert Greene*, ed. A. B. Grosart, London and Aylesbury, 1881–6. 15 vols.
Hauvette 1903	H. Hauvette, *De Laurentio de Primofato*, Paris, 1903.
Hauvette [1909]	H. Hauvette, *Les plus anciennes Traductions Françaises*, Paris [1909].
H.L.Q.	*Huntington Library Quarterly*, 1926–.
J.E.G.P.	*Journal of English and Germanic Philology*, 1903–.

Lowndes   W. T. Lowndes, *The Bibliographer's Manual*, London, 1834. 4 vols. New ed. H. G. Bohn. London, 1857–64. 6 vols.

Marillier   H. C. Marillier, *Dante Gabriel Rossetti*, London, 1901.

Marshall   R. Marshall, *Italy in English Literature, 1755–1815*, New York, 1934.

M.L.N.   *Modern Language Notes*, 1886–.

M.L.R.   *Modern Language Review*, 1906–.

M.P.   *Modern Philology*, 1903–.

O.E.D.   *New English Dictionary on Historical Principles*, ed. Murray *et al.* Oxford, 1888–1933.

O.V.   *Opere volgari di Giovanni Boccaccio*, ed. I. Moutier, Florence, 1827–34. 17 vols.

P.M.L.A.   *Publications of the Modern Language Association of America*, 1884–.

Page   F. Page, *Patmore, A Study in Poetry*, Oxford, 1953.

Pinkerton   *A General Collection of the best and most interesting Voyages and Travels*, ed. J. Pinkerton, London, 1808–14. 17 vols.

R.E.S.   *Review of English Studies*, 1925–.

Root   Chaucer, *Book of Troilus and Criseyde*, ed. R. K. Root, Princeton, 1926.

Schelling   F. E. Schelling, *Elizabethan Drama, 1558–1642*, London, 1908. 2 vols.

Scott   M. A. Scott, *Elizabethan Translations from the Italian*, Boston and New York, 1916.

Shedd   *The Complete Works of Samuel Taylor Coleridge*, New York, 1884, ed. W. G. T. Shedd. 7 vols.

Skeat   *The Complete Works of Geoffrey Chaucer*, ed. W. W. Skeat, Oxford, 1894–7. 7 vols.

S.O.B.D.   [Thomas Moore], *Spirit of Boccaccio's 'Decameron'*, London, 1812.

S.P.   *Studies in Philology*, 1906–.

S.T.C.   *A Short-Title Catalogue of books printed in England, Scotland, Ireland and of English books printed abroad 1475–1640*, London, 1926.

T.L.S.   *Times Literary Supplement*, 1902–.

Utley   F. L. Utley, *The Crooked Rib*, Columbus, 1944.

Waller and Glover   *The Collected Works of William Hazlitt*, ed. A. R. Waller and A. Glover, London, 1902–6. 13 vols.

Weiss   R. Weiss, *Humanism in England during the fifteenth century*, Oxford, 1941.

Welby   *Complete Works of Walter Savage Landor*, ed. T. E. Welby, London, 1927–36. 16 vols.

Wilkinson   *Two Tracts Affrican and Mensola . . . and Newes and Strange Newes from St. Christophers*, ed. C. H. Wilkinson, Oxford, 1946.

INTRODUCTION

BOCCACCIO'S literary career opened when after some initial opposition on the part of his father he was allowed to leave Florence for Naples. In this new environment of popular gaiety and courtly splendour he showed little inclination for the business career planned for him by his stern parent. On the contrary, he appears to have fallen in love with a lady whom in a series of works he calls Fiammetta. According to tradition, she was Maria d'Aquino, the natural daughter of King Robert of Anjou, a romantic association now regarded with scepticism.[1] Consequently, it is doubtful whether it was Maria d'Aquino that prompted him to tell in Italian the French romance of Floris and Blanchefleur under the title of the *Filocolo*. Its immaturity is indicated by its abuse of digressions and descriptions. Nevertheless, it has various interesting features, including the assembly in Book IV of a number of ladies and gentlemen who sit in a circle on a meadow under a shady tree near the cool water of a spring and debate thirteen questions relating to love. The scene, which in some measure anticipates the *Decameron*, has a parallel in the *Ameto*, an eclogue pervaded with moral and religious symbolism under the influence of Dante.

More important than the *Ameto* is the *Filostrato* where Boccaccio is far more himself. The story of Troilo and Griseida is animated by his passion for Fiammetta, and again in the *Teseida* the narrative is strongly coloured, it would seem, by his own feelings. In the *Amorosa Visione* he writes once more under the influence of Dante, though even in this serious poem, where Fiammetta hovers in the background, it is evident that the ascetic outlook of Dante was completely alien to his imitator. When he comes to *Fiammetta*, Boccaccio analyses the feelings of a woman betrayed and abandoned by her lover; in short, the situation here is the counterpart of that in the *Filostrato*. Here, however, the form is autobiographical, and an attempt is made to heighten the importance of the heroine's lament by the introduction of classical lore and the use of a dignified, oratorical prose style. In the *Ninfale Fiesolano* Boccaccio returns to verse and unites the love-story of Affrico and Mensola, a shepherd and a nymph dedicated to the service of Diana, with the rivalry of this goddess and Venus. After a short-lived joy the lovers are parted. Affrico in despair commits suicide; Mensola

---

[1] A. Chiari, *Indagini e Letture*, 2nd series, Florence, 1954, pp. 41–2.

B

is punished by Diana who transforms her into the river that still bears her name, just as Affrico's grandfather for a like offence had been turned into the river Mugnone. The background of hills and streams and villages is one that Boccaccio knew and loved, and he conveys admirably the charm and beauty of the landscape. On the other hand, he is less successful when he tells how Pruneo, the son of Affrico and Mensola, became the founder of Fiesole, and grafts the early history of that city and Florence on to the love-story.

It was Florence and the neighbouring countryside which was again in Boccaccio's mind when, after the devastating outbreak of the plague in 1348, he used it as a setting for the *Decameron*, his great masterpiece. There followed the *Corbaccio*, in which his wounded pride took vengeance on a widow who had rejected with scorn his attentions and poured out abuse not only on this Florentine but on the whole sex. Finally, he turned to the compilation of his Latin works, *De casibus virorum illustrium*, *De claris mulieribus*, *De montibus* and *De genealogia deorum*, on which his humanistic zeal built weighty monuments.

I

THE LATIN WORKS

IT was above all these compilations that earned for Boccaccio great renown as a scholar in the latter part of the Middle Ages. His fame was based in part on the encyclopædias of classical knowledge, *De montibus* and *De genealogia deorum*. Both were translated into Spanish, only the latter into French. Neither was rendered into English, but they were certainly known in humanistic circles. John Whethamstede, elected abbot of St. Alban's in 1420, quotes *De genealogia deorum*[1] and his protector, Humphrey, duke of Gloucester, possessed the two works.[2] However, it was above all *De casibus virorum illustrium* and *De claris mulieribus* that exalted his reputation to a remarkable height. For Pedro Lopez de Ayala, chancellor of Castille, who began a translation of the first of these, he was 'el maestro', and a Toledo edition of a translation of this work in 1511 calls Boccaccio 'un doctor famoso'.[3] Similarly, Fernan Mexia in his *Libro yntitulado nobillario*[4] describes him as the 'famoso filosofo',[5] and for Georges Chastellain, the historiographer to the dukes of Burgundy, he is 'le noble docteur Bocace'.[6] Pierre Faivre, the first translator of *De casibus* into French[7] thought him a 'tres-excellent historien'. In keeping with this attitude is the advice given to the student of 'English politicks', in a fifteenth-century manuscript that belonged to the earl of Leicester, to read 'Seneck and John Bocasse'.[8] The *De casibus* became a guide for rulers. It provided abundant illustrations of the errors that kings and princes should avoid.[9] The magnificent manuscript copies still extant prove

[1] W. F. Schirmer, *Der englische Frühhumanismus*, Leipzig, 1931, p. 96; Weiss, p. 31, n. 8. Whethamstede's *Granarium* was modelled on *De gen. deorum*. The title *De genealogia deorum* has been preferred to the form *De genealogiis deorum*, as the former is the one most often used by older English writers.

[2] Weiss, p. 64.

[3] A. Farinelli, 'Note sulla fortuna del Boccaccio in Ispagna nell' Età Media', *Archiv*, 1905, cxiv, p. 410, n. 2 and again in Farinelli, i, p. 95.

[4] Seville, 1492.

[5] *Archiv*, cxv, p. 368 and Farinelli, i, p. 149.

[6] *Oeuvres*, ed. K. de Lettenhove, Brussels, 1863–6, vii, p. 143.

[7] Bruges, 1476.

[8] MS Rawlinson A 338 in the Bodleian Library. Cf. R. Tuve, 'Spenser's Reading: The *De claris mulieribus*', *S.P.*, xxxiii, no. 2, 1936, p. 147, n. 1.

[9] Philip II of Spain had no less than five manuscript copies (cf. *Archiv*, cxiv, p. 403, n. 4 and Farinelli, i, p. 103, n. 1).

how lively was the interest that it aroused,[1] and it is characteristic that in 1422 Alonso of Cartagena should complete the version of Ayala for the benefit of the heir to the throne of Portugal.[2] It was therefore natural that the duke of Berry should encourage Laurent de Premierfait[3] and that Humphrey, duke of Gloucester, should command Lydgate to translate *De casibus*.

For the men of the fifteenth century Boccaccio was the great moralist, comparable to Boethius and Seneca. Chastellain saw in him 'le docteur de patience en adversité'.[4] This conception was given practical application when Charles of Orleans, during his twenty-five years of captivity in England after the battle of Agincourt, occupied himself with the treatise of Boccaccio,[5] and when, after the assassination of John the Fearless, duke of Burgundy, in 1419, his widow also found solace in this account of the misfortunes of others.[6] But Chastellain regarded Boccaccio as something more than an aid to endurance. Addressing the author, he declared 'tu incites les courages à vertus en délaissant les vices', which has its parallel in Premierfait's statement that Boccaccio's works:

> A vertu font chemin, de mal font devoyer.[7]

To this Premierfait adds that

> Tel auteur adonc doit avoir ou ciel partage,[8]

a sentiment echoed in the assurance of the author of *Celestina* that Christ will receive him into his glory.[9]

Boccaccio had the approval of the Church everywhere. In Spain friars vied with canons and bishops in their eulogies,[10] and *De casibus* and *De claris mulieribus* were quoted side by side with the book of Genesis and the works of Saint Augustine.[11] In France Claude Witart,

---

[1] Cf. Bergen, i, pp. xiv–xv. Two manuscripts of Premierfait's translation in the British Museum are of special interest. Royal MS. 14 E.v was executed, probably at Bruges, for a king of England [Edward IV?] whose arms, with Yorkist badges, occur frequently in the borders. The statement of P. Durrieu, *Le Boccace de Munich*, 1909, that it belonged definitely to Henry VII appears to have no foundation. On the other hand, Royal MS. 20 C.iv has on f. 1 the joined initials HR, which are presumably those of Henry VII.

[2] *Archiv*, cxiv, pp. 404–5 and Farinelli, i, p. 105.

[3] There were two editions of this version, 1484 and 1494. The earlier rendering of Pierre Faivre also ran to two editions, 1476 and 1483. Cf. *Gesamtkatalog*, vol. iv, items 4432, 4433, 4434, 4435.   [4] *Oeuvres*, p. 98.

[5] L. V. de Lisle, *Le Cabinet des MSS. de la Bibliothèque Nationale*, Paris, 1868–1881, i, p. 106.

[6] Henry Martin, *Le Boccace de Jean sans Peur*, Brussels, 1911, p. 2.

[7] Hauvette [1903], p. 26, n. 2.   [8] Ibid.

[9] *Archiv*, cxiv, p. 397 and Farinelli, i, p. 91.

[10] *Archiv*, cxiv, p. 401 and Farinelli, i, p. 99.

[11] C. B. Bourland, 'Boccaccio and the *Decameron* in Castilian and Catalan Literature', *Revue Hispanique*, xii, p. 18.

the nephew of an archdeacon, dedicated his translation of *De casibus* in 1578 to the bishop of Soissons, declaring that those who read it would derive from it doctrine conducive to their salvation, since it was not only full of philosophy but also replete with very Christian instruction leading to the life everlasting;[1] in England Robert Flemyng, who became dean of Lincoln in 1452, was a reader of *De claris mulieribus* and *De casibus*,[2] and the latter was in the possession of John Russell, elected bishop of Lincoln in 1480.[3]

1. *De casibus virorum illustrium*

Nearly a third of the manuscripts containing Chaucer's *Monk's Tale* refer to it, either at the beginning or the end or both, as *De casibus virorum illustrium*,[4] but it is uncertain whether or not this association, implying as it does, a parallel between *De casibus* and the tale, is derived from Chaucer himself. On the other hand it is obvious that the *Monk's Tale* lacks the dream machinery and the moralising aim of the original.[5] And if the text of the various tragedies is examined it is evident that not one is taken in its entirety from Boccaccio. Only the last stanza of 'Zenobia' can be traced back to him with some confidence. Yet, strangely enough, the poem advises the reader to consult 'maister Petrak' about Zenobia.[6]

By contrast there is no mystery about Lydgate's *Fall of Princes*.[7] The monk of Bury was at one with the numerous ecclesiastics of Spain who appreciated the edifying purpose of *De casibus*, and the humanistic Humphrey, duke of Gloucester, thought him well fitted to render Boccaccio's famous work into English. It was at his patron's suggestion that Lydgate wrote the envoys which enlarge on the various episodes of the *Fall of Princes*. Quite apart from these commentaries, in accordance with the duke's wishes, he related at length the story of Lucrece, despite the fact that in doing so he exposed himself to a comparison with his master Chaucer, a possibility which he otherwise prudently avoided. For this purpose he used the declamation on Lucrece by Petrarch's friend, Coluccio Salutati, and it may well be that

[1] Hauvette [1909], p. 132.   [2] Weiss, p. 104.   [3] Ibid., p. 177.
[4] R. K. Root in *Sources and Analogues of Chaucer's Canterbury Tales*, ed. W. F. Bryan and G. Dempster, Chicago, 1941, p. 615.
[5] R. W. Babcock, 'The Medieval Setting of Chaucer's *Monk's Tale*', *P.M.L.A.*, 1931, xlvi, pp. 210–11.
[6] R. K. Root, op. cit., pp. 616, 632–5.
[7] For an account of Lydgate see the following: E. Koeppel, *Laurents de Premierfait und John Lydgates Bearbeitung von Boccaccios De Casibus Virorum Illustrium*, Munich, 1885; H. Bergen, Introduction to *Fall of Princes* (1923), op. cit.; F. Brie, 'Mittelalter und Antike bei Lydgate', *Englische Studien*, lxiv, 1929, pp. 261–301; W. F. Schirmer, *John Lydgate: Ein Kulturbild aus dem 15 Jahrhundert*, Tübingen, 1952.

the manuscript containing this Latin narrative came from Duke Humphrey's library. Thus Lydgate became associated with the Italian Renaissance, and spoke, though not a classical scholar, with reverence of the great names of antiquity. In particular, he wrote eloquently in praise of Cicero and, where his source had paid a brief tribute to Athens, he dwelt on its cultural importance for the whole world.[1]

> For in that cite, pleynli to termyne,
> Off the seuene artis, as doun from on hedspryng,
> Ther ran out ryuers and stremys off al cunnyng.
>
> (i, 4254–6)

The efforts of Ptolemy II to accumulate knowledge also won Lydgate's admiration, and it is a true book-lover who describes the burning of the great library at Alexandria as 'ful gret pite'.[2] The ancient world attracted him in many ways, and even though he was impatient to press on with his translation, he could not refrain from interpolating an account of Roman triumphs[3] and a description, based on Aulus Gellius, of the different kinds of crown awarded by Rome for martial deeds.[4] For the writers of the past he cherishes a profound respect:

> as to me, it is a thyng odible,
> Thynges tenpugne, awtentik and olde,
> Which notable clerkis in ther daies tolde.
>
> (iii, 2266–8)

This does not mean that he felt under an obligation to follow them precisely. Even Boccaccio he modified as he thought fit, and as for Laurent de Premierfait's version of *De casibus* on which he relied, Lydgate allowed himself considerable freedom of treatment. This applied especially to any passages that were offensive to his patriotic sentiment. Thus when Boccaccio in speaking of the fate of King John of France refers to the English as 'inertissimis adque pauidis et nullius valoris hominibus' which is echoed by Premierfait's 'hommes faillis & vains & de nulle valeur', Lydgate defends the prowess and the chivalry of his countrymen and of Edward, the Black Prince, while he roundly condemns Boccaccio for his partiality. However,

> His fantasie nor his oppynioun
> Stood in that caas of non auctorite:
> Ther kyng was take; ther knihtis dide flee;
> Wher was Bochas to helpe at such a neede?
> Sauff with his penne he made no man to bleede.
>
> (ix, 3178–82)

Not content with this disapprobation, Lydgate turns everything in

---

[1] All quotations are taken from Bergen's edition.
[2] vi, 2588.   [3] iv, 526–74.   [4] iv, 239–315.

favour of the English, passing over the retention of John in captivity, despite the payment of his ransom by the French, and suppressing Premierfait's dark hints about the sinister mode of the king's death. Somewhat earlier in the last book Lydgate had felt a similar discomfort. Boccaccio had declared that the kings of France outshone the princes of the West as the sun outshines the stars, and Premierfait had followed him. Somewhat erroneously Lydgate relates this eulogy to France itself and then maintains that it was a biased view originating, not in Boccaccio, but in

> oon Laurence, which was a translatour
> Of this processe, to comende Fraunce;
> To preise that lond set al his plesaunce.
>
> (ix, 1886–8)

One can understand that such praise would hardly be to the taste of Humphrey, duke of Gloucester, the great-grandson of Edward III, and it was but natural that he and Lydgate should be so sensitive at a moment when English prowess in France had been gravely affected by Joan of Arc. Certainly, when Premierfait did use the encounter of Boccaccio with Dante to interweave an encomium of Paris, Lydgate omitted it. At the same time he ignored the French translator's attempt to enhance its cultural importance and his assertion that the *Divine Comedy* was derived from the *Roman de la Rose*.[1] Yet another omission occurs in the account of the portents that precede the outbreak of the civil war between Julius Caesar and Pompey. Among those was the birth of children with tails, 'come sont aulcuns anglois'.[2] This widespread gibe of the mediæval world was too much for Lydgate![3]

For his part he considered himself at liberty to adopt the same propagandist tactics as Premierfait. Hence his insertion of a eulogy of England from London to the Cotswolds and from York to Canterbury.[4] However, Lydgate is moderate in his patriotism. He speaks in the highest terms of King John of France who 'quit hym lik a manli kniht'[5] and lies buried at St. Denis 'with othir worthi kingis'.[6] Moreover, when he mentions Henry V, the patron of his *Troy Book*, he indulges in no panegyric of his victorious career but presents him as one whose aim was peace between England and France.[7] It is true that Lydgate gives only the English view of the rights and wrongs of the wars with France, but in general he had no liking for war. Once at

---

[1] Cf. ix, 2522 ff. [2] Cf. vi, 2331.

[3] It caused an affray at Messina in 1190 when the English crusaders under the command of Richard I, enraged at being called 'caudati', attacked the inhabitants. The king in consequence seized the town. Cf. J. S. P. Tatlock, *The Legendary History of Britain*, Berkeley and Los Angeles, 1950, pp. 505–7 and Ch. xxiii, notes 81–3.

[4] viii, 2685–95. [5] ix, 3191.

[6] ix, 3203. [7] i, 5969–73.

least, in a mood of detachment, he pauses to consider its causes and ponders whether it is due to the influence of the stars or to

> wilful rage
> As atween Romeyns & folkis of Cartage.

$$(v, 424-5)$$

It remains a mystery to him, but he sees that it brings little profit to either side. Conquerors like Cyrus, Sisera and Marpesia may win martial fame, but sooner or later they come to grief, and for an epitaph on Pyrrhus, Lydgate writes:

> Loo, heer the eende of folkis rekeles
> That folwed werre & list nat lyue in pes!

$$(iv, 3897-8)$$

The glory of the victor is but fleeting, for

> Conquest bi werre lastith but a whyle,

$$(i, 1531)$$

and,

> off al werre deth is the fyn parde.

$$(i, 5892)$$

In keeping with this attitude is the distaste that Lydgate here and there exhibits when he encounters some of the grim episodes in which *De casibus* abounds. He omits many of the savage struggles between Marius and Sulla,[1] limits the details of the mob's ferocity towards Andronicus[2] and cuts down the account of the torture and mutilation of Hanno by the Carthaginians.[3] When women and children are concerned, Lydgate's sentiments are equally conspicuous. He condenses the tale of Atreus and Thyestes[4] and suppresses various particulars in the account of Marius's cruelty towards the women of the Cimbri.[5] The same procedure may be observed in the story of the ravishing of the Levite's wife by the Gibeonites, when Lydgate refers the reader to the Book of Judges[6] for the complete relation of these hideous events.

It is not surprising that the gentle monk of Bury was able to partake of Jocasta's distress when King Laius commanded that his son Oedipus should be put to death in the forest:

> Litil wonder thouh she felte smerte!
> To all women I reporte me,
> And onto moodres that be tendre off herte,
> In this mater iuges for to be.
> Was it nat routhe, was it nat pite,
> That a pryncesse and a queen, allas,
> Sholde knowyn hir child deuoured in such cas!

$$(i, 3221-7)$$

[1] vi, 1093 ff.   [2] ix, 1457-77.   [3] iii, 4201-4.
[4] i, 4012-53.   [5] vi, 1065-78.   [6] iii, 1510-26.

In some ways the situation of Queen Althaea was still more painful, and Lydgate enters into her dilemma. Her son Meleager having presented to Atalanta the head of the boar he had killed, slew his two uncles that had deprived her of it. The task of avenging them fell to Althaea, and Lydgate shares the conflict in her heart.[1]

The task imposed on Althaea was all the more grievous, because in Lydgate's opinion women as a whole are disposed to show mercy, not to exact vengeance. Nevertheless, beneath their angelic appearance some are as cruel as wolves or lions or tigers.[2] Lydgate also maintains that women cannot keep a secret, that they are full of duplicity, and are treacherous and fickle.[3] On another occasion the story of Orpheus and Eurydice is used by him for a gibe at the bondage of married men. Some in Orpheus' place would not have sorrowed but

> thanked God, that broken was the cheyne
> Which hath so longe hem in prisoun bounde,
> That thei be grace han such a fredam founde.
>
> (i, 5808–10)

He is again in a satirical mood when he recalls that Chaucer was requested by the queen to write the lives of nineteen good women but could not find so large a number.[4] All these reflections are in keeping with the common mediæval attitude to women[5] and with that of Boccaccio in particular.[6] Like him Lydgate admitted that there were some good and innocent women, while insisting that they were to be revered precisely because they were so few.[7] Yet there is a difference between *De casibus* and the English version. When Boccaccio composed it, he was still smarting under the ridicule of the young widow whom he had wooed and whom he had attacked so furiously in the *Corbaccio*. Something of this temper still lingered in his chapter 'Adversus nimiam credulitatem'[8] where the whole sex is declared to be 'insatiabili libidine semper ardens'. Lydgate is less explicit regarding this charge and glides away from the accusation of libidinousness to talk with his tongue in his cheek about the wifely patience of Englishwomen.[9] And when Boccaccio's smouldering wrath bursts into flame in the chapter 'In mulieres', Lydgate is more balanced and more restrained.

> It is no resoun tatwiten women all,
> Thouh on or too whilom dede faile.
> It sittith nat, nor it may nat auaile,
> Hem to rebuke that parfit been & goode,
> Ferr out off ioynt thouh sum other stoode.

---

[1] i, 4964–8.
[2] i, 2515; iii, 2469–71; vi, 68.
[3] i, 6352–6; i, 6373–7; i, 5153–9; i, 5503–9.
[4] i, 330–6.
[5] Cf. F. L. Utley, *The Crooked Rib.*
[6] 'omnes fugiendas censeo'.
[7] i, 1812–13, 2843–9.
[8] Book i.
[9] i, 4728–46.

And I dar seyn, that women vertuous
Been in the[r] vertu off price mor comendable,
That ther be summe reknyd vicious,
And off ther lyuyng founde also onstable.
Goode women auhte nat be partable
Off ther trespas nor ther wikked deede,
But mor comendid for ther womanheede.

(i, 6646–50; 6665–71)

He has no personal animus against the sex and rejects Boccaccio's advice to flee them all.

Sexual passion was distasteful to Lydgate, and he is ill at ease in touching on illicit associations. Thus if Boccaccio describes how Antiochus escapes through the aid of a 'meretricula', Premierfait has no objection to calling her 'vne femme publique', but Lydgate glosses over her occupation by terming her 'a woman that lyued in pouerte'. Again, whereas Boccaccio displays an interest in Arsinoë, despite her misdeeds, Lydgate is hostile and condemns 'fals lust of sensualite'. The evil life of Messalina and Caligula evidently appeared to him unsavoury, and various details are omitted. So too Lydgate found the incestuous passion of Byblis for her brother repugnant and compressed his account into a few lines. Most odious of all in his eyes was the vice of homosexuality, and he either deletes all mention of it from his version,[1] or expresses his disgust at the 'foul & outragous' theme and the 'horrible deede'.[2]

This greater severity is also visible whenever the actions of ecclesiastics are touched on, for Lydgate is always concerned lest any discredit should fall on the Church. In this respect he differs notably from Premierfait who does not hesitate to point out the abuses prevalent in his own day. Thus in his picture of the golden world he declares that he is living in an age of pride, avarice and lust, when the morals of churchmen from the highest to the lowest are corrupt. Lydgate rejects this and a similar criticism in the ninth book. And if he has to admit that an individual pope like John XII led a vicious life, he is careful not to reproduce Premierfait's generalisations about the pride, sloth, and ribaldry of other bishops of Rome. He even goes so far as to replace the story of Joachim, high priest of the Jews, by that of Uzziah, because he is embarrassed by such an evil ecclesiastic, though he was not a Christian.

On the other hand, he loves to dwell on those rulers in former times who were staunch champions of the Church, like the Emperor Constantine and Theodosius. The latter in particular is praised, because

[1] In connexion with Vitellius (vii, 978), Ptolemy Philopator (v, 862–5) and Alexander, brother of Olimpias, the last of these perverts being struck out of the narrative (iii, 4760).   [2] vii, 720–1.

To the cherche he meekli did obeye,
[Lik] Goddis kniht did lowli his penaunce.

(viii, 2080–1)

But supreme among these ancient sovereigns imbued with the Christian spirit was Arthur, and as Lydgate wishes to idealise him, he is compelled to alter his relationship to Modred. According to Boccaccio and Premierfait, Modred was a son of Arthur by a concubine, but Lydgate, anxious to present Arthur as flawless in every way, makes Modred his cousin.

There is yet another facet of Lydgate's religious outlook. He tried to shun any parallel between Christians and pagans. Thus when Cartalus, bishop of Tyre, offers tithes to Hercules, the English version speaks of the performance of a sacrifice

Aftir the rihtis of ther paynym wise.

(iii, 3911)

Naturally, Lydgate declines to accept Premierfait's suggestion that God intervened on behalf of the ruthless Gaius Marius and, however much he may admire Cicero's eloquence, he will not hear of the claim that he was divinely inspired. Quite consistently, he has no equivalent to Boccaccio's wrathful outburst after Cicero's death: 'O Deus bone. Vbi indignatio iusta? Vbi ignis edax? Vbi fulmen? Vbi telluris hiatus?', for that implied that God should have inflicted condign punishment on Pompilius for the slaying of Cicero. Lydgate never forgets that the Romans were pagans, and even when he laments the fall of Rome, he condemns her for idolatry and holds her up as a warning example. As for Julian, who having seen the light, yet renounced Christianity and relapsed into the darkness of paganism, Lydgate treats him with the utmost rigour and consigns him to hell, where he is 'dampned with Sathan depe in peyne'.

In view of Lydgate's orthodoxy it is remarkable that he dismissed so briefly Boccaccio's denunciation of the Jews in his chapter 'In Iudæos Pauca'. On the other hand, he was most stern towards English heretics and praised Henry V, because

To stroie Lollardis he sette al his labour

(i, 5967)

and his patron, Humphrey, duke of Gloucester, since

heretik dar noon come in his siht,

(i, 410)

and

in this land no Lollard dar abide

(i, 403)

under his sway. He is equally hostile towards the Knights Templar, exhibiting none of the distress which Boccaccio had felt and refusing any admiration for their constancy in the hour of death. For Lydgate it sufficed that the action against them had papal sanction.

Conservative by temperament and also by reason of his dependence on patronage, he had little good to say of any one who caused upheaval in the state. Again and again he points the lesson that nothing is more to be deplored than civil discord, for

> thilke werris be most infortunat,
> Whan blood with blood, lat no man deemen othir,
> List [to] werreie, as brother ageyn brother,
>
> (iii, 4884–6)

and

> Kyngdamys deuyded may no while endure.[1]
>
> (i, 3822)

An abundance of material from the legendary dissension of Arthur and Modred and the civil wars of Rome to recent events in France enabled Lydgate to develop his theme.

A factor not to be ignored in the consideration of such problems is the attitude of the people. Lydgate distrusts the commons, accusing them of fickleness and ingratitude. Thus he comments on the exile of Themistocles:

> In trust off comouns is no perseueraunce:
> As wynter [&] somer be dyuers off ther hewe,
> So be thei dyuers in chaung off pryncis newe.
>
> (iii, 2203–5)

His bias may also be seen in his account of Coriolanus, when he declares that his banishment was without cause and suppresses all reference to the quarrel between plebeians and patricians.

For his part Lydgate has an instinctive dislike of the ordinary man who tries to obtain political power, since

> Froward techchis been euer in cherlis founde
>
> (iv, 2701)

and so

> thestat of politik puissaunce
> Is lost wher-euer knaues haue gouernaunce.
>
> (iv, 2673–4)

Those who aim at a higher rank than pertains to them are apt to fall victims to pride or to become cruel and vengeful. And so in speaking of Spartacus, Lydgate asks:

> What thyng mor cruel in comparisoun
> Or mor vengable of will & nat off riht,
> Than whan a cherl hath domynacioun![2]
>
> (vi, 778–80)

[1] He expatiates on this in relating the dissensions among the Trojans. Cf. *Troy Book*, ed. H. Bergen, London, 1906–35, iv, 4506–37.

[2] Cf. his remarks on Philippa Catanensi, ix, 3025–8.

However, to some extent he had come under the influence of the humanistic tradition which insisted on the merit of the individual in contrast to hereditary rank. Wealth and power, he asserts, are no means to attain nobility unless they are accompanied by virtue, and it is a man's deeds that alone can prove that he is noble. Rank by itself is not enough, for

> ofte tyme vertu nor gentilesse
> Come nat to heires bi successioun,
>
> (vi, 596–7)

and ultimately it is God that ordains who shall possess nobility. This quality is bestowed only on the meek and god-fearing, and such a man, if born in a humble position, does deserve to be exalted:

> who list hymsilf to knowe,
> And is be grace enclyned to meeknesse,
> Thouh he fro pouert in streihtnesse brouht up lowe
> And is be vertu reised to worthynesse,
> With sceptre of pes & suerd of rihtwisnesse
> Indifferentli his doomys demenyng,—
> Such oon is able to be cleped a kyng.
>
> (v, 2831–7)

From this passage the conclusion might be drawn that such a man would be justified in ousting a vicious ruler. Yet that was far from Lydgate's intention. No one was less of a revolutionary than he. In this he diverges considerably from Boccaccio who regarded the princes of his age with contempt and aversion. Lydgate goes out of his way to avoid anything that might undermine the position of a monarch. Thus in speaking of Machæus, duke of Carthage, he omits the fact mentioned by Premierfait that in Carthage all dignities and offices were elective[1] and he sets aside the contention in the French translation of Boccaccio's chapter 'In Fastosam Regum superbiam' that in the beginning kings and other princes were chosen by the consent of the people to protect and defend them and that the failure of a ruler to carry out his obligations relieved his subjects of their duties to him.[2] For a writer like Lydgate, closely bound as he was to a patron of royal descent, it was impossible to accept the view that allegiance could be cast off in this fashion, and so he introduces the concept of the state as a body, every part interrelated and every part having its function.[3] However, Lydgate emphasises again and again the necessity for a sovereign to care for the people. If he rules well, they will obey. He turns *De casibus* into a manual of advice. Princes should choose wise counsellors.

---

[1] iii, 3886 ff.

[2] Again in iii, 1373 ff. he omits the statement in Premierfait that princes were formerly elected by the consent of the people and suppresses the opinion that the lechery of a ruler frees them from their obligations.   [3] ii, 827–903.

They should take as their guide, not their wives or rash young men, but reason. They should eschew pride, lust and avarice, judge calmly and show mercy. Lydgate admonishes the exalted reader to do reverence to the Church and to observe God's precepts. All evils recorded by Boccaccio were due to lack of religion; the warning is given that

> Ye be no goddys, ye be but men mortal,
>
> (ix, 3486)

and that

> Deth spareth nouther hih blood nor hih lynages,
>
> . . . . .
>
> Transitoire been heer your pilgrymages.
>
> (vi, 1751, 3)

Nevertheless, there remained a problem of government, for what was to happen if all these sage counsels were neglected? Boccaccio had his remedy, which was to plot and conspire, to take up arms and oppose by force an enemy of the people. In his eyes it was not only necessary but holy to do so, since there was hardly any sacrifice more acceptable than the blood of a tyrant.[1] Premierfait went still further and declared that it was the most acceptable of all, and he repeats this in speaking of Machæus, duke of Carthage:

la seigneurie dun tel homme ne doit estre soufferte / ains le doit len sacrifier & occire / car le sang dun tyrant est sacrifice plaisant & aggreable a dieu.

Inevitably, in view of his position, Lydgate was constrained to reject this justification of tyrannicide. All he will admit is that the people of Carthage thought such a sacrifice pleasing to their gods. His solution was to wait until God should remove the tyrant. Repeatedly he states that while God may show forbearance for a time, he will in the end chastise the evil ruler and preserve innocence and reward the poor for their long patience. Yet there is some confusion in his thought, since he recognises elsewhere that human beings will be the agents of retribution:

> God wold nat suffre he sholde long endure,
> Graunteth no tiraunt to haue heer no long lyff;
> For be sum myscheef or sodeyn auenture
> Thei deien be moordre, with dagger, suerd or kniff.
>
> (viii, 1758–61)

Yet however inconsistent this may seem, it is clear that his whole bent was to uphold the view that

> To moordre a prince, it is a pitous thyng.[2]
>
> (vi, 2941)

---

[1] 'In Fastosam Regum superbiam'.

[2] Cf. his remarks on the murder of Agamemnon (*Troy Book*, ed. Bergen, v, 1136–47).

There is also some inconsistency in Lydgate's attitude towards the deities of the ancient world. Sometimes he refers to the punishment inflicted by them for sacrilege, but on the other hand in dealing with the sacrilege of Xerxes in the temple of Apollo at Delos he speaks of 'God' and 'goddis' in the same breath. Yet elsewhere he differentiates between the Christian God and the gods of other faiths, and he is especially opposed to any form of idolatry. In narrating the fate of Hostilius he says:

> His false goddis myhte hym nat auaile,
> Iubiter, Saturnus nor Venus.
> Lat al Christene defie such rascaile;
> For to our feith thei be contrarious.

> > (iii, 778–81)

Again the account of the deification of Romulus calls forth the comment:

> Loo, heer off paynymys a fals opynyoun,
> To Cristes lawe contrarie and odious,
> That tirantis sholde for fals oppressioun
> Be callid goddis or named glorious,
> Which bi ther lyue wer founde vicious:
> For this pleyn trouthe, I dar it riht weel tell,
> Thei rathere be feendis ful deepe in hell.

> > (ii, 4208–14)

As one might expect, he casts doubt on the value of the oracle of Delphi, but he carries his scepticism even into the Biblical story of the witch of Endor. However, after declaring it to be contrary to reason, he is seized with fear of being branded as unorthodox and commits the matter to divines.

In his survey of the misfortunes that overtake mankind so grave a writer as Lydgate was impelled to ask what was their ultimate cause. Like his contemporaries he attributes them in many cases to the influence of the stars. Thus he wonders whether or not the marriage of Oedipus to Jocasta was brought about by some unfavourable constellation, and in speaking of Astyages he recalls that when such an influence has affected human destiny, some hold that no man can avert it. Again, referring to Alexander of Epirus, he asserts that the period of life of a prince cannot be altered,

> For whan heuene of deth hath set a date,
> No mortal man eschewe may his fate.

> > (iv, 1602–3)

At times fate and stellar influence seem almost interchangeable in Lydgate's mind, but in some passages his outlook is almost pagan, as when, having rebuked the Parcae for cutting the thread of Alcibiades' life, while sparing the undeserving, he concludes:

> Alcibiades is passed into fate,
> Liht of knihthod lith clipsed in the shade;
> The Parchas sustren to soone sette his date,
> Of hih noblesse to make the laurer fade.
> Lacedemonoys of his deth wer glade,
> Funeral fyr his bodi hath deffied,
> For hih prowesse his soule stellefied.

(iii, 3676–82)

Such an atmosphere as we breathe here differs from that which normally envelops Lydgate's work. As a rule he lets the reader clearly understand that God controls all things and that his will cannot be altered. It is significant that in the following lines he confronts those scholars who believe in Fate with those divines who subordinate Fate to the power of God:

> But O allas, al fatal purueiaunce
> Kepith his cours, as summe clerkis seyn;
> But the writyng off doctours, in substaunce,
> And these dyuynes replie ther ageyn,
> And afferme thoppynyoun is in veyn
> Off hem that truste on fate or destyne:
> For God aboue hath the souereynte.

(i, 4971–7)

Lydgate often associates Fortune with Fate or Destiny, and once more he is careful to point out that the operations of Fortune are likewise restricted by God. Consequently, he denounces those who declare Fortune to be a goddess, for it is contrary to reason, and they are 'bestiall folk', since God endowed man with reason and intended him to have the free choice of good. Hence he makes Boccaccio in his dialogue with Fortuna ridicule fools who in adversity blame her:

> as sumtyme seith a theeff,
> Whan he is hangid: 'it was his destyne'—
> Atwitith Fortune his iniquite,
> As thouh she hadde domynacioun
> To reule man bi will ageyn resoun.

(vi, 283–7)

It is futile, he contends, to attempt to shuffle out of personal responsibility in this fashion,

> For ther is no synne but it be voluntarie

(vii, 403)

and

> Synne ay requereth vengaunce at his tail.
> God off Fortune taketh no counsail.

(iii, 193–4)

Not only in its ideas but also in its technique *The Fall of Princes* diverges considerably from *De casibus*. It takes no interest in the person of Boccaccio himself and ignores the prologue in which he sets forth his purpose, as it does the author's explanation of his object in presenting the story of Philippa Catanensi.[1] Lydgate cared nothing for the fact that her life was based on what Boccaccio had heard and seen. He was equally indifferent to the dramatic episodes that Boccaccio introduced between his divers lives, just as he interwove at the end of each day of the *Decameron* descriptive scenes in which the narrators figured against a pleasing natural setting. Lydgate had no idea of the artistic variety which such a pause created. In one or two places also he is singularly clumsy in narrative technique. Thus Atreus in addressing 'Bochas' quotes the author himself: 'As seith Bochas', 'myn auctour writ the same'. So too Lydgate ruins the effect of the tale of Oedipus, when he makes Apollo disclose to him, not only the fact that he will marry his mother but also that her name is Jocasta. On the other hand, he does attempt to relieve the monotony of an unbroken series of narratives by the use of a letter from Canace to her brother and by the employment of dialogue. However, the problem to which Lydgate addressed himself above all else was that of compression. The Latin original was succinct, as Boccaccio in his prologue had claimed it would be. But it had been expanded to unwieldy dimensions by Premierfait. In addition, Lydgate had to satisfy the desire of his patron for moralising envoys. We can observe how, as he went along, he felt obliged to reduce their number. However, that did not remove the chief difficulty, and he had to prune his French model drastically. First, he excised the references with which Premierfait studded his translation. It is but rarely that one remains.[2] He also avoids repetition of a story:

> For as me semeth, it wer a thyng in veyn,
> Thyng onys told to telle it newe ageyn
>
> .   .   .   .   .   .
>
> Sithe it is told, what sholde it mor auaile?[3]
>
> (iv, 202–3, 207)

He deletes matter which is superfluous, such as a chapter on the familiar mediæval theme of dreams, and although a zealous churchman he discards a lengthy account of the origin of the Papacy, beginning with the fall of Adam and continuing through the Incarnation and Redemption.[4] Descriptions such as those of Numidia and Bactria suffer the same fate. Some figures are thrust out of the book; others are dismissed summarily, and a whole series of emperors is packed into some two hundred lines.[5]

---

[1] In Book ix he omits the whole of Premierfait's Ch. xxv.
[2] v, 1481–2.
[3] Cf. v, 2611–3.
[4] ix, 1065 ff.
[5] viii, 204–420.

C

Inevitably such condensation reacted on Lydgate's style, and he himself was conscious of the result:

> This litil chapitle, as toforn is seene,
> Rehersid hath & toold in wordis pleyn
> Of emperour[e]s almost ful fourteene.
>
> (viii, 421–3)

Yet if his style is sometimes bald, it is not without ornament. Here and there he makes use of antithesis and the repetition of a word or phrase. Thus he writes of Samson and Delilah:

> He mente trouthe, & she was variable,
> He was feithful, and she was ontrewe,
> He was stedfast, and she was onstable,
> His trust ay oon; she loued thynges newe:
>
> (i, 6441–4)

and contrasts Paradise with the world into which Adam and Eve were driven:

> There is delit, and heer is sorwe [&] care,
> There is ioie, and heer is heuynesse,
> There is plente, and heer is euel fare,
> There is helthe, and heer is gret siknesse,
> Heer trouble ay meynt with onseur gladnesse,
> Ther is ay blisse and eternal glorie,
> And heere no merthe but fals & transitorie.[1]
>
> (i, 666–72)

Imagery also serves to enliven Lydgate's narrative. Some of it is conventional but at other times he includes scenes from everyday life such as the galled horse, bending his back when touched, and the snail shrinking its horns, the new-shorn sheep, the bear torn to pieces by dogs, the leper 'coorbid bak & chyne', the gambler casting his dice, the smith's forge belching black smoke, the gushing conduit, the carver making a fair image on his timber, and painted tables and walls. And when Lydgate appeals to the reader not to judge him too harshly, he contrasts his own dull work with that of the illuminator of manuscripts:

> Off gold nor asewr I hadde no foysoun,
> Nor othir colours this processe tenlvmyne,
> Sauff whyte and blak; and they but dully shyne.
>
> (ix, 3398–400)

He gives us a homely glimpse of the ass, so reluctant 'whan men hadde haste to gon', of medicinal herbs, and of salves applied to festered sores. Unusually vivid is the image of the unexpected resurrection of a dead man at his funeral:

[1] Cf. ii, 1856–9; iv, 2304–10; vi, 9–12, 54–70.

This ioye was lik a feeste funerall,
In folk of custum that doon ther besi cure
To brynge a corps, which of custum shall
Haue al the rihtis of his sepulture,
And in this tyme, of sodeyn auenture
To lyf ageyn restored be his bonys,
Causyng his freendis to lauhe & weepe attonis.

(viii, 1380–6)

Lydgate's eye continually rests on the countryside and the weeds among the corn. He also tells of Boreas, which 'yong[e] sheep & blosmys greueth ille', of the 'bakwynter' in May that in the midst of the nightingale's song blasts the freshness of summer. So too the new buds and primroses, all too swiftly losing their fresh hues, and the flowers cut down by the mower's scythe in June, are made to serve as emblems of changing fortune.

However, it is above all the imagery of light that interests Lydgate. His great men and women are compared to lamps and lanterns and lodestars, or to the sun which with its splendour dims the star and the moon. This radiance is most conspicuous of all in Lydgate's account of King Arthur:

Yit was ther neuer seyn so briht a sonne,
The someres day in the mydday speere
So fress[h]li shyne.

(viii, 2857–9)

In one passage he combines the symbol of a pilgrimage used by Boccaccio with his favourite imagery of light and darkness:

I stood chekmaat for feer whan I gan see
In my weie how litil I hadde runne;
Lik taman that failed day & sunne,
And hadde no liht taccomplisshe his viage,
So ferr I stood a-bak in my passage.

The nyht cam on, dirked with ignoraunce,
Mi witt was dull be cleernesse to discerne
In rethorik for lak off suffisaunce,
The torchis out, & queynt was the lanterne.

(iii, 52–60)

Far more frequent than such a picture of the benighted wayfarer is the repeated image of the sun eclipsed by cloud, mist or rain, as a symbol for the overthrow of power or the swallowing up of fame in the shadows of oblivion. The numerous passages in which this imagery appears leave no doubt that Lydgate was drawing on his own experience of 'wattri shours'.[1] It is true that one can here and there trace a

---

[1] He was well aware, of course, that his master Chaucer had used the weather to indicate a change of fortune for the better as in *Troilus and Criseyde* (iii, 1060–1). On occasion, Lydgate does the same (ix, 2949–51). However with him, sun, cloud, rain and darkness are far more often employed to suggest a change for the worse.

source of inspiration in Premierfait, but there is a world of difference between the prosaic statement 'les nyeubles de l'air ne peuuent obscurcir les rays du soleil' and Lydgate's

> Thouh it so falle sumtyme a cloudi skie
> Be chacid with wynd affor the sunne briht,
> Yit in effect it lasseth nat his liht;
>
> (vi, 2971-3)

where there is a lively movement that springs from personal observation. As a rule, however, Lydgate writes independently, especially when he draws his favourite picture of a bright morning growing overcast:

> But longe or eue dirknesse ther doth appeere,
> Thoruh cloudi reynes & mystes long durable.
>
> (iv, 1984-5)

It is a native speaking with the caution born of long experience of the fickle English climate who says:

> The faire day men do preise at eue.[1]
>
> (ix, 2024)

This familiarity with rain and wind and storm reappears in conjunction with that delicate appreciation of the beauty of flowers which is so characteristic of Lydgate. Prompted by Premierfait's description of youth blossoming until in old age it becomes pale, grey and bent, he recreates the passage in this fashion:

> al beute shal waste a-wey & fade
> Lik somer flours in ther most excellence,
> That growe on hillis & lowe doun in the shade:
> The rose, the lilie, whan thei be most glade,
> Vpon ther stalkis—ther preef is alday seyn—
> Been beten doun with a stormy reyn,
>
> (v, 58-63)

and again one has the impression of a sight actually seen. The power to create a striking picture is likewise felt in another place where Lydgate touches on this theme, though here the flower imagery is subordinate:

> Beute declynyth, his blosmys falle doun;
> And lite and litil be successioun
> Cometh croked elde onwarli in crepyng,
> With his potent[2] ful poorli[3] manasyng.
>
> (i, 767-70)

The elegiac strain in Lydgate can be powerful as well as pathetic. He writes of the fall of Rome with dignity, especially in the seven

---

[1] Cf. ix, 1695-701.　　　[2] 'crutch'.　　　[3] 'indigently'.

stanzas cast in the 'Ubi sunt' form where he contrasts the fame, greatness and splendour of Rome with its later state of ruin and decay.[1]
It is true that the poet later imposes on his theme a didactic conclusion,
but such a moral is not surprising in the orthodox ecclesiastic in quest
of a solution to the mystery of the fluctuations in human happiness.
Yet Lydgate the man remains keenly aware of the pain and loss that
they bring in their train. It is a hard world that he portrays; seldom
does it witness a change for the better. What is more characteristic of
The Fall of Princes as of Boccaccio's *De casibus* is the mingling of bliss
with bitterness. The sense of the mutability of life inspires notable
lines, among which some of the most eloquent are those on Marcus
Manlius:

> What myhte auaile his noblesse in bataile?
> Bies[2] of gold, crownes of laureer?
> His riche platis or his vnkouth maile,
> His myhti sheeldis, that shon so briht & cleer?
> Or his tryumphes, songe ferr & neer,
> Or his victories for the cite wrouht?—
> In his gret myscheeff[3] auailed hym riht nouht.
>
> (iv, 505–11)

It was above all as the translator of *De casibus* that Lydgate became
famous, so that a scribe of the fifteenth century thought it quite
natural to add to 'De casibus virorum illustrium' in the Huntington
manuscript of the *Monk's Tale*[4] Lydgate's translation, 'The Falle of
Princis'. Similarly, we encounter him in Caxton's prologue to *King
Arthur*, published in 1485. The printer refers the reader to 'thystorye
of bochas in his book de casu principum',[5] which suggests a translation
of Lydgate's title into Latin rather than that given by Boccaccio.
Reference is made once more to Boccaccio in a manuscript of about the
middle of the fifteenth century,[6] but on investigation it is found that
the writer is drawing on Lydgate.[7] In the course of his treatise in verse
on the ten commandments, derived from Robert Mannyng of Brunne's
Handlyng Synne, he speaks of Semiramis:

> Bochas rehersys off wyffes many on
> whych to þere husbans wer contraryus
> Among all oþer he wrytes off on

---

[1] ii, 4460–585.
[2] 'torques', 'collars'.   [3] 'misfortune', 'distress'.
[4] Cf. W. McCormick, *The Manuscripts of Chaucer's Canterbury Tales*, Oxford, 1933,
p. 543.
[5] *The Prologues and Epilogues of William Caxton*, ed. W. J. B. Crotch, London, 1928,
p. 93.
[6] MS. Arundel 20 in the British Museum.
[7] Attention is drawn to this by W. Farnham, 'England's Discovery of the Decameron', *P.M.L.A.*, 1924, xxxix, p. 155. The corresponding passage in Lydgate
occurs in i, 6630–6. Cf. Bergen, vol. i, p. 187.

> semeiyanus[1] hyr name off cunyng vycyous
> quene off assyry he callyd hyr thus
> whych wold no man any wysse denye
> with hyr crokyd instinct to encresse & multyply.[2]

A little later the poet quotes Boccaccio as his authority for an incident in the life of Pasiphae:

> ffor as bochas in his wrytyng berys wytnes
> quene passiphe had a chyld full ffeyr,
> hyr husband not knowyng by no lyknesse
> but that the chyld was hys verye eyr
> hys trust was gode and off no dyspeyr.
> for sum husbandes as poyttes haue compylyd
> whych moste trustes sonnest are begylyd.[3]

But here too Lydgate is the immediate source.[4]

The two writers were continually linked together, as when Benedict Burgh[5] in his poem in praise of Lydgate introduces 'the lauriate bocase'.[6] The association was prolonged from the fifteenth century into the sixteenth by the editions of *The Fall of Princes*, from that of Pynson down to that of Wayland.[7] In the last of these an envoy is added by Greneacres 'vpon Iohn Bochas',[8] in which, after alluding to the sorrowful contents of the book, he addresses Proserpine in these terms:

> Admitte this Bochas for a manne of thine
> And though hys habite blacker be than sote
> Yet was it made of thy monkes hode.
> That he translated in English of Latine,
> Therfore now take him for a man of thyne.

At the end of a few copies of Wayland's edition the title-page of the first edition of *A Mirror for Magistrates* has survived.[9] This serves as a reminder that it was meant to be an extension of *The Fall of Princes*. The idea of such a continuation of *De casibus* was not peculiar to England. In fifteenth-century Spain the marquis of Santillana, a contemporary of Humphrey, duke of Gloucester, and like him a great humanist, presents Boccaccio in his *Comedieta de Ponça* as the consoler of four unhappy women, Leonora, dowager queen of Aragon, Maria, queen of Navarre, Blanca, reigning queen of Aragon and the

---

[1] A corruption of 'Semiramis'.

[2] Fol. 50b, col. 2. This same stanza occurs with little variation in Peter Idley's *Instructions to his Son*, ed. C. D'Evelyn, Boston and London, 1935, ii, 1805–11. For other examples of *The Fall of Princes* being used for anti-feminist controversy, cf. Utley, pp. 192–3, 211, items 185 and 220.　　　　　[3] Fol. 55a, col. 1.

[4] Bergen, vol. i, p. 74; i, 2703–9.　　　　　[5] Died in 1483.

[6] Cf. Lydgate and Burgh's *Secrees of old Philisoffres*, ed. R. Steele, London, 1894, p. xxxi.

[7] Pynson (1494 and 1527), Tottel (1554), Wayland (1555?).　　　　　[8] Fol. 219a.

[9] Cf. Campbell, Intro. pp. 5–7 and J. W. Cunliffe in *Cambridge History of English Literature*, 1909, iii, pp. 193–4.

Infanta Catherina, who bewail the disastrous battle off the island of Ponza in 1425. Boccaccio replies to them in Italian and promises to record their misfortunes.[1] In the same way Boccaccio appears in the *Tragedia de la insigne Reyna Isabel* by Don Pedro, constable of Portugal.[2] So too Georges Chastellain has a vision in which Boccaccio commands him to write down the sorrowful history of Margaret of Anjou, the widowed queen of Henry VI of England.[3] However, *A Mirror for Magistrates* was intended to be on a far larger scale. As Baldwin the editor, stated:

Whan the Printer had purposed with hym selfe to printe Lidgates booke of the fall of Princes, and had made priuye thereto, many both honourable and worshipfull, he was counsailed by dyuers of theim, to procure to haue the storye contynewed from where as Bochas lefte, vnto this presente time, chiefly of suche as Fortune had dalyed with here in this ylande:[4]

At least one of the seven scholars whom Baldwin approached, George Ferrers, wanted something more comprehensive. He said:

I meruaile what Bochas meaneth to forget among his myserable princes, such as wer of our nacion, whose numbre is as great, as their aduentures wunderful: . . . But as it shoulde appeare, he beynge an *Italien*, mynded most the *Roman* and *Italike* story, or els perhaps he wanted our countrey chronicles.[5]

This patriotism is characteristic of the age, and although in the first edition Baldwin and his friends decided to limit themselves to the original plan, in later editions more and more figures were introduced until in 1610 the whole scheme was complete.

Inevitably, if the fortunes of men living after Boccaccio and Lydgate were to be discussed, the place of the old writers had to be taken by some one else, and so the characters address Baldwin. However, this device is not always adhered to. Henry, duke of Buckingham, speaks to Sackville, and Sir Nicholas Burdet to John Higgins. Between the lives there are prose links when the committee deliberates about who shall appear next, and occasionally even discusses a contradiction in the chronicles. In one instance John Tiptoft, earl of Worcester, himself comments on Fabyan and Hall![6] There is consequently less unity than in Boccaccio. However, *A Mirror for Magistrates* has one advantage over *The Fall of Princes*. Moralising envoys are discarded, and only in the edition of 1587 do they recur at the end of each life up to Caius Julius Caesar.

---

[1] C. B. Bourland, loc. cit., pp. 20–1.
[2] *Archiv*, cxv, p. 387, n. 1 and Farinelli, i, p. 184, n. 1.
[3] See *Le Temple de Bocace*, in the *Oeuvres*, vii, pp. 75–143.
[4] The text printed here is that given by Campbell, p. 68.
[5] Cf. Campbell, pp. 69–70.
[6] An obvious anachronism, since this well-known humanist died in 1470.

In 1574, when John Higgins published sixteen, or in some copies seventeen, pre-Christian lives, he adopted new machinery. He opens with a description of the waning of summer, the fall of the leaves and the approach of the cold after the manner of Sackville's *Induction*. Then he relates how one evening early in winter, as he is reading *A Mirror for Magistrates*, Morpheus brings him to a hall. From 'a duskish Ile' at the end of the hall Morpheus summons the Britons who one by one relate to the poet all their misfortunes with great lamentation. The general scheme is akin to that of Boccaccio and Lydgate. On the other hand, in 1578 Thomas Blennerhassett proceeds differently. There is neither procession nor lamentation. The poet is not addressed, but each story has an induction, spoken by 'Memorie' and 'Inquisition', and at the end of the induction each character in turn is called on to unfold his tale. In 1587 the lives are mainly by John Higgins, and when he uses envoys, it is partly for moralising comment, partly as a link in the narrative. To that extent they replace the figure of Morpheus. Some of the speakers implore the poet to write their lives. On the whole his technique here shows a greater conformity to the pattern of Lydgate. In 1610 Richard Niccols filled in the gaps left by his predecessors and the design was completed. He took a hint from Blennerhassett and let 'Memorie' summon the new characters, and from Higgins's introduction of 1574 he borrowed and elaborated the winter setting. In a lengthy induction he describes a walk in a desolate landscape. The trees are covered with icicles and hoar-frost; the nightingale and the birds of spring are gone:

> None but the Red-brest and the Wren did sing the euen away,
> And that in notes of sad record for summers late decay.[1]

The sun sets, the mists rise, and darkness descends. One feels that although this picture is but a prelude to the poet's vision of men of bygone days, it is inspired by a genuine love of the joys and beauties of the countryside.

Throughout the long evolution of *A Mirror for Magistrates* the figure of Boccaccio is never far away, sometimes in the company of Lydgate, sometimes alone. Thus in 1587 King Brennus says:

> And let what *Bochas* writes and *Higgins* here doth pen,
> As myrours shew what good wee gate, to warre with *Delphos* men,[2]

and Julius Caesar wishes his deeds to be recalled once more,

> Although by *Bocas* I haue whilom told my mind,
> And *Lydgate* haue likewise translated wel the same.[3]

---

[1] Cf. *A Mirror for Magistrates*, ed. J. Haslewood, London, 1815, ii, p. 547.
[2] Cf. Campbell (Add. Parts, 1946), p. 279.　　　　　　　[3] Ibid., p. 290.

So too in *Churchyards Challenge* (1593), containing the tragedies of Jane Shore, the earl of Morton, and Sir Simon Burlei, the poet, who already had connexions with *A Mirror for Magistrates*, makes Burlei reproach Baldwin for omitting him and beg Churchyard to commemorate his name:

> Did Boccace liue, or Lidgate write againe,
> Some hope were left, my lanterne should haue light:
> If any one, that had a Poets vaine,
> Knew halfe my life, or had my case in sight,
> In colours fine, I should bee paynted right.
> But gaping graue, and gnawing wormes below,
> Snapt Bocace vp, and Lidgate long agoe.
>
> (p. 26)

A similar appeal is made to Sir David Lyndesay by David Beaton, cardinal and archbishop of St. Andrews, after his murder in 1546. Lyndesay's poem may have appeared in 1548, in which case it preceded the first edition of *A Mirror for Magistrates*. The author tells how

> Nocht Lang ago, efter the hour of pryme,
> Secreitly sittyng in myne Oratorie,
> I tuk ane Buke, tyll occupye the tyme,
> Quhare I fand mony Tragedie and storie,
> Quhilk Ihone Bochas had put in memorie,
>
> (Prologue, 1–5)

when suddenly Beaton appeared and spoke to him:

> Rycht sure I am, war Ihone Bochas on lyue,
> My tragedie at lenth he wald dyscryue.
> Sen he is gone, I pray the tyll indyte
> Off my Infortune sum Rememb[e]ra[n]ce,
> Or, at the leist, my Tragedie to wryte,
> As I to the sall schaw the Circumstance.[1]
>
> (27–32)

It was another assassination which in a roundabout fashion again brought Boccaccio to the notice of English readers. On 17 April 1617 the young Louis XIII had Concini, the favourite of the queen-regent Marie de'Medici, murdered, and his widow, the notorious Leonora Galigai, executed a few weeks later. Pierre Matthieu, looking round for parallels for the fall of royal favourites, in the same year published *Aelius Sejanus, histoire romaine* and *Histoire des Prosperitez Malheureuses, d'une femme Cathenoise, grande Seneschalle de Naples*. The second of these was derived from *De casibus*, Book ix,[2] supplemented by

---

[1] Cf. *The Works of Sir David Lindsay of the Mount*, ed. D. Hamer, Scottish Text Society, 1931–4, 4 vols., i, pp. 130–1.

[2] Lydgate had, of course, dealt with the startling career of 'Philippa Catanensi'. Cf. Bergen, ix, 2805–3056.

G. A. Summonte's *Istoria della città e regno di Napoli*.[1] The assassination of George Villiers, duke of Buckingham, on 23 August 1628, turned the thoughts of English writers to Matthieu's work. In 1628 two translations of the one book were printed in Paris under the title, *The powerfull favorite, or the life of Aelius Sejanus*, but it was not until 1632 that Sir Thomas Hawkins published his *Vnhappy Prosperitie Expressed in the Histories of Ælius Seianus and Philippa the Catanian*. He followed his source closely[2] and was too cautious to comment freely on the sudden falls of favourites, but the lesson was plain for every man. The application was easily made to the case of Buckingham when he read Matthieu's generalisation about the fate of Philippa:

It is a tragicall effect of the inconstancy of Fortune no lesse cunning in her Deceits, than giddy in her Favours. She could not raise this woman from a more despicable degree, nor precipitate her from an higher, To shew, The Ascent to great Prosperities is of Glasse, the Top a Terror, and Descent a Precipice.[3]

Matthieu's final words are also in a vein that the author of *De casibus* might not have found unpleasing:

In all this we must conclude, that ill successe waiteth on unjust prosperity, that there is not any wickednesse which beareth not its paine and repentance; that he who perpetrateth one, expects the opportunity of another, that whilst the Worlds Theater lasteth, Fortune thereon will play her Tragedies, and will make it appeare, she flatters those she meanes to stifle.[4]

Certainly this moralising strain is in keeping with the attitude of Lydgate and much of *A Mirror for Magistrates*. Even more completely mediæval, however, is a passage in *Churchyards Challenge*. The poet draws from 'the tragedie of the Earle of Morton' a lesson not only on the instability of life but also on the need to despise this world in anticipation of heaven:

> Loe, lookers on, what staie remains in state.
> Loe, how mans blisse, is but a blast of winde:
> Borne vnto bale, and subiect to debate,
> And makes an ende, as destine hath assignde,
> Loe heere as oft, as Morton comes to minde,
> Dispise this worlde, and thinke it nothing straunge:
> For better place, when we our liues doe chaunge.
>
> (p. 25)

The old tradition died hard, and there are lines in the Induction to the 1610 edition of *A Mirror for Magistrates* which closely resemble those of Churchyard, at least in their emphasis on the instability of all

---

[1] Cf. M. A. Hortis, *Studi sulle opere latine del Boccaccio*, Trieste, 1879, p. 128, n. 2, and Henri Hauvette, 'Un chapitre de Boccace et sa fortune dans la littérature française' in *Bulletin Italien*, Bordeaux, 1903, vol. iii, no. 1, pp. 1–6. The name 'Summonte' was inaccurately given as 'Summoto'.

[2] He reproduces the error 'Summoto'. A second edition appeared in 1639.

[3] Cf. 1639 ed., p. 295.

[4] Cf. 1639 ed., p. 406.

things earthly. The decay of the beauties of summer, Richard Niccols declares,

> Did shew in state there was no trust, in wealth no certaine stay,
> One stormie blast of frowning chance could blow them all away.[1]

Yet when he turns to read *A Mirror for Magistrates*, his thought undergoes a development. He now speaks, not so much of swift falls from power as of Death the leveller, and his verse acquires a quality that looks forward some thirty years to Shirley's famous poem 'Of Death'. Gazing at his book, he says:

> There, as in glasse, I did behold, what day before did show,
> That beautie, strength, wealth, worlds vaine pompe, and all to dust do go;
> There did I see triumphant death beneath his feet tread downe
> The state of Kings, the purple robe, the scepter and the crowne;
> Without respect with deadly dart all Princes he did strike,
> The vertuous and the vicious Prince to him been both alike.
> Nought else they leaue vntoucht of death except a vertuous name,
> Which dies, if that the sacred nine eternize not the same.[2]

However, such a passage can hardly redeem the prosiness or obliterate the monotony of *A Mirror for Magistrates* as a whole. Niccols' edition did not sell;[3] it no longer met the needs of the age. Only one year after its publication Dekker declared in the prologue to *The Roaring Girle* that

> Tragick passion
> And such graue stuffe, is this day out of fashion.

No wonder that as the reign of Elizabeth merged in that of James, *A Mirror for Magistrates* was satirised or ridiculed.[4] Nevertheless, this continuation of Boccaccio's *De casibus* had left a palpable mark on English historical poems and English historical drama.[5] Towards the

---

[1] Quoted from the edition of 1610. Cf. Haslewood, op. cit., ii, p. 548.
[2] Ed. of 1610, p. 557. Cf. Haslewood, ed. cit., ii, p. 549. Cf. Niccols' lines in the Induction to *Englands Eliza*, printed along with *A Mirror for Magistrates* in 1610:

> The Prince and Swaine to death are both alike,
> No ods are found when he with dart doth strike.
> (p. 874)

Something akin to this can, of course, be traced back to Lydgate, though he places the emphasis on the indifference of Death to all men, whatever their station:

> with his darte he maketh doun to fall
> Riche and poore, hem markyng sodenly:
> His vnwar strook smyt[eth] indifferently,
> From hym refusyng fauour & al meede,
> Off all estatis he takith so litil heede.
> (*The Fall of Princes*, ed. Bergen, i, 3790–4)

[3] Cf. J. W. Cunliffe, loc. cit., p. 198.   [4] Ibid., p. 199.
[5] Cf. W. Farnham, *The Medieval Heritage of Elizabethan Tragedy*, Berkeley, 1936; E. M. W. Tillyard, *Shakespeare's History Plays*, London, 1944; W. F. Schirmer, 'Glück und Ende der Könige in Shakespeare's Historien.' (*Arbeitsgemeinschaft für Forschung des Landes Nordrhein-Westfalen*, Heft **22**, pp. 7–18.)

end of the seventeenth century it would seem that the original work had fallen into desuetude. At any rate, the reference to it as 'a Compend of the Roman Historie' by Sir James Turner, soldier and scholar, indicates that he had little idea of its contents.[1] The day of *De casibus* was done.

2. *De claris mulieribus*

This work, which Boccaccio had dedicated to the Countess Andreina degli Acciaiuoli, also enjoyed a great reputation in Europe. A Spanish translation was made in the fifteenth century and was printed at Saragossa in 1494,[2] one year before the Castilian version of *De casibus*, another edition following in 1520.[3] In France an anonymous version has been preserved in a manuscript dated 1401, and in a modified form this was published by Antoine Vérard at Paris in 1493, apparently under the patronage of Anne, queen of France. It was reprinted in 1538 and a new translation was printed in 1551.[4] The Latin text was reproduced at Louvain, Strassburg and Ulm,[5] and when this was turned into German about 1473 by Heinrich Steinhövel, it was widely read, four editions being called for before 1500,[6] four others following in the sixteenth century.[7] Steinhövel dedicated his work to Eleanor, duchess of Austria, the daughter of James I of Scotland, the first initial of the dedication showing her coat of arms, a lion wearing a crown.[8]

 In the fifteenth century the association of *De claris mulieribus* with *De casibus* was extremely close. Thus it was claimed by Vérard that the book offered not only the virtues and eulogies of noble and illustrious women but also their 'fortunes and infélicités', and he also declared that Boccaccio's aim was to prove the instability and variation of Fortune. Though not guilty of such a misconception, the author of an English translation,[9] probably made somewhere between 1440 and 1450,[10] was also familiar with *De casibus*. In his introduction he refers to

---

[1] MS. in my possession—written about 1690. [2] *Gesamtkatalog*, iv, item 4491.
[3] Cf. Bourland, loc. cit., p. 12, and *Archiv*, cxv, p. 570 and Farinelli, i, p. 152.
[4] Cf. Hauvette [1909], pp. 124–7, and Hauvette [1903], p. 106, n. 2; also *Gesamtkatalog*, iv, item 4490.
[5] *Gesamtkatalog*, iv, items 4483 to 4485.   [6] Ibid., items 4486 to 4489.
[7] *Boccaccios De claris mulieribus deutsch übersetzt von Stainhövel*, ed. K. Drescher, Tübingen, 1895, pp. xi–xiv.   [8] Cf. Drescher's edition, p. ix.
[9] Add. MS. British Museum, 10304, ff. 2a–46b. Quotations are taken from the manuscript. The line references are to G. Schleich's edition, *Die mittelenglische Umdichtung von Boccaccios 'De claris mulieribus'*, Leipzig, 1924. An account of the poem had previously been given by J. Zupitza, 'Über die mittelenglische Bearbeitung von Boccaccios De claris mulieribus' in *Festschrift zur Begrüssung des fünften allgemeinen Neuphilologentages in Berlin 1892*, pp. 93–120.
[10] Cf. J. Raith, *Boccaccio in der englischen Literatur von Chaucer bis Painters Palace of Pleasure*, Munich, 1936, p. 74.

> Iohn Bokase / so clepyde is his name
> That wrote the fall of pryncys stronge & bolde
> And into englissh / translate is the same.
>
> (16–18)

He adds:

> An odyre he wrote vnto the laude & fame
> Of ladyes noble / in prayse of all wymen
> But for the rarenes / few folke do it ken.
>
> (19–21)

From this it may be concluded that *De claris mulieribus* was not nearly so well known as *De casibus* had become through Lydgate. The poet was anxious to make good this deficiency, all the more because he felt it unjust that no author except Boccaccio had written solely about women, whereas many had devoted books to men. However, he trusted that his labour would receive the patronage of some noble princess,

> For poetys ben of litell reputacion,
> That of estatys haue no sustentacion.
>
> (27–8)

At the close he expresses a hope that he may still find encouragement, so that the whole work may be completed:

> If it fortune to be acceptable
> And please the herers / forth I wyll procede
> To the residue of ladyes notable;
> But fyrste of all / to se howe this shall spede
> I will take counsell / ere it go on brede
> leste that I eyre the bareyn se banke
> And gete me more of laboure than of thanke.
>
> (1786–92)

Apparently no counterpart of the distinguished continental patronesses or of Humphrey, duke of Gloucester, was forthcoming, and so out of Boccaccio's one hundred and five lives only twenty-one were translated. The first section consists of ten, most of whom are goddesses. Then follow eleven whom the poet assembles from various parts of the book on the ground that they were 'by their dedys laudable', though it is difficult to see how he can include Circe and Medea on this ground. However, he had a sense of design. After translating Boccaccio's prologue he proceeds to the stories, linking them together as well as he can, and rounds off the whole with a brief conclusion.

That he was a scholar is obvious. He was well acquainted with Latin, and his pride in this is reflected in his identification of himself with those who are indebted to Carmenta for her invention of Latin letters:

> So vnto vs / that were in cunnynge blynde,
> Of all latyne she is the firste fowndress.
>
> (1503–4)

Sallust he used on occasion, Ovid more often, and most frequently, Virgil. In the life of Mantho he takes the opportunity to mention that the town of Mantua was called after her, in order that he may pay a tribute to

> the noblest poet
> Virgyle Maro / that euer men herd of ʒet.
>
> (1420–1)

That this is not just lip-service is shown by the numerous passages in which he amplifies Boccaccio's lives with the aid of the *Æneid*.

It has been suggested that the poet was an ecclesiastic, because he knows the meaning of the name Eve, and mentions Moses as the inventor of Hebrew letters.[1] Certainly, he displays many signs of piety, as when he indicates a period in this fashion:

> Long toforn cryst and mary virgynall flour
>
> (824)

and again

> Both forn and after that cryst from deth did ryse.
>
> (840)

Similarly, he says of the sybil Erythrya that she

> Wonderys thyngys made in prophecy
> Of cristen feithe and of our lorde Ihesus,
> The whiche is a grete strength to vs
> And to the Ivys vtter confusyon
> That byleve not the Incarnacyon
>
> (1116–20)

and at the close he reiterates that it brought commendation to all women that in Erythrya

> found was swyche vertue
> And suyche cunnynge to speke of criste Ihesu.
>
> (1161–2)

The same emphasis may be observed in a passage on the prophetic power of Almathea which, he says, expanding Boccaccio, she had

> Of hym that is of rightwysness the son
> The which all men doth enlumyne
> Withoute whoos grace no thinge we can kon
> Of oure own selfe / nere ʒit ymagyne.
>
> (1177–80)

From time to time there are clear indications that the poet meant his translation to have a special appeal to women, which was but natural in view of his desire to obtain a princess as his patron. Thus in the account of Juno, he draws an intimate parallel between ancient and modern times which discloses his intention:

[1] Cf. Schleich's edition, p. 105.

> And, lyke as cristen wymen, grete with chylde,
> Whan their labours & throwys drawen nere
> Cryen on Mary Ihesus modyre mylde
> Help lady / that I vnbownden were
> So the gentyls / as poetys don vs lere
> Callyd on Iuno for helpe & socour
> Goddess of byrth / in euery sele & hour.
>
> (540–6)

Once more he has a female audience in mind when he laments at some length the fading of Eve's beauty after the Fall, and then addresses his listeners directly:

> Remembre thys / ye ladyes souereyne
> Evys bewte wytt and womanhede
> Excedyd Dido Criseyde & Heleyne
> Thof they were famouse as ȝe shall after rede,
> Ȝyt she & they / all now be idede
> ffor dethe no thynge spareth vpon lyfe
> But at the laste / all he dothe down dryfe.
>
> (358–64)

He does this also at the end of the life of Medea, where in emphasising the evil consequences of her original infatuation for Jason, he utters this warning:

> Take hede all virgyns & withdrawe your sight
> ffrom lascyuyous & wanton ȝonge personys
> Be not famylyer / nowdir be daye ner nyght
> For certenly / it shall repent ȝow onys.
>
> (1380–3)

It was perhaps because he did not look with favour on uncontrolled passion that he ignored Sappho's unhappy love and concentrated on her poetic genius. Having referred to her invention of the Sapphic measure, which he considered a most notable achievement, he says:

> In a woman this is worthy praysynge
> ffor men wold thynke them self thank worthy
> Now adayes / if they were so crafty.
>
> (1447–9)

His admiration for Carmenta is even greater, since she had pre-eminence

> By litrale studye in latinyte.
>
> (1452)

The scholarly poet, who esteemed skill in the Latin tongue so highly, thought her deserving of reverence, since this was the sphere of man rather than woman. Such an attitude may seem unduly condescending, but it was understandable in the fifteenth century. For intellectual power in the other sex he had a genuine respect, especially when, as in Minerva, it was combined with purity,

> ffor all on vertue sett was hir affeccion
> Euer bydynge styll on perfeccyon
> A pure vyrgyne to hir lyves endyng
> To flessly lustys neuer consentyng.

(746–9)

It was the chastity of Camilla, no less than her courage that attracted the poet. He treats her with sympathy from the beginning, and as he describes the hard lot of the motherless child, a note of tender pity is heard. In the account of her death in battle he draws on Virgil to illustrate the insidious guile and cowardly behaviour of her slayer, Arruns, and ends his narrative with this moving passage:

> Down she fell emongys hir meyne
> Dede to the ground with sorough & weylynge
> And forthwith hir host gan turn bak & fle
> Vpon horsbake / as fast as they myght flynge
> Camilla the quene / dede home caryynge
> And beryed hyr with many a wepynge teere
> ffor neuer ʒitt was suyche on reygnynge there.

(1086–92)

No difficulty arose about the question of a patron when Henry Parker, Lord Morley, undertook his translation of *De claris mulieribus* some time between 1534 and 1547. Of high rank, he was sent on a mission in 1523 to confer the Order of the Garter on the Archduke Ferdinand and while he was at Nürnberg his portrait was drawn by Dürer.[1] He steered his way skilfully through the troublous years of Henry VIII's reign, despite the fact that he was the father-in-law of Anne Boleyn's brother. It was to the king that he dedicated his version of the first forty-six chapters of Boccaccio's work, and, as the prologue shows, it was meant as a New Year's gift. How warily a person of such eminence had to tread may be gathered from a change in the wording of a short passage in the life of Sappho. In his version it runs:

and hyr name sett emongste the moste renomyde poetes, whiche surely is more laude to hyre then the diademe to sum kynges, or the bysshopps myters, or the conquerours lawrell braunches.[2]

The alteration lies in the words 'sum kynges', for Boccaccio had spoken of kings in general, without any qualification. The modification was clearly meant to avoid any possible cause of offence to the 'imperiall dignyte' of Henry VIII.

---

[1] Cf. *M.L.R.*, 1945, xl, p. 129. H. G. Wright, 'Sir Henry Parker, Lord Morley, and Albert Dürer'.

[2] Cf. *Forty-six Lives translated from Boccaccio's 'De Claris Mulieribus' by Henry Parker, Lord Morley*, ed. H. G. Wright, London, 1943. E.E.T.S. Orig. series 214, p. 155.

Morley was well informed not only about the classics but also about the work of Dante, Petrarch and 'John Bocas of Certaldo'. He was acquainted with Boccaccio's sonnet on Dante[1] and was aware who wrote the *Decameron, De genealogia deorum, De casibus* and *De claris mulieribus*. In presenting the forty-six lives from the last of these to the king, Morley had in mind his humanistic leanings and likewise 'the right renomyde and most honorable ladyes' of his court. He expressed the hope 'that it shulde be well acceptyde to theym to se and reede the meruelouse vertue of theyr oune sexe, to the laude perpetuall of theym'. However, recalling that among Boccaccio's famous women some deserved notoriety rather than praise, he hastened to add:

albeit, as Bocas wrytethe in hys proheme, he menglyssheth sum not verey chaste emongste the goode, yet hys honeste excuse declarethe that he dyd it to a goode entent, that all ladyes and gentlewomen, seynge the glorye of the goode, may be steryde to folowe theym, and seynge the vyce of sum, to flee theym.[2]

The translation, which is probably based on the Latin text of the edition printed at Louvain in 1487 by Egidius van der Heerstraten, is reasonably accurate and conveyed to the illustrious circle of Henry VIII and his court a good idea of the more important figures in *De claris mulieribus*, even if the style flowed less smoothly than that of Boccaccio.

It is possible that the conception of Chaucer's poem *The Legend of Good Women* (ca. 1385) was suggested by Boccaccio, though it can hardly be proved. On the other hand, in *The Siege of Thebes*, which is supposed to be related to the Canterbury pilgrims on their homeward journey, Lydgate makes specific reference to *De claris mulieribus* as one of the authorities for the life of Ipsiphyle:

> Lok on the book that Iohn Bochas made
> Whilom of women with rethorikes glade;
> And directe be ful souereyn style
> To fayre Iane the queene of Cecile.[3]
>
> (3201–4)

In the sixteenth century it was not forgotten, and Sir Thomas Hoby thought it worth his while to buy Giuseppe Betussi's Italian version

---

[1] 'Dante Alighieri son, Minerva oscura.' Vide post, p. 363.

[2] *Forty-six Lives, etc.*, p. 3.

[3] Later (3506–16) he declares that Ipsiphyle was forgiven by her husband, 'Thogh Iohn Bochas þe contrarie telle'. Lydgate was wrong in saying that Boccaccio dedicated his work to Johanna, queen of Sicily. This was his original intention, but in the end he dedicated it to the Countess degli Acciaiuoli, as is shown by the prefixed epistle. On the other hand, the last chapter deals with Queen Johanna, and in his conclusion Boccaccio alludes to this 'tam clara regina'. Lydgate's error is repeated by Lord Morley (cf. *Forty-six Lives*, p. 3 and Addenda, p. 191).

D

when he was at Venice in 1554.[1] Spenser was also familiar with *De
claris mulieribus* and used it for his *Faerie Queene*. There is reason for
saying that the relationship of Artegall to Radigund is considerably
affected by that of Hercules to Iole,[2] and it is possible that the gloss of
'E.K.' on Flora in the *Faerie Queene* as on Chloris in the *Shepheardes
Calender* harks back to the same source.[3] Without doubt the tale of
Camiola in Painter's *Palace of Pleasure*[4] was derived from *De claris
mulieribus*. He inserted it between tales of revenge and cruelty to
provide a contrasting example of a woman in whom 'the vertue of
Liberality glistered lyke the morning Starre after the Night hath cast
of his darke and Cloudy Mantell', and he introduced an allusion to
Boccaccio (and perhaps to himself!) when he made Camiola assert:
'The renoumed wryters of eche coũtrey will place me amõgs the ranke
of yᵉ noblest dames'. In its turn Massinger's play, *The Maid of Honour*
(1632), was inspired by Painter.[5] But the original work was still read

[1] The copy is in my possession. It is the Venice edition of 1547, the first having
appeared there in 1545. On the title-page are Hoby's signature and the motto 'Tendit
in ardua virtus'.

[2] Cf. R. Tuve, 'Spenser's Reading: The *De Claris Mulieribus*', *S.P.*, 1936, xxxiii,
pp. 150–9. The confusion of Iole with Omphale as the cause of Hercules' degradation
was pointed out by A. E. Sawtelle, *The Sources of Spenser's Classical Mythology*, New
York, 1896, p. 63. W. P. Mustard claimed that it reached Spenser through Tasso
(cf. *M.L.N.*, 1905, xx, p. 127). According to H. G. Lotspeich, however, (*Classical
Mythology in the Poetry of Edmund Spenser*, Princeton, 1932, pp. 72–3) the nearest
parallel to Spenser is to be found in Boccaccio's *De genealogia deorum*. D. Bush,
Mythology and the Renaissance Tradition, Minneapolis, 1932, p. 91, indicates the
possibility of a borrowing either through Tasso or Boccaccio.

[3] R. Tuve, loc. cit., pp. 161–2.

[4] ii, no. 32. Cf. Marcus Landau in *Zeitschrift für vergleichende Litteraturgeschichte*,
ed. Max Koch, neue Folge, Berlin, 1893, vi, p. 414. The medium through which it
reached Painter was the French version of *De claris mulieribus* printed at Lyons in
1551, as has been proved by Robert Hamilton who gave me this information.

[5] Quite independently of Painter, however, Massinger at one point sketches an
English background. In Act I, Sc. 1, Bertoldo says to his natural brother, Roberto,
king of Sicily, who is trying to dissuade him from an expedition against the duchess
of Sienna:

> if examples
> May move you more than arguments, looke on *England*,
> The Empresse of the European Isles,
> And unto whom alone ours yeelds precedence,
> When did she flourish so, as when she was
> The Mistresse of the Ocean. Her navies
> Putting a girdle round about the world,
> When the *Iberian* quak'd, her worthies nam'd;
> And the faire flowre Deluce grew pale, set by
> The red Rose and the white.

The allusion to the defeat of the Spanish Armada in this passage is an obvious
anachronism. Even more notable is the intrusion of Shakespeare into a theme from
Boccaccio, when Roberto uses Puck's words to Oberon (*A Midsummer Night's Dream*,
II, i, 175). In a general way the anomaly is recorded by A. Ott, *Die italienische Novelle
im englischen Drama von* 1600 *bis zur Restauration*, Zurich, 1904, pp. 48–9.

at the beginning of the seventeenth century, as is proved by Thomas Heywood's reference to it as one of his authorities for Pope Joan in his *Gunaikeion* (1624).[1]

However, of more general importance than these individual borrowings is the contribution, direct and indirect, that *De claris mulieribus* made to the controversy that raged over the merits and demerits of women. In Italy, where women of the upper classes at the time of the Renaissance were on a footing of equality with men and received the same instruction as men and were consequently well versed in classical subjects,[2] Boccaccio's treatise had many admirers and imitators,[3] even though others found an abundance of material for condemning the weakness of the opposite sex.[4] From Italy the debate spread to Spain, France, Germany and ultimately to England. It was perhaps a sign of the times when *The boke of the Cyte of Ladyes*, a translation of a work by Cristine de Pisan which owed its inspiration to *De claris mulieribus*, appeared in 1521. Beyond any question was the interest shown in the *De nobilitate et præcellentia foeminei sexus declamatio* by Henricus Cornelius Agrippa who took a leading part in the dispute. It was translated repeatedly into Italian, and there were several English versions.[5] One of the Italian translations was that of Lodovico Domenichi, *La nobiltà delle donne*, which was used by William Bercher for *The Nobility of Women*, 1559.[6] Thus in this roundabout way *De claris mulieribus* provided material for those who wished to eulogise women. However, it was not forgotten that in his *Corbaccio* he had attacked the opposite sex ferociously, and Domenichi mentions him among the anti-feminists. Bercher does not give his name, but to any one familiar with the controversy Boccaccio would surely occur on reading 'whatsoever they be that slander wymen they be rewarded at one tyme or at another and of them that knowe what reason is are not to be harde'.[7] Bercher might say what he would, but the author of *The Scole House of Women* (1560) knew full well that Boccaccio had

---

[1] p. 376.

[2] Jacob Burckhardt, *Die Cultur der Renaissance in Italien*, Basle, 1860, pp. 391–2.

[3] For an account of its influence in Italy, France, Spain and Germany see L. Torretta in *Giornale storico della letteratura italiana*, 1902, xl, pp. 35–65.

[4] Cf. Utley, op. cit., pp. 67–74; A. Farinelli, loc. cit., pp. 373–87; R. Warwick Bond in the introduction to his edition of W. Bercher's *The Nobility of Women*, 1559; in Germany the *Clarissimarum feminarum laudatio* by A. von Eyb drew on Italian sources, among them probably Boccaccio, and this work was translated into German by Nicolaus von Wyle.

[5] D. Clapam, *A Treatise of the Nobilitie of Woman Kynde*, 1542; H[ugh] C[rompton], *The Glory of Women; or a looking-Glasse for ladies*, 1652; H[enry] C[are], *Female Pre-eminence; or the Dignity and excellency of that sex, above the male*, 1670, and E. Fleetwood, *The Glory of Women*, 1652.

[6] Ed. R. Warwick Bond, Roxburghe Club, 1904.

[7] Op. cit., p. 103. Cf. p. 173, note in the same work.

spoken with two voices on the subject of women, and supported his own satire by an appeal to 'Bochas'.[1] The author of a ballad written about the same time,[2] which scarifies the alleged weaknesses of women, also cites Boccaccio, along with Guido delle Colonne, as a witness:

> In Bocas an Guydo I rede and fynde,
> Thatt wemen of verrey nature and kynde
> Be subtyll and unstedfaste of mynde;
> But I will say nothinge.

These carping critics, however, did not prevent Thomas Salter in 1574 from including *De claris mulieribus* in a list of works suitable for reading by women. He recommended that they should turn to

the holie Scripture, or other good bookes, as the bookes of *Plutarche*, made of such renowmed and vertuous women as liued in tyme paste, and those of *Boccas* tendyng to the same sence.[3]

In one way or another, therefore, *De claris mulieribus*, like *De casibus* was brought into close relationship with the life and thought of the English reader.

3. *De genealogia deorum*

As a handbook of mythology the third of Boccaccio's important Latin works was invaluable for scholars and writers. One sign of this is the publication in the fifteenth century of five editions of the Latin text in Italy and one in Germany, some of them with *De montibus* attached.[4] It was also well known in England, though not translated as in France[5] and in the sixteenth century in Italy.[6] Humphrey, duke of Gloucester, had a copy,[7] and there was one in the Royal Library of Scotland in 1578.[8] Lydgate alludes to it and borrows from it in *The Fall of Princes*[9] and *The Siege of Thebes*.[10] One passage in the second of

---

[1] Fol. D, iiia:

> ye shall fynde, many a reason
> The pryde of women, to deface
> For theyr mislyuyng.

[2] Cf. H. E. Rollins's *Analytical Index*, S.P., 1924, xxi, no. 1207. He identifies this poem with the ballad 'But I wyll say nothinge', entered to Thomas Colwell in 1564–5. The text of the poem is given in *Songs and Ballads, with other short Poems, chiefly of the reign of Philip and Mary*, ed. T. Wright, London, 1860, pp. 163–5.

[3] In *A Mirrhor made for all Mothers, Matrones, and Maidens, intituled the Mirrhor of Modestie*, quoted by L. B. Wright, *Middle-Class Culture in Elizabethan England*, Chapel Hill, 1935, p. 106.

[4] Cf. *Gesamtkatalog*, iv, items 4475 to 4480.

[5] Printed in 1498 and again in 1531.   [6] By Giuseppe Betussi, Venice, 1547.

[7] Vide ante, p. 3.   [8] Cf. Dibdin, iii, p. 246.

[9] Cf. E. Koeppel, *Laurents de Premierfait und John Lydgates Bearbeitung von Boccaccios 'De casibus Virorum Illustrium'*, Munich, 1885, pp. 59–60.

[10] Cf. the edition of A. Erdmann and E. Ekwall, London, 1911–30, ii, pp. 100, 102, 105–6, 108–9, 110, 123–4, 127, 128 and 132.

these works is of exceptional interest. It occurs in the account of the death of Lycurgus, king of Thrace. Having reported that because he mingled water with his wine, Bacchus broke his limbs and drowned him in the sea, Lydgate goes on:

> But the trouth ʒif ʒe lyst verryfie,
> Rede of goddes the Genologye,
> Lynealy her kynrede be degrees,
> I-braunched out vpon twelue trees,
> Mad by Bochas de certaldo called,
> Among Poetys in ytaille stalled,
> Next Fraunceys Petrak swyng in certeyn.

(3537–43)

Caxton also had recourse to *De genealogia deorum* for his *Recuyell of the Historyes of Troye* in 1475[1] and for his *Historie of Jason* in 1477.[2] Evidently he regarded Boccaccio's statements as authoritative and relied on them to amplify his information. This reputation was maintained in the sixteenth century, and it may be taken for granted that many English teachers followed the advice of Erasmus in *De Ratione Studii* to learn from *De genealogia deorum*.[3] Its high standing may also be seen from Sir Thomas Hoby's purchase of Betussi's Italian translation when he was at Venice in 1554.[4] The learned 'E.K.' had recourse to it when commenting on *The Shepheardes Calender* in 1579,[5] and there may be traces of it in the *Faerie Queene*, Greene's *Frier Bacon and Frier Bongay*, the anonymous *Selimus*, Jonson's *Alchemist* and Richard Barnfield's poems.[6] In 1624 Thomas Heywood in his *Gunaikeion* points to it as a source for the tale of Althaea and Meleager,[7] and Sir James Turner[8] still looks up to it with respect.

A figure which finds its way into English literature from *De genealogia deorum* is Demogorgon, though sometimes one has to reckon with the possibility that Lucan was the source. Occasionally he enters by a devious route. Thus Abraham Fraunce in *The Third part of the Countesse of Pembrokes Yuychurch: Entituled Amintas Dale,*[9] when speaking of 'the great and terrible God of heauen and earth,

---

[1] Cf. the edition of H. Oskar Sommer, London, 1894, pp. 3–4, 39, 50, 60, 215, 246, 271, 284, 396.
[2] Cf. *The Prologues and Epilogues of William Caxton*, ed. W. J. B. Crotch, London, 1928, pp. 34–6.
[3] Cf. T. W. Baldwin, *William Shakspere's small Latine and lesse Greeke*, Urbana, 1944, i, p. 84.
[4] In my possession. It is the Venice edition of 1553. The title-page bears Hoby's signature and the motto 'Tendit in ardua virtus'.
[5] Cf. W. P. Mustard, 'E.K.'s Classical Allusions', *M.L.N.*, 1919, xxxiv, pp. 197–8, 202.
[6] Cf. C. G. Osgood's introduction to *Boccaccio on Poetry*, Princeton, 1930, p. xliv.
[7] p. 354.
[8] Vide ante, p. 28.
[9] London, 1592.

accompanied only with Æternitie & Chaos'[1] cites Leo Hebræus[2] as his
authority and seems quite unaware of Boccaccio's work. Again Samuel
Rowlands[3] refers to 'Leo Hebreus', though as the phrasing shows, he
is merely repeating what Fraunce had said. At first sight Ben Jonson
in *The Alchemist*[4] appears to know more about 'Boccace' as the ultimate source of this information, but modern enquiries have traced
his knowledge of Demogorgon to Robert Vallensis who in his turn does
signal back to 'Boccatius'.[5]

An earlier play[6] that introduces the kindred theme of magic is
Greene's *Frier Bacon and Frier Bongay*, in which Bacon declares that
he could have circled England with a wall of brass,

> But proud *Asmenoth* ruler of the North,
> And *Demogorgon* maister of the fates,
> Grudge that a mortall man should worke so much.[7]

The allusion is not precise enough for one to maintain with certainty
that Greene knew *De genealogia deorum*, but we can be more confident
about Spenser. No doubt he had come across the name in the first of
the *Cinque Canti* ascribed to Ariosto.[8] But Demogorgon, the wise
prince, who controls the fairies and every five years summons them to
assemble in council in a sunlit temple on a lofty mountain, has none of
the sombre background that is typical of the scenes in which he figures
in the *Faerie Queene*. How different in its suggestion is the picture of

> the bottome of the deepe *Abysse*,
> Where *Demogorgon* in dull darknesse pent,
> Farre from the view of Gods and heauens blis,
> The hideous *Chaos* keepes.[9]

The linking of Demogorgon with the three 'fatall Sisters' in the neighbouring lines is in keeping with the account in *De genealogia deorum*.[10]
That is also true of his association with Night, when Duessa goes to

[1] Fol. 4a.

[2] Ibid. Leo Hebræus or Leone Ebreo was born about 1460 at Lisbon and died in
Italy some sixty years later. His account of Demogorgon, which appears in the second
of his *Dialoghi d'Amore*, is based on that of Boccaccio, but without acknowledgement.

[3] *Martin Mark-All, Beadle of Bridewell; His defence and Answere to the Belman of
London*, London, 1610. See p. 30 in the Hunterian Club reprint of 1874.

[4] Acted in 1610. Cf. Act II, Sc. i.

[5] Cf. *Ben Jonson*, ed. C. H. Herford, Percy and Evelyn Simpson, Oxford, 1925–52,
x, p. 72.

[6] Chambers, iii, pp. 328–9, dates it about 1589.   [7] Act IV, Sc. i.

[8] The description of the contrast between 'Duessa sunny bright' and 'griesly
Night' (*F.Q.* Bk. I, Canto v, St. 21) may well be influenced by that between Alcina
and Invidia (I, 42). So too the account of Ate, Duessa's companion, and her abode
resembles that of the Albergo dell'Invidia (Bk. I, Sts. 38 ff.).

[9] *F.Q.* Bk. IV, Canto ii, St. 47.

[10] H. G. Lotspeich, op. cit., pp. 58–9. Cf. also *F.Q.*, iv, p. 182.

Hell in order to cure Sansfoy and, addressing Night, recalls that she
was begotten 'in Daemogorgons hall' and saw 'the secrets of the world
vnmade'.[1] The very spelling of the name in this passage indicates that
Spenser had in mind Boccaccio's etymology which related it to δαίμων.[2]
The third occasion on which the poet mentions Demogorgon is in
connexion with Archimago:

> He to his study goes, and there amiddes
> His Magick bookes and artes of sundry kindes,
> He seekes out mighty charmes, to trouble sleepy mindes.

> Then choosing out few wordes most horrible,
> (Let none them read) thereof did verses frame,
> With which and other spelles like terrible,
> He bad awake blacke Plutoes griesly Dame,
> And cursed heauen, and spake reprochfull shame
> Of highest God, the Lord of life and light;
> A bold bad man, that dar'd to call by name
> Great *Gorgon*, Prince of darknesse and dead night,
> At which *Cocytus* quakes, and *Styx* is put to flight.[3]

Here the poet identifies 'Demogorgon' with 'Gorgon', as Boccaccio,
following Lucan had done.[4] Taken in conjunction with the passages
already quoted, this heightens the probability that Spenser had *De
genealogia deorum* before him.

About the time when the lines about Archimago were published,[5]
Marlowe's *Dr. Faustus* was first performed.[6] Here too the magician,
deeply versed in books, sets about his conjuration as night approaches.
He too is 'a bold bad man' who rejects the Holy Trinity,[7] utters dread
incantations and, along with the infernal powers, invokes Demogorgon. Neither in the poem nor the play does Demogorgon arise, but
in response to the spell 'Legions of Sprights' are summoned from
'deepe darknesse dred' in the one, and in the other, Mephistophilis.

Shortly after *Dr. Faustus* the anonymous *Selimus* appeared.[8] It
contains a reference to 'Black *Demogorgon*, grandfather of night', but
when Baiazet proceeds to speak of his 'firie hall' and his control over
'all the damned monsters of black hell',[9] the dramatist appears to
wander from Boccaccio's conception. There is a similar vagueness,

[1] *F.Q.* Bk. I, Canto v, St. 22.
[2] Cf. H. G. Lotspeich, *F.Q.*, i, pp. 191–2.   [3] *F.Q.* Bk. I, Canto i, Sts. 36–7.
[4] Cf. H. G. Lotspeich, *F.Q.*, i, p. 191.   [5] 1590.
[6] According to Chambers, iii, p. 423, and J. Bakeless, *The Tragicall History of
Christopher Marlowe*, 1942, i, 274–7, in 1588–9. On the other hand, F. S. Boas,
in his edition of the play, London, 1932, p. 11, favours the date 1592; W. W. Greg,
Marlowe's 'Doctor Faustus', 1604–1616, 1950, pp. 3–10, fixes it during the twelve
months following the spring of 1592.
[7] Act I, Sc. iii.   [8] 1594.
[9] Cf. *Selimus*, ed. W. Bang and W. W. Greg, Malone Society, 1908.

when Richard Barnfield in his *Cassandra*[1] lets Phoebus set forth a claim

> That he from *Demogorgon* was descended:
> Father of th'Earth, of Gods and men commended.[2]

Sir Walter Raleigh speaks only in general terms when in his *Historie of the World*, having referred to the chaos that existed before the creation, he declares that from 'this lump of imperfect Matter had the ancient Poets their inuention of *Demogorgon*'.[3] So too, when Momus in Thomas Carew's masque, *Coelum Britannicum*,[4] in a jocular fashion traces his descent as in a Welsh genealogy: 'My name is Momus-ap-Somnus-ap-Erebus-ap-Chaos-ap-Demogorgon-ap-Eternity', we cannot be sure that he had read Boccaccio. But at least his courtly audience at Whitehall must have been familiar with the general tradition. In the same way Milton assumes this knowledge on the part of the reader of *Paradise Lost*,[5] when he relates how Satan, venturing from Hell towards the World, plunges into the nethermost Abyss and there beholds Chaos and Night, and standing by them

> Orcus and Ades, and the dreaded name
> Of Demogorgon.

In detail there may be some poetic manipulation here, but the whole passage, including the description of strife and discord, indicates that, whatever the immediate source of Milton's knowledge, he was most likely inspired by *De genealogia deorum*. By contrast, Dryden's connexion with Boccaccio in the sphere of mythology is of the most tenuous kind. He evidently associated Demogorgon with night, as may be seen from his adaptation of *The Flower and the Leaf*, where the fairies normally appear only under cover of nocturnal darkness:

> when the moon arises, none are found;
> For cruel Demogorgon walks the round,
> And if he finds a fairy lag in light,
> He drives the wretch before, and lashes into night.
>
> (492–5)

If the awe-inspiring Demogorgon is here abased to the petty task-master of the fairy world, in Shelley's *Prometheus Unbound* he is assigned a part worthy of, though different from that which Boccaccio gave him. The poet, with his innate capacity for myth-making, has grafted the story of Demogorgon on to that of Prometheus and Jupiter. Demogorgon is 'a tremendous gloom', and the mighty portal to his realm is 'like a volcano's meteor-breathing chasm'. To reach his

---

[1] Printed in 1595, in *Cynthia. With certaine Sonnets, and the Legend of Cassandra.*
[2] Cf. Montague Summers' edition of *The Poems*, London, n.d., p. 72.
[3] Book i, Ch. i, Section 5.   [4] Acted 1634.   [5] Cf. ii, 959–67.

cave the way goes down 'through the gray, void abysm', and there a veiled form sits on an ebony throne. When the veil falls, darkness radiates from the shapeless figure. This tallies in a general way with the conception of *De genealogia deorum*. On the other hand, in Shelley's version Demogorgon is the child of Jupiter who holds universal sway, until at the moment of his overthrow the 'awful shape' of Demogorgon appears before his throne and in reply to the tyrant's question, 'What are thou?' says:

> Eternity. Demand no direr name.
> Descend, and follow me down the abyss.
>   . . . we must dwell together
> Henceforth in darkness.

(III. i. 52–5)

Here are audible echoes of the Boccaccian tradition combined with something strange, but elsewhere Shelley's imagination creates an entirely new role for Demogorgon as in the scene[1] where in oracular language, sometimes clear, sometimes cryptic, he replies to Asia's enquiries about the origin of the world and of good and evil. It is he, finally, who reveals that only eternal love can triumph over fate and time, chance and change. And after the triumph of love and the destruction of tyranny, to which these words are a prelude, it is left to Demogorgon in the closing lines of the drama to announce to man and the whole universe the victory of gentleness, virtue, wisdom and endurance. Thus Shelley develops Demogorgon into one who knows not merely the secrets of the world before its creation, but also the supreme mystery of the future, and the grim figure of the earlier myth becomes the mouthpiece of the poet's own visionary philosophy. Whether the channel through which Shelley became familiar with Demogorgon was the *Faerie Queene* or *Paradise Lost*, or whether like some of his contemporaries,[2] he had read Betussi's translation, nowhere is he treated with greater originality than in *Prometheus Unbound*.

It could hardly be expected that a work devoted primarily to the accumulation of knowledge about the gods of classical antiquity would exercise a perceptible influence on critical theory in England. However, it has been recognised what an important part the *De genealogia deorum* played in stimulating fifteenth-century writers to abandon the mediæval conception of poetry as rhetoric skilfully turned into verse.[3] Boccaccio's discussion of poetry in Books xiv and xv brought

---

[1] Act ii, Sc. 4.   [2] Vide post, pp. 337, 361.

[3] Cf. *Boccaccio on Poetry : Being the Preface and the Fourteenth and Fifteenth Books of Boccaccio's 'Genealogia Deorum Gentilium'*, ed. C. G. Osgood, Princeton, 1930. See also J. W. H. Atkins, *English Literary Criticism, Medieval Phase*, Cambridge, 1943, pp. 171–5.

about this change when he asserted that truth lay hidden beneath the
poet's allegory. The effect of this view is seen in Stephen Hawes'
Passetyme of Pleasure, when he declares in his dedication to Henry
VII:

> vnder a colour a truthe maye arise
> As was the guyse in olde antyquyte
> Of the poetes olde a tale to surmyse
> To cloke the trouth.[1]

He reiterates this statement in Chapter IX and denounces the blind-
ness of the ignorant who are unable to appreciate the underlying
meaning of the poetry:

> But rude people opprest with blyndnes
> Agaynst your fables wyll often solysgyse
> Suche is theyr mynde suche is theyr folysshnes
> For they byleue in no maner of wyse
> That vnder a colour a trouthe may aryse.[2]

But these lines[3] are an obvious rendering of a passage in Chapter XIV
of *De genealogia deorum*.[4]

One of the clearest formulations of Boccaccio's attitude occurs when,
after speaking of Æneas' journey to see his father in Hades, he asks
how anyone can believe that Virgil wrote these lines without a meaning hidden beneath the veil of myth.[5] His words are echoed by Gavin
Douglas in 1553 in his translation of the *Æneid*. In its sixth book, he
maintains, Virgil showed himself to be a high philosopher,

> And, wnder the cluddes of dirk poetry
> Hid lyis thair mony notable history.
> For so the poetis be ther crafty curis,
> In similitudis, and vnder quent figuris,
> The suthfast mater to hyde and to constrene . . .[6]

As his authority Douglas cites 'Ihone bochas, in the genologie of
goddis'.

It is unusual to find a reference so specific as this, but it is not
unreasonable to assume that *De genealogia deorum* continued throughout the sixteenth century to assert the independence of the poet's
function and his significance as an interpreter of truth. Though other
similar compilations appeared, Betussi's Italian translation of Boccaccio's work ran to ten editions in the hundred years that followed its

---

[1] Cf. W. E. Mead's edition, London, 1928, ll. 50–3.
[2] Ibid., ll. 792–6.   [3] Continuing to l. 805.
[4] Cf. C. W. Lemmi, 'The influence of Boccaccio on Hawes's *Pastime of Pleasure*',
R.E.S., v, pp. 197–8.
[5] 'sub fabuloso velamine'.
[6] Cf. *The Poetical Works of Gavin Douglas, Bishop of Dunkeld*, ed. J. Small, Edinburgh, 1874, 4 vols., ii, p. 9.

publication in 1547.[1] It is difficult to disentangle these later encyclopædias from that of Boccaccio, but there is at least one place in Sidney's
Apologye for Poetrye, where a prompting from *De genealogia deorum*
appears almost certain,[2] and if his familiarity is thus established, it
would follow that some of his arguments in favour of poetry are ultimately derived from this source. In Bacon's *De sapientia veterum* the
task of analysing his interpretations of the classic deities is equally
complex, but as in Sidney's *Apologye* there is good reason to believe
that the author had recourse to Boccaccio.[3]

Once the habit of finding an allegory everywhere has been acquired,
it may lead to strange conclusions in the hands of any one gifted with
a lively imagination. Inspired by a highly controversial spirit, Gabriele
Rossetti[4] built up an amazing edifice of anti-papal teaching that he
found covered beneath the veil in Boccaccio's writings. This was the
last and the most peculiar legacy of *De genealogia deorum*.[5]

[1] Cf. C. W. Lemmi, *The Classic Deities in Bacon*, Baltimore and London, 1933, p. 1.
[2] *Elizabethan Critical Essays*, ed. Gregory Smith, i, pp. lxxviii–lxxix, 206 and 406,
note.
[3] Cf. C. W. Lemmi, op. cit.   [4] Vide post, pp. 361–2.
[5] It has been claimed by W. H. Schofield that a minor work of Boccaccio, his eclogue
'Olympia', influenced *Pearl*. His view was not accepted by I. Gollancz (cf. his ed. of
Boccaccio's Olympia, London, 1913, pp. 49–50) or E. V. Gordon (cf. his ed. of *Pearl*,
Oxford, 1953, p. xxxv).

II

THE MINOR ITALIAN WORKS

1. The *Corbaccio*, *Ameto*, and *Amorosa Visione*

THOUGH *De genealogia deorum* was not translated into English, it left its mark on English literature in various directions. The same can hardly be said of the *Corbaccio*. Humphrey, duke of Gloucester, possessed a Latin version made for him by Antonio Beccaria,[1] but the work seems to have been little known, except in a general way as a manifestation of the anti-feminist tradition. The *Ameto* and the *Amorosa Visione* also remained untranslated as they did in France. It has been suggested that Chaucer was acquainted with the former, but the evidence is not convincing.[2] Perhaps it was known to 'E.K.' who in the epistle to Spenser's *Shepheardes Calender* recalls how many poets, including Boccaccio, wrote pastorals before they had attained their full power. However, as the *Ameto* is not mentioned by name, there is an element of doubt, even if Spenser's commentator was aware of Boccaccio's importance for the Renaissance pastoral.[3] Still more dubious is the attempt to associate Chaucer with the *Amorosa Visione*,[4] whereas its connexion with Hawes' *Passetyme of Pleasure* is more firmly established.[5]

2. The *Teseida*

The *Teseida*, which glanced back to the ancient world and related a love-story rooted in the age of chivalry, was calculated to appeal strongly to the mediæval reader or listener. In Spain it was popular though not translated,[6] and in France there were three versions in the fifteenth and sixteenth centuries.[7] It caught Chaucer's eye and left its

---

[1] Cf. W. F. Schirmer, *Der englische Frühhumanismus*, Leipzig, 1931, p. 44, and Weiss, pp. 45–6. Beccaria's stay in England lasted from 1438–9 to 1445–6, as is shown by Weiss, *Giornale Storico della letteratura italiana*, 1937, cx, pp. 344–6.

[2] Cummings, pp. 33–42.

[3] The *Ameto* was discussed by J. C. Walker, *An historical and critical essay on the revival of the drama in Italy* (1805). Cf. Marshall, p. 346.

[4] Cummings, pp. 13–32.

[5] C. W. Lemmi, 'The Influence of Boccaccio on Hawes's *Pastime of Pleasure*', *R.E.S.*, 1929, v, pp. 195–6.

[6] *Archiv*, cxvii, pp. 114–15, and Farinelli, i, pp. 246–7.

[7] Hauvette [1909], pp. 50–67.

stamp on his *House of Fame, Anelida and Arcite* and the *Parlement of Foules*. However, it is in his *Knight's Tale* that the effect of the *Teseida* is most fully seen.[1] The chief problem that confronted him was to fit the story into the scheme of the *Canterbury Tales*. The *Teseida* was long and leisurely in its movement, and obviously a faithful adaptation would have made the *Knight's Tale* unduly prominent. Even as it stands, this tale takes up twice as much space as the narratives of the Clerk, The Man of Law, the Merchant and the Wife of Bath, which are the only ones to attain anything like the same proportions. Yet Chaucer had reduced the *Teseida* from nearly ten thousand lines to less than a quarter of its original length. To achieve this feat of condensation much was omitted. Classical lore which Boccaccio, in his enthusiasm for the ancient world, had introduced so freely, is sacrificed. The bare minimum is told of Teseo's campaign against Thebes. Various processions, visits to temples and pagan rites are discarded. The ceremony of Palemone's marriage to Emilia offered another opportunity for ruthless excision. So did the account of the festivals and tournaments organised by Palemone and Arcita while awaiting the arrival of their supporters. The sixth book of the *Teseida* enumerated all who were invited to come and even recorded those who were unable to do so. On other occasions in the next two books similar lists are given, but, apart from the chief protagonists, Chaucer mentions only Emetreus and Ligurge. The seventh book is not only condensed but also recast. After Boccaccio's Teseo had given instructions for the combat, there are repeated delays. By contrast, when Theseus has laid down the conditions, the company rides to the lists, the combatants enter, the gates are shut, the trumpets sound, and at once the fight begins. After the accident to Arcita the compression of events is equally notable;[2] similarly, his death is related without any of the numerous details in the original.

At an earlier stage Chaucer dispensed with the wanderings of Arcita in exile and simplified the action in other respects. His version knows nothing of the plan which enabled Palemone to escape by disguising himself, at the suggestion of his servant Panfilo, in the clothes of the physician Alimeto, or of his stay at an inn where he is provided with a horse and armour. Again, after the duel in the wood Chaucer makes the rivals set out at once for Thebes, instead of riding back to Athens where they are cared for and treated with honour in the palace, and, their possessions restored, lead a life which for its splendour and generosity wins the sympathy of the Athenians. As a result of all these changes the *Knight's Tale* has fewer personages than

[1] Cf. R. A. Pratt, 'Chaucer's Use of the *Teseida*', *P.M.L.A.*, 1947, lxii. pp. 598–621.
[2] Book ix, stanzas 13–49, i.e. 296 lines, are reduced to six lines.

the *Teseida*. Panfilo and Alimento become anonymous; Ischion, the great physician whom Teseo summoned to examine Arcita, vanishes, and Acate, the intended husband of Emilia whose premature death left the field open for Arcita, fails to emerge.

The characters that do remain are not unaffected. Ippolita, who in the *Teseida* had shown herself a dutiful and submissive queen but at the tournament had revealed some of the martial ardour of an Amazon, becomes a mere lay-figure. Teseo also undergoes some modification. Boccaccio had portrayed him as a great warrior who defeated the Amazons and the tyrant Creon and at the tournament watched the combatants with the eye of an expert. At the same time there is a gentler strain in Teseo. So engrossed does he become in his love for Ippolita that he tarries in Scythia until Peritoo reproaches him for deferring his return to Athens where such glorious tasks await him. In striking contrast to the callousness of Creon towards his enemies, Teseo sees to it that in accordance with custom the tyrant is cremated and that his ashes are placed in a temple at Thebes. Moreover, he gives orders that none of the holy places are to be violated by his plundering followers. He is the most humane of victors. The dead are buried, and the battlefield is searched, so that all the wounded may receive medical care. He does debate within himself whether Palemone and Arcita ought not to be put to death, but he has their wounds seen to as if they had been his own men, and, though they are heavily guarded, they are lodged in a room in the palace, with servants to wait on their pleasure. When Peritoo has obtained the release of Arcita, Teseo bestows gifts upon him—an action as thoughtful as it was generous, since Arcita had lost everything. Again the scene in the wood reveals the innate magnanimity of Teseo. On discovering the lovers Teseo courteously enquires who they are, and then, conquering his wrath, with great politeness thanks them for their explanation of how they came to love the same woman and who she is. His tolerant attitude towards them is not incredible, since he has but recently known an infatuation himself. His kindly treatment of them at Athens, his loving care for the wounded Arcita and his consideration for the defeated combatants complete the portrait of a singularly attractive personality.

Chaucer's Theseus has fewer shades in his character. It is above all the stern ruler who is depicted, and no opportunity is lost of exalting his dignity. The Theban women fall prone before him, and those who petition him to spare Palamon and Arcite kneel in his presence. Again before the combat his importance is enhanced. In Boccaccio he joins his nobles in the palace and on enquiring whether the combatants have arrived, is informed

No, signor mio, ma e'verranno tosto.[1]

(*O.V.* vii, st. 100, l. 8)

Chaucer is careful to avoid any such casual treatment, and his Theseus is not kept waiting.[2]

> Duk Theseus was at a window set,
> Arrayed right as he were a god in trone.

(A. 2528–9)

Instead of Theseus announcing the conditions of the combat himself, a herald does so with due ceremony:

> An heraud on a scaffold made an ho,
> Til al the noyse of the peple was y-do
> And whan he saugh the peple of noyse al stille,
> Tho showed he the mighty dukes wille.

(A. 2533–5)

As a general Theseus is far more ruthless towards Thebes and its inhabitants. The city is demolished, and the imprisonment of Palamon and Arcite is rigorous. Nothing is said of attendants, and the grimness of the prison is emphasised:

> The grete tour, that was so thikke and strong,
> Which of the castel was the chief dongeoun.

(A. 1056–7)

In Boccaccio the prisoners' chamber had a window which Arcita, in spite of his fetters, was able to open. On the other hand, Palamon and Arcite lie in darkness[3] and must obtain the consent of the gaoler before they can leave the dungeon and go to an upper chamber, whence they can see the garden. Even then, it is through thick and square iron bars. When Arcite is released, only the conditions imposing the death-penalty if he violates them, are related. This impression of severity is confirmed by the episode in the wood. Theseus at once spurs his horse forward and stops the fight. On learning who the combatants are, he forthwith declares that they must die. And though he afterwards relents, it must be admitted that his tolerant attitude towards the lovers is much less comprehensible than in the *Teseida*.

If Theseus has fewer facets to his character than his counterpart, that is still truer of Emelye. In Boccaccio she is given considerable prominence. In particular, he traces the gradual awakening of her

---

[1] References for quotations from the *Teseida*, which is contained in vol. ix of the *Opere volgari*, are by book, stanza, and line.

[2] All quotations from the *Knight's Tale* are taken from Skeat.

[3] This may be deduced from the reference to the dungeon and also from the later account of Palamon's captivity in A. 1451–2:

> In derknesse and horrible and strong prisoun
> This seven yeer hath seten Palamoun.

love for Arcita. At the beginning of the poem she is a mere child, and the fact that she is being watched from the window does nothing but flatter her vanity. As she catches sight of Arcita riding away into exile, she feels compassion. When he returns to Athens, she is still too young to know the meaning of love, but she is proud to find that she alone can penetrate his disguise and wonders what has made him run such risks. The episode in the wood again brings her to the fore. It is she who first chances upon the combatants and through some of her attendants calls Teseo to witness the spectacle. After the disclosure of the identity of the two protagonists and the revelation that it is she whom they love, Emilia is embarrassed and at the same time feels distress at the sight of their wounds. When Teseo tells her that she will marry one of them, she blushes but remains silent. As the company returns to Athens, Emilia rides in their midst, and that is symbolical of the importance attached to her. She is mentioned by name among those who welcomed the rivals, and before the combat Arcita publicly declares his love for her, while Palemone regards her as a goddess. During the combat it is the sight of Emilia that inspires Arcita with fresh energy and determination. Her own reactions as she watches the fluctuations of the struggle are also described. It becomes clear that she is now capable of love, but she does not yet know which of the combatants to choose. However, she is intensely moved. Unlike Teseo and Ippolita she finds the battle 'Orribile . . . rea e dura', because she reflects that her beauty is the cause of so much bloodshed, on account of which so many will curse her. Then suddenly after the victory of Arcita her love turns to him.

The accident that befalls Arcita provides still more proof of her affection. Fear seizes her as she sees him fall, and she is assailed by the conviction that like all others she must taste the bitterness as well as the joy of love. Filled with grief at the sight of his face covered with dust, blood and sweat, she cannot repress her tears. Bashfully she begs him to take comfort. She assures her 'dolce sposo' that she will always be with him. The triumphal procession concentrates the eyes of all Athens upon her, and as she sits beside Arcita, gracious and pleasing, the object of universal admiration, she knows a measure of happiness. But it is short-lived. Before long, Arcita's strength begins to fail, and she is plunged into despair. It is vain for him to urge her to marry Palemone after his death. She cannot forget her 'caro sposo' and, like one frantic, she kisses him and falls prone in a swoon. A curse seems to weigh upon her, and rather than bring misery to Palemone as she has done to Arcita, she prays that Jove will remove her from this life. In spite of this passionate outburst, when Arcita is dead, she controls her emotion and with Palemone performs the last offices. At the pyre she contends with her feelings and, though she faints, struggles to her feet, only to swoon again after throwing her rings and ornaments into the fire. For a time her sorrow is extreme, and when Teseo urges her to marry Palemone, she sits mute, with bowed head, until he has to ask her whether she has heard. At first she will not let herself be persuaded but in the end yields to his arguments. It must be conceded that, in spite of her hesitation, the interval appears somewhat brief. But as if to justify the change, Boccaccio had analysed Palemone's feelings towards Emilia at some length after the overthrow of Arcita, and Palemone's unshakable devotion to her had been made clear when he refused to follow her advice to marry some other Greek beauty. In this way too Emilia gains in prominence, and at the close she is once more in the foreground amid the festivities and the wedding procession in Athens.

On the other hand, in Chaucer, Emelye plays a relatively obscure part. After the one glimpse of her in the garden she practically disappears until Arcite becomes her page, and at the scene in the wood she does nothing but join with other women in petitioning Theseus to have mercy on the two knights. Apart from her prayer to Diana she remains a mere puppet who flits past the reader for a moment at the tournament and the funeral pyre, until she is united to Palamon at the close. Chaucer makes no effort to trace the gradual growth of her love for Arcite, the one indication being given in a single line, coupled with a sceptical generalisation about women.[1] Similarly, he suppresses the important passage in which Boccaccio had defined the attitude of Emilia to Palemone and the unswerving affection of the latter. As a result of this and other omissions the acceptance of Palemone by Emilia seemed to Chaucer too sudden and therefore unconvincing. So after the combat he sent the Greek kings home, and in the *Knight's Tale* it is only after the lapse of a number of years that they reassemble and press for the marriage.[2]

Another feature that Chaucer had to sacrifice is the analysis of the heroine's varying moods. Nothing is shown of her passionate devotion, and in her grief she is an entirely conventional figure who shrieks and faints and has to be carried away. She is not a thinking being who wonders whether she does not bring disaster upon all to whom she is plighted, and so she exhibits no reluctance to marry Palamon. An angel hovering in the background, a colourless abstraction, she lacks the individuality and the humanity of Emilia.

Just as Boccaccio dwells at length on the emotions of the heroine, so

---

[1] A. 2681–2.
[2] He uses the same prolongation to explain a change of attitude in Criseyde. Vide post, pp. 95–6.

E

he elaborates those of Palemone and Arcita. In particular, he describes how the former, still captive in Athens, alternates between joy and grief, weeping and sighing over his lot, yet gathering confidence at the very thought of escape. His sorrow over his defeat is also fully depicted, while the accident to Arcita leaves him alternating between regret and hope. Still more carefully does Boccaccio note the mutations in Arcita's mind. His lamentation when he leaves Athens and, gazing sadly up towards Emilia on her balcony, rides away amid wind and rain, is not easily forgotten. It leaves behind something of the poignant desolation felt by the reader at Troilo's visit to the empty house of Griseida, and one is again reminded of Troilo's longing for his absent love when Arcita stands on the shore at Egina and exclaims, as the wind blows towards him from Athens,

> Questo fu ad Emilia molto presso.[1]
>
> (*O.V.* iv, st. 32, l. 8)

And suddenly, hearing of the untimely death of Acate, an irresistible surge of longing prompts him to defy the prohibition of Teseo against his return. Once in Athens, he is glad to be near Emilia and yet unhappy because she is unaware of his love. Hence his habit of retiring to a wood, where, lying under a pine by a stream, he is wont to sigh:

> io amo, e non son punto amato,
>
> (*O.V.* iv, st. 68, l. 2)

and with the name of Emilia on his lips falls asleep. Of all these states of mind the *Knight's Tale* has little or nothing.

Another feature that is developed more clearly in the *Teseida* is the friendship of Palemone and Arcita and its durability, in spite of all the antagonism generated by their love for Emilia. In Boccaccio this antagonism emerges but slowly. At first their friendship is unshaken. Together they watch day by day for the appearance of the heroine in the garden, and when bad weather keeps her indoors, they are united in grief. Together they sigh and weep, together they find relief by composing verses in her honour. In fact, they are fellow-sufferers rather than rivals in love. It is significant that Arcita, on his liberation by the intervention of Peritoo, should return to take leave of his friend and that he should confide to him a message for Emilia, if ever he should meet her. For his part, Palemone can hardly bear the thought of separation from Arcita.

> senza te in doglioso tormento
> Rimango, lasso, tristo ed iscontento.
>
> (*O.V.* iii, st. 77, ll. 7–8)

---

[1] Cf. *Filostrato*, book v, st. 70 and *Troilus and Criseyde*, book v, 671–2.

When Arcita is to set forth, they are so overcome that their servants have to lift them up and rebuke them for this excess of sentiment. Thereupon they kiss each other and say farewell with broken voice.

It is in the wood that they meet again, and though in the meantime Palemone has felt some jealousy of Arcita, when he chances upon his friend sleeping peacefully, he has not the heart to wake him. After the dawn-song of the birds has roused Arcita, Palemone greets him kindly; they rejoice together and relate their experiences. Not until they fall to speaking of Emilia do their tempers begin to rise. Even then each calls the other his dear friend, and it is only after a long discussion, when neither will give way, that Arcita unwillingly dons his armour and the struggle opens. In this Palemone receives a blow on the head and falls from his horse, whereupon with the utmost solicitude Arcita takes off his helmet, lays him tenderly on the grass and flowers and laves him with water. At first his efforts seem to be in vain, and Arcita laments his brave companion and recalls how reluctant he had been to fight with him. In his distress he regrets that he ever loved.

With the arrival of Teseo, their friendship is again demonstrated. In reply to the duke's enquiry, Arcita says that they are two knights who for love are testing their valour. Only when pressed does he reveal who he is. But he screens his opponent. The latter must speak for himself. Then Palemone discloses his name. So far nothing has been breathed about the lady for whom they are contending, and it is only when cornered by Teseo's interrogation that Palemone makes known the whole affair. He confesses that he has done wrong and deserves death, but he is silent about the infliction of any penalty on Arcita. Before the tournament at Athens, while awaiting the arrival of their supporters, they live in complete harmony. Their former amity is restored and whatever either wishes, is agreed to by the other. After the combat, even though he is keenly aware of the humiliation of defeat, Palemone induces his friends to walk willingly in the triumphal procession, in order to give consolation to the injured Arcita. The old friendship is nowhere more poignant than when the dying hero asks to see, hear and touch his friend and companion and declares that the one offence of which he has ever been guilty is to have taken up arms against him. In accordance with Arcita's request Palemone helps to perform the last offices for Arcita, and at his obsequies sacrifices in the fire not only arms and jewels but also his hair and beard. So fervent is his devotion that in spite of his passion for Emilia he fears that in marrying her he would wrong his dead friend, and it takes all the arguments of Teseo and the Greek kings to dispel his misgivings.

By comparison the friendship of Chaucer's heroes seems formal and superficial rather than deep and intimate. Their rivalry for the love of Emelye at once leads to a quarrel, and the violence of their temper begets a fierce hostility. The jealousy of Palamon is more volcanic than any such emotion in his Boccaccian counterpart.

> Ther-with the fyr of Ielousye up-sterte
> With-inne his brest, and hente him by the herte
> So woodly, that he lyk was to biholde
> The box-tree, or the asshen dede and colde.
>
> (A. 1299–302)

It is true that at the first encounter in the wood Arcite promises to bring food, drink and bedding to Palamon and that next day they help each other to arm

> As freendly as he were his owne brother.
>
> (A. 1652)

But this hint of friendship is less notable than the abuse with which Palamon had assailed his rival as he burst out of the bushes, and we are left with the impression that he will stick at nothing. Little surprise is felt therefore when he immediately betrays their secret to Theseus, declares that Arcite has long befooled him and, having thus incited Theseus, demands death not only for himself but for Arcite as well. Nor does the *Knight's Tale* describe any restoration of friendship or exhibit all the numerous instances of personal devotion in which the *Teseida* abounds.

However, the obscuring of the reconciliation between love and friendship is not the only effect of Chaucer's attempt at condensation on the relationship of Palemone and Arcita. The relative importance of the two figures is transformed. It seems likely that Boccaccio sympathised with Arcita as he did with Troilo. In each poem Fortune intervenes to cut short the happiness of love, and, as has already been indicated, there is an affinity between some episodes in the *Filostrato* and the *Teseida*. In any case, Arcita is more conspicuous than his rival. Significantly, it is he who first sees Emilia, and after he has been liberated, far more attention is paid to his state of mind than to that of Palemone. Before the tournament Arcita addresses Emilia and later harangues his supporters at length. Much less space is given to Palemone, and his thoughts and words are reported indirectly. Equally striking is the full account given of Arcita's exploits, whereas Palemone's achievements are found in two lines tacked on to the eulogy of his opponent. In the *Knight's Tale*, the process of abridgement undermines the dominant position which Boccaccio had bestowed on Arcita. Not only that, but Chaucer tries of set purpose to win sympathy for Palamon by extending the period of his captivity in a gloomy dungeon to no less than seven years.[1] In addition, he makes some changes which help in a positive manner to enhance the standing of Palamon. At the very beginning it is Palamon who first catches a glimpse of Emelye, and during the tournament the mode of his defeat tends to emphasise his valour in a way unknown to the *Teseida*. There, in fact, Palemone is overcome in a rather ignominious fashion. His arm is bitten by the steed of Cromis; he falls to the ground and, as soon as he has been dragged from the horse's mouth and out of the fray, Arcita disarms him. By contrast, Chaucer's Palamon is severely wounded by Emetreus, but even so strikes him from his saddle and, in spite of Palamon's condition, it takes twenty men to overpower him. Moreover, Chaucer takes good care not to submit him to the humiliation of the triumphal procession, and he transforms Teseo's tribute to the combatants as a whole into an apologia for Palamon:

> Soothly ther was no disconfiture,
> For falling nis nat but an aventure;
> Ne to be lad with fors un-to the stake
> Unyolden, and with twenty knightes take,
> O persone allone, with-outen mo,
> And haried forth by arme, foot, and to,
> And eek his stede driven forth with staves,
> With footmen, bothe yemen and eek knaves,
> It nas aretted him no vileinye,
> Ther may no man clepen it cowardye.
>
> (A. 2721–30)

Perhaps Chaucer felt that if Palamon's marriage to Emelye was to be justified, something had to be done to elevate his position. At any rate, the shifting of the balance in his favour is unquestionable.

Though many of the alterations that have been considered must be ascribed to the need for compression, Chaucer did not perform his task mechanically but left himself free to add where he wished. In some of these passages his realistic temper found vent. One of the most striking examples is the unflinching recital of the medical effects of Arcite's wounds, the symptoms and the remedies vainly applied, culminating as it does in the grim humour of the lines:

> Nature hath now no dominacioun.
> And certeinly, ther nature wol nat wirche,
> Far-wel, phisyk! go ber the man to chirche!
>
> (A. 2758–60)

Another glimpse of real life is afforded by the reference to the decoration of Athens with cloth of gold before the tournament and the picture of the crowd discussing the chances of the combatants. Boccaccio had

---

[1] Cf. p. 47.

told of the great barons debating the point, but Chaucer turns it into a vivid popular scene:

> Somme seyden thus, somme seyde it shal be so;
> Somme helden with him with the blake berd,
> Somme with the balled, somme with the thikke-herd;
> Somme sayde, he loked grim and he wolde fighte;
> He hath a sparth of twenty pound of wighte.
>
> (A. 2516–20)

The preparation for the tournament also furnishes an animated picture of contemporary life which owes very little to the *Teseida*.[1] Here are all the colour and pomp of mediæval chivalry. Knights, squires, yeomen and armourers are conjured up before our eyes; helmets, shields, lances, hauberks and coats of mail. Everywhere there is bustling activity, the clatter of hoofs, the clink of armour, the clang of hammers, and the sound of pipe, trumpet, clarion and drum.[2] Such was the scene that Chaucer had in mind when he wrote:

> Ye knowen wel, that every lusty knight,
> That loveth paramours, and hath his might,
> Were it in Engelond, or elles-where,
> They wolde, hir thankes, wilnen to be there.
> To fighte for a lady, *benedicite*!
> It were a lusty sighte for to see.
>
> (A. 2111–16)

In spite of the Greek setting, it was possibly some English tournament[3] that Chaucer recalled from his own experience when he evoked the vision of the ancient world. The same may be true of his description of Arcite making a garland of woodbine and hawthorn-leaves and the rising sun drying

> in the greves
> The silver dropes, hanging on the leves.
>
> (A. 1495–6)

Certainly, the passage which relates how Arcite, clad as a poor labourer,

---

[1] 'The fomy stedes on the golden brydel / Gnawinge' was derived from 'E spumanti li lor freni rodiensi' (*Teseida*, vii, st. 97, l. 3) and it is possible that 'Con selle ricche d'ariento e d'oro' (ibid., vii, st. 97, l. 2) suggested

> herneys
> So uncouth and so riche, and wroght so weel
> Of goldsmithrie, of browding, and of steel.

[2] Essentially such a description had the same interest for Chaucer's mediæval audience as the description of the hero's armour in *Sir Gawain and the Green Knight* or that of the Trojans in Lydgate's *Troy Book*, iii, 44 ff.

[3] It has been suggested by Johnstone Parr, 'The Date and Revision of Chaucer's *Knight's Tale*' (*P.M.L.A.*, 1945, lx, 317–24) that this may have been the one held by Richard II in London in May, 1390, Chaucer as Clerk of the King's Works being actively concerned with the preparations. The hypothesis is interesting, even if one does not regard Parr's conclusions as indubitably established.

enters the service of Theseus, would doubtless appeal to Chaucer's contemporaries. From the bald statement in the *Teseida* that he was lodged with the duke, Chaucer develops the following:

> To the court he wente up-on a day,
> And at the gate he profreth his servyse,
> To drugge and drawe, what so men wol devyse.
> And shortly of this matere for to seyn,
> He fil in office with a chamberleyn,
> The which that dwelling was with Emelye.
> For he was wys, and coude soon aspye
> Of every servaunt, which that serveth here.
> Wel coude he hewen wode, and water bere,
> For he was yong and mighty for the nones,
> And ther-to he was strong and big of bones
> To doon that any wight can him devyse.
>
> .   .   .   .   .
>
> And thus, with-inne a whyle, his name is spronge
> Both of his dedes, and his goode tonge.
>
> (A. 1414–25; 1437–8)

These lines are quite in the tradition of English romance and to some listeners at any rate may well have had a familiar sound.

Chaucer made other additions of a philosophical nature. Thus when Arcite is released from prison, only to find himself banished from Athens and debarred from seeing Emelye, he exclaims:

> Allas, why pleynen folk so in commune
> Of purveyaunce of God, or of fortune,
> That yeveth hem ful ofte in many a gyse
> Wel bettre than they can hem-self devyse?
>
> (A. 1251–4)

His point is that it is futile for human beings to go in quest of happiness when all is ordered for the best by divine wisdom. Palamon, on the other hand, questions the justice of the fate meted out to him. Arcite has been allowed to regain his liberty; he remains a prisoner. He denounces the cruelty of the gods who are indifferent to the lot of mankind. Indeed, he asserts that man is worse off than an animal:

> whan a beest is deed, he hath no peyne;
> But man after his deeth moot wepe and pleyne,
> Though in this world he have care and wo.
>
> (A. 1319–21)

The explanation he leaves to the theologians. It is Egeus, the old sage, who corrects Palamon. He is well aware of the sorrows of life:

> This world nis but a thurghfare ful of wo,
> And we ben pilgrimes, passinge to and fro;
> Deeth is an ende of every worldly sore.
>
> (A. 2847–9)

It is the last line which is a repudiation of Palamon's assertion. The typical mediæval metaphor of the pilgrimage with its Christian associations evokes the world of bliss after death. Thus we are led to a passage in the speech of Theseus:

> Why grucchen we? why have we hevinesse,
> That good Arcite, of chivalrye flour
> Departed is, with duetee and honour,
> Out of this foule prison of this lyf?[1]
>
> (A. 3058–61)

For his part, Theseus has no doubts about the wisdom of the 'firste moevere', even if his purpose is not clear. There is a meaning and an order in the world.

Evidently, in the *Knight's Tale* as elsewhere, Chaucer is preoccupied from time to time with the problem raised by the sufferings of mankind. The sudden death of Arcite in the moment of victory is one of those reversals of fortune which fascinated the Middle Ages. However, though it may be a tragedy in accordance with Lydgate's usage, one may question, even if everything in the poem is taken into account, whether an accident caused by the shying of a horse warrants the opinion that 'the view of the universe taken by the Tale is a tragic view, and the condition of man presented by the teller is also tragic'.[2] Moreover, one may well ask whether Chaucer is so profoundly moved by the events of this story as by those of *Troilus and Criseyde*. His attitude to the heroine and her admirers differs greatly from that displayed towards the Trojan lovers. The swift transition of Arcite from mirth to reverie evokes a smile at

> thise loveres in hir queynte geres,
> Now in the croppe, now doun in the breres,
> Now up, now doun, as boket in a welle.
>
> (A. 1531–3)

And when the occasion presents itself, Chaucer interpolates these lines on the folly of Palamon and Arcite:

> But this is yet the beste game of alle,
> That she, for whom they han this Iolitee,
> Can hem ther-for as muche thank as me;
> She woot namore of al this hote fare,
> By God, than woot a cokkow or an hare!
> But al mot been assayed, hoot and cold;
> A man mot been a fool, or yong or old.
>
> (A. 1806–12)

---

[1] In the last line there may be an echo of the form of words used for the rite of burial in Chaucer's day. In the Westminster Missal it ran: 'suscipe animam serui tui. N. quam de ergastulo seculi huius uocare dignatus es' (cf. Henry Bradshaw Society, iii, 1286).

[2] Cf. W. Frost, 'An Appreciation of Chaucer's *Knight's Tale*' (R.E.S., 1949, xxv, p. 299).

The implications of the second passage, uttered by Theseus, have some affinity with the attitude of his namesake in *A Midsummer Night's Dream*.[1] The first quotation, spoken by the author, blends in tone with the other, and it would seem that Chaucer, even if he sympathised with Palamon, nevertheless viewed the doings of the two rivals with detached amusement. Assuredly, when disaster overwhelms Arcite, he gives no sign that his feelings were so deeply engaged as in the misfortunes of Troilus. Perhaps this explains why, in touching on the death of Arcite, he introduced the macabre humour already pointed out. It is also possible that for the same reason he transferred the lofty episode in the *Teseida* describing the flight of Arcita's soul to the passing of Troilus and replaced it by the whimsical jocularity that deliberately sacrifices all solemnity:

> His spirit chaunged hous, and wente ther,
> As I cam never, I can nat tellen wher.
> Therfor I stinte, I nam no divinistre;
> Of soules finde I nat in this registre.
>
> (A. 2809–12)

As Chaucer left the theme that he derived from the *Teseida*, it was more a tale of action than a psychological study. Attention was focused on the conflict between Palamon and Arcite. To that extent it was better suited to the Knight who might be expected to know more of duels and tournaments than of the intricate movements of the human heart. How far Chaucer had this in mind when making his adaptation, one can only surmise. What is certain is that the *Knight's Tale* is more compact, more organically coherent, swifter and richer in sudden dramatic situations, but that it is inferior in tracing gradual developments and in subtle characterisation.[2] It would be as foolish to expect that the *Teseida* could be compressed into the mould of the *Knight's Tale* without loss as it would be to suppose that *Clarissa Harlowe* could be faithfully reproduced as a short story.

Thanks to Fletcher's dramatisation of Chaucer's tale in *The Two Noble Kinsmen* and Dryden's adaptation in his *Fables*, the work of Boccaccio was indirectly perpetuated. Dryden spoke of the *Knight's Tale* in his preface, declaring that he preferred this 'Noble Poem' to all Chaucer's other stories. Indeed, he ranked it as perhaps not much inferior to the *Iliad* and the *Æneid*. He goes on:

[1] Act V, Sc. i.

[2] It is no doubt true that Chaucer made some effort to distinguish between Palamon and Arcite, but opinions have differed sharply about the interpretation of their characters. Cf. H. N. Fairchild, 'Active Arcite, Contemplative Palamon', *J.E.G.P.*, 1927, xxvi, pp. 285–93, and A. H. Marckwardt, *Characterisation in Chaucer's 'Knight's Tale'*, University of Michigan Press, 1947. R. A. Pratt, while recognising some differentiation, does not consider that it goes very far. Cf. *P.M.L.A.*, 1947, lxii, pp. 615–16.

I had thought for the Honour of our Nation, and more particularly for his, whose Laurel, tho' unworthy, I have worn after him, that this Story was of *English* Growth, and *Chaucer*'s own; But I was undeceiv'd by *Boccace*; for casually looking on the End of his seventh *Giornata*,[1] I found *Dioneo* (under which name he shadows himself) and *Fiametta* (who represents his Mistress, the natural Daughter of *Robert* King of *Naples*) of whom these Words are spoken. *Dioneo e Fiametta gran pezza cantarono*[2] *insieme d'Arcita, e di Palamone*: by which it appears that this Story was written before the time of *Boccace*; but the Name of its Author being wholly lost, *Chaucer* is now become an Original.[3]

Dryden's error was corrected by John Farmer in *An Essay on the Learning of Shakespeare* in 1767, and from that time on Boccaccio was recognised as the composer of the *Teseida*. His authorship was mentioned by Thomas Russell[4] in a footnote to his sonnet 'To Boccaccio', in 1789. However, he gave no sign of having read the poem, and Leigh Hunt, writing in his essay 'May Day' in 1820, lamented that

we never had the happiness of meeting with that very rare work. The Italians have so neglected it, that they have not only never given it a rifacimento or re-modelling, as in the instance of Boiardo's poem, but are almost as much unacquainted with it, we believe, as foreign countries.

Nevertheless, through the medium of Chaucer, he perceived something of Boccaccio's power and maintained that the tree must have been a 'fine old enormity' which could supply such inspiration.[5] Hunt's complaint about the neglect of the *Teseida* was not unfounded,[6] though Antonio Montucci's *Italian Extracts* (1806) did contain a passage describing the defeat of the Amazons by Theseus.[7] However, Antonio Panizzi did something to remove Hunt's criticism, for in 1830 he dealt at length with the *Teseida* and the *Knight's Tale*, incidentally defending Boccaccio against Tyrwhitt and Warton.[8] His essay was studied by J. C. Hobhouse who in this way became familiar with the 'plot' of the Italian original.[9]

[1] That is, of the *Decameron*.
[2] The first edition has a misprint which is here corrected.
[3] Cf. *The Works of John Dryden*, ed. Scott-Saintsbury, Edinburgh, 1885, xi, 239.
[4] Cf. *Sonnets and Miscellaneous Poems*, Oxford, p. 6. My attention was drawn to this sonnet by J. Raith, op. cit., p. 141. Vide post, p. 277.
[5] *The Indicator*, no. xxix. Vide post, pp. 352–3.
[6] In 1801 Friedrich von Schlegel also laments that he has been unable to find a copy of the complete work and has had to rely on the prose excerpt of Granucci (cf. 'Nachricht von den poetischen Werken des Johannes Boccaccio', *Vermischte kritische Schriften*, Bonn, 1877, pp. 6 and 11).
[7] Cf. Marshall, p. 311. In the second edition of Montucci (1818) it occurs on pp. 223–4. Montucci recognises that it is not well known and praises it highly.
[8] *Orlando Innamorato di Bojardo: Orlando Furioso di Ariosto: With an essay on the romantic narrative poetry of the Italians*, i, pp. 159–90.
[9] *Italy*, London, 1859, p. 242.

3. The *Filostrato* •

Whereas Chaucer omitted to state who was the creator of the *Teseida*, he ascribed the *Filostrato* to 'Lollius'. In both cases it is likely that the manuscript at his disposal failed to mention Boccaccio. There is a similar erroneous attribution of the poem, this time to Petrarch, in the translation made by Louis de Beauvau between 1442 and 1445.[1] As he was in the service of René, king of Sicily, the journey of this seneschal of Anjou to Italy imparted to him the same stimulus as to Chaucer, and the parallel becomes closer when we recall that he was sent by his master as an envoy to Pope Pius II,[2] just as Chaucer was entrusted with missions to the cities of Genoa and Milan. Once again it was a piece of good fortune that this admirable early work of Boccaccio fell into the hands of the great English poet.[3]

Unlike Louis de Beauvau, who translated with tears in his eyes, because he was smitten with the same grief as the love-sick Troilus, Chaucer was able to approach the *Filostrato* with a certain detachment. This contrasts notably with the strong autobiographical element in Boccaccio's poem, the very basis of which is his separation from Fiammetta. In the 'Proemio' he tells the lady to whom it is dedicated that whenever she hears Troilo weep and lament the departure of Griseida she will recognise his own voice, tears, sighs and anguish, and whenever she reads of the beauty and good qualities of Griseida, she is to understand that it is really herself who is meant. He therefore chooses her as his Muse, since it is the grief caused by her leaving him that has led him to relate the woeful tale of Troilo, for in so doing he is revealing himself through the pains of others.[4] About half-way through the poem Boccaccio appeals once more to this lady to have pity on him and by her return give back to him the ease of which she has bereft him.[5] Finally, he bids his book go to this gentle lady and, pointing to its author's utter misery, induce her to come and solace him who is happy only in her presence.[6] This insistence is notable and accounts for Boccaccio's portrayal of dawning love, the joy of its consummation, the bitterness of parting and the hope of reunion. He sought above all to convey these moods, and there is a passionate lyrical strain in his narrative. In these circumstances he was less

[1] Hauvette [1909], pp. 19–26.   [2] Ibid., p. 23.

[3] The *Filostrato* and *Troilus* are compared in detail by R. Fischer, *Zu den Kunstformen des mittelalterlichen Epos*, Wiener Beiträge, ix, 1899, pp. 217–30. For a valuable interpretation of *Troilus* see W. P. Ker, *English Literature: Medieval*, London, 1912, Ch. ix.

[4] *O.V.* i, st. 2–5. The *Filostrato* occupies vol. xiii of the *Opere volgari*. Subsequent quotation references are by book, stanza, and line.

[5] *O.V.* iv, st. 23–5.   [6] *O.V.* ix, st. 5–7.

concerned to depict human character. Hence the minor figures are sketched but lightly, and for the most part his eyes are concentrated on the lovers. Even in their relations, however, not everything is explained, and in particular the reasons for the betrayal of Troilo by Griseida are left somewhat obscure.

On the other hand, Chaucer addresses 'moral Gower' and 'philosophical Strode', and at the beginning invokes Tisiphone, one of the Furies, whom he regards as a fitting Muse for a story of tragic love. Free from any preoccupation with his own sentiments, he is able to watch the actions of all the characters and analyse them with a steady, penetrating gaze. Significant in this respect is the light thrown on Hector by Chaucer's addition of his reply to the proposal to exchange Griseida for Antenor:[1]

> 'Sires, she nys no prisoner', he seyde;
> 'I not on yow who that this charge leyde,
> But, on my part, ye may eftsone hem telle,
> We usen here no wommen for to selle'.

> (iv, 179–82)

However, the share of Hector in the action was too small for Chaucer to do more than emphasise his dignity and manliness, but in Diomede he had more scope. Boccaccio had conceived of this figure as a cunning seducer who contents himself at his first meeting with noting the distress of Troilo and Griseida and only later with a cautious, gradual approach ventures to become more personal, and finally leads up to a declaration of love. Yet it is strange that one so experienced should at the end of this speech blush and with trembling voice lower his eyelids and avert his gaze. Such genuine and involuntary embarrassment is hardly compatible with the deliberate calculation of a wily man of the world. And surely he is not at all astute when he bids Griseida, longing for Troilo and her native town, to abandon the false love of the Trojans, and disparages her fellow-citizens as crude barbarians, little to be esteemed in comparison with the Greeks who are superior to all other nations. It would seem as if Boccaccio in his humanist zeal for Hellenic civilisation had lost sight of the fact that such boasts as these would be calculated to repel Griseida by their nationalistic arrogance.

Chaucer's Diomedes is more consistent in every way. He has all the ease in love-making of one

> that koude more than the Crede
> In swich a craft.

> (v, 89–90)

---

[1] All quotations are taken from *The Book of Troilus and Criseyde*, ed. R. K. Root, Princeton, 1926.

and embarks on the wooing of Criseyde at their very first encounter, with all the audacity and self-assurance of a man versed in dealing with women. But he is as shrewd as he is daring and avoids any tactless criticism of the Trojans. After vowing on his honour as a knight that he is anxious to please Criseyde, he promises that she will readily find among the Greeks one as loyal and as kind as any Trojan. Thereupon, taking a step forward, he begs her to treat him as a brother and then, after emphasising the common bond between Greeks and Trojans, in that all serve the god of love, declares himself

> Youre owene aboven every creature.
>
> (v, 154)

This is coupled with asseverations that he has never talked thus to any woman before and cannot frame his words aright, for want of instruction in such matters:

> I lovede nevere womman here biforn
> As paramours.[1]
>
> (v, 157–8)

But he gives a pledge to devote himself to her alone and, anticipating that she may be taken aback by this unexpected declaration, he claims that such instances of instantaneous love are not unknown and implores

> That ye me for youre servant wolde calle,
> So lowely ne so trewely yow serve
> Nil non of hem, as I shal, til I sterve.
>
> (v, 173–5)

In spite of this veneer of courtly love, Diomedes is merely pursuing his own unscrupulous designs. The intrigue is for him a mere pastime, and even if he is not altogether successful, he thinks that it will at least shorten the journey.[2] However, his speech to Criseyde is such a masterpiece of plausibility, that she is impressed by 'this sodeyn Diomede' and, in the end, overcome by his artful persuasion.

---

[1] Cf. Benoît de Ste. More, *Le roman de Troie*, ed. L. Constans, Paris, 1904–12. (All quotations are made from this edition.)

> Onques d'amer ne m'entremis,
> N'amie n'oi ne fu amis
>
> (ll. 13527–8)

and

> Mainte pucele avrai veüe
> Et mainte dame coneüe:
> Onc mais a rien ne fis preiere
> De mei amer en tel maniere.
> Vos en estes la premeraine,
> Si sereiz vos la dereraine.
>
> (ll. 13561–6)

[2] v, 94–6.

Still more remarkable is the development that Pandaro undergoes at Chaucer's hands. As Boccaccio portrays him, he is a disillusioned young man who has loved without finding happiness and esteems women lightly. Devoted to the interests of Troilo, he would sacrifice his own sister to him, and, though he does not relish the function of a go-between, he arranges the meeting of his friend with Griseida. As a man of the world he foresees the result of her treachery long before Troilo, but refrains from disabusing him. When it can no longer be concealed, he suggests that the battlefield may solve all these troubles and shares its dangers with Troilo to the last. Chaucer's Pandarus has some affinities with his Boccaccian prototype in that he too is presented as a disappointed lover. He laments that no one has cast a friendly look upon him, he weeps and wails, and at intervals he takes to his bed for grief. But such passages are inconsistent with his outlook elsewhere. How can one take his sentimental melancholy seriously when he jests repeatedly about his love to Criseyde? Thus when she asks to be told

> How ferforth be ye put in loves daunce,
> (ii, 1106)

the reply comes:

> 'By god', quod he, 'I hoppe alwey byhynde.'[1]
> (ii, 1107)

This humour of Pandarus is a trait for which there was but the slightest of hints in his counterpart. His geniality and high spirits are infectious; his jovial laughter echoes through the early part of the poem. To Criseyde, especially, he succeeds in imparting some of his cheerfulness; she laughs with still greater gusto. Sometimes his attitude to her is one of jocular familiarity, as when he visits her on the morning after her first encounter with Troilus at his house. But more characteristic is a vein of sly humour. Thus he joins the invitation to his home 'to speke of love aright' with the seemingly innocent remark,

> For ther have ye a leiser for to telle.
> (iii, 200)

Equally characteristic is his comment after the fainting Troilus has been placed in Criseyde's bed and has recovered from his momentary weakness. As Pandarus retires with his candle to the fireside, he says:

> for aught I kan espien,
> I nor this candel serven here of nought;
> Light is nat good for sike folkes yen.
> (iii, 1135–7)

---

[1] Cf. also ii, 1165–9.

And a moment or two later, perceiving Criseyde in her lover's embrace, he murmurs, as he prepares to withdraw to his own room,

> if ye be wise,
> Swouneth nat now, lest more folk arise.
>
> (iii, 1189–90)

Yet whether his manner be boisterous or subdued, under the humorous exterior Pandarus hides a steely resolve to break down Criseyde's resistance. In doing so, since Chaucer has transformed him from Criseyde's cousin into her uncle, he combines authority[1] with tenderness. There is no reason to doubt his assurance of his affection and his reluctance to grieve her, and his distress at the sight of her tear-stained face on hearing that she is to be exchanged for Antenor is patently sincere. Nevertheless, his devotion to Troilus is still greater. He sympathises with him on seeing how he suffers from his undeclared and unreciprocated love, and although he may feel a pang of compunction at the thought of betraying his niece, he soons thrusts aside his hesitation, because he believes that every woman is at heart a rake and all she needs is a favourable opportunity:

> vice
> No womman drat, if she be wel avised.
>
> (iii, 327–8)

In keeping with this maxim, he sees no wrong in offering not only his own sister, as his prototype had done, but also Eleyne, the wife of Troilus' brother Paris, as a means of slaking his friend's passion.[2] It is typical of his mentality that he should imagine that Troilus is at first unwilling to disclose whom he loves, lest Pandarus should steal the lady from him. This hedonist plunges into his intrigue with all the zest of the hunter in pursuit of his quarry:

> A ha! . . . here bygynneth game.
>
> (i, 868)

> Lo, hold the at the triste cloos, and I
> Shal wel the deer unto thi bowe dryve.
>
> (ii, 1534–5)

He bustles to and fro with all the eagerness of a hound on the trail.

> He shof ay on; he to and fro was sent;
> He lettres bar . . .
>
> (iii, 487–8)

This joyful zeal distinguishes him from Pandaro, though they have in common other traits such as an emotional nature that finds an outlet

---

[1] This holds good, even if we do not regard him as an elderly man, a view unwarranted by the text. Cf. J. S. P. Tatlock, 'The People in Chaucer's *Troilus*', *P.M.L.A.*, 1941, lvi, p. 95. [2] Cf. i, 676–8; 860–1.

in tears. Yet here again a distinction must be drawn. In the scenes
common to Chaucer and Boccaccio Pandarus evinces more restraint
and dignity.[1] Because he is less lachrymose, he is in a better position
to rebuke Troilus for his folly in thinking that by shedding tears he
can ever hope to win a woman. So too he summons Criseyde to action,
instead of giving way to idle tears:

> What helpeth it to wepen ful a strete,
> Or though ye bothe in salte teeris dreynte?
>
> (iv, 929–30)

Nevertheless, when it suits his purpose, he can use tears with considerable effect. Especially is this so when he wants to excite pity in Criseyde.
In presenting Troilus to her he cannot refrain from glancing at her
hardness of heart.

> Therwith it semed as he wepte almoost.
>
> (iii, 64)

Previously, when pleading with her not to make Troilus die of grief,
he throws himself into his task with such earnestness that the tears
burst from his eyes, and later in order to reinforce his friend's appeal

> Pandare wep as he to water wolde.
>
> (iii, 115)

On such occasions as these Pandarus plays his part with an air of
conviction. He is indeed an excellent actor. With what a sorrowful
mien does he hang his head after reminding Criseyde of the melancholy truth that her beauty must soon decay, and how grave is his
manner as he keeps up the pretence of Troilus' illness and bids the
attendants stand back quietly while Criseyde enters the patient's
room! Another scene in which his natural bent for acting finds expression is the one where Criseyde first kisses Troilus. Her uncle's delight
is doubtless genuine enough, but his way of showing it is somewhat
theatrical:

> Fil Pandarus on knees, and up his eyen
> To hevene threw, and held his hondes hye.
>
> (iii, 183–4)

---

[1] Cf.

> Pandare myghte nat restreyne
> The teeris from his eyen for to reyne.
>
> (iv, 872–3)

and

> Pandaro, ch'avea
> Con Troilo pianto il giorno lungamente,
> Le lagrime dolenti non potea
> Tener, ma cominciò similemente,
>
> .   .   .   .
>
> A pianger con costei dogliosamente.
>
> (*O.V.* iv, st. 101, ll. 1–6)

This histrionic capacity is a great asset in the execution of his design. Still more valuable is the thoroughness with which this wily intriguer lays his plans. With the meticulous deliberation of a general contemplating a campaign, he works out his scheme in its smallest details. Unlike his counterpart in the *Filostrato*, he never sets things in motion until he has prepared the ground carefully. At the very outset, after promising to help Troilus, he

> went his wey, thenkyng on this matere,
> And how he best myghte hire biseche of grace,
> And fynde a tyme therto, and a place.
>
> For everi wight that hath an hous to founde
> Ne renneth naught the werk for to bygynne
> With rakel hond; but he wol bide a stounde,
> And sende his hertes line out fro withinne
> Aldirfirst his purpos for to wynne.
>
> (i, 1062–9)

In the same way he gives Troilus most precise instructions about his demeanour as he rides past Criseyde's house and about the letter that he is to send her, cunningly adding that he is to blot it a little with his tears. With equal minuteness he unfolds to Troilus his stratagem for bringing the lovers together at the house of Deiphobus, and one must admire the ingenuity of his device. Troilus feigns sickness and apparently in a high fever retires to his chamber amid the consternation of Deiphobus and his retinue. After dinner next day Pandarus consents to allow Troilus to see visitors:

> But wel ye woot, the chaumbre is but lite,
> And fewe folk may lightly make it warm.
>
> (ii, 1646–7)

Plausibly he suggests that only Deiphobus and Eleyne should enter at first and with air of mystery hints that Troilus has some matter of national importance to communicate. Then, having permitted them to speak to the patient and arranged for them to be occupied elsewhere, he summons Criseyde and her attendants, all of whom believe that Deiphobus and Eleyne are still with Troilus and that she will briefly ask for his support against Poliphete in their presence. The proprieties being thus observed, the attendants are ordered to wait outside for fear of disturbing the feverish Troilus, and Criseyde enters. Thanks to such skilful management, Pandarus carries the interview to a successful issue. No sooner is it over than he is already looking ahead to the next stage of his enterprise—the meeting at his own house. On this, the crucial moment, he bestows all his pains:

F

> For he, with gret deliberacioun,
> Hadde every thyng that herto myghte availle
> Forncast, and put in execucioun,
> And neither left for cost ne for travaille.
>
> (iii, 519–22)

However, such precision alone would not account for Pandarus' triumph in swaying Criseyde to yield. One has the impression of his wider experience and his intellectual superiority to all the others in the poem. More genial than Iago he feels a like joy in pulling the threads of the intrigue and befools Deiphobus with the same scornful delight as the ensign displays towards Othello. Pandarus is no sentimentalist and has no sympathy for a languishing lover. A practical man of the world, he spurs Troilus on to action and rouses him time and again from his dejected lethargy. No dreamer himself, he does not understand how others can trust in the portents of 'swich ordure'. He is essentially a realist, and it is characteristic that when he keeps his longing friend company as they pace the walls of Troy, he does not forget to tell him when it is time to dine![1] Guided by hard common-sense, this sceptical roué cannot refrain from a gibe at the solemn manner of Troilus as he is about to enter the room of Criseyde:

> thow wrecched mouses herte!
> Artow agast so that she wol the bite?
>
> (iii, 736–7)

Such diffidence as that of Troilus is incomprehensible to one who moves so confidently to his goal and allows nothing to prevent him from attaining it. He lies without hesitation and invents the stories of Poliphete and of Horaste with all the glibness and speciousness of frequent practice. Most unscrupulous of all is his conduct to Criseyde. When inviting her to his house, he vows that Troilus will not be there, swears by all the gods that his statement is true and wishes that he may suffer all the torments of hell if it proves false. Finally, when he has escorted Troilus to her bedchamber, he declares that Troilus, impelled by jealousy, has contrived to find a secret way into the house.

More than anything else, however, it is Pandarus' understanding of human nature that makes him so dangerous. Knowing as he does the knightly courage of Troilus, he stirs him from his lethargy by playing on this with the suggestion that fear of the Greeks has turned his thoughts to religion. So too he never loses sight of Criseyde's timidity and tender-heartedness and is careful not to rouse her fears.

---

[1] It is the same practicality as that of Speed in relation to the love-sick Valentine (*The Two Gentlemen of Verona*, ed. A. Quiller-Couch and J. Dover Wilson, Cambridge, 1921, II, i, 156–60).

When Troilus rides past her house, Pandarus instructs him to fix his
eyes on himself and not to linger. In making any request to his niece
he always reassures her. Thus at the beginning he merely asks her to
be more amiable to Troilus; she need not bind herself by any promise.
At a later stage he asserts that Troilus wants nothing but to serve her
and maintain her honour. Realising her dislike of gossip, Pandarus
seeks to prove that she has nothing to apprehend on that score. When
he enters her room by night, he warns her not to cry out and then
calms her by saying that none can hear and, moreover, he will go as
soon as he has told his tale. Immediately afterwards he reveals the
presence of Troilus in the house, but adds in the same breath that his
coming is unknown to any one else. There can be no harm in her
seeing him, and Pandarus will be there all night. Whenever she shows
signs of alarm, he soothes her with honeyed words, linked with a
touching reminder of their kinship.

In his attempts to persuade Criseyde, Pandarus never fails to work
upon her tender feelings. His prototype had touched on Griseida's
sensitiveness about the swift fading of beauty, and this argument likewise figures in the discussions with Criseyde. But it is a theme of
trivial importance compared with the appeal to her gentle heart.
From the outset Pandarus insists that Troilus's life is in danger and
that she will have to shoulder the responsibility for his death. He
cannot bear to repeat to her the words of the woeful Troilus; so painful
is the topic that, were he to do so, he would swoon. At times he trades
upon her affection for himself and asserts that unless she relents, he
too will die. As a climax to numerous previous entreaties, with what
pathos he depicts the sorry case of his friend:

> This is so gentil and so tendre of herte,
> That with his deth he wol his sorwe wreke;
> For trusteth wel, how sore that hym smerte,
> He wol to yow no jalous wordes speke.
> And forthi, nece, or that his herte breke,
> So speke youre self to hym of this matere.
>
> (iii, 904–9)

Conspicuous also is the use that Pandarus makes of surprise to
influence Criseyde. Thus when he has been protesting how innocuous
his proposals are, he suddenly exclaims:

> Ther were nevere two so wel ymet,
> Whan ye ben his al hool, as he is youre;
> Ther myghty god yit graunte us see that houre.
>
> (ii, 586–8)

Naturally, Criseyde retorts that she has spoken nothing of the kind.
Pandarus agrees and lets the matter rest, but he is well pleased to have

planted the idea in her mind.[1] Criseyde is even more completely taken aback when he is escorting her to the room of Troilus in Deiphobus' house and she is under the impression that she is to request his help against Poliphete. On the very threshold, however, without any preface Pandarus whispers:

> Nece, I conjure, and heighly yow defende,
> On his half, that soule us alle sende,
> And in the vertue of corounes tweyne,
> Sle nat this man, that hath for yow this peyne.
>
> (ii, 1733–6)

Even more startling is the dramatic fashion in which he produces Troilus, whom he has declared to be in another room of the house, at her bedside and belies the smooth assurances given only a few seconds earlier.

Nothing could better demonstrate the untrustworthiness of Pandarus or the tactics by which he combines the gradual approach with sudden leaps forward to the goal. He is in truth a master of intrigue, as quick-witted as he is careful in planning and as prompt to take advantage of an unforeseen opening as to develop well-laid schemes. Thus the unexpected appearance of Troilus riding in the street causes Criseyde involuntarily to start back from the window at which she and Pandarus are sitting. Pandarus begs her not to go in, lest Troilus should think she wishes to avoid him. Her reply, 'Nay, nay', and her blushes betray her inclinations, and Pandarus is not slow to make the most of this opportunity. Knowing that she is not indifferent to Troilus, he later tries to win her over to his proposal by saying that she cannot care for Troilus or she would not put his life in jeopardy as she is doing, which wrings from her the blunt confession:

> Had I hym nevere lief! By god, I weene
> Ye hadde nevere thyng so lief.
>
> (iii, 869–70)

Pandarus at once seizes on the admission to reinforce his pleas on behalf of Troilus. His readiness of mind and his practicality are again illustrated when he has so unexpectedly brought Troilus to Criseyde. At this sudden appearance she is so utterly embarrassed that she is speechless. It is an awkward position, and the tactful Pandarus tries to hide her confusion by a playful remark:

> nece, se how this lord kan knele!
>
> (iii, 962)

He gains a little more time for her to recover by hurrying off for a cushion on which Troilus, who is clad only in a shirt and furred cloak,

[1] ii, 589–97.

may kneel. However, he is nowhere more entirely master of an emergency than when his friend, without warning, collapses in a dead faint at the bedside of Criseyde. For the moment all his elaborate plans seem to have come to naught. In vain his disposal of her attendants in the room outside that of their lady, in vain his choice of a night of rain and storm, in vain his precautions to secure privacy. But he rises to the occasion and, thrusting the unconscious Troilus into Criseyde's bed, works at the same time upon her dawning admiration and her sense of pity. The situation is retrieved, and Pandarus at long last has triumphed.

The pithy, colloquial language of Pandarus makes him a more familiar figure than in the original. On the other hand, Chaucer's presentation of Troilus tends to idealise him. As has been pointed out by a number of scholars,[1] the poet was under the influence of the courtly love code, and his conception of his hero's relation to Criseyde was coloured by its outlook. This is true up to a point, though the characters are never mere types conforming to a rigid scheme. The effect is nowhere more clearly visible than in the portrayal of Troilus himself. There was, of course, some trace of the courtly outlook in the *Filostrato*. Griseida is a haughty lady and Troilo her subject and servant; the necessity for keeping their love secret is asserted, because they are surrounded by eager slanderers; and in accordance with tradition, the coming of dawn is hateful, Troilo cursing its approach. Finally, there is a suggestion of the transforming power of love:

> Tu fai cortese ognuno e costumato
> Chi del tuo fuoco alquanto è infiammato.
>
> (*O.V.* iii, st. 77, ll. 7–8)

In particular, its effects are seen in the redoubling of Troilo's martial energy which makes him the terror of the Greeks:

> e questo spirto tanto altiero
> Più che l'usato gli prestava amore,
> Di cui egli era fedel servidore.
>
> (*O.V.* iii, st. 90, ll. 6–8)

In other respects, however, Boccaccio differs considerably from the troubadours. His Troilo is a lover as well as a servant, and the terms 'amadore' and 'servidore' are interchangeable. Love being less idealistic, it may wane in time as the result of absence from 'la cosa

---

[1] Cf. W. G. Dodd, *Courtly Love in Chaucer and Gower*, Boston, 1913, pp. 129–208; R. K. Root, *The Poetry of Chaucer*, Boston, 1922, pp. 102–21; T. A. Kirby, *Chaucer's 'Troilus': A Study in Courtly Love*, Louisiana State University, 1940. In England C. S. Lewis has discussed the question at length in 'What Chaucer really did to *Il Filostrato*', *Essays and Studies*, xvii, pp. 56–75 and in *The Allegory of Love*, Oxford, 1936 and 1938. In his article 'The People in Chaucer's *Troilus*' (vide ante, p. 63) J. S. P. Tatlock challenges the view that Chaucer was so much affected by courtly love.

amata'. More significant still, though nominally the faithful servant of Griseida, Troilo criticises and abuses her. He may ponder for a moment whether he is to blame for her desertion, but concludes that it is she who is false and disloyal. She is 'la nostra fraudolente donna', and he reproaches her bitterly for her broken pledges. Theoretically he recognises that the servant should refrain from complaint of his lady's actions and momentarily he may acquiesce with an air of humility, but he leaves no doubt that he thinks her in the wrong. Devoured by suspicion and his jealousy at her failure to return, Troilo is far from assuming that she is on a plane above all ordinary mortals. On the contrary, he places himself in the seat of the judge but magnanimously promises, if she will return, to forgive her without exacting any penalty. Again he threatens to kill himself, observing that though he will suffer, hers will be the shame for having consigned one so innocent to an obscure death. As long as he hopes that Griseida will come back to Troy, his reproaches are courteous; but when he is sure that she will not, he pours forth a torrent of denunciation and vows to kill Diomedes, not merely as an act of vengeance, but as the best means of grieving one so full of deceit and lies.

Perceiving the warring elements in Troilo, Chaucer set himself to depict a hero conforming more whole-heartedly to the code of courtly love. In the first place he elaborates various features that were merely outlined in his source. The brief references to the antagonism of the dawn towards the rapturous lovers are developed into an *alba*.[1] Similarly, the new martial vigour that Troilus displays under the stimulus of love is emphasised:

> And this encres of hardynesse and myght
> Com hym of love, his ladies thank to wynne,
> That altered his spirit so withinne.
>
> (iii, 1776–8)

The mere promise of help from Pandarus in his wooing of Criseyde is enough to make Troilus start from his bed, leap on to his steed and work havoc among the Greeks. In other respects he undergoes a change that amounts to a transformation. Instead of scoffing at love, haughty and aloof in his bearing, he wins universal popularity for his affability, no less than for his valour. After the achievement of his desires Troilus' happiness finds expression in his love of dress and festivities and in his extensive generosity, so that

> swich a vois of hym was and a stevene
> Thorughout the world, of honour and largesse,
> That it up rong unto the yate of hevene.
>
> (iii, 1723–5)

[1] iii, 1450–63.

It is as though the youthful gaiety and delight in colour that character-
ise Chaucer's Squire were blended with the courtesy and martial
prowess of the Knight. As in Boccaccio the lovers have to reckon with
the serpent tongues of the envious, and one passage is entirely typical
of the troubadour convention when Criseyde, contemplating flight
from the Greek camp by night, exclaims:

> No fors of wikked tonges janglerie;
> For evere on love han wrecches had envye.
>
> (v, 755–6)

When they meet in public, the lovers are always on their guard lest
they should reveal their secret to those standing by, and Troilus,
despite his passion, never gives a hint of his feelings. Even when he is
amazed by the decision to exchange Criseyde for Antenor, he utters
not a word. His chief concern is for her honour; his own interests
must be subordinate:

> syn that I am hire knyght,
> I moste hire honour levere han than me
> In every cas, as lovere ought of right.
>
> (iv, 569–71)

Along with this zealous care for her reputation there goes an ardent
devotion. On the whole Troilus thinks of himself as a servant rather
than a lover. It is true that he longs for the physical consummation of
his love, but apart from the encounter at Pandarus' house, little is said
of fleshly delights. We shall search in vain for any such cry as that of
his prototype:

> Or foss'io teco una notte di verno,
> Cento cinquanta poi stessi in inferno.
>
> (*O.V.* ii, st. 88, ll. 7–8)

More typical is Troilus' declaration to Criseyde

> god hath wrought me for I shal yow serve,
>
> (iii, 1290)

which is an exact parallel to the words of Gaucelm Faidit about his
relationship to his lady:

> Dieus mi fes per far son mandamen.[1]

Troilus again and again reveals his wish to serve Criseyde as her man,
her knight, who like the vassal owes obedience to his superior in all
humility and faithfulness. His attitude is defined at length when he
begs to be allowed to place himself under her orders:

---

[1] Cf. F. Diez, *Die Poesie der Troubadours*, Leipzig, 1883, p. 128, n. 6.

In trouthe alwey to don yow my servise,

As to my lady right and chief resort,
With al my wit and al my diligence;
And I to han, right as yow list, comfort,
Under youre yerde, egal to myn offence,
As deth, if that I breke youre defence;
And that ye deigne me so muche honoure,
Me to comanden aught in any houre;

And I to ben youre, verray, humble, trewe,
Secret, and in my peynes pacient;
And evere mo desiren fresshly newe
To serve, and ben ay ylike diligent;
And with good herte, al holly youre talent
Receyven wel, how sore that me smerte.

(iii, 133–46)

Above all it is this quality of patience that helps to bring Troilus nearer than Boccaccio's hero to the ideals of courtly love, even when he is subjected to the greatest strain. Jealousy is alien to him, and though on the occasion of the meeting at Pandarus' house he has to corroborate his friend's tale to Criseyde, he is ill at ease. His explanation is therefore lame and faltering, and as soon as possible he apologises for his supposed jealousy and pleads to be forgiven. More characteristic of him is his assumption that Criseyde's failure to return to Troy is due to some fault in himself. In his letters he beseeches her to come and keep her pledge, but does not upbraid her. Even after receiving her final reply, he is reluctant to believe any ill of the woman whom he has served so loyally. At last, however, the bitter truth becomes obvious. Yet there is a singular gentleness in his recognition of the painful facts. Whereas his prototype had perceived that a new love was the cause of Griseida's lies, Troilus understands that she

Nas nat so kynde as that hire oughte be,
(v, 1643)

and the treachery denounced by Troilo is toned down to 'hire hertes variaunce' (v, 1670). Troilus may wonder for a moment why God does not punish Criseyde, but the only reproach that he permits himself to address to her is the dignified and restrained remark, 'I have it nat deserved' (v, 1722).

What does hurt him to the quick is her lack of loyalty; which is but natural, since loyalty is the very core of his being. So conspicuous is it that Pandarus, in enumerating his good qualities, mentions his loyalty first, and Criseyde confesses that this trait helped to win her heart. For one so steadfast there can be no question of forgetting. Like Troilo, he is haunted by the image of his lady, but whereas his self-centred counterpart complains because he cannot drive it from his mind, Troilus loves her as before. Assured that he has not long to live, he gives orders for his cremation and the sending of his ashes to Criseyde.[1] It certainly never occurs to him as it does to Troilo, that he might grow accustomed to separation from her. Even before the actual parting he sees in Death the only solution, and he adjures those lovers who may pass his tomb to remember him,

> For I loved ek, though ich unworthi were.
>
> (iv, 329)

This diffidence is yet another trait that differentiates him from Troilo. Sometimes it assumes the form of an excessive modesty springing from a consciousness of the uncouthness of the Trojans compared with the polished Greeks, but more often it arises from a sense of his personal inferiority to the lady he worships. So great is the distance between them in his esteem that he is alarmed at the mere prospect of speaking to her of love. His confusion is akin to that portrayed by Bernard de Ventadour who, on seeing his lady, betrays his emotion in eyes, hue and visage and trembles with fear like the leaf in the wind.[2] Troilus lies repeating what he intends to say but on her approach is overcome by a sudden embarrassment and forgets all his carefully planned speech. Blushes alternate with pallor, as with downcast eyes and trembling voice he twice falters 'mercy, mercy, swete herte!'

The scene in Criseyde's bedchamber when Troilus suddenly faints with emotion may also be interpreted in the light of the troubadour tradition. It is likely that the episode was suggested to Chaucer by the incident related in the *Filostrato* when Troilo, after listening to the discussion in the Trojan assembly about the exchange of Griseida, swoons with anxiety.[3] By transferring the event to the earlier stage in the relations of the lovers Chaucer provided yet another illustration of the emotional upheaval experienced by the hero in the presence of his lady which the poets of courtly love had so often dwelt upon.

He may well have had another reason. The swoon of Troilo in public savours of weakness, whereas that of Troilus, exhausted by long waiting

---

[1] v, 309–15.

[2]
> Cant eu la vei, be m'es parven
> als olhs, al vis, a la color,
> car aissi tremble de paor
> com fa la folha contra'l ven.

Cf. *Bernart von Ventadorn : Seine Lieder*, ed. C. Appel, Halle, 1915, no. 31, ll. 41–4.

[3] He is brought round by his brothers who bathe his face and rub his pulse. The same treatment is applied by Pandarus and Criseyde.

> Therwith his pous and paumes of his hondes
> They gan to frote, and ek his temples tweyne.
>
> (iii, 1114–15)

in suspense close to the woman he loved so ardently, might be more readily excused. This supposition is all the more probable because again and again Chaucer strives to make Troilus more manly than his counterpart. The hero of the *Filostrato* was marked by an emotionalism and a sentimentality which scarcely harmonised with his martial fame, and there are many signs that Chaucer was aware of this incompatibility. At the close of the poem he is careful to warn the reader that he has been concerned to portray Troilus in love and that in consequence those who might wish to know of his warlike deeds should turn elsewhere. Guido delle Colonne and Benoît de Ste. More were doubtless the authorities uppermost in Chaucer's mind. For them the love of Troilus and Briseida was a mere episode occurring during a truce in the Trojan war and serving as a relief from the numerous battle scenes. They depicted him as a great warrior and leader, second only to Hector, and in their narrative, after his brother's death, Troilus naturally steps into his place as the champion of the Trojans. In Benoît especially Troilus is the flower of chivalry and rates knightly honour higher than anything in the world. It is clear that Chaucer was affected by this conception. Hence, even though he disclaims any attempt to show this aspect of his hero, he introduces various passages with the express intention of revealing his exploits in combat. He is presented as a paragon of chivalry,[1] and we are given more than one glimpse of him as he puts the Greeks to flight, the account of Pandarus being especially vivid.[2] But the most graphic passage is that which pictures his return from the battlefield with all the marks of the fray upon him, to the jubilant acclamation of the people of Troy.[3]

Having witnessed such a scene, Criseyde rightly praises Troilus for his manliness,[4] and there are various allusions to this quality, whether it is displayed in action or in the repression of his grief. Nowhere is his self-control more remarkable than when it has become certain that the happiness of the lovers is to be shattered by Criseyde's departure from Troy. His farewell is described thus:

> whan he saugh that she ne myghte dwelle,
> Which that his soule out of his herte rente,
> Withouten more, out of the chaumbre he wente.
> (iv, 1699–701)

The suggestion of suffering too acute for words is in striking contrast to the tearful parting narrated by Boccaccio. There is a similar strength in Troilus' quiet acceptance of the inevitable, once he has been assured that he may expect to see Criseyde again within ten days, an attitude very different from the feeble lamentations of Troilo on this occasion.

---

[1] v, 835–40.   [2] ii, 193–203.   [3] ii, 624–44.   [4] iv, 1674.

Yet Troilus' acquiescence is not a weak passivity. It is typical of him
that he longs for action and plans to carry off Criseyde before she has
been handed over to the Greeks. Indeed, but for his fear that she might
be killed in the struggle,

> He hadde it don, withouten wordes more.
> (v, 56)

Nothing distinguishes Troilus more sharply from his prototype than
this dislike of wordiness. His songs and his letters to Criseyde are much
briefer,[1] and in this restriction of sentiment and lyric utterance the
Chaucerian intention to portray him as a man of action whose speech
tallies with his deeds, becomes manifest, and his assurance to Criseyde

> At shorte wordes, wel ye may me leve;
> I kan no more, it shal be founde at preve
> (iv, 1658–9)

reflects his character faithfully. To one so little given to eloquence and
rhetorical ornament the advice of Pandarus to Troilus when composing his first letter that he should eschew the repetition of a word,
however excellent in itself, must seem pointless. On the other hand,
it does apply to Troilo, as may be seen from the corresponding letter
written by him:

> *Tu sola* puoi queste pene noiose,
> Quando tu vogli, porre in dolce pace;
> *Tu sola* puoi l'afflizion penose,
> Madonna, porre in riposo verace;
> *Tu sola* puoi con l'opere pietose
> Tormi il tormento che sì mi disface;
> *Tu sola* puoi, siccome donna mia,
> Adempier ciò che lo mio cuor disia.
>
> Dunque, *se mai* per pura fede alcuno,
> *Si mai* per grande amor, se per disio
> Di ben servire ognora in ciascheduno
> Caso, qual si volesse o buono o rio,
> Meritò grazia, *fa'ch'io* ne sia uno,
> Cara mia donna; *fa'ch'io* sia quell'io,
> Che a te ricorro, sì come a colei
> Che se' cagion di tutti i sospir miei.
> (*O.V.* ii, st. 101–2)

It seems that Chaucer had observed this habit of Troilo, of which
other examples may be found in the *Filostrato*,[2] and had placed the

---

[1] His song in iii, 1744–71 takes up four stanzas, and that in v, 638–44 one, in contrast
with Boccaccio's sixteen and five (iii, st. 74–89 and v, st. 62–6); his letters (ii, 1065–84
and v, 1317–421) take up three and fifteen stanzas respectively, as against eleven and
twenty-four in Boccaccio (ii, st. 96–106 and vii, st. 52–75).
[2] *O.V.* v, st. 54–5; vii, st. 34–5 and 59; viii, st. 12–13.

admonition in the mouth of Pandarus, without considering that it was not required by a hero on whom he had bestowed simplicity and directness of speech in keeping with a man of action.

Perhaps it was for this reason that Chaucer modified or suppressed an image that Troilo uses about himself when, seeking Griseida's favour, he exclaims:

> Io tornerò, se tu fai donna questo,
> Qual fiore in nuovo prato in primavera.
>
> (*O.V.* i, st. 56, ll. 1–2)

and later,

> Non fu mai rosa in dolce primavera,
> Bella, com'io a ritornar diposto
> Sono.
>
> (*O.V.* v, st. 37, ll. 4–6)

Clearly, Chaucer felt uncomfortable about the association of a virile warrior with a spring flower and a rose. Therefore he substituted

> For was ther nevere fowel so fayn of May,
> As I shal ben.
>
> (v, 425–6)

The change is significant, the image of Boccaccio suggesting a passive beauty, that of Chaucer an active energy. This accords well with his conception of Troilus. From the beginning we are made to perceive his power of leadership when he strolls about the temple, glancing at the ladies and followed by other youths,

> as he was wont to gide
> His yonge knyghtes.
>
> (i, 183–4)

Afterwards he shows himself capable of taking the initiative, whereas Troilo is incapable of doing anything without a hint from his friend. Apparently it is Troilus' idea to get rid of Deiphobus and Eleyne, while he converses with Criseyde, by handing to them documents that he has received from Hector. At the end of his interview with her, as he hears them returning from the garden, he keeps up the pretence of his illness by groaning heavily and dismisses them on the plea that he needs rest. In all this, though, of course, Pandarus arranges the meeting at the house of Deiphobus, Troilus receives no outside help. Similarly, when he has heard of Pandarus' scheme for bringing him together with Criseyde at his own house, Troilus quite independently circulates a report that if he is missed, night or day, it is to be understood that he has gone to sacrifice at the temple of Apollo, in order to learn when the Greeks will flee next, and he is not to be disturbed. Finally, when the exchange of Criseyde for Antenor has been agreed upon, he forms some sort of plan.[1] With a companion so experienced as Pandarus, Troilus is naturally inclined to rely on his counsel, but he is not without resources of his own. Certainly he is no mere yes-man, waiting to be told what to do and is altogether unlike the hesitant hero portrayed by Boccaccio:

> Volendo e non volendo or questo or quello,
> Intra due stava il timido donzello.
>
> (*O.V.* iv, st. 16, ll. 7–8)

When Troilus does conceive of a scheme, he is shrewd and practical. However passionately he may be in love, he has a streak of hard common sense. In persuading Criseyde to flee with him, he does not overlook the need for the means of subsistence. Troilo is satisfied to look forward to a romantic world of vague delight; Troilus is business-like in the extreme:

> And vulgarly to speken of substaunce
> Of tresour, may we bothe with us lede
> Inough to lyve in honour and plesaunce,
> Til into tyme that we shal ben dede;
> And thus we may eschuen al this drede.
>
> .   .   .   .   .
>
> And, hardily, ne dredeth no poverte,
> For I have kyn and frendes elleswhere,
> That, though we comen in oure bare sherte,
> Us sholde neyther lakken gold ne gere,
> But ben honoured while we dwelten there.
>
> (iv, 1513–17; 1520–4)

Such a man as this is not likely to become the prey of his emotions. Consequently, Chaucer sought in various ways to moderate the excessive display of feeling in which Troilo indulges repeatedly. One sign is his suppression of the kisses which his hero on several occasions bestows upon Pandarus. Sometimes he omits all reference to them; elsewhere he substitutes some other mode of expressing Troilus' sentiments. Thus when Pandarus brings the good news that Criseyde will favour Troilus, instead of kissing him again and again, he holds up his hands to express his joy and gratitude. Similarly, on seeing his friend after the night of his meeting with Criseyde at Pandarus' house, Troilus falls on his knees, whereas in Boccaccio we read:

> con disio gli si gittò al collo:
>
> .   .   .   .   .
>
> E nella fronte con amor baciollo.
>
> (*O.V.* iii, st. 56, ll. 4–6)

Even more striking is the greater restraint imposed by Chaucer

---

[1] iv, 169–75.

upon his hero in the expression of his grief or disappointment. Troilo is everlastingly emitting sighs and shedding tears, complaining of the fires of love which martyrise his soul and consume him to the point of death, or lamenting his unhappy lot. He is a languishing and a wailing lover who alienates our sympathy by his futile and maudlin self-pity. Chaucer resolutely set himself to modify this feature of the Boccaccian hero's character, always keeping in mind that he was not only a passionate lover but also a warrior. He limits the sighs, tears, sobs and complaints and more than once gives a glimpse of the fiery vigour of Troilus, as when he tersely declares

> I wol my selven sle, if that ye drecche[1]
>
> (iv, 1446)

or after pouring imprecations on Calchas exclaims:

> wolde blisful Jove, for his joie,
> That I the hadde where I wolde in Troie!
>
> (iv, 335–6)

When Troilus is assailed with grief, it is not allowed to attain exaggerated proportions. His words to the absent Criseyde are more concerned with her happiness than with his own misery:

> For ther nas houre in al the day or nyght,
> Whan he was there as no wight myghte hym heere,
> That he ne seyde: 'O lufsom lady bryght,
> How have ye faren syn that ye were heere?
> Welcome, ywis, myn owne lady deere.
>
> (v, 463–7)

In comparison Troilo seems an effeminate weakling:

> E non passava sera nè mattina
> Che con sospiri costui non chiamasse,
> O luce bella, o stella mattutina;
> Poi, come s'ella presente ascoltasse,
> Mille fiate e più, rosa di spina
> Chiamandola che ella il salutasse,
> Pria ch' e' ristesse sempre convenia,
> Il salutar col sospirar finia.
>
> (O.V. v, st. 44, ll. 1–8)

Criseyde's failure to return throws Troilus into a state of profound dejection, and he shuns all society and refuses food and drink. Yet in all this there is no trace of the lachrymose self-indulgence displayed by his prototype. Nor would Chaucer's reader ever suspect, when the despairing hero soberly contemplates suicide, what a wild outburst in the

---

[1] Cf.

> Nè veggio bene ancor com'io mi passi
> Senza doglioso ed amaro languire,
> Sentendo te altrove.
>
> (O.V. iv, st. 140, ll. 4–6)

original had been rejected by the English author. Boccaccio shows us Troilo in a state of hysterical excitement; he tries to stab himself and is only prevented from doing so by sheer force. He loses all self-control and in spite of his unbounded fury appears weak and unbalanced. He sits down 'piangendo', and when Pandaro has rebuked him, he answers with tears in his voice, his words continually interrupted by sobs.

If Troilo is undignified here, there are other scenes in which the violence of his emotion is somewhat comic. It is difficult to repress a smile at the sight he presents as he falls prone on his bed and bursts into tears after confessing to Pandaro his love for Griseida. Chaucer would have none of this. Nor did he retain the passage in which the woeful Troilo is visited first by his brother Deifebo and then by a crowd of solicitous Trojan women, who flock into his chamber and try to banish his sorrow, the whole culminating in a family quarrel when Cassandra ventures to sneer at Griseida. Other passages there are which Chaucer does not reject outright but which he transforms in such a way that they cease to be ridiculous. Thus when Pandaro comes to consult with his friend after the decision to hand over Griseida to the Greeks has been made, Boccaccio relates that

> Troilo, tosto che veduto l'ebbe,
> Gli corse al collo sì forte piangendo,
> Che bene raccontarlo uom non potrebbe;
>
> .   .   .   .   .   .
>
> E in cotal guisa, null 'altro facendo
> Che pianger forte, dimoraro alquanto
> Senza parlar nessuno o tanto o quanto.
>
> (*O.V.* iv, st. 44, ll. 1–8)

Chaucer mentions that on entering the chamber, Pandarus 'ful tendreliche wepte' and stood gazing with folded arms at 'this woful Troilus' and 'his pitous face'. He also adds that

> This woful wight, this Troilus, that felte
> His frend Pandare ycomen hym to se,
> Gan as the snow ayeyn the sonne melte,
> For which this sorwful Pandare, of pitee,
> Gan for to wepe as tendreliche as he.
>
> (iv, 365–9)

But he does not let the friends weep on each other's neck. Moreover, the introduction of the simile lends a certain poetic quality that somehow elevates the scene. The same holds good of another passage that concludes Troilus' rebuttal of Pandarus' arguments to the effect that he should forget Criseyde and bestow his love on some other woman. In Boccaccio both men burst into tears and, in spite of Pandaro's attempts to console him, Troilo weeps copiously. Chaucer on this occasion tolerates no rivalry in shedding tears, makes Troilus more subdued in his grief and again achieves a poetic effect by means of a simile.

> This Troilus in teris gan distille,
> As licour out of a lambyc ful faste;
> And Pandarus gan holde his tonge stille,
> And to the ground his eyen down he caste.
>
> (iv, 519–22)

A like procedure is adopted in the scene where Troilus meets Criseyde after the grievous tidings of their coming separation have become known. Here is certainly nothing to excite the reader to laughter. Chaucer tries to distract attention from the abundance of their tears and sobs and sighs by emphasising their bitterness, as may be seen from these lines, which may nevertheless be faintly ironical at the close:

> Tho woful teeris that they leten falle
> As bittre weren, out of teris kynde,
> For peyne, as is ligne aloes or galle.
> So bittre teeris weep nat, as I fynde,
> The woful Mirra thorugh the bark and rynde.[1]
>
> (iv, 1135–9)

It is obvious that even after all the changes made by Chaucer, Troilus is no strong, silent man. He is still so much given to a display of feeling that he merits Pandarus' reminder that the shortest way to success in love is not to wallow and weep like Niobe the queen. But Chaucer tones down the grosser effects and on occasion employs more subtle ways of suggesting emotion—Troilus' sudden outburst of song at the prospect of being reunited to Criseyde, his loving memory of the voice of Criseyde singing to him from the past, his deathly pallor, his inability to sit quietly on his horse, the furious pace at which he rides, or his restless pacing to and fro upon the walls of Troy, the sudden frosty chill at his heart when he sees his lady's empty house.

One may wonder whether Chaucer was satisfied with Troilus after he had undergone so much manipulation. Though the modern English reader may find him still too prone to emotional display, there is no reason to surmise that his creator would agree, for the severe convention of to-day is not of long standing, as the scene of Nelson's death

---

[1]
> Di lagrime bagnati tutti quanti,
> E volendo parlarsi non potieno,
> Sì gl'impedivan gli angosciosi pianti,
> E'singhiozzi e'sospiri, e nondimeno
> Si baciavan talvolta, e le cascanti
> Lacrime si bevean.
>
> (O.V. iv, st. 115, ll. 2–7)

serves to remind us.[1] In another respect, however, he may well have felt some misgiving. There were moments in the intrigue against Criseyde when the conduct of Troilus hardly seemed worthy of an ideal knight. He stooped to subterfuge, deceit, and the violation of solemn assurances. These passages, of Chaucer's own invention, present Troilus in an unfavourable light, and so what the poet had gained by an attempt to exhibit his hero as the epitome of chivalry, as modest[2] as he is valiant, is nullified by such shifty proceedings. It is a sign of Chaucer's discomfort that he tries to forestall adverse comment. He declares, perhaps half in jest, that he will not be astonished,

> if it happe in any wyse,
> That here be any lovere in this place
> That herkneth, as the story wol devise,
> How Troilus com to his lady grace,
> And thenketh, 'so nolde I nat love purchace'.
>
> (ii, 29–33)

But he replies that customs vary in different countries and that one cannot expect that everywhere love should be made as in England by formal visits and declarations!

The predicament from which Chaucer sought to escape in this fashion was of his own creation. It arose from amplifications of the original not unconnected with the character of Criseyde. However, before attempting to discuss Chaucer's portrayal of her, it is well to understand how Boccaccio had drawn her counterpart. Griseida belongs to a group of similar figures in his writings, all of them young widows urged on by 'la rabbiosa furia della carnale concupiscenza'.[3] Of these Dido is one, and in *De claris mulieribus* he goes so far as to condemn all women who marry a second time on the pretext that they cannot resist the soliciting of the flesh. In his earlier work, *The Decameron*, the point of view is not that of the severe moralist, as may be seen

---

[1] It is of interest to note that in *Morte Arthure*, which was written between 1350 and 1400 and therefore belongs to Chaucer's period, Sir Gawaine weeps for his men and Arthur, on finding Sir Gawaine dead, swoons and weeps profusely. His grief is so immoderate that Sir Ewayne rebukes him:

> It es no wirchipe i-wysse to wryng thyne hondes,
> To wepe als a womane it es no witt holdene!
> Be knyghtly of contenaunce, als a kyng scholde,
> And leue siche clamoure for Cristes lufe of heuene!
>
> (3977–80)

[2] Witness his embarrassment at the acclamations of the crowd:

> he wex a litel reed for shame,
> Whan he the peple upon hym herde cryen,
> That to byholde it was a noble game,
> How sobreliche he caste adown his eyen.
>
> (ii, 645–8)

[3] Cf. *L'Ameto-Lettere-Il Corbaccio*, ed. N. Bruscoli, Bari, 1940, p. 219.

G

from three young widows who are the heroines of their respective tales.[1] Among them Elena of Florence[2] is notable, because, like Griseida, she is determined not to fetter herself in wedlock again but to spend her time gaily in the company of whatever gallant she may choose.[3] There is also an essential similarity between Ghismonda[4] and Griseida, each of them a resolute personality bent on satisfying her desires, though Griseida is cast in a less heroic mould and has not to battle against the will of a savage father. In Griseida's sensuality lies the secret of the ease with which Pandaro induces her to accept his proposal on behalf of Troilo. She offers some objection, asserting that she is still mourning her dead husband and will continue to do so all her life. Yet only six stanzas later her resistance is overcome, the decisive factor being Pandaro's argument that her beauty will soon fade, either through old age or death.

In her later reflections, she maintains that there is no reason why she should not love while still young. Others do this; to follow their example can be no sin. So her decision is:

> Adunque vigorosa
> Ricevi il dolce amante, il qual venuto
> T'è fermamente mandato da Dio,
> E sodisfa'al suo caldo disio.
>
> (*O.V.* ii, st. 74, ll. 5–8)

Her love for Troilo, as she herself candidly admits, is simply a means to quench the fire within her; even before she has met him, she is already indulging in amorous delight in anticipation:

> or foss'io nelle braccia
> Dolci di lui, stretta a faccia a faccia!
>
> (*O.V.* ii, st. 117, ll. 7–8)

She has therefore made up her mind to yield and in her reply to his letter indicates this openly. It is true that when Pandaro next approaches her, she talks of loving Troilo like a brother, but a moment later she abandons all opposition and sends a message to say that she will comply with Troilo's wishes. Without delay he comes to her house, is admitted by her in person, and their passion is consummated in a scene that is frankly sensual.

Griseida is therefore a somewhat too merry widow, and it can occasion no surprise that such a woman should transfer her affection to Diomede. Boccaccio does not explain her motives in any detail because he probably considered that the reason for her conduct was manifest. However, in the summary of Diomede's qualities which Griseida ponders before surrendering herself to him, one is significant

---

[1] ii, 2; iv, 1; viii, 7.   [2] viii, 7.   [3] Cf. *Filostrato*, ii, st. 69–74.   [4] iv, 1

After mentioning his robust physique and handsome appearance, Boccaccio adds:

> E ad amor la natura aveva prona.
>
> (*O.V.* vi, st. 33, l. 5)

Clearly, he thought of Griseida as a sensual creature, which accounted for the rapidity with which she allowed Diomede to supplant Troilo and her lack of subsequent regrets. This behaviour seemed to him to warrant his general condemnation of young women at the close of the poem for their inconstancy and libidinousness.

It was, however, not only in Boccaccio that Chaucer found a portrayal of the relations of Troilus and Criseyde. Older still were the accounts given by Benoît de Ste. More and his successor Guido delle Colonne, and these are also valuable for the appreciation of Chaucer's interpretation.[1] Guido was a prosaic individual with a strong moralising bent and a violent prejudice against women. He never loses an opportunity of denouncing their folly, and he indulges in such generalisations as

> omnium enim mulierum semper est moris vt cum inhonesto desiderio virum aliquem appetunt, sub alicuius honestatis uelamine suas excusationes intendant[2]

and

> sicut de forma ad formam procedere materie notum est, sic mulieris concupiscentia dissoluta procedere de uiro ad uirum, uti esse creditur sine fine.[3]

The attitude of such a writer to Briseida is decided in advance. He regards her merely as one of a species and not as an individual. Consequently, he omits many details that throw light on her psychological development and reveal the struggle between good and evil in her nature. Guido is blind to the subtler shades of characterisation because he does not want to see. If he finds her described as

> Simple e aumosniere e pitose,[4]

he suppresses the line, for it does not fit into his scheme. For the same reason he will hear nothing of the tears shed by the Trojan ladies at her departure, nor of her own genuine grief on being separated from these friends and from her lover. Nor does he appreciate the mixed feelings with which Briseida receives the steed won by Diomedes from Troilus, nor the importance of the later return of the horse to the

---

[1] His dependence on Joseph of Exeter's poetical paraphrase, *Frigii Daretis Ylias*, must also be taken into account, as has been proved by R. K. Root, *M.P.*, 1917, xv, pp. 1–22. The work had a great reputation in the Middle Ages. It was still read in the Renaissance period, being first printed at Basle in 1558 under the title *Daretis Phrygii . . . de Bello Trojano . . . libri sex* and again in 1583.

[2] *Historia destructionis Troiae*, ed. N. E. Griffin, Cambridge, 1936, Liber ii, p. 18.

[3] Griffin's ed., Liber ii, p. 17. [4] Benoît, l. 5288.

victor and the gift of her sleeve to be worn as a favour in a tournament. He does not grasp the significance of these incidents as milestones on the road of estrangement. The whole business is for him quite simple. Briseida's action is only what is to be expected and invites no comment, unless it be to emphasise her evil ways. He loses no chance of slipping in a condemnatory phrase such as 'propter suas illecebras',[1] and having loaded the dice against her by making her love for Troilo begin to abate on the very first day of her arrival in the Greek camp, he proceeds to add:

Quid est ergo quod dicatur de constancia mulierum, quarum sexus proprium in se habet ut repentina fragilitate earum proposita dissoluantur et hora breuissima mutabiliter uariantur? Non enim cadit in homine uarietates et dolos earum posse describere, cum magis quam dici possit sint earum uolubilia proposita nequiora.[2]

Determined as he is to present Briseida only as a type of female callousness and perfidy, Guido takes good care that his reader shall never learn anything of her heart-searching, her regrets and repentance. In his hands she tends to become a mere abstraction.

Very different is the treatment of the story in the *Roman de Troie*. It is true that like Guido, Benoît regards the siege of Troy as the main theme and introduces the love-element primarily as a contrast to the inevitable monotony of the numerous battle-scenes. But his mind is more supple, and he sees clearly into the working of the human heart. His Briseida is well liked by all the Trojans. Priam alone would gladly see her leave Troy, but that is merely because he is animated by hostility to her father; he praises ungrudgingly her nobility, virtue, wisdom and beauty. The rest of the royal family regret her departure, and many people bid her a sorrowful good-bye. For her part, she is no less grieved and leaves them with tears and cries and sadness in her heart. At her final parting from Troilus she is even more intensely moved:

> La danzele cuide morir
> Quant de celui deit departir.
>
> (ll. 13495–6)

She vows that all her life she will never be the friend of another, and Benoît says nothing to imply that her assurances of fidelity are less sincere than those of Troilus. Yet he has no great faith in the steadfastness of women. Their sorrow is of brief duration; they weep with one eye and smile with the other. They soon change their mind, and even the wisest of them is foolish. A woman who has loved for seven years will forget in three days.[3]

Although Benoît makes no comment, his account of the magnificent and costly robes that Briseida took with her from Troy,[4] following as

---

[1] Griffin's ed., Liber viii, p. 85. [2] Ibid., Liber xix, p. 166.
[3] ll. 13441–6. [4] ll. 13329–409.

it does without a break the description of the bitter nocturnal parting from Troilus, was most likely intended to suggest a calculating strain in her. However that may be, it is certain that on the way to the Greek camp she already begins to appear less attractive. Her rejection of Diomede's advances savours of worldly wisdom, and we become aware of a hard, rational strain in her. She argues that she does not know him well enough and that it would be rash of her to love him so quickly. She must also consider her reputation. But what alienates sympathy most of all is her mention in the same breath of the grief she feels at the loss of her friend and her wealth. One is struck also by the fact that, while she maintains that she is in no mood for love and hopes that God will not implant any such emotion in her, she goes so far as to say that, were it to happen, there was no one whom she would care for more than Diomede. In keeping with this attitude is her failure to show any displeasure when, unnoticed by others, he steals one of her gloves.

The same unfeeling element in her character as has already appeared emerges again when she meets Calchas. At first she is, like him, over-joyed and responds to his kisses and embraces, yet a moment later she is mingling reproaches for his treason with a lament over the forfei-ture of his riches and possessions. The change is so abrupt that it points to a lack of balance in her nature. We are therefore prepared for the discovery that the meeting with the Greek princes tends to make Briseida relinquish her original intention, and before the fourth evening she has given up her plan for returning to Troy. Benoît comments on this instability and grimly adds that it is the loyal who pay for it. However, the process is gradual, and Benoît traces skilfully the various stages. The next of these is reached when Diomede, having dismounted Troilus, presents his horse to Briseida. In her reply she cannot refrain from telling him that if he loves her, he should spare her people, and with obvious pride in Troilus' prowess she warns the donor what a requital he may expect from such a knight. Neverthe-less, she ends by saying that since he loves her, she would be wrong to hate him. She will therefore not hate him, though she does not love him. From now on Diomede suffers the agony of his unreciprocated passion, and though he often pleads with her, she remains obdurate. At this juncture there is still no question of any relenting on her part. Indeed, Benoît remarks that she grew three times harder, for such is the nature of women. Diomede's renewed petitions only strengthen this sense of power:

> E mout se fait joiose e liee
> De ço qu'il est si en ses laz.

(ll. 15174–5)

However, at last she decides to give him one of her silken sleeves to bear as a pennant on his lance. This is the first positive mark of favour that she has bestowed upon Diomede, and Benoît stresses its importance; for henceforth her love for Troilus is broken, and he will await her in vain.

Yet it is not until many months later, in fact not until some years after her departure from Troy, that Briseida yields to Diomede. By the irony of fate it is Troilus himself who brings it to pass. During the fifteenth battle he wounds Diomede severely and Briseida takes pity on him. Thoroughly disillusioned by now, Troilus assumes that she has already given herself to Diomede and predicts that before the siege is over, she will betray him too, and he will have to keep a sharp look-out, if he is not to share her with others.

> Ne s'est ancor pas arestee,
> Dès que li mestiers li agree.
>
> (ll. 20097–8)

These bitter words are heard both by Greeks and Trojans, and repeated far and wide. But in spite of Troilus' accusations, it was only after Diomede had been wounded that Briseida bestowed her love upon him:

> Dès ore est tote en lui s'entente,
> Dès or l'aime, dès or l'en tient.
>
> (ll. 20216–17)

> Dès or puet om aparceveir
> Que vers lui a tot atorné:
> S'amor, son cuer e son pensé.
>
> (ll. 20226–8)

However, Benoît is not content to end the story thus. In a long soliloquy he makes Briseida reveal all the warring emotions within her. She is far from happy, for she knows that she will be held in evil repute:

> De mei n'iert ja fait bon escrit
> Ne chantee bone chançon.
>
> (ll. 20238–9)

The women of Troy will find fault with her, for she has brought shame upon them, and her treachery will always be a cause of reproach to them. She admits that she is false, fickle and foolish, and her heart is too changeable. Her friend was the best that any one could have; she ought to have loved him and hated those who sought to harm him, instead of which she has bestowed her love on his worst enemy. Consequently, she will for ever be despised. All this would never have happened, if she had not left Troy. Never did her heart then even contemplate change. But among the Greeks she was without friends, and she felt the need for someone to dispel her sorrow. Yet in spite of these attempts at self-justification, her heart grieves and bleeds; she often weeps and wishes that she could forget what she has done. She prays God to prosper Troilus, for she is filled with remorse. Harassed by her memories and the pangs of regret, she nevertheless realises that she must face the situation. Repentance avails nothing; there is no remedy. Henceforth she must give her mind to Diomede, so that each may have joy in the other. She ends by declaring that her proud bearing towards him has gone and she is prepared to do his will.

With the examples of Guido and of Benoît before him Chaucer could see which was to be avoided and which provided the more fruitful way of interpreting Boccaccio's heroine. His Criseyde is a pleasing figure with long, slender fingers and fair hair bound with a thread of gold. Her voice is agreeable, and everything about her of a feminine delicacy. Far from being tall and powerful in body, she is of medium height, and no one was ever 'lasse mannyssh in semynge'. In disposition she is harmonious and well balanced. There is no trace of morbidity in her grief for her dead husband, and in spite of her rejection of Pandarus' invitation to join in the celebrations of the coming of May and her protest that it would be more fitting for her to pray in a cave and read saints' lives, she is still full of zest and gaiety. Whereas we hear little of the 'piacevole riso' of Griseida, the sound of Criseyde's laughter echoes through the early part of the poem, and it is hearty laughter, the unrestrained mirth of a young and healthy creature.

This normality is reflected in her love for Troilus, into which the motives that animate Boccaccio's heroine do not enter. One of the chief factors to sway her is her admiration of his qualities, and not so much Pandarus' argument about the passing of beauty. She extols him not only for his valour but also for his ethical supremacy, a combination which, as she points out, is seldom found in one person. In the first place she is attracted to him neither by his royal birth nor his warlike fame, but by his

> moral vertu, grounded upon trouthe,
> (iv, 1672)

which enables his reason to bridle his passion. In such words there is nothing that smacks of the facile voluptuary or the superficial wanton, an impression that is confirmed by the slowness with which she yields to Troilus and Diomedes, no less than by her motives in delaying. Of her prototype Pandaro had claimed that she was more honest than other women, but his assertion is belied by her actions. On the other

hand, when Pandarus speaks of Criseyde as 'vertuous . . . al' and
'of vices cleene', when he maintains that

> the name as yit of hire
> Among the peple, as who seyth, halwed is;
> For nevere was ther wight, I dar wel swere,
> That evere wiste that she dide amys,
>
> (iii, 267–70)

we are willing to believe him, partly because of her conduct until that
point in the tale, partly because of the high esteem in which she is held
by the noble Hector. As Deiphobus tells,

> I have herd hym, o tyme and ek oother,
> Speke of Cryseyde swich honour, that he
> May seyn no bet.
>
> (ii, 1452–4)

Deiphobus himself as well as Eleyne praises her, both for her good
breeding and her admirable qualities. The poet too commends her,
as being polite and 'sobre . . . and wys'.

An amatory poem is hardly the place in which to look for sagacity,
yet Criseyde does contrive to display it. Most conspicuously it appears
in her comment on the futility of lamentation without action:

> if a wight alwey his wo compleyne,
> And seketh nought how holpen for to be,
> It nys but folie and encrees of peyne
>
> (iv, 1255–7)

and in her decision to ignore popular clamour,

> For whoso wol of every word take hede,
> Or reulen hym by every wightes wit,
> Ne shal he nevere thryven.
>
> (v, 767–9)

Quite apart from this, she evinces, if not wisdom, at any rate a distinct
shrewdness. The confusion of Troilus on the occasion of their meeting
at Deiphobus' house does not escape her notice, and her questions
about his supposed jealousy of Horaste are so penetrating as to embar-
rass her lover.

The incident of Horaste brings to light another aspect of her
fundamental seriousness. She had prized Troilus especially for his
loyalty and assumed that he would credit her with an equal fidelity.
What hurts her therefore in his feigned jealousy is the mere idea that
he should think her capable of disloyalty. Fidelity had in fact been a
postulate for her love from the very beginning and on their parting
she makes the most solemn vows, praying that if she is false, she may
be consigned to hell. This emergency is but the test to which she had
looked forward when she declared to Troilus:

> I emforth my connyng and my might,
> Have, and ay shal, how sore that me smerte,
> Ben to yow trewe and hool with al myn herte;—

> And dredeles, this shal be founde at preve.
>   (iii, 999–1002)

Ironical as this may seem in the light of later events, no doubt should be cast on the sincerity of her promise. Chaucer gives his guarantee:

> treweliche, as writen wel I fynde,
> That al this thyng was seyd of good entente;
> And that hire herte trewe was and kynde
> Towardes hym, and spak right as she mente;
> And that she starf for wo neigh, whan she wente,
> And was in purpos evere to be trewe.
>   (1415–20)

It is evident therefore that Criseyde's intentions were unimpeachable. How then are her subsequent fickleness and betrayal to be explained? First, it may be observed that Chaucer was not altogether lacking in sympathy with what Guido and Benoît had said of women's instability. We may recall the remark that he interposes in the *Knight's Tale* when Emelye, seeing Arcite victorious, began to look upon him with approval:

> For wommen, as to speken in comune,
> They folwen al the favour of fortune.
>   (A. 2681–2)

Accordingly, he depicts Criseyde as weak, drifting along under the impulse of Fortune, with the result that her purpose is nullified. In character as in physique she has less strength than Griseida, and whereas the latter abandons Troilo for Diomede in the deliberate pursuit of sensual desire, the inconstancy of Criseyde arises from an infirmity to which many factors contribute. One of the first signs of Chaucer's plan is seen in his systematic suppression of references in the *Filostrato* to the heroine's haughtiness. The first time that he comes across the epithet 'altiera', he tones it down to 'with ful assured lokyng and manere', and though he does admit a little later 'somdel deignous', he afterwards removes all trace of imperiousness. What a contrast, for example, is the patient acquiescence with which she leaves Troy, to the fiery indignation of Griseida!

> whan she redy was to ride,
> Ful sorwfully she sighte, and seyde: 'allas!'
> But forth she moot, for aught that may bitide;
> Ther nys non other remedie in this cas;
> And forth she rit ful sorwfully a pas.
>   (v, 57–61)

After such an exhibition of passivity one is not surprised to find that she excuses her failure to return as being due to 'the goddes ordinaunce'.

In her attitude to her father she reveals a similar lack of spirit. She goes so far as to wish him bad luck for her share in his misfortune, but she indulges in no such fierce and violent denunciations as Griseida. Either she says nothing at all of 'mio padre malvagio' or contents herself with exclaiming

> O Calkas, fader, thyn be al this synne!
>
> (iv, 761)

She speaks with some contempt of his reported ability to expound Apollo's words and suggests that his interpretation is governed by his own cowardice, but when she meets him face to face, she politely declares that she is glad to see him and in her manner is both 'milde, and mansuete', whereas Griseida, though not openly hostile, displays no such complaisance. Finally, Criseyde even tells Diomedes that she is obliged to Calchas for the arrangement of the exchange—a statement which would seem incomprehensible but for the feebleness arising from the courtesy of the well-bred lady and the dutifulness of the daughter.

To her other relative, Pandarus, she is also deferential. It is true that she is attached to him as her friend and counsellor, but there are passages in which she clearly looks up to him as a senior kinsman who is to be treated with respect and whose word is law. In the first of these she is eager to learn what the news is, about which he has just dropped a hint, but she refrains from pressing him:

> uncle myn, I nyl yow nat displese,
> Nor axen moore that may do yow disese.
>
> (ii, 146–7)

The second relates how she accepts his invitation to supper in spite of some misgivings:

> she graunted with hym for to go
> Withoute await, syn that he hire bisoughte,
> And, as his nece, obeyed as hire oughte.
>
> (iii, 579–81)

To Troilus, once he has become her lover, her subordination is still more complete:

> what so ye me comaunde,
> That wol I don.
>
> (iv, 1294–5)

This side of Criseyde's nature places her at a disadvantage when she has to handle an unexpected crisis and come to a rapid decision unaided. Pandarus knows this well and repeatedly adopts shock tactics to gain his ends. Time and again he succeeds, but nowhere is her helplessness more patent than when he startles her by bringing Troilus to her bedside as if by magic.

> But, lord, so she wex *sodeynliche* reed!
> Ne, though men sholde smyten of hire heed,
> She myghte nat a word aright out brynge
> So *sodeynly*, for his *sodeyn* comynge.[1]
>
> (iii, 956–9)

A similar procedure is followed by Diomedes. His counterpart in the *Filostrato*, seeing the rage of the haughty Griseida as they wend their way to the Greek camp, confines himself to watching her and waits four days before making any advances. On the other hand, the sight of Criseyde's meekness incites Diomedes to act at once. His proposal, as they ride from Troy, is truly remarkable. Yet Criseyde's surprise combines with her habitual courtesy to inspire, not a tart rebuff, but an answer that encourages him to persist in his attentions. Thus the inability of the weak and clinging lady of high rank to cope with such a situation marks one stage in her progress towards the ultimate betrayal.

Another cause of weakness in Criseyde is a trait in her character that C. S. Lewis[2] has insisted on—her timidity. This goes far beyond any such feature in the conventional courtly lady, for her apprehensiveness is accentuated by her isolation. A trace of it is found in Boccaccio, but it relates only to her position as an exile among the Greeks. Thus he describes how she shrinks from asking whether the reports that she is to be exchanged are true—'per paura', and in the Greek camp weeps over her plight, because 'con cui dolersi non avea'.[3] But Chaucer sees her as a pathetic, lonely figure from the outset. She is a widow, surrounded by powerful adversaries like Poliphete; her father has fled to the enemy. Chaucer therefore applies to her the words that Boccaccio had reserved for her later troubles:

> allone
> Of any frend to whom she dorste hir mone.[4]
>
> (i, 97–8)

The treachery of Calchas affects profoundly one who is both sensitive and devoted to her native city, and though she is respected by Hector and the Trojan leaders and can enjoy social intercourse with them and Pandarus and her three nieces, Chaucer conceives of her as lacking intimates to whom on her own initiative she can confide her difficulties.

---

[1] Italics added. [2] *The Allegory of Love*, Oxford, 1938, pp. 185–90.
[3] Vide post. [4] Vide ante.

How lonely she is in society is brought out by the scene in the temple when Troilus becomes enamoured of her. Boccaccio speaks of her as being 'nel tempio presso alla porta' and may well have intended to convey that Griseida, having arrived late or being anxious to leave early, was no very devout worshipper. At any rate, he gives no indication of any particular significance in this phrase. Chaucer, on the other hand, adds words that are pregnant in their implication:

> she stood ful lowe and stille allone,
> Byhynden other folk in litel brede,
> And neigh the dore, ay under shames drede,
> Simple of atire.
>
> (i, 178–81)

And why should she thus be haunted by the fear of disgrace? Because of her father's disloyalty to Troy. There could surely be no more effective picture of one in dread of ostracism, deliberately keeping to the back of the temple, shrinking into herself, and even by the plainness of her garb,[1] trying to withdraw from the public eye. This loneliness is dispelled for a time by her love for Troilus, but when she has to face the prospect of leaving him, it returns with a sharper edge than before, and with true insight Chaucer makes her call upon her dead mother, uttering as she does so a wail of helpless anguish. Well might she look forward with dismay to leaving Troy, for quite apart from her distress at the separation from her lover, she had no cause to like the Greeks. Indeed, they had always been a bogey to her:

> I am of Grekes fered so that I deye.
>
> (ii, 124)

The outlook for a solitary woman in a camp of warriors was not reassuring, especially as any kind of violence always filled her with alarm. It is typical of her that when contemplating suicide, she rejects the use of weapons,

> syn neither swerd ne darte
> Dar I noon handle.
>
> (iv, 771–2)

Similarly, the sight of Troilus' sword wrings from her an involuntary cry of fear, and Pandarus' threat to kill himself has an overwhelming effect:

> Criseyde, which that wel neigh starf for feere,
> So as she was the ferfulleste wight
> That myghte be . . .
> She gan to rewe and drede hire wonder soore.
>
> (ii, 449–51; 455)

---

[1] The context makes it unlikely that by this reference to the simplicity of her attire widow's weeds are meant.

With supreme skill Chaucer has portrayed her fluttering sensibility and the panting alternation in her of hope and terror; her need for reassurance from Pandarus and her recovery of confidence when the tact and loyalty of Troilus are proved. The poet reveals that her anxiety to conceal their love-affair is not just a part of the troubadour convention—the desire to avoid scandal—but an inherent dislike of publicity. How sensitive and highly strung she is may be seen from the sudden panic that seizes her when Troilus rides past and Pandarus has to beg her not to flee from the window, or again from her tremulous alarm when she is kept on tenterhooks, awaiting Pandarus' news:

> Beth naught agast, ne quaketh naught; wherto?
> Ne chaungeth naught for feere so youre hewe.
>
> (ii, 302–3)

Even when she is by herself, the mere thought of yielding to Troilus brings on such an access of fear that she almost falls. In keeping with this is her impulse, on hearing that Poliphete is bringing a legal action against her, to let him have his way, regardless of the rights or wrongs of the case, for enough will still remain for her, and she will be left in peace. What is to be expected of so timorous a creature as this when circumstances have snatched her away to the Greek camp? It is indeed remarkable that she should contemplate an attempt at escape, and that in spite of her fears of being taken as a spy or, still worse, of falling into the hands of some ruffianly Greek soldier, she should conquer her apprehensions and resolve to set forth the following night. In the end, however, her courage evaporates. The words of Diomedes about the parlous state of Troy and the fact

> that she was allone and hadde nede
> Of frendes help
>
> (v, 1026–7)

cause her to hesitate and finally to give up the design.

Allied to Criseyde's quivering sensibility is her tender-heartedness, for

> nevere mo ne lakkede hire pite.
>
> (v, 824)

This emotion is, however, something more than the attribute bestowed by mediæval convention on a heroine, and the wily Pandarus is quick to exploit the possibilities that it opens up for his intrigue. Hence in pleading for Troilus, her uncle is careful to point out that if Troilus dies of unreciprocated love, he will join his friend in death. Again and again he plays on this string until she is swayed by the knowledge that

> myn emes lif is in balaunce,
>
> (ii, 466)

and so she agrees to show Troilus some measure of kindness. The appeal to her tender heart never fails, especially when it is combined with physical weakness or suffering. The spectacle of Troilus at Deiphobus' house, supposedly exhausted by a fever and yet struggling to rise and kneel before her, awakens all her womanly solicitude. Still more is her sense of pity aroused, after Pandarus' harrowing recital of Troilus' agonies, when he swoons at her bedside. Everything is forgotten—her shyness, her reserve, her caution—as she seeks to revive him by various means and finally, when all else fails, by her kisses. And just as this tenderness leads to the consummation of Troilus' desires, so it is the decisive factor that makes her yield to Diomedes. By a tragic irony it is the compassion kindled in her as she gazes upon and tends the wounds received by Diomedes at the hands of his rival that persuades her to bestow her love upon him. As Chaucer, following Guido delle Colonne, tells us:

> I fynde ek in stories elleswhere,
> Whan thorugh the body hurt was Diomede
> Of Troilus, tho wepte she many a teere,
> Whan that she saugh his wyde wowndes blede;
> And that she took to kepen hym good hede,
> And for to hele hym of his sorwes smerte
> Men seyn, I not, that she yaf hym hire herte.
> (v, 1044–50)

With all her gentleness and weakness, Criseyde never yields easily, even when her inclination impels her to do so. Her resistance to the suit of Troilus is prolonged. This may be partly because, as C. S. Lewis has emphasised, Chaucer wished to follow the convention of courtly love. But it is also because this reluctance is an essential part of her maidenly modesty, for in spite of the fact that she is a widow, she exhibits an almost virginal bashfulness. With all the insight of a Richardson, Chaucer traces the series of events by which her scruples are slowly overcome. A whole succession of incitements—the love-song of Antigone in the garden, the ecstasy of the nightingale, Criseyde's dream about the eagle, the eulogies of Troilus by the guests at Deiphobus' house, the spectacle of the hero returning in triumph from the fray—arouses first her interest and then her affection. The activities of Pandarus too have a large share in stimulating her love. His task is arduous, for she is always unwilling to commit herself irretrievably. Even when she has admitted to Pandarus in the nocturnal scene that she loves Troilus, she wishes to postpone seeing the supposedly distraught hero till the morrow, and it is only after another heart-rending appeal that she consents to speak to him that night. At the same time she begs Pandarus to safeguard her honour and tries to rise from the bed. It is clearly not her intention to yield at this juncture, and only the unexpected swoon of Troilus and their subsequent bodily nearness lead to her surrender. How long this gradual development took, Chaucer does not state, but he hints that it was a lengthy affair:

> I sey nat that she so sodeynly
> Yaf hym hire love.
>
> (ii, 673–4)

On the contrary, it was only

> by proces and by good servyse,
> He gat hire love, and in no sodeyn wyse.
>
> (ii, 678–9)

Evidently then their slowly growing intimacy must have extended over a considerable portion of the three and a quarter years during which the love of Troilus and Criseyde burgeoned and flowered.[1]

The phases of the evolution which culminated in Criseyde's desertion of Troilus are not marked with the same elaboration, but there are indications that Chaucer thought of the betrayal as the result of a gradual progression. Such specific references to time as there are all tend to imply a longer duration than that envisaged by Boccaccio, even though the actual difference in the two versions may be relatively small. While awaiting the return of Criseyde, Troilus and Pandarus stay a week with Sarpedon, instead of five days; after her arrival in the Greek camp ten days elapse before Diomedes approaches her, whereas in the *Filostrato* this occurs on the fourth day, and though the 'monthes tweyne' of her absence to which Troilus alludes in his letter may not appear much more than the forty days of the original, to him it seems 'longe tyme agon' and not 'poco tempo'. The attitude of Criseyde herself strengthens the impression that her submission to the will of Diomedes took place at no early date. Certainly, when he makes his astounding declaration on the way to the Greek camp, the grief-stricken heroine pays little heed and listens but absent-mindedly:

> Criseyde unto that purpos lite answerde,
> As she that was with sorwe oppressed so
> That, in effect, she naught his tales herde,
> But her and ther, now here a word or two.
> Hire thoughte hire sorwful herte brast atwo.
>
> (v, 176–80)

And though she is too gentle and too courteous to administer a rebuke,

---

[1] Troilus tells Pandarus (iii, 360–2) that it was April when he was sick to death through love for Criseyde; Pandarus goes to inform her about May 3rd (ii, 50–6); it is the first week in August when the Trojans ask for an armistice and agree to exchange Criseyde for Antenor (iv, 31–2), but this is in the third year after Troilus fell in love with her (v, 8–14).

her reply is politely evasive. Chaucer admits that her resolve to escape to Troy is not long maintained, but it does persist for fully two months, which is much more than is to be gathered from Boccaccio's 'tosto'. Moreover, whereas the *Filostrato* attributes the change of plan to the ascendancy of her 'novello amadore', Chaucer avoids any definite statement to show that Diomedes had already won her affection. For the same reason, when the Greek resumes his entreaties, though she replies as becomes a well-bred lady, she is far from giving him

> Lieta speranza di quel che cercava.
>
> (*O.V.* vi, st. 13, l. 8)

Pursuing the same tactics as when pressed by her uncle, she tries to gain time by asking for a postponement of any further discussion until the next morning. For the moment her words are studiously vague:

> Paraunter thanne so it happen may,
> That whan I se that nevere yit I say,
> Than wol I werke that I nevere wroughte.
>
> (v, 991-3)

Her promise that if she were to favour any Greek, it should be Diomedes, does not amount to much in view of the horror with which she regards the enemies of Troy. And her conclusion:

> I sey nat therfore that I wold yow love,
> Ny sey nat nay.
>
> (v, 1002-3)

is clearly an effort to temporise, for even if she goes so far as to present Diomedes with a glove, her mind is still bent on her native city, as is proved by her exclamation immediately after:

> O Troie town,
> Yit bidde I god, in quiete and in reste
> I may yow sen, or do myn herte breste.
>
> (v, 1006-8)

When she is left to ponder over her fate, it is significant that what is uppermost in her thoughts is her isolation and helplessness. There is no suggestion of a new passion. However, at their next interview Diomedes does succeed in banishing her grief and later receives from her various presents, including a steed and a brooch that had been given her by Troilus. All this is intended to mark Criseyde's gradual turning away from her old lover, until the climax is brought about by the sight of Diomedes' wounds inflicted by the Trojan champion. However, Chaucer insists that this point was reached only after a considerable interval:

For though that he bigan to wowe hire soone,
Or he hire wan, yit was ther more to doone.[1]
(v, 1091–2)

Finally, as another extenuating feature of her conduct, the poet mentions that Criseyde is filled with acute remorse. When her liaison with Diomedes is accomplished, she knows no happiness:

For I have falsed oon, the gentileste
That evere was, and oon the worthieste.
(v, 1056–7)

She is tormented, not only by the thought of her treachery to one who was the embodiment of loyalty, but also of the infamy into which she has plunged herself and all her sex. At the same time she recognises that there can be no going back, and the irrevocability of her action blinds her eyes with bitter tears.

From the analysis of Criseyde's character emerges with absolute transparency Chaucer's conception of her as weak rather than vicious. He may deplore that she was 'slydynge of corage' and criticise her lack of delicacy in bestowing on Diomedes the brooch given to her by Troilus, but sees in her no essential depravity. With the sure hand of a master he traces the way in which the schemes of Pandarus in conjunction with a series of incitements achieve her union with Troilus, and how the unforeseen exchange combines with isolation and loneliness to make her the prey of the glib and astute woman-hunter Diomedes. The part of external events in this development is notable. As in Shakespeare's great tragedies circumstances operating on an infirmity of character produce a disastrous result.

Such intervention from without in human affairs was evidently much in Chaucer's mind.[2] Hence the numerous and extensive passages on Fortune, which are of a magnitude far beyond the brief, occasional allusions in the *Filostrato*. No doubt, they were to the taste of the mediæval reader. Yet their scope and frequency point to something more than an attempt at mediævalisation. The translator of the *De consolatione philosophiæ* obviously had a personal interest in the question, and further proof is found in his repeated preoccupation with the omens conveyed by dreams. Nor is it without deliberate purpose that when Chaucer first introduces Criseyde to us, she is listening to one of her attendants reading aloud from the romance of Thebes. She has heard

how that king Layus deyde,
Thorugh Edippus his sone,
(ii, 101–2)

[1] Cf. 'But theron was to heven and to doone' (ii, 1289), when Criseyde resists Pandarus' overtures.
[2] Cf. W. C. Curry, 'Destiny in Chaucer's *Troilus*', *P.M.L.A.*, 1930, xlv, pp. 129–68.

H

and is just about to pass to the account of the sudden end of Amphiaraus in an earthquake. These were remarkable illustrations of the influence of Fate on human beings,[1] and the more one appreciates Chaucer's artistic sense and in particular his use of tragic irony, the more one becomes convinced that his choice of the romance of Thebes on this occasion was an integral part of the design of his poem. Was not Tydeus a prominent figure in the story of Thebes, his indirect share in the untimely death of King Lycurgus' son being but one among various notable examples of the effects of Destiny in that romance? And was not Diomedes the son of Tydeus?—Diomedes who, after the violent intervention of Fate in the love affair of Troilus and Criseyde had shattered their happiness, was the instrument to complete the work of destruction. In this fashion Criseyde's own fortunes were associated with the romance of Thebes, which may explain the disproportionate amount of space allotted to that subject in the fifth book, at a juncture when the poem should be hastening to its close. In any case, it is likely that Chaucer wished to suggest that in Criseyde's lot was to be seen yet one more instance of the way in which the 'executrice of wyerdes' was wont to operate. The lengthy speech of Troilus on 'necessitee' and free-will is therefore not an excrescence, but an essential feature of the work, and though Criseyde is too facile in ascribing her treachery solely to the thrusting on of Destiny, Chaucer seems to have thought that her action was bound up with one of the great universal mysteries. So he succeeds in making us feel, as we witness the bitter regret of Criseyde over her loss of Troilus that

> The worste kynde of infortune is this:
> A man to han ben in prosperitee,
> And it remembren whan it passed is.
>
> (iii, 1626–8)

To one thus caught in the grip of Fate Chaucer had no desire to refuse his sympathy, especially as her sorrow was due in some degree to that pity which 'renneth sone in gentil herte'. The spectacle of weakness unable to cope with adversity excited in him, not scorn or condemnation, but insight and compassion. That is why, before he narrates Criseyde's desertion, he anticipates the hostility of her critics:

> Allas! that they sholde evere cause fynde
> To speke hire harm! and if they on hire lye,
> Iwis, hem self sholde han the vilanye.
>
> (iv, 19–21)

[1] Lydgate comments on the death of Amphiaraus as being due to the irresistible hand of Fate:

> Only of fate which no man can repelle,
> þe erth opnede and he fille doun to helle.
>
> (*Siege of Thebes*, 4033–4)

For his part, as he openly declares after her deed has been told, he looks upon her as one deserving commiseration. She is a 'sely womman' whom he has no wish to rebuke more than the tale warrants, and he continues:

> Hire name, allas, is punysshed[1] so wide,
> That for hire gilt it oughte ynough suffise.
> And if I myghte excuse hire any wise,
> For she so sory was for hire untrouthe,
> Iwis, I wolde excuse hire yit for routhe.
>
> (v, 1095–9)

Taking this view, Chaucer found no room for any generalisations about the frailty of women. On the contrary, he suppressed not only Troilo's early gibes at the fickleness of the sex which turns like the leaf in the wind but also the passage at the end of the *Filostrato* in which Boccaccio repeats the charge in the same words, along with that of an inherent sensuality:

> Virtù non sente nè conoscimento,
> Volubil sempre come foglia al vento.[2]
>
> (*O.V.* viii, st. 30, ll. 7–8)

The general trend of Chaucer's poem would not permit of such a summing up; his conclusion had perforce to be altogether different. A hint of what he is leading up to is given by Criseyde when, on hearing that she is to be torn away from Troilus, she exclaims:

> Endeth thanne love in wo? Ye, or men lieth,
> And al worldly blisse, as thynketh me.
> The ende of blisse ay sorwe it occupieth,
>
> (iv, 834–6)

which conveys so poignantly the bitter-sweet, not only of love, but of all human happiness. These words are echoed in the comment of Chaucer himself:

> Swych fyn hath false worldes brotelnesse!
>
> (v, 1832)

All is unstable, all is vanity; joy and happiness are fleeting.

> Swich is this world, whoso it kan byholde;
> In ech estat is litel hertes reste;
> God leve us for to take it for the beste!
>
> (v, 1748–50)

---

[1] Variant reading 'publisshed'.
[2] Cf. a passage in the *Corbaccio*:

Mobili tutte e senza alcuna stabilitá sono: in una ora vogliono e svogliono una medesima cosa ben mille volte, salvo se di quelle, che a lussuria appartengono, non fossono; per ciò che quelle sempre le vogliono.

(*L'Ameto-Lettere-Il Corbaccio*, ed. cit., p. 216)

How is that to be done? Not by delivering, as Boccaccio had done, a warning to young men to control their passions and beware of women, but by directing all young people, men and women alike, to fix their eyes on God, the embodiment of enduring love:

> O yonge fresshe folkes, he or she,
> In which that love up groweth with youre age,
> Repeyreth hom fro worldly vanyte,
> And of youre herte up casteth the visage
> To thilke god that after his ymage
> Yow made, and thynketh al nys but a faire
> This world, that passeth soone as floures faire.
>
> (v, 1835-41)

This passage accords with the overpowering emotion that seized Chaucer as he set himself to relate the disastrous turn in the love of Troilus and Criseyde. He writes trembling with fear, contemplating the scene earnestly, not cynically. Similarly, the laughter of Troilus, as his soul looks down from on high after death, is not the mocking laughter of disillusionment but that of the detached spectator who from afar can survey life as a whole and see the folly of human agitation in the pursuit of blind desire. It is Fortune that derides those she overthrows, but Fortune and the Parcae are subordinate to Jove, and at the close Chaucer refers his listener to the all-powerful deity, as he directs him to 'the first moevere' at the end of the *Knight's Tale*. In each case behind apparent caprice and disorder is an assurance of purpose and order.

Hence the love-story of Troilus and Criseyde, though they are perhaps neither of them really tragic characters, is seen by Chaucer as part of the mystery of human existence. He makes it something more than a lyrical cry of amorous exaltation, something more than a tale of courtly love, something more even than a penetrating study in the psychology of seduction. In his hand it acquires a greater depth and a wider perspective, so that while in some ways more mediæval than Boccaccio's romance, his version has that universality which is the sure sign of great literature.

Through the medium of Chaucer the story of Troilo and Griseida entered on a long and complicated history which need hardly be considered in detail in a survey of the influence of Boccaccio in England.[1] Suffice it to say that in Robert Henryson's powerful *Testament of Cresseid* there is still a trace of sympathy for her, but the moral of her punishment with leprosy for her offence is brought out unforgettably, and more and more in the sixteenth century she was regarded

[1] See H. E. Rollins, 'The Troilus-Cressida Story from Chaucer to Shakespeare' *P.M.L.A.*, 1917, xxxii, pp. 383-429.

as the type of the fickle wanton. This is clearly the Shakespearian conception, even though Shakespeare's play ends inconclusively. This strange ending tempted Dryden to try his hand at improving Shakespeare, though in doing so he merely obscured the central theme, the fickleness of Cressida. Wordsworth, in his 'Troilus and Cresida', an adaptation of part of Chaucer's poem, has no ethical preoccupation. The scene that appealed to him most powerfully was that describing the emotion of Troilus as he stands before the deserted house of the heroine after her departure from Troy. It is beyond all doubt one of the finest passages in *Troilus and Criseyde*, and one is inclined to ask whether, as Wordsworth wrote his version in 1801, there lingered some memories of his own parting from Annette Vallon. However that may be, in this poem as in the *Lyrical Ballads* of this period, he seized on the elemental human passion here depicted with such intense pathos. This adaptation, linking as it does Boccaccio, Chaucer and Wordsworth, bears out the claim made in the 1802 revised version of the famous Preface (1800) to the *Lyrical Ballads* that

in spite of difference of soil and climate, of language and manners, of laws and customs: in spite of things silently gone out of mind, and things violently destroyed; the Poet binds together by passion and knowledge the vast empire of human society, as it is spread over the whole earth, and over all time.

4. The *Filocolo*

Boccaccio's first romance, the *Filocolo*, was far too long and rambling to attract a translator either in England or Spain, though a German version was printed at Metz in 1499 and again in 1500.[1] France had to wait until 1542, when Adrien Sevin's rendering achieved great popularity, which was perhaps due in part to the fact that the *Filocolo* was based on the French tale of Floris and Blanchefleur. However, the possibility had already been grasped of detaching a section of the romance and giving it an independent existence. The episode in question describes how the hero Florio, having been deprived of Biancofiore by her parents, in the course of his quest for her is driven to Naples by a storm. Outside the city he and his friends, on passing a garden where there is a joyous company, are invited to enter. Later, in the heat of the day, Fiammetta requests the strangers to join her and her attendants. Seated in a circle round a fountain, they choose Fiammetta as their queen. Each of the thirteen in turn sets forth a problem on love. This is solved by Fiammetta; then the speaker dissents from her view; and thereupon Fiammetta answers the challenge and defends her opinion. When evening comes, the merry-

---

[1] *Gesamtkatalog*, iv, items 4470 and 4471.

making is resumed, and at nightfall the company returns to Naples, where Florio takes leave of Fiammetta. All that was needed to develop this into a separate entity was to provide it with an introduction or argument, relating briefly the events that brought Florio to Italy. This appears to have been done first in the *Treize elegantes demandes damours*, published in Paris in 1531 and twice reprinted.[1] In Spain we find *Trece questiones muy graciosas*, printed in 1546, 1549 and 1553.[2] The corresponding English version appeared in 1567 under the title *A pleasaunt disport of diuers noble personages* which was reprinted in 1571 and 1587 as *Thirteene most plesant and delectable questions, entituled a disport of diuers noble personages*.[3] The initials of the translator 'H.G.', have been thought to stand for Humphrey Gifford and Henry Grantham, but the latter interpretation is the more probable. The translation, which owes nothing to its French or Spanish counterparts but was influenced by the relevant portion of Sevin's rendering of the whole *Filocolo*, follows the Italian text with considerable fidelity, though Grantham's command of the language is sometimes imperfect. Here and there we chance upon a happy phrase such as 'golden sleep' for 'dolce sonno' or 'weather beatẽ mates' for 'naufraghi'. But leaving such phrases aside, the translation combines the inevitable charm of the best Elizabethan prose with the richness and stately movement of Boccaccio's *Questioni*. These qualities are reflected, for instance, in the description, at the close, of how the company departed and Philocopo with a dignity of speech befitting the chivalrous formality of a knight addressing a queen in her court, bade farewell to Fiammetta:

Thence was heard of al sides the pleasant instruments, and the aire resounding of amorous songs, no part of the Garden was without banketting: wherein they all abode merily all that day, euen to the last houre: but night being come vpon them, and the starres shewing forth their light, it semed good to the Lady, & to them al, to depart & to returne to the citie, wherein being entred, Philocopo takyng his leaue, thus sayde vnto hir: Most noble Fiametta, if the Gods shoulde euer graunt me, that I were myne own, as I am an others, without doubt I shoulde bee presently youres, but bicause myne owne I am not, I can not gyue my selfe to an other: Howe be it forsomuch as the miserable heart coulde receyue strange fier, so muche the more it feeleth thorow your inestimable worthinesse to bee kindled, and shall feele alwayes and

---

[1] Hauvette [1909], pp. 3–4.

[2] P. Rajna, 'L'Episodio delle Questioni d'Amore nel Filocolo del Boccaccio', *Romania*, 1902, xxxi, pp. 28–32; C. B. Bourland, loc. cit., p. 14; *Archiv*, cxvi, p. 96, n. 2, and Farinelli, i, p. 244, n. 2.

[3] *Short-Title Catalogue*, items 3180 to 3182; W. C. Hazlitt, *Hand Book to Poetical and Dramatic English Literature*, 1867, p. 42, item 6b, mentions a fourth of which only the title-page is said to be preserved in the Bagford papers in the British Museum. Nothing appears to be known of this edition otherwise. In 1927 there appeared a reprint with an introduction by Edward Hutton.

incessauntly, with more effect shal desire neuer to be forgetfull of your worthinesse. She thãked Philocopo gretly of this curtesy at his departure, adding that it would please the Gods quickely to bryng a gracious peace to his desires.

In spite of Grantham's assertion that the reading of the book 'shal bring pleasure and delight', he is obviously not much concerned with the good stories that it contains, two of which were told again in the *Decameron*. He gives no sign either of grasping the relation between the framework for linking tales in the earlier and the later work, or of appreciating the skilful design and perfect symmetry of the *Questioni*. Nor is he aware of its possible autobiographical interest, for the simple reason that little was known by the Elizabethans about Boccaccio's life. Like his contemporaries, Grantham thought far more of him as a moralist and scholar than as a man and artist. Hence the importance in his eyes of the subject-matter, which 'being therwithall duely considered shall gyue sundrie profitable Lessons meete to be followed'. Of course, the theme of love in itself was calculated to appeal to the reader, but the problems were presented in a form highly congenial to an age which was still not too far removed from the mediæval *débats* and which delighted in the use of the dialogue for presenting opposed points of view. It is evident that at the back of Grantham's mind was the recollection of *De casibus*, *De claris mulieribus*, and *De genealogia deorum*, as may be seen from his tribute to Boccaccio as one 'of no smal credit with the Learned, for those his sundry well written workes'. For him Boccaccio was above all the scholar, a conception which is reflected in the designation of the author on the title-page as 'Poet Laureat', a term which did not acquire its present meaning in England until the age of Dryden but was conferred on writers before that time chiefly to recognise their learning.[1] It has been maintained that vestiges of the *Filocolo* can be discovered in Chaucer's *Troilus and Criseyde*, but this opinion has been treated with scepticism.[2] On the other hand, it is quite obvious that *The Flower of Friendship* which

---

[1] Cf. H. G. Wright, 'The Elizabethan Translation of the "Questioni d'Amore" in the *Filocolo*', *M.L.R.*, 1941, xxxvi, pp. 289–303.

[2] Cf. Cummings, pp. 4–12. Scholars have also supposed an indebtedness of the *Franklin's Tale* to the *Filocolo*, which in part turns on the supposed debt of *Troilus and Criseyde* to the latter. Among the many notable students of Chaucer who have debated the question, for the sake of brevity only a few can be mentioned. W. H. Schofield, *P.M.L.A.*, xvi, pp. 405–49, believes that Chaucer used, not the *Filocolo*, but a lost lay. Cummings supports him. Rajna, *Romania*, xxxii, pp. 204–67, argues in favour of Chaucer's indebtedness to Boccaccio; J. L. Lowes, *M.P.*, xv, 689–728, treats the case thus presented with his customary insight; G. Dempster and J. S. P. Tatlock, in *Sources and Analogues*, p. 376, consider it highly probable. F. N. Robinson shares this view, but in the notes to the poem in his edition of Chaucer pares away much of the supposed evidence. In these circumstances the hypothesis must be regarded as plausible but not proved.

was published in 1568,[1] one year after Grantham's translation had appeared, owed something to the English version of the thirteen questions.[2] The book tells how a company of distinguished friends, including 'M. Lodouic Viues, and an old Gentleman called M. Erasmus' considered the best way of spending their time. Bowls and archery were proposed, but

M. Pedro nothing at all lyking of such deuises, wherein the Ladies should be left out, said: y[t] he wel remembred how Boccace & Countie Baltizer with others recoũted many proper deuises, for exercise, both pleasaunt & profitable, which (quoth he) were vsed in y[e] courts of Italie, and some much like to them, are practised at this day in the English court, wherein is not only delectation, but pleasure ioyned with profite, and exercise of the wit.

The reference to the custom of Elizabeth's court is all the more notable, because Edmund Tilney, the author of *The Flower of Friendship*, was afterwards to become Master of the Revels, and dedicated his work to the Queen. His reference to Castiglione obviously applies to *The Courtier*; that to Boccaccio envisages the contents of *A pleasaunt disport of diuers noble personages*. Tilney's imitation is not in the least mechanical. It is true that just as Ascaleone is first chosen king and then, at his suggestion, Fiammetta is elected queen, so 'Maister Pedro di luxan' is asked to preside, whereupon he proposes that they shall accept Lady Julia as their sovereign. But in other respects the narrative goes its own way, for the topics are considered on successive afternoons, and on the first it is Pedro who airs his views on the duties of a husband, on the second, Lady Julia who expounds the obligations of a married woman. There are other traits which lend great charm to Tilney's little book, but these are inspired by the *Decameron*.[3]

Brian Melbancke in his *Philotimus* (1583) is less concerned with originality of structure than with the discovery of a good story. He found two among the thirteen questions, nos. 4 and 12, and in the preamble to the latter we hear an echo from Grantham:

The Queene of a companie in a merrie meeting of gallants for disporte, hauing this question propounded . . .

Both stories are condensed, and the tone is crude. It is obvious that in spite of Melbancke's euphuistic style they were meant for a public very different from that envisaged in *The Flower of Friendship*.

No great interval elapsed between the publication of *Philotimus* and the composition of Lyly's *Loves Metamorphosis*.[4] The transformation of the nymphs Nisa, Celia and Niobe by Cupid for their hardness of heart has been traced back to an episode in the seventh book of the

---

[1] It was much read. Other editions in 1571 and 1577.
[2] Noted by Scott, p. 21.   [3] Vide post, p. 481.   [4] Not published till 1601.

Filocolo, with which Lyly has interwoven the story of Erisichthon's metamorphosis in Ovid.[1] There is a parallel in Robert Greene's *Alcida*,[2] where three nymphs undergo a like transformation. The perplexing problem that faces the scholar is therefore to determine whether Lyly was following Greene or Greene, Lyly. If the date 1588–9 be accepted as that when Lyly's play was written, it would seem that the credit for the notion of harking back to Boccaccio must go to Greene.[3] On the other hand, if it be assumed that *Loves Metamorphosis* was written as early as 1585–6,[4] then it is Greene who is the debtor to Lyly. In either case we have here yet another example of the infiltration of classical conceptions into Elizabethan literature through the medium of Boccaccio.[5]

5. *Fiammetta*

One can only speculate what Chaucer would have made of *Fiammetta* if it had come into his hands, but it was late in reaching England. In Spain it was translated early, perhaps at the beginning of the fifteenth century, and found its way into print at Salamanca in 1497 and at Seville in 1523. It was widely read until it was placed on the Index in Spain in 1631.[6] In France it was slow to arrive, and the first version gave only six chapters, but it at once became popular. Two editions appeared in 1532 at Paris and Lyons, and a third in 1541. A new translation of the whole work was made in 1585 by Gabriel Chappuys and printed along with the Italian text.[7]

It was perhaps as a result of this bilingual rendering that *Fiammetta* began to arouse enthusiasm in England, for it was in 1585 that Paulus Jovius observed how 'Courtiers are inwardly rauished in vewing the Picture of *Fiametta* which Boccace limned'.[8] In any case, two years later Bartholomew Young published his *Amorous Fiammetta*,[9] probably using for this purpose the Italian text of an edition printed either in 1558 or 1565.[10] The mere fact that the book was dedicated to such

---

[1] V. M. Jeffery, *John Lyly and the Italian Renaissance*, Paris, 1928, pp. 84–91.

[2] Published 1588.

[3] René Pruvost, *Robert Greene et ses romans*, Paris, 1938, pp. 315–17.

[4] T. W. Baldwin, *Shakspere's Five-Act Structure*, Urbana, 1947, pp. 517–25.

[5] The *Filocolo* afterwards was little known. An attempt has been made to prove that Keats used it for 'The Eve of St. Agnes' (cf. H. N. MacCracken, in *M.P.*, 1907, v, pp. 145–52) but this is unconvincing. A. Montucci included some passages from it in his *Italian Extracts* (cf. 2nd ed., 1818, pp. 297–303, 305–7, 308–11).

[6] *Archiv*, cxvi, pp. 79–80; and Farinelli, i, pp. 209–11; also Bourland, loc. cit., p. 13.

[7] Hauvette [1909], pp. 33–43.

[8] *The Worthy tract of Paulus Iouius*, sigs. 4 verso–5.

[9] Reprinted with some modernisation, London, 1929.

[10] Cf. H. G. Wright, 'The Italian Edition of Boccaccio's *Fiammetta* used by Bartholomew Young', *M.L.R.*, 1943, xxxviii, pp. 339–340.

a well-known figure as Sir William Hatton[1] and that the translator was a member of the Middle Temple suggests that it was thought likely to appeal to cultured and influential circles. The translator included in his work the epistle of Gabriele Giolito which declared that *Fiammetta* was amongst the finest prose of 'that most excellent & learned Clarke, Master John *Boccace*', and Thomas Newman in his dedication, though he refers deprecatingly to the book as only prose, nevertheless did not fail to extol Boccaccio as 'a famous Poet'. There was indeed an abundance of material, particularly in the seventh book, where Fiammetta's sufferings are compared with those of the famous lovers in classical antiquity, to satisfy the craving of the age for the background of the ancient world. Here was Boccaccio the scholar, but as in so many of his works, the learning is blended with the theme of love. In one sense *Fiammetta* is complementary to the *Filostrato*, the latter a story of the betrayal of Troilo by the faithless Griseida, the other a tale of the desertion of Fiammetta by Panfilo. In both works the anguish of soul is powerfully depicted by the hand of a master in the understanding of the human heart, an insight which may well have its origin in his own experience. Such anguish was calculated to appeal to a generation that found delight in Petrarch, and it is significant that on the title-page of *Amorous Fiammetta* the translator quotes from one of his sonnets[2] the words

bel fine fa, chi ben amando muore

which he repeats in Spanish at the end of his translation and again in French after the table of contents. This is a significant reminder that the translation appeared just before the great outburst of sonnet-writing in England in the last decade of the sixteenth century. In Bartholomew Young's mind there was a palpable connexion between the love-theme of the Petrarchan sonnet and that of *Fiammetta*. At the same time the translator thought it necessary to lend a moral purpose to the story. Giolito, addressing the ladies of Castale in Monferrato had asked:

Because contayning in it the sighes, the teares, & prolonged miseries of an enamoured yong Gentlewoman forsaken of her Louer, who doth not conceiue this very same to be set foorth as a soueraigne example, and sole instruction for you all.[3]

And so he admonishes them:

---

[1] Nephew of Sir Christopher Hatton, Lord Chancellor and favourite of Queen Elizabeth (cf. *D.N.B.*, xxv, p. 162). Christopher Hatton himself is associated with Boccaccio. Vide post, p. 178.

[2] Book x, 110. Cf. *Le Rime di Francesco Petrarca*, Rome, 1821, i, 330.

[3] Dedication, para. one.

Reade it therefore, & dyscoursing amongst your selues the dolorous cõplaints of that miserable and haplesse Ladye *Fiammetta*: by her desastrous and aduerse Fortune, learne you (fayre Ladyes) to be wyser and better aduysed.[1]

Thomas Newman was quick to seize on this interpretation and present the book as a warning against undisciplined passion. His words are echoed on the title-page:

Amorous Fiammetta. Wherein is sette downe a catologue of all and singuler passions of Loue and iealosie, incident to an enamored yong Gentlewoman, with a notable caueat for all women to eschewe deceitfull and wicked Loue, by an apparant example of a *Neapolitan* Lady, her approued & long miseries, and with many sounde dehortations from the same.

Young did not go quite so far as Chappuys who considered that his readers would draw from his version the lesson that they should devote themselves entirely to the love of God and find no perfect pleasure except in their Creator.[2] Nevertheless, the moral conclusion of the English translation, however peculiar it might have seemed to Boccaccio, would have won the approbation of Samuel Richardson. But the time was not ripe in England for the psychological novel in prose. Young's translation may well have enjoyed some success on its publication, but *Fiammetta* found no imitators. The temper of the literary world underwent a change as the sixteenth century drew to a close. Petrarch gave way to Hall and Donne, and the spirit of romance began to quail before the lash of satire.

It is also probable that as the years passed by, Young's style was found too ornate and too full of artifice. It is also verbose to an extraordinary degree. Adjectives are piled up. Some are inserted, so that 'sonno' becomes 'sweet sleepe', 'bugie', 'plausible lies' and 'casi', 'bitter chaunces'; others are doubled, so that 'sozze' is rendered by 'foule and lothsome', 'tempestuosi' by 'boysterous and tempestuous', 'sottile' by 'subtile and Sophisticall'. Nouns and verbs are duplicated in the same way. In general, the turn of phrase is cumbrous, as may be seen from the rendering of 'per lunga usanza' as 'by tract of long time and custome', of 'stimolati da molti disii' as 'procured and maintained by innumerable pricking desires', and a simple combination like 'atti diversi' is inflated to the dimensions of 'diuers dryfts, manie meanes, and sundry flights'. Of course, this expansion is not without purpose. It arises from a desire for balance and alliteration. But the effect is to slow down the movement of Boccaccio's prose, as may be gathered from a comparison of

nella vaga puerizia tratta, sotto reverenda maestra qualunque costume a nobile giovane conveniente apparai

(*O.V.* ch. i, p. 3)

---

[1] Dedication, para. two.

[2] Hauvette [1909], pp. 42–3.

with

in my yong and tender yeeres, brought vppe vnder a reuerend and sage
Matrone, I easilie learned euerie good qualitie, which was most conuenient
and commendable for anie yong and noble Woman.

(page 1)

This style seems all the more unnatural, because it is employed in an
attempt to convey the grief of a broken-hearted lover. Nevertheless, it
is likely that Young's contemporaries admired its opulent decoration
and stately harmony. In the long run, however, when taste changed
in favour of simple and direct style, such mannered writing went out
of fashion. Whatever the cause or causes, *Amorous Fiammetta* was
not reprinted[1] and left no successors.[2]

6. The *Ninfale Fiesolano*

Neither in France nor in Spain was the *Ninfale Fiesolano* appreciated
to anything like the same extent as *Fiammetta*. A translation is known
to have been in the possession of the marquis of Santillana but now
seems to have disappeared, and in France the only rendering was that
of Antoine Guercin, printed at Lyons in 1556. This fell into the hands
of Jo. Goubourne, and he turned it into English. The version of this
otherwise unknown writer was published by an obscure printer,
William Blackman, in 1597. An account of the book with a transcrip-
tion of the title-page was given by J. Payne Collier.[3] He did not state
where he had seen this copy, which seemed to have disappeared, until
it was revealed that it was in the library of Worcester College, Oxford.[4]
Goubourne dedicated his book to 'Maister Frauncis Verseline' who
belonged to a family of Venetian glass-makers named Verzellini. The
father, James or Jakob, enjoyed the support of Sir William Cecil, and

[1] Until the edition of K. H. Josling, London, 1929.

[2] It has been suggested by W. D. Briggs that there is a vague recollection of
Fiammetta in the *Faerie Queene*, iii, 2 (cf. *Matzke Memorial Volume*, Stanford University,
1911, pp. 57–61). In the nineteenth century some passages were given in A. Montucci's *Italian Extracts* (2nd ed., 1818, pp. 312–15). His comment is characteristic of
his age:

> The subject of this highly interesting poetical novel is the illicit love of a married
> lady, called Fiammetta; and although a few lines of it are devoted to painting the
> transitory charms of pleasure; yet her torturing disappointment and long repentance
> are represented so lively throughout the work, that it cannot but inspire its readers
> with detestation for the crimes of Fiammetta, and deeply implant in their bosoms a
> love for that virtue, which is the firmest tie of human society, namely, *conjugal
> fidelity*.

[3] *A Bibliographical and Critical Account of the Rarest Books in the English Language*,
London, 1865, i, p. 13.

[4] It was edited by C. H. Wilkinson for the Roxburghe Club in *Two Tracts Affrican
and Mensola . . . and Newes and Strange Newes from St. Christophers*, Oxford, 1946.

from 1574–5 on he figures, sometimes with his son Francis, in contemporary records.[1] These facts are of interest, as they show that Goubourne's patron was an Englishman of Italian descent who had some taste for the literature of Italy.

In his dedication Goubourne admits that he has relied on a French text, and the title-page is equally candid:

Newly translated out of Tuscan into French by Anthony Guerin, domino Creste.
And out of French into English by Io. Goubourne.

The name of the French writer calls for comment, since in the Lyons edition it is given as 'Antoine Guercin du Crest'. Evidently 'Guercin' has been carelessly read as 'Guerin' and 'du' as 'do', that is, 'domino'. The phrase 'Newly translated' is also peculiar when it is borne in mind that Guercin's rendering was over forty years old. It is simply the literal and thoughtless equivalent of 'Nouuellement traduit'.

This is characteristic of Goubourne's procedure. Seldom does he display any independence. It is true that he discards the title 'Le Nymphal Flossolan', perhaps thinking it unintelligible to an English reader, and replaces it by the sub-title, at the same time lending to it a more seriously emotional note:

A Famous tragicall discourse of two louers, Affrican, and Mensola, their liues infortunate loues, and lamentable deaths . . .

Yet immediately afterwards he returns to Guercin with the words 'A History no lesse pleasant then full of recreation and delight', the tone of which seems incongruous after the earlier part of the title. In other respects, however, Goubourne is almost invariably a slavish imitator. He was probably unaware that the *Ninfale Fiesolano* was a poem of four hundred and seventy-two stanzas. Like Guercin he writes in prose, divided into chapters, the sole difference being that the French version has nineteen chapters, the English only eighteen, because the first of Guercin, an epistle desiring the favour of his lady, was not the work of Boccaccio, and so, not unreasonably, was left unnumbered by Goubourne.

Wherever Guercin diverges from the original, the English translation follows suit. Thus the names 'Affrican', 'Alcumena' and 'Senadeche' are taken, not from 'Africo', 'Alimena' and 'Sinedecchia', but from their counterparts in the French text. Most conspicuous of all is the name 'Flossolan'. At first Guercin had translated 'Fiesole' by 'Flossole' but later he replaced it by 'Flossolan', his equivalent for the corresponding adjective, 'Fiesolano'. Perceiving the discrepancy, Goubourne everywhere uses 'Flossolan'. The work ends, in accordance

[1] Wilkinson, p. xxv, notes 1 and 2.

with Guercin's example, by applying this strange form to the book itself: 'Thus endeth Maister Iohn Bocace to his Flossolan', the very structure of which is a clumsy adaptation of 'Icy se taist M. Jean Boccace, et fait fin à son Flossolan'.

Hauvette's penetrating analysis[1] of Guercin's methods enables us to watch how Goubourne accepts his omissions, abbreviations, additions and errors. More important than such minutiæ, however, is the transformation that is brought about in various aspects of the poem. It has been universally recognised that one of its most pleasing features is the tenderness with which Boccaccio portrayed the relationship between the hero and his parents, their anxiety for his welfare when he is oppressed by the cares of love, and their grief at his death. The first of these is abridged, and in the episode where they perform the last rites for Affrican, the victim of Diana's wrath, instead of burying his remains by the side of the river, the parents unfeelingly cast his ashes into the water. Another incident which in Boccaccio was full of intense pathos depicts the arrival of the aged Senadeche with the orphan child of Affrican and Mensola, so that she may entrust it to the sorrowing grandparents. Something of its emotional power still lingers, but much has been lost.

The figure of Mensola also falls short of the delicacy and innocence of the original. This nymph, dedicated to the service of Diana, had fled before the young shepherd and in a fit of anger had shot an arrow at him and the next moment had uttered a cry of warning. In the French version and consequently in that of Goubourne this subtle indication of the dawn of love is ignored. Instead, Mensola slackens her pace so that she may satisfy her curiosity about the pursuer. Later, when she discovers that she is with child, she displays a worldly wisdom and a sensual ardour that are alien to her namesake in the *Ninfale Fiesolano*.

It may be that these elements in her character spring from a conception at the back of Guercin's mind of Diana and her nymphs as the counterparts of an abbess and her nuns. He even goes so far as to present Diana as holding a chapter. That being so, he was perhaps inclined to associate the story of Mensola with tales of amorous living in monasteries and convents in which the literature of the late Middle Ages abounded. This is all the more probable because, as Hauvette has demonstrated, Guercin was familiar with the *Decameron*.[2]

Boccaccio's poem was an expression of violent passion but at times in Guercin's hands this deteriorated into a tasteless lasciviousness. All the same he experienced some qualms. He thought it necessary to turn a blind eye to the opening stanzas in which Boccaccio extols

[1] Hauvette [1909], pp. 43–9.   [2] Ibid., p. 47, n. 6.

love and to add a passage which, as Goubourne renders it, explains that sacred love for his lady

hath caused me to aduenture this present trauaile: and take pen in hand, to discourse an Historie verie auncient, but pleasant, full of delight and worthy your hearing: to the ende that each one knowing the subtill sleights of Cupid, might learne to eschew his Darts, and sharpe pointed arrowes, yielding at the first a poysoned sweete, pleasant, and inuisible: but once wounded, the sweetnes becomes meere rage, bereauing him of sence, memory, and vnderstanding that feeles it: And with like care to extinguish the hote burning and pestilent fier of that Goddesse his Mother, sole enemie to Chastitie.[1]

Thus Boccaccio's paean becomes an admonition. As if this were not enough, an appeal is addressed to all amorous ladies to defend the translation:

vouchsafe to shield me against the enuious backbiters, that by their venomous pearcing and detracting tongues, I be not deemed to haue written of a thing base and vnprofitable.[2]

The carping critics are again rebutted in the epistle to the reader, and in reply to the accusation that the work is devoid of profit, the author declares that he will not heed the brutishly minded:

I care not, seeing my translation I present not to them, but to euery gentle mind affecting vertue.[3]

Such a claim would indeed be difficult to uphold, but it is symptomatic of the uneasiness that Guercin felt after tampering with Boccaccio's poem. Goubourne may well have shared this discomfort, but his slavish fidelity conceals any personal reaction. If we are in the dark about his attitude to the ethical problem involved, we can at least discern that he was not much concerned about the origin of Florence and its association with Fiesole, a matter of profound interest to Boccaccio. As a result there is a visible tendency for him to hasten through this part of the narrative and reach the close. It is, of course, true that Boccaccio was primarily attracted to the love-story and that although he was now remote from Naples and could view with detachment his youthful passion, the knowledge of the bitterness of parting still lingered and enabled him to enter into the grief of the shepherd and the nymph after their brief hour of happiness. For Goubourne this was also the central theme, and the mythological background with its rivalry of Venus and Diana merely of secondary value. Yet through the medium of Guercin the charm of the pastoral setting with its clear streams and cool valleys penetrated to him. His style is marked by the same quest for alliteration as that of Bartholomew Young, but he writes with ease

---

[1] Dedication to Author's 'Mistris'.
[2] Ibid.   [3] 'To the Readers Health'.

as in the following passage that describes Affrican's fruitless search for Mensola:

As he thus reasoned with himselfe, he beheld certaine young Maides of meruailous beauty, sporting them selues in midst of a thicket within that Valley, whom he thought to surprize before they wist: And as one that seekes to catch the Cricket or Grashopper of the Groue, so went he softly stealing among the bushes, to a rowe of Chesnuts there growing: In the shadow whereof he espyed three Damsels, their heads decked with greene Chaplets, reposing their weary bodies at the feete of those Trees, deuising together, and sweetly singing in the shade.[1]

Another such graceful picture is drawn when the arrival of Diana is described:

in a Valley large, plaine, and very dilectable, in the middest whereof was a Pond, the water therein discending from a siluer spring in the height of the Mountaine, bordering the East side of the Vally, ranne with a sweete and delectable murmure: which passed for a space by the Plaine, letted by the rootes of sundry great Trees, staide it selfe in forme of a little Lake. The water discending from the Fountaine, by the fresh force thereof had decked the place where it passed, with sundry sorts of sweet hearbes and flowers.[2]

The scene is pleasing in itself, but it has an additional value as a first sketch of the 'Valle delle donne',[3] so that even if Goubourne's *Famous tragicall discourse* soon sank into oblivion, at least it contained an artistic anticipation of a notable scene in the *Decameron*.

[1] Wilkinson, fol. 13.   [2] Wilkinson, fol. 4.
[3] At the end of Day VI of the *Decameron*, vide post, pp. 344, 350, 351, 357, 402.

III

THE DECAMERON IN
THE FOURTEENTH, FIFTEENTH, AND
SIXTEENTH CENTURIES

THE *Decameron* as a whole does not seem to have become known in Western Europe until the fifteenth century. France was earliest in the field when Laurent de Premierfait, who lacked any acquaintance with Italian and had to rely on the aid of a friar, Antonio d'Arezzo, produced a translation in 1414. It was printed in 1485 by Antoine Vérard and though arbitrarily mutilated by Vérard, ran to eight editions between 1485 and 1541. Still more popular was the racy and accurate version of Antoine le Maçon. Within seventy years of its publication in 1545 nineteen editions appeared in Paris, Lyons, Amsterdam and Rotterdam. As was the case with Boccaccio's Latin works, royal personages took an interest in the *Decameron*. A copy of Premierfait's rendering was presented to the duke of Berry, third son of King John the Good and brother of Charles V; and it was Queen Margaret of Navarre, sister of Francis I, who encouraged le Maçon to undertake his task, and it was to her that his work was dedicated.

In Spain the *Decameron* in its entirety was translated into Catalan in 1429, and another manuscript of the middle of the century contains fifty stories in Castilian. The first printed edition was published at Seville in 1496, and four others followed in the next century. In Germany a translator[1] who used the pseudonym 'Arigo' produced a version which was printed at Ulm about 1473 and at Augsburg in 1490. It continued to enjoy great popularity in the sixteenth century[2] and left a deep mark on Hans Sachs.[3] In Holland, where the humanistic movement was strong as in southern Germany, fifty tales were

---

[1] Now thought to be Heinrich Leubing. Cf. K. Drescher, *Arigo, der Übersetzer des Decamerone und des Fiore di Virtu*, Strassburg, 1900. For the text of the translation see *Decameron von Heinrich Steinhöwel*, ed. A. von Keller, Stuttgart, 1860.

[2] For a brief account of the west European translations of the *Decameron* see H. G. Wright, *The First English Translation of the 'Decameron'*, Upsala, 1953, pp. 8–10.

[3] J. Hartmann, *Das Verhältnis von Hans Sachs zur sogenannten Steinhöwelschen Decameronübersetzung*, Berlin, 1912.

I

translated by Dirck Cornhert, a notable figure of the Dutch Renaissance, in 1564, and in 1605 the remaining fifty were published in the rendering of Gerrit Hendricx van Breugel.

England had to wait until 1620 for a complete translation[1] but, of course, in one way or another news of the *Decameron* had arrived long before then. In view of Chaucer's familiarity with Italian, an advantage denied to most of his countrymen for many a long day, there has been a natural inclination to assume that he must have read the work, it being argued that this was all the more likely because of his probable meeting with Boccaccio in 1373. However, such a meeting is just as dubious as the supposed visit of Milton to Galileo.[2] Moreover, there is no convincing internal evidence that Chaucer had read any of the tales or that the framework for his *Canterbury Tales* was suggested by that of the *Decameron*.[3]

If there are such strong reasons against Chaucer's acquaintance with the *Decameron*, there can be no doubt about the interest taken in it by Humphrey, duke of Gloucester. He possessed a copy of Premierfait's translation, and the manuscript presented to him by the earl of Warwick with a note in Humphrey's autograph is still in the Bibliothèque Nationale.[4] The work continued to be read in the highest circles and, turning northwards to Scotland, we find 'The decameron of Bocas' in the Royal Library in 1578.[5] In the humbler ranks of society also it attained a certain diffusion in the course of the sixteenth century. Thus Sir Thomas More's personal servant, Walter Smyth, in his will bequeathed to John More, his master's only son, Chaucer's tales and 'Boocas', which was probably the *Decameron*.[6] Again it can be surmised with some likelihood that it was one of the distractions of Gabriel Harvey while an undergraduate at Oxford. He describes how he devoured

> All kynde of bookes, good and badd,
> Sayntish and divelish, that are to be hadd.

[1] Vide post, p. 191.

[2] Cf. Piero Rebora, 'Milton a Firenze', *Nuova Antologia*, October, 1953.

[3] The question is discussed, with references to other contributions to this topic, by R. K. Root, 'Chaucer and the *Decameron*', *Englische Studien*, 1912, xliv, pp. 1–7; W. F. Schirmer, 'Boccaccios Werke als Quelle G. Chaucers', *Germanisch-Romanische Monatsschrift*, 1924, xii, pp. 289–93; W. Farnham, 'England's Discovery of the *Decameron*', *P.M.L.A.*, 1924, xxxix, pp. 123–39; Mario Praz, 'Chaucer and the great Italian writers of the Trecento', *The Monthly Criterion*, 1927, vi, pp. 141–50; R. A. Pratt and K. Young, 'The Literary Framework of the *Canterbury Tales*' in *Sources and Analogues of Chaucer's 'Canterbury Tales'*, ed. W. F. Bryan and G. Dempster, Chicago [1940], pp. 11–20.

[4] MS. Fr. 12, 421. Cf. K. H. Vickers, *Humphrey, Duke of Gloucester*, London, 1907, p. 437.

[5] Dibdin, iii, p. 246.

[6] Cf. A. W. Reed, *Early Tudor Drama*, London, 1926, p. 154.

Alternating between grave and gay, he is seen one moment poring over Cicero's *Orations* and Aristotle's *Politics*, and then

> Within a daye or twoe immediately followinge,
> At Petrarche and Boccace I must haue a flynge.[1]

After wrestling with Cicero and Aristotle, Boccaccio might well seem an agreeable relaxation. Yet he, as well as Petrarch and Dante, offered difficulties to the English scholar, and to provide for the needs of the latter William Thomas, who had stayed at Padua, drew up the *Principall rules of the Italian Grammer* and added 'a Dictionarie for the better vnderstandynge of *Boccace, Petrarcha,* and *Dante*'.[2] An edition of the *Decameron* in Italian was licensed to John Wolfe on 13 September 1587,[3] though no copy is at present known. The authorisation by Archbishop Whitgift may appear remarkable, but the reputation of Boccaccio as a humanist still was high, and the renderings into Latin of the tales of Grisild,[4] Guiscardo and Ghismonda,[5] Titus and Gisippus,[6] and Cimone[7] by Petrarch, Bruni and Beroaldo were not forgotten. The archbishop could have justified the study of the last of these stories, as was done by an anonymous writer at the end of the century who mentions Boccaccio and Plato[8] side by side as exponents of the view that love can make a man 'gentle, debonaire and vertuous' or 'so ciuill gentle, conformable, valiant and renowned, as no one could equall him in all graces and good partes beseeming a Gentleman'.[9]

However, not all humanists were agreed about Boccaccio, and some notable figures at home and abroad condemned tales and romances. Vives, whose work on *The instruction of a Christen woman* appeared in English about 1540, criticises such popular reading as Amadis and Tristan, Lancilot du Lake, Floris and Blanchefleur, Pyramus and Thisbe, Guy of Warwick and Bevis of Southampton, and the *Euryalus* of Æneas Sylvius, later Pope Pius II. The *Decameron*, like Poggio's *Facetiæ*, was severely censured by Vives.[10] So too Roger Ascham in *The Scholemaster* in 1570 denounces *Morte Arthure* and incidentally, the episodes of 'Sir Launcelote' and 'Syr Tristram'. He then continues:

---

[1] *Letter-Book*, ed. E. J. L. Scott, Camden Society, Series II, No. 33, 1894, pp. 133–4.
[2] See the edition of 1562. The work was first published in 1550.
[3] Cf. Scott, p. 91 and Arber's *Transcript*, ii, p. 221. Scott points out as a notable fact that in the same year the publication of Bartholomew Young's translation of *Amorosa Fiammetta* was sanctioned by the bishop of London.
[4] Vide post, pp. 116–22, 196, 307.   [5] Vide post, pp. 123, 131.   [6] Vide post, p. 154.
[7] Printed about 1498. Cf. *Gesamtkatalog*, item 4437. Vide post, pp. 194, 264.
[8] The reference is to the 'Conuiuium', i.e. the *Symposium*.
[9] *Fancies ague-fittes, or beauties nettle-bed*, 1599. My attention was drawn to this work by Wilkinson, p. xxi.
[10] Cf. *Opera*, Basle, 1555, ii, p. 658.

And yet ten *Morte Arthures* do not the tenth part of so much harme, as one of these bookes made in *Italie*, and translated in England. They open, not fond and common wayes to vice, but such sutle, cunnyng, new, and diuerse shiftes, to cary yong willes to vanitie, and yong wittes to mischief, to teach old bawdes new schole poyntes, as the simple head of an English man is not hable to inuent.[1]

It is true that Ascham does not specify the *Decameron*, but it must have been on his list, for shortly after he contrasts unfavourably 'a tale in Boccace' with a story of the Bible.

One year earlier this point of view is presented with even greater vehemence in the English translation by J. Sandford of the German philosopher Henricus Cornelius Agrippa's work, which in its English dress was called *Of the Vanitie and vncertaintie of Arts and Sciences.* He too rejects as dangerous such tales of love as those of Lancelot and Tristram and condemns Æneas Sylvius, Dante, Petrarch, and above all Boccaccio, who

hath wonne himselfe the price or palme of bawdes chieflye in those bookes, whiche he entituled Le cento Nouelle: whose examples, & doctrines, are nothinge els, but very subtill deceites of bawdries.[2]

This trend of opinion, which judged all literature exclusively by moral values, was not without some effect in governing the choice and treatment of tales from the *Decameron*.

1. Tales in Verse derived through French and Latin

Though Chaucer's *Clerk's Tale* is ultimately derived from the *Decameron*, it is based on an anonymous French prose translation of the Latin version made by Petrarch and on the revised draft of the text as it left the great humanist's hand shortly before his death in 1374.[3] What with the changes introduced by Petrarch and those resulting from Chaucer's modification, the story differed in some respects from that of Boccaccio.[4]

---

[1] 1570 ed., fol. 27.   [2] 1569 ed., fol. 98.

[3] For an account of the French versions, see E. Golenistcheff-Koutouzoff, *L'histoire de Griséldis en France au XIVe et au XVe siècle*, Paris, 1933. Through the medium of Petrarch's version the story was also carried to Germany, where it was printed separately, several editions appearing in the period 1470–80 (cf. *Decameron von Heinrich Steinhöwel*, ed. A. von Keller, Stuttgart, 1860, p. 685). Similarly the Spaniard knew it in Petrarch's version and ascribed it to him (cf. Farinelli, i, 32–6). For an account of the widespread popularity of the story of Grisild in many countries, and not only in the Middle Ages, see K. Laserstein, *Der Griseldisstoff in der Weltliteratur*, Weimar, 1926.

[4] Cf. J. B. Severs, 'The Clerk's Tale' in *Sources and Analogues of Chaucer's 'Canterbury Tales'*, pp. 288–91, and *The Literary Relationships of Chaucer's 'Clerkes Tale*, New Haven and New York, 1942.

Here and there a detail is added which lends an air of veracity to the narrative. The gems for Grisild are 'set in gold and in asure'; the wedding procession moves away with all the young nobles of Walter's retinue, to the accompaniment of 'many a soun of sondry melodye'; the revelry that follows continues until sunset, and the festivities after the reconciliation 'til on the welkne shoon the sterres light'. The poet depicts Grisild as a casual spectator, who, curious to see the new marchioness, intends to stand with other village-maidens and who, when called by Walter

> sette doun hir water-pot anoon
> Bisyde the threshfold, in an oxes stalle.[1]
>   (E 290–1)

Yet even if these traits added here and there enable the reader to see people and places more clearly, Chaucer was still more concerned with the minds of human beings. The tale itself presented a theme dear to Boccaccio—the existence of nobility of soul in the lowest ranks of society. Chaucer accepted this, as is shown by the remarks on 'gentil-esse' in *The Wife of Bath's Tale*,[2] which were inspired by the classical tradition that had been handed on to Dante.[3] However, that did not mean that he idolised the people. Even though he recognised the person of exceptional qualities, he could not refrain from a generalisation which gives a different turn to Petrarch's text when he makes the Clerk declare that 'the peple have no greet insight in vertu'.[4] If Chaucer's critical attitude suddenly gleams forth here, it is openly displayed to condemn the fickleness of the masses in their quest of novelty which leads them to approve their lord's plan to replace Grisild by a younger wife:

> Your doom is fals, your constance yvel preveth,
> A ful greet fool is he that on yow leveth!
>   (E 1000–1)

Chaucer belonged to those who, like the sober folk in the city, despised such incalculable gusts of popular feeling. How then does he present Walter, the capricious husband of Grisild? It was no easy task to discover enough sympathetic qualities in him to reconcile the reader to the happy ending of Boccaccio's tale. Indeed, Dioneo, the narrator of the story in the *Decameron*, exhibits him as one who, far from illustrating the theme of liberality or magnificence which had been laid down for the tenth day, was guilty of 'una matta bestialità'. Chaucer tries to suggest some essential goodness in Walter when the latter,

---

[1] Quotations from the *Clerk's Tale* are taken from Skeat.
[2] Skeat, D 1109–204.
[3] Particularly in the *Convivio*. Cf. B. J. Whiting, *The Wife of Bath's Tale* in *Sources and Analogues of Chaucer's Tales*, pp. 265–6.   [4] E 242–3.

moved by his wife's constancy, casts his eyes downward and when, as a prelude to his disclosure of the truth, in an access of remorseful tenderness he calls her 'dere wyf'. Yet on the whole Chaucer contrives to stir our feelings against Walter by the insertion of such words as 'sturdy' ('harsh'), 'wikke' and 'boistously' ('roughly').[1] More plainly he shows his bent when the Clerk maintains:

> I seye that yvel it sit
> Tassaye a wyf whan that it is no nede,
> And putten her in anguish and in drede,
>
> (E 460–2)

a sentiment which he later reiterates.[2]

A similar procedure can be noted in the sketch of Walter's servant who obeys his commands to carry off first the daughter, then the son from Grisild. The choice of words 'he stalked him ful stille' to describe his entrance into her chamber is significant. Equally menacing is his silence when Grisild pleads for her children. But his expression is eloquent of an intention to slay the girl, and the way in which this 'ugly' servant lays hands on the boy is still 'worse, if men worse can devyse'.

The total effect is to sway the sentiment of the reader in favour of Grisild and against the ruler who abuses his power. The tale, as related by Boccaccio and Petrarch, depicts a feudal society, where the marquis has absolute power over his subjects. However, in Chaucer's hands their submission to his will implies an even wider gap between them and their lord. Their spokesman, addressing Walter, feels that he is guilty of some presumption in asking for an audience and begs that he may not be treated with disdain. And when Walter yields to their request and fixes a date for his marriage, Chaucer depicts them obediently and reverently kneeling down to thank him. This emphasis of Chaucer makes it all the more natural that a mere girl, the daughter of the poorest of the poor in a little village of this community, should share in the unquestioning deference to every wish of their lord. When Walter calls, she adopts the same posture as other superior members of society had done:

> doun up-on hir knees she gan to falle,
> And with sad contenance kneleth stille,[3]
>
> (E 292–3)

and indoors she is so amazed at his presence that her face grows pale. Although her consent is formally asked by Walter, the possibility of a refusal is even less likely in the environment depicted by Chaucer than

---

[1] sturdy, E 698; wikke, E 785; boistously, E 791.

[2] E 621–3.

[3] See also E 949–52.

in that of Boccaccio. In addition, Chaucer lends to her vow of unswerving obedience a greater solemnity. Grisild does not merely promise, but
swears unfailing acceptance of Walter's every wish, and the word is
reiterated to stress its importance. In this way a stronger moral obligation is implied, the upholding of which has a basis in Grisild's strength
of mind.

However, while Chaucer by these slight modifications seeks to
account for Grisild's dutifulness, he is clearly anxious lest she should
appear a mere automaton. He emphasises what he finds in his source
about her fundamental humility which preserves her from haughtiness
or pride in the hour of prosperity[1] and helps her to maintain her pledge
to her lord. She performs all that she is told to do, and even goes
beyond all that was demanded when in her mean array she mingles
with the throng that presses towards the gate to welcome the new
marchioness. Consequently, there is every justification when the
Clerk's praise, implying as it does that she rivals Job, culminates in the
eulogy:

> Ther can no man in humblesse him acquyte
> As womman can, ne can ben half so trewe
> As wommen been.

(E 936–8)

Moreover, Chaucer introduces a personal quality into the relationship of Walter and Grisild which is more intimate than that of lord
and vassal. At the outset he sees to it that she is treated with respect.
There is something repugnant in the feudal despotism with which, in
the original, Walter orders Grisild to be stripped of her clothes and
robed anew in the presence of all and sundry. Petrarch saw no reason
to modify this episode which in his version takes place on the threshold
of the cottage. In relating the incident Chaucer speaks vaguely of the
disrobing 'right there', but Grisild in restrospect says that it occurred
'in my fadres place'. This greater delicacy on Chaucer's part was
meant to remove any obstacle to the development of affection between
her and Walter. That this affection, far from being diminished by her
trials, had actually grown, may be seen from her declaration that she
will always love him best.[2] It is this attachment which explains her
sudden outburst:

> O gode god! how gentil and how kinde
> Ye semed by your speche and your visage
> The day that maked was our mariage!
>
> But sooth is seyd, algate I finde it trewe—
> For in effect it preved is on me—
> Love is noght old as whan that it is newe.

[1] Cf. E 927–31.   [2] E 973.

> But, certes, lord, for noon adversitee,
> To dyen in the cas, it shal nat be
> That ever in word or werk I shal repente
> That I yow yaf myn herte in hool entente.
>
> (E 852–61)

It is this passionate recollection which introduces a note of indignant protest into her request not to be sent home naked from the court:

> Ye coude nat doon so dishoneste a thing
>
> (E 876)

and explains the dignified entreaty combined with tender reproach in her words:

> Lat me nat lyk a worm go by the weye.
> Remembre yow, myn owene lord so dere,
> I was your wyf, thogh I unworthy were.
>
> (E 880–2)

Here it is the wife who speaks, and the same heightening of emotion is perceptible when the instincts of the mother are stirred. Chaucer follows the essentials of the story, but his Grisild seems a more lifelike figure when she pleads with Walter's servant and bids her child farewell.[1] At the close, when the feelings of the wife and the mother are awakened at one and the same time and she faints for joy, the Clerk touches his readers with his exclamation:

> O, which a pitous thing it was to see
> Hir swowning, and hir humble voys to here!
>
> (E 1086–7)

Still more powerful is the effect of Grisild's own words,[2] as she gazes at her children and then suddenly faints for the second time. There is no such access of feeling in Boccaccio who was here more concerned with outward events than the inner life. The first swoon was introduced by Petrarch; but the second was added by Chaucer, to exemplify the power of maternal love. This is revealed when, as she falls, she seizes her children and holds them in a convulsive grasp even when she has lost consciousness.[3] Not content with this, Chaucer works upon his audience by describing the overpowering effect on the spectators as well:

> O many a teer on many a pitous face
> Doun ran of hem that stoden hir bisyde;
> Unnethe abouten hir mighte they abyde.
>
> (E 1104–6)

Such a scene made Grisild more warmly human, when at long last the rigid control of her feelings was broken down by the sudden impact of events. Perhaps it also served to gratify Chaucer's sense of irony.

---

[1] E 547–60.   [2] E 1093–8.   [3] E 1100–03.

Only a short time before Grisild had interceded for the new marchioness on the ground that she could not endure an ordeal so well as one of tough peasant stock; and now, taken off her guard, she herself is overcome by the cumulative strain.

However, all other considerations were subordinate to the main purpose, to offer a conspicuous example of courage in adversity. Here was an illustration of the workings of fortune, raising the heroine to the heights of joy only to cast her down again.[1] In this respect the fate of Grisild resembled that of many another figure known to Boccaccio, but it differed in her final restoration to happiness. Under the influence of Petrarch, Chaucer again and again throws into relief the strength and tenacity which enabled

> this humble creature,
> Thadversitee of fortune al tendure.
> (E 755–6)

Walter tries to portray her sorrows as 'the strook of fortune or of aventure', and the people who accompany her after her expulsion from the court throw the responsibility on Fortune whom they curse most heartily. Consequently her ultimate triumph warrants the lesson

> that every wight, in his degree,
> Sholde be constant in adversitee.
> (E 1145–6)

This gives a turn to the story which was not found in Boccaccio. However, though Chaucer was aware that there was a problem in the sufferings of mankind, as the parallel that he draws between Job and Grisild indicates, he asks no questions. He does not attempt to probe the mystery and does not even dwell upon it as in *Troilus and Criseyde*. It is enough for him to cast a passing glance and then proceed to the conclusion of the Clerk—God inflicts on mankind the scourge of adversity

> And for our beste is al his governaunce;
> Lat us than live in vertuous suffraunce.
> (E 1161–2)

Such a pious philosophy is altogether in keeping with the character of the narrator. Even in the Prologue to the tale Chaucer singles out those features in the Clerk which make his choice of the career of Grisild as his theme the most natural thing in the world. It is, in truth, a revelation of his inmost self. He rides along

> as . . . stille as dooth a mayde,
> Were newe spoused, sitting at the bord.[2]
> (E 2–3)

---

[1] E 810–12.   [2] Prologue to *Clerk's Tale*.

His tale is that of a quiet maiden by a quiet scholar whose voice is as
benign as that of Grisild herself. Absorbed in study, he eulogises, not
only Petrarch, the nominal author of the story, but also 'Linian' or
Giovanni di Lignano, another man of learning. And it is characteristic
of his gravity that by way of preface to the 'mery tale' for which the
Host had asked, he should add:

> But deeth, that wol nat suffre us dwellen heer
> But as it were a twinkling of an yë,
> Hem bothe hath slayn, and alle shul we dyë.
> (E 36–8)

The ending of the story harmonises perfectly with the character of
the Clerk, for with unconscious irony he ends by preaching, which
the Host had begged him at all costs to avoid!

Not only did Chaucer select a tale which was consistent with the
personality of the narrator, he also fitted it into the framework of the
surrounding tales. Whereas the last tale of the *Decameron* came but ill
from the lips of Dioneo and, as Boccaccio himself realised, hardly tallied
with the general theme prescribed for the tenth day, Chaucer contrives within the limits of the *Clerk's Tale* to prepare the way for its
successor. It is true that, as he was unlimited by any specified theme,
his task was easier than that of Boccaccio. Nevertheless, one must
admire the ease with which Chaucer prepares the descent from the
world of lofty idealism to that of earthy passion in the *Merchant's
Tale*. He begins when in his account of the prosperity in marriage of
Walter's son, the Clerk observes:

> Al putte he nat his wyf in greet assay,
> (E 1138)

and this leads on to the statement, for which there is no warrant in
Petrarch or Boccaccio, that

> This world is nat so strong, it is no nay,
> As it hath been in olde tymes yore.
> (E 1139–40)

There is a faint ripple of humour on the surface of this grave tale,
which becomes a smile when the scarcity of Grisilds in modern times
is related,[1] and culminates in the ironical laughter of Chaucer's envoy.
The transition to the world of 'Ianuarie' and 'May' is complete.

So masterly was Chaucer's narrative that no other mediæval
English writer attempted to compose a tale in verse on the subject of
Grisild. But his influence is palpable in the *Legenda Sismond*, the
work of Gilbert Banester, Master of the Children of the Chapel Royal

---

[1] E 1164–9.

from 1478 to 1486.[1] In one manuscript the poem is even attached to Chaucer's *Legend of Good Women,* and the portrait of Sismond contains obvious borrowings from *The Booke of the Duchesse*:

> She was white, ruddy, fressh and lowely hewyde,
> In all hyr body wes nat o wikkyd syng,
> And euery day hyr fayrnes anewyd,
> For it wes sadde, demwre and benynge;
>
> .   .   .   .   .
>
> Hardly hyr tonge shulde none hurt nor enpayre.
>
> Hyr eloquens was spokyn with so mylde speche,
> With sad contenance, thus may I expresse,
> That, forsoth, she was a werreye lywys leche.[2]
>
> (50–4, 63, 64–6)

Banester alludes to 'Bocas in cent nouellys',[3] which suggests, with other evidence, that he relied upon a French version, and this in turn was based upon the Latin version of Leonardo Bruni, made in 1436 or 1438. The English version deals more fully than the original with the characters of Tancred, Ghismonda and Guiscardo and their relations with one another. Tancred is shown as a great ruler whose fame is spread far and wide. His daughter, here called Sismond, is marked by loyalty, steadfastness and gentleness, and the depth of her nature is revealed by the intensity of her emotion at the death of her husband. Tancred for his part is also capable of tenderness, and his decision that Sismond shall never marry again is dictated by pity as well as by affection. The bond between father and daughter is made more solemn and more intimate by a deliberate pledge which Sismond gives him at this moment. This feature was clearly meant to provide another reason for his anger at her later conduct, but it does confront the narrator with a difficulty, since Banester hardly explains adequately her change of mind.

As for Guistard, he has undergone a notable idealisation. The sharp-witted page of Boccaccio is now a young squire whose perfect manners and good breeding recall the squire in Chaucer's prologue to the *Canterbury Tales.* He is a polished gentleman who seems an

---

[1] For a detailed account of the manuscripts and of the poem see *Early English Versions of the Tales of Guiscardo and Ghismonda and Titus and Gisippus from the Decameron,* ed. H. G. Wright, London, 1937, E.E.T.S., Orig. Ser. 205; and Josef Raith, *Boccaccio in der englischen Literatur von Chaucer bis Painters Palace of Pleasure,* Munich, 1936, pp. 77–80. See also W. H. G. Flood, *Early Tudor Composers,* Oxford, 1925, pp. 13–16.

[2] Quotations are from MS. Add. 12524 as printed in Wright's edition. Cf. *The Booke of the Duchesse,* ll. 904–6, 916–18, 930–1, 925–6, 919–20. This borrowing was first noted by J. Raith, op. cit., p. 79.

[3] This is the reading of MS. Rawlinson C. 86. That of MS. Add. 12524, 'Bocase in kent' is obviously corrupt.

admirable representative of the land which, as Banester tells us, Tancred kept free 'from fylthy vice'. Conscious of his humble birth, he maintains a fitting modesty and regards himself as 'one off the lest'. The English version discards the device of the letter in the reed by means of which the heroine communicates with him in the *Decameron*. Instead, after a cautious preamble, Sismond openly confesses her love. Unlike his counterpart, Guistard is dumbfounded and receives the news with blushing diffidence. As the story unfolds, the tendency to idealise develops into a bent for moralisation. Banester would clearly have disapproved of the passion of the lovers in the *Decameron* and presents Guistard and Sismond as being 'in grete syn'. At the same time he insists that Sismond wished

> To haue lyffid in the law of matermony,
> (238)

but she now finds that her pledge, so rashly given in an access of grief, is an impassable barrier, and the bitter truth causes her to weep a hundred times.

After the discovery Sismond's attitude again differs notably from that of her prototype. She still retains her filial respect and is less fiercely defiant. Outwardly firm, even to the point of offering to die instead of Guistard, she is not cast in the same stern mould as Ghismonda. After she has taken the poison, there is a glimpse of human frailty, and on her death-bed she is seen

> Tremelyng and quakyng, fast drawyng after breth.
> (511)

The pathos of the situation is enhanced when Tancred, who had been not a possessive but a loving parent, now overwhelmed with grief, utters a great cry and falls dead, unlike his counterpart, who lives on to repent his cruelty and inter the lovers in one tomb.

However, the English version does shift the responsibility for this fatal event on to Tancred. Sympathy is given to Guistard and Sismond, and at the close Tancred is openly condemned and the omnipotence of love proclaimed:

> For, certys, of trew lufarys it is the gyse,
> Vhen there trouble and vexacioune is moste sore,
> They woll love yche other in more hertily wyse
> Ane hundreth fowlde then euer they dyd afore;
> Youth will to youth and lofe to lufe euermore.
> (575–9)

But Tancred had done worse than thwart the course of love; he had been 'ayeyenst spowsail' and so was morally culpable. Having exonerated Guistard, Banester expresses a hope that

> hys feithfull entencioune
> Vas the cause off hys endelese saluacioune.
>
> (594–5)

Though he is more doubtful about Sismond, in view of her desire for
marriage, her sufferings, and her final contrition (of which nothing
has hitherto been said), he entertains hope for her soul also,

> For off feith and treuth of all lufarys suremountyng
> She was, and a m[i]roure to women all,
> Ensample of treue and stedfast lowe gyffyng.
>
> (604–6)

The poem finds in the sorrowful ending yet another example—that
of the power of Fortune. In the last resort it was Fortune that was the
cause, since she brought to pass the death of Sismond's husband, then
brought new joy into her life through Guistard, and finally plunged
all into disaster.[1] How much this interpretation appealed to the
fifteenth century may be perceived from one of the manuscripts in
which the story is preserved.[2] Here the tale is given a prologue which
comments thus:

> The wykked daunger and envyous ielosye
> Be ay redy in co[r]ners to espye,
> Wyth myschef doing theyre vtmost deuour
> All treve louers to parte and disseuyr,
> As ye shall here þe lyke case
> Betwene ij louers don as it was.
> Fortune caused þe herty love betwene þaym;
> Alas! and at þe last fortune discouerd thaym,
> And this causeth me to be wondir heuy
> That she nad preserued thaim secretly,
> For I wis, fortune, and yf [ye] had liste,
> This mater had neuyr be knowen nor wiste.
> O lady Venus, þe hygh and myghty goddesse,
> Ye shulde haue kythed your gentilnesse,
> Fortune and ye all myghte haue sauyde,
> Whose corsis now lyeth in thayre chestes grauyd.[3]

The manuscript brings into close connection two other poems which
reveal a fundamental kinship of outlook. The second, which is the
immediate forerunner of the story of Guistard and Sismond, denounces
the treachery of Fortune. Two lines epitomise the argument:

> In wel beware þe wysely,
> For fortune turneth sodenly.[4]

The first was written by Lydgate at the command of Queen Catherine
as she walked in the meadows that had just been mown, and in his

---

[1] Cf. ll. 83–4, 210, 239–42, 339–40 and 441.
[2] Rawlinson C. 86 in the Bodleian.
[3] Cf. Wright's ed., Intro., pp. xiii–xiv.   [4] Ibid., Intro., p. xiii.

hands the scene becomes a symbol of the fickleness of Fortune. Nothing fair may continue long, for with a turn of her wheel she destroys all beauty, and in contrast to this world, where all is uncertain and subject to perpetual transmutations, Lydgate points to the unchanging glories of the celestial city. In the same way the poem preceding the lovers' tale combines an admonition with praise of the joys of heaven:

> Then caste away þy croked appetyte
> Of worldely welth þat may þe not avayle;
> In hevenly love I counceyle þe delite,
> Here to gete it with þy true trauayle;
> Yf þou do þus, of blis þou maist not fayle.
> Geve god þy hert; many maner wyse
> Now blissed is he, þis worlde þat can despise.[1]

Read in this context, the conclusion of the tale of Guistard and Sismond, preoccupied as it is with the salvation of their souls, is seen in a new light. For Banester and for Englishmen of the fifteenth century it had an atmosphere altogether different from that in which the 'lieta brigata' lived and moved.

It would seem also as if Banester failed to appreciate the humanistic tradition that animates the lengthy speech in which Boccaccio's heroine defends her choice of Guistard, on the ground that personal merit should count for more than high rank. Her pleas, which are remarkable for their democratic bias, are reduced to

> what is noublenesse but vertue, parde?
> (379)

Whatever Banester's reasons, in his version the powerful equalitarian arguments of the original almost disappear. It was left for a later writer to expound what he had virtually ignored.

In the latter part of the fifteenth century Boccaccio's tale found another English interpreter whose work is preserved in a manuscript[2] and in the volume *Certaine Worthye Manuscript Poems of great Antiquitie*, which was printed in London in 1597 and dedicated 'To the worthiest Poet Maister Ed. Spenser'.[3] There are many parallels between this anonymous version and that of Banester, which point to a common source. This was probably the French form of the tale mentioned earlier, but there is certainly direct borrowing from Banester. Thus the conclusion is derived from him.

The unknown author was a scholar, familiar with literary devices, who adorns his verse with images which distinguish his work from Banester's plain and simple style. He draws on Nature, jewels, navigation and warfare, and on occasion from a more homely environment.

---

[1] Cf. Wright's ed., Intro., p. xiii.
[2] R. 3.19 at Trinity College, Cambridge.   [3] Reprinted at Edinburgh in 1812.

He sees his characters in a mediæval setting and affords a glimpse of contemporary life, as when he pictures those who sally forth from the castle in the morning, some to hawk, some to hunt, and some to labour, and alludes to the way in which an event might be recorded in verse and travel far and wide:

> For with gentyls and mynstrellys hyt was a comon song,
> So that euery man in all the contrey rownde
> Spake of the infortunat love of Gunstard and Sismound.[1]
>
> (607–9)

Similarly, he tells of her golden surcote, furred with precious ermine, and shows her picking flowers in the castle garden to make a garland for dancing in. The natural background and the changing seasons are related to the story, and the love-theme, conceived as part of the universal rejuvenation, is invested with grace and beauty:

> In the mery season of somer, [feyre] and hote,
> When euery thyng revyueth by course of nature,
> And wynter with hys frosty berde and hys frysyd cote
> Ys put in to exyle, and may no lengor dure,
> Then somer yeueth hys lyuerey with hys besy cure,
> New clothyng all the erthe in a lusty grene,
> Embroudyd full of floures ryght fresshly besene.
>
> (386–92)

The outward manifestations of emotion also catch the poet's eye. He sees Gunstard blench and tremble with fear on his arrest, Tancred turn white with wrath, and Sismond wring her long and slender fingers or sit motionless, pale and wan, with deathlike countenance. At greater length he describes the heroine's troubled sleep after the seizure of her lover and the fearful vision that rose before her eyes. He is clearly tempted to tarry over the dream in Chaucerian fashion but the example of Boccaccio recalls him from this excursion. Nevertheless, elsewhere he does pause to consider various points such as the precautions of the lovers and the reason for the death of Sismond's husband, which the original had ignored for the sake of economy. So too he devises a better pretext than was to be found in the *Decameron* for Sismond's dismissal of her attendants and retirement to her chamber.

Above all, however, he devotes his attention to the portrayal of the characters. There was in Boccaccio's Ghismonda more than a suggestion of a masterful, scheming woman, bent on satisfying her lust, and in Guiscardo of a youth somewhat too shrewd in amorous matters. The anonymous poet, though at this point he does not modify the tale

---

[1] MS. R. 3. 19, Trinity College, Cambridge. Quotations and line references are based on Wright's edition.

as Banester had done, was anxious, like him, to idealise the relations of his lovers. In his version Gunstard notes in his mistress various signs that she is in love, but he has no idea with whom:

> Tyll onys he fortunyd to stond before that lady,
> And she beholdyng hym with dedly pale fase,
> Nat spekyng a worde, she gaue a gret sygh,
> And anon with that she gan withdraw hyr ygh,
> Castyng downe hyr loke fer in to the ground;
> So womanly shamefast she stood a gret stound.
>
> (198–203)

Now Gunstard understands and does his utmost to please his lady. But he hardly dares to believe in his good fortune; joy and doubt alternate, until he is convinced that she does love him, though no word has passed between them. Yet if after all he is mistaken, he is resolved to persevere in his service.

The letter sent by Sismond, a feature retained from the *Decameron*, is used to throw light on her character. In the interest of speedy narration Boccaccio had said nothing of its contents; on the other hand, the English poet uses it to dispel any impression of a cunning schemer, as may be perceived at the very beginning:

> I send vnto yow gretyng with loue and hert entier,
> Nat bold by rehersayll my counsell to detect
> For dredefull shamefastnes; wherfore thys messyngere
> Shall do all thys entyrpryce, whos countenaunce and chere
> Changeth for no shame; therfore these lettres blake,
> I pray yow, dysdeyne yow nat to rede theym for my sake.
>
> (254–9)

And there is real delicacy of insight in the picture of her, as she hesitates over her signature:

> She wrot ther: 'By your owne' and made no mencyon
> Of hyr name, ne no more, tyll aftyr a gret stound,
> And then, with sore syghyng, she addyd 'Sismound'.
>
> (313–15)

In the great crisis Sismond, who, as in Banester's version, wishes to plead with Tancred for her lover's life, greets her father, not with defiance, but with reverence and humility. However, she is presented in a new light after she has received visible evidence of Tancred's cruelty, for she then refuses to send him any reply whatsoever. Another innovation is the silence of Gunstard, for very shame, when first rebuked by Tancred. The poet also tries to provide a motive to justify Tancred's conduct, when he explains his anger as springing in part from resentment at the prospect of one whom he had rescued from beggary, holding sway over his lands. However, the narrator's sympathies are all with the lovers. In particular he understands the anguish of Sismond and on her death bursts into an exclamation of grief:

> Allas! my wofull pen soroweth for to wryte
> Thys lamentable ende for thys tragedy.
> Who cowde without wepyng thys matyr endyte,
> To se so feyre a creature to dy so wrechydly,
> Of bewte feyrest and welle of curtesy?
> (911–15)

This attitude assumes another form in the comment which is added after Gunstard has been arrested and the raging Tancred has brushed aside his excuse:

> So was hys mynde with malyce and yre obnub[i]lat.
> Alas! where malyce regneth, ther may non excuse avayle;
> A gret abusyon hyt ys a ruler to be impassionat;
> O ye worthy prynces! therfore, to whom of hygh estat
> The gydyng ys commyttyd of noble regyons,
> Well ye ought to take hede to rule your pa[ssyo]ns!
>
> Committeth nat wylfully sensualyte,
> Agayn the ryghtfull conscience of reson to put restreynt;
> Beth nat rulyd only by myrthe and volunte,
> Oppressyng by [m]yght and power theym that be weke and feynt,
> Wherby your noble fame ys oftyn hurt and atteynt;
> Hyt causeth also the pepyll in tyme of your dystresse
> To draw from yow theyr fauour and herty feythfulnesse.
> (464–76)

This passage is notable, for it not only reveals the author's condemnation of Tancred, but goes much further and extends beyond the scope of the tale. In fact, it embodies a warning to all tyrants that they may forfeit the loyalty of their subjects. One cannot help wondering whether the writer has not his eye on the events of Richard III's short and bloody reign.

In these lines one can hear at times the monitory voice of Lydgate in *The Fall of Princes*, and the poet's utilisation of the tale to remark on the instability of human happiness and the vagaries of Fortune proves that the two writers shared the general outlook of the age. Early in the poem there is an ill omen in the brief lament that cruel destiny so often changes joy into mourning, and again and again, in a plangent counterpoint, the narrator describes the sudden caprices of Fortune, 'more variaunt and flyttyng then ys the mutabyll mone' and denounces her duplicity and inconstancy as she

> by hyr vnstable centyr
> Plongeth estates gret downe from hyr whele full fer,
> When she lyst of daunger to swarve and repent hyr.
> (730–2)

And Sismond herself curses Fortune and reminds one of Romeo's[1] challenge to fate, when she cries:

> All thy gret malyce holy I defy.[2]
>
> (618)

In this matter the anonymous writer agrees with Banester, but he differs from him in his wholehearted support of the humanistic tradition that underlay Sismond's defence of her love for one inferior to her in rank. Whereas his predecessor had turned aside uneasily from this part of her speech, he develops the arguments placed in her mouth by Boccaccio:

> Furst when oure modyr Eue brought forth Abell and Caym,
> Who cowde prefer hymself of byrth or of lynage,
> And of theym tweyne infauntes, who cowde a tytyll claym
> In gentyll blood, in noblenes, or in hygh parage?
> That tyme was no dyfference betwyxt gentylman and page,
> But euery man was fayne to put hym in deuour
> Hys lyuyng for to gete with swetyng and gret labour.
>
> Of all thys tyme was no man bound ne vndyr seruage,
> No man by seruyce vndyr subieccyon,
> Tyll when the pepyll gan to revell and rage,
> Guydyng theymsylf by wyll and nothyng by reson,
> Offendyng the lawe by theyr transgression,
> That of ryght and iustice they must be correct
> Of oon that was theyr souuerayn and they to hym subiect.
>
> But he that shuld be rewler and haue regency
> May nat of ryght be suche on as ys a transgressour;
> Agayn all dew ordyr [of nature] hyt ys, truly,
> That vyce shuld syt above and be a gouernour;
> But when that vertu, connyng, gentilnes, honour,
> He ys of ryght prouyd to be a souerayn,
> All though hys byrth be poore, thys ys the certayn.
>
> On this wyse was Moyses and Gidion also,
> The noble Duke Iosue, by god hymsylf elect,
> And scrypture reherseth many mo,
> Whyche a[t] theyr byrth were pore and deiect,
> Yet were they for theyr vertu chosyn [to] direct
> And to gyde the pepyll; so, shortly, thys ys trew,
> That ther ys no gentylman but oonly by vertew.
>
> (743–70)

Yet this conviction does not prevent the translator from combining

---

[1] *Romeo and Juliet*, ed. J. Dover Wilson and G. I. Duthie, Cambridge, 1955. V. i. 24.

[2] For references to Fate and Fortune see ll. 26, 211–17, 371–8, 410–13, 617–19, 689–96, 729–32 and 873–5.

his humanistic idealism with contempt for the fickleness of 'the comon vnstabyll vulge',[1] thus aligning himself with Chaucer.

This version is not devoid of interest. It keeps with some fidelity to Boccaccio's story which saw nothing essentially wrong in the frank satisfaction of sexual passion. Consequently, the attempt to blend with this attitude the point of view of Banester, who set out with an ethical bias and modifies the tale accordingly, was bound to fail. As with two starkly differing materials there is a violent clash, and the suture is visible. In some ways the greater elaboration is an advantage, but it is gained only by retarding the swift movement of Boccaccio.

Nevertheless, this rendering is far superior to that of William Walter who was a servant of Sir Henry Marney, the chancellor of the Duchy of Lancaster. His *Guystarde and Sygysmonde*, which was printed by Wynkyn de Worde in 1532, has survived in a copy, believed to be unique, belonging to the duke of Devonshire. It is based on the Latin translation of Leonardo Bruni, already mentioned, which enjoyed great popularity, especially after the invention of printing, for in the years between 1470 and 1500 no fewer than seventeen editions appeared. The text used by Walter was probably one of the editions that came from the press of the Cologne printer, Kornelius von Zieriksee.[2] Walter is content to relate in a straightforward fashion and makes few changes, but he abridges the address of Sygysmonde to her father, omitting the allusion to sovereigns who have risen from obscurity to eminence and deleting anything which would imply a lack of filial dutifulness on her part. At the close in the traditional manner of mediæval poetry he adds a pious prayer for the souls of the lovers. A few other alterations are no doubt deliberate, but more often his departure from Bruni seems to be the result of carelessness or lack of proficiency as a Latin scholar. His chief weakness, however, lies in his diffuseness and verbosity, which contrast with the simplicity and directness of Bruni and the concentration of Boccaccio. Nowhere can this be seen better than in the stanza spoken by Guistard in reply to Tancred's reproach. His prototype had uttered the famous words: 'Amor può troppo più che nè voi nè io possiamo'. From Walter's hands the answer emerges thus:

> The true louer answered pyteously
> Vnto Tancrede sayenge syr for certayne
> The harde chaunce of loue no man can deny
> It is greater than is the power humayne
> From it I coude my selfe in no wyse refrayne

[1] The speaker is Sismond, but she is probably echoing the translator's own sentiment (cf. l. 722).

[2] Cf. *Early English Versions of the Tales of Guiscardo and Ghismonda and Titus and Gisippus*, pp. lviii–lxiv.

Your puyssaunce may not vnto loue compare
Loue is so greate that it wyll no man spare.[1]
(274–80)

Walter has few resources as a translator and little skill in verse.

Nearly a quarter of the poem was contributed by Robert Coplande, Wynkyn de Worde's assistant. He wrote a prologue and an envoy as well as a running commentary on the tale. This industrious printer uses the story chiefly as a warning against idleness, for it was this defect in the upbringing of Sygysmonde which in his opinion was the root of all her troubles.

Fedde deyntely / no maner werke to vse
Whiche caused ydelnesse / for to habonde
And vnto pleasure / set onely for to muse
Daunce / songe / and play / she dyd not refuse
Whiche thynges assembled / engendred delyte
Of naturall lust / to do her appetyte.
(16–21)

Coplande approved of the story only in so far as it provided the reader with a warning against sensual delight and the follies to which it leads. Yet with all his gravity and prudence he cannot deny his sympathy altogether. He admires the lovers' constancy and the readiness of Sygysmonde to suffer death, at the same time as he condemns Tancred for his ferocity and lack of balance. Moreover, while he emphasises the responsibility of the characters for the sorrow that descends upon them, like other narrators of the period, he also blames

Vnstable fortune / tomblynge as the see
Thã yse more slypper / frosen after rayne
(239–40)

who has betrayed them, as she had done so many other lovers, from Dido and Æneas to Arcite and Emelye, and from Paris and Helen to Troilus and Criseyde.

Still this worthy printer felt that Walter could be better employed than in dealing with such a theme and recalls his promise to write a book

Whiche is of substaunce worthe many of this
And more worthy / of mater excellent.
(619–20)

It is likely that Walter agreed with the gist of Coplande's criticisms as may be seen from his attack on idleness in the prologue to *The Spectacle of Louers*. Possibly the new work of which he had spoken

---

[1] Line references to Walter's *Guystarde and Sygysmonde* are from Wright's edition *Early English Versions*, etc.

was *Tytus and Gesyppus* which appeared from the press of Wynkyn de Worde and is extant in a copy, seemingly unique, in the possession of the duke of Devonshire. From the theme of love Walter turns to that of friendship, which throughout the Renaissance made so strong an appeal in literature.[1]

His rendering is derived from the Latin version of Philippo Beroaldo, first published at Bologna in 1491. As in his earlier translation, Walter is unable to appreciate the structural continuity of the original, and his work is correspondingly defective. This indifference to the niceties of artistic composition is once more displayed in the harangue of the Athenians by Titus, as it had been in the speech of Sygysmonde to Tancred. The masterpieces of Boccaccian rhetoric meant little to Walter, who saw in them an impediment to the narrative, and he lays rough hands on them in an attempt at condensation. Again, as in *Guystarde and Sygysmonde*, he alters the ending. It becomes a lament on the growth of avaricious egoism, and a panegyric of friendship culminates in criticism:

> But now a dayes amyte dothe decay
> Eche man couetyth his synguler profet
> Vpon perylles they do forecast alwaye
> That by a frende they do but lytell set
> All theyr delyte is ryches for to get
> Ingratitude wo worthe vnto the
> Whiche doost exclude both loue & amyte.[2]
>
> (806–12)

Other slight modifications crop up from time to time. Thus on occasion Walter shows an awareness of a contrast between the customs of England and the practice of the lands which are the scene of the tale. Consequently, he comments on Greek wedding rites and substitutes hanging for crucifixion.

However, the translation is not an intelligent adaptation, for it is often inaccurate and sometimes obscure. Nor is the verse satisfying, for Walter was an unskilled craftsman whose fumbling for expression results only in baldness or verbosity.

As the date of publication of Walter's *Tytus and Gesyppus* is not known, it cannot be established whether or not Sir Thomas Elyot's version[3] owed anything to it. *The Gouernour*, when it was printed in 1531, was meant to be a serious work, and the tale was introduced to provide relief, while at the same time conducing to friendship. It is

---

[1] For an account of the fortune of Boccaccio's tale see L. Sorieri, *Boccaccio's Story of Tito e Gisippo in European Literature*, New York, 1937.

[2] Text of quotation and line references from Wright's ed., cf. p. 174.

[3] This is discussed at this point, although it is prose, because it is so closely related to tales in verse in this section.

possible that Elyot was acquainted with Beroaldo's translation,[1] but the rendering is so free that it is difficult to give absolute proof. His version has many distinctive features. Humanist as he was, he could not refrain from letting Titus embellish his speech to the Athenians with allusions to Greek myth and epic—Jupiter, Leda and Europa, the exploits of Hercules and his subjection to Deianira, the love of Paris for Helen and the siege of Troy. At the same time with an eye on the English reader, like Walter, he thought it advisable to explain Greek wedding customs. He also considered it only fitting that a series of secret meetings should precede the betrothal of Gisippus and Sophronia, and when the marriage takes place, there is feasting, the agreements are read and signed, and the dowry is fixed.

More important, however, is Elyot's handling of the speeches. Once he lets Titus expound to Gisippus his state of mind arising from his passion for Sophronia, whereas Boccaccio merely gives the gist of it in reported form. But far more common are instances of Elyot's policy of abridgement. Thus he omits the long debate that Titus has with himself on becoming enamoured of Sophronia, the speech in which he declares that he will either conquer his love or perish, and that in which, in response to the entreaties of Gisippus, he reluctantly consents to accept the betrothed of his friend. The effect of this last omission is to make Gisippus pass straight on to outline his plan without waiting to hear the opinion of Titus, and as a result Titus becomes almost a nonentity. Moreover, the elimination to a large extent of the conflict between Titus's desires and his scruples robs the story of much of its dramatic quality. This loss is made all the more acute by the removal of the episode in which at the last moment Titus is seized with compunction at the thought of taking his friend's bride and has to be importuned once more by Gisippus. Another scene discarded by Elyot is that in which Sophronia, on learning of the deception practised on her, indignantly retires to complain to her kinsmen. The suppression of her protest makes her even more of a puppet than in the original.

Nor is this the only place where the characterisation in Elyot is inferior to that of Boccaccio. Thus when Titus has confessed to Gisippus how passionately he loves Sophronia, in Boccaccio, Gisippus

---

[1] Cf. Sir Thomas Elyot, *The Boke named The Gouernour*, ed. H. H. S. Croft, London 1880 and J. Raith, op. cit., pp. 101–2. As J. C. Maxwell points out, C. T. Good analysed Elyot's departures from Boccaccio in *M.L.N.*, 1922, xxxvii, pp. 1–11, and attempted to trace them back to Petrus Alphonsus' *Disciplina Clericalis*. There can be no doubt that the versions of Walter and Elyot along with the original helped to make Titus and Gisippus well-known examples of friendship. Allusions to them are numerous (cf. *M.P.*, 1910, vii, p. 580). The tale left its mark on the early part of Lyly's *Euphues* (cf. S. L. Wolff, 'A Source of *Euphues*', *M.P.*, 1910, vii, pp. 577–85).

hesitates for a moment. Elyot, however, depicts him as accepting the situation with a readiness which seems all the more incredible when a few lines farther on Gisippus confesses that his delight in Sophronia's company surpassed all that he derived from his inherited possessions. The lack of subtlety here shown comes out again in the tendency to exaggerate emotion. For example, when Gisippus thinks himself to have been recognised and ignored by Titus, instead of departing in wrath as in the *Decameron*, he swoons and has to receive aid from the bystanders. So too, whereas Boccaccio describes how he falls asleep, worn out with grief, Elyot tells how he 'with wepinge and dolorous cryenge bewayled his fortune'. Once again Elyot grasps after the more palpable in drawing a picture of the boyhood of Titus and Gisippus. The kinship between them was purely spiritual, but Elyot is not content with that. In spite of the fact that they were in no wise related, the one being a Roman and the other an Athenian, he would have us believe that they were so much alike that their parents could hardly distinguish one from the other, and that it was necessary for laces of different colours to be hung round their necks.

Another feature of Elyot's narrative is the tendency to present Titus and Gisippus, not as private individuals of high rank, but as public figures of national importance. Consequently, instead of haranguing the relatives of Gisippus and Sophronia, Titus addresses all the nobility of Athens. He declares that he has been sent for by the authority of the senate and people of Rome and he warns his listeners that if harm befalls Gisippus, he will return at once 'with the inuincible power of the Romanes'. In Rome, Gisippus is brought for trial, not before the praetor Marcus Varro, but before the senate, and it is the senate which orders his release. So too, when Gisippus resolves to go back to Athens, instead of marrying the sister of Titus and living happily ever after with his friend, in Elyot's version Titus assembles a great army with the consent of the senate and the people, and Gisippus is restored to wealth and dignity. Apart from the fact that Walter had made Titus threaten to return with an army and inflict vengeance there is no parallel for these developments.

Elyot likewise introduces some changes of minor significance. He enumerates the qualities of Sophronia and emphasises the love of Titus' mother for her son by referring to the importunity with which she insists on his return to Rome. The necessity for his departure is made so urgent that the very next day after the union of Titus and Sophronia has been consummated, he discloses to the Athenians that he has taken the place of Gisippus. Praising his friend, he maintains that such generosity, far from deserving blame, entitles him to a statue or an image of gold, and he offers him then and there one half of his possessions. Certain traits are likewise added to the character of Gisippus. A devotee of philosophy, he is reluctant to marry, lest it should interfere with his studies, and when his misfortunes have reduced him to despair, his philosophy alone deters him from suicide. There is indeed a singular high-mindedness about him, which is shown again when he decides to remain in Athens because he believes that his counsel can be of service to his native city.

In the Roman section of the story there are some details which are distinctive. Thus, when Gisippus is waiting outside the residence of his friend, both Titus and Sophronia come out, and to this extent the failure to recognise him is rendered less credible than when Titus alone passes him by. However, in Elyot's version he does ultimately identify Gisippus by 'a litle signe in his visage'. On leaving the house of Titus in despair, Gisippus wanders till he comes, not to a cave, but to an old barn; and whereas in Boccaccio the two thieves enter the cave and Gisippus witnesses the one murder the other, in Elyot the murder is committed elsewhere and the criminal, seeking refuge in the barn and perceiving Gisippus's knife, takes it away, stains it with the dead man's blood, and puts it in the hand of the sleeping Gisippus. In Boccaccio, Gisippus is weaponless, a point on which Titus seizes at the trial in order to exculpate him; but Elyot, having deprived Titus of this plea, has to fall back on a vague phrase about reasons and arguments by which Titus affirmed that he himself was guilty.

In 1562 there was published *The most wonderful and pleasaunt History of Titus and Gisippus* by Edward Lewicke,[1] which was based upon Elyot's version. He makes a few alterations. Perhaps for the sake of brevity he omits the marriage formalities and says nothing of Titus' favourable reception on his return to Rome, his happy married life and honourable career. Evidently too he considered that it was improbable that Gisippus should renounce Sophronia without an inward conflict, and so he omits Elyot's description of Gisippus as 'nothynge sorowfull all though that he hartely loued the mayden', just as he earlier inserted the qualifying phrase:

> Although he sorowed at the chaunce.
>
> (244)

Again he leaves out Gisippus's swoon and his weeping and wailing and dolorous crying, possibly because this seemed to him incompatible with the mentality of one versed in philosophy. Such a modification was justified, but it is unfortunate that at the trial Lewicke cut away

---

[1] Printed in Wright's edition of *Early English Versions of the Tales of Guiscardo and Ghismonda and Titus and Gisippus from the Decameron*, pp. 175–216. Line reference to this edition.

the passage in which Elyot had carefully prepared the recognition, so that after Gisippus is led to the bar, Titus

> Lept from the bench incontinent.
> And downe vpon his knees he fell.
> (819–20)

However, neither these omissions nor a few minor additions can obscure the complete subservience of Lewicke. He repeats Elyot's very words and even borrows his marginal notes. By inclination he was verbose, as may be seen from his note on the rhinoceros where he talks of 'the nostrilles of his nose' and says that 'this beast is as big as an Elephant and is naturally an enemye to the Elephant'.[1] It is not surprising therefore to find that he swells out Elyot's text inordinately, so that on one occasion ten words, of which six are monosyllables, are expanded into a whole stanza.

Nor is he aided by the eight-line octosyllabic stanza, rhyming *ababbcbc*. This is difficult enough for any one with such scanty poetic resources, but his task is rendered still more arduous by the attempt to carry on the final rhyme of each stanza into the next. Such a scheme was beyond his capacity. He has recourse to padding and colloquialisms, and his groping for rhymes is painful. The result is prosy and monotonous. Lewicke's technique was inadequate, and although he clearly wished to make a romantic tale still more romantic, he failed completely.

The conception of Boccaccio's tale as a romance was perhaps at the back of the mind of Edward Jenynges when he turned it into verse in 1574. *The Notable Hystory of two faithfull Louers named Alfagus and Archelaus. Whearein is declared the true fygure of Amytie and Freyndshyp,* is divided into ten chapters, each with a separate heading. The story is in fact none other than that of Titus and Gisippus. Alfagus, the son of Lypodus, a Roman knight, is sent to Carthage, then famous for its learning, and grows up with Archelaus, the son of Olympus, the chief ruler of the city. The heroine is named Andromyca. The new garb is but thin, and the old one underneath becomes visible on two occasions. The first is when Alfagus addresses the nobles of Carthage. He begins by saying:

> My freindes & nobles of Carthage[2]

but continues:

> This loue hath brought perpetuall fame
> and eke great commendacion,
> Vnto this Citie and also
> vnto the Grecians nacion.[3]

---

[1] Cf. Wright's ed., p. 181.   [2] Sig. G. ii.   [3] Ibid.

Later, Alfagus tells his audience:

> I do perceaue you wonder much
> ye noble Athenes now
> To heare of thes.[1]

The attentive reader cannot but be puzzled by this Hellenic intrusion into an African city, and he may also find it odd when Alfagus, describing his love, refers to the Carthaginian poets who have written of Jupiter, Leda and Europa, the exploits of Hercules and his subjection to Deianira, the love of Paris and Helen and the siege of Troy. If he has Elyot's version at hand, he will realise from this last passage, if he has not done so before, that Jenynges is yet another versifier who has relied on the adaptation of the tale in *The Gouernour*.

Like his immediate predecessor, he often gives the reader a mere paraphrase of Elyot's text. But though his words are often very close to those of the prose version, he shows more independence than Lewicke. He indicates the approach of dawn as Chaucer had done in the *Clerk's Tale* by an allusion to the twinkling stars. So too he pictures the dawn itself:

> The early mornynge in the east
>   began then[2] to vnlose,
> Her purple gates and shewed her house
>   deckt red with many a Rose.
>
> The twynklynge stars withdrew a non
>   which by the mornyng starre,
> Lyke as the Captayne of an hoste,
>   is lead both nye and farre:
> So he abydeth last of all
>   within the heauenlye watche
> And Phebus with all the haste he maye,
>   his matters doth dispatche.[3]

Jenynges was not altogether satisfied with Elyot's portrayal of the lovers' relations. He adds a brief wooing scene, at the end of which Andromyca gives her consent to Archelaus, and he prepares the way for Alfagus' infatuation. From the moment his friend had spoken of her, he had longed to see her, and when the time comes for him to meet her, he is so eager that he rises at dawn and wakens Archelaus. Another development is the contrivance of a scheme to substitute Alfagus for Archelaus and the instruction of Alfagus in the part that he has to play. This is all the more remarkable, because at this point Elyot says 'To make the tale shorte' and hastens on to the marriage. However, Jenynges is never in a hurry and ignores hints regarding

---

[1] Sig. G iv.   [2] Text 'them'.   [3] Sig. G i.

brevity. Thus he deals at length with the wedding night. Alfagus
is hidden in the wall of the bridal chamber, and from his point of
observation he watches Archelaus dismiss those who have escorted
Andromyca and himself. Then on a pretext he leaves the room and
gives the signal to Alfagus who takes his place.

The departure of Alfagus for Rome gives rise to a tender leave-
taking, for which there is again no foundation in *The Gouernour*.
All Elyot had to say was 'Titus with his lady is departed towardes the
citie of Rome'. But Jenynges adds this passage:

> Farewell my most deare freind for now
>   frome you I must depart,
> Farewell my louyng mate in whom
>   I alwayes set my harte:
> Although in person I be gone
>   yet haue mee still in mynde,
> If euer of me you stande in neede
>   a sure freind shall you fynde.
>
> Archelaus kyssed Alfagus then
>   whome he loued as his lyfe,
> He kyssed eke the Ladye fayre
>   which should haue ben his wyfe.[1]

The subsequent journey of Archelaus to Rome is used by Jenynges
to work upon the feelings of the reader. Elyot after a prefatory remark
—'what shall nede a longe tale?'—had summed up the hardships of
Gisippus as 'moche payne / colde / hunger / and thurste'. On the
other hand, Jenynges exploits the opportunity to the full and, by a
strange anachronism, presents Archelaus as a palmer who begs for
alms in rain and sheds tears at his misery. The emotion is again heightened when Archelaus is passed by Alfagus without recognition, and
his lament is expanded from two or three lines to several stanzas.
There is a similar emphasis when Alfagus expresses his longing for
death. Another such lengthy display of feeling occurs when the friends
are reunited. Moreover, at the close Jenynges cannot resist the temptation to indulge in sentiment. After the trial Elyot had brought the tale
to a swift end, but in the last chapter Archelaus 'showethe *Alfagus* all
hys troubles and myserye, who sorowfully lamented hys case'. We
therefore are compelled to hear how Archelaus recapitulates his experiences for the benefit of his friend, a repetition which is singularly
inartistic, as it delays the narrative unduly. But Jenynges is still bent
on appealing to the reader's feelings. He analyses the two friends'
reactions after the account of all that has happened. Alfagus is overcome with distress at his failure to recognise the wanderer:

[1] Sig. I ii.

> But when Archelaus sawe hys freinde
>   Alfagus to relent,
> And inwardly with doulfull teares
>   his neclygence repente:
> Moste louyngly imbraced hym,
>   and sayde my freynde be styll,
> Leaue of your sorowfull syghes ye make
>   your vysage for to spyll.
>
> The thyngs which nowe are past & gone
>   no man may call agayne,
> Why hurte you now your selfe therfore
>   and weepe with greuous payne.[1]

Finally, there is a parting scene which, though not formally, is a repetition of the earlier farewell when Alfagus set out for Rome. In eight stanzas the friends declare their eternal friendship, and Archelaus gives Alfagus his blessing and takes his leave:

> With that he caste his armes abrode
>   hys freinde for to receaue:
> He kyssed him sweetlye then and sayde
>   farewell my hartes delyght,
> Farewell my louyng frende on whom
>   I thynke both daye and nyght.[2]

Even now, the parade of sentiment is not quite ended, for Jenynges has still to relate how

> Alfagus kyssed hym also
>   with the lyke salutacyon.[3]

However superfluous some of these innovations may seem, not all the changes made by Jenynges are open to criticism. There is a certain vividness in his account of the merchant who was surprised by the thief lying in wait behind a bush:

> And sodenly the man he tooke
>   who thought no harme ne ill,
> And not contented with his goods
>   foorthwith he dyd hym kyll.[4]

The spectacle of the officers searching every hollow tree for the criminal and afterwards binding him hard and fast with ropes also lends interest. There was likewise something to be said for Jenynges' elaboration at the trial scene of Elyot's bald statement that 'Titus denyed it / and affirmed with reasons and argumētes / that he was the murderer / & nat Gysippus'. Jenynges believed in more specific detail, and there can be no doubt that Alfagus' confession of his murder of the man against whom he had a grievance carries conviction:

[1] Sig. N ii.   [2] Sig. N iv *verso*.   [3] Ibid.   [4] Sig. K iii *verso*.

> For as in that place all alone
>   a huntynge I dyd ryde,
> By euell aduenture in the waye
>   the man there I espyed:
> And thynkyng that no better tyme
>   I myght auenged bee,
> But then when as we were alone
>   And no man els to see.
>
> I drewe my sworde without delaye
>   and vnto him I sayde,
> Thou vyllayne nowe to fynde the here
>   I am ryght well apayde:
> And therwithall on hym I layd
>   without respect or care,
> That sodenly his deadly wounde
>   he had or I was ware.
>
> Which when I sawe out of the waye
>   I drewe hym by and by,
> I tooke my horse in all the haste
>   and homwardes faste did flye.[1]

The presentation of the characters as they speak lends to this scene a dramatic quality. Nor is this an isolated instance. Time and again, when Elyot uses reported speech, Jenynges gives the actual words and, even if he sacrifices something in terseness, he gains in directness. He employs a stanza containing four broken fourteeners, rhyming *aabb*, and in his hands the medium has some fluency. Certainly, even if he is no great artist, he is superior to Lewicke.

Nothing is known about him except what can be gleaned from the book itself. In his address to the reader he states that he has employed his pen with it 'on many idle daies', which suggests that it was written as an agreeable diversion rather than as a means of earning a living. The title-page alludes to it as 'Much pleasaunte and delectable to the Reader', but in the address the emphasis is on the benefit that it will confer. The author is in fact a serious writer who looks askance at tales of chivalry and claims to offer something better:

> Many yonge wyts desyre for to read
> Hystoryes olde, in Meeter delectable,
> Of dyuers good Knyghtes and such as be dead,
> Leauyng behynde them a fame much commendable,
> Yet is the readynge therof nothinge profitable,
> But in this small treatice a man maie beholde,
> How freyndshyp is better then syluer or golde.[2]

This gravity of purpose is revealed in another way. Though the

---

[1] Sigs. L iv–L iv *verso*.   [2] Sig. A iii *verso*.

praise of friendship is his chief concern, Jenynges loses no opportunity of commenting on the instability of human fortunes. He not only seizes on every allusion to Fortune by Elyot, but adds others of his own, and in addressing the reader he draws this lesson from the story:

> oft times by fortune it comith to passe
> A man now in welthe and great prosperytie,
> Is brought in a momit[1] much worsse then he was
> Standinge in peryll and great extremytie:
> Freyndshyp oft times then faileth verely.[2]

Yet in his opinion God is always superior to Fortune, and so when Archelaus in relating his experiences laments that

> fortune with her fatall wheele
> my good lucke dyd enuye,[3]

Jenynges introduces Alfagus as offering consolation because under divine guidance all has turned out well:

> My freind Archelaus Alfagus sayde
> to god gyue prayse alwaye,
> Who hath you helped in your cares
> vnto this present daye.[4]

It is a conclusion akin to that of Chaucer's pious Clerk after his tale of adversity surmounted.

2. Tales in Verse derived from the Italian Text

As the sixteenth century advanced, translators were forthcoming who could go straight to Boccaccio[5] when writing their tales in verse. The earliest of such stories is probably *A pleasant and delightfull History, of Galesus Cymon and Iphigenia*, the author's name being given on the title-page as 'T.C.' The only copy at present known, which is in the Bodleian Library, is undated. However, the printer is Nicolas Wyer, whose activities lasted from 1556 to 1560, which offers some idea of the date of publication. Another clue, however, is given by a passage in the account of Cymon's voyage. It runs thus:

> The restles Tide, that beares his Barke
> with waltryng waues on Sea:
> Rowes wambling foorth: w[t] hope & mirth
> were fedde his Mates and he,

---

[1] This unusual word might be taken at first sight for a corrupt form of 'moment'. However, C. T. Onions suggests that it is either a misprint for 'minuit', a variant of 'minute', or a cross between 'moment' and 'minuit'.

[2] Sig. A iii.   [3] Sig. L ii.   [4] Sig. N ii *verso*.

[5] Cf. E. Koeppel, *Studien zur Geschichte der italienischen Novelle in der englischen Litteratur des sechzehnten Jahrhunderts*, Strasburg, 1892.

Away, the meerie Mariner hales,
    deuyding fomyng streames:
The braggyng Boy, hies vp to toppe
    of Mastes loftie Beames.
The waueryng Flag for Ioy is vaunst,
    the Seas begyn to swell:
And he in hope amidst the stormes,
    of surgyng Seas do[1] dwell.[2]

This is obviously related, though exactly how it is difficult to say, to
a passage in the second part of *The Mirror for Magistrates* which
was published by Thomas Marshe in 1563. Lord Hastings' description
of his flight overseas from Lynn is similar to the one just quoted, the
only difference being that it pictures the seamen waiting in the calm
bay after the tide has ebbed:

    The restles tyde, to bare the empty baye,
    With waltryng waves roames wamblyng forth. Away
    The mery maryner hayles. The braggyng boye,
    To masts hye top vp hyes. In signe of ioye
    The wauering flagge is vaunsd. The suttle Seas
    Theyr swellyng ceasse: to calmest even peace
    Sinkth down theyr pride. with dronkennes gainst al care
    The Seamen armed, awayte theyr noble fare.[3]

The address to the reader defends the usefulness of such tales on the
ground that they are 'as a moste cleare Glasse, for imitacion, of ordering, and institution of mannes life'. Though the simile is common in
this period, it seems likely that here too the poet had in mind *The
Mirror for Magistrates*. His address is also important because in the
course of a picturesque appeal for the reader's support against hostile
critics he declares that this is his first book:

I craue . . . that thou would stoppe with an Iron Barre, and Bolte of Brasse
the belchyng Nosethrils of RHINOCEROS subtyll Snowte, and his raging, furious
howling, cōpesce, and mitigate with perpended Iudgement. And lastly, that
thy friendly worde, breathyng & blowyng: a coole, & gentle blaste, of Golden
Ayre, maye happelie yeld, vnto my first fruits, a calme and fauourable winde.[4]

    Boccaccio's tale, the first of the fifth day, contained repeated allusions
to Fortune, and it was an obvious choice for one who had encountered
so many variations on this theme in *The Mirror for Magistrates*.
The title of the poem speaks of it as describing the fickleness of
Fortune, and in his address the author tells the reader that he may see
in it 'the mutabylytie, fickle state of Fortune'. In the course of the
narrative her caprice is again emphasised until at the end she relents.

---

[1] Possibly a misprint for 'to'.   [2] Sig. B iv.
[3] Campbell, 1938, p. 273.   [4] Sigs. A ii *verso*–A iii.

But the 'Argument', surveying the whole story, shows most clearly how large this conception looms in the author's mind:

> see how wauering Fortune turnes,
>   with euery blast of winde:
> First, gentle face, then frowning frets,
>   she casts on longyng minde.
> From lowryng lookes, to smilyng cheere
>   she eftsoones flittes againe:
> The lingring louer thus she feedes,
>   with hope his loue to gaine.
> And then from top of whirlyng wheele,
>   she throwes him in the suddes:
> The captiue thence to raunsome then,
>   with aide in haste she scuddes.
> And graunts at length his wisshed pray
>   and onely hartes delight:
> Which he enioyed against the force,
>   of forreine foes despight.[1]

However, for the reader the poem was also of interest because it illustrated 'the puissant force of ragyng loue', and, as the 'Argument' proves, the author's sympathy was with its power to redeem Cymon from boorish stupidity and turn him into a normal being. It would even appear from the lines:

> Beholde how Reason yeldes to loue,
>   and Vertue geueth place[2]

that in the clash between reason, as embodied in Galesus and his insistence on the fulfilment of the solemn contract to Pasimonde, and passion as represented by Cymon, the poet's heart went out to the infatuated lover.

This was due in part at least to the transformation of Cymon at the beginning of the tale. Though Boccaccio never speaks of the court, by frequent reference 'T. C. Gent.' develops his theme into a contrast between the country clown and the courtier. Cymon is changed from one who refuses 'to leade a Courtiers lyfe' and stubbornly insists on following the plough, to one who is a match for 'Courtly Gentlemen' and even outdoes 'Courtiers all'. Moreover, the beauty of Iphigenia is adorned 'with Courtly grace', and at the sight of this 'to Courte in haste, he hyes'.

The early relations of Cymon and Iphigenia also undergo a modification. On the one hand, his sufferings in love are intensified, and she becomes the scornful maiden who

> spewd foorth spiteful taūting glikes
>   at him, with frownyng face[3]

---

[1] Sig. A iii *verso*.   [2] Ibid.   [3] Sig. A viii.

and even went so far as to bar her father's gate with might and main against Cymon. The story halts while a picture is drawn of the hero brooding in his country cabin. So much is the narrator preoccupied with this emotional state that later in the narrative he expands a few words of Boccaccio[1] as follows:

> And now with diligence, to prooue
>   his vowed Loyaltie:
> With mightie hande, for to withstande,
>   her partynge from his eye.
> For thee, (he said) I frie and swelt,
>   in Fornace, of desire:
> For of a Beaste, to manly shape
>   thou madste mee to aspire.
> Yf that the Gods wyll graunte, that I
>   to wyfe, may thee enioye:
> And thy Societie, to embrace,
>   that shall my cares destroye,
> And doubtlesse, would I thinke in ioye,
>   to passe my goulden yeares:
> And for to leade an Angelles lyfe,
>   amongst the Princelie Peeres,
> And certes, Death shall ende my dayes,
>   with dint of bloudie knife:
> But I, in spite of hatefull foes,
>   wyll winne thee to my wyfe. [2]

It may well be that the author felt some resentment against Iphigenia, which would explain why he relates in realistic fashion how she was 'gulffde wᵗ gripyng fittes' during the storm. At any rate, he had not overlooked her exceeding cruelty in his version, and so at the end he harks back to her former attitude:

> For when the stormes of cancred hate,
>   were ouerblowen and past:
> And scorneful spight, had spewde his gall
>   on Seas by whyrlynge blaste,[3]

Iphigenia at length yielded readily to Cymon, so that they lived happily after. The poet likes strong effects, whether he is portraying the agonies of love or a storm at sea. Equally he enjoys a fight and throws himself with rough vigour into the combat on board the ship of Rhodes. Here, and even more elsewhere, he delights in the addition of detail. This is most conspicuous in the account of the sudden appearance of Cymon and his friends at the wedding banquet:

---

[1] 'ora è tempo di dimostrare, o Efigenia, quanto tu sii da me amata. Io son per te divenuto uomo, e, se io ti posso avere, io non dubito di non divenire più glorioso che alcuno Iddio; e per certo io t'avrò o io morrò' (*O.V.* vol. iii, p. 22).

[2] Sig. B iii *verso*.   [3] Sig. D ii *verso*–D iii.

L

then enter they with force:
The suppyng Chãber, where the Brides,
   refreshd with foode their Corse.
Amongste them, other Ladyes sate,
   by order, in degree:
At royall Table, richely dight,
   and garnishde sumptuouslie.
With massie Bowles, of golden Cuppes,
   bedecte with Pearle, and Stone:
With other Gẽmes, APOLLOS[1] beames
   not muche vnlike that shonne.
And furnishde well with speciall cates,
   and daintie Princelike fare.[1]

In general he shows more energy than subtlety, which combines with his parade of classical lore and words like 'amenitie', 'formositie', 'pulchritude', 'fulgent' and 'equipollent' to corroborate his statement that he was a novice in the art of poetry. It is perhaps also a sign of his struggle with his broken fourteeners that he employs so many adjectives to fill up his line and in particular that he has a taste for those of two syllables as in 'his knaggy Staffe', 'the shrillie windes', 'hugie Trees, with loftie toppes', and 'her Fathers hugie Gate'.

In artistic power the translator falls far short of Boccaccio. This is shown again in the lines which round off the story:

And thus they passde their happy dayes,
   in neuer diynge blysse:
Of whiche, I craue of God, for aye
   good Ladies neuer misse.[2]

However, this ending suggests that he had noted Boccaccio's habit in certain tales of concluding with a generalisation which expresses a desire for himself and others of the same happiness as befell those whose fate he had just narrated. The poet had also observed how Panfilo now and then turned to address the ladies in his audience as 'dilettose Donne' or 'piacevoli Donne'. Unfortunately, in this isolated tale the mention of these 'good Ladies' is out of place. Nevertheless, this awkward ending indicates that the translator had an eye for Boccaccio's skill, though he could not apply what he had learnt.

The second example of a single verse tale translated direct from the *Decameron* is *A notable Historye of Nastagio and Trauersari* which was published in 1569. The author is 'C.T.' and like 'T.C.' he embellishes his work with Italian mottos and quotations. It is possible that he too was familiar with *The Mirror for Magistrates*. Thus after Guido and his dogs have hunted and mutilated the beautiful lady of Ravenna, we read that she

---

[1] Sigs. C viii–C viii *verso*.   [2] Sig. D iii.

fast began to runne.
with hedlong flight, towardes swelling seas,
Like pellet shott from gonne.[1]

As she is in the heart of the forest, her precipitous course towards the
sea catches our attention. The association of flight with gunfire and
the sea is to be found in the life of Lord Hastings. The passage occurs
only forty lines after that borrowed by 'T.C.',[2] when Hastings' ship,
having put to sea from Lynn, is sighted and pursued by the Flemings:

Forth flyeth the bark, as from the vyolent goonne
The pellet pearsth all stayes and stops eft soone.[3]

It is therefore likely that the author had *The Mirror for Magistrates*
in mind when, in the address to the reader, he speaks of his poem as
'this little glasse', and just as the famous work was essentially didactic,
so 'C.T.' paints

a liuelye paterne of cruell tirannie: with a dewe reuenge for the same, iustly
ordained by the deuine powers.[4]

In addition to the desperate passions of the lovers caught in the snares
of Venus, the reader may see

a mirror of prodigalitie and sea of louers wastfull expences, wherby thou
maist learne to measure thy selfe, with the bushell of reason, and to kepe an
ordinarie meane',[5]

for

Examples are written, to the ende, that men should folow the good, & learne
to eschew the ill.[6]

There was a fundamental affinity between the story of Nastagio and
the obdurate lady and that of Cymon and Iphigenia as presented by
'T.C.', though there was no need for any transformation in the
relationship of Nastagio and his love, for as it is depicted in the
Decameron, it is that of the faithful lover and the scornful lady. In
each tale we witness the triumph of the lover by somewhat unorthodox
methods.

This clearly interested 'C.T.' as much as it appealed to 'T.C.' and
indeed the parallels between the two men are so close as to suggest
that they are one and the same.[7] This is all the more probable, because

---

[1] Sig. B ii *verso*.   [2] Vide ante, p. 143.   [3] Campbell, p. 274.
[4] Sig. A ii.   [5] Sig. A ii *verso*.
[6] Sig. A ii *verso*. This is closely akin to William Painter's statement in the dedication of the first volume of *The Palace of Pleasure* to the earl of Warwick that its
contents 'may render good example for all sortes to follow the best, and imbrace
the vertuous, contrariwise to reiect the worste, and contempne the vicious'.
[7] This view is held by J. Raith, op. cit., p. 95.

the translator relates that Nastagio saw his lady at court, and tells of his kinsmen's advice to quit 'the courtly traine' and of his resolve

> to leaue the court,
> and her, that did allure,[1]

whereas in Boccaccio there is no hint that she occupies such a position. Thus the translator toys with the contrast between court and country, as has been explained in connexion with Cymon. Again one cannot help noticing that a passage is inserted to illustrate the emotional state to which Nastagio is reduced by his frustrated love. He tries to distract his thoughts in various ways:

> And there he dailye spent the time
> in chase of grieslye beastes:
> Sometime in Hawking, and somtime,
> at wittie playe of chestes.[2]

On other occasions, like Cymon, he broods in solitude:

> Sometime he toke delight, to walke
> (as louers do) alone:
> To desert dales, to mountaines hie
> and places eke vnknowne.
> There to vnlode his carefull minde,
> of thousand corsies past:
> To tell the trees, and knaggie rockes.
> howe loue his heart agast.[3]

The development of Boccaccio's account of the savage punishment inflicted by Nastagio and his hounds reveals a delight in physical action akin to that displayed in the picture of Cymon's fight with the Rhodians, and there is the same love of detail in the description of the feast prepared by Nastagio as in that of the banquet at the wedding of Pasimunda and Ormisda:

> Nastagio made a sumptuous feast,
> and spared not for cost:
> Of meate, he had great plentie, both
> of boyled, bakde, and rost.
> Of other Iuncketts, he had store,
> for suche a dynner, mete:
> And when the bidden guests were come,
> He frindly did them grete,
> And welcomde them, in order all,
> eche one, in his degre:
> And to his cruell mistris, shewde,
> a face, of frindly glee.[4]

There is less classical decoration than in the earlier poem and a

---

[1] Sigs. A iv *verso*–A v.   [2] Sig. A v *verso*.
[3] Ibid.   [4] Sigs. B iv–B iv *verso*.

greater use of simile. But the same recourse to adjectives can be traced which now and then leads to such a pleonastic passage as this:

> he seemde to heare,
> a greuous lamenting.
> And dolefull skrikes, and groning cries,
> sent forth from carefull brest:
> Of wofull damsell, vexde with grefe.[1]

Finally, there is the same partiality for disyllabic adjectives as in 'knaggie rockes', 'with shrilly voice', 'that hugie woode' and 'with swiftie foot'.

Whatever the shortcomings of 'T.C.' and 'C.T.' from an artistic point of view, they did at least widen the choice of tales from the *Decameron*. This process is carried a stage further by George Turbervile in his *Tragical Tales*. He appears to have been well acquainted with the work and at the end of a poem addressed to his friend Spencer quotes the words 'Sola miseria è senza inuidia', spoken by Filostrato in the preamble to the fourth day. It was above all the stories of this day that attracted Turbervile, and of the seven stories based upon the *Decameron* in his *Tragical Tales*,[2] no less than five were taken from it. Coming as they did from a group for which the theme was love that ended disastrously, they fitted in admirably with his scheme. The other two also have love as their subject, and if not tragic, they have at least a serious aspect. In this lay their appeal to Turbervile, a grave poet, who describes how he approached his task:

> I to reading *Boccas* fell,
> and sundrie other moe
> *Italian* Authours, where I found
> great stoare of states in woe,
> And sundrie sortes of wretched wights:
> some slayne by cruell foes,
> And other some that through desire
> and Loue their lyues did lose:
> Some Tyrant thirsting after bloud,
> themselues were fowly slayne:
> And some did sterue in endlesse woes,
> and pynde with bitter payne.
> Which gaue me matter fitte to write:
> and herevpon it grewe
> That I this Tragicall deuise,
> haue sette to open viewe.[3]
>
> (fol. 11 *recto*)

t is evident that he read the *Decameron* with an eye on the instruction

[1] Sig. A vi.
[2] Nos. 1, 3, 4, 6, 7, 9 and 10 were derived from *Dec.* v, 8; x, 4; iv, 9; iv, 4; iv, 5; v, 7 and iv, 8 respectively.
[3] Quotations and references from first edition.

to be gained. How alien his outlook was to that of Boccaccio may be
seen from his attitude to the story of Gerbino, the grandson of Guiglielmo, king of Sicily. Urged on by his love for Gostanza, the daughter
of the king of Tunis, Gerbino violates the safe-conduct granted by
Guiglielmo for her passage to the king of Grenada and is put to death.
For Boccaccio this was but one more example of the omnipotence of
love. His intention was to awaken sympathy for the lovers, and so
Filomena, who tells the next tale, is filled with compassion for their
untimely fate. But Turbervile regarded the story mainly as a legal
and political problem, and in the 'Argument' he points out that in
spite of Guiglielmo's affection for his grandson, the latter was sentenced
to death, because

> He did prefer his lust before the lawes.
>
> (fol. 80 *verso*)

Love is no excuse for piracy. In the 'Envoy' Turbervile insists on the
need for implicit obedience on the part of subjects, since monarchs
derive their authority from God. As *Tragical Tales* appeared in 1587,
shortly after the Babington plot and the execution of Mary, queen of
Scots, his remarks on the supreme power of a reigning monarch have
a peculiar interest:

> Who works against his soueraigne Princes word,
> And standes not of the penaltie in awe,
> Well worthy is to feele the wrathfull sword,
> And dye the death appointed by the law:
> No fauour is to such offendours due,
> That, eare they did amisse, the mischiefe knew.
>
> For Princes willes are euer to be wayde,
> The statutes are the strength and stay of all,
> When lawes are made, they ought to be obayde,
> What royall Peeres, by pledge, or promise: shall
> At any time confirme to friend or foe,
> Must stable stand, the law of armes is so.
>
> For they are second Gods in earth belowe,
> Assignde to rule and strike the onely stroke,
> Their crownes and scepters, be of perfect shew,
> That all estates are vnderneath the yoke:
> What they shall say, or doe in any case,
> By dutie ought to take effect and place,
>
> Wherefore who dares aduenture vp so hie,
> And proudly presse to alter kings decres,
> Not fearing what may light on them thereby,
> Nor forcing what they shall by folly leese:
> Of law deserue the hardest point to byde,
> For scorning those whom God appoyntes to gyde.
>
> (fols. 90 *verso*-91 *recto*)

Precisely because Guiglielmo repressed his own feelings and carried out the law, Turbervile expresses his admiration, for justice is the supreme requirement in a king. Any attempt to act contrary to the established order can only lead to chaos. Hence

what Peeres, and Princes once haue wild,
No subiect should endeuour to vndoe:
For kings will looke to haue their hestes fulfild,
And reason good that it should aye be so.
As beastes obey the loftie Lyons looke,
So meane estates must puysant Princes brooke.

Ill fares the barke amid the broyling seas,
Where euery swayne controlles the maisters skill,
And each one stires at helme him selfe to please,
And folowes not the cunning Pylots will:
So realmes are rulde but badly, where the base
Will checke the chiefe, that sit in highest place.

(fol. 91 verso)

Another story in which Turbervile modifies the emphasis is that of Gentile and Catalina. In the Italian original what is most stressed is the generosity of Gentile in restoring her to Nicoluccio after he has found her in the tomb, supposedly dead. The fact that Gentile had previously sought to win her love, and had only desisted when she rejected his advances, was of minor importance in Boccaccio's tale. Turbervile, for his part, exalts her as a model of virtue who scorns all 'masking mates' hovering about her husband's gates. As for Gentile, he illustrates the evil courses to which uncontrolled youthful passion may lead, and he is considered blameworthy even though he later mended his ways. His conduct is therefore presented, not as an example of liberality or magnificence, but as a warning to forsake blind fancies.

If Turbervile takes up this position here, it is only to be expected that in the tale of Rossiglione and Guardastagno he should refuse all sympathy to the lovers, whereas Boccaccio clearly expected that their story would awaken pity.[1] Even if Guardastagno had betrayed a friend who had trusted him completely, the treacherous attack of Rossiglione, no less than his sadistic cruelty in making his wife eat her dead lover's heart, is singularly repellent. However, Turbervile ignores these unpleasant features in Rossiglione's actions, passes over his conscience-stricken flight and says nothing about the grief and lamentation of the whole countryside. For him the story is one of illicit love and breach of trust. He dwells at length on the generous nature of Rossiglione and maintains that Guardastagno's crime was all the more unpardonable, because he betrayed his friend. However, fleshly lust blinds men to all other considerations:

[1] See the introductory words of Dioneo who relates it.

> see, how synne once seasing on the minde
> Doth muffle man and leades him quight away:
> It makes him passe beyond the boundes of kynde,
> And swerue the trade where truth and vertues lay,
> Refusing friendes, reiecting lawes, and right,
> For greedy care to compasse foule delyght.
>
> (fols. 70 *verso*–71 *recto*)

At the same time Turbervile blames the lady whom he places among such women as entice to lewdness by their looks, gesture and speech. The sensual, he concludes, are as untrustworthy as the ambitious, but the passion in each case brings retribution:

> marke yet well the sause that doth ensue,
> Such stolne flesh, is bytter as the gall,
> Great are the plagues to such disorders due,
> From skyes reuenge and fearefull scourge doth fall:
> The dome diuine although it suffer long.
> Yet strikes at last, and surely wreakes the wrong.
>
> (fol. 71 *recto*)

It is on this grim note of divine vengeance that Turbervile ends, and the reader is thus admonished:

> Note here the fruites of treason and of lust:
> Forbeare the like, for God is euer iust.
>
> (fol. 71 *verso*)

The problem of the love of Girolamo and Salvestra offered more difficulty to a man of Turbervile's mentality. It is true that Salvestra had a husband, that Girolamo pursued her with his ardent confessions of love after her marriage and that he died of grief at her side. Yet there was no breach of wedlock; Girolamo and Salvestra had known each other from childhood; and he had only with reluctance been parted from her by the attempts of his mother and his guardians to forestall what they regarded as an unsuitable match. Up to a point Turbervile looks with favour on Girolamo whose fidelity was thwarted by the interference of these worldly-wise seniors. He asserts that love is irresistible and to allow monetary considerations to stand in the way is the height of folly; in his opinion this was the lesson that Boccaccio wished to drive home:

> in this tale the Florentine doth showe
> The great mishaps by such restraint that grow.
>
> (fol. 143 *recto*)

However, there are qualifications to this doctrine of love's omnipotence. It must not be allowed to break the bonds of marriage. And so, after all, Turbervile cannot help condemning Girolamo for not abandoning all thought of Salvestra on his own initiative. Again he warns men against lust and against women who are false to their husbands. Yet strangely enough, with an entire lack of consistency he denounces Catalina violently for her cruelty to Girolamo. In his eyes she is the epitome of the hard-hearted mistress:

> Couldst thou alow thy frend so hard a hap
> As by thy syde amid his sute to see
> Him die the death and all for loue of thee?
>
> (fol. 143 *verso*)

Finally, with a complete disregard of his insistence on the inviolability of marriage, he admonishes his women-readers:

> Draw hether dames and read this bloody fact
> Note wel the fruite of frowardnes in loue
> Peruse the plague of her that pyty lackt
> See how in that she pleasd the gods aboue
> Example take your rygor to remoue.
>
> (fol. 143 *verso*)

In Turbervile's handling of the tale of Lorenzo and Lisabetta, though no question of wedlock is involved, there is also a vacillation. He glosses over the fact that Lorenzo had loved others before Elizabeth by stating vaguely that

> He then began to leaue
> His forraine haunt at game abroade,
>
> (fol. 93 *verso*)

but he does not conceal the sensual character of their relationship. Nor does he overlook the fact that the 'leacher' Lorenzo played 'so vile a part' in defiling the sister of his masters. Consequently, he ends the narrative, not with the fragment of a pathetic folk-song, but with all the rigour of a moralist:

> Loe here the lotte of wicked loue,
> Behold the wretched end
> Of wilfull wightes, that wholy doe
> On *Cupides* lawes depend.
>
> (fol. 100 *recto*)

Nevertheless, in the Envoy he relaxes something of his severity and towards the heroine, at any rate, displays a certain tenderness. He felt that the brothers were at fault for not providing her with a husband long before she fell in love with their employee, and their later conduct seemed to him as foolish as it was cruel.

If Lorenzo as a hero caused Turbervile some embarrassment, the behaviour of Pasquino in the ninth tale did not seem to him in any way open to criticism. Nor did he find any serious moral or ethical problem in the relations of the lovers. However, there was a social question, and he feared that the women among his readers might object to a tragic tale which took as its theme such humble folk as a spinner and the servant of a woolmonger. Hence he meets their objection by emphasising the universality of love, which knows no distinction of class or rank:

> The minde is all that makes: or marres the thing,
> *A Carter loues as whotly as a King.*
>
> <div align="right">(fol. 130 <i>recto</i>)</div>

In the remaining tale, that of Nastagio's love for the daughter of Paolo Traversaro, on whom Turbervile bestows the name Euphymia, the translator had no need to apologise on the score of the characters' social position, for all belonged to distinguished families of Ravenna. The story, previously rendered by 'C.T.', relates how Nastagio used the spectacle of the ghostly Guido degli Anastagi, pursuing with his hounds the cruel lady who had wronged him, to terrify the obdurate Euphymia into accepting his proposal of marriage. Turbervile's heart is on the side of Nastagio, but he cannot refrain from shaking his head at the hero's impetuosity and his lavish expenditure to gain Euphymia's favour. Being for the most part an advocate of reason even while he recognises the force of love, he despises those who persist in wooing a flint-like woman. He is all the more dubious about Nastagio's wisdom in continuing to press his suit, because he realises that Euphymia, whatever explanation she herself may put forward for her tardy compliance with his wishes, only yields in the end through fear lest the same fate may overtake her as befell Guido's lady. This is no satisfactory basis for happiness.

Most of all, however, Turbervile is preoccupied with Euphymia's hardness of heart. The time-honoured theme of the cruel mistress was a favourite with him, as is illustrated by the frequency with which it appears in his own poems. Indeed, it amounts almost to an obsession, as may be seen from its altogether unwarranted intrusion into the tale of Girolamo and Salvestra. Here he takes advantage of the story to admonish all haughty mistresses:

> You stately Dames, that peacocklyke do pace,
> Through pride abusing such as are your thralls,
> Enforcing them for lacke of better grace,
> Vnto their bane, which sundrie times befalles,
> Not finding salue to cure their griefull galles:
> *Euphymias* plagues imprinte in heedeful mynde,
> And looke for like, if you be found vnkynde.
>
> <div align="right">(fol. 34 <i>verso</i>)</div>

On the whole, Turbervile's translation is tolerably accurate. In no case, however, does he tie himself down to a close translation; he loves to fill in detail which Boccaccio with his keen sense of economic narration habitually omits. He also likes to dwell upon the emotional state of his characters, whether it be a Nastagio in despair at the failure of his advances, Euphymia prostrate with fear at the sight of Guido and his hounds, or Guardastagno and Rossiglione, the one rejoicing at the prospect of seeing his mistress and the other plotting revenge. No doubt this interest accounts for the insertion of a letter from Euphymia to Nastagio, explaining her former and her present attitude to him. But in a sense it is irrelevant, because her explanation is untrue and consequently is afterwards rejected by the translator himself. In any case, it is far too long, occupying as it does, over one third of the story.

The idea was unfortunate, since it interrupted the flow of the tale. On this point Turbervile was remarkably insensitive, altogether failing to perceive one of the chief merits of Boccaccio as a narrator. Another sign that points in the same direction is his description of Nastagio as gazing at the chase of the lady by Guido and his hounds for the space of an hour. The addition of speeches, such as that of Nastagio to his friends at Chiassi or that of Euphymia's maid on handing over her mistress's letter, also tends to slow down the pace of the narrative. Further, Turbervile is fond of introducing parenthetical comment, generalisations on love, and tags to indicate some habit or practice. Recourse to aphorisms and employment of similes and classical parallels contribute still more to swell out the story, and with purposeless verbosity two or three lines are turned into long passages that dissipate the savour of Boccaccio.

At the same time it must be admitted that, according to his lights, Turbervile was a conscious craftsman, as can be perceived from his deliberate exploitation of alliteration and his manipulation of metre and stanza. Nevertheless, it cannot be said that he is in any way outstanding. He had some idea of technique, but little sense of poetry. At best his style is pedestrian and on occasion of a ludicrous flatness. The account of Nastagio roaming about the pine-woods near Chiassi, absorbed in grief at his unrequited love:

> So long he staide, as dinner time drew neare,
> Which he forgot, not minding bellye cheare,
> (fol. 16 *verso*)

is singularly unfortunate. Nor is Turbervile any more successful in picturing the sorrow of Girolamo:

> It greeude the Marchant to the guts
> That he was so forgote,
> (fol. 135 *verso*)

or the despair of Salvestra at his death:

> Not stintyng till she came vnto
> The body where it lay,
> And being there she gaue a shoute,
> And yelded forth a bray.[1]

(fol. 140 recto)

In spite of his failings Turbervile is not without interest as a representative of the Elizabethan age. Indirectly he reflects its strong sense of social distinctions and its fondness for 'degree'. He also mirrors the feeling of instability that marked the period and upholds without questioning the necessity for accepting the commands of divinely appointed sovereigns. Further, just as his contemporaries took delight in *De casibus* and *The Fall of Princes*, because they depicted the fluctuations in the lives of the great, Turbervile selected from the treasure-house of the *Decameron* seven tales to illustrate the caprices of Fortune. All else he passes by, as if it had no attraction for him. He pays no heed to stories of mirth-arousing pranks or amorous gallantry, for he is a grave observer of the actions of men and women, and his outlook differs vastly from that of the youthful Boccaccio. Hence in his comments on the seven tales, which are love-stories as well as examples of the working of Fortune, even though he talks often and long about the power of Cupid, he is careful to insist on the claims of morality and to utter a warning that those who are carried away by passion will inevitably be punished. There must be order in the lives of individuals as well as in affairs of state. His *Tragical Tales* are ultimately an extension of Lydgate's *Fall of Princes*, and from the monk of Bury Turbervile learnt the regrettable habit of diluting the story and appending to it a moralising commentary in the form of an 'Envoy'.

Obviously there was much in the *Decameron* that so severe a moralist could not appreciate, incapable as he was of understanding that Boccaccio's aim was not to provide lessons for the conduct of life, but merely to entertain. Equally Turbervile failed to grasp the ease, the swiftness and the economy of the Italian original. The craft of concentrated narration he was unable to acquire, and the art of translation in verse demanded a subtlety and sensitiveness beyond his powers.

3. Tales in Prose based on the French or Italian

The theme of love is again fully represented in *The Forrest of Fancy* by 'H.C.' which was published in 1579, but the mood is not tragical.

---

[1] The connexion between Turbervile and Boccaccio was first fully analysed by E. Koeppel in 'George Turbervile's Verhältniss zur italienischen Litteratur', *Anglia*, 1891, xiii, pp. 42–71.

The author, who is a young man, explains in his address to the reader that his object has been to procure his pleasure and profit, and so he has brought together in one volume a number of pieces in verse and prose which he has written 'at idle times', to sharpen his wits and shake off sloth. These pieces, which he considers 'to be fitte for the present time, and agreable with the mindes of moste men', contain two tales from the *Decameron*.[1] It is evident from the names of the characters and from traces of the moral generalisations in the translation of le Maçon that 'H.C.' used this intermediary.[2] From allusions to the tale of the earl of Angiers and to that of Nastagio, it is clear that the author's knowledge extended beyond the stories that he related. However, if he knew the *Decameron* as a whole, he made no attempt to imitate his model by employing a framework or a linking device.

The broadening of interest displayed in the choice of these two tales had already been revealed by William Painter's selection in *The Palace of Pleasure* which had appeared in 1566–7 in two volumes. He knew Girolamo Ruscelli's edition of the *Decameron*[3] and studied his 'pretie notes', but he also drew extensively on the translation of le Maçon.[4] Painter had a great admiration for 'eloquent and gentle Boccaccio' and considered that his work, 'for his stile, order of writing, grauitie, and sententious discourse, is worthy of intire provulgation'. Nevertheless, some of the tales seemed to him to deserve condemnation to perpetual prison, and so he confined himself to ten in the first volume[5] and six in the second.[6]

In undertaking his translation Painter was to some extent animated by patriotism, and among others he probably had le Maçon in mind when he spoke to Sir George Howard of

the passing diligence of other Coũtreys, by curious imbelishing of their states, with the troublous trauaile of their brain, and laborsome course of penne, Who altogether imploye those paines, that no Science lurke in corner, that no Knowledge be shut vp in cloisters, that no Historie remain vnder the maske and vnknowne attire of other tongues.[7]

---

[1] iii, 5 and v, 7.

[2] From v, 7 this moral is drawn: 'Whereby is signified the diuers dangerous and troublesome accidentes that dayelye happen vnto vs, by the power of loue, and frailty of fortune, the only tormenters of mans life'. This corresponds to the following passage in le Maçon's version: 'Pour signifier les diuers trauaux & perilleux accidens causez par ces deux tant puissans Seigneurs Amour & Fortune Tyrans de la vie humaine'. On the question of the moralising in later editions of le Maçon, see H. G. Wright, *The first English translation of the 'Decameron'*, Upsala, 1953, pp. 185–8.

[3] Venice, 1552.

[4] Cf. H. G. Wright, 'The Indebtedness of Painter's Translations from Boccaccio in *The Palace of Pleasure* to the French Version of le Maçon', *M.L.R.*, 1951, xlvi, pp. 431–5.

[5] i, 3, 8, 10; ii, 2, 3, 4, 5, 8; iii, 9; iv, 1.

[6] i, 5; viii, 7; x, 3, 4, 5, 9.

[7] Vol. ii, 1567. Epistle.

He was confident that the tales in the first volume would afford pleasure to the reader. He declared that

they recreate, and refresh weried mindes, defatigated eyther with painefull trauaile, or with continuall care, occasioning them to shunne and auoyde heauinesse of minde, vaine fantasies, and idle cogitations. Pleasaunt so well abrode as at home, to auoyde the grief of Winters night and length of Sommers day.[1]

Indeed he claims that their appeal is universal at all times and in all places. However, Painter is also careful to emphasise the more enduring benefit that may be derived from them. From this point of view he eulogises his second volume as 'a very Court & Palace for all sorts to fixe their eies therein, to view the deuoires of the Noblest, the vertues of the gentlest, and the dueties of the meanest'.[2] He was uneasily aware that the 'pleasant discourses, merie talke, sporting practises, deceytful deuises, and nipping taũtes'[3] of the first volume, though exhilarating, hardly merited commendation on such lofty grounds. In particular, he was concerned about those which seemed 'to intreat of vnlawfull Loue, and the foule practises of the same'. Yet even from those, he told the earl of Warwick, some profit might accrue:

both olde and yong may learne howe to auoyde the ruine, ouerthrow, inconuenience, and displeasure, that lasciuious desire, and wanton will, doth bring to the suters and pursuers of the same.[4]

In his address to the reader Painter mentions individual tales in the first volume and indicates the lessons that were to be drawn from them:

Is the noble man affected to vnderstande what happie ende, the vertue of Loialtie and fidelitie doth cõduce, the Earle of Angiers may be to him a right good example? Will Gentlemen learne how to prosecute vertue, and to profligat from their minde, disordinate Loue, and affection; I referre them to the historie of Tancredi. . . . Is not the marchaunt contented with his goodes already gotten, but will nedes goe seke some other trade: let him note and consider the daungers wherein the aduenturer Landolpho was? Is he disposed to sende his factor beyonde the seas, aboute his affaires, let him firste bid him to peruse Andreuccio, and then cõmaund him to beware of Madame Flordelice. . . . If scornefull speach or flouting sport doe flow in ripe wittes and lauish tongues of womankinde, let them beware they do not deale with learned sorte, least Master Alberto with Physicke drogues . . . do staine their face.[5]

Such didacticism was far removed from the spirit of the *Decameron*, and it limited Painter's selection. No less than thirteen of his total of

---

[1] Vol. i, 1566. Epistle to Reader.   [2] Vol. ii, 1567. Preface to Reader.
[3] Vol. i, 1566. Epistle to Earl of Warwick.
[4] Epistle to Earl of Warwick, vol. i.   [5] Epistle to Reader, vol. i.

sixteen are taken from Days 1, 2 and 10. Days 3, 4 and 8 are each represented by one only; Days 5, 6, 7 and 9 are ignored. After this rigorous exclusion Painter was still not content. For the benefit of the reader he commented whilst he narrated. He was particularly concerned about sexual passion, and so in the tale of Rinaldo he replaces the sensual delight of the lovers by a condemnation of 'this lecherous ladie, burnyng inwardlie with amourous desire'.[1] Crafty beings like Helena are a reminder of the wiles of women, and Painter warns the reader, 'what lothsom lustes do lurke vnder the barke of fading beautie, what stench of filthie affection fumeth from the smoldring gulf of dishonest Loue, what prankes such Dames do plaie for deceite of other and shame of themselues'.[2] On the other hand, 'Master Gentil of Carisendi' is praised for his triumph over his passion. By contrast, the lust of the king of France is denounced, and the marchioness of Monferrato is commended as 'a noble creature, so well bedecked with vertue as with beautie'.[3] But it is the tale of Dianora which gives rise to the most elaborate eulogy of chastity, combined with an admonition not to endanger it by rash promises. At the close the author intervenes once more to laud Ansaldo because he 'repressed his wanton minde, and absteined frõ that, which God graunte that others by like example may refraine'.[4]

However, there were other matters in Boccaccio's tales on which Painter seized, besides the control of sexual passion. The story of Mithridanes and Nathan prompted the narrator to stigmatise the envy of the latter and to exalt the generosity of the former. This last quality is emphasised in Painter's remarks on 'Master Thorello and Saladine'. Supported by Cicero's *De Officiis*, he draws a picture of what hospitality ought to be and has been in England, with a nostalgic lament over its decline in his own age:

I deeme it so worthie to be frequented in noble men and all degrees, as their palaces and great houses should swarme with guests, and their gates clustring with whole multitudes of the poore to be satisfied with relief. Such hath bene the sacred vse and reuerent care of auncient time. Such hath bene the zealous loue of those, whose fieldes and barnes, closets, and chestes haue bene stored and stuffed with worldely wealth, that comparing that golden age, glistering with pietie and vertue, to these our worsse than copper days, cancred with all corruption, we shall finde the match so like, as darke and light, durt and Angell golde.[5]

In other respects too Painter had his eye on contemporary England. He knew the power of the court and those who belonged to it. Consequently, he tones down the sweeping criticism involved in the tale of Ermino Grimaldi and restricts it to 'some of the Courtiers of oure age'.

---

[1] Vol. i, fol. 67 *verso.*   [2] To the Reader, vol. ii.
[3] Vol. ii, fol. 114 *recto.*   [4] Vol. ii, fol. 118 *recto.*   [5] Vol. ii, fol. 129 *recto.*

Similarly, he made a slight but significant change in the story of 'The King of England's Daughter'. In the original he read her request to the Pope to bless her marriage to Alessandro in these terms:

e la vostra benedizion ne doniate, acciocchè con quella, sì come con più certezza del piacere di colui del quale voi siete vicario, noi possiamo insieme all' onore di Dio ed al vostro vivere e ultimamente morire.

(O.V. vol. i, 132)

Fearing that this might be construed as favouring Papal supremacy, he therefore modified the passage to read thus:

and that you would giue vs your benediction, to the intent wee maie liue together, in the honour of God, to the perfection and ende of our life.[1]

On a lower plane also Painter makes an adjustment to blend with an English setting. Thus in the tale of 'Mistresse Helena', when she hears the 'cicale' from the tower in the heat of the July sun, he translates it by 'crickets' and adds 'Butterflies' and 'humble bees', and after she has been carried down, she receives 'warm drinks and meates' instead of 'pan lavato'.

In general, however, Painter's rendering is faithful enough, thanks in no small degree to the aid that he received from le Maçon. His estimate of his capacity was modest, and in translating from French and Italian he claimed to do no more than 'to expresse the sense'. Here and there he adds a metaphor and adorns his style with doublets which produce an undesirable tautology, but on occasion he can be terse and racy. There is far more learned embroidery in the second book than in the first, and the latter volume also contains more synopses and more general observations, especially by way of preface to a tale. This feature is also accompanied by an increase in didacticism. On the whole, there is a greater self-consciousness. The result is not always happy. In one respect, however, the second volume shows a heightened artistic awareness. That is in the feeling for design. There is little coherence in the first volume, though at the end of the story of 'Master Alberto of Bologna' Painter reveals an appreciation of Boccaccio's habit of introducing comment by the characters at the end of a tale. He speaks in person thus: 'I (in the name of Panfilo Filostrato and Dioneo,) by way of intreatie doe beseech ye Ladies, Pompinea, Fiãmetta, Philomena, and other gentlewomen . . .'.[2] Since the story is detached from the framework of the *Decameron*, the references to these characters is pointless, but at least it shows that Painter was not blind to the technique of Boccaccio. In the later volume, however, the preamble to 'The Marchionisse of Monferrato' harks back to the preceding tale of Euphimia of Corinth. In 'Mistresse Helena of Florence

[1] Vol. i, fol. 72 *recto*.   [2] Vol. i, fol. 64 *recto*.

there is a cross-reference to an earlier story: 'Philenio was more pitifull ouer the three Nimphes & faire Goddesses of Bologna, whose History you may read in the xlix. Nouell of my former Tome'.[1] The opening of 'Mistresse Helena' points the contrast with that of Salimbene and Angelica: 'Diuerte we nowe a litle from these sundrie happes, to solace our selues with a merie deuise, and pleasaunt circumstance of a Scholers loue, and of the wily guily subtilties of an amorous Widow of Florence',[2] and the close looks forward to the succeeding tale of Camiola and Rolande: 'But now turne we to another widowe that was no amorous dame, but a sober matrone . . .'.[3] Such transitions are obvious and, taken as a whole, *The Palace of Pleasure* lacks co-ordination. Nevertheless, there is some reason to believe that Painter was aware of Boccaccio's sense of design, though he was unable to rival it.

4. Collections of Tales and Romances in Prose, derived from an unknown Source

There are other collections of tales and romances in prose which have drawn upon the *Decameron*, though they have been manipulated in such a way that it is impossible to say through what channel they reached the English writer. The earliest of these is probably *The Sack-Full of Newes*. It has survived only in an edition of 1673, but it was entered in the Stationers' Register in 1557,[4] and in his well-known *Letter from Kenilworth* in 1575 Robert Laneham mentions that his friend Captain Cox owned the book.[5] *The Sack-Full of Newes* contains twenty-two stories, the third of which is based on the seventh tale of the seventh day. As the work belongs to the category of jest-books, its appeal is simple and direct, and it is characteristic of its popular aim that the story borrowed from the *Decameron* should have as its theme the outwitting and cudgelling of an elderly husband. There is no attempt to build up a framework for the collection, and the various tales are unconnected. Boccaccio's tale is reduced to its bare essentials, and the process that it has undergone may be seen at once if we compare the original opening with that of the Elizabethan version: 'There was an old man that could not well see, who had a fair young wife, and with them dwelt a young man'.[6]

The tale that comes next but one before this in the *Decameron*

---

[1] Vol. ii, fol. 377 *recto*.   [2] Vol. ii, fol. 376 *recto*.   [3] Vol. ii, fol. 391 *recto*.

[4] Cf. E. Arber, *A Transcript of the Registers of the Company of Stationers of London, 1554–1640*, i, fol. 22.

[5] Cf. F. J. Furnivall, *Captain Cox, his Ballads and Books*, London, 1871, p. lxvi.

[6] Cf. *Shakespeare Jest-Books*, in *Old English Jest-Books*, ed. W. C. Hazlitt, London, 1864, ii, p. 169.

M

experienced similar treatment in *The Schoolemaster or Teacher of Table Phylosophie*, which was printed in 1576 and again in 1583. This curious production, ascribed to Thomas Twyne, first discusses food, drink and table manners and suggests topics of conversation such as 'why doth the yolke of an egge which is layd in the full of the moone, and in the light therof, scoure spottes out of cloath?' Then in the fourth book it introduces a number of 'honest Iestes' which are meant 'to be vsed for delight and recreation, at the boord among Company'. Twyne makes some attempt to group his jests and places the story taken from Boccaccio under the heading 'Of Knights, or Souldiers'.[1] Later he brings together 'many mery iestes of Sisters',[2] and in this connexion relates almost in skeleton form the second tale of the ninth day. Its picture of abuses in monastic life was accepted only too readily by the Protestant England of Queen Elizabeth. This may be seen not only from Twyne's work but also from a passage in William Warner's *Albions England*,[3] which appeared in 1589. It is spoken by Robin Hood when criticising the world on which he and his companions have turned their backs. He cites the tale of the abbess and the nun as an example of its rottenness, and to suit his own purpose Warner makes the nun's offence even worse than in the original.

There was an anti-ecclesiastical flavour about two tales in *Tarltons newes out of Purgatorie*.[4] The first of these is the tale of Fra Alberto,[5] but the chief figure is called 'Fryer Onyon', the name of the hero of *Dec*. vi, 10. On the other hand, Lisetta remains unchanged. The scene is transferred from Venice to Florence, and when the friar leaps out of the window, he falls, not into the Grand Canal, but into a narrow lane where he is sorely bruised. Consequently, when he takes refuge, his account of how he had fallen among thieves is plausible. There are minor variations in this intrigue, but the only one of any importance is the appearance of the friar's brethren when he has been exposed and derided. At the sight of him, naked in the market-place, 'they couered their shauen crownes with their cooles, and went home with a flea in their eares'. The bias here is especially marked, but it is also visible in the second anti-ecclesiastical story, that of the vicar of Bergamo. This is Boccaccio's tale of Fra Cipolla,[6] but having already used the name 'Fryer Onyon', the author avoids it here. He prefaces Boccaccio's tale with that 'Of the frere that stale the podyng'.[7] Thus the two stories directed against the friars are welded together. The main character, the vicar of Bergamo, is a boon companion, noted for

---

[1] Ch. 8.   [2] Ch. 40.   [3] Book v, Ch. 27.
[4] Ed. J. O. Halliwell, Shakespeare Society, 1844. The date 1590 is assigned to the work by *C.B.E.L.*, i, p. 713, but the *Index* merely describes it as belonging to the sixteenth century. Quotations are from the 1590 edition in the B.M.
[5] *Dec.* iv, 2.   [6] *Dec.* vi, 10.   [7] No. 70 in *A Hundred mery Tales*.

his readiness to spend his time playing cards all day with his parishioners for a pot or two of ale. In the end, 'his score growing very great,
and much chalke vpon the post', the owner of the inn demands payment, and they come to blows. Bent on revenge, the vicar forbids his
flock to go to the alehouse to eat hot puddings before mass and thus
deprives the hostess of a profitable source of income. Finding that his
ban is ignored, he raids the tavern and puts to flight all whom he
finds there. The alewife is punished and the prohibition enforced.
Anxious to make some amends to his parishioners, the vicar ponders
what he can do. One day when travelling towards Pisa he meets a
stranger who has certain feathers 'of a byrd called Apis Indica, which
were long and large, of the colour of golde, and were so bright as
scarse one could looke against them: such before were neuer seene in
Italie'. He buys one and decides to exhibit this to his flock as belonging
to the wing of the angel Gabriel. At this point the connexion is made
with the tale of Fra Cipolla, the two men who substitute coals for the
feather being of those who had taken offence at the vicar's interference
with their consumption of puddings. The trick is played, not at the
inn, but at the vicar's house with the aid of his servant. The only other
change is the allusion to the relics of British saints instead of the fantastic creations in the original. Thus the vicar tells of 'Saint Dunstones
tonges', a cure for catarrh, Saint Winefrid's girdle, an aid to the eye-
sight, and Saint Asaph's beads, a remedy for the palsy.

One has the impression that even though the narrator is speaking of
Bergamo, he has in mind an English scene. The same atmosphere is
created in another tale, that of Signor Bartolo, a gentleman of Venice,
and his cook Stephano,[1] especially when we read that Stephano 'was
the chief gallant of all the parish for dancing of a Lincolnshire horne-
pipe in the Churchyard on sondaies'. Again there seems to be a great
distance between Currado Gianfigliazzi who is wont to ride out with
his hounds and hawks in quest of game, and Bartolo who keeps cranes
in his yard as if they were poultry. The fourth tale from the *Decameron*[2]
keeps closer to Boccaccio's version, apart from the removal of the scene
to Lyons and the bestowal of names such as 'Monsieur Perow' and
'Pier' in keeping.

Despite their popular tone, the stories in *Tarltons newes* are not so
bare in their simplicity as those in *The Sack-Full of Newes*. They too are
akin to the category of jests, but the narrative is fuller, and the author
is more sophisticated. He is not above introducing a Latin phrase like
'Cætera quis nescit?' and occasionally indulges in literary decoration
as when he writes: 'the Palme will grow straight though it bee neuer so
depressed; and a wanton will bee a wanton, were shee married to

---

[1] *Dec.* vi, 4.   [2] *Dec.* vii, 6.

Cupid'. He is not unfamiliar with the balanced sentence and so in his preamble, when he describes how he had mourned the death of Richard Tarlton, he continues: 'yet at last, as the longest Sommers day hath his night, so this dumpe had an ende'. This introduction illustrates his sense of design, which binds the collection together. He relates that he had intended to go to the theatre on Whit Monday but on arriving there found 'such concourse of vnruely people' that he preferred to walk in the fields. And so he went to 'the backside of Hogsdon' and, feeling the sun hot, rested in the shade of a tree and, falling asleep, dreamt that Tarlton appeared to him and recounted his experiences in purgatory, the various characters whom he encountered having punishment inflicted on them, according to their offences. Friar Onyon is tormented with wasps, Stephano sits with a crane's leg in his mouth, and the vicar of Bergamo with a coal in his. Tarlton is the connecting link, and he appears once more at the close. He tells how he was appointed to play jigs to the ghosts all day on his tabor, with the result that he performs better than in his lifetime. When he demonstrates his skill, the sound of the tabor awakens the author, and the book is ended.

The Cobler of Caunterburie (1590) has also an English background, the narrators of the tales being passengers in a boat which sets out from Billingsgate for Gravesend. In his preamble the author mentions that he had meant to travel in a tilt-boat, which was provided with an awning, but seeing that there was no danger of rain, he stepped into a barge and, the tide having ebbed and a wind sprung up, the watermen hoisted sail and laid aside their oars. Among the passengers is a gentleman who pulls *Tarltons newes* out of his sleeve and one of the others disparages it because most of the stories 'are stolne out of Boccace Decameron'. The author of *The Cobler of Caunterburie* must have written this with his tongue in his cheek, since four of his own tales are derived in some measure from Boccaccio. The one told by the Gentleman describes in its early part how Sir Rowland, a scholar of Cambridge, falls in love with a woman who is already engaged and how she, for the amusement of her betrothed, lets him wait in the yard of her house on a cold night until he is half-dead with cold. The parallel with Helena and Rinieri[1] is obvious. The following tale, that of the Scholar, is appropriately devoted to passionate love. It is the story of Gianni di Procida and Restituta,[2] with certain modifications. Under the influence of another tale,[3] that of Gostanza and Martuccio, the scene is transferred from Palermo to Tunis, but what is more

---

[1] *Dec.* viii, 7.   [2] *Dec.* v, 6.
[3] *Dec.* v, 2. Cf. H. Gassner, 'The Cobler of Caunterburie', *Englische Studien*, 1894, xix, p. 455.

notable is the shift in emphasis which lends a romantic quality to the relations of Iacomin and Katherine. When they meet unexpectedly after their separation, Katherine is on the point of swooning and later 'after a volly of sighes, quencht with teares, they began to discourse their fortunes'. Not only is the emotion heightened but the tale is developed into an example of the workings of true love. Even before they are married, Katherine speaks as if they were man and wife, and when they are sentenced by the king to be burnt at the stake, far from grieving and trembling for their lives as in the *Decameron*, they 'were no whit dismaied at this newes, but imbracing & kissing each other, comforted themselues in this, y^t they should as they liued together so die together, & y^t their soules nor bodies should neuer part'. In short, both in its insistence on the caprices of Fortune and in the elevation of the sentiment, there is a perceptible affinity with some of the Elizabethan tales in verse.

The author was conscious of the feeling that he had imparted to the theme and describes how an old wife was moved to tears. However, by way of relief she tells a story which returns to the type favoured in the jest-books. It is a combination of the first and eighth tales in the seventh day of the *Decameron*, and once again a man is outwitted by the cunning of a woman. The last story shows the same delight in overreaching the simple-witted, and just as Ferondo is duped by the abbot,[1] so the farmer of Wickam is baffled and derided by his English counterpart.

The author of *The Cobler of Caunterburie* was not without learning, but he aimed at a popular audience. His book was a gallimaufry, intended to please every one.

When the Farmer is set in his chaire turning (in a winters euening) the crabbe in the fier, heere hee may heare, how his sonne can read, and when he hath done laugh while his bellie akes. The old wiues that wedded themselues to the profound histories of Robin hood, Clim of the Clough, and worthy syr Isenbras, may here learne a tale to tell amongst their Gossippes.[2]

However, the construction is lucid and coherent. A short introduction pictures the scene and the narrators; there are suitable transitions from one story to another, and of set purpose the first and the last refer to a prior and an abbot respectively. To some extent *The Cobler of Caunterburie* was indebted to Chaucer for its pattern, but the writer's familiarity with the *Decameron* suggests that Boccaccio's sense of form was not without a contributory effect.

On a higher literary plane is George Whetstone's work entitled *An Heptameron of Ciuill Discourses*, which appeared in 1582. As the title indicates, it was modelled to some extent on the *Heptaméron* of

---

[1] *Dec.* iii, 8.   [2] Epistle to the Reader.

Margaret of Navarre. In each case the narrative is connected with travel, though the similarity is not very close. Indeed, Whetstone has shown some originality in that the scene, unlike that of the *Heptaméron* and the *Decameron*, is indoors, the time of the year being Christmas. In the introduction the traveller describes at some length how he had gone astray in a forest when he saw through the trees the lights of a stately palace. He received a polite welcome, but as he thought this was merely Italian courtesy, he asked the way to Ravenna. However, when he saw the inscription 'Entrate, e ben venuto' over an entrance, he made his way to the great hall,

the Skreene wherof, was curiously fronted with clowdy Marble, supported on euery side the passadges, with stately Pillers of Geate: and ouer the three Portalles, stood the Images of two men: the one of Allablaster Marble, bare headed, representing the vertue of welcome: the other of blewe Marble, attyred lyke a Cooke, and by him were artifycially painted, Pheasants, Partriges, Capons, & other costly Cates, as the Figure of Bountie.[1]

From here he passed into a great chamber,

richly hung with Tapistrie: yᵉ Roof wherof, was Allablaster plaister, embost wᵗ many curious deuises in gold[2]

and so on to a bed-chamber, which had a 'fayre prospect into a goodly Garden, beautified, with such rare deuises, as deserued to be compared with the earthly Paradice of Tiuoly'. This palace with its Italian background recalls the *Decameron* rather than the monastic setting of the *Heptaméron* in southern France; in its ornate beauty, comparable to 'the statelynesse of Cardinall Furnesæs Pallace,[3] buylded & beautified, with the ruinous Monumentes of Rome, in her pride', it has all the richness of the Renaissance at its height.

With the discussion of fixed topics for each of its seven days it combines the narration of stories. The fourth day, which has marriage as its theme, introduces 'The aduenture of Fryer *Inganno*'. In this tale the foolish Venetian, Madonna Lisetta, is replaced by a country woman named Farina, who dwells somewhere in the Apennines. Farina listens with the same credulity to the guileful Inganno as Lisetta does to Frate Alberto.[4] But the development is different, for in Whetstone's version God intervenes 'to punish his lewde intent, & to preserue her from sinnyng through ignoraunce'. It is the very simplicity of Farina that contributes to this end. Overjoyed by Inganno's promise, she seeks to have church bells rung, but the priest, 'glad to take one of those Beggers in a Pitfall, that with glorious lyes, had robbed him of his Parishioners deuotions', disabuses her. Under his

---

[1] Sigs. B *verso*–B ii.   [2] Sig. B ii.

[3] This is perhaps a garbled form and may refer to the beautiful Palazzo Farnese, built by Alessandro Farnese, Pope Paul III.   [4] *Dec.* iv, 2.

guidance an ugly maid is substituted for Farina, and the friar is surprised with her as the provost of Fiesole was with the hideous Ciutazza.[1] Inganno is not only exposed to mocking laughter but is stripped and laid in nettles, and next afternoon a funeral procession is formed 'with a hundred Torches, Tapers, and other waxen lyghtes'. The intention is to bury Inganno alive, and only the intercession of the friars saves him. By this union of two of Boccaccio's tales, Whetstone earns the title of 'Morall', bestowed on him in a eulogy at the beginning of the book, and his tale of Inganno is not out of harmony with that of Promos and Cassandra which follows immediately after. However, if mercy is shown to Inganno, he is not depicted as in any way penitent, for the tale ends thus:

The poore Fryer discharged from the handes of these vngentle people, learnea afterwardes to be more warie: but for all this punishment, was nothinge the honester. For amonge men of his Habit, remayneth an opynion, that the faultes, whiche the Worlde seeeth not, GOD punnisheth not.[2]

The hostility which is implicit here becomes more open in *The Spanish Masquerado* by Robert Greene. Appearing in 1589, it utters a cry of triumph over the destruction of the Spanish Armada and blends patriotism with Protestant fervour. In view of the excommunication of Queen Elizabeth by Pius V in 1570 Greene's anti-papal tone is not surprising. He derives support for his attack on the papacy and the cardinals from Boccaccio, and it is to his authority that he again appeals when he denounces

The rest of the rascal Rable of the Romish church as Monkes, Friers, and dirging Priestes, . . . sitting banquetting with the fair Nunnes, hauing store of daintie Cates, and wines before them, stall-fed with ease, and gluttony

and

the iolly fellowes that once in England liued like Princes in their Abbeies and Frieries. . . .[3]

The events of 1588 did not conduce to dispassionate opinions, and it was with some glee that Greene pointed to Boccaccio's tales of Frate Alberto[4] and Frate Cipolla[5] as examples of 'pranks, abhominable to rehearse'.

However, Greene used Boccaccio for other ends than the exploitation of political and religious passion. In his romances he seized on tales from the *Decameron* to exemplify the power of love. This is in

---

[1] *Dec.* viii, 4.   [2] Sig. N ii.
[3] Edition of 1589, sig. C 3 *verso*; Grosart, v, pp. 265, 266. The latter reference is to the text as reprinted in Grosart, *The Life and Works of Robert Greene*, 15 vols., 1881–6.
[4] *Dec.* iv, 2.   [5] *Dec.* vi, 10.

fact the theme of the second day's discourse in *Morando, The Tritameron of Loue*, which was first published in 1584. As an illustration
Morando alludes to the first tale of the fifth day.[1] The scene is transferred from Cyprus to Lacedemonia, and it is when passing through
the streets that the hero is affected by 'the glittering beautie' of the
fair lady which transforms him from a clown to a courtier. Morando
sums up thus:

who rightlie can deny that loue is not the cause of glory, honour, profit and
pleasure which happeneth to man, and that without it he can not conuenient-
lie liue, but shall run into a thousand enormities. Whereof I conclude, that
not to loue, is not to liue: or els to lead a life repugnant to all vertuous qualities.[2]

Five years later Greene returned to this theme in his *Ciceronis Amor.
Tullies Loue*.[3] The scene is now moved into the country outside Rome,
and as in the preceding romance it is only the early part of Boccaccio's
tale that Greene draws on. Fabius, the counterpart of Cimone, is the
son of the wealthy senator Vatinius, and his transformation is linked
to the love affairs of Lentulus and Tully, Terentia and Flavia. After
listening to the recital of an ode by a shepherd the two ladies, accompanied by Cornelia, retire to a grove and are overtaken with sleep.
It is here that the oafish Fabius contemplates Terentia and becomes
enamoured of her. However, her choice has fallen on Cicero, though
she is unable to give any reason for it, 'because loue is not circumscript
within reasons limits'.[4] Finally, the senate intervenes, and Fabius
marries Cornelia. In this respect Greene departs from Boccaccio and
turns the violent, possessive and unscrupulous emotion of Cimone into
a romantic tale 'of the most purest passion that is inserted into the
heart of man'.[5]

A similar bent is visible in *Perimedes the Blacke-Smith*, published in
1588. The blacksmith of Memphis and his wife tell tales of an evening.
That of Perimedes on the first evening is based on the sixth tale of
Boccaccio's second day, and on the second Delia follows with another
which comes immediately after that of Cimone in the *Decameron*. But
Greene, as elsewhere, was not content with the concentrated narrative
of the original. This may be seen particularly when the hero Alcimedes
takes the king by the hand and, presenting him to his troops, harangues
them in an impassioned oration. The episode terminates thus:

therefore Gentlemen, God and our Right, and with that he put spurs to his
horse, and gaue a furious and valiant onset vpon the enemy.[6]

---

[1] The form 'Chimon' used by Greene indicates that he relied on the text of
le Maçon.   [2] Edition of 1587, sig. E 2 *verso*; Grosart, iii, p. 92.
[3] This romance was popular. Nine editions appeared between 1589 and 1628.
[4] Edition of 1597, p. 72; Grosart, vii, p. 216. The text reprinted by Grosart is that
of the 1589 edition.   [5] p. 57; Grosart, vii, p. 189.
[6] Edition of 1588, sigs. E *verso*–E 2; Grosart, vii, p. 53.

The central feature of *Philomela*, printed in 1592, is the chaste and faithful love of the heroine, the daughter of the duke of Milan, who is married to Count Phillippo Medici, the cousin of the duke of Venice. Phillippo is tormented by jealousy and persuades his friend, Giovanni Lutesio, to put her to the test. This he does, but without success. However, the frantic Phillippo denounces them to the duke of Venice, and with the aid of two suborned slaves convinces all Venetians of the injury done to him. After the trial Philomela is banished and goes to Palermo under the name of Abstemia. Phillippo sets out for Milan, where the duke casts him into prison, but when one of the slaves confesses the truth, Lutesio is set free and Venice invaded. Phillippo is brought to judgement and banished to Palermo. Filled with remorse, he enters a grove and contemplates death. It so happens that Arnoldo Strozzo, the son of the duke of Palermo, wishing to visit secretly a young gentlewoman who lives at some distance from the city, exchanges clothes with a slave in the grove and bids him return to Palermo. However, a rival of Arnoldo, named Petro Salmo, mistaking the slave for the master, kills him and mangles his face beyond all recognition. Arnoldo's page, finding the body, gives the alarm. Phillippo is caught in the grove, rapier in hand, and is arrested. By permission of the gaoler Philomela sees him and knows that the prisoner is her husband. At the trial before the duke of Palermo there is a situation modelled on that at the close of the tale of Titus and Gisippus. Husband and wife vie with each other in claiming to have committed the crime, to the amazement of all present. But the disclosure of their innocence is made, not by the murderer, but by Arnoldo who returns just in the nick of time. Nevertheless, in this case all does not end well. Phillippo is carried away in a swoon and within two hours 'in an extasie he ended his life', and Philomela remains a widow, so famous for her constancy that after her death she is solemnly buried in the church of St. Mark. It is therefore only in a minor degree that Boccaccio enters into this Euphuistic romance. Like the others that have been discussed, it is marked by a love of eloquence and fine writing and delights in romantic love with a high moral tone. Greene's declaration that 'A womans honestie is her honour, and her honour the chiefest essence of her life' is typical of his attitude in *Philomela*, and equally characteristic is his warning to Lutesio that 'adulterie . . . is commended in none, condemned in all, and punnished in the end either with this worldes infamie or heauens anger'.[1]

As others had woven tales from the *Decameron* together, in *Philomela* Greene blended a Boccaccian story with different narrative material.

---

[1] Edition of 1592, C 2 *recto*; Grosart, xi, p. 130. *Philomela* was also reprinted by S. E. Brydges in *Archaica*, vol. i, 1815.

This mingling of plots had its counterpart in his plays, and narrator and dramatist followed this practice throughout the Elizabethan period. Indeed, as will be seen later, it was continued in seventeenth-century drama, so that *Philomela* itself provided one strand in Robert Davenport's *The City-Night-Cap*.[1] In general playwrights found in Boccaccio a rich vein of inspiration.

5. The Ballad

There is palpable evidence in some of the Elizabethan adaptations of tales from the *Decameron* of a desire to satisfy popular taste. It was therefore but natural that the same class should be catered for in ballads. Chaucer's *Troilus and Criseyde* was thought to offer suitable material, as may be seen from the poem of seventeen stanzas preserved in a manuscript which has been dated about 1557–65.[2] It is an interesting example of the way in which a literary work of the first magnitude could be stripped of all subtlety and reduced to the barest outline for the sake of action. The tone is that of the tavern, not that of a nobleman's hall.

Another ballad, of which we can say that it has passed through the hands of an intermediary, is 'Of the faithfull friendship that lasted betweene two faithfull friends'. This is by Thomas Deloney and appears in *The Garland of Good Will*.[3] It has been suggested[4] that he drew on Elyot's version, and there can be no doubt that this is so, as is shown by the peculiarities that it shares with Elyot's adaptation.[5] These features may have come to Deloney either from *The Gouernour* or at one remove from Lewicke's *Titus and Gisippus*. In any case, he had not Boccaccio before him. Deloney knew exactly what was suited to the reader whom he had in view. He eliminated the eloquent speeches and the spiritual struggles of the two friends in order to concentrate on the incidents of the tale. The last stanza serves to illustrate his dependence on Elyot and his skill in achieving the simple, popular style:

> In rich array he clothed him,
>   as fitted his degree:
> And helpt him to his lands againe,
>   and former dignity.

---

[1] Vide post, pp. 238–40.

[2] Ashmole 48 in the Bodleian. Cf. H. E. Rollins, *M.L.N.*, 1919, xxxiv, p. 347. The poem is included in *Songs and Ballads, with other short Poems, chiefly of the reign of Philip and Mary*, ed. T. Wright, London, 1860, pp. 195–7.

[3] First printed in 1631, but, as it would seem, entered in the Stationers' Register in 1593. Cf. *The Works of Thomas Deloney*, ed. F. O. Mann, Oxford, 1912, pp. 562–3.

[4] By F. O. Mann, ibid., p. 573.   [5] Vide ante, pp. 133–6.

The murtherer he for telling truth,
    had pardon at that time:
Who afterwards lamented much,
    his foul and grieuous crime.[1]

Deloney was equally successful with his ballad 'Of patient *Grissel* and a Noble Marquesse' which likewise figures in *The Garland of Good Will*. However, as entries in the Stationers' Register prove, ballads on this theme were in existence as early as 1565–6, and Deloney may simply have worked over an older version.[2] Again there is notable condensation, and everything is done to expedite the narrative. Thus to avoid any delay or repetition, instead of the two children being born at intervals, they are depicted as twins. Everything which is not indispensable is discarded. The one person named is Grissel; the marquis is referred to only by his title, so that he becomes a mere representative of the nobility; Grissel's father Janicula disappears; no places are specified. The total effect is to transform the story into a fairy-tale without a local habitation, its appeal being akin to that of Cinderella. Much emphasis is laid on the poverty of fair Grissel and the consequent hostility of the nobility:

Her country russet was chang'd to silke & veluet
    as to her state agreed.
And when that she was trimly tired in the same
    her beauty shined most bright:
Far staining euery other braue & comely Dame
    that did appeare in her sight,
Many enuied her therefore,
Because she was of parents poore,
    and twixt her Lord & she great strife did raise:
Some saide this and some said that,
Some did call her beggars brat,
    and to her Lord they would her oft dispraise.[3]

The happy ending therefore involves not only the restoration of the heroine to a place of honour, but also the triumph of virtue and beauty over malice and prejudice.[4]

It may be surmised that directly or indirectly the story of Grissel came from Chaucer. In the case of another ballad that ultimately goes back to the first tale of the fourth day it is impossible to decide by what channel Boccaccio's Guiscardo and Ghismonda made their entrance

---

[1] Cf. Mann, ut supra, p. 345.   [2] Ibid., p. 575.   [3] Ibid., p. 347.

[4] The ballad remained popular right into the eighteenth century, sometimes printed by itself, sometimes inserted into a prose framework, an introduction and a conclusion, each of two small chapters. This is distinct from *The Ancient True and Admirable History of Patient Grisel*, which is entirely in prose. Cf. *The History of Patient Grisel*, Percy Society, No. 18, London, 1842, which contains the ballad in its prose setting and the separate prose version. The latter alone is reprinted with a useful introduction by H. B. Wheatley, Villon Society, London, 1885.

into this very different sphere. Nor are we able to date the poem with any precision. However, this love-story was well known in the fifteenth century, and Bruni's Latin version[1] carried it far and wide. In Spain pictures of the hero and heroine were even used to decorate the face cards in a player's pack,[2] and in Elizabethan England Thomas Peend ranked it with the greatest love-tales of the world,[3] and Barnaby Rich similarly referred to it along with Pyramus and Thisbe and Romeo and Juliet.[4] Among the people it had an attraction not less than that of patient Grissel, because in both there was a disparity in rank between the lovers. In fact, the social gap is made still wider in the ballad by presenting Guiscardo, here plainly styled William, as a kitchen-boy in the service of a great king, which renders a story already romantic still more so.[5] In some versions there is a faint echo of the name 'Ghismonda' in 'Lady Dysmal' or 'Lady Diamond', whereas in others she figures as 'Daisy', 'Dayesie" or 'Dysie'.[6] The terseness and abruptness of the dialogue are most characteristic:

> They hae taen out this bonnie kitchen-boy,
>   And killd him on the plain;
> His hair was like the threads o gold,
>   His een like crystal stane;
> His hair was like the threads o gold,
>   His teeth like ivory bane.
>
> They hae taen out this bonnie boy's heart,
>   Put it in a cup o gold;
> 'Take that to Lady Daisy,' he said,
>   'For she's impudent and bold;'
> And she washd it with the tears that ran from her eye
>   Into the cup of gold.
>
> 'Now fare ye weel, my father the king!
>   You hae taen my earthly joy;
> Since he's died for me, I'll die for him,
>   My bonnie kitchen-boy.'
>
> 'O where is all my merry, merry men,
>   That I pay meat and wage,
> That they could not withhold my cruel hand,
>   When I was mad with rage?

---

[1] Vide ante, pp. 123, 131.   [2] C. B. Bourland, loc. cit., p. 24.

[3] In *Newe Sonets, and pretie Pamphlets*, 1565. It was also included in his *Deuises in* 1581.

[4] In *A Right Exelent and pleasaunt Dialogue betwene Mercury and an English Souldier*, 1574.

[5] Cf. F. J. Child, *The English and Scottish Popular Ballads*, Boston, 1894, v, pp. 29–38 and *English and Scottish Popular Ballads*, ed. H. C. Sargent and G. L. Kittredge, Boston and New York, 1904, p. 583.

[6] Cf. Sargent and Kittredge, p. 583.

'I think nae wonder, Lady Daisy,' he said,
  'That he brought your body to shame;
For there never was man of woman born
  Sae fair as him that is slain.'

This version, taken down from the recollection of a lady in Kirkcaldy, was published in 1859,[1] but the ballad lingered on and was recorded as 'Lady Diamond' by Gavin Greig,[2] who was related to Robert Burns and to Edvard Grieg, the Norwegian composer.

6. The Drama

Like the ballad-writers, the dramatists of the sixteenth century on the whole turned to the more serious tales in the *Decameron*. As early as 1547–9 Ralph Radcliffe, a schoolmaster at Hitchin, wrote *De patientia Griselidis* for performance by his boys. About 1566 John Phillip also gave the tale dramatic form, and the play may have been acted by the children of Paul's.[3] Strongly influenced by the morality, *Patient Grissell* shows Reason and Sobrietie contending with the Vice, here called Politicke Perswasion, for control over the marquis, and the ultimate victory of the power of good as it is embodied in the heroine. The preface is significant:

> Let *Grissills* Pacience swaye in you, wee do you all require,
> Whose Historye wee vnto you, in humble wise present,
> Beseechyng God, wee alwayes maye in trouble bee content:
> And learne with hir in weale and woe, the Lord our God to praise.[4]

This note is heard again the first time that she comes on the stage and sings a song inspired by submission to the will of God. This piety is in fact inherited from her parents. Her mother, an invention of the dramatist, appears when in the throes of death in order to declare:

> throughe Christ my only iustificasyon,
> I striue ageinst sinne, death and, damnacyon,
> And euen amidste the bitter pangs of death,
> Whose gripes most sharp semd to close my breath,
> I appele to Christ for mercy and grace,
> Trustinge amonge his saintes in the heauens to haue place.
> (328–33)

Grissell's father Ianickell is no less devout. He is confident that even

---

[1] W. E. Aytoun, *The Ballads of Scotland*, 2nd ed., 1859, ii, p. 173.

[2] Cf. *Last leaves of Traditional Ballads and Ballad Airs collected in Aberdeenshire by the late Gavin Greig and edited . . . by Alexander Keith*, Aberdeen, 1925, p. 213. Greig died in 1914.

[3] E. K. Chambers, ii, pp. 13–14.

[4] Cf. Preface, ll. 17–21. All quotations and line references are based on the Malone Society reprint, ed. R. B. McKerrow and W. W. Greg, 1909.

though he is left alone after the loss of his wife and the marriage of his daughter, God will provide for him:

> Hee is my Rocke, my stafe, my stay, my trust and perfect guid.
>
> (762)

His parting words to Grissell as she sets out for the palace are:

> Set Gods feare before thyne eyes good Grissell.
>
> (826)

Yet his firmness crumbles when she is sent home again in humiliation, and he begins to rail against Fortune. Grissell, however, never falters. The marquis himself perceives that

> She feareth God, she dreads his name, she leades a Godly life,
>
> (392)

and she rejects Ianickell's laments about the turning wheel of Fortune:

> Blame not Fortune for my ouerthroe,
> It was the will of God, that it should be so:
> And what creature liuing, can withstand his prouidence,
> This Crosse is to trye vs, as hee doth his elect.
>
> (1767–70)

So confident is she of divine protection, that Ianickell, 'perplexed with woe' though he is, gradually is won over to acquiescence. In short, Boccaccio's tale of patient Griselda begins to bear some likeness to the trials of Job.

However, the religious element is often tinged with didacticism. Indigence holds up Grissell as a model of true obedience, and the heroine turns aside from her own affairs to urge children to give to their parents due obedience and admonishes them in this fashion:

> Flye selfwill, which doth stoubbernes ingender,
> To honor your Parents do dayly remember.
>
> (599–600)

Her insistence on the undesirability of 'filthie speach' and 'crooked language' is echoed by her father when he converses with Gautier while his daughter is being arrayed in her new and rich attire. Perhaps a little prematurely the two men talk about the education of the prospective children. Ianickell gives this advice:

> Restraine in them, swearing, and all vngodlynes,
> Chastice and ponish them, lest sinfull infection,
> Alure them to all mischife and wickednes.
>
> (789–91)

Gautier is entirely of his opinion and agrees that

> in tender yeares, while youth is greene and fresh,
> All lewd inormities a Rod maye redresse.
>
> (808–9)

Sobrietie takes up the tale and drives home the lesson:

> Children chasticed in Infancie, in aige flie sinne,
> But if Parents cloake their godlesse conuersacion,
> In the end to contemne their superiours they beginne,
> Thefore (sic!) correction bringeth them to good educasion.
>
> (816–19)

Thus the dramatist digresses from the theme to indulge in generalisations about the evils to be shunned by the young and the obligation of
parents to exercise rigorous discipline.

Just as this lesson in pedagogy springs ultimately from the admirable
qualities of Grissell, so her virtues by contrast give rise to another type
of didacticism, satire on the foibles of women. Gautier's reluctance to
marry provides Politicke Perswasion with an opportunity for a cynical
picture of wedlock:

> I hard many a one saye,
> That the first daie for weddinge all other doth excell,
> For after they haue had not one merie daie.
>
> (183–5)

Later he attacks women on the ground of their love of expensive dress
and beauty lotions:

> The pride of some dames make the husband beare an empty purse
> They must be trimmed after the trickest fassion,
> Fyne watters must be bought for beawties preseruasyon,
> There heare with abodkin muste be curld after the fynest guise,
> Ther Neates toungs with peakes must hange ouer ther eyes,
> And to make them seeme proper headid, fyne caps they haue,
> Such as will scantly couer the crowne, I thinke as God me saue,
> But to make them syt cleane I swere by Saynt tan,
> They cut of ther heare, as I am an honist man.
>
> (371–9)

Even more vigorous is his denunciation of wives who either scold or
burst into tears if they do not get their way:

> Sume of them I tell you will be stoberne and vnkynde,
> Denye them of ther willes and then ye mar all,
> Ye shall see what there after is like for to fall,
> Ether brauling, iaulynge, sknappinge, or snarringe,
> Ther tounges shall not cease but alwaies be iarringe,
> Or els they will counterfait a kind of hipocrisye,
> And symper lyke a fyrmentie pot, the finger shalbe in there eye
> Theyle saie, loue is forgotten though my loue be showne,
> I see you loue another better then your owne,
> Tush, tush, I know full well theire meaninge and intent
> They be the craftiest cattell in Cristendome or kent.
>
> (423–33)

This social satire is a continuation of the morality tradition, and the choice of the Vice as the medium of criticism is not inappropriate. But he has other functions in the play. It is he who opens with a prologue. This is a fantastic affair which has little relation to the central theme. Politicke Perswasion describes a visit that he paid to Heaven where he saw Venus milking a cow and St. Peter frying pancakes for Jupiter. The following day he mounted a strange horse which threw him off and cast him down to Hell. He was placed at Beelzebub's table, but the servitors were such 'Crabtree facst knaues' that he was terrified. Rescued by an angel, he was placed on the horse and again thrown off. This time he nearly broke his neck on Westminster Hall but was rescued by Charing Cross and the weathercock on St. Paul's, and the cross in Cheapside played on a bagpipe for joy at his escape. This excursion into the realm of wonder was doubtless intended to appeal to a London audience, but is detached from the story of Grissell. However, after Grissell's marriage the Vice has a most important role, for it is he who induces Gautier to impose the series of afflictions upon her. Boccaccio had not attempted to explain why the marquis behaved as he did. The idea merely came into his head. Chaucer had contented himself with condemning his conduct without probing his motive. Phillip, however, felt that some agency was needed to account for this sudden change in Gautier's attitude. He finds it in the Vice who determines to sow dissension:

> I will not cease priuely her confusion to worke,
> For vnder Honnie the prouerbe saith poyson maye lurke:
> So though I simulate externally Loue to pretend,
> My loue shall turne to mischife, I warrant you in the end.
>
> (897–900)

He is the born mischief-maker and finds mirth in stirring up trouble. He is not a villain, for he is swayed by the goodness of Grissell, but with a perversely joyous impishness he continues to afflict her:

> I am kyn to a woman in all poynts ile haue my will.
>
> (1230)

However, Phillip's explanation is no explanation at all. Politicke Perswasion was but a servant, newly admitted to his master's presence. Yet he acquires such power over the marquis that the passionately devoted husband succumbs, at once and without a struggle, to his promptings. Only an audience familiar with the convention of the Vice could readily accept this outcome. As an attempt to rationalise the behaviour of the marquis, however, it is a failure.

In fact, Gautier is even more incomprehensible than in Boccaccio for Phillip has portrayed him as a romantic lover, filled with a passion quite alien to his prototype, which renders his sadism incredible. A the same time he does show signs of humanity, especially when he is anxiously awaiting news of the birth of his son. Again when Grissell is to return home, he addresses her as 'my deare and espoused mate', and when she is informed of his intention to marry another wife, her dutiful acceptance shakes him, and he feels that his conduct is disgraceful. Only the intervention of Politicke Perswasion prevents him from abandoning his plan. Yet at the close he thinks it enough to tell Grissell that he has merely wished to try her patience.

In this part of the play the Nurse, another figure created by Phillip, has an important task. Since her mistress was prevented by the story from offering any great resistance to Gautier, that function is assigned to her. In two scenes she pleads for the children. On the first occasion, when Gautier and Grissell are present, she reminds him of the commandment 'Thou shalt not kyll' and warns him that God will exact vengeance. She declares that even wild beasts care for their offspring and offers to flee into exile and care for the child, if only it may be spared. On the second occasion she is singing a lullaby when Dilligence enters with drawn sword to take the infant away. Again it is through her that the voice of humanity is heard; this time she goes so far as to denounce Gautier's tyranny. Rumor is also introduced to condemn his cruelty, and Vulgus exclaims:

> Woe be to this Marquis, ye curssed bee his dayes.
>   (1717)

Gautier's sister, to whom the children are sent secretly, is no new figure, but Phillip relates her not only to the action but also to this humane strain of feeling, when she displays an almost maternal joy at the sight of the little girl whose coming dispels the grief of her widowhood.

Mainly by the addition of new figures, Grissell's mother, Politicke Perswasion, the Nurse, the Midwife and also by the development of others in the tale, Phillip has eked out his material and adapted the story to the stage. The use of songs lends variety and serves the same purpose. The insertion of a lengthy wooing scene is also significant, for Ianickell's initial opposition to Gautier's desire and Grissell's reluctance to marry out of her humble sphere prove that, as in the Nurse scenes, Phillip had grasped the importance of conflict in drama. He has also enough artistic skill to group his characters in different ways in the two appearances of the Nurse in defence of her charges. There is no mechanical repetition. Phillip likewise appreciates the value of contrast. Thus the scene in which Grissell's mother piously fixes her eyes on her approaching death and goes out leaning on Grissell's shoulder is followed by one devoted chiefly to satire on women.

N

Pathos is again dominant when we see Grissell mourning her loss and rejoicing in the thought of her mother in Heaven. Sharply opposed in tone is the earthiness of the next scene where two lackeys quarrel, using foul language and blasphemous oaths.

However, the play is not without defects. The prologue is irrelevant, and the action is slow in getting under way. Phillip packed a good deal of his filling material into the early part of the play, so that what with the death of Grissell's mother, the lengthy wooing scene and the extensive satire on women, considerably over one third of the 2120 lines are spoken before Grissell leaves her home. In the handling of time Phillip is also somewhat unsuccessful. At l.877 Gautier sets out with her to the palace; four lines later Politicke Perswasion indicates that she is pregnant, and in l.947 her daughter is born. This is quite in keeping with the tradition of mediæval drama, where time is symbolical, but the modern reader will hardly think that Phillip has shown mastery in creating the 'willing suspension of disbelief'. From the dramatic point of view there was also a disadvantage in letting the audience know that the two children are not murdered, but safe and sound in their aunt's keeping. The element of surprise is therefore lacking, and the tension is reduced, for the excitement of the audience is limited to an anticipation of the disclosure of the truth to Grissell. Another defect is the ostentatious parade of classical learning that marks the play. It becomes disconcerting when attributed to a simple peasant like Grissell. Finally, there is the cramping didactic purpose of the dramatist which subordinates drama to edification and converts a play into a homily.

One of the songs in *Patient Grissell* is set 'to the tune of Damon & Pithias'[1] which underlines the popularity of friendship as a theme in the literature of the period. This subject was used by Ralph Radcliffe in his *De Titi et Gisippi amicitia* (1547-9) and again in a play, *Titus and Gisippus*, acted at court by the children of Paul's on 17 February 1577.[2] Unfortunately, neither of these dramatic versions of Boccaccio's tale has been preserved. From the serious we pass to the tragic in *Gismond of Salern*[3] which was acted before Queen Elizabeth, the date generally accepted being 1567-8. The authors, Robert Wilmot and four of his friends, including Christopher Hatton, the future Lord Chancellor,[4] were members of the Inner Temple. In adjusting Boccaccio's story of Tancred, Guiscardo and Ghismonda for the stage

---

[1] *Damon and Pithias*, by Richard Edwardes, was produced in 1565 and printed in 1571.

[2] Chambers, iv, pp. 93 and 152.

[3] Printed in *Quellen des weltlichen Dramas in England*, ed. A. Brandl, Strassburg 1898, pp. 539-95 and in *Early English Classical Tragedies*, ed. J. W. Cunliffe, Oxford 1912, pp. 161-216.   [4] Vide ante, p. 106

they added a number of minor characters. Iulio is the loyal captain of
the guard who carries out orders like an automaton. Renuchio, a
gentleman of the Privy Chamber, while obeying the king's command
with equal fidelity, displays a greater sensitiveness and humanity.
Gismond's aunt Lucrece is her confidante. To her she discloses her
most intimate feelings but is advised by Lucrece not to disregard the
king's wishes. Finally, a minor part is given to Claudia, who describes
Gismond's mental unrest without realising that love is the cause.

Classical lore is applied with more discrimination than in *Patient
Grissell*. It is brought in to emphasise the fact that this is a tragedy of
love, and it enhances the dignity and solemnity of the passion. Cupid
appears in the very first scene which is coloured by Dolce's *Didone*.[1]
His intervention kindles the ardour of the lovers and the opposition of
Tancred. In this way he takes 'sharp reuenge on earthly wightes'.
The revenge theme, here merely glanced at, is invested with a more
sinister atmosphere when Megaera emerges to bring

> Vengeance and blood out of the depest helles.
>   (IV. i. 1)

Entering the palace, she throws her stinging snakes into the breast of
Tancred and Gismond and thus leads each to cause the death of the
other. Her function is essentially moral:

> Furies must aide, when men will ceasse to know
> their Goddes: and Hell shall send reuēging paine
> to those, whome Shame frō sinne can not restraine.
>   (IV, i. 42–4)

Like Megaera, the Chorus of four gentlemen of Salerno shows clear
signs of Senecan inspiration. Its comments at the end of each of the
first four acts are of a general kind—the instability of fortune, the
inconstancy of most women, the power of love and the need for virtue
in lovers. In Act V, Sc. i, however, it deals with the particular and
condemns Tancred's cruelty. Gismond has moments when she is
animated by the spirit of revenge. She has something of a Medea in
her when she contemplates burning her father with his court and
palace, and if she in the end refrains, it is only because her death will
inflict greater woe and so avenge Guishard. There are elements of
horror in the original tale which are in keeping with the Senecan
model, and these are exploited by the dramatists. Thus Gismond
receives the golden cup containing the lover's heart, weeps into it,
poisons herself and dies in the presence of the audience. Guishard's
death takes place off stage, but Renuchio's account in all its gory
detail is in the Senecan tradition. Lastly, the horror is increased

[1] Cf. J. W. Cunliffe, 'Gismond of Salerne', *P.M.L.A.*, xxi, pp. 442–50.

when Tancred is made to commit suicide, though this is related in an epilogue.

Of the three chief protagonists, Guishard is the least prominent but the most successful. His position has been exalted so that there is no such disparity between the 'Counte Palurine' and Gismond as existed between Boccaccio's lovers. Nevertheless, he is modestly aware of her higher rank. He never attempts to deny his guilt and, as the executioners approach, he faces them with a courage as dauntless as his devotion was chivalrous. So favourably is he portrayed that one has the impression that the sympathy of the young dramatists instinctively went out to him, even if, according to their principles of virtue, Guishard's conduct was faulty. Equally, one feels that they regarded Tancred with dislike, though he had been wronged. He is a selfish and possessive parent who is governed by personal motives. It is the lust for revenge, not the need to uphold the law, which impels him, and he is a most unworthy agent for the upholding of those moral powers that Megaera was intended to represent. Not only is he an unwise ruler but undignified as well, ranting and raging and shedding floods of tears.

As the title of the play indicates, *Gismond of Salern in Loue* regarded the heroine as even more important than Tancred. The whole of the first act is devoted to the portrayal of her widowhood. Stress is laid on her intense sorrow at the death of her husband and her wifely devotion to his memory. Evidently the dramatists were anxious to create a favourable impression at the start; but the effect of this marital piety, which was unknown to Boccaccio, is to render the suddenness of her infatuation with Guishard less comprehensible. Equally alien to her prototype is Gismond's meek submissiveness. To this extent she resembles Patient Grissell. But whereas Grissell typifies obedience to her husband as well as to her father, the problem as posed here is solely that of filial obedience. In the tale the conflict was that between a daughter's duty to a royal parent and a deep-rooted natural desire. Here the issue is obscured by the dramatists' moral aim, and as a result Gismond appears tame and colourless in the first three acts. After the discovery of her relations with Guishard, the scene in which she is rebuked by Tancred lacks the fire of the corresponding scene in the tale. This is partly because the sequence of events has been altered, so that in the play this episode precedes the appearance of the arrested Guishard. Consequently, she is without the emotional stimulus which his seizure had provided in Boccaccio. Again, Guishard having been elevated to the rank of an earl, Gismond is deprived of the equalitarian argument so effectively used in the tale and as a result of the dramatists' wish to preserve decorum, she does not try to justify her love on the ground of sexual need. In fact, it is not until the last two scenes that she exhibits anything of Ghismonda's spirit, and even then she hardly reveals the same unwavering resolution and strength of mind.

In form the play is also defective. There is an excessive number of soliloquies, and the characters utter their speeches like marionettes. The dialogue is wooden, and the use of rhyme restricts the movement of the verse.

It was therefore not surprising that in 1591 Robert Wilmot should publish a revised version, *The Tragedie of Tancred and Gismund*, 'polished according to the decorum of these daies'.[1] His alterations are extensive. Claudia is omitted, but two other Furies, Alecto and Tysyphone are added. Iulio, instead of being captain of the guard, becomes Lord Chamberlain, Renuchio taking over his post as commander. The Chorus now consists of four maidens in attendance on Gismund. Its functions are more comprehensive. Here and there it intervenes in the action, and on three occasions it sings a song.

Music is used in conjunction with the dumb shows that present the events of the following acts or link two acts together. In one dumb-show there is a dance; in another a storm of thunder and lightning breaks, as the Furies rise from Hell; in the last Guiszard is taken from beneath the stage, a strangling cord is placed around his neck, and he is haled forth. Renuchio brings in a cup of gold and in it a bloody heart, reeking hot.

The taste for the spectacular exemplified here is manifest also in the dance performed by the three Furies and in the throwing of Megaera's snake on Tancred, an incident not witnessed by the audience in *Gismond of Salern*. The coming of Cupid at the beginning of the play is shown as a descent from Heaven in a cradle of flowers, while he leads by silken cords the allegorical figures of Vaine Hope and Brittle Joy on his left and Faire Resemblance and Late Repentance on his right. There is also an increase of stately ceremony and pageantry in connexion with Tancred.

In general, there is far more bustle and animation. Wilmot has learnt to appreciate the importance of movement and of gestures to express emotion. The death of Gismund, which in the earlier version took place in her chamber, presumably a mere recess, is now enacted on the open stage after the performance of a preparatory ritual. So too the king orders Iulio to carry out his last wishes and, having torn out his eyes, kills himself on the stage.

Wilmot also displays a keener sense of construction. He links the various scenes together and recognises the dramatic value of surprise. His dialogue is more natural and flexible, and the partial abandonment of rhyme in favour of blank verse gives him far greater ease and freedom.

[1] See the edition of W. W. Greg, Malone Society, 1914.

The characters likewise underwent some modifications. The one who is least changed is Guiszard. He is conceived of as a prince,

> a man right wise,
> a man of exquisite perfections.
>
> (III. i. 600–1)

Thus his rank is exalted and his qualities are magnified. But as the title of the play suggests, Wilmot was especially concerned with Tancred. He does everything possible to stress any trait that would entitle him to the affection of his daughter. His advanced age is mentioned to create pathos, and his love is no longer the possessive affection of a self-centred parent but a genuine love. His distress after Gismund has taken poison, conveyed as it is in simple words, is poignant in its sincerity:

> What has thou done? oh let me see thine eyes,
> Oh let me dresse vp those vntrimmed locks,
> Looke vp, sweet child, look vp mine only ioy,
> Tis I thy father that beseecheth thee:
> Reare vp thy body, straine thy dying voice
> To speake to him, sweet *Gismund* speake to me.
>
> (V. iii. 1740–5)

Not only is Tancred more human, he is also more dignified. When rebuking Guiszard, he no longer sheds copious tears, and when he rejects Iulio's plea for clemency, he has a kingly utterance. Wilmot has done everything he could to augment his authority by hedging him about with courtly etiquette, so that even Gismund approaches him with the utmost humility and, as she lies dying, does not forget to call him 'your maiestie' as well as 'Father'. However, it is not only by means of such formality that Tancred inspires greater reverence In his actions he is mindful of his duty as a monarch. It is his responsibility to enforce the law, and he knows that he is not merely a parent but also the head of the state. In his painful dilemma he asks:

> shall iustice not preuaile?
> Shall I (a king) be proued partiall?
> How shall our Subiects then insult on vs,
> When our examples (that are light to them)
> Shalbe eclipsed with our proper deedes?
>
> (IV. ii. 1032–6)

Gismund is also modified to some extent, though not so much in the early part of the play. It is true that at first she appears somewhat bolder when explaining to Lucrece her desire for re-marriage, but in dealing with her father she is a timid and submissive figure. However after her appeal to his paternal instincts has been rejected, her temper undergoes a change for which nothing has prepared the spectator

She is fierce, resolute and bitter. Nothing can deter her from suicide, even though she knows that she will be damned for the offence. And just as Macbeth later was to declare 'I gin to be aweary of the sun', so she cries:

> now doth my soul begin
> To hate this light
>
> (v. ii. 1720–1)

and in her despair vows that

> Hel is on earth, yea hel it selfe is heauen
> Compar'd with earth.
>
> (v. ii. 1728–9)

Thus at the close she displays all the energy and firmness of Boccaccio's heroine, but nothing is done to prepare for this transformation which remains as unconvincing as the swift transition from the mourning widow to the passionate lover.

In revising the play Wilmot was hampered by his didactic preoccupation. The moralizing strain of the version of 1567–8 is heard still more loudly. Partly he aims at the conduct of Tancred which culminates in his suicide, 'to his owne reproch, and the terror of all other hard hearted fathers'. But above all he raises his hand to warn the spectator of the disaster that must ensue from actions such as those of Gismund. He lets Tancred denounce his daughter as a 'cursed strumpet' and by contrast his Chorus sings the praises of the Virgin Queen, thus blending courtly compliment with moral edification. As a clergyman he was concerned lest he should be criticised for dabbling in the writing of plays. He therefore warded off any unfavourable comment by pointing to the example of Beza and Buchanan and by claiming that in the original play he and his friends had agreed in 'commending vertue, detesting vice, and liuely deciphering their ouerthrow that suppresse not their vnruly affections'. As for his own version, he would have none of the 'scurrilous words' that blemished so many amorous poems and asserts that his

purpose in this Tragedie, tendeth onely to the exaltation of vertue, & suppression of vice, with pleasure to profit and help al men, but to offend, or hurt no man.[1]

Consequently, he saw no reason why he should not dedicate it to two ladies and recommends it either for performance or reading in winter, because

the perusing of some mournfull matter, tending to the view of a notable example, will refresh your wits in a gloomie day, & ease your wearines of the louring night.[2]

---

[1] Address to 'the Gentlemen Students of the Inner Temple'.
[2] Dedication to Lady Marie Peter and Lady Anne Graie.

Such was the fate of Boccaccio's tale when it fell into the hands of scholarly Englishmen, the first draft being certainly influenced by Dolce and probably by Antonio Cammelli, the second possibly deriving some ideas from Federico Asinari.[1]

In the interval between the composition of these two versions Sir Henry Wotton's *Tancredo* had been performed at Queen's College, Oxford. According to Izaak Walton, Wotton was on friendly terms with Alberico Gentili, professor of civil law, who may well have stimulated his interest in Italian. It is known that in later years he was acquainted with Salviati's notes on the *Decameron*,[2] but it is impossible to establish his familiarity with them when he wrote his tragedy on the injunction of the provost for the private use of the members of Queen's. The disappearance of the play itself is unfortunate, for it would have been of considerable interest to note how far Wotton had been guided by Salviati. Evidently it was suitably edifying in tone, for Walton states that it

> was so interwoven with Sentences, and for the Method and exact personating those humours, passions and dispositions, that the gravest of that society declared, he had, in a sleight employment, given an early and a solid testimony of his future abilities.[3]

Further, Walton records that Baptista Guarini 'thought it neither an uncomely nor an unprofitable employment for his age'.

While Oxford bent its eyes towards the tragic possibilities of the *Decameron*, Cambridge exploited it for comedy. In this respect two Latin plays, acted at St. John's College, probably in March 1578–9, and in 1580 respectively, sowed a seed which was to yield an abundant harvest on the popular stage in the seventeenth century. The first is usually known as *Hymenaeus*,[4] though the manuscripts in which it is preserved give no title. One member of the cast was Abraham Fraunce, and it was he who wrote the second comedy, *Victoria*, of which he presented a copy to his benefactor, Sir Philip Sidney.[5] The source of *Hymenaeus* is indicated by the author in the prologue:

---

[1] For an account of plays, English and foreign, on the theme see *Ghismonda*, ed. H. G. Wright, Introduction, Manchester, 1944.

[2] He drew up a list of Italian authors some time after 1628, in which there appear 'The Annotations of Salviati upon the Decameron of Boccaccio'. Cf. *The Life and Letters of Sir Henry Wotton*, ed. L. P. Smith, Oxford, 1907, ii, pp. 484–5. I owe this reference to Wilkinson, p. xx, n. 2. On the importance of Salviati's edition of the *Decameron* and his marginal notes, cf. H. G. Wright, *The first English translation of the 'Decameron'*, pp. 129–64.

[3] Cf. 'Life of Henry Wotton' in *Lives by Izaak Walton*, World's Classics, ed. G. Saintsbury, 1927, p. 100.

[4] Ed. G. C. Moore Smith, Cambridge, 1908.

[5] The manuscript, preserved at Penshurst, was edited by G. C. Moore Smith in Bang's *Materialien zur Kunde des älteren englischen Dramas*, xiv, Louvain, 1906.

Nam huic comœdiæ dedit olim materiam
plus trecentis hinc annis in Decamero Bocatius,
cum chirurgum Rogerus inhoneste falleret.[1]

The last line proves that it was the tenth tale of the fourth day that
formed the basis of the play and also that the dramatist disapproved
of the deception of Mazzeo della Montagna by Ruggieri da Jeroli.
On moral grounds therefore the intrigue between Mazzeo's wife and
the dissolute gallant, Ruggieri, undergoes a change which is even more
drastic than that made by the English translator of the *Decameron*
in 1620. In fact the alteration is so considerable that the prologue says.

> hæc a Bocatij fabula longe magis est alia,
> quam a Colace Menandri Eunuchus Terentij.[2]

The dramatist replaces the original main characters by Alfonsus, the
old father of Julia, and her three wooers, Erophilus, Fredericus and
Pantomagus, a doctor. Erophilus is a young man who has been sent by
his father Ferdinandus, a man of rank in Venice, to study at Padua.
Alfonsus favours Pantomagus who is known to be wealthy, whereas he
disapproves of Erophilus, regarding him as a dissolute stranger. On the
other hand, Julia has lost her heart to Erophilus. Their love is a romantic passion, and in the prologue Hymenaeus enlists the sympathy of
his young Cambridge audience against a mercenary marriage and in
favour of an idealistic union:

> Hanc nuptiarum pestem impeditum venio,
> solus enim optime cognovi incommoda,
> ex isthoc fonte impuro quæ profluunt.
> Accedo igitur opitulatum Juliæ,
> vt illa illum sibi habeat coniugem,
> quem amat, et a quo redamatur maxime.[3]

Alfonsus watches so vigilantly over Julia that Erophilus feels inclined
to carry her off by night. But much as she loves him, she shrinks from
deserting her father and from exposing both Erophilus and herself to
slander. She therefore advises him not to act rashly. When Alfonsus
has turned Erophilus away from his house, the lover goes to his friend
Camillus who proposes that, as Alfonsus is giving a banquet to cele-
brate his birthday, and some masquers are to perform dances, Erophilus should go with them. Thus in disguise he defies the hostility
of Alfonsus and contrives to speak at length with Julia. The guests
having departed, Alfonsus is taken ill, and an operation which Pantomagus was to have performed on him is postponed. That night, with
the aid of Julia's maid Amerina, Erophilus is admitted to see his love.
All at once he loses consciousness and appears to be dead. Amerina

---

[1] Cf. G. C. Moore Smith's ed., p. 2.   [2] Ibid., p. 2.   [3] Ibid., p. 1.

suggests that he should be stabbed repeatedly, so that it may seem as if he had been killed in a brawl. However, Julia will have none of this, and in the end the two women are helped by Erophilus' servant Pantaleo to place the body in an empty chest standing outside a neighbouring house. Pantaleo, lamenting this unhappy end of chaste love, sets out for Venice to inform Ferdinandus.

Shortly after, Bargulus and Clopetarus, who are normally highway-men in league with an innkeeper, but on this occasion are plain burg-lars, come in with goods stolen from the house of a merchant. They deposit these in the chest and carry it off to their room at the inn. There Erophilus revives and a clamour breaks out. The innkeeper calls loudly, and the magistrate investigating the burglary arrives. At first Erophilus is under suspicion because he declares that his mind is a complete blank. However, the burglars confess, and after the arrival of Ferdinandus the inquiry is pursued further, and all the facts are elicited. Pantomagus had left behind a phial containing opium which was intended for the operation. Amerina had placed this with other bottles in Julia's room and she, thinking it contained rose-water, gave it to Erophilus to quench his thirst. Alfonsus, on hearing that Ferdi-nandus is a man of distinction and on receiving apologies from Ero-philus, agrees to the marriage.

By this modification a different atmosphere is created from that in the *Decameron*. The chastity of the lovers is insisted on again and again, and the immoral 'Stadico' inquiring into the crime is replaced by a businesslike magistrate.

To offset the serious element in the romantic part of the play, comic effects are introduced by means of the wooers, Fredericus and Panto-magus, who were added by the dramatist mainly for this purpose. Fredericus is described early in the play as 'potator egregius'. He is typical of the period, since his countrymen had the reputation of being heavy drinkers. After the banquet he comes out of the house with aching eyes and head; everything seems to be turning round, and he sees the gods and goddesses drinking at a feast. 'Heus quo ruit mundus' he asks, and he has a strong desire to lie down. Evidently this character was calculated to appeal to the undergraduate audience, and equally popular in its aim was his habit of mingling Dutch phrases now and then with his Latin. His rival Pantomagus is also a farcical figure. As a wooer he is diffident and has to be assured by his servant Gothrio that he has a royal gait and that his hair, face, voice, dress and bearing are those of a lover. His absurd behaviour at the banquet makes him a laughing-stock. Moreover, though he allows himself to be persuaded by Gothrio that people call him the god of medicine, he is a char-latan, for he is more interested in cabbalistic art than in Galen and

Hippocrates and applies the remedies of a sixteenth-century quack called Burcot.

This relation of the play to the contemporary world is seen also in the transference of the action from Salerno to Padua. When Boccaccio wrote, Salerno was still famous for its medical school, and the *Regimen Sanitatis Salerni* had carried its name all over Europe. But long before the Elizabethan age its repute had declined, and Padua was better known in the English universities. Incidentally, the change had the advantage that Ferdinandus could be brought rapidly from Venice which was only twenty miles away. The process of adaptation is seen again when the role of the two usurers, whom Boccaccio had chosen on account of their evil reputation in the Middle Ages to steal the chest by night, is taken over by highwaymen. In one other respect the dramatist contrived to interest his Cambridge audience. A passage in Act IV, Sc. ii, assigns to the innkeeper a criticism of the students of Padua:

> Est adeo in hac civitate quoddam genus hominum
> imperiosum, superbum, argutum, sophisticum,
> quos vno verbo scholares nominant.[1]

He adds that the hostility of the townsmen to these keen-witted but penniless fellows is not confined to Padua—a point that would certainly not be lost on the audience at St. John's.

In its blending of romance and comedy *Hymenaeus* is typically Elizabethan. As a play it is far superior to Fraunce's *Victoria* which is long and involved. The plot deals with the relations of Victoria, the wife of Cornelius, to her lovers Fidelis and Fortunius. Onophrius, the teacher of Fidelis, is also in love with her and in the pursuit of his designs hides in a tomb where Cardinal de Cusa is buried. In Act III, Sc. viii, Onophrius is found there by two vagabonds, Pyrgopolinices and Terrapontigonus, who force him to join them in rifling the tomb. As in *Dec.* ii, 5,[2] they open the tomb and force him to descend. He hands up to them first the mitre, then the vestments, but asserts that he cannot find the cardinal's precious ring. They close the tomb, and he remains there until Frangipetra, a soldier, opens it again. He declares that he fears neither the living nor the dead, but flees when Onophrius calls 'Alecto', exclaiming 'hoc est iura mortuorum violare'. This insistence on the crime of sacrilege, which is not mentioned in Boccaccio's tale, is a notable feature of the scene. Before he is compelled to go below, Onophrius begs to be spared, because he shrinks from the thought of wronging the dead and violating their tombs. There follows a vivid description of his cries after he has been shut in:

[1] Cf. Moore Smith's ed., p. 42, and note, p. 82.
[2] The source was pointed out by E. Koeppel, *Anglia Beiblatt*, 1906, xvii, pp. 365–70.

ô, ô, ô, ô furiæ, ô stridor dentium, et ingens
luctus, et inferni metuendus carceris horror.
ô vermes et ossa, ô caro putrida,
heu rapit Pluto, rapit Proserpina.[1]

After he has escaped, his mind is full of the monsters and furies that he
has seen, so that he can hardly speak of it all. Nevertheless, he carries
off the ring as a reward for his labour and in this respect differs in no
wise from Andreuccio of Perugia.

The episode is but a minor feature of the play, but it is of interest,
since it shows that this tale of low life in Naples had already begun to
attract the attention of English dramatists.

[1] Cf. G. C. Moore Smith's edition in Bang's *Materialien zur Kunde des älteren englischen Dramas*, vol. xiv (1906), p. 55.

IV

THE DECAMERON IN
THE SEVENTEENTH CENTURY

IN the course of the seventeenth century Boccaccio's reputation as a writer of fiction grew steadily, and the pre-eminence of the *Decameron* became more and more firmly established. In a manuscript of about 1690[1] there is a translation by Sir James Turner of the lines on his tomb at Certaldo:

> John's Ashes and his Bones doe ly
> Within this tombe of Stone
> His Soule exempt from Labour, Sits
> Before Gods Blessed throne,
> My ffather hight Boccaccio
> In Certald borne was I,
> My Studie was Sueet Poesie,
> Heere Spechles now I Ly.

This application of 'Poesie' to imaginative composition is confirmed by a passage in Edward Phillips's *Theatrum Poetarum*,[2] where Boccaccio is described as 'a most generally known and Extolled *Florentine* Writer, and worthily rank'd among the Poets', among other works because of the *Decameron*. Sir William Temple upheld him as one of the 'great Wits' among the moderns,[3] and John Evelyn, similarly considering his ingenuity, refers to him as 'witty'.[4] William Wotton, echoing Dryden's glowing tribute to the melodious quality of the Italian tongue and his remark that 'The Language has in a manner been refin'd and purify'd from the *Gothick*, ever since the time of *Dante*',[5] declares that it 'is so very musical that no Art can mend it' and then proceeds to define Boccaccio's share in its development:

in *Boccace*'s Time, . . . in the earliest Dawnings of Polite Learning in these Western Parts of the World, *Italian* was a formed Language, endued with that peculiar Smoothness which other European Languages wanted; and it

---

[1] In my possession.
[2] London, 1675, Section ii, 'Eminent Poets among the Moderns', p. 60. Phillips's words were repeated without acknowledgement by T. Pope Blount, *De Re Poetica*, London, 1694, in the section 'Characters and Censures', p. 29.
[3] *On Ancient and Modern Learning*, London, 1690.
[4] *Memoirs*, under the year 1674.   [5] In the preface to *Albion and Albanius*.

has since suffered no fundamental Alterations, not any, at least, for the better, since in the *Dictionary* of the Academy *della Crusca, Boccace*'s Writings are often appealed to in doubtful Cases which concern the Niceties of the Tongue.[1]

It was above all the *Decameron* that was notable in this connexion and it is significant that as far back as 1605 Sylvester in his translation of Du Bartas had rendered 'Le Toscan est fondé sur le gentil Bocace' as 'On mirthfull *Boccace* is the *Tuscan* plac'd'.[2] A commentary on Du Bartas, translated by Thomas Lodge, interprets the purport of this line as follows:

He maketh also mention of the *Tuscan* tongue, because that amongst diuers of the Italians, it is the most complete Language, whether we speak of the *Luckquois*, the *Milanois*, the *Geueuois*,[3] the *Venecian*, or others which are not so pure and refined, as the *Florentine* and *Tuscan* are: *Iohn Boccace* wrote many yeeres since, but very wittily and purely, as his *Decameron* . . . and other his bookes, so dearely beloved by the children of this world do declare.[4]

Both for its part in the evolution of the Italian language and for its own intrinsic qualities the *Decameron* won the support of men of letters, and there is every reason to believe that the opinion of Isaac Bullart cited by Thomas Pope Blount[5] was representative of the prevailing attitude not only of French, but also of English writers in the seventeenth century. He says:

That the most considerable of all *Boccace*'s Works was his *Decameron*, which had been receiv'd with the Universal Applause of all *Italy*; and that it was so well approv'd of in Foreign Parts, that it was Translated into almost all Languages; and that the more it was suppress'd, and censur'd, by reason of some severe Reflections upon the Monks, the more it was desir'd, and sought after.

Indirectly this wide popularity is reflected in Hobbes's *Decameron Physiologicum* (1678) and *The Spanish Decameron* (1687), the one consisting of ten dialogues on scientific problems, each occupying a chapter, the other of 'Ten Novels'. More directly it is to be traced in Burton's long enumeration of winter recreations.[6] Among these he includes the tales of Boccaccio, which, along with other similar stories, 'some delight to hear, some to tell, all are pleased with'. Sir Thomas Browne, writing at the end of the *Religio Medici*[7] on the theme of the

[1] *Reflections upon Ancient and Modern Learning*, 1694. Cf. *Critical Essays of the Seventeenth Century*, ed. J. E. Spingarn, iii, p. 205.

[2] *Bartas His Deuine Weekes & Workes*. The second week, p. 431.

[3] There is probably a misprint here for '*Geneuois*'. Perhaps the dialect of Genoa is intended.

[4] *A Learned Summary Upon the famous Poeme of William of Saluste Lord of Bartas* London, 1621, part 2, p. 192.

[5] *De Re Poetica*, Section ii, 'Characters and Censures', p. 29. Pope Blount also quotes Bullart in his *Censura celebriorum authorum*, Geneva, 1694, p. 439

[6] *The Anatomy of Melancholy* (1621), ed. A. R. Shilleto, London, 1903–4, ii, p. 93

[7] London, 1642.

happiness to be found in God, declares that all else that the world terms happiness is to him no more than a story from Pliny or Boccaccio, 'an apparition or near dilusion, wherein there is no more of Happiness, than the name'.

In part at least the appreciation of the *Decameron* was due to the appearance of a translation in 1620,[1] long after it had been made accessible in other countries.[2] This encountered some initial difficulties, for after it had been sanctioned by the bishop of London, approval was withdrawn by the archbishop of Canterbury. However, his consent was ultimately obtained, and this version, which was in all likelihood the work of John Florio, had other editions in 1625, 1634, 1657 and 1684. The woodcuts of the first edition, repeated in some of the later editions, were derived from the French translation of le Maçon printed at Lyons in 1558, and these enhanced the appeal of the text.[3]

The English translator, who was familiar not only with the French rendering[4] but also with the expurgated text of Lionardo Salviati, displays earnestness and piety, and condemns sexual excesses and irregularities. His moralised version is often marked by an emotional and a dramatic quality as well as by a partiality for significant detail. This vividness is strengthened by a considerable range of stylistic effects from the simple and racy to the elaborate and ornate. The translator makes extensive use of balance, and his work has a well-defined rhythm. These unite with a complicated and skilfully devised system of alliteration to leave a deep impression on the ear. So artistic a creation, even though it departs from the more economical and less ornate narrative style usually employed by Boccaccio in the *Decameron*, long continued to attract readers, and the omission or toning down of some passages open to criticism enabled it to reach a wide circle in England.

1. Collections of Tales in Prose and Verse

It is, of course, not always possible to say whether or not those writers who drew on the *Decameron* after 1620 had this translation before hem, because its characteristic features are often blurred in the process

[1] Reprinted in *The Tudor Translations* in 4 vols., London, 1909, with an introduction by E. Hutton. The text used is that of the second edition for Part 1 and that of the irst for Part 2.

[2] Cf. H. G. Wright, *The first English translation of the 'Decameron'*, Upsala, 1953.

[3] These woodcuts were evidently found so ornamental that they were used for illustration when the work in question had nothing to do with the *Decameron*. My riend C. H. Wilkinson draws my attention to the title-page of Robert Greathead's *The Testament of the Twelve Patriarchs the Sons of Jacob*, 1674, which shows the woodcut at the top on the right of the title-page of the 1620 translation (Part I), and to he title-page of *The Murmurers. A Poem*, 1689, where similarly the woodcut in the middle on the right of the title-page of the 1620 version (Part I) is used.

[4] Probably in the Paris edition of 1578 or 1579.

of adaptation. This applies particularly to drama but also to such a work as *Westward for Smelts*, which likewise appears to have been first published in 1620.[1] This collection of tales is given a framework which, however, has nothing to do with that of the *Decameron*. In fact, it is entirely English in character. It would seem as if the author had kept an eye on the design of *The Cobler of Caunterburie*.[2] Here too a journey along the Thames helps to link the tales together, but an attempt is made to lend some originality to the device by sending the boat up the river, instead of down. The writer describes how a waterman bargains with a company of 'Westerne Fishwiues' who, 'with their heads full of wine, and their purses ful of coine', were homeward bound. They agree to his terms, the boy lays the cushions, and having passed the troublesome places, 'where the Wherries runne to and fro like Weauers shuttles',[3] they reach Lambeth. At this point the waterman, seeing the fishwives begin to nod, sings a song to rouse them, and they afterwards tell a series of tales.

The second of these, related by a woman from Stand on the Greene, obviously has some affinity with the ninth tale of the second day of the *Decameron*. The relationship is so tenuous that at first one is inclined to doubt the existence of any direct contact. However, it has been pointed out[4] that all the other stories in the collection except one are based on Italian 'novelle', and this makes it likely that the author could read Boccaccio's tale of Ambruogiuolo and Bernabò in the original. If the English writer had read the original, he introduced some notable changes, as will appear from the following synopsis:

The events of the story take place during the Wars of the Roses. The wager is laid, not among merchants, but among gentlemen at a London inn, where one of them has come on business from Waltam. The villain proceeds to Waltam and, espying the lady in the fields, kisses her by way of salutation in accordance with the English custom of the day, 'a thing no modest woman can deny'. On the pretext of having a message from her husband, he gains access to the house, feigns illness, secretes himself beneath her bed, and when she and her maid have retired to rest, creeps out, picks up the gold crucifix that she was wont to wear near her heart, steals away and rides off to London next morning. Her husband is convinced of her guilt and in despair joins the army of Henry VI. He sends his servant George to bring her to Enfield where he prepares to kill her, but refrains when her entreaties convince him of her innocence. She disguises herself as a boy and is taken into Edward IV's service as a page. After the king's victory at Barnet she searches the battlefield for her husband. Instead she finds the villain and when tending his wounds sees her crucifix. He gives her the crucifix, saying that his conscience pricks him. Finding her husband

---

[1] It was not registered until 15 January 1620.   [2] Vide ante, pp. 164–5.
[3] Quotations from the copy at Trinity College, Cambridge.
[4] By J. Raith, *Die Historie von den vier Kaufleuten. Die Geschichte von der vertauschten Wiege*, Leipzig, 1936, p. 16.
[5] Cf. Cressida's reception by the Greek leaders, *Troilus and Cressida*, Act IV, Sc. v. See also Erasmus, *Epistolae*, ed. P. S. Allen, Oxford, 1906, i, pp. 238–9.

prisoner, she has him brought to court. There, when confronted with the man whom he has wronged, the villain confesses his crime. The king leaves it to Mistress Dorrill to settle accounts with her husband, and when she has forgiven him, the king sentences the villain to pay treble the amount of the wager and to one year's imprisonment. Husband and wife then return home and, having presented the money to George, live happily ever after.

Such a summary is enough to indicate how notably this tale differs from that of Boccaccio. At the same time it offers some parallels to Shakespeare's *Cymbeline*,[1] but it is quite possible that these are derived from the play rather than the other way round.[2]

Another collection of tales is *The Tincker of Turvey*, published in 1630. It is a modification of *The Cobler of Caunterburie* which by certain alterations seeks to impart an air of novelty. The epistle which acts as preface is somewhat different, though towards the end there is some resemblance to the 'Coblers Epistle'. It opens with 'The Tinkers Song'. Then follow 'The Description of the Tinker' and 'The Tinkers Tale' which tells how a rich country pedlar is cozened by three people and deceives them again. For the rest, the two collections agree, except that after the Scholar's Tale there comes the Seaman's Tale which rounds off the group. Thus the omission of the Old Wive's Tale and the Sumner's Tale involves the sacrifice of Boccaccian material.

2. Individual Tales in Prose and Verse

More stories from the *Decameron* are interwoven in Henrie Stephen's *A World of Wonders* which appeared in 1607.[3] Three are introduced to illustrate 'the wicked wiles, deuised by our wanton wenches and light-skirted huswiues'.[4] Two others have an anti-clerical bent. One of them is the tale of the abbess and the priest,[5] the other that of Fra Cipolla.[6] It may be suspected that the Protestant propagandist also had a hand in the chapter 'Of man-slaughters and murthers committed by the Popish Cleargie'. In the account of the war between the duke of Brabant and the earl of Guelderland for the duchy of Limburg, in the course of which the bishop of Cologne was taken prisoner and committed to the custody of the earl of Mount for the space of seven years, we learn how, when the bishop was released, the earl, who accompanied him as far as Deutz on the Rhine, was ambushed by the

---

[1] Cf. W. F. Thrall, 'Cymbeline, Boccaccio, and the Wager Story in England', ;.P., 1931, xxviii, p. 116, n. 42.

[2] Cf. J. Raith, *Die Historie von den vier Kaufleuten*, p. 16.

[3] This is a translation of *L'Introduction au traité de la conformité des merueilles ancien- aes auec les modernes* by Henri Estienne, 1566.

[4] *Dec.* vii, 3 (Book i, pp. 106–7); vii, 6 (Book i, p. 107); iii, 3 (Book i, p. 110).

[5] *Dec.* ix, 2 (Book i, pp. 180–1).   [6] *Dec.* vi, 10 (Book ii, pp. 350–1).

O

bishop's men and in his turn thrust into prison. Here his treatment bore some similarity to the punishment of Ambruogiuolo,[1] for the bishop caused an iron cage to be made,

which in sommer was annointed ouer: with hony and set in the open Sunne, lodging the poore Earle therein, there to be assaulted by flies (you may well imagine how.)[2]

The same bias is to be observed in one of the tales to which Burton alludes in *The Anatomy of Melancholy*. It occurs in a passage denouncing monks and confessors, because 'under colour of visitation, auricular confession, comfort, and penance, they have free egress and regress, and corrupt God knows how many'. To illustrate his argument, he uses one of the tales cited in *A World of Wonders*.[3] Equally characteristic of this age of fierce religious controversy is Burton's attitude towards the story of the three rings.[4] Instead of concluding from it the need for tolerance, he denounces Boccaccio, along with Giordano Bruno, Machiavelli and Pietro Aretino, as an atheist.[5] However, his interest in the *Decameron* is not confined to the sphere of religious controversy. Thus when he speaks of the transforming power of love and beauty, he deals at length with the early part of the tale of *Cimon and Iphigenia*.[6] Indirectly it is the appreciation of beauty that leads Henry Peacham also to the *Decameron*. In *The Compleat Gentleman*, which was printed the year after the first edition of Burton's work, he mentions various Italian painters. Of these

Buffalmacco was scholar to *Taffi*, and as excellent in his profession, so was he merry and of pleasant conceit: wherefore hee was familiar with *Bruno* and *Calandrino*, rare Artists and of his owne humour, many of whose iestes are recorded by Boccace.[7]

[1] *Dec.* ii, 9 (Book i, p. 198).
[2] Cf. Henri Estienne, op. cit., 1566, Book i, p. 320. See also *The Stage of Popish Toyes*, p. 33.
[3] *Dec.* ix, 2. Cf. *The Anatomy of Melancholy*, ed. A. R. Shilleto, iii, p. 148.
[4] *Dec.* i, 3.
[5] iii, p. 445. The climate of the seventeenth century was not congenial to it. Not until Lessing's *Nathan der Weise* appeared in 1779 was this story used by a great writer to discuss differences of religious faith in a more tolerant spirit. However, a French metrical version was published at Dublin in 1721. 'Les Trois Anneaux', which an entry in pencil in the B.M. copy ascribes to 'René Mace', follows 'Les Trois Justaucorps . . . Tiré de l'Anglois du Révérend Mr. Jonathan Swif' (sic!). Bound up with this Dublin volume is *Recueil de Pieces Serieuses, Comiques, et Burlesques,* 1721 (no place of publication), which also contains the above tale in French, but here (p. 225) it is attributed to 'Monsieur de J . . . S . . .'. Whoever was responsible for the appearance of 'Les Trois Anneaux' in Dublin must have seen a point of contact between Boccaccio and Swift, even though there is no connexion between *A Tale of a Tub* and the story, and the fierce irony of the one differentiates him from the easy-going scepticism of the other.
[6] *Dec.* v, 1. It was apparently known to him through the translation of Beroaldus the Latin form of Beroaldo. (Cf. *The Anatomy of Melancholy*, ed. cit., iii, p. 200. Vide ante, p. 115.   [7] Ch. xii

The satirist too found material in the *Decameron*, as may be seen from *The Knave of Clubbes* (1609) by Samuel Rowlands.[1] One of the portraits that he draws, entitled 'A Cuckold', is derived from the tale of Madonna Isabella, Leonetto and Lambertuccio.[2] Often written in a vigorous, colloquial style, it transforms Boccaccio's figures into contemporary types. Leonetto is the courtier, Lambertuccio the swaggering captain who breathes fire and fury at the very thought of his rival:

> I would make incission in his guts,
> And carue his carcasse full of wounds and cuts.
> (sig. E *recto*)

But this tale in verse sounds a harsher note than the original, as may be seen from the opening line:

> A Citty wanton full of pride and lust.
> (sig. D4 *recto*)

The voice of the satirist is heard again at the close when Rowlands puts words into the mouth of the courtier which, though they are fitting enough, coming as they do from one whose life has been saved by a quick-witted woman, are nevertheless meant to be interpreted ironically, since she has betrayed her husband:

> More louing far in heart then men you be,
> Extending your affections bounteous, free,
> Most affable and pittifull by nature,
> The worlds euen supreame all excelling creature,
> Fond men vniustly doe abuse your names,
> With slandrous speeches and most false defames,
> They lye, and raile, and enuies poyson spit,
> But those are mad-men that doe offer it,
> They that inioy their wit and perfect sence,
> Wil hate the hart should breed a thoughts offence
> Accounting it a womans greater honor,
> To haue a senceles foole exclaime vpon her.
> (sig. E2 *recto*)

Characteristic though this tale is of the interest in shrewd wantons who beguile their husbands, and popular though this story and others like it were in seventeenth-century drama, there was not lacking an occasional appreciation of the nobler qualities of human nature. It is perhaps not without significance that in 1683 William Winstanley revived Elyot's version of Titus and Gisippus in an abridged and

---

[1] First printed as *Tis Merry when Knaves Meet*, of which no copy seems to be extant. *The Knave of Clubbes* was first printed in 1609; other editions followed. Quotations are from the B.M. copy which, according to *S.T.C.*, is to be dated [1611] but, according to B.M. Catalogue [1615?].

[2] *Dec.* vii, 6. Cf. *A World of Wonders*.

modernised form,[1] and in 1694 Walter Pope included among his *Select Novels* the tale of Patient Grissell,[2] just at a time when the drama was swinging away from tales of amorous intrigue to themes of pathos and sentiment.

3. The Drama

(a) *Tragedy*

The story of Guiscardo and Ghismonda still continued to appeal to dramatists in the seventeenth century. Among these was William Percy, a contemporary of Sir Henry Wotton at Oxford. In 1602 he wrote *A Forrest Tragaedye in Vacunium* which, like his other plays, seems to have been intended for amateur performance in the household of his brother, the earl of Northumberland, though his directions prove that he wrote it with an eye on the boy actors, the Children of Paul's.[3]

The opening is derived from *Il Sacrificio*, which was produced in 1531 at Siena and derived its name from the sacrifice to Cupid of sonnets written by the Academy of the Intronati. However, in view of the tragic nature of his theme, Percy introduces famous tragic lovers whose sorrowful end is related. These lovers appear again at the close of each act, and in two choruses each lover declaims a few lines on the power of love, on his or her own fate, or a comment on the play. Considerable use is made of music, the waits playing when these ancient lovers cross the stage, and the 'consort' accompanying the chorus when they are speaking.[4]

There are points of contact with *Gismond of Salern*, by Wilmot and his friends, as is shown by the careful analysis of the play,[5] and no student of Boccaccio has any difficulty in recognising the source of inspiration when in Act II, Sc. i the heroine Fulvia confides to her black attendant Rhodaghond that she has arranged for her lover Affranio to come to her:

> There stands abutting to our Castell wall
> A hidden vault with bushes ouergrown
> That they do couer the whole Mouth of him,
> whereto abutting, at our chamber foote,
> standeth a doore by reason of his site,
> These many yeares, worne out of memory.[6]

---

[1] Cf. Wilkinson, p. xviii, n. 4. It was also printed in Winstanley's *Historical Rarities and curious Observations Domestick & Foreign*, London, 1684, pp. 273–87.

[2] It came to him, however, through Petrarch's later version of Boccaccio's tale.

[3] An account of the plot was first given by H. N. Hillebrand, *H.L.Q.*, 1938, I, no. 4. p. 409. A detailed study of the play, its sources and literary qualities was made by M. H. Dodds, 'A Forrest Tragaedye in Vacunium', *M.L.R.*, 1945, xl, pp. 246–58.

[4] Cf. M. H. Dodds, loc. cit., p. 248.   [5] Ibid., p. 250

[6] Quotations are from the manuscript in the Henry E. Huntington Library.

In Act III, Sc. 2 Fulvia welcomes Affranio, and their conversation leaves no doubt regarding the intimacy of their relations. However, an observer, Tremellio, is present, concealed in much the same way as Tancred, and after the departure of the lovers, he starts up furiously and vows revenge. In the final scene Fulvia looks forward to being reunited with Affranio, even as Ghismonda rejoices at the prospect of her soul encountering that of Guiscardo after death.

However, there are some notable features in the main plot that have been overlooked. In the *Decameron* there were two stories that were rich in Senecan material, though that of Guiscardo and Ghismonda contains more significant dramatic potentialities. In each case savage revenge is inflicted for a wrong done, by tearing out the heart of the offender. Tancred places the heart, still whole, in a golden cup which his servant presents to Ghismonda. In the other story, that of Rossig-glione and Guardastagno,[1] the former bids his cook take the heart which he declares to be that of a boar but is actually that of Guardas-tagno and serve it that evening. The heart is minced, and the wife of Rossiglione eats it in a way that is not unfamiliar to readers of Seneca's *Thyestes*. It occurred to Percy that he might unite the two stories to form the main plot of his tragedy.

His heroine is not a widow like Ghismonda, nor is she a princess. Consequently, all the arguments by which Ghismonda justifies her conduct to Tancred are eliminated at one stroke. No question of dis-parity of rank arises, for even if Fulvia is the daughter of a marquis, Affranio is of noble birth and owns a castle adjacent to that of Tremellio. The conflict therefore springs, not from filial disobedience but from the disloyalty of a wife and the violation of friendship. The opening scene emphasises the cordiality of this relationship between the two neighbours, for Tremellio entreats Affranio to stay on and spend the time in hunting. It is the treachery of his friend that rankles so with Tremellio, as we perceive from his cry:

> ne're so foule a Fact from freind to freind,
> Neuer so vile an Act from Man to Man,
>
> .   .   .   .   .
>
> was this a Recompense for that deare loue
> which I haue borne thee from thyne Infancye!
> (III. ii)

As soon as he has made the discovery, he gallops away after Affranio and, like Rossiglione, lies in ambush, though unlike him, without attendants. He leaps out, kills him, and cuts out the heart with his hunting-knife. It is now that we perceive the full import of Percy's description of Tremellio among the dramatis personae as 'A Knight

---

[1] *Dec.* iv, 9. Vide ante, pp. 151–2.

apparrelld in greene and with wood knif', the array in which he appears in the first scene. The forest is the background which dominates Percy's mind, as the title of the play *A Forrest Tragaedye in Vacunium* discloses.

The two Boccaccian stories join again in Act V, Sc. v, though Percy introduces some modifications. He would have none of the gruesome meal that Rossiglione offered his wife. Instead, Tremellio gives her the choice between killing herself with his knife that so recently has slain Affranio or of drinking the wine from a cup of gold into which the powdered heart of Affranio has been poured. She rejects the second alternative and, taking the knife, stabs Tremellio to death; then, squeezing a poisoned citron into the cup, she drains it and dies, unrepentant, crying:

> I come, Affranio, Affranio, I come
> And with this drink I drinke my soule unto thee.

The only other characters present, Rhodaghond and Jeptes, follow her example and die.

These two figures form part of the sub-plot invented by Percy. The hero is Amadour, a Frenchman, the heroine Florimel, the daughter of Fulvia. She has a second suitor, Clodio, an Italian, but she prefers Amadour. Jeptes is her tutor, and when Clodio discovers that Amadour is his rival, he obtains from Jeptes a poisoned citron which he presents with many professions of friendship to Amadour. When Amadour has been secretly married to Florimel, in all innocence he satisfies her desire for fruit by giving her the citron. She is taken ill and Amadour now realises that it was his life that was aimed at. When Clodio enters, Amadour runs him through with his rapier. Florimel expires and Amadour dies of grief. Jeptes is filled with remorse for his share in these events, and so it is appropriate that he should take poison at the close. If Rhodaghond does the same, it is because, when her mistress in a gust of anger struck her in the presence of her lover Jeptes, she betrayed Fulvia by calling Tremellio back from the hunt and thus exposed the lovers. So she also expiates her treachery by means of the poisoned cup.

No doubt the episode of the poisoned citron was suggested by an incident that occurred in France three years before the play was written, when Gabrielle d'Estrées, the principal mistress of Henry IV, whom the king wished to marry, was poisoned by a lemon.[1] Apart from this topical interest, however, the sub-plot serves a useful purpose by amplifying the rather slender material of the main plot and by delaying the catastrophe. Despite its final tragic nature, at intervals an element of light relief is provided, and Percy shows some ability

[1] Cf. M. H. Dodds, loc. cit., p. 253.

in creating dramatic contrast. Nevertheless, the play as a whole has but few æsthetic qualities, so that *A Forrest Tragaedye in Vacunium* is chiefly remarkable as an example of the interweaving of two tales from the *Decameron* with a sub-plot to illustrate the force of Jeptes' question to Fulvia:

> Think you Blood shall not be requit with blood?

The theme of Guiscardo and Ghismonda was again embodied in dramatic form by an anonymous writer whose work is contained in Add. MS. 34312 in the British Museum. The play bears no title but has for convenience' sake been called *Ghismonda*[1] after the heroine. The manuscript is undated, but the text shows clear traces of the translation of the *Decameron* that first appeared in 1620. Another clue is provided by the description of one of the characters as 'a chrono-masticall courtier'. The word 'Chronomastix' was employed by George Wither in *Britain's Remembrancer* in 1628[2] but had already become known to the public through Ben Jonson's *Time Vindicated* which was printed in 1623. One may therefore conclude that *Ghismonda* must be later than 1620 and perhaps after 1628.[3] A note to the epilogue states 'Scriptum p Capellanum tuum deuinct- & deuotissimum'. Since the MS. was at one time in the possession of the Dolben family and since David Dolben was bishop of Bangor from 1631 to 1633, it is possible that the play was written by him and transcribed by his chaplain Hugh Williams, or that it was the work of Hugh Williams himself. At any rate, the author was a man of learning and interested in religious matters, for he touches on purgatory and papal infallibility, on confession and absolution, martyrdom and canonization; and the problem of the conditions under which a vow is binding, no less than the advice of a spiritual director, came within the scope of his consideration.

Like Wilmot and his friends, the author of *Ghismonda* deals at length with the widowhood of the heroine. From the beginning he tries to depict her as fundamentally serious. Accordingly she feels such intense grief at the death of her husband that she vows never to marry again. This is a cause of anxiety to Tancred. He is therefore happy to entertain a proposal from the duke of Capua that his son Felix shall marry her, for in this way he hopes to dispel her unhappiness. However, by this time she has become attracted to Guiscardo, and when it seems likely that he will be sent on a mission to Capua, she gives him a hint of her affection. When Guiscardo has received the king's orders,

---

[1] *Ghismonda*, ed. H. G. Wright, Manchester, 1944.
[2] Attention was drawn to this by N. Orsini, *Studii sul rinascimento italiano in Inghilterra*, Florence, 1937, p. 62.
[3] The suggestion that it may be as late as 1665 (cf. *Ghismonda*, Introduction, p. 2) I now consider unlikely (cf. *R.E.S.*, 1947, xxiii, p. 358).

Ghismonda resolves to declare her love. To do this she uses the device of the letter in the cane, but displays more awkwardness than skill in the process. On reading the invitation to visit her that night through a 'vent-loope', concealed by briars beneath the window, Guiscardo tells the king's messenger that he cannot go until the spring. It is this strange answer, not mere chance, that arouses Tancred's suspicion. On information given by one of his courtiers about a stray remark that he had heard Ghismonda make to Guiscardo, he proceeds to her room. Concealing himself, he falls asleep. He awakens to see Guiscardo kissing the princess and, unlike his prototype, lets his anger get the better of him. He shoots at them with his pistol and when he misses, rushes towards them with his sword, only to stumble and fall. He ignores Ghismonda's protestations that no serious offence has been committed. Guiscardo is arrested and beheaded on the stage; the executioner makes his exit with the body in order to remove the heart.

The scene in which the cup of gold is handed to Ghismonda echoes the words of the corresponding passage in the English translation of 1620. But there are some innovations. She sends a request by a courtier that she may be buried with Guiscardo, a superfluous addition, because she herself later begs her father to grant this favour. She does not fill the golden cup with her tears and, on the other hand, in the cabinet containing the poison she discovers a letter from Guiscardo that inspires her eulogy of his virtues. More important, before clasping the heart to her bosom, she wraps it in her veil, the black hue of which symbolises her grief, and its white lining Guiscardo's nobility.

The death scene lacks the tranquil dignity and awe-inspiring solemnity of the original, for the waiting-woman shrieks and Ghismonda cries and groans as she lies in the throes of death. Tancred utters futile expressions of remorse which he carries to such a pitch that he declares not only Ghismonda, but also Guiscardo to be a martyr.

Ghismonda's eloquent speech, in which she defends her conduct and justifies her choice of Guiscardo in the tale, for various reasons finds no place here. The excision of this central feature reduces the dramatist's material considerably, and he has to find means of eking it out. As the princess does not give the letter to Guiscardo until Act IV and as the lovers are not discovered until Act V, the problem arises how to fill in the first three acts. Much attention is paid to Ghismonda's state of mind. She has no one in whom she can confide, for Mistress Minks, her waiting-woman, moves on a different plane from her virtuous mistress. They are as far apart as Juliet and her Nurse. However, from discussions between Tancred and his courtiers, Guiscardo, Gabriello, Pasquino and Glausamond, we learn much about Ghismonda's attitude. Guiscardo and Glausamond are sent to comfort the

disconsolate widow, and a considerable part of the second act is taken
up with their visit. Most of the third act is devoted to the proposal
brought by the Capuan ambassador, to comment on Ghismonda's
reaction and to the solemn conclave of Tancred and his councillors
which ends with the decision that Guiscardo shall depart as an envoy
to Capua.

However, the dramatist needed still more material and so he introduced an under-plot. This relates to a dispute that breaks out between
Pasquino and Gabriello when the former steals out of the tavern where
they have been drinking and leaves Gabriello to pay the bill. This
practical joke which gives rise to a controversy that recurs at intervals
was intended to provide some slight relief from the serious main plot.
It also served to illustrate the general unscrupulousness of the courtiers,
among whom by contrast Guiscardo stands forth pre-eminent, even
as Ghismonda shines by the side of the venal and corrupt Mistress
Minks.

The incidental criticism of court life is another feature of the play.
Tancred himself censures it, and Pasquino is the embodiment of the
ambition that exults over the downfall of a fellow-courtier. Nothing
could be more callous than his words to Guiscardo when the executioner bears in the scaffold:

> Here's the place you'r like to leaue your head at.[1]
> (Act V)

But the most interesting of the subordinate figures about the court is
Glausamond. He is a cynic, with no high opinion of his fellow-mortals
of either sex. The perfect courtier, he makes it his chief object to
please his master, for

> None can thriue now without a brazen face.[2]
> (Act I)

He loves to talk in cryptic phrases, conveying his meaning by hints
and veiled allusions, because he knows the danger of open speech in a
court. The age is such that a measure of dissimulation is essential:

> The dayes we liue in
> Are now preposterous grown, the time come agayne,
> When 'twas a grace to lie, sin to speake playne.
> Tell a man of his faultes, because you loue him,
> You lose him quite, therby so moue him
> To anger and impatience that hee'le greeue
> To se you in his sight and not beleeue
> What your good wishes told him. Comend a gull,
> Whose father di'd but lately, leaueing him full

---

[1] Wright's ed., p. 177.   [2] Ibid., p. 125

Of that which drawes attendanc, and 't is great odds
Hee'le prize you as the heathens did there gods,
Call you his genius, thanke your kind wordes to him,
Although by these faire speaches you vndoe him.
If you'r toe conscientious to lie,
You must goe liue alone, for company
You're like to haue but little.[1]

(Act II)

The fact that despite his cynicism Glausamond risks his own interests
by pleading with the raging Tancred on behalf of the lovers makes him
an attractive figure, but it does not imply that his satirical comment on
his period was insincere or unwarranted.

In portraying the chief figures of Boccaccio's tale the dramatist
had less freedom than in creating an entirely new figure like Glausamond, but he contrives to manipulate them in an original way. To
Guiscardo he allots a more important part than any other writer had
done previously. As in various plays, English and Italian, Guiscardo
rises in the social scale. Here he is a peer of the realm and a member
of the king's council as well as Ghismonda's gentleman-in-waiting.
He enjoys the confidence of Tancred who praises his honesty and trustworthiness, and at the beginning he is loyal enough to the king. But
when Ghismonda bestows upon him unmistakable signs of her favour,
his sense of duty to his sovereign weakens. Indeed, he goes so far as
to shun the mission as Tancred's envoy to Capua in order that he may
be near Ghismonda. It is only when disaster has overtaken him that
he stands forth in his full strength and nobility. Now there is no
dilemma, and his way is clear. His chief concern is that the honour of
the princess may be unstained, and he begs that if any one is to be
punished, it shall be himself. He faces execution bravely, protesting his
innocence to the last.

In spite of the tyrannical role that Boccaccio had assigned to the
king, the dramatist treats him with considerable sympathy. He is
shown as the victim of his office. Hedged round with courtly deference,
he lives in isolation and finds it difficult to ascertain the truth. Even
his daughter is an enigma. He is genuinely anxious for her welfare,
and unlike his prototype is by no means a possessive father. It is his
desire to remove her melancholy that leads him to approve her
marriage to Felix of Capua, and every step that he takes in the matter
is carefully weighed. The same sense of responsibility appears when
suspicion falls on Guiscardo. He refrains from precipitate action, and
it is only when he has seen the lovers kissing and embracing that he
loses his self-control. It has to be remembered, however, that Guiscardo
had been his right-hand man, so that his conduct seemed doubly

[1] Wright's ed., pp. 133-4.

traitorous to the king. Momentarily Tancred hesitates when Glausamond demonstrates the flimsy nature of the evidence, but in the end he resolves to put Guiscardo to death, for even if he were innocent, his audacity might have led him to aspire to the throne. The king therefore proceeds on his course, undeterred by Ghismonda's threat of suicide which he does not take seriously. Yet even now he is not devoid of magnanimity and orders for Guiscardo the death of a nobleman, not of a felon, and at the close his natural generosity reasserts itself. Full of remorse, he commands that the lovers shall be interred together:

> Such martirs neuer were before;
> No story doth record where such a paire
> Did die so good, so inocent, so faire.[1]
>
> (Act V)

Though Boccaccio recognised that fate had dealt harshly with the lovers, he could never have subscribed to such an ending. But his tale had been transformed in the English translation of 1620, so that the relationship of Guiscardo and Ghismonda never went further than the exchange of chaste and modest kisses. Taking his cue from this passage, the dramatist portrays Ghismonda as a model of chastity who leaves an impression of unblemished purity, not only on Tancred and Guiscardo, but also on the cynical Glausamond and the unprincipled Pasquino. Consequently, he is able to show the love scene on the stage. It is a harmless affair in which Guiscardo sings a song commending Ghismonda's virtues.

Not content with this, the play seeks to convince the spectator of her saintliness. This emerges clearly when Guiscardo describes her discourse with him about her oath never to marry again. He speaks of her with veneration, as if she were something holy:

> She stopt, and, as it weare a saynt that thought
> The aire was too corrupt to entertayne
> The breath her voice expel'd, forthwith she sayd:
> 'Heauen shall resolue this scruple, and repentance
> Make this spott white by dayly exercise'.[2]
>
> (Act I)

However, even with the alterations made in Boccaccio's tale, this saintliness is difficult to maintain. Ghismonda never lacks a certain earthly shrewdness. Even amid her mourning for her husband, she introduces a qualification in her oath never to marry again which enables her to escape from the vow if she finds another as good as the first. Again in the use of the cane there is an element of astute calculation; her encouragement of Guiscardo to disobey Tancred and her arrangement of the rendezvous are the actions of a fallible mortal,

---

[1] Wright's ed., p. 184. [2] Ibid., p. 121.

and the archness, not to say slyness, of her manner during the interview does not suggest holiness.

More in keeping with the spirit of her Italian prototype is the heroic courage of Ghismonda in the latter part of the play. She does not flinch from death but, confronting Tancred, boldly declares:

> though I haue a body feminine,
> I'le shew a spirit that is masculine.
>
> .   .   .   .   .
>
> I'm but a woman, yet made of the mould
> That Cesar was.[1]
>
> (Act V)

Hearing this, Tancred confesses that she talks 'like an emperor', and Glausamond admires her as an 'heroick wench'. Even if Ghismonda is only a partial success, it is interesting to see also how the dramatist evokes from Boccaccio's story those heroic qualities that Dryden also was to elicit in 'Sigismonda and Guiscardo'.[2]

The author of *Ghismonda* discards the apparatus of classical tragedy, and there is no clear indication that he was acquainted with Italian plays on this theme. On the whole his work appears to be in the popular English tradition, though it has various traits which suggest that it was unlikely to be acceptable in the ordinary theatre. It has some original ideas but its poetic merit is slight.

The Atheist's Tragedie (1611) by Cyril Tourneur, which is a tragedy of a very different order, also drew on the *Decameron*.[3] Here truly is a world of utter villainy, cunning exulting in its triumph over innocence, and perfidy rejoicing in the power of its subtle contriver. Horror is piled upon horror—ghostly visitations, murder to the uncanny accompaniment of the howling dog and the screeching owl, and nocturnal intrigues in a churchyard with skulls as a pillow for a pair of lovers. The forces of evil appear omnipotent until vengeance is inflicted on the villain, not by one of his victims but by himself.

It might be thought that Boccaccio's light-hearted tale of gallantry would be singularly out of place in such surroundings, and indeed in its original form it could hardly have been made an integral part of a play so dark and menacing. Yet Tourneur manages to do this. However, he limits it to a sub-plot, a minor episode, and at the same time lends to it a different quality.

This under-plot is derived from the sixth tale of the seventh day, which relates how Isabella, being dissatisfied with her husband, turns

---

[1] Wright's ed., p. 173.   [2] Vide post, p. 270.

[3] Cf. G. Langbaine, *The Lives and Characters of the English Dramatick Poets*, 1698, p. 505, and E. Koeppel, *Quellen-Studien zu den Dramen Ben Jonson's, John Marston's und Beaumont's und Fletcher's* (Münchener Beiträge, Heft xi), Erlangen and Leipzig 1895, p. 138.

her affection towards Leonetto, but is at the same time harassed by the attentions of Lambertuccio. One day during the absence of her husband she receives Leonetto, but he has barely arrived when Lambertuccio appears on the scene. Isabella's embarrassment is heightened by the return of her husband. The device by which she extricated herself from this dilemma is an example of the ingenuity displayed by women in the tales of this day. Her counterpart in the play, Levidulcia, the wife of Belforest, is the very embodiment of lust. She encourages a mere servant in the most brazen fashion and has just persuaded the reluctant Fresco, when he has to hide behind the arras, because Sebastian, the younger son of the villain D'Amville, appears at the door. Sebastian is coarse and virile, a man whose bluntness matches her own shamelessness. They are interrupted by Belforest. Like Lambertuccio, Sebastian draws his sword and feigns to have pursued Fresco. After he has gone, Fresco emerges, invents a long story of which there is nothing in the *Decameron*, and departs. But the play cannot allow this theme to end gaily. Levidulcia and Sebastian are resolute in the pursuit of their passion. They are surprised once more by Belforest. In the ensuing struggle both men are slain, and Levidulcia, suddenly, perhaps too suddenly, overcome with remorse, stabs herself. The lasciviousness of Sebastian and Levidulcia is clearly intended as a contrast to the nobility of Charlemont and the purity of Castabella. At the same time they offer a parallel to the malevolence of D'Amville. In a different sphere and on a lower level the scheming and treachery of Levidulcia match his, and even as retribution overtakes D'Amville when he dies by his own hand, so justice is done when she commits suicide. In this way Boccaccio's story was assimilated to the sombre background of English revenge tragedy.

A tale from the *Decameron* is again used in the under-plot of Thomas Southerne's *The Fatall Marriage* which was first produced and printed in 1694. The main plot deals with the intrigue of Carlos, the younger son of Count Baldwin, against his elder brother Biron who, having married Isabella against the wishes of his father, has incurred his displeasure, and after his departure for the wars is generally believed to have fallen in battle. Carlos is aware that Biron is alive but a slave, yet for his own ends he keeps the news from the count. After years of mourning, Isabella, faced with poverty and distress for herself and her child, agrees to wed the devoted Villeroy. Immediately after the marriage Biron returns and is killed by Carlos and his men. Isabella, torn by conflicting emotions, goes mad and kills herself. Even if these events now appear somewhat theatrical, they have considerable power.

It was the serious plot in which Southerne was chiefly interested, and he wrote it with an eye on Mrs. Barry, who took the part of

Isabella. But he added 'a little taste of comedy', as he himself declared, to satisfy 'the present humour of the town'. One of the elements in this comic plot is derived from the eighth story in the third day of the *Decameron*. As Boccaccio told it, this had an anti-clerical bias, since it showed how an abbot in the pursuit of his designs against the wife of the jealous Ferondo, drugged the latter, and had him buried in a tomb of the monastery, where he was flogged periodically for ten months and induced to believe that he was in purgatory. In the end, he was drugged once more, revived and allowed to return home, cured of his jealousy. The theme of the jealous husband was popular in seventeenth-century drama, but Southerne modified the part of the abbot and at the same time moralised the plot. Fernando, as he calls the husband, is on bad terms with his wife, his daughter Victoria and his son Fabian. It is the last of these, who is supposed to have turned religious, that leads the intrigue against Fernando. The abbot and the friars know what is afoot and countenance Fabian's scheme by allowing him to wear the habit of their order, but they are not active participants. Fabian drugs his father at the wedding feast of Villeroy and Isabella and carries him off to a tomb in the burying-place in the monastery, where he receives a sound thrashing, and as he himself afterwards related:

I thought I was alive in Purgatory; and stood in't a good while; but there's no contending with the Devil in his own Dominions you know; I was forc't to confess my self, at last, as dead as a Herring.

(IV. i)

He regains consciousness and emerges from the tomb, just as the procession of supposed mourners is passing by. His joy and bewilderment at finding himself in the land of the living are well depicted. In fact, he is so glad to be alive that he will consent to anything that his family desires and renounces all his former suspicions.

The under-plot is meant to provide comic relief, the tomb episode occurring between the wedding of Villeroy and Isabella and the return of Biron which leads to the tragic ending. Thus the comic burial of Fernando is not without an ironic effect, since it is so soon followed by a series of disasters that culminate in the death of Villeroy, Biron and Isabella. To that extent it can be defended, but when Garrick revived the play in 1757, he omitted Fernando, Fabian and Victoria and rejected the comic scenes which seemed to him indelicate and immoral. The play was recast according to the sentimental bent of the age.

(b) Comedy

Just as a favourite theme of the sixteenth century, the story of Guiscardo and Ghismonda, was revived in the seventeenth for the purpose
of tragedy, so the well-known tale of Griselda found its way into the
comedy of the period. 'The Plaie of Patient Grissell' was entered in
the Stationers' Register on 28 March 1600 and was in all likelihood
produced in February or March of that year, though not printed till
1603.[1] Even if it resembles Chaucer's *Clerk's Tale* in some respects,
it diverges in others, so that it is impossible to say in what form the
last tale of the *Decameron* was known to the collaborating dramatists,
Chettle, Haughton and Dekker.

The tale is of the romantic kind that appealed to the Elizabethan
audience, and the wooing of a beautiful peasant girl by a marquis who
afterwards married her, had something in common with the wooing
of fair Margaret, the daughter of the keeper of Fressingfield, by Lacy,
earl of Lincoln, in Greene's *Frier Bacon and Frier Bongay*. Like
Grissill, Margaret underwent an ordeal before her happiness was
obtained. It is true, that was before she went to court and it was a trifle
compared with the trials of Grissill; but in a general way one can see
why the dramatists turned to this subject. However, in one sense the
unshakable devotion of a heroine that inspired unending patience did
not offer promising dramatic material, since her reaction can almost
be predicted when she has to face a new sorrow. Though this weakness
is inherent, the dramatists try to avoid monotony by inventing trials
for Grissill. The marquis compels her to pick up his glove and to
kneel down and tie the shoes of his faithful servant Furio. She has
to serve his courtiers, Mario and Lepido, with wine, bowing to them
as she does so, and just before she is restored to happiness, she is
obliged to carry a heavy load of wood into the castle.

An attempt is made to humanise the marquis. By asides, confidential
conversations and by his appearance in disguise, which, of course,
according to the convention of the Elizabethan stage, is impenetrable,
we learn how ardently he loves both Grissill and his children and how
he himself suffers, so that at times he is on the point of abandoning
his plan. But even if the play does something to make him more
pleasing, his cruelty is not explained, any more than in the tale, and
appears to spring from an unaccountable caprice.

A whole series of characters is used to comment on his strange
conduct. Furio carries out his orders faithfully, even though his heart

[1] Chambers, iii, p. 292. The play was edited for the Shakespeare Society, 1841, by
J. P. Collier, and in the *Dramatic Works of Thomas Dekker*, ed. Fredson Bowers,
Cambridge, 1953, vol. i. Quotations and line references are based on this latest
edition.

bleeds. But when he has to part the mother from her children, his assumed harshness is discarded and he yields to her entreaties to be allowed to feed them, saying 'I would I were rid of my miserie, for I shall drowne my heart, with my teares that fall inward'.[1] Grissill's father is as patient as Grissill herself. He acquiesces, for he feels bound to obey his lord in all things, but near the end, when the marquis asks whether he is happy, the old peasant replies:

> Who can be glad when he indureth wrong?
> (v. ii. 102)

His son Laureo, a figure unknown to Boccaccio, is less submissive. A scholar who has spent nine years at the university and has achieved nothing, he is dissatisfied with the world at large:

> Oh I am mad,
> To thinke how much a Scholler vndergoes,
> And in th'ende reapes naught but pennurie.
> (i. ii. 141–3)

He therefore protests against the whims of the marquis and does not hesitate to speak of his tyranny. He sits reading and brooding over his wrongs and finally, in the presence of the marquis himself, throws down the wood that he has been carrying on his back and declares:

> I haue cast downe my burthen not my loade,
> The loade of your grosse wrongs lyes heere like leade.
> (v. ii. 63–4)

Yet despite the indignation at injustice which here bursts forth, there is nowhere in the play a revolt against the existing order. From the beginning, Janicola's servant Babulo had seen in the marriage a violation of the norm which could not endure. He says 'beggers are fit for beggers, gētlefolkes for gētlefolkes: I am afraid yͭ this wŏder of yͤ rich louing yͤ poor, wil last but nine daies'. And Janicola maintains that 'bond-men must serue' and 'Great men are gods, and they haue power ore us'. Even Laureo apologises to the marquis in the end:

> Pardon me my gratious Lord, for now I see,
> That Schollers with weake eyes, pore on their bookes,
> But want true soules to iudge on Maiestie:
> None else but Kings can know the hearts of Kings,
> Hence foorth my pride shall fly with humbler wings.
> (v. ii. 214–18)

Nevertheless, the effect of the criticism of the subordinate figures is to suggest that the marquis has inflicted a grievous wrong, as he himself openly confesses. Only two characters support him throughout, Mario and Lepido, the pliant courtiers. They are mere time-servers

[1] iv. i. 139–40.

who are satirically presented and fittingly punished by their dismissal from court.

The dramatists make the serious plot attractive by turning Janiculo and his household into Elizabethan workmen. They are basket-makers, and when the marquis, disguised as a member of this craft, declares that he will resist the forcible separation of the children from their mother, Babulo exclaims 'Oh rare, cry prentises and clubs', a call known to every Londoner. The early morning scene in Janicola's cottage with its air of brisk and cheerful industry is strongly reminiscent of the similar scene in *The Shoemaker's Holiday*. Just as Eyre wakes up and sets to work the womenfolk and the journeymen, so Janicola rouses Grissill and Babulo. The last of these is closely related to Firk and Hodge, and Eyre's cry 'haste to work' is echoed by Janicola's: 'lets faster worke: time apace weares'. The theme is taken up again in the charming lyric 'Art thou poore yet hast thou golden Slumbers' with its chorus:

> Worke apace, apace, apace, apace:
> Honest labour beares a louely face,
> Then hey noney, noney: hey noney, noney.
> (i. ii. 101–3)

Another aspect of this humble life is shown in the scene where we see Grissill seated, while Ianicola to the accompaniment of Laureo's lute sings the lullaby 'Golden slumbers kisse your eyes', as he rocks the cradle made by Babulo.

The dramatists felt that they needed something more than these poetic glimpses of workaday life to offset the painful episodes of the main plot. In various ways they provide humour to lighten the spectacle of Grissill's sorrows. Even Furio, who is an intensely serious figure, raises a laugh when he is saddled with Grissill's two infants and laments his inexperience in handling children. More important is Babulo, whose function is often that of a clown, jesting and criticising under the cover of his wit. In addition there is a gull, the foppish Signor Emulo, who is described thus:

one of those changeable Silke gallants, who in a verie scuruie pride, scorne al schollers, and reade no bookes but a looking glasse, and speake no language but sweet Lady, and sweet *Signior* and chew between their teeth terrible words, as though they would coniure, as complement and Proiects, and Fastidious, and Caprichious, and Misprizian, and the Sintheresis, of the soule, and such like raise veluet tearmes.
> (ii. i. 54–60)

Emulo in person shows his fondness for grandiloquent language and magnificent attire in his account of a duel that he fought. When he finds himself unappreciated, he resolves to leave Italy for ever, but

P

his condemnation is rejected by Farneze, who exclaims in defence of his native land:

away you ideot: *Italy* infects you not, but your owne diseased spirits: *Italy*? out you froth, you scumme, because your soule is mud, and that you haue breathed in *Italy*, you'll say *Italy* haue defyled you: away you bore, thou wilt wallow in mire in the sweetest countrie in the world.

(III. ii. 92–6)

Thus the gallant, the butt of so much contemporary ridicule, is made an object of satirical contempt. Far more genial is the presentation of his opponent in the duel, Sir Owen ap Meredith, who has strayed into the domains of the marquis of Saluzo. He woos and marries a widow called Gwenthyan[1] who is a cousin to the duke, her first husband having brought her from Wales. Both she and Sir Owen talk broken English, which seems all the more impossible because Rice or Rees, Sir Owen's servant, who is obviously meant to be a Welshman, speaks English quite normally. However, the Elizabethan spectator was not likely to cavil at such an anomaly and was evidently as well pleased as with the Anglo-Dutch jargon of Hans in *The Shoemaker's Holiday*. Among themselves Sir Owen and Gwenthyan often talk Welsh, and in spite of the distorted form in which it appears in the printed version, it is obvious that Dekker, or whichever of the other two collaborators was responsible for this part of the play, had derived it from a pure Welsh source. This use of dialogue in a foreign tongue may be compared to some extent with that of French by Catherine when she is wooed by Henry V. But the effect in *Patient Grissill* acquires additional piquancy from the altercations between Sir Owen and Gwenthyan, for she is even more hot-tempered than himself, and valiant though he is, he cannot control her. He complains that her tongue goes jingle-jangle, better and worse than bells when the house is on fire, and that she chides and brawls and scolds and scratches terribly, so that he feels inclined to take to his heels and run to Wales. As he himself sadly admits:

> Sir *Owen ap Meredith* can rightly tell,
> A shrewes sharpe tongue is terrible as hell.

(III. ii. 278–9)

One of the liveliest scenes in the play is that which depicts her revenge on her husband[2] when in an attempt to assert his authority he tears her superb and expensive new ruff. Knowing that Sir Owen has invited the marquis and his attendants to dine at his house, she calls in the beggars to partake of the food and drink and, arrayed in the rags of a beggar, receives Sir Owen and his guests. Everything has been devoured, and the kitchen, strewn with the fragments of the

---

[1] Obviously a corruption of the Welsh name 'Gwenllian'.   [2] Act IV, Sc. ii

repast, looks 'like the end of some terrible battle'. But 'the best sport is to see the scullians, some laughing, some crying, and whilst they wipe their eies they blacke their faces', the cooks cursing their lady and some praying for their lord. The relations of Sir Owen and Gwenthyan are the counterpart of those between the marquis and Grissill, but the roles are reversed. It is Sir Owen who has to undergo a series of trials until at the close Gwenthyan adopts a conciliatory tone, at the same time warning him not to be too proud and triumphant!

The sub-plot has an important function. Its episodes, interposed between the painful, even heart-rending scenes of the main plot, afford relief and also help to create the illusion of passing time which is necessary for the story of Grissill. The married life of Sir Owen and Gwenthyan is like a commentary in dramatic form on Chaucer's warning:

No wedded man so hardy be tassaille
His wyves pacience, in hope to finde
Grisildes, for in certein he shall faille![1]
(E 1180–2)

The portrayal of these two Welsh people is a caricature, but it is good-natured. Indeed, Sir Owen, brave, quick-tempered and patriotic—
'By Cod *Wales* is better countrie then *Italies*, a great teale so better'
—is akin to Fluellen, and it is significant of his popularity that the last words of the play are placed in his mouth, as he expresses the hope that if the audience love Gwenthyan, they will love him as he loves them too, and so with a Welsh greeting he bids them good-night. The intrusion of these characters into the old tale might well have seemed strange to Boccaccio, but the medley was deliberately calculated by dramatists who understood the art of satisfying their patrons in the Elizabethan theatre.

The marriage of a noble to one of lower rank is the central theme of the story of Beltramo and Giletta, the ninth tale of the third day in the *Decameron*, which constitutes the main plot of Shakespeare's *All's Well that Ends Well*. The original story is one of highly romantic love, on to which is grafted the problem of the relative value of noble descent and personal merit. This topic is of such widespread interest that it is worth while considering the background before examining the play in detail. The question had been discussed by the ancients and from them had been handed on to Boethius, Dante and Chaucer. The development of humanism in Italy and the growth of the mer-chant class, not least in Florence, created a lively preoccupation with the subject.[2] Boccaccio, perhaps actuated to some extent by personal impulses, was by no means indifferent to it, and in the fifteenth

---

[1] Skeat's text.
[2] Jacob Burckhardt, *Die Cultur der Renaissance in Italien*, Basle, 1860, pp. 355–65.

century it was frequently debated, one of the best known contributions being the *Controversia de Nobilitate* of Bonaccorso da Montemagno. This attracted attention in the great civic centres of humanism in south-west Germany and was soon translated. A French version by Jean Mielot also appeared, and this was turned into English by John Tiptoft, earl of Worcester, and printed by Caxton in 1481.[1] This humanistic tradition manifested itself again in *Il Nennio* by Giovanni Battista Nenna, which was translated in 1595 by William Jones.[2]

[1] MS. Harl. 4402 in the British Museum not only contains Mielot's version but is itself a collection of debates and verse on nobility. Cf. A. W. Reed, 'Fulgens and Lucres', *T.L.S.*, 3 April 1919, p. 178.

[2] The fact that it was dedicated to the earl of Essex indicates that such discussions were not in any sense opposed to the aristocratic principle. Even Mary, queen of Scots, when it suited her purpose, would argue in favour of the man 'de bas estat, pauvre en biens, mais généreus d'esprit' (cf. A. Labanoff, *Lettres . . . de Marie Stuart*, 1844, vii, 298–9 and J. E. Neale, *Queen Elizabeth*, 1934, p. 140). The general aristocratic tone of Elizabethan England is unquestionable. Yet, looking at Europe as a whole and the powerful mercantile communities in which the arguments about personal merit and hereditary rank found congenial soil, it is natural to ask whether or not they were purely theoretical. Here it may be observed that despite the division of society into well-defined classes during and after the Middle Ages, the structure was not absolutely rigid. Even in the mediæval period there was some movement (cf. A. Law, 'The English *Nouveaux-Riches* in the fourteenth century', *Transactions of the Royal Historical Society*, New Series, 1895, ix, pp. 49–73). Thus William de la Pole, a merchant of Ravenser Odd and Hull, who married the daughter of another merchant named John Rotenhering, became notable as the founder of the great house of the earls and dukes of Suffolk (*D.N.B.*, xlvi, p. 48). The Church provided another opening for some able men of humble birth like Baldwin, archbishop of Canterbury, and Robert Grosseteste, bishop of Lincoln, and after the exodus of foreign priests during the Black Death there were still more opportunities, so that complaints were made of the promotion of sons of cobblers and even of serfs to the office of bishop (*Pierce the Ploughman's Crede*, ll. 744–57). In fact, the spread of education was such that the House of Commons in 1391 petitioned Richard II to prevent the children of serfs being sent to school in order to alter their social status (cf. J. E. G. de Montmorency, *State Intervention in English Education*, Cambridge, 1902, p. 27), an appeal that was rejected. The most spectacular rise to power through the medium of the Church was, however, seen in the career of Cardinal Wolsey. After the dissolution of the monasteries a good many merchants founded important families. In this connexion the family of Henry Cromwell, *alias* Williams, of Huntingdonshire is of interest. The descendants of 'a Putney ale-brewer and innkeeper' offer a good example of 'that flexibility in the English aristocratic system which permitted new families to spring suddenly from obscurity to wealth and splendour' (cf. J. E. Neale, *The Elizabethan House of Commons*, London, 1949, p. 48). And A. F. Pollard (*Factors in Modern History*, London, 1907, p. 41) writing on 'The Advent of the Middle Class' remarks that 'the great ministers of Tudor times, the Cromwells, the Cecils, the Walsinghams, all spring from the new middle, and not the old feudal, classes; and Queen Elizabeth herself was great-grand-daughter of a London merchant'. The alteration in economic values in the course of the sixteenth century strengthened the social position of the merchant classes, which is reflected in literature. On the subject of the change in social conditions and the relationship of 'virtue' to nobility see R. Kelso, *The Doctrine of the English Gentleman in the sixteenth Century*, Urbana, 1929, pp. 16 and 23–7. For an outline of the influence of the humanistic tradition see A. W. Reed's paper on 'Chivalry and the Idea of Gentleman' in *Chivalry*, ed. E. Prestage, London, 1928, pp. 207–28.

The theme of nobility had taken dramatic shape on the Continent in a play of Sixt Birck, a native of Augsburg who passed many years at Basle, and in England, first in Henry Medwall's *Fulgens and Lucres*, which was inspired by Bonaccorso, and later in two interludes, *Godly Queene Hester* and *Gentleness and Nobility*.[1] However, the play that stands nearest to *All's Well* in subject-matter is Bernardo Accolti's *Virginia*, of which the earliest edition appeared in 1513, for it too is drawn from Boccaccio's tale of Giletta. It has been suggested that Shakespeare was acquainted with the Italian play, but this seems highly improbable. The usual assumption is that he found his theme in Painter's *Palace of Pleasure*, but there are grounds for thinking that he came across it in the French version of Antoine le Maçon[2], which may have been brought to his attention when he was lodging with Christopher Montjoy, a Huguenot refugee.[3]

In his story Boccaccio does not make any of the characters, whether Giletta herself or any one else, expound the claims of the woman of merit. It is mentioned that she has beauty, wisdom and wealth, but there are no speeches to justify a marriage between people of different rank. This may appear strange, for elsewhere Boccaccio discloses his point of view. A striking example occurs in the *Filostrato* when Troilo defends Griseida against Cassandra's objections on the ground of her inferior rank:

> Che più, donna Cassandra, chiederete
> In donna omai? il suo sangue reale?
> Non son re tutti quelli a cui vedete
> Corona o scettro o vesta imperiale;
> Assai fiate udito già l'avete,
> Re è colui il qual per virtù vale,
> Non per potenza: e se costei potesse,
> Non cre'tu ch'ella come tu reggesse?
>
> (*O.V.* vii, st. 99, ll. 1–8)

And in the first tale of the fourth book of the *Decameron* he dwells at length on this topic when he lets Ghismonda, the daughter of the prince of Salerno, uphold her choice of Guiscardo, 'a man of very humble origin, but pre-eminent for native worth'. In a long and eloquent speech she maintains that 'whoso with merit acts, does plainly shew himself a gentleman'. She therefore rebuts the charge that she has demeaned herself, for though Guiscardo is poor, 'many

---

[1] Ed. A. C. Partridge and W. W. Greg, Malone Society, 1950.
[2] Cf. H. G. Wright, 'The Indebtedness of Painter's Translations from Boccaccio in *The Palace of Pleasure* to the French Version of le Maçon, *M.L.R.*, 1951, xlvi, pp. 431–5 and 'How did Shakespeare come to know the *Decameron*?', *M.L.R.*, 1955, lix, pp. 45–8.
[3] Cf. S. Lee, *A Life of William Shakespeare*, London, 1916, pp. 276–7.

kings, many great princes, were once poor', and 'poverty, though it take away all else, deprives no man of nobility'.[1]

In *All's Well* Shakespeare has deprived the heroine of the wealth that Giletta possessed and reduced her to 'a poor physician's daughter'.[2] It is obvious that he was fully capable of reducing her fortune in order to throw her personal qualities into relief, but if he was familiar with the French version of le Maçon, he might well have read the words of Ghismonda in the tale that was next but one after that of Giletta. If this was so, he could hardly fail to be impressed by her speech, one of the most famous in the whole *Decameron*, in which the insistence on the merit of the individual in contrast to rank or riches finds such memorable expression. Though this is conjectural, it is certain that Shakespeare embodies in a vital way Boccaccio's point of view, and brings out by various means what is implicit in the tale. He invents the old countess of Roussillon, Bertram's mother, who has no prejudices about rank, approves of the marriage and condemns her son's misprising of Helena. When she learns of his desertion of her, she declares that he is her son no longer. Another new character is the old courtier Lafeu. He shares the countess's high opinion of Helena and finds it incomprehensible that any young man should fail to seize the opportunity to marry her and later, on hearing of her supposed death, he praises her as

> a wife
> Whose beauty did astonish the survey
> Of richest eyes, whose words all ears took captive,
> Whose dear perfection hearts that scorned to serve
> Humbly called mistress.
>
> (v. iii. 15–19)

Lafeu's attitude is supported by the conversation of the two French lords in the Florentine camp, from which it is evident that Bertram is considered much to blame for abandoning Helena. The other French nobles are quick to appreciate her qualities, and Shakespeare has devised Act II, Sc. iii, expressly to show their eagerness to marry her.[3]

There is then virtual unanimity about the qualities of Helena and about the desirability of securing her in marriage. Only Bertram stands aloof, and in his stubborn aristocratic pride he is as far apart from his fellow-noblemen as Coriolanus from the other patricians. In order to bring out still more clearly Bertram's folly Shakespeare ascribes

---

[1] J. M. Rigg's translation.

[2] All quotations from *All's Well* are taken from the edition of A. Quiller Couch and J. Dover Wilson, Cambridge, 1929. For a discussion of the play see M. C. Bradbrook 'Virtue is the true Nobility. A Study of the Structure of *All's Well that Ends Well*' *R.E.S.*, New Series, 1950, i, pp. 289–301.

[3] Cf. J. Dover Wilson's interpretation of this scene in the previously-mentioned edition of *All's Well*, p. 146.

without any hint from Boccaccio, the virtue of humility to his father. The king notes this quality in the old count:

> Who were below him
> He used as creatures of another place,
> And bowed his eminent top to their low ranks,
> Making them proud of his humility . . .
>
> (I. ii. 41–4)

This humility is a trait of Helena herself. She thinks of Bertram as a star shining above her and compares herself to the Indian that worships the sun. She is fully conscious that hers is but a 'low and humble name', and even when Bertram has treated her with discourtesy, she still speaks of him as 'my dearest master'. Though she does not lack courage, she is not a forceful, virile creature in relentless pursuit of her quarry. Her words to Bertram, when she chooses him in the presence of the king, are full of tact:

> I dare not say I take you, but I give
> Me and my service, ever whilst I live,
> Into your guiding power . . .
>
> (II. iii. 105–7)

After the betrothal she maintains this attitude and asks of Parolles what Bertram's wishes are:

> In every thing I wait upon his will,
>
> (II. iv. 55)

and to Bertram himself she declares,

> Sir, I can nothing say,
> But that I am your most obedient servant.
>
> (II. v. 73–4)

Nowhere does Helena appear more attractive than just before she and Bertram separate, he to go to Florence, she to Roussillon. He is curt to the point of rudeness and talks in short, abrupt phrases and churlishly rejects her timid plea, so discreetly conveyed, for a parting kiss.

It is true that the modern reader or spectator, living in a very different society, will find Helena almost too submissive to her lord, but her humility is dignified in comparison with the grovelling self-basement of Accolti's Virginia. It may also be objected against Helena that the substitution trick which she plays on Bertram is hardly compatible with the qualities ascribed to her elsewhere.[1] But this is, of course, merely part of the machinery derived from a mediæval tale that belonged to the incredible world of romance, and in any case the

---

[1] For a defence of the role of Helena see Emile Legouis, 'La Comtesse de Roussillon', *English*, 1937, i, pp. 399–404.

total impression of Helena is not one of her excessive astuteness as in Virginia. More disturbing in some ways is the excessive familiarity of the virtuous Helena with Parolles, the chief figure in the not very successful sub-plot that Shakespeare added to provide a few moments of laughter as a distraction from the serious plot. But his heart was not in Parolles as it had been in Falstaff. Even Bertram, who, in associating with such a person as Parolles, shows the same lack of discernment as elsewhere, cuts a sorry figure, for Helena is exalted at the expense of her husband. As a whole therefore, in view of its unsatisfactory hero and inferior sub-plot, *All's Well* is not one of Shakespeare's greatest comedies. The old romance is not blended to perfection with the problems of reality.

It is the question of merit and nobility, as it is embodied in Helena, which lends an air of gravity to the play. This is implicit in Boccaccio's tale, even as it is in *Patient Grissell*, and one indication of its significance is the pronouncement of the king, the head of an aristocratic society, when Bertram with supercilious mien declines the royal proposal:

> 'Tis only title thou disdain'st in her, the which
> I can build up . . . Strange is it, that our bloods,
> Of colour, weight, and heat, poured all together,
> Would quite confound distinction, yet stand off
> In differences so mighty . . . If she be
> All that is virtuous (save what thou dislik'st,
> A poor physician's daughter) thou dislik'st
> Of virtue for a name; but do not so:
> From lowest place when virtuous things proceed,
> The place is dignified by th' doer's deed:
> Where great additions swell's, and virtue none,
> It is a dropsied honour: good alone
> Is good, without a name; vileness is so:
> The property by what it is should go,
> Not by the title . . . She is young, wise, fair;
> In these to nature she's immediate heir;
> And these breed honour: that is honour's scorn,
> Which challenges itself as honour's born,
> And is not like the sire: honours thrive,
> When rather from our acts we them derive
> Than our foregoers: the mere word's a slave,
> Deboshed on every tomb, on every grave
> A lying trophy, and as oft is dumb
> Where dust and damned oblivion is the tomb
> Of honoured bones indeed.
>
> (II. iii. 120–44)

This is the very essence of the humanist tradition, and Shakespeare knew that he could count on the interest of those among his audience who were familiar with it, while at the same time this point of view could not fail to gratify the citizens of London.

Blurt Master-Constable. Or the Spaniards Night-Walke, which was entered in the Stationers' Register on 7 June 1602 and printed that year, belongs approximately to the same period as *All's Well*. It too has a romantic main plot, the scene being laid in Venice, whither Fontenella, a Frenchman, has been brought as a prisoner of war. He manages to escape to the house of Imperia, a courtesan, and Violetta, who has married him secretly, follows him there. The courtesan serves as a link with the sub-plot, in which Lazarillo de Tormes, a Spanish soldier of fortune, becomes infatuated with her. Lazarillo is an absurd figure who is made to look even more ridiculous by the treatment that he receives from Imperia. She promises to satisfy his desire at midnight, and in the meantime he is escorted to a room. He is warned that the house is haunted and that strange sounds of music and singing and laughter are sometimes heard, but that he is not to move or be afraid. However, when he listens to music and singing, he does move, and when a Spanish pavan is played, he dances, then lies down to sleep, only to fall into a cesspool, to the accompaniment of the mocking laughter of Frisco, Imperia's servant. He contrives to get out and appears before the house, shivering, but Frisco responds to his entreaties for his clothes with abuse. He leaves Lazarillo who vows that he will be revenged, but amid his fury is arrested by Blurt.

This sub-plot is derived from one incident in the adventures of Andreuccio of Perugia on his visit to Naples in the fifth tale of the second day of the *Decameron*, which belongs to the group that finds pleasure in outwitting the simple or inexperienced. Frisco is not a bully like Scarabone Buttafuoco but he relishes the success of the trick. The transformation of Andreuccio into a Spaniard was calculated to satisfy an audience with whom his countrymen were unpopular. The replacement of the contrivance of the tale by the mechanism of the trap-door was a necessary adjustment to the needs of the stage, and there was a certain justice in the choice of the Spanish pavan that leads to Lazarillo's downfall. As the name Lazarillo de Tormes indicates, the author of the play was familiar with Spanish picaresque literature,[1] and the element of farcical comedy, combined with a glimpse of the underworld, was clearly to the taste of the Elizabethan playgoer. The same bent was to be displayed a year or two later in *Measure for Measure*, where Mistress Overdone and Pompey, her servant, appear in Vienna with Elbow, the constable. So too along with Imperia and Frisco we find Blurt Master-Constable and his attendant Slubber.

[1] *Lazarillo de Tormes* had been translated by David Rowland in 1586, and the second part by 'W.P.' in 1596.

Reminiscent as they are of Dogberry and Verges, they help to remind us that despite the foreign setting the dramatist was here depicting one stratum of contemporary English society.

John Marston's *Parasitaster, or The Fawne* (1606), on the other hand, has Italian figures and relies for its success chiefly on the skilful plot. It is based on the third tale of the third day of the *Decameron* in which an amorous woman under cover of confession dupes a stupid friar and uses him to act unwittingly as a messenger to her lover. But instead of the middle-class environment of Florence, in which city the husband is a merchant of woollen goods, *The Fawne* transports the spectator to the court of Hercules, duke of Ferrara, and a widower, who wishes to marry his son Tiberio but finds him unwilling. Tiberio is sent to woo for his father Dulcimel, daughter of Gonzago, duke of Urbin. The princess detests the thought of marrying an elderly man and falls in love with Tiberio, to whom she manages to convey her feelings through the involuntary agency of her father, in much the same way as the friar is used by Boccaccio. At first Tiberio feels nothing but astonishment, but when he receives a letter that he is supposed to have written to her and a scarf that he is accused of having sent, he begins to perceive Dulcimel's hidden meaning. However, it is his reluctance to have dealings with women that differentiates him from his counterpart in the *Decameron*. On reading the letters he exclaims:

> O quick deuicefull strong braind *Dulcimel*
> Thou art to full of witte to be a wife,
> Why dost thou loue, or what strong heat gaue life
> To such faint hopes? O woman thou art made
> Most only of, and for deceit . . .
>
> (III. i)

This reluctance, based on distrust of all women, is reinforced by his unwillingness to abuse his father's trust in him. The two obstacles are put in a nutshell, when he asks

> shall I that euer loathde,
> A thought of woman, now begin to loue,
> My worthy fathers right, breake faith to him that got me
> To get a faithless woman?
>
> (III. i)

However, after a struggle he falls in love with her, and, as later in Dryden's 'Sigismonda and Guiscardo', the intrigue ends with their marriage by a priest. Duke Hercules, who in disguise as Faunus has witnessed the growth of his son's affection, gives his blessing.

Thus a successful amorous intrigue, with a continuation of illicit love, is transformed into a play of true love that culminates in matrimony. But *The Fawne* is not simply a moralisation of a tale in which an astute woman by the keenness of her wits achieves her aim. It retains the interest of this sharp intellect, but the plot is enriched by the reluctance of Tiberio to marry and to prove unfaithful to Hercules. Further, there is the healthy unwillingness of a young woman to accept an old widower, so that she is justified in seeking to avoid a social abnormality. Hence the play has an inward as well as an outward morality that distinguishes it from the carefree hedonism of Boccaccio's story.

In *Cupid's Whirligig*, entered in the Stationers' Register on 29 June 1607 and printed that year, Edward Sharpham returned to the tale of Isabella, Leonetto and Lambertuccio which had been used by Tourneur.[1] Once again the story is worked in as a sub-plot, but the whole play is a comedy. The leading figure is Sir Timothy Troublesome, so frantically jealous that the slightest thing sets him aflame. His wife, who is perpetually harassed by his suspicions, is beyond reproach, and the early part of the play seeks to show how all attempts to win her from her husband fail. In the fourth act Captain Wouldly tries to make love to her, but every time that she says her husband is coming, the typical swaggering captain changes his tone and wants to hide. He has just been put out of the way when Master Exhibition enters. The latter belongs to the Inns of Court and is making love in a barbarous legal jargon when the return of Sir Timothy is announced. He is overcome with fear, and it is Lady Troublesome who suggests what he is to do. On her advice he draws his sword and says nothing to Troublesome except that he will be revenged in another place. Wouldly is found quaking and trembling, for he is an arrant coward, and Lady Troublesome explains that he was pursued by Exhibition into the house. Troublesome thanks her, invites Wouldly to supper, and promises to escort him home.

These incidents follow the original story in all essentials, but there is a modification in that Wouldly is the first to enter, whereas his counterpart, the blustering Lambertuccio, is the second. The reason for this change is that Sharpham, who was anxious to make the situation as farcical as possible, thought that more laughter could be created by depicting Wouldly as the craven who has to be rescued from an ignominious plight. In point of fact, there is not much to choose between the two lovers, for the one is as panic-stricken as the other. The pedantic legal speech of Exhibition is another comic device and at the same time helps to establish the play in its English environment. As in Boccaccio, it is the keen-witted woman who controls events, but her character is transformed, since she is a chaste wife, harassed by unwelcome suitors and tormented by that favourite figure in the comedy of the period, the jealous husband.

[1] Vide ante, pp. 204–5.

When Shakespeare was looking round for a subject in 1609, he had no inclination to paint contemporary manners but preferred to treat a romantic theme. He recalled the second day of the *Decameron* which dealt with the fortunes of those who after various adventures attained unexpected happiness. There was, indeed, no lack of romance in the ninth tale of Zinevra who, after the foolish wager of her husband Bernabò with Ambruogiuolo had brought about their separation, wandered about until, in disguise, as a trusted soldier of the Soldan she extorted a confession from her traducer and had him put to death. Shakespeare too placed his heroine in the service of a great commander, the Roman general Lucius. However, the setting of her troubles is not Genoa, Acre and Alexandria, but the palace of Cymbeline, in ancient Britain, and the mountains of Wales. Yet even though the play differs notably from the tale in these respects, Shakespeare was familiar with the whole story. The punishment of Ambruogiuolo by smearing his body with honey and then tying him to a stake until he was devoured by swarms of flies, wasps and gadflies is recalled in the threat of Autolycus to inflict a similar death on the shepherd's son.[1]

There are many similarities between the plot of the early part of *Cymbeline* and Boccaccio's narrative. In each case, when the wager is laid, a formal pact is drawn up and signed. Iachimo has the trunk ready in which he is to lie concealed, just as Ambruogiuolo has a chest at hand. Imogen has a waiting-woman, Zinevra a little girl. In both versions the bedchamber is illuminated, so that the intruder is able to look round. Iachimo is tempted but represses his passion for the sake of his scheme, and the same is true of Ambruogiuolo. Both men observe the pictures, the situation of the room, both carry away objects of value, and both note a mole under the breast of the sleeper.[2] The villain's proofs in the play and in the narrative are given in the same sequence, and both husbands are bent on vengeance. There is also a parallel in the disguising of the heroine with the aid of her servant. In Boccaccio he hands over his doublet and hood in exchange for her clothes; in the play with somewhat greater delicacy Pisanio produces a bag containing doublet, hat and hose which he has brought with him in anticipation.[3]

---

[1] *Shakespeare The Complete Works*, ed. C. J. Sisson; *The Winter's Tale*, IV. iv. 811–20.

[2] *Cymbeline*, II. ii. 37, 'On her left breast': II. iv. 134, 'under her breast'. It is discrepancies such as these that harass Shakespeare scholars. The use of 'on' instead of 'under' in the first instance was probably on metrical grounds. In the second instance 'left' was perhaps omitted, because 'right proud' follows in the next line. All quotations are taken from *Shakespeare The Complete Works*, ed. C. J. Sisson.

[3] There are some features which differentiate *Cymbeline* from Boccaccio's tale, and these have caused a vast amount of speculation about Shakespeare's source. The wager story is widespread, and Gaston Paris tried to group these many different versions in *Romania*, xxxii, pp. 481–551, but in *Miscellanea di studi critici edita in onore*

However, of necessity the tale underwent a transformation because it was linked to the reign of Cymbeline and the invasion of Britain which inspired a succession of patriotic outbursts[1] that associate this late work with the earlier ones on English history. It is Cymbeline who gives his name to the play, and the fate of his Queen and her son is linked with that of his daughter Imogen and her missing brothers. In this way the adventures of the heroine become far more involved than those of Zinevra. But Pisanio's words

> Fortune brings in some boats that are not steer'd
> (IV. iii. 46)

may be applied both to Imogen and Zinevra and contain in brief the theme enunciated for the second day of the *Decameron*.

The royal birth of Imogen had important consequences. It raised her and inevitably Posthumus too from the mercantile atmosphere of the tale. The exposition in the opening scene shows this clearly. Posthumus is 'a poor but worthy gentleman', descended from a family of famous soldiers. His father Sicilius had won glory and honour in war, and his two brothers had died sword in hand. Left an orphan, he had been brought up and made a gentleman of the bedchamber by Cymbeline. Imogen 'esteemed him and his virtue' and

---

di *Arturo Graf*, Bergamo, 1903, he had already modified his views. To some extent he was under the influence of R. Ohle, *Shakespeares Cymbeline und seine romanischen Vorläufer*, Berlin, 1890, whose arguments were refuted by H. R. D. Anders, *Shakespeare's Books*, Berlin, 1904, pp. 60–4. Alois Brandl, in his article 'Imogen auf den Aran-Inseln', *Shakespeare Jahrbuch*, 1917, liii, pp. 13–34, attempted a new analysis of the versions of the wager story. Considerable importance was attached to the contributions of Brandl and Gaston Paris by W. F. Thrall in 'Cymbeline, Boccaccio, and the Wager Story in England', *S.P.*, 1931, xxviii, pp. 107–19. This thorough survey discusses at length the hypothetical relationship of *Cymbeline*, *Westward for Smelts* and *Frederyke of Jennen*. The author is inclined to postulate an old play used by Shakespeare, though he is unwilling to commit himself. J. Raith, *Die Historie von den vier Kaufleuten*, Leipzig, 1936, which contains the text of *Frederyke of Jennen* and a concise and lucid introduction, is suspicious of the lost play theory and devotes himself chiefly to the relationship of Boccaccio and Shakespeare. For want of definite proof about this old play, it seems advisable to pursue this course, for, as Thrall recognises, the tale in the *Decameron* 'remains the most satisfactory analogue'. In some measure the whole discussion is connected with the problem of Shakespeare's knowledge of Boccaccio. It has generally been assumed that for *All's Well that Ends Well*, he must necessarily have had recourse to Painter's *Palace of Pleasure*, but this is erroneous (cf. H. G. Wright, 'How did Shakespeare come to know the *Decameron*?', *M.L.R.*, 1955, xlix, pp. 45–8). There is a possibility that when *Cymbeline* came to be written, Shakespeare no longer had access to the *Decameron* as when he wrote the earlier play and consequently eked out his knowledge by means of *Frederyke of Jennen*. No convincing reason exists for thinking that *Cymbeline* is indebted to *Westward for Smelts* (vide ante, pp. 192–3).

[1] Cf. the words of Posthumus (II. iv. 15–26) which act as a prelude to the great scene of defiance (III. i). Later comes the passage (IV. iv) in which Guiderius, Arviragus and old Belarius resolve to share in the resistance, and v. i, in which Posthumus prepares for the battle.

> By her election may be truly read
> What kind of man he is.
>
> (I. i. 53–4)

The situation resembles in some measure the choice of Guiscardo by
Ghismonda, and though Posthumus was of gentle birth, the king felt
justified in calling him 'Thou basest thing'.[1] The sense of the gap in
rank between Imogen and Posthumus is expressed with even greater
energy by Cloten:

> For
> The contract you pretend with that base wretch,
> One bred of alms, and fostered with cold dishes,
> With scraps o' th' Court, it is no contract, none.
> And though it be allowed in meaner parties—
> Yet who than he more mean?—to knit their souls,
> On whom there is no more dependency
> But brats and beggary, in self-figured knot;
> Yet you are curbed from that enlargement by
> The consequence o' th' crown, and must not foil
> The precious note of it with a base slave,
> A hilding for a livery, a squire's cloth,
> A pantler, not so eminent.
>
> (II. iii. 117–29)

This is the haughty disdain of Bertram for Helena, multiplied tenfold.
However, a reply is forthcoming. Imogen rejects this point of view,
as the king had done that of Bertram, and Posthumus is eulogised in
the opening scene by the two gentlemen, as Helena had been praised
by the nobles of France.

Thus one of the central features of *Cymbeline* is the justification of
Posthumus who ultimately proves his worth by his deeds. But first of
all he has to atone for the error into which he falls. In anticipation of
the final reconciliation Shakespeare depicts Posthumus in as favourable
a light as possible. However, we are given a glimpse of his passionate
nature when, in praising Imogen's chastity, Posthumus himself
declares:

> Me of my lawful pleasure she restrained,
> And prayed me oft forbearance.
>
> (II. v. 9–10)

He is a full-blooded soldier, and his soldierly qualities, which in the
end redeem him, have much to do with his downfall at the hands of
Iachimo. When he is banished, as if by a natural instinct, he makes his
way to Philario, his father's old comrade-in-arms. As in the tale it is
at a feast[2] in Philario's house at Rome that he encounters a number of
strangers, but whereas in Boccaccio the whole company consists of
Italian merchants assembled at Paris, those whom Posthumus meets

---

[1] I. i. 125.   [2] See Iachimo's words in v. v. 155.

include not only Iachimo, but also a Frenchman, a Dutchman and a Spaniard, a group which is partially reminiscent of the Italian, French and Spanish merchants in *Frederyke of Jennen*.[1] Shakespeare's Dutchman and Spaniard do not utter a word, but the Frenchman has a dramatic function to perform in that he recalls a dispute between Posthumus and another Frenchman at Orleans when Imogen was declared to be 'more fair, virtuous, wise, chaste, constant, qualified, and less attemptable, than any the rarest of our ladies in France'. As Posthumus himself admits, this quarrel at Orleans sprang in some measure from the impetuosity of youth. At Rome he is more sedate and displays more self-control, 'sitting sadly' and 'calm as virtue'.[2] He is also more discreet and tactful, not seeking in any way to detract from the charms of women in other countries.[3] Nevertheless, it is the Frenchman's account of Posthumus' conduct at Orleans that spurs Iachimo on to issue his challenge. The dialogue marks the gradual rise in Posthumus' irritation, until Philario interposes a quiet appeal, 'Let us leave here gentlemen', when it seems as if Posthumus would be appeased. However, the lull is only momentary, and as Iachimo goads him still further, it is clear that his quick temper is roused. He begins to talk of the punishment that Iachimo would deserve after the failure of his attempt, and when Philario again interposes an entreaty: 'Gentlemen enough of this; it came in too suddenly, let it die as it was born', his words fall on deaf ears. A moment later the wager has been laid. From this scene, which is admirable in its concentration, Posthumus emerges, not as a foolish hothead, but as one driven to exasperation by the cynical disbelief of Iachimo.

On the occasion of the second meeting in Philario's house,[4] the Frenchman whose dramatic task was done, and the Dutchman and Spaniard who never had any, are discarded. Philario alone remains with Posthumus and Iachimo. At the beginning of the scene Posthumus is confident. The account of the bedchamber is far more detailed than that given in Act II, Sc. ii, for with true artistic instinct Shakespeare avoided any mechanical repetition, and the new descriptions of the tapestry and the chimney-piece have been saved for this crisis. The figures of Antony's encounter with Cleopatra on the Cydnus and of chaste Diana bathing have an oblique relevance to the accusation made by Iachimo, and his story acquires a specious air of truth. Nevertheless, Posthumus remains calm, but as Iachimo continues with his inventory, he begins to doubt. 'This is her honour!' he cries, but a moment later he thinks clearly again. However, this lucidity of judgement is soon beclouded, and the ocular proof of the bracelet completes

---

[1] Cf. J. Raith, *Die Historie von den vier Kaufleuten*, pp. 107–10.
[2] Iachimo's words in v. v. 160, 174.   [3] Ibid., 173.   [4] II. iv.

the destruction of his faith. It is true that Philario's intervention and admonition to patience have a temporary effect, but it is short-lived, and, as at the first meeting, Philario's second exhortation is swept aside, and Posthumus's rage overflows all bounds. As a soldier he thinks of action:

> O that I had her here, to tear her limb-meal.
>
> (II. iv. 147)

which echoes Othello's cry: 'I will chop her into messes'. All restraint is lost, and in the following scene he denounces all women as false and treacherous. A long period of repentance follows, and bitter remorse atones for the suffering that his too quick temper has inflicted on Imogen. In the last scene he still speaks with the same violence, but it is now directed against himself, and his anguish is only dispelled by her forgiveness.[1]

In portraying Posthumus, Shakespeare also developed the importance of Iachimo. In his hands the original Italian becomes a Machiavellian villain, even though the period is that of Augustus Cæsar, so that there is nothing improbable in Iachimo's statement that the trunk carried into Imogen's room contains rare plate and jewels, a gift for the emperor. However, the feeling that animates Shakespeare is the Renaissance Englishman's conviction that Italy was a land abounding in women beautiful but dangerous, and in men subtle of intellect and cunning beyond measure. Even when making his confession, Iachimo is conscious of his mental superiority:

> mine Italian brain
> Gan in your duller Britain operate
> Most vilely.
>
> (V. v. 196–8)

Certainly, he is adroit in his dealings with Posthumus, who in all his straightforward soldierly honesty is at the mercy of the more nimble-witted Iachimo. Nor is it only Posthumus who is deceived, but Imogen also, for her innocence is exploited with the same skill by the astute Machiavellian who changes his ground with the utmost dexterity. Yet even if Iachimo is a shrewd and cynical man of the world, he is no Iago. It would seem as if early in the play Shakespeare had decided that Iachimo should be spared at the close, and so at the end of Act II, Sc. iv, when Posthumus has rushed out and Philario has cried:

> Let's follow him, and pervert the present wrath
> He hath against himself,

Iachimo, as if anxious to avoid any mishap to Posthumus, says: 'With all my heart'. The two meet again as antagonists on the battlefield in

---

[1] V. v. 210–25.

Act V, Sc. ii, when Iachimo is disarmed by a Briton who, unknown to him, is Posthumus. He is burdened with a sense of guilt:

> I have belied a lady,
> The Princess of this country, and the air on't
> Revengingly enfeebles me.
>
> (v. ii. 2–4)

His defeat in single combat combines with his repentance to induce in Posthumus a mood of magnanimity:

> Live,
> And deal with others better.
>
> (v. v. 419–20)

The part of Imogen also underwent a notable development by Shakespeare. In Boccaccio's tale she is almost a nonentity until Bernabò resolves that she shall die. On the other hand, in the opening scene of the play, by her bold defiance of her father, she reveals that strength of mind which is one of her distinctive traits, and on the occasion of her first interview with Iachimo her chastity expresses itself in a prompt recoil from his infamous proposal. The bedchamber scene reinforces this impression, when, before falling asleep, she prays for protection from 'the tempters of the night'. The twofold mention of classical lore with its allusion to Tarquin and Tereus emphasises her innocence and the danger to which she is exposed. It is as if Shakespeare could not bear the thought of this peril, and so the period of her sleep extends only from midnight to four o'clock, when the darkness gives place to the light of a summer dawn, and terror melts away at the sound of Cloten's aubade.

The fact that Pisanio, unlike Zinevra's servant, does not accompany his master abroad but remains in attendance on Imogen is of considerable significance. It enables Shakespeare to omit a scene which might otherwise have been necessary in order that the servant should be instructed to return and lure his mistress away from home to a lonely place suitable for her murder. But it is also important, because Pisanio, having witnessed her sorrow at Posthumus' absence and the pressure brought to bear on her to marry Cloten, can testify to her loyalty. Consequently, on receiving Posthumus' letter ordering him to put Imogen to death, he at once rebels, whereas his counterpart in the tale complies readily enough.

If Shakespeare by various devices has lent greater prominence to Imogen's chastity, he has also emphasised her courage. Whereas Zinevra is not called upon to face a crisis until she is left alone to begin her wanderings, Imogen shows a stout spirit in the very first scene and continues to do so to the end. It is as though Shakespeare had made the courage of Zinevra in the latter part of the tale permeate the play. Unlike her prototype she sheds no tears when Pisanio discloses Posthumus' command. On the contrary, instead of pleading for mercy she begs him to draw his sword and dispatch her quickly. When he suggests the expedient of the disguise, she is prompt in her determination:

> This attempt
> I am soldier to, and will abide it with
> A prince's courage.
>
> (III. iv. 185–7)

As these lines indicate, the knowledge of her royal birth sustains and animates her with a firm resolve to be worthy of her rank. She faces privation and hardship without faltering:

> hardness ever
> Of hardiness is mother,
>
> (III. vi. 21–2)

and although at heart she shrinks from the sword, she draws it and, conquering her natural hesitation, plunges into the darkness of the cave. Thus Shakespeare creates one of the most attractive of his heroines—chaste and loyal, brave and undaunted by misfortune. Her supposed death in the mountains of Wales has, of course, no place in the original tale but it enables Shakespeare to invest her with the poetry of flowers, even as he had done with Juliet and Ophelia. Arviragus vows to deck her grave with 'pale primroses' and 'azured harebell', while 'female fairies' who haunt the wilds cast over it their protecting spell.

In this way, even though the core of the play consists of the clash between good and evil in human nature, *Cymbeline* acquires a certain detachment by the removal of the scene to ancient days and remote places. At the same time the mountain solitudes help to introduce a discussion on the merits and demerits of the simple life in contrast with the sophisticated world of the court. Belarius, who speaks from knowledge born of suffering, is the advocate of the rural life. But Guiderius is in doubt:

> Haply this life is best,
> If quiet life be best.
>
> (III. iii. 29–30)

In the end both he and Arviragus, with all the eagerness of youth, are bent on exploration, whatever Belarius may say. It is the same problem as is presented in a slightly different form when Prospero leaves his magic island at the call of duty to return to what in the eyes of Miranda is a 'brave new world'.

By raising this question, which was one that was much debated in the seventeenth century, Shakespeare provided yet another source of interest. His romantic tragi-comedy was therefore no less to the taste of his audience than Ben Jonson's portrayal of contemporary life in *The Devil is an Ass*, which also draws on the *Decameron*, adapting episodes from two tales to an English setting. Attention is focused on Fabian Fitzdottrel,[1] a Norfolk squire and a typical 'gull' of the period, who, while close-handed in small matters, is so credulous that he falls a victim to unscrupulous projectors. It is through his love of fine attire that he is linked to the sub-plot, in which Wittipol, a young gallant, and his friend Manly are prominent. In Act I, Sc. ii and iii, Jonson has recourse to the fifth tale of the third day, where Francesco Vergellesi allows Ricciardo to speak to his wife on condition that he is to be present, in return for which Vergellesi is to have his handsome palfrey. In secret he orders his wife to remain mute, whatever Ricciardo may say. At the interview, when no answer from the lady is forthcoming, Ricciardo perceives that a trick has been played on him and with ready wit he replies in her name, suggesting how they can meet in the absence of Vergellesi. Jonson makes a number of important changes. First, the reward is altered. It would seem as if Jonson, having read that Ricciardo was a foppish gallant, substituted for the horse a valuable cloak, since Fitzdottrel's desire to possess splendid attire accords better with the dramatist's interpretation of him as a 'gull'. Another alteration concerns Wittipol's presence in the same room when Mrs. Fitzdottrel is instructed to remain mute. If he nevertheless exclaims 'I taste a trick in't' in conformity with the tale, this is probably not due to a blunder on Jonson's part[2] but to an assumption that the audience would understand that Wittipol was supposed not to have overheard. A new stipulation is added in the play—that the wooer is to remain at a distance of one yard from the lady.

In the first scene the compact is made; in the second the interview takes place. On the latter occasion the characters of Fitzdottrel and Wittipol are set forth clearly, and they are less shadowy than their prototypes. Some light is also thrown on Mrs. Fitzdottrel, for even if she says nothing once the interview has begun, and unlike her Italian counterpart neither by sighs nor glowing eyes responds to Wittipol, beforehand she complains that her husband is making her an object of derision as well as himself, and afterwards she compares herself to one in a cage. Jonson likewise creates a certain tension when Fitzdottrel imposes a time-limit of a quarter of an hour reckoned by the watch that he holds in his hand. As an experienced dramatist he also recognises that the long speech of the wooer in the tale must in some way be made

---

[1] The name suggests rusticity and stupidity, since the dottrel was a symbol of foolishness (cf. *O.E.D.*, iii, p. 610).
[2] Cf. W. S. Johnson in his edition of the play, New York, 1905, p. xlvii.

more dramatic. Consequently, he interposes remarks by Manly and Fitzdottrel, chiefly the latter, who interrupts from time to time, especially when Wittipol abuses him and when, speaking as if he were Mrs. Fitzdottrel, he proposes an assignation. Fitzdottrel, chafing and fuming, has to be restrained by threats to strip him of his cloak if he keeps on breaking in. As a result the monologue develops into a dialogue which enlivens the scene. In addition, Jonson appreciates the need for movement. In contrast to the tale, where Ricciardo remains seated beside the lady, the play depicts Wittipol as changing his position. When he speaks in the name of Mrs. Fitzdottrel, he puts Manly in his own place and addresses him. Moreover, when he goes back to his place, the watchful Fitzdottrel bids him keep his ground, that is, not pass the rush on the floor which he had fixed as the bound at the beginning.

The precise form in which the intrigue is to be carried on is not settled at the interview as in Boccaccio. As Jonson wanted to extend the sub-plot, he introduced in Act II, Sc. i an episode from the third tale of the third day, that of the dull-witted friar.[1] Mrs. Fitzdottrel sends a message to Wittipol by Pug, the stupid devil who gives the play its name, that he is to cease paying his attentions to her from the window of the chamber in Lincoln's Inn that faces her gallery. In the next scene Wittipol has taken the hint and appears in Manly's room. His eloquent wooing culminates in the famous lyric, which contains the lines:

> Haue you seene but a bright Lilly grow,
> Before rude hands haue touch'd it?
> Haue you mark'd but the fall of the Snow,
> Before the soyle hath smuch'd it?[2]

The lines are not only beautiful in themselves, but they suggest that the woman to whom they apply is worlds apart from the amorous intriguer of the tale and so they have a decisive significance in the unfolding of the plot. The rest of the play is in keeping with this picture of immaculate purity, for in Act IV, Sc. iii the heroine explains to Wittipol that, before they were interrupted, she had meant to ask him to be her friend, but not her lover. Urged on by Manly, he agrees to her request and helps to prevent her husband from ruining her fortunes by his credulity. Thus Jonson adapts Boccaccio's tale with considerable skill to form an element in an English comedy which laughs at folly and inculcates virtue.

There is no certainty about the date when 'The Triumph of Honor' and 'The Triumph of Love' were composed, since *Four Plays in One*

[1] Vide ante, p. 218.
[2] Cf. *Ben Jonson*, ed. C. H. Herford, Percy and Evelyn Simpson, vol. vi, 1938, p. 20

of which they form a part was not printed till 1647. However, as they are generally ascribed to Beaumont, who died in 1616, they may be considered at this point. It has been maintained[1] that 'The Triumph of Honor' is derived from the fifth tale of the tenth day of the *Decameron* but the name of the heroine, Dorigen, and the nature of the test imposed on Martius, the removal of rocks, indicate that it is inspired by Chaucer's *Franklin's Tale*. On the other hand, 'The Triumph of Love' is a free dramatic version of the seventh tale of the fifth day. The scene is transferred from Sicily to Milan, where the usurping duke of Mantua holds sway. Gerrard, whose parents were killed in the attack on Milan, has been brought up by Randulpho, the brother of Benvoglio, who in his turn has cared for Ferdinand, another youth of unknown parentage. The circumstances in which Gerrard has come to love Benvoglio's daughter, Violante, are ignored in the play, whereas the tale dwells at some length on the relations of Pietro and Violante. In both cases Violante is discovered to be with child. The lovers' fault is excused to some extent in the tale by the chance that isolated them from others, whereas in the play there is an attendant, Dorothea, who furthers the intrigue, and the whole affair appears more sophisticated in spite of Violante's declaration:

> Heaven doth know,
> If ever the first Lovers, ere they fell,
> Knew simply in the state of innocence,
> Such was this act, this, that doth ask no blush.[2]

In fact, Beaumont's exposition is not altogether satisfactory because he is anxious to hasten on to all the complications with which he has packed this one-act play. Benvoglio decides that Ferdinand shall marry Violante. Ferdinand is filled with joy but this is changed to despair when Gerrard reveals to his friend, who has pledged secrecy, how matters stand. From a dumb-show, to which Beaumont has recourse because of the severe limits imposed upon the action, the spectator learns that a friar has married Gerrard and Violante, another innovation by the dramatist. She withdraws, Gerrard walks in meditation, and an infant is presented to him. Ferdinand, distraught with grief, inadvertently discloses his friend's secret to Benvoglio. The enraged parent makes his way to the new duke who has succeeded the dead usurper. Again there is a dumb-show in which duke Rinaldo hears Benvoglio's demands for justice, whereupon Ferdinand, having been made by Benvoglio to take an oath, is handed a cup by Dorothea and departs. The play is then resumed. Ferdinand brings a letter from

[1] This is rejected by E. Koeppel, *Quellen-Studien*, p. 49 and n. 4.
[2] Cf. *The Works of Beaumont and Fletcher*, ed. Waller and Glover, 10 vols., vol. x, 1912, p. 513.

Benvoglio to Violante in which she is urged to drink of the poisoned cup, but he himself tries to drain it. However, when he fails to do so, Violante drinks the rest, and both lie dead. This is in striking contrast to the corresponding scene in the tale, where the messenger brutally abuses Violante with foul words, when offering her the alternative of poison or the sword. However, Beaumont is preparing a startling close. For whereas in the tale the servant is suddenly interrupted after Pietro's high rank has been revealed and all ends happily, the play maintains the suspense for some time. Gerrard is seen in the presence of the executioner and makes a manly farewell speech, when his aunt Cornelia discloses that she is the missing wife of the duke, that Gerrard and Ferdinand are his sons, Gerrard being the elder. Simultaneously Dorothea confesses that she put opium, not poison, in the cup, and at once Ferdinand and Violante awake. The discovery is followed by a series of broken ejaculations which one has difficulty in taking seriously.

Duke Cor.	Son, Daughter.
Ferd.	Father, Mother, Brother.
Ger.	Wife.
Viol.	Are we not all in Heaven?
Ger.	Faith, very near it.
Ferd.	How can this be?
Duke	Hear it.[1]

The lovers receive the duke's blessing, and Dorothea is rewarded for disobeying orders, in that she is married to Ferdinand, who is not allowed to utter a word.

It is obvious that Beaumont's purpose was to adapt a tale to the stage. Finding it too slight, he expanded his material by the introduction of a rival lover with a considerable paraphernalia of attendants, servants and guards and built up a series of complications which are unexpectedly resolved at the close. Thus a romantic story is developed into a world that is quite fantastic.

In Fletcher's play *Monsieur Thomas*, probably written some time between 1610 and 1616, there is again a clash between love and friendship. Valentine, a man of middle age, intends to marry his ward Cellide. He introduces to her Francisco, a young friend whom he has met. Francisco becomes passionately fond of her and is so tormented by the conflict between his affection for her and his friendship for Valentine that he falls ill. In the end it turns out that Francisco is Valentine's son, who had been lost at sea among the Genoa galleys, so that the way is prepared for Francisco to marry Cellide. Fletcher enlivens the play with a number of comic scenes. In some of the most amusing he satirises the doctors who come to diagnose the cause of

[1] *Works of Beaumont and Fletcher*, ed. cit., vol. x, p. 333.

Francisco's illness. However, the chief source of laughter is in the sub-plot which concerns Thomas, the son of Sebastian. Thomas is a scape-grace who has been abroad and hence is called 'Monsieur'. He is now supposed to be a reformed character, but while this is pleasing enough to Mary, the niece of Valentine, it irritates his father, Sebastian. Quite unlike the usual sober-minded father who grieves over an unruly son and rejoices at his reformation, Sebastian now thinks of Thomas as a poor-spirited creature unworthy to be his heir. Thomas is in a dilemma, and the play extracts good comedy from the scenes in which, as a supposed model of sobriety, he tries to win Mary, and the contrasted scenes in which, to satisfy his parent, he indulges in wild pranks with his companions Hylas and Sam. For one of his escapades (Act V, Sc. ii) Fletcher probably used the fourth tale of the eighth day. Thomas, dis-guised in the clothes of his sister Dorothea, contrives to enter Mary's house, but Mary, having been warned by Dorothea, lures him into a bed with a negro girl whom he believes to be Mary. He is afterwards exposed to derision, just as the provost of Fiesole is with the hideous Ciutazza. Of course, the incident is freely adapted, but as Fletcher knew his *Decameron* well, there are good grounds for accepting this parallel. The suggestion[1] that in Act III, Sc. iii and Act IV, Sc. ii there are reminiscences of the fourth tale of the seventh day and the second story of the ninth, cannot be dismissed out of hand. One might also surmise that even though the circumstances differ in some respects, the illness of Francisco and the visit of the doctors is to be found in embryo in that of Giachetto Lamiens, the son of the marshal of England.[2] It is the existence of these incidents in the same play, tenuously though they may seem to be attached to the original, that strengthens the case for Fletcher's indebtedness. Certainly, in the *Decameron* there was matter congenial to the languishing love-element in the main plot and to the battle of wits in the under-plot, in which a man is outdone by a woman. Through the escapades of Thomas and his roystering companions Fletcher gives us a picture of contemporary manners and adapts Boccaccio to English surroundings.

Closely related to *Monsieur Thomas* in its general design is *Women Pleas'd*, though here the scene is laid in Florence, and the only obvious English traits are morris-dancers and Bomby, a Puritanical cobbler, who is hostile to Maypoles, sports and dancing. The main plot relates to Silvio, who has as his rival the duke of Siena. They both seek to marry Belvidere, the daughter of the duchess of Florence. The duchess favours the duke of Siena and exiles Silvio, but when the duke, think-ing himself affronted, declares war on Florence, it is Silvio who gains the victory for the Florentines. He has been aided by a deformed

---

[1] E. Koeppel, *Quellen-Studien*, pp. 95–6.   [2] *Dec.* ii, 8.

enchantress who after the battle requires that he shall grant her wish when she makes it known. In the presence of the duchess she demands that he shall marry her. Reluctantly he agrees, and on the wedding-day she removes her disguise and stands forth as Belvidere. With this romantic plot goes a sub-plot in which the leading figure is Isabella, the wife of Lopez, a miserly jeweller, who half-starves Isabella and his servant Penurio. They are leagued against him, Isabella with the connivance of Penurio seeking consolation elsewhere. It is in this connexion that Fletcher has recourse to the *Decameron*. Two scenes are based on tales in the seventh day. The first is the sixth tale which had already been popular with Tourneur and Sharpham. In Act II, Sc. vi, Claudio corresponds to Leonetto, and Bartello, the captain of the citadel, to Lambertuccio. They enter in the same order as in the tale, and make their exit in the same fashion as in Boccaccio. It is, of course, Isabella who invents the story that is told to her husband. However, Fletcher departs in one particular from the original. Lopez is suspicious and does not trust Claudio, who is much too handsome for his taste. In Act III, Sc. iv Fletcher interweaves the eighth tale. Here Isabella falls asleep as she is waiting for Rugio. She has tied a string to her finger, so that he may signal to her. Lopez returns unexpectedly and falls into a towering rage. As in the tale Isabella substitutes her maid for herself while Lopez has gone out for a moment, and when he returns, it is Jaquenet whom he thrashes in the dark. He leaves the house to bring her relatives, only to find Isabella unhurt. The tables are turned on him, and they depart uttering threats. But once more Fletcher introduces a change in the attitude of Lopez. He is not brow-beaten and bemused like his prototype and, after they have gone, asks her to explain her scheme. She does so convincingly, but not truth-fully, for she asserts that it was Bartello whom she was expecting. This prepares the way for Act IV, Sc. iii, where Bartello visits her again. Once more he is interrupted and has to take refuge by climbing up the chimney. A moment later Lopez enters with Rhodope, Bartello's wife. When Isabella has left them, Lopez kisses Rhodope and begins to talk of love, all within earshot of Bartello. The situation is an obvious adaptation for stage purposes of that in the eighth tale of the eighth day. In the end, alarmed by the outbreak of war, Lopez has the chimney searched for the jewels that he has hidden there, and Bartello is discovered.

Fletcher skilfully joins together three unconnected stories, the link being the shrewd character of Lopez which enables him in the third of these scenes to triumph over Bartello. The under-plot as a whole pictures a world of sexual passion and coarse speech that stands out against the unswerving devotion and lofty idealism of Silvio and

Belvidere in the main plot. Bartello is an important figure, since he is the chief means of attaching the two plots to each other. A development of Lambertuccio, he becomes in Fletcher's hands something more than the swaggering captain. Despite his boisterous and jaunty assertion of his youthfulness, he is old and fat, and in his gullibility recalls the later Falstaff. He has neither wit nor resourcefulness in a crisis, as one may see from the farcical episode in which he squeezes his way up the chimney. This incident is as ludicrous as anything in *The Merry Wives of Windsor*. The contrast between the earthy preoccupations of this very unmartial soldier and the high-hearted valour of Silvio suggests that Fletcher had in mind Falstaff and Prince Henry, so that in working on the material from the *Decameron*, by a devious route he again associates Boccaccio with Shakespeare.

Whereas lust and nobility are contrasted in *Women Pleased*, they are pitted against each other in *The Knight of Malta*, which was first acted before 1619. The scene is laid in Malta, and the background is the struggle of the Knights of the Order of St. John against the Turks. Montferrat, one of the knights, carried away by his passion for Oriana, the sister of Valetta, the Grand Master of Malta, forgets his vows of chastity. When she rebuffs him, he accuses her of loving a Turk and of betraying military information to him. Valetta sentences her to death, but Gomera, a Spanish aspirant to knighthood, defends her in combat, and her innocence is established by his victory. Gomera marries her but cannot repress his jealousy of Miranda, an aspirant to membership of the Order, who has won fame by his exploits. Although Miranda has always loved Oriana, Gomera's suspicions are unfounded. Oriana, who is with child, is so overcome with emotion that she faints, and Gomera believes that she is dead. Her black attendant, the lover and the agent of Montferrat, to further her own designs administers a sleeping potion, and Oriana is buried in the temple of St. John. It is at this point that Fletcher makes use of an episode in the fourth tale of the last day of the *Decameron*. There Messer Gentile Carisendi enters the tomb of Madonna Catalina and kisses the face of the dead woman. Even in these surroundings his passion has not vanished altogether, and it is impossible not to feel repugnance at this situation. Fletcher's handling shows greater delicacy. Miranda, who is about to enter the Order of St. John, visits the church to prepare himself spiritually for the ceremony of knightly dedication. His purpose therefore is pure and devout; he is about to take a vow of chastity. Nor does he come alone. He is accompanied by a fellow-soldier, Norandine. There is no question of his kissing Oriana, for he is unaware that she is dead, and only when she groans and awakens, do the others find her. Miranda kneels to offer a prayer of gratitude before he conveys her to the fort that he commands. When she has given birth to a son, Miranda is about to arrange for her return to her husband, but at the last moment is sorely tempted by his passion, which is intensified when she confesses that she has always loved him. However, in a famous speech (Act V, Sc. i) Oriana diverts his thoughts from earthly love to the spiritual and heavenly. Ultimately, in the presence of Valetta and the knights she lets fall her veil and Gomera is united to his wife and child. The play ends with the expulsion of Montferrat from the Order and the solemn admission of Miranda, after he has vowed

> ever to defend
> The virtuous fame of Ladies, and to oppugne
> Even unto death the Christian enemy.

There are characters in this play that remind us of other typical Fletcherian figures. Gomera, though admirable in some ways, is the jealous old husband, and Norandine, bluff and frank, has no exalted view about the relations between men and women. Above him in nobility stands Miranda. Yet even he has moments when he falters, just as Messer Gentile does, but both overcome their frailty and offer an example of restraint and generosity. Thus the figure of Miranda is inspired by Messer Gentile, though Fletcher, through the agency of Oriana, lifts the old theme to a higher plane and at times imparts a religious note which is alien to the tale and rare in his own work.

Another play in which Fletcher is said to have had a hand, along with Jonson and Middleton, is *The Widdow*, which has been dated 1615 or 1616. Two stories from the *Decameron* are used in connexion with Philippa, the young wife of an old judge, Brandino. She is enamoured of Francisco and, just as the heroine of the third tale of the third day sends the stupid friar as a messenger to her lover, Philippa dispatches Brandino to Francisco with a letter asking for a rendezvous, which the young man is said to have addressed to her, but which is really written by Philippa. Thus Francisco is apprised of her attitude towards him. He declares that he had merely wished to test her constancy and so to clear her name of slander. Brandino accepts the explanation and invites him to his house. Francisco is about to continue the intrigue when he is arrested with his friends Attilio and Ricardo, the last of whom is a suitor to Valeria, a widow, and has aroused the hostility of a rival. Francisco is bailed out by Brandino who presses him to use his house.

Soon afterwards he is attacked and wounded by thieves. The same night Martia, disguised as a man, Ansaldo, is also set upon and robbed. In the meantime, Philippa to her intense annoyance has been waiting in vain. Seeing a light in her house, Ansaldo, who has been stripped to his shirt, gazes up at it. Francisco, whose experience has shaken him, begins to ponder:

> these wenching businesses
> Are strange unlucky things, and fatall fooleries,
> No mar'l so many gallants die ere thirtie,
> 'Tis able to vex out a mans heart in five year,
> The crosses that belong to't . . .
>
> (III. i)

He catches sight of Ansaldo and, thinking that he sees a ghost, is filled with superstitious alarm. His conscience pricks him, as he considers Brandino's recent kindness and the friendship that had existed between him and his father.

> What ere it be, it is made strong against me
> By my ill purpose. For 'tis mans own sin
> That puts on armour upon all his evils,
> And gives them strength to strike him: were it less
> Then what it is, my guilt would make it serve;
> A wicked mans own shadow has distracted him:
> Were this a business now to save an honour,
> As 'tis to spoil one, I would pass this then,
> Stuck all hels horrors i'thee: now I dare not.
> Why may't not be the spirit of my Father
> That lov'd this man so well, whom I make haste
> Now to abuse? And have been cross'd about it
> Most fearfully hitherto, if I think well on't;
> Scap'd death but lately too, nay most miraculously;
> And what do's fond man venture all these ills for,
> That may so sweetly rest in honest peace?
> For that which being obtain'd, is as he was
> To his own sence, but remov'd neerer still
> To death eternall: what delight has man
> Now at this present, for his pleasant sin
> Of yesterdaies committing? 'las, 'tis vanish'd,
> And nothing but the sting remains within him.
>
> (III. i)

While he is thus watching, Ansaldo decides to knock. Philippa, thinking that it is Francisco, is overjoyed. She is amazed to hear that it is not, but when her maid Violetta commends the beauty of Ansaldo, she consoles herself. The situation is obviously inspired by that of the second tale of the second day of the *Decameron*, where the lady of Castel Guiglielmo, frustrated in her expectation of seeing the Marquis Azzo, consoles herself with Rinaldo who has been robbed by highwaymen and stripped to his shirt. Ansaldo, like Rinaldo, is provided with a suit of clothes, but here the play diverges, for Ansaldo declares that he must leave at once on an urgent errand, and Philippa is baulked once more. Later she arrays Ansaldo as a woman, thinking to deceive her husband. But the laugh turns against her when Ansaldo's sex is revealed and Francisco, falling in love with Ansaldo—Martia, wants to marry her.

The treatment of the material from the *Decameron* in this play is remarkable. One need only compare it with the handling of similar tales in Fletcher's under-plots to realise how greatly it differs. The gravity of the tone, the earnest philosophising about sin and death, the sensitiveness to the pricking of conscience and the awareness of the tranquillity that comes from a mind untroubled by guilt, are incompatible with the Fletcherian attitude, as indeed they are with the carefree gallantry of Boccaccio.

It is the interest in the struggle between desire and chastity that inspires *The Two Merry Milke-Maids*, printed in 1620 as the work of ' I.C.', which is said to stand for John Cumber, one of the actors of the Revels by whom this comedy was performed before James I.[1] The heroine is named Dorigene, which recalls Chaucer's *Franklin's Tale* and ' The Triumph of Honor'.[2] But the plot indicates that the author, in spite of the change of name from Dianora to Dorigene, was following the fifth tale of the tenth day in the *Decameron*. The play opens with a pastoral setting which at once creates an atmosphere of romance. Julia and Dorigene have dressed up as milkmaids, and the latter in this rustic attire wins the heart of 'John Earnest, Duke of Saxonie'. After their marriage Dorigene is visited by Dorilus, the brother of Julia. He had previously wooed her, and one day she had promised in jest that he should have his will, if ever she became a duchess. He is still infatuated with her, yet far from purposing to keep her to her word, merely intends to look upon her and bear his loss. However, on learning from Dorigene that she has always loved and still loves him, and has married the duke only because in this way the fortunes of her impoverished father might be restored, he declares:

> You haue afresh kindled the fire againe,
> And I must die a Martyr in your loue.
>
> (II. i)

The situation is not unlike that of Oriana and Miranda,[3] but Dorigene is no Oriana, and the mood is deprived of any exaltation when Julia coldly remarks that if the worst comes to the worst with her brother, it is ' but a foolish Louer cast away'. In the end Dorigene imposes on him the task of obtaining:

> A Garland of the rarest Flowers on Earth,
> The choicest to the Eye, and to the Sent,

---

[1] Schelling, i, p. 439.
[2] Vide ante, p. 229.   [3] Vide ante, pp. 233–4. Cf. *The Knight of Malta*, v. i.

Set with such Fruits the season of the yeere
Affoords not in this Clyme, And it must haue
The vertue of continuing euer fresh,
As long as you remaine constant in loue.

(II. i)

It is possible that the dramatist substituted the garland for Boccaccio's magic garden, because it was better suited to the capacity of the
stage at that time. But the magician invoked is altered for another
reason. The introduction of John Ernest, duke of Saxony, a contemporary ruler, was no doubt prompted by the popular marriage of
Princess Elizabeth to the Elector Palatine,[1] and the transference of
the scene from northern Italy to a German court led the dramatist to
Wittemberg,[2] so well known to English theatre-goers through Marlowe's *Dr. Faustus* and Shakespeare's *Hamlet*. It is therefore a friend
of Dorilus named Bernard who has acquired a knowledge of magic
through his studies at Wittemberg who provides the garland.

This is handed to her in the second scene of Act II. Dorigene is
dumbfounded; the duke, seeing her distress, enquires its cause. He
finds her story convincing but thinks that it may be a wile and so, in
accordance with the familiar dramatic device of the period, he decides
to test her. He therefore bids her fulfil her promise, his attitude being
that of some cynical gallant:

I prythy

Make no scruple of't then other Women:
It is a Cryme, that not one Night i' the yeere,
But some where or other such a Fault is made,
Nor lookes the Wife the next day worse for it.

(II. ii)

Dorilus is overcome by the duke's offer which he refuses, for he is
swayed not only by his sense of the duke's generosity but also by his
realisation of his obligation of loyalty to his ruler.

The play has now reached the end of Act II, and the author has to
find material for three more acts. The duke, worked upon by a scheming lord, Raymond, has an access of jealousy. He runs his sword
through Dorilus and sends Dorigene to prison. But Dorilus is aided by
Bernard, who has given his friend a ring to make him invisible. At the
trial of Dorigene, he defends her, as a spirit, with such force that the
duke perceives that he has wronged her. In Act IV, however, he has
another bout of jealousy but Raymond, who is taken ill, confesses and
clears Dorigene. In spite of this penitence, he tries to ravish Julia and
is condemned to death. Dorigene begs for pardon, and the duke

---

[1] Schelling, i, p. 437.

[2] The form used in the play, probably owing to an English confusion of Wittenberg
with Wirtemberg, now Würtemberg.

consents with some reluctance. Thereupon Raymond again repents, and at the close Dorilus regains the favour of his lord.

The repeated jealousy of the duke and the repeated alternation of villainy and repentance in Raymond are obviously employed to eke out the plot, and the greater use of the magic element than in the tale can be accounted for in the same way. The elevation in rank of the chief characters provides scope for the favourite theme of loyalty to the monarch, and similarly Gilberto of Udine is transformed into the jealous husband of seventeenth-century drama. In this process something of Boccaccio's purpose—to offer examples of notable generosity—is lost. The duke acts as he does, partly to try his wife, and whereas the magician demanded his price and then renounced his claim because of the generosity of Gilberto and Ansaldo, Bernard aids Dorilus out of friendship, requiring and relinquishing nothing. Consequently, the conflict, so sharply defined at the beginning of the play, weakens into a succession of incidents without essential cohesion.

Robert Davenport's tragi-comedy, *The City-Night-Cap*, which was licensed in 1624, again has the chaste wife who is put to the test by a jealous husband. Lorenzo is married to Abstemia, the sister of the duke of Venice. Though he himself urges his friend Philippo to try the fidelity of Abstemia, he becomes convinced of her guilt and abuses and kicks her until she swoons. Even one of his attendants ventures to reprove him: 'You are too violent, my Lord'. The duke of Verona judges the case. Philippo is banished, and Abstemia is to be divorced. But the duke of Venice intervenes, and there is a new trial, at the end of which Lorenzo is banished, his office and revenues being granted to Philippo. In the meantime, after a bewildering profusion of incidents, Lorenzo and Abstemia are brought together again in a way that is reminiscent of Boccaccio's tale of Titus and Gisippus. Lorenzo has been searching vainly for Abstemia and in despair draws his sword and is about to kill himself. At this moment he is seized and accused of a murder that has been committed. Longing for death, he pleads guilty. Now Abstemia enters and, recognising her husband, declares that she committed the crime. Lorenzo denies it, and as they vie with each other like Titus and Gisippus in claiming to be the culprit, they are sent to prison, where they are reconciled.

There now follows a situation which offers a parallel to the famous scene where Isabella visits Claudio in gaol in *Measure for Measure*. Antonio, the son of the duke of Milan, who holds under arrest the real malefactor, offers to free Lorenzo, if Abstemia will sacrifice her honour. Lorenzo weakly agrees, but she asks how he could live afterwards in such disgrace. Antonio insinuates that she only appears virtuous. Once her husband is hanged, she will prove less difficult. Lorenzo, inflamed

by jealousy once more, believes that she has some cunning scheme to
get him out of the way and exclaims:

> Oh slie hypocrisie!
> Durst ye but now die for me? good heavens! die for me!
> The greatest act of pain, and dare not buy me
> With a poor minutes pleasure![1]
>
> (Act V)

To this Abstemia replies:

> No, Sir, I dare not; there is little pain in death,
> But a great death in very little pleasure:
> I had rather, trust me, bear your death with honour,
> Then buy your life with baseness: as I am expos'd
> To th'greatest battery beauty ever fought,
> Oh blame me not, if I be covetous
> To come off with greatest honour; if I do this
> To let you live, I kill your name, and give
> My soul a wound; I crush her from sweet grace,
> And change her Angels to a furies face:
> Try me no more then, but if you must bleed, boast
> To preserve honour, life is nobly lost.
>
> (Act V)

As Davenport drew on Boccaccio for one incident in his portrait of
the virtuous Abstemia, so he had recourse to him for a woman who by
her misconduct was to emphasise Abstemia's nobility. It is Dorothea,
her waiting-woman and the wife of Lodovico, who acts as a foil by
her wanton disposition. She has cast her eyes on one of Lodovico's men
called Francisco. As in the seventh tale of the seventh day Madonna
Beatrice dupes her husband Egano in the pursuit of her intrigue with
Anichino, so Dorothea beguiles Lodovico. He is sent on a fool's errand
to the garden, and Dorothea befools him so completely that he praises
her chastity as he goes. The waiting Francisco cannot refrain from
saying:

> Well now I see, as he who fain would know
> The real strain of goodness, may in her read it;
> Who can seem chaste, and can be what she seems:
> So, who would see hells craft, in her may read it,
> Who can seem too, but not be what she seems:
> In brief, put him to school (would cheat the de'l of 's right)
> To a dainty smooth-fac'd female hypocrite.
>
> (Act II)

He afterwards explains that he only took advantage of his lord's
absence to try Dorothea and, feigning regret that his action may be
misconstrued, he threatens to fall on his sword, so that Lodovico is
convinced of his loyalty. However, Lodovico does not go on being
deceived like his prototype Egano, who becomes a mere laughing-stock.

[1] Quotations from 1661 edition.

The truth comes out. Francisco is condemned to ride through Verona, facing the hindquarters of a donkey and holding its tail as a bridle. Dorothea is sent to 'the Monasterie of Matrones'.

Davenport's general plan was not novel, as he himself admitted, but he keeps a firm hand on the central theme. The antithesis between the two chief woman characters in the main and the sub-plot is neatly maintained, and with genuine comic irony he makes Lodovico eulogise his supposedly virtuous wife at the expense of the supposedly faithless Abstemia. The design of the play is completed by the words of the duke of Milan at the close:

> bad women,
> Are natures clouds eclipsing the fair shine;
> The good all gracious, saint-like and divine.
>
> (Act V)

Italy is also the setting of Massinger's comedy, *The Guardian*, first performed in 1633. It has an intricate plot, one element of which owes something to the tale in the *Decameron* that follows immediately after that of Egano and Beatrice.[1] Severino, a nobleman banished and living as a bandit chief, returns to his home, only to find that his wife Jolante has a lover for whom she has provided a banquet. He binds her while he goes into another room, carrying tapers with him, to study his vengeance. The waiting-woman Calypso takes Jolante's place, and Severino enters saying

> It is a deed of darkness, and I need
> No light to guide me.
>
> (Act III)

He stabs Calypso in the arms and cuts off her nose. She bears it without betraying her mistress. When he has gone, Calypso retires and Jolante resumes her place. Severino returns with a taper and to his astonishment discovers her unharmed. She asserts that Heaven has heard her prayers and restored her as a miraculous proof of her innocence. The similarity with Boccaccio's story applies only to the latter part, and though there is the same keen-witted dupery as in the tale, the episode in *The Guardian* is much more savage and brutal.

John Jones's tragi-comedy, *Adrasta: or, the Woman's Spleene, and Loves Conquest*, which was never acted, was printed in 1635. The main plot deals with the theme of virtuous and faithful love. Lucilio, the son of Duke Orsino and his wife Adrasta, is devoted to Althea, a lady of noble rank. In spite of all attempts to dissuade him, Lucilio refuses to give up Althea. Adrasta plots against her life, but Lucilio helps her to

[1] Vide ante, p. 232, where its use in Fletcher's *Women Pleased* is pointed out. However, Langbaine, op. cit., 1698, p. 356, errs in calling it 'Day 8. Nov. 7', instead of vii, 8. His error is repeated by Scott, p. 95.

escape and takes her place in prison. He is about to be put to death, when his identity is discovered. He is banished, but ultimately he and Althea are reunited and gain the consent of the duke and duchess.

As a contrast the sub-plot depicts the passion of Damasippus, who is described as 'a lecherous Stoike', for Mistress Frailware, the wife of the Constable. In Act III, when Lucilio is in Frailware's custody, Damasippus, at the suggestion of the ubiquitous and mischievous Page, visits Mistress Frailware. The Page informs the Constable of what is afoot, and on his prompting the representative of the law decides to repay Damasippus in kind by inviting Mistress Abigail, his wife, to supper. Consequently, Damasippus and Mistress Frailware are surprised as they are sitting down to their meal. There is just time to hide Damasippus before the Constable enters with Mistress Abigail. The newcomers sit down to enjoy the excellent supper but Mistress Frailware, saying that she feels unwell, withdraws to her room. Damasippus, as he lies hidden, now hears Frailware making advances to his wife and has the mortifying experience of learning that she had many times wished him in his grave. At this point the Page enters, disguised as a fiddler, and plays to them. Abigail is unwilling to listen but agrees to do so, saying: 'I can endure anything for your sake sweet M. *Frailware*'. At this Damasippus, who apparently is in a chest on which the others are seated, stirs uneasily, startling Frailware as he does so. When he emerges, the Page suggests that as a punishment his beard shall be shaved off.

It is possible that in the construction of *Adrasta* John Jones was influenced by Fletcher's *Women Pleased*, where the eighth tale of the eighth day was also used in the sub-plot.[1] However, the story of Zeppa and Spinelloccio is far more easily recognised in the plot relating to Frailware and Damasippus. Nevertheless, in adapting the narrative to the dramatic form, an important change was made by the introduction of the mischievous page, whose presence at the meeting of Frailware and Abigail as well as his proposal to punish the offending Damasippus moralise the episode. There is nothing original in *Adrasta*, and one can only subscribe to Langbaine's remark: 'This Play the Actors refus'd, and I think with Justice; it being very indifferently written'.[2]

On a higher literary plane is *The Siedge: or, Love's Convert*, a tragi-comedy which has been dated 1637.[3] It is the work of William Cartwright who held the office of proctor in the university of Oxford. The scene is laid in Byzantium which is besieged by Misander, the

[1] Vide ante, p. 232.   [2] Op cit., p. 281.
[3] Schelling, ii, p. 607. G. B. Evans, *The Plays and Poems of William Cartwright*, Madison, 1951, p. 355, suggests that it was seen by King Charles during the royal progress in 1636 or a few months later in London on the occasion of the court performance of *The Royal Slave*.

R

tyrant of Thrace. He demands that a virgin shall be sent to him from the city. Leucasia is ordered by her father to go and kill the tyrant in his sleep. In his tent she falters and upsets a lamp. Misander, awaking, stabs her, but later, overcome by her eloquence, makes her his queen. To offset this serious plot in which a lustful tyrant is converted into a virtuous husband, Cartwright interweaves with it an under-plot. This is of a comic nature, but free from all bawdiness.

It depicts how Pyle, a rich widow of Byzantium, is importuned by her suitors, upon whom she imposes various commands. Philostratus is ordered to shut himself in a coffin in the temple, and he enters in a winding-sheet, grumbling as he does so:

> I have not seen the inside of a Temple
> These twelve Months til this time, & now I come
> Commanded too: Hell's in this damned Widdow.
> What doth she mean to make me lye in a Coffin?
> I am not fit for Death, although I think
> I'm very forward towards it: Somthing in
> My Bones doth tell me so.
>
> (v. v)

In the next scene Prusias, dressed like an angel, enters with a 'Caduceus' in one hand and a taper in the other. He is uneasy at the thought of spirits haunting the temple but hopes that his rod and candle will ward them off. However, when he seats himself on the coffin which he is supposed to guard, he is terrified by a sudden rumbling. There follows a scene in which Nicias slinks in and takes up his position behind a pillar as an observer, while Callimachus who is to carry away the coffin, appears in the guise of a Fury. The fears of Nicias, Prusias and Callimachus are admirably portrayed in this passage:

> *Nic.* Lord! how my hand doth shake. I set down one thing,
> Then blot it out again I know not how.
> Pray *Jove* he doth not sent me! If he hath
> But any Nose, he hath th'Advantage of me.
> *Pru.* Heav'n bless me! Yonder's one I'm sure's no Angel.
> O my prophetick words! that I should promise
> T'encounter with a Fury!
> *Cal.* Hold! yond's something
> That is not one of us: I would I were
> A very Fury now indeed, and had
> All qualities belonging to my shape.
> The first thing that I'd do, should be to make
> My self invisible. Widdow, you must pardon me;
> Sure I shall fall into a Thousand peeces
> If that this shaking leave me not the sooner.
> I vow I'm not afraid for all my fooling—
> I—I—must on—

Pru. Good heaven! hee's coming towards me:
    How blew my Candle burns! I see his feet,
    Th'are cloven ones for certain.
Cal. Y-y-yet I dare not—
    'Tis safest to retire, my joints are loose all,
    And yet I can scarce move 'em.
Nic. He hath found me,
    He is upon the Train: how his Nose shakes
    As he snuffs up the Ayre!
Cal. My Teeth do ch-ch-ch-chatter
    As schoolboys in cold weather.
Pru. Heav'n defend me!
    How he doth gnash his teeth, and make hell here!
    I would I were i' th' Coffin at a Venture.
Nic. All my left side's grown stupid. I'm half stone;
    I feel a numness steal o'r all my limbs:
    I shall augment the number of the Statues.
    It will be *Niobe Nicias* presently.
Cal. Being it is an Angel, 'twill not hurt me.
    I will make towards it however.
Pru. Now,
    Now he comes open-mouth'd; Lord, what a smoak
    He belcheth like a Furnace! look! he claps
    His tail between his Legs, as dogs are wont
    When they will do shrewd turns; 'tis a sly Spirit;
    They'l never leave their cunning.
Cal. Hee'l not suffer me
    To talk long with him, hee's so us'd t'*Ambrosia*,
    And to's Perfumes, which hee'l not find here sure.
Pru. O!—   *Cal.* O!
Pru. You—   *Cal.* You—
Pru. Your Honour—   *Cal.* Blessed Spirit—
Pru. Yes.   *Cal.* I—must have—that—Body—there.
Pru. You can
    Lay no claime—unto him—he is not—yours—
Cal. He is our due.
Pru. How can you prove't?
Cal. Dare you
    Dispute with him that first invented Logick?
Pru. No, no, I am no Scholar, I'm a Captain.
Cal. You must not guard the dead then, he must down.
                           (v. vii)

The dispute is abruptly ended when Philostratus, rising out of the coffin, casts off Prusias, and he and the others scatter in terror. Philostratus, running out, meets Misander and his attendants. It is evident that this scene in the temple was inspired by the first tale of the ninth day of the *Decameron*, where Madonna Francesca de' Lazzari dispatches her wooers, Rinuccio Palermini and Alessandro Chiarmontesi, on an errand akin to that of Pyle's suitors, though the episode is modified considerably in order to harmonise with the change of setting from Pistoia to Byzantium.

In Act V, Sc. viii Leucasia enters with her train and a priest. Then Pyle arrives and is compelled to select one of the suitors, her choice falling on Nicias. The two plots are thus linked together at the close. Earlier too they are connected when Pyle, aspiring to become queen, is induced to take part in a plot against Misander. There are serious, even threatening moments in the main plot, and the under-plot affords comic relief. The seventh scene of the last act in particular presents the farcical situation skilfully, and here at least Cartwright shows that even if he was not a remarkable dramatist, he had a sense of humour.

In Richard Rhodes's comedy, *Flora's Vagaries*, which was acted at the Theatre Royal in November 1663 and at court on 14 February 1667[1] the popular third tale of the third day in the *Decameron* again plays an important part. However, the relationship of deceiver and deceived is that of daughter and father, not that of wife and husband. Otrante, who is kept under the closest supervision by her father, has fallen in love with Lodovico, who had been instrumental in rescuing her when she was carried off by Francesco. As Lodovico is a woman-hater, she calls in friar Domenico and persuades him to carry a message to her rescuer. He is to say that she rejects Lodovico's letters, which, of course, he has never written, and to give him a bracelet which he is supposed to have presented her with. To make doubly sure that her meaning is understood Otranto asks her cousin Flora to explain to Lodovico her initiative in wooing him. This is an addition by Rhodes to eke out the material of the tale. In Act III he inserts still more padding. Grimani dresses up as a friar,[2] hoping to discover the secrets of his daughter and niece. But they are aware of his plan and in their confession abuse Grimani roundly till he can restrain his fury no longer and betrays himself, whereupon they declare that the spurious friar must be ill. At the end of the act Otrante again dispatches Friar Domenico to Lodovico with a letter that he is accused of having written. By means of this letter she conveys to Lodovico that her father is to go out that afternoon. Further, she will hang a scarf out of her window and if he knocks gently at her gate, he will be admitted. It is possible that the device of the scarf as a signal was suggested by the fifth tale of the third day, as it appears in the English translation of 1620.[3] In the end Lodovico and Otrante reveal everything to Friar Domenico,

---

[1] Cf. A. Nicoll, *A History of Restoration Drama*, Cambridge, 1923, pp. 305, 371. It was printed in 1670. As a curiosity it may be noted that even in the uncongenial Restoration atmosphere the story of 'Patient Grissel' still lingered on, and that Pepys in his diary records having seen a 'puppet-play' of this name on 30 August 1667.

[2] Perhaps suggested by *Dec.* vii, 5.

[3] Cf. H. G. Wright, *The first English translation of the 'Decameron'*, p. 68.

who with great complaisance agrees to marry them, and Grimani has
to recognise the 'fait accompli'.

However, this conclusion is not reached without considerable resistance on the part of Lodovico. When his friends urge him to comply
with Otrante's wishes, he says querulously:[1]

> Must I then forgo my Liberty, and effect the
> Title of a good womans-man, the Woman is handsom,
> that is the truth on't, and she will have me love
> her, who can help it, what must be, must be.
> (Act II)

But in Act III, Sc. iii he still hesitates: 'Curse on these Women, I am
strangely tempted, yet I won't be in Love'. When he receives the
message about the scarf, he exclaims:

> The World, the Flesh, and the Devil met in
> Women. Honest she cannot be, that's impossible,
> she knows I cannot love her well enough to marry
> her, besides no honest Woman would e're have
> made her Confessor her Pander.
> (Act III)

Nevertheless, at last he is convinced that Otrante is virtuous and is
won over.

Evidently Rhodes felt the need to show a gradual transformation of
Lodovico's attitude. He gains time for this process by expanding the
original tale through the episode of Flora as messenger and that of
Grimani as confessor, and the overcoming of Lodovico's reluctance
lends novelty to the old tale.

This is again employed by Sir Francis Fane in his *Love in the Dark,
or the Man of Bus'nesse* which was acted at Drury Lane in May 1675[2]
and printed that year. However, here it is a jealous husband, Cornanti,
who keeps his wife Bellinganna in seclusion, so that only her confessor
Scrutinio can see her. She makes use of Scrutinio, as the lady of
Florence employs the stupid friar, to take a message to Trivultio, a
gentleman of Milan, in which he is accused of having attempted her
honour and afterwards molested her with music beneath her window
looking on the Strada Nuova. Trivultio understands the hint, and soon
arrives at her house with a boy who plays while he sings. Such an
adventure appeals to him as 'an enterprise fit for a great Spirit'. He
has a chance to marry Aurana, a wealthy lady, but he regards the
match as 'a Golden Trap'. He decries marriage and exclaims:

> Matrimony! for Heaven's sake name it not.
> I do not love to hear the sound of Fetters.
> (II. i)

So he prefers freedom.

---

[1] Quotations from the edition of 1670. [2] A. Nicoll, op. cit., p. 363.

In view of this attitude he is induced far too easily to reconcile himself to marriage with Aurana. This is after Bellinganna grants access and then proceeds to entreat him to woo Aurana. Bellinganna succeeds in persuading him to do so. However, though the connexion between Trivultio and Bellinganna turns out to be harmless enough, they decide in Act III to cure Cornanti of his jealousy. Bellinganna places her husband with six or seven bravoes in ambush in a garden. Then Trivultio appears, and she addresses him in the most seductive fashion, but he repels her and moves his cane as if he were beating her violently. Cornanti is cured of his suspicions and ejaculates 'Such a Wife and such a Friend!' This incident was probably an adaptation of the popular tale of Beatrice and Egano.[1] But here the husband, though misled for his own good, is not betrayed by Bellinganna.

So far as the action goes, *Love in the Dark* is not immoral. The gallant does not have his will. Bellinganna is not unchaste, and Trivultio puts on the bonds of wedlock, despite his original aversion. However, the sudden change is unconvincing. It is impossible to resist the feeling that what most truly reflects the temper of the period is the declaration of the early Trivultio: 'A man had need to have his wits about him, in this quick-sighted Philosophical Age, wherein whoring is improv'd to a liberal Science'.[2]

This preoccupation of those who frequented the Restoration theatre is mirrored by Aphra Behn's comedy, *The Rover: or, the Banisht Cavaliers*, which was first performed at the Duke's Theatre in Dorset Garden in March 1677[3] and printed that year. The scene is Naples in carnival time, and the theme is the amorous adventures of a number of Englishmen. Those of Blunt, a simple-minded country gentleman, are derived ultimately from the tale of Andreuccio of Perugia[4] and more immediately from *Blurt Master-Constable*.[5] Having left his companions lest they should follow him, Blunt is decoyed to the house of Lucetta. He is impressed by its richness and naïvely believes her statement that the mere sight of him has captivated her. Her jealous husband is supposed to be away from home. Nevertheless, in the following scene she bids him put out the light to avoid suspicion. The bed on which she is lying descends, and as Blunt is groping about in the dark, he falls through a trap-door into a sewer. His rich clothes, gold watch, well-filled purse, diamond rings and gold bracelet fall into the hands of Lucetta and her confederates. Blunt is furious at his own simplicity and, as he climbs back on to the stage, covered with dirt, makes this comment on his folly:

[1] Vide ante, p. 239.
[2] Act I, 1675 ed., p. 14.   [3] A. Nicoll, op. cit., p. 353.
[4] *Dec.* ii, 5.   [5] Vide ante, p. 217.

I am got out at last, and (which is a Miracle) without a Clue—and now to Damning and Cursing!—but if that wou'd ease me, where shall I begin? with my Fortune, my self, or the Quean that couzen'd me—what a Dog was I to believe in Woman? oh Coxcomb—Ignorant conceited Coxcomb! to fancy she cou'd be enamour'd with my person! at first sight enamour'd!—oh, I am a cursed Puppy! 'tis plain, Fool was writ upon my Forehead! she perceiv'd it!—saw the *Essex* Calf there—for what Allurements cou'd there be in this Countenance? which I can indure, because I'm acquainted with it—oh, dull silly Dog! to be thus sooth'd into a Couzening! had I been drunk, I might fondly have credited the young Quean!—but as I was in my right Wits, to be thus cheated, confirms it I am a dull believing *English* Country Fop—but my Camrades! death and the Devil! there's the worst of all—then a Ballad will be Sung to Morrow on the *Prado*, to a Lousie Tune of the Enchanted 'Squire, and the Annihilated Damsel.

(III. ii)

There is in these three scenes of the third act the same farcical comedy as in *Blurt Master-Constable*, but, as Blunt's power of self-criticism indicates, even if he is gullible, he is not an utter simpleton. When his infatuation is abruptly terminated, he displays a robust common sense. As a country squire he is the butt of the keen Restoration intellect, but at the same time he is accorded a measure of sympathy which was denied to Lazarillo de Tormes, for after all he is a stout supporter of the Stuart dynasty and among his possessions that fall into the hands of Lucetta is a medal of the king.

To satisfy the same kind of interest as that to which Aphra Behn had appealed, Thomas Durfey wrote his comedy *Squire Oldsapp: or, the Night Adventurers*, which was also produced at the Dorset Garden Theatre, some nine months after *The Rover*.[1] The scene is moved, however, from the Neapolitan underworld to England. The four leading figures in a complicated plot are Squire Oldsapp, credulous, old and infirm, who keeps Madam Tricklove as his mistress 'for the credit on't'. She favours a town gallant called Welford and arranges a meeting with him, but, owing to a misunderstanding, another lover, Henry, is taken to her. In Act IV, Sc. iii, in order to elude the vigilance of the jealous Oldsapp, Henry is to wait in the street until Tricklove gives him a signal. Lest she should fall asleep, she ties a string leading from the balcony into the street, and to the string a bell is attached. When all is quiet, Henry is to ring the bell. This part of the play is obviously adapted from the eighth tale of the seventh day of the *Decameron*. The rest of the episode modifies the original story considerably. When Oldsapp stumbles over the string, he is on the alert. Consequently it is he, not Tricklove, who opens the door to Henry. Oldsapp calls for lights, and while they are coming, Tricklove's servant Pimpo replaces Henry who is escorted to a hiding-place. When the lights are brought,

[1] Cf. A. Nicoll, op. cit., p. 361.

Pimpo pretends to be drunk, and Tricklove explains that he had been given permission to make merry with some friends, and the contrivance of the bell was solely to prevent his creating a disturbance by knocking.

Linked to this episode there now follows another derived from the seventh tale of the seventh day. When Pimpo has reeled off the stage, Tricklove makes a feigned confession. She pretends to be expecting Welford and says that she has agreed to meet him in the garden. Oldsapp is therefore induced to put on Tricklove's night attire, wait until Welford appears and then thrash him soundly. Barely has Oldsapp gone, when Welford presents himself to Tricklove. She is taken aback but quickly devises how to get rid of him. He is to behave as if he thought Oldsapp really was Tricklove, and to thrash him soundly for unfaithfulness. The ruse is successful, and in the first scene of Act V the jealous Oldsapp has been drubbed into the belief that Welford is his loyal friend.

There is an element of farce in the scene where Pimpo acts as if he were drunk, but the play as a whole concentrates on the intrigue. The combination of the two tales provides two lovers, one of whom is outwitted, just as Oldsapp is duped. The jealous old man gets no sympathy, despite the pitiless beating inflicted on him. In this world his sixty-three years merely emphasise his folly, and no sentiment is wasted on him. The interest is focused on the battle of wits, and the last words of the play, spoken by Tricklove, are significant:

> to forge plots in an extremity,
> Let every Mistress learn of me.

It was at the theatre in Dorset Garden that Durfey's comedy, *The Royalist*, was acted in January 1682,[1] and it was printed in that year. Here the author harks back to the ninth tale of the seventh day, that of Lidia, Nicostrato and Pirro, but the setting is Cromwellian England, not ancient Greece. Camilla, the wife of Sir Oliver Oldcut, chairman to the committee of sequestrations, is secretly loyal and attracted to Sir Charles Kinglove, 'the Royalist, one of the King's Colonels at *Worcester*-Fight, a Lover of Monarchy and Prerogative'. To test her love for him, Sir Charles imposes three conditions. The demands in the original story that the favourite hawk of Nicostrato shall be killed and that Lidia shall pull a tuft of hair from his beard are discarded. They are replaced by the requirement that Camilla shall arrange for Kinglove to kiss and embrace her in the presence of Oldcut and also to strike her husband three times on the nose. Further, whereas in the original tale Lidia has to extract a sound tooth from

---

[1] A. Nicoll, op. cit., p. 361.

Nicostrato, in the play Kinglove claims two teeth. The reason for the last change is that the scene is made more amusing, for when the surgeon, having removed one good tooth and palmed off a hollow one to show Sir Oliver, is trying to pull out the second, Oldcut himself snatches it from his mouth and sees that it is sound. Thereupon he complains bitterly that from now on he is 'doom'd never to bite any thing harder than a Custard' and swears that he will murder the surgeon.

Not only does Durfey create this farcical episode but he avoids carrying the pear-tree incident to the limits of the tale. Moreover, the intrigue of Camilla, unlike that of Lidia, is not developed as had been agreed, for Kinglove discovers that the page who has followed him in all his misfortunes is really a lady named Philippa, and his affection is directed towards her. This play about Cavalier and Puritan, though hostile to Cromwell's party, ends on a note of reconciliation. By the Protector's commands Kinglove's sequestered lands are restored to him, and he can look forward to his marriage to Philippa with an easy mind.

The adaptation of material from the *Decameron* to an English environment is illustrated once more in *The London Cuckolds* by Edward Ravenscroft. This comedy, which was produced at the theatre in Dorset Garden in November, 1681[1] and printed in 1682, introduces Wiseacre and Doodle, two aldermen of London, and Dashwell, a London attorney, all of whom are duped by their wives and thus give the play its title. The most interesting of the women is Eugenia, Dashwell's wife, who is the typical keen-witted contriver of intrigues. Her admirer Loveday visits her when Dashwell is absent, but they are interrupted by the unexpected return of the husband. She hides Loveday by drawing the curtains round her bed, seats herself on a cushion and pretends to be at her devotions. After Dashwell has gone, a second interruption occurs. It is Ramble, 'a great Designer on Ladies', who comes to see her at her request. But this is an awkward coincidence, and Eugenia is anxious to get rid of him, though he is reluctant to depart. While they are still parleying, Dashwell reappears. Now Ravenscroft harks back to the sixth tale of the seventh day in the *Decameron*. Eugenia tells Ramble to draw his sword and threaten to be in pursuit of some one. But Ravenscroft makes the scene more tense than any other English dramatist who had exploited such a situation. Ramble is too zealous in playing the role of the infuriated pursuer. Eugenia and her servant Jane both vow that no one is there, but Ramble keeps them on tenterhooks while he searches every corner. Then he throws open the curtains of the bed and discloses Loveday.

[1] A. Nicoll, op. cit., p. 370.

Eugenia has the presence of mind to swoon. Ramble controls his feelings, but as he withdraws, cannot refrain from exclaiming 'Oh false, damned false woman'.

It still remains for Eugenia to pursue her intrigue with Loveday. At this stage Ravenscroft draws on the seventh tale of the seventh day. Eugenia tells her husband that Loveday is importuning her and has asked her to meet him in the summer-house in the garden. She persuades Dashwell to put on her night-attire and await the arrival of Loveday. In due course he is soundly thrashed by Loveday who feigns to be inflicting punishment on Eugenia for thinking him capable of such an action towards 'so worthy a Gentleman' as Dashwell. For his part, Dashwell can only say 'I am convinc'd it was very well meant' and 'he did it but to try my Wife for my sake'.

This is beyond doubt the least moral of the Restoration comedies that use the *Decameron* wholly or in part for their plots. The women have no trace of virtue and acquiesce only too readily in the betrayal of their husbands who in their turn, while they see through their pretexts, appear to accept the situation. The atmosphere is created in the opening scene when Wiseacre and Doodle discuss the manners of their time. Wiseacre declares: 'Girles now at sixteen are as knowing as Matrons were formerly at sixty, I tell you in these days they understand *Aristotle*'s Problems at twelve years of age', to which Doodle replies: ' 'Tis true indeed, nothing in the nature of man or woman is a secret to them . . . O to say the truth 'tis a very forward knowing age'.

In view of the tone then prevailing in the theatre, it is interesting to see how Durfey revised Shakespeare's *Cymbeline* in *The Injured Princess, or the Fatal Wager*, which was acted at Drury Lane Theatre about March 1682[1] and published the same year. The new title suggests which part of the play attracted Durfey. It is the relationship of the jealous husband to a faithful wife whose fidelity is subjected to a test. It may be observed that Imogen is renamed Eugenia, like the central figure of *The London Cuckolds*, and Durfey allows the spectator at times to gain the impression that she is an intriguer of the same type. This is conveyed by Pisanio, who in *The Injured Princess* is slow to be convinced of her innocence. Hypocrisy and deceit are suggested by his exclamation:

> Oh Woman, Woman!
> Who ere cou'd learn thy deep Philosophy,
> Or fathom thy unsounded Sea of Craft?
> That look of her's has power to cause sound Faith
> Revolt, and make men fancy her a Saint.
>
> (III. iii)

---

[1] A. Nicoll, op. cit., p. 361.

And when she faints, it is as if he had the swoon of Ravenscroft's Eugenia in mind, for he says:

> There is another Fetch of female Policy,
> This Swouning: I have known a Woman swound
> At the puking of her Monkey, or feign sorrow
> To see her Husband's nose bleed. Craft, Craft, damn'd Craft:
> I'le not believe 'um.
>
> (III. iii)

Naturally, Durfey's Pisanio could not be allowed to show the same tenderness to Eugenia, as his counterpart had done to Imogen. Hence these lines are omitted:

> O gracious lady,
> Since I received command to do this business,
> I have not slept one wink.
>
> (*Cymbeline*, III. iv. 101–3)

Accordingly, he provides no disguise for her and leaves her somewhat churlishly. He refrains from killing her but is still disposed to believe her disloyal to her husband:

> from this moment
> Expect no further service; for Heaven forbid,
> The least grain of my Love shou'd fall on her,
> Whose blameful Levity wrong'd my dearest Friend.
> Thus then I turn away, and all alone
> Within this gloomy melancholy Desart,
> Leave you to Fortune: If you are innocent,
> That Innocence protect you; but if guilty,
> As I must doubt you are, let Thunder
> Punish the hated Falshood.—Fare ye well.
>
> (III. iii)

Nevertheless, as she continues her entreaties, despite himself he is strangely moved. Yet even now this emotion does not shake his conviction of her guilt:

> my heart
> Bleeds for ye, altho' your abhorred Crimes deserve no pity.
>
> (III. iii)

This persistent suspicion of the loyalty of women is one of the most striking features of Durfey's adaptation. It came natural to one who had presented scheming women in his own plays and was conversant with them in the work of his contemporaries.

It followed that Durfey had difficulty in presenting Eugenia as a woman animated by the powerful indignation that springs from innocence. It is significant that he abridges Imogen's long speech,[1]

---

[1] Act III, Sc. iv, 66–101.

in which she derives strength and courage from the knowledge that she has always been true. In its place he inserts half a dozen lines. Here Eugenia's asseveration has nothing like the same force and fades away into a pathetic wail:

> I swear
> I am not guilty, yet do not wish to live
> *Vrsaces* being false. Come, strike my Lord,
> Strike the innocent Mansion of my Love, my heart,
> And give a hapless, much wrong'd Woman, rest,
> As lasting as her woes.
>
> (III. iii)

This tendency to self-pity becomes more and more apparent as the play develops. The energy of Imogen's words,[1] almost martial in their brevity, evaporates in the corresponding lachrymose passage of *The Injured Princess*, where the sentiment is heightened by the horror of the background:

> Alas I know not where I am! The Place
> Is ruthless, wild and uninhabited;
> No friendly Path leads to a neighbouring Village,
> But all untrod and savage, like the Covert
> Of some rude Satyr; here only Nettles grow, and Ivy
> That clings to th'dismall Ewe;[2] and in yon Rock,
> The dreadful spotted Toads and poysonous Serpents
> Will hourly fright me in this horrid Place,
> For I shall die with Fear!
>
> (III. iii)

She moans over her plight and in contrast to Imogen's terse reply 'Amen! I thank thee' to Pisanio's good wishes at their parting, pours forth this stream of rhetorical lamentations:

> Oh wretched state!
> Oh misery! If Vertue be thus us'd,
> How are the vicious punish'd? What shall I do,
> And whither shall I turn? As some poor Slave,
> Accus'd of Crimes which he had never done,
> Is from his angry Patron's Favour thrown.
> Hated altho' he faithfully did serve,
> Is cast on some wild Beach to pine and starve.
> In vain bemoans himself, and makes defence,
> In vain sighs, weeps, and tells his Innocence.
> Sits madly on some Rock, his Eyes to flow,
> Mourns his hard Fate, but knows not where to go.
> So I unskilful what strange Course to run,
> Must perish here, by faithless man undone.
>
> (III. iii)

---

[1] Act III, Sc. iv, 168–70, 182–7.   [2] That is, of course, 'Yew'.

Once her wanderings have begun, Eugenia complains of hunger and fatigue, and before she enters the cave bewails her wretched plight and prays to Heaven for mercy.

Another notable feature of *The Injured Princess* is the omission of the lyrics 'Hark! hark! the lark at heaven's gate sings' and 'Fear no more the heat o' the sun', and the lament of Arviragus over Fidele. Evidently Durfey did not appreciate the beauty of these passages. Fairies and flowers were not to his sophisticated taste, and the exquisite fancy which pictured the robin covering the grave with moss in winter was lost upon him.

It is certain that the changes introduced by Durfey were in keeping with the attitude of the Restoration theatre-goers, but his decision to make them may have been influenced by his knowledge of Boccaccio. From his tales in verse[1] we may conclude that he was acquainted with the *Decameron* in the English translation of 1620, and it is legitimate to assume that he read the tale of Bernabò and Genevra in that form. There was no poetic strain in the tale, but there was in the words of Ambruogiuolo all the suspicion of women which emerges from Durfey's adaptation. Such a writer as he could not fail to approve Ambruogiuolo's declaration to Bernabò:

I am sure thou beleeuest, and must needes confesse it, that thy wife is a woman, made of flesh and blood, as other women are: if it be so, shee cannot be without the same desires, and the weaknesse or strength as other women haue, to resist such naturall appetites as her owne are. In regard whereof, it 's meerely impossible (although shee be most honest) but she must needs do that which other women do: for there is nothing else possible, either to be denied or affirmed to the contrary . . .[2]

Surely this is the very essence of the Restoration gallant's philosophy. As for the marked element of pathos in Eugenia's character, this too already existed in Boccaccio. At first Genevra lacks courage. She shrinks from the sword and weeps. Indeed, the translator of 1620 also shows her as kneeling and wringing her hands. It is this pathetic, helpless woman that Durfey develops, whereas Shakespeare had laid his emphasis on her toughness and resolution in distress, which were suggested by the heroine who in her later adventures became a soldier in the Soldan's retinue and exacted retribution from her traducer.

Characteristic of the late seventeenth century in various ways is *The Lover's Stratagem, or Virtue Rewarded.* It is found in MS. Rawl. poet. 18 in the Bodleian Library[3] and is based on the 1620 English

[1] Vide post, pp. 277–84.
[2] Quoted from the first edition of 1620. Cf. *The Decameron*, ed. E. Hutton, ii, p. 207.
[3] The text is given with an important introduction and full notes in the edition of Alfredo Obertello, Genoa, 1952.

translation of the *Decameron*.[1] The manuscript dates back to the last quarter of the century or possibly to the early eighteenth century. However, there is some internal evidence that is more precise. An allusion to Dryden's *All for Love*,[2] which was acted at Drury Lane in December 1677 and printed in 1678, shows that the play must be later, and the use of the word 'Sbiries',[3] first recorded in its English form in the *London Gazette* in 1687[4], may perhaps be another clue. Evidently the anonymous author belongs to that group of dramatists who between 1680 and 1700 display a greater consciousness of moral values.[5] The choice of the fifth tale of the tenth day, which was devoted to outstanding examples of liberality or magnificence, was in itself notable, for it had only once previously been handled in dramatic form, and that was as far back as 1620 in *The Two Merry Milke-Maids*. The changing outlook is reflected in the prologue which opens thus:

> Long has yᵉ Husband here been Ridicul'd,
> Long made a Cuckold, and too often ffool'd,
> and all because that Vice yᵉ Stage has Rul'd.
> Can you for once fforgive a Modest Play,
> show it by Gracing of us with your Stay.[6]
>
> (1–5)

The dramatist

> has this Day a loving Couple drawne,
> Such Counterparts they on each other ffawne.
> and tho' yᵉ ladie's Driven to Distresse,
> She comes off Bravely that you must Confesse;
> In Such a Manner Scarce was known before,
> Just when She was design'd to be a Whore.
>
> (14–19)

---

[1] This is proved by the names of places. The play reads 'Udina' instead of 'Udine' and whereas Boccaccio spoke of 'Frioli', the English translator referred to 'Fretu lium' which was 'better knowne by the name of *Forum Iulij*', an error reproduced by the dramatist. The same is true of names of persons. The woman employed as a go between in the *Decameron* is simply 'una femmina'. The 1620 version, which dislike all vagueness, calls her 'Mistresse Maquerella', and 'Macquerella' appears in the play. The English translation is fond of using titles and for Boccaccio's plain 'Gilberto substitutes 'Signior Gilberto', and again the playwright follows suit. There are other parallels too. Ansoldo is described in the Dramatis Personae as 'a Noble Baron' which reflects 'a noble Baron' of 1620 rather than 'un nobile e gran barone'. Boccaccio had related the persistence with which the wooing of the lady was conducted 'spesso per sue ambasciate sollicitandola'. The translator conveyed this by 'daily solicitings, Letters, Ambassages and Love-tokens'. In the play the words 'daily' and 'letters each day' indicate that the Italian text was not the immediate source. Finally 'ffragrant fflowers' for Boccaccio's 'fiori' can be traced back to the 1620 version which, with the same delight in alliteration as is shown in 'Mistresse Maquerella' and in many other ways, inserted the adjective.

[2] Act II, Sc. ii.   [3] Act V, Sc. iv

[4] See *O.E.D.*, viii (S–Sh), p. 155.

[5] Cf. A. Nicoll, op. cit., pp. 244, 252–3.

[6] Quotations are from the MS. References are to Obertello's edition.

It is a kind of thing that he could not well pass by, for even if it looks as if the tale were a lie, ' 'tis Such as Boccace Told '. The play therefore offers a perfect pattern of marriage, but at the same time, the author confesses that he has had to make concessions to the taste of his period:

He Spoiles ye Tale to Gratifie ye Age,
Since Baudy's ye Decorum of ye Stage.
(28–9)

In order to amplify the story for the needs of a five-act play the dramatist adds a number of characters. In addition to Gilberto, his wife Dianora and her admirer Ansoldo, he introduces Labona, sister to Dianora (who is wooed by Abafto, a kinsman of Ansoldo) and Roberto, brother to Dianora and the lover of Bellinda. She is a sister of Rodolpho, a kinsman of Gilberto. The two pairs of lovers are contrasted with the happy married couple. Both Labona and Bellinda are coy, the latter being the antithesis of romance and not eager to rush into matrimony. The protracted wooing of these young lovers serves to fill in the intervals between the episodes in the action relating to the three chief figures. Abafto is linked to this plot, because he hopes to become Ansoldo's heir and so promises to further his designs on Dianora. Thus a conflict arises within him, for he realises that he may in this way ruin his hope of winning Labona. Rodolpho is the faithful supporter of Gilberto and seeks to foil Ansoldo's plans. To further his purpose he obtains information from the Steward, who in his turn receives news of what is going on in the household from the Curate who is Gilberto's chaplain. It is Rodolpho who warns Gilberto when Dianora has been induced to break her plighted word, if Ansoldo can produce a garden with all the flowers of May in 'Nipping January', and it is he who contrives that Gilberto and himself shall be present at the interview when she persuades Ansoldo to forego his claim. The messenger sent by Boccaccio's ardent lover to Dianora is developed into a typical figure of seventeenth-century drama, the attendant of Dianora and the agent of Ansoldo, whose name Macquerella is an indication of her wanton, mercenary disposition. The magician is provided with a servant Rumbulo, who at the close of the play is married to Macquerella after she has been dismissed from Gilberto's service.

Comedy is provided in the very first scene by 'a Great Rabble in Drunken postures with Wine and Glasses in their hands. Some Drinking Some ffilling', but this lively opening also helps in the exposition, as they are in Gilberto's house, celebrating his wedding anniversary. They appear again in Act V to inspect the garden that the magician has caused to spring up. As they are debating how it has been created, he undertakes to make them dance with absolute regularity. He causes ethereal music to play, and they are delighted to find that their movements are perfect. One even declares that he will no more be called a clown by his wife, now that he can dance so finely. But when the magician bids them try without his aid, they are all out of step. Panic seizes them and they hasten away, one calling out 'ffarewel Mephestophilus'. However, this crowd scene is an essential part of the action, filling as it does the interval between Dianora's hearing about the magic garden and her arrival there.

The magician has a more important function than in the tale, practically the whole of Act IV and a part of Act V being devoted to his work. As Boccaccio presented the situation, Gilberto agreed that Dianora should keep her promise to Ansoldo. This consent is depicted as an act of generosity, but at the same time the tale does not attempt to disguise the fear of the magician which also sways Gilberto. On this account as well as on ethical grounds his action is therefore open to criticism. It is evident that the dramatist was conscious of this weakness, and so, when Dianora goes to Ansoldo, he describes her conduct as being determined by the magician, against her will. The necromancer is a striking figure. He refuses payment in advance for his work, and this prepares the way for his generosity at the end of the play when he annuls the bond signed by Ansoldo for two thousand ducats. Everything is done to make him impressive. His servant Rumbulo comes ahead of him and scares Ansoldo's servant Peter for his curiosity in prying into the magician's books. Donning a painted bullock's hide with two large gilt horns, he pursues Peter, who takes refuge with Ansoldo and Abafto, trembling with fear, so that 'his knees Salute each other like Two old friends at parting'. The scene provides farcical comedy, but it also helps to define the attitude of Ansoldo and Abafto who treat sceptically the reports in circulation about the magician's powers. However, various incidents lead them to change their views, with the result that when the ceremony of the bond is performed, the status of the magician is greatly enhanced. He has previously declared that it will not be possible to furnish the wondrous garden completely with jessamines and greens in one day, but that it will be quite ready by noon of the next day. His haste because there is so much to be done, lends a sense of urgency to the fourth act, and there is an animated scene when at his demand Ansoldo sends many people to level the ground, equipped with pickaxes and shovels. This bustle is followed by the solemn moment when the garden is called into being. The magician has dismissed Rumbulo and is seen alone. He strikes the ground repeatedly with a white wand and conjures up Merlyn and asks for his aid. The necromancer is a Spaniard, but the dramatist finds nothing

anomalous in his evocation of a British magician, for he is concerned
only with the spectacle that follows. Merlyn's ghost rises out of the
stage and after seeing the bond, sinks down again, while a cloud of
smoke ascends to warm the air. Then spirits hover about the sky, some
bringing greens, others flowers, which they fix in the ground. Next
demons rise and dance, and a song is sung in parts by the spirits and
demons, after which a garden suddenly springs up, the spirits fly away
and the demons sink down, bringing the fourth act to a close. In Act V
the spirits appear once more and sing a song 'in Recitativo' to accompany Abafto, Labona, Roberto and Bellinda, as they walk about the
garden. By means of the music and the spectacle, which shows in
passing what advances had been made in stage machinery in the
Restoration age,[1] the author transmutes fear into grace and beauty.

As a contrast the Curate and the Steward are meant to emphasise
the sordid aspect of everyday life, and at the same time are allotted a
minor role in the action. The Curate is an avaricious parasite and a
dissembler, caring little for morality, if only appearances are preserved.
But the Steward is a more robust figure. He is a shrewd man of the
world who sees through the Curate, and when he notes the parson's
eager interest in the possibility of his death, observes: 'I may Remember you, if when I do depart you give a heave, & dissipate Some
Thoughts wch may molest me'.[2] He takes a cynical view of all mankind
and of women in particular. A professed libertine, he enjoys life and
above all delights in duping dull husbands. He is prepared to admit that
Gilberto and Dianora are happy, but it is typical of him that he puts
the worst possible construction on the relations of Dianora and Ansoldo.
His conviction that every woman is at heart a rake emerges clearly
in a conversation with Rodolpho about Dianora:

Rod.   I Cannot Think, but that She's honest.
Stew. She's a woman!
Rod.   Must She be therefore ffalse.
Stew. have Patience & you'l See.
Rod.   If She be false then all her Sex are damn'd. for in
       appearance Honour is her center. besides She has a
       Man that cannot brook Such usage.
Stew. Cæsar & Pompey did. & woman wil be woman Stil.

(III. ii. 89–96)

The Steward and, in a lesser degree, the Curate reflect the Restoration
atmosphere, and it is as if they were discussing a dashing gallant of the
period, when they speak of Ansoldo:

Cur.   Wel I Protest these hansome Men with ffair Estates
       & verst in foreign Modes that tel their Story wel
       have ways to Conquour where they Court

[1] Cf. A. Nicoll, op. cit., pp. 35–49.   [2] III. ii. 161–2.

S

> *Stew.*   Sure 'tis an Il Return upon his ffriend. but these
> Accomplisht Men Ruine more women then al yᵉ
> vanities yᵉ world can ffurnish.
>
> (III. ii. 130–5)

It was perhaps such passages as these that the Prologue had in view when it deplored the bawdy element that the author had felt constrained to foist on Boccaccio's tale in order to satisfy the contemporary theatre-goer. However, no doubt it also alluded to the figure of Ansoldo who is developed into an intriguing gallant. His prototype had gone no further than to send messages by means of a woman, but Ansoldo is shown as a close friend of Gilberto and exploits this intimacy by installing an agent as the attendant of Dianora, so that she may arrange meetings between them. These take place in the absence of Gilberto on business, an incident of which the tale knows nothing. Ansoldo prides himself on his skill in writing letters that have a double meaning and is confident of his success for

> Women that are ffair, are Sildome Dul.
>
> (II. i. 8)

At the interview he brushes aside Dianora's objections. If the affair is discreetly managed, no one need know. Moreover,

> Were yᵉ Thing new or very rarely done,
> that were another Case but this is Cõmon.[1]
> I Take not from him ought that is his own.
> I only Borrow that wᶜʰ I Restore
> to him again. no Damage does accrew . . .
>
> (II. ii. 125–9)

When Dianora tells him to hold off his hands or she will call for aid, he demands:

> wil you comply, I cannot brook denial.
>
> (II. ii. 138)

She remains firm and, taking up a hint in the tale,[2] she urges him to direct his attention to his military career:

> Bred up in Armes, persue your wonted Course
> purchase new Honour to your growing ffame.
>
> (II. ii. 157–8)

She reminds him of great generals of the ancient world whose love affairs led them astray:

> Mark Anthony did yᵉ like losse Sustain,
> by lodging in that ffair Egyptians Armes.
> He thereby lost yᵉ Empire of yᵉ world.
>
> (II. ii. 165–7)

---

[1] Cf. the attitude of the Duke in *The Two Merry Milke-Maids.*

[2] 'per arme conosciuto', which is rendered 'actiue in Armes' in the 1620 translation.

To which Ansoldo, with an obvious allusion to Dryden's *All for Love,*
replies:

> And 'twas wel lost to gain yᵉ Prize he had.
> (II. ii. 168)

When Ansoldo again meets Dianora in Act III, he redoubles his
importunities. She appeals to his reason and points out that for the sake
of a fleeting pleasure he will breed a lasting quarrel and that such
conduct is sinful. But he is in a state of feverish excitement, and although she temporises, he threatens force, so that in the end she agrees
to comply with his wish, provided that he creates in midwinter a
garden full of spring flowers. When, to her dismay, it is completed, in
Act V she pleads with him to be generous and spare her, but he remains
adamant and bids her receive him that night.

Till now Ansoldo has been the cunning and experienced lecher, but
there have been occasions when uneasiness came over him at the
thought that he was violating Gilberto's hospitality. He stifled his
conscience temporarily, but it revives in the nocturnal scene when
he meets Dianora for the third time. They both believe that they are
alone, but in reality Gilberto and Rodolpho are hidden in the room.
Dianora declares that she is there, not of her own volition, but impelled
by the power of magic. She comes as a victim led to sacrifice and begs
him not to take advantage of a woman, but he tells her that she might
as well 'preach to a Pirate to release his prize'.[1] There follows a prolonged discussion, and the tension is heightened by the running commentary of Gilberto and Rodolpho which mirrors the fluctuating
emotions of the speakers. At one moment they think that she will
yield. Then, as she reinforces her appeal by reminding Ansoldo how
Gilberto had saved his life when he was seized by the 'Sbiries'[2] for
wounding a young count, their hopes rise again. But soon the listeners
once more have the impression that she will give way, when suddenly
she breaks away from Ansoldo and says:

> I Thought ffriendship like yours had been Imortal, & wil
> you for a Momentary pleasure forfeit that Sacred Name.
> (v. iv. 271–2)

Then, seeing how this affects Ansoldo, she redoubles her pressure:

> I am your ffriends
> Seignior Gilbertos wife your ffellow Traveller, your School
> Companion. your very self in all thats good. yᵉ Man to
> whom you Stand So much obleig'd.
> (v. iv. 274–7)

Though a hint of Ansoldo's indebtedness to Gilberto has been given

---

[1] v. iv. 235.   [2] Italian police.

previously, the dramatist skilfully holds back the full extent of his obligation till this crisis. As Dianora plies him with arguments thick and fast, he is seized with shame and renounces his plan. At the close of the play he acts on her earlier suggestion and declares his intention to quit the court of Venus and go off to the next campaign, where perhaps a bullet will end his career. Thus virtue triumphs and the profligate reforms.

The play is brisk and lively and, apart from a certain obscurity about the doings of Rodolpho, well constructed. The dramatist shows his ability to adjust a mediæval tale to the needs of the contemporary stage, and in so doing reflects the period of transition from the Restoration theatre to a more decent type of drama.

V

THE DECAMERON
IN THE EIGHTEENTH CENTURY

ONE sign of the continued interest in the *Decameron* was the appearance of new translations. The first of these was published in 1702 and was said to be 'accommodated to the Gust of the present Age'. It is based on a French edition, printed at Amsterdam in 1697 and again in 1699.[1] The address to the reader explains that these tales 'being often obscure, by reason of the multiplicity of words; and three hundred and fifty Years, also making a great alteration in the gust of Men, to render them more entertaining, it was absolutely necessary to abridge them, dress them after the modern Fashion, leave out the superfluous repetitions, and sometimes not only alter intire Periods, but to change the whole Structure'.

The original form of the *Decameron* is certainly discarded. The 'Proemio' and 'Conclusione' are omitted. Each tale is a separate unit, and no attempt is made to link either the stories or the various days together.[2] The doings of the narrators and the rural background are ignored. Some songs are omitted, but others are retained, even though this creates a certain awkwardness in view of the alterations in the framework.[3] The songs themselves are in the manner of the period, as may be seen from the following:

> Near to a gentle purling Crystal Spring,
>   Whose fertile Streams enrich'd the Neighb'ring Ground,
> The teeming Earth did fragrant Flowers bring,
>   Which Flora in her richest Robes had Crown'd;
> Fit for a mournful Lover's sad Retreat,
> There wretched Cloe did lament her Fate.
>
> Whilst of bright Cynthia I a Follow'r was,
>   No anxious thoughts disturb'd my peaceful Breast,
> Through obscure Groves regardless I did pass,
>   My innocence secur'd my Ease and Rest;
> Till I grew fond of Pleasures which soon cloy,
> Enslave our Souls, and all our Peace destroy.

---

[1] With engravings by Romain de Hooge.

[2] This makes it possible to transfer the fifth tale of the third day, so that it becomes Novel L.

[3] Cf. Part II, p. 202.

> For I! poor Cred'lous Nymph! alas! Poor I!
> Was Charm'd by a false Swains deluding Voice,
> Whose graceful Mien would please a Deity;
> All o're our Plains they did applaud my Choice;
> But now too late, to my great grief, I find
> Him more unconstant than the Waves and Wind.
>
> Great Cupid, to your Vassal Pity shew,
> It's your own Interest, though the Cause is mine,
> When devout Votaries thus suffer, who
> Will venture to burn Incense at your Shrine:
> Bad is th'Exchange we make of Liberty
> For Scorn, disdain and abject Slavery.[1]

The regularity and the condensation of these stanzas are paralleled by
the balance and epigrammatic quality of the prose, as may be seen
from the preamble to Novel XXI: 'It is a great mistake to think that as
soon as a young Girl has put on the Veil, that she has neither Passion
nor Desires, and breaths nothing but Piety and Devotion. The Heart
cannot be changed so easily as the Habit'. One notes here a critical
attitude towards the monastic system, and in numerous places the
translation displays an anti-clerical bias. It emerges in the address to
the reader and, very clearly, in the following observation prefixed
to the tale of Fra Alberto di Imola:

> As there is nothing more sacred amongst Men than Religion, so there is
> nothing that is more abused to base and sinister ends. This is the Cloak, that
> is generally worn, to hide the most villainous Actions, and this prophane
> Liberty is in a great Measure owing to the Clergy themselves.[2]

This version enjoyed some success, and in 1712[3] a second edition
was called for. However, by 1741 it was felt that a new translation was
desirable which could claim greater fidelity to Boccaccio. The translator[4] speaks with scorn of the two older English renderings, 'for such
liberties are taken every where in altering every thing according to the
people's own taste and fancy, that a great part of both bears very little
resemblance to the original'. He used the Italian text and, apart from the
omission of the 'Proemio' and 'Conclusione', presented the *Decameron*
to the English reader in a more accurate form than had hitherto been
known,[5] though he carries out a certain amount of expurgation.[6]

---

[1] Part II, p. 203.   [2] p. 172

[3] The British Museum Catalogue records an edition of 1722, but on inspection I
found that this was really the edition of 1712, the numeral having been tampered
with by some one or other. A correction has been made in the Catalogue, for it is
clear that an edition of 1722 does not exist.

[4] He is said to have been Charles Balguy. Cf. *D.N.B.*, Art. 'Balguy'.

[5] According to W. Roberts, *The Earlier History of English Bookselling*, London
1889, p. 127, the lists of John Nicolson, Robert Knaplock and Samuel Ballard include
one containing 'all the novels of Mr. John Boccace' with cuts. I have never seen this

[6] For example, iii, 10 and ix, 10 are omitted.

In addition to these translations, editions of the Italian or French
text with numerous illustrations by famous artists like Gravelot,
Boucher, Cochin, Eisen and Moreau were published with the London
and Paris imprint in 1757, 1757–61 and 1768.[1] Another edition of the
Italian text with the London and Leghorn imprint was issued in 1789.
Other editions published in London only were those of 1762 (editor
Vincenzio Martinelli) and 1774. There was also the *Scelta di Novelle di
Giovanni Boccaccio*, edited by G. Giannini (1791), which contained
twenty-eight tales. But the most important of all the London editions
was that of 1725 which was reissued in 1727. It was a reprint of the
famous Giunti text published at Florence in 1527. It had not only
many patrons in high society but also such persons as Sir Hildebrand
Jacob, the dramatist, Richard West, the eminent constitutional lawyer
and man of letters, Joseph Smith, the British Consul at Venice who in
1729 himself prepared an edition of the *Decameron*, and Dr. Richard
Mead, the famous physician who attended Pope and also, like Smith,
was a great bibliophile.

The poet Gray had a copy of the London edition of 1725 and in his
notes mentioned the authors, 'Chaucer, Shakespeare, Dryden, Fontaine,
Moliere, Pope, etc., who have been indebted to Boccaccio, with the titles
of the Poems, Tales, etc. which have originated with the *Decameron*.'[2]
Topham Beauclerk, Dr. Johnson's friend, had a fine collection of
Boccaccio's writings. In addition to *De casibus* and *De claris mulieribus*
in Betussi's version and most of the Italian works, it included six copies
of the *Decameron* in French, Spanish, Italian and English.[3] Eminent
writers such as Sterne and Gibbon likewise included the work in their
libraries,[4] and in the historian's opinion Boccaccio's fame rested on the
Decameron.[5]

In a roundabout way his reputation was enhanced by those of his
tales which were retold by La Fontaine in his *Contes et nouvelles*. Some
of them were translated in 1705 in *Miscellaneous Poetical Novels or
Tales, Relating Many pleasing and instructive Instances of Wit and
Gallantry in Both Sexes: Suited to the Belle-Humeur of the Present Age*.[6]
A different translator was at work in the *Tales and Novels in Verse*,
London, 1735[7] and *The Spectacles* in 1753.

[1] Henri Cohen, *Guide de l'amateur de livres à gravures du XVIIIe siècle*, 6e éd. par
S. de Ricci, Paris, 1912, pp. 158, 160, 161.

[2] Cf. W. Powell Jones, 'Thomas Gray's Library', *M.P.*, 1937–8, xxxv, p. 261.

[3] This was the translation of 1620 in the second edition of 1625. Cf. *Bibliotheca
Beauclerkiana*, p. 83, nos. 2649 to 2662.

[4] Gibbon had an edition published at Amsterdam in 1761.

[5] *The Decline and Fall of the Roman Empire*, London, 1900, vii, p. 120.

[6] The plates at the beginning of each tale are taken from the French edition of La
Fontaine's *Contes et Nouvelles*, Amsterdam, 1701.

[7] Reprinted at Edinburgh in 1762.

The critics also concerned themselves with Boccaccio and were all the more readily drawn to his writings because he belonged to the same period as Chaucer. Pre-eminent among these was Dryden. As a critic of Boccaccio he was handicapped by his ignorance of the *Filostrato* and the *Teseida*. He was also at fault in thinking that Petrarch, not Boccaccio, first wrote the tale of Griselda. Nevertheless, he was aware of Boccaccio's importance in the development of Italian prose and of the 'familiar style, and pleasing way of relating comical adventures' which he shared with Chaucer. A writer in *The Monthly Review* in 1768,[1] agreed with Dryden in praising his style:

> It must be acknowledged that he possessed the talent of story-telling in the highest perfection; nothing, in this respect, can be conceived more natural, perspicuous, or elegant; his words seem made on purpose for what he describes.[2]

He goes on to picture Boccaccio's surprise at the popularity of a work that was far from being his main preoccupation and his astonishment, had he been told:

> your Latin and Italian works will remain buried in the dust of libraries, whilst your Decameron, printed upwards of two hundred times, translated into all the languages of Europe, read by every body, shall procure you the title of the Cicero of Tuscany, and the Father of the Italian Language![3]

Despite his enthusiasm, he was aware that the *Decameron* had its censurers and felt constrained to defend it on the grounds that it was meant only for amusement and that the circumstances of the time when it was composed justified the occasional freedom of its tone.[4]

Dr. Johnson would hardly have welcomed this argument if we may judge by his comment on the tales from Boccaccio in Dryden's *Fables*. As a scholar he tolerates 'Sigismonda and Guiscardo' for the celebrity of the story, and 'Cymon and Iphigenia' because he knew that a Renaissance humanist of repute like Beroaldo had set his stamp upon it, but he abstains from all praise. As for 'Theodore and Honoria', he concedes that it affords opportunities of striking description, but qualifies this slight approval with the complaint that 'it contains not much moral'.[5] It is evident, that if examined from this point of view, the *Decameron* could not hope to pass his severe scrutiny. However, his attitude was at least governed by zeal in the pursuit of truth. On the other hand, when Boccaccio had penetrated through the medium of Dryden into the realm of art, Charles Churchill's attack on Hogarth's painting, 'Sigismonda mourning over the heart of Guiscardo',[6] was animated by no general philosophical consideration. In any case, the

---

[1] Vol. xxxix.   [2] p. 559.   [3] p. 560.   [4] pp. 560–1.
[5] *The Lives of the most eminent English Poets*, London, 1781, ii, pp. 174–5.
[6] Now no. 1046 in the Tate Gallery.

stir thus caused,[1] no less than the picture itself, served to heighten
Boccaccio's fame, and this was yet further enhanced by Sir Joshua
Reynolds's painting, 'Cymon and Iphigenia'.[2]

1. Tales in Verse

Even if Dryden spoke of Boccaccio mainly as a diverting writer, the
three tales that he included from the *Decameron* in the *Fables* in 1700
were all of a more serious kind.[3] It is certain that Dryden knew the
original text, for in his preface he quotes in Italian the allusion to the
story of Palamone and Arcita as it was sung by Dioneo and Fiammetta
at the end of the seventh day. The translations themselves also suggest
that Dryden had the Italian version before him,[4] and a passage in the
dedication of the *Æneis* in 1697[5] proves that he read the 'Conclusione'
which was omitted in the English translation of 1620. On the other
hand, there are abundant traces of this earlier rendering in Dryden's
work,[6] and it is evident that he used the two texts concurrently.

Dryden's task was not rendered any easier by his age and physical
condition. He was approaching seventy and suffered from various
complaints. In a letter to Mrs. Steward, dated 2 February 1699 he says:
'betwixt my intervalls of physique and other remedies . . . I am still
drudging on'.[7] Again in the preface to the *Fables* he speaks of being
'a cripple in my limbs' and the illness which interrupted his enterprise.
It is to these troubles that the poet refers in the opening lines of
'Cymon and Iphigenia':

> Old as I am, for Ladies' Love unfit,
> The Pow'r of Beauty I remember yet,
> Which once inflam'd my Soul, and still inspires my Wit.
>
> (1–3)

and in 'Sigismonda and Guiscardo' the grief of the aged Tancred, to
which the English translator of 1620 had given a new poignancy, is
intensified by Dryden in a passage to which there is no counterpart in
Boccaccio:

> To what has Heav'n reserv'd my Age? Ah! why
> Should Man, when Nature calls, not chuse to die,
> Rather than stretch the Span of Life, to find
> Such Ills as Fate has wisely cast behind,

---

[1] The *Epistle to William Hogarth* ran to four editions in 1763.
[2] Now in Buckingham Palace.
[3] *Dec.* iv, 1, v, 8 and v, 1.
[4] For a full discussion see the forthcoming edition of Dryden's *Poems* by James
Kinsley. Quotations from the *Fables* in the following pages are from the first edition.
[5] Cf. Dryden's *Essays*, ed. W. P. Ker, Oxford, 1926, ii, p. 231.
[6] See the edition of Dryden's *Poems* by James Kinsley.
[7] *The Letters of John Dryden*, ed. C. E. Ward, Duke, N.C., 1942, p. 109.

> For those to feel, whom fond Desire to live
> Makes covetous of more than Life can give!
> Each has his Share of Good; and when 't is gone,
> The Guest, tho' hungry, cannot rise too soon.
>
> (325–32)

But old age and illness were not the only handicaps with which Dryden had to contend. The revolution of 1688 had sealed up his sources of income and he was only too well acquainted with poverty. Even earlier in the reign of Charles II he had lived in straitened circumstances and on the death of that king in 1685 had gone so far as to insert in the 'Threnodia Augustalis' a hint that writers had not received their full due:

> Tho' little was their Hire, and light their Gain,
> Yet somewhat to their share he threw.
>
> (377–8)

At a time when royal patronage meant so much, when poets 'must live by Courts, or starve',[1] Dryden was predisposed to sympathise with poverty. Consequently, when Sigismonda reproaches Tancred for his failure to recognise the merit of Guiscardo, she goes beyond anything that her prototype had said:

> 'tis not Baseness to be Poor;
> His Poverty augments thy Crime the more.
> Upbraids thy Justice with the scant Regard
> Of Worth: Whom Princes praise, they shou'd reward.
> Are these the Kings entrusted by the Crowd
> With Wealth, to be dispens'd for Common Good?
> The People sweat not for their King's Delight,
> T'enrich a Pimp, or raise a Parasite;
> Theirs is the Toil; and he who well has serv'd
> His Country, has his Countrys Wealth deserv'd.
>
> (547–56)

The last four lines in particular have a personal note and it is manifest that Dryden had his eye on contemporary society rather than on Boccaccio's tale.

In yet another respect the *Fables* reflect the conditions of his age. The publication of Jeremy Collier's *Short View of the Profaneness and Immorality of the English Stage* in 1698, just when Dryden was engaged on the *Fables*, made him sensitive to the charges directed against him. In the preface he replies to Collier and again in the introduction to 'Cymon and Iphigenia', where he writes:

> What needs he Paraphrase on what we mean?
> We were at worst but Wanton; he's Obscene.
>
> (21–2)

[1] Epilogue to *The Pilgrim*, 1700.

Yet despite his rejoinder, Dryden felt himself obliged to take account of Collier's accusations. It is this awareness which explains the nature of the tales selected from the *Decameron*. Hence Dryden's declaration: 'I have written nothing which savors of immorality or profaneness.' He then adds, as if after all he had some misgivings, that if perchance there was anything wanton, it was due to inadvertence. It is possible that he had in mind ll. 156–80, ll. 230–2 and ll. 245–51 of 'Sigismonda and Guiscardo'.[1] These passages have a sensual quality that is not due to Boccaccio, but to Dryden. On the other hand, a concession is made by the introduction of a priest who celebrates the marriage of the princess and the squire. Yet this is but a veneer of morality, and Dryden continues to speak and to think of them as lovers and to bestow on them his sympathy. Consequently, it comes as a surprise when the poet, contrary to his express intention in the preface not to point the moral for fear of becoming tedious, imposes on the tale an instructive ending:

> Thus she for Disobedience justly dy'd;
> The Sire was justly punish'd for his Pride:
> The Youth, least guilty, suffer'd for th'Offence,
> Of Duty violated to his Prince.

> (750–3)

This cold summing up clashes with the rest of the poem and, so far as the hero and heroine are concerned, runs counter to Dryden's earlier attitude.

Such a dissonance is in the last resort due to the hostile influence of Jeremy Collier, and Dryden's preoccupation with the current of opinion that he had set moving also explains a number of changes in 'Cymon and Iphigenia'. Thus one observes a somewhat greater restraint than in Boccaccio's description of the sleeping Iphigenia. Still more important is the alteration in the relationship of Cymon to her. In the original, her father Cipseo, when arranging for her marriage with Pasimondo, is merely behaving like an honourable man who keeps his promise, and the hero has no warrant for carrying off the solemnly plighted lady except his own passion. For Boccaccio that was the only justification needed, since 'Amor vincit omnia', a view which is set forth elsewhere by Guiscardo with moving simplicity in his reply to the reproachful Tancred: 'Amor può troppo più che nè voi nè io possiamo'. However, Dryden grows uneasy and adopts various devices to exonerate Cymon. Prejudice is stirred up against Pasimond in the reader's mind by the statement that Iphigenia is 'to wed a foreign spouse'. On the other hand, he is attracted towards Cymon when he discovers that fate has proved an obstacle to the hero's happiness, in

---

[1] In the text of the tale he is called 'Guiscard'.

that 'tho' better lov'd', he was unable to declare his affection. Cymon himself is able to reject Pasimond's demand for the completion of the marriage contract as a 'lawless Bargain' and to represent this as null and void, since

> The Parent could not sell the Daughter's Love.
> (299)

The later reiteration of this attitude when he maintains that he deserves Iphigenia far more than Pasimond:

> to whom your formal Father ty'd
> Your Vows; and sold a Slave, not sent a Bride
> (316–17)

transforms the story into a romantic exploit in which the irresistible ardour of youth triumphs over the sordid calculations of age.

Dryden prudently decided not to attempt to justify the conduct of Lysimachus in carrying off Cassandra, the bride of Ormisda. As the magistrate of Rhodes, elected to administer the law, he committed a doubly heinous offence. He makes no attempt to exculpate himself but admits that he has no title to Cassandra and that in fleeing with her from Rhodes he is asserting that might is right, whatever others may say. Dryden refuses to condone this rape and introduces a passage, at variance with Boccaccio, to condemn Lysimachus:

> This Youth proposing to possess, and scape,
> Began in Murder, to conclude in Rape:
> Unprais'd by me, tho' Heav'n sometime may bless
> An imipous Act with undeserv'd Success.
> (467–70)

Quite apart from this concern with moral issues which with some probability may be ascribed to the intellectual climate of his age, Dryden comments on various features of contemporary life. He expresses the dislike of a standing army when he shows his distrust of the 'men inur'd to blood and exercis'd in ill' who executed Tancred's orders for the murder of Guiscardo, for

> (Slaves to Pay)
> What Kings decree, the Soldier must obey:
> Wag'd against foes; and, when the Wars are o'er,
> Fit only to maintain Despotick Pow'r:
> Dang'rous to Freedom, and desir'd alone
> By Kings, who seek an Arbitrary Throne.
> (596–601)

In a less serious vein Dryden introduces the forces of the Rhodian who, after satisfying themselves that they outnumber Cymon and his shipwrecked followers, proceed to attack them. This enables him to poke fun at the militia of the day:

> The Country rings around with loud Alarms,
> And raw in Fields the rude Militia swarms;
> Mouths without Hands; maintain'd at vast Expence,
> In Peace a Charge, in War a weak Defence:
> Stout once a Month they march a blust'ring Band,
> And ever, but in times of Need, at hand:
> This was the Morn when issuing on the Guard,
> Drawn up in Rank and File they stood prepar'd
> Of seeming Arms to make a short Essay,
> Then hasten to be Drunk, the Business of the Day.
> (399–408)

Here Dryden is in a genial mood, but perhaps less so in an oblique criticism of the Church of England because of its failure in a crisis to uphold its doctrine of passive obedience.[1] There are other shrewd thrusts of a more general kind which are prompted by Boccaccio's tales. Thus the withdrawal of Theodore from Ravenna affords an opportunity for a comment on the parasitical companions who hindered his tranquil communion in the forest:

> He would have liv'd more free; but many a Guest,
> Who could forsake the Friend, pursu'd the Feast.
> ('Theodore and Honoria', 70–1)

And the unscrupulous action of Lysimachus inspires the epigram:

> The Great, it seems, are privileg'd alone
> To punish all Injustice but their own.
> (471–2)

The satirical portraits of individuals, an art in which Dryden had long excelled, are not less notable. That of Cymon, before his understanding had been awakened by love, is clear and sharp of outline:

> He look'd like Nature's Error; as the Mind
> And Body were not of a Piece design'd,
> But made for two, and by Mistake in one were join'd.
>
> .   .   .   .
>
> The more informed, the less he understood,
> And deeper sunk by flound'ring in the Mud.
> (58–60, 63–4)

The same keen barbs are placed at the disposal of Tancred when he wishes to express his contempt of Guiscard:

> A Man so smelling of the Peoples Lee,
> The Court receiv'd him first for Charity;
> And since with no Degree of Honour grac'd,
> But only suffer'd, where he first was plac'd:
> A grov'ling Insect still; and so design'd
> By Natures Hand, nor born of Noble kind:
> A Thing, by neither Man nor Woman priz'd,
> And scarcely known enough, to be despis'd.
> (317–24)

[1] ll. 423–4.

Indirectly Dryden here draws another portrait, that of Tancred himself, the haughty monarch, incapable of appreciating anything but aristocratic lineage. From the beginning he is depicted as a ruthless tyrant. Even the account of the cave is used to suggest a ruler abusing his power and anxious for his safety. Oppressed by care, he suffers from insomnia, and when he has surprised his daughter with Guiscardo, this 'Royal Spy' appears sinister and malevolent, as he retires unseen,

> To brood in secret on his gather'd Spleen,
> And methodize Revenge.
>
> (257–8)

He is the 'gloomy Sire', the 'sullen Tyrant', whose repressed anger finally finds vent in 'a bloody Sacrifice'. At the same time he is not without dignity, and Dryden rejects as inappropriate Boccaccio's comparison of the weeping Tancred to a child that has been severely thrashed. However, he is never allowed to gain our sympathy. It is true that for a moment, by a projection of his own personality, Dryden brings home the pathos of old age, but any impulse in favour of Tancred is soon dispelled. In the final scene, when Sigismonda lies dying, we have no description such as that given in the English translation of 1620 of the 'teares streaming downe his reuerend beard', for that might soften the reader's heart towards the penitent king. Indeed, all that we learn of this manifestation of his remorse is from Sigismonda's curt words: 'Restrain thy tears', and as death draws near, she ignores his very presence.

Even if he is unattractive, Tancred is a striking figure, whereas Guiscardo, though pleasing, is relatively insignificant. Boccaccio had described him as a servant, so that the wrath of his master was understandable. In Dryden, however, he is said to be

> Of gentle Blood; but one whose niggard Fate
> Had set him far below her high Estate.
>
> (49–50)

This statement regarding his rank was no doubt inspired by the application of the word 'Gentleman' to him in the English version of 1620, but it does make Tancred's contemptuous denunciation of his plebeian status appear unreasonable and inconsistent. In other respects Dryden does little with this character, except to place in his mouth a bold reply when he is haled before the king.

In Sigismonda Dryden sees in the early part of the tale one who is typical of her sex, keen-witted and full of subtle devices:

> What will not Women do, when Need inspires
> Their Wit, or Love their inclination fires!
>
> (127–8)

But later the woman is transformed into the heroine. Dryden adds a trait here and there. Thus Sigismonda receives the goblet with a severe smile, and, after she has taken the poison and lain on her bed, she refuses to open her eyes. In this way the impression of her indomitable, inflexible will is heightened.

Dryden has certainly done justice to Sigismonda and created a memorable heroine, but in their way Honoria and Iphigenia are equally striking. These are women of a less virile type, akin to Sigismonda in her early stage, but incapable of her heroic fortitude. Dryden's attitude to women in general is suggested by his remark on Honoria's meditation as she considers the possibility of yielding to Theodore's suit:

> Her Sexes Arts she knew, and why not then,
> Might deep Dissembling have a Place in Men?
>
> (397–8)

The upshot was that

> She with no winding turns the Truth conceal'd,
> But put the Woman off, and stood reveal'd.
>
> (408–9)

The decision was arrived at as the result of fear, and Dryden exhausted all his resources in tracing the mental anguish that Honoria endured after seeing the pursuit of the lady by the spectral horseman and his hounds:

> At ev'ry little Noise she look'd behind,
> For still the Knight was present to her Mind:
> And anxious oft she started on the way,
> And thought the Horseman-Ghost came thundring for his Prey:
> Return'd, she took her Bed, with little Rest,
> But in short Slumbers dreamt the Funeral Feast:
> Awak'd, she turn'd her Side, and slept again;
> The same black Vapours mounted in her Brain,
> And the same Dreams return'd with double Pain.
>   Now forc'd to wake, because afraid to sleep,
> Her Blood all Fever'd, with a furious Leap
> She sprung from Bed, distracted in her Mind,
> And fear'd, at ev'ry Step, a twitching Spright behind.
> Darkling and desp'rate with a stagg'ring pace,
> Of Death afraid, and conscious of Disgrace;
> Fear, Pride, Remorse, at once her Heart assail'd,
> Pride put Remorse to flight, but Fear prevail'd.
> *Friday*, the fatal Day, when next it came,
> Her Soul forethought the Fiend would change his Game,
> And her pursue, or *Theodore* be slain,
> And two Ghosts join their Packs to hunt her o'er the Plain.
>
> (359–79)

In his analysis of her conflicting emotions and the portrayal of the fears working on her overheated imagination Dryden is masterly.

When he comes to depict Iphigenia, the emphasis on the artfulness of women is even stronger. It appears in two scenes, the first of which concerns the removal of Iphigenia by Cymon from the ship on which she was sailing to Rhodes for her marriage to Pasimond. In the original she sheds tears of genuine distress and Dryden retains this display of emotion. But as he had altered the tale and depicted her love for Cymon, he explains her tears as a cloak to disguise her true feelings:

> To seeming Sadness she compos'd her Look;
> As if by Force subjected to his Will,
> Tho' pleas'd, dissembling, and a Woman still.
>
> .   .   .   .   .   .
>
> Faintly she scream'd, and ev'n her Eyes confess'd
> She rather would be thought, than was Distress'd.
>   (309–11, 320–1)

The second scene is that of the storm. In the *Decameron* the heroine weeps and, quite justifiably, curses the passion of Cimone which has brought her to this pass. But again Dryden seeks to describe a more complicated state of mind. He does so in a brilliant passage where Iphigenia's fluttering fears and shifting emotions are analysed with a skill that is mingled with contempt:

> Sad *Iphigene* to Womanish complaints
> Adds pious Pray'rs, and wearies all the Saints;
> Ev'n if she could, her Love she would repent,
> But since she cannot, dreads the Punishment:
> Her forfeit Faith, and *Pasimond* betray'd,
> Are ever present, and her Crime upbraid.
> She blames her self, nor blames her Lover less,
> Augments her Anger as her Fears increase;
> From her own Back the Burden would remove,
> And lays the Load on his ungovern'd Love,
>
> .   .   .   .   .   .
>
> That for his daring Enterprize she dy'd,
> Who rather not resisted, than comply'd.
>   Then impotent of Mind, with alter'd Sense,
> She hugg'd th' Offender, and forgave th' Offence,
> Sex to the last.
>   (349–58, 364–8)

There are many signs that the author of the *Fables* not only possessed insight into human nature but also the power to present characters as active figures in a play. Sometimes the description of the setting recalls the stage. For example, there is the pavilion of Theodore in the forest

> With Flow'rs below, and Tissue over-head.
>   (258)

Again we are reminded of stock dramatic figures, when Sigismonda conveys her message to Guiscardo with the utmost caution,

> for fear to be betray'd
> By some false Confident, or Fav'rite Maid.
> (90–1)

The bow with which he receives it is but in keeping with the need for action in the theatre. Repeatedly Dryden the dramatist comes to the aid of Dryden the translator and introduces movement that is lacking in Boccaccio. Thus in the final scene of 'Sigismonda and Guiscardo' Tancred opens the curtains round his daughter's bed, only to reveal her lying with firmly closed eyes. And when Theodore's guests withdraw, the courteous host says farewell to them all but passes by Honoria unheeding. Another feature that Dryden introduces is the ceremonious behaviour of Tancred and Sigismonda in the presence of her attendants. He kisses her cheek and blesses her as she kneels before him.

Facial expression is not overlooked as a means of disclosing personality. Who can forget Cymon with his 'stupid Eyes, that ever lov'd the Ground' or the spectacle when

> The slavering Cudden, prop'd upon his Staff,
> Stood ready gaping with a grinning Laugh?
> (179–80)

The anger of the spectral knight is suggested by the flashing flames of his ardent eyes and by his fierce stare. No wonder that the spectator quails before this menacing figure:

> Stern look'd the Fiend, as frustrate of his Will,
> Not half suffic'd, and greedy yet to kill.
> (193–4)

Similarly, the uneasiness of Honoria is augmented when she has noted the stern look of her lover, as if he were hatching some deep design.

Dryden also expresses emotion by a sigh or a groan[1] or by some other outward manifestation. The pent-up wrath of Tancred finds an outlet in his 'lonely walking by a winking Light', sobbing, weeping, groaning and beating his withered beard. The anxiety of Sigismonda, as she lies vainly waiting for the arrested Guiscardo, is equally convincing. She

> long expecting lay, for Bliss prepar'd,
> List'ning for Noise, and griev'd that none she heard;
> Oft rose, and oft in vain employ'd the Key,
> And oft accus'd her Lover of Delay.
> (292–5)

As an experienced dramatist, Dryden knew full well the importance

---

[1] 'Sigismonda and Guiscardo', ll. 639, 650.

T

of keeping things moving on the stage, and that holds good of groups as well as individuals. Consequently, when the baffled crowd of Rhodians arrive at the harbour, only to see Lysimachus and Cymon sailing away, instead of standing about as in Boccaccio, in Dryden's version they hurl their darts until the fugitives are out of range.

It is perhaps in his descriptions that Dryden the poet is most free to range at will. In 'Sigismonda and Guiscardo' he does not find much scope for his mastery in this sphere, though the account of the dimly-lit rift in the mountain-side gives some idea of what he could achieve. On the other hand, the use of light-imagery in 'Cymon and Iphigenia' to relate the gradual dawn of intelligence in the hero[1] is a remarkable performance, and the picture of the sleeping Iphigenia, invested with all the grace of an ancient goddess, is among the most exquisite poetry that Dryden ever wrote. If this passage is outstanding in its languorous charm, the dramatic representation of the storm is outstanding in its vigour:

> Scarce the third Glass of measur'd Hours was run,
> When like a fiery Meteor sunk the Sun;
> The Promise of a Storm; the shifting Gales
> Forsake by Fits, and fill the flagging Sails:
> Hoarse Murmurs of the Main from far were heard,
> And Night came on, not by degrees prepar'd,
> But all at once; at once the Winds arise,
> The Thunders roul, the forky Lightning flies.
> In vain the Master issues out Commands,
> In vain the trembling Sailors ply their Hands:
> The Tempest unforeseen prevents their Care,
> And from the first they labour in Despair.
> The giddy Ship, betwixt the Winds and Tides
> Forc'd back, and forwards, in a Circle rides,
> Stun'd with the diff'rent Blows; then shoots amain,
> Till counterbuff'd she stops, and sleeps again.
>
> (327–42)

In 'Theodore and Honoria' the descriptions occupy a place of special importance. The brief account of the spring scene in the forest where the disconsolate lover wanders has a lyrical quality. The song of the birds provides

> Musick unbought, that minister'd Delight
> To Morning-walks, and lull'd his Cares by Night.
>
> (62–3)

There is again a rare melody in the lines that follow shortly after:

> 'Twas in a Grove of spreading Pines he stray'd;
> The Winds within the quiv'ring Branches plaid,
> And Dancing-Trees a mournful Musick made.
>
> (78–80)

[1] ll. 117–23, 139–48.

Using the pathetic fallacy, Dryden associates the doleful mood of Theodore with these sombre surroundings.

However, the most powerful effects are those created by the description of the hunt. It has to be borne in mind that Dryden takes from the English version of 1620 and ultimately from Salviati the interpretation of the chase as a diabolical illusion intended to lead astray the soul of man.[1] Thus the spectral horseman is a demon or the devil himself. Consequently, regarding him as no ordinary ghost, Dryden lets his imagination play on the ominous silence and then the convulsion of Nature that foretell his approach towards the solitary Theodore:

> While list'ning to the murm'ring Leaves he stood,
> More than a Mile immers'd within the Wood,
> At once the Wind was laid; the whisp'ring sound
> Was dumb; a rising Earthquake rock'd the Ground:
> With deeper Brown the Grove was overspread:
> A sudden Horror seiz'd his giddy Head,
> And his Ears tinckled, and his Colour fled.
> Nature was in alarm; some Danger nigh
> Seem'd threaten'd, though unseen to mortal Eye:
> Unus'd to fear, he summon'd all his Soul,
> And stood collected in himself, and whole;
> Not long: For soon a Whirlwind rose around,
> And from afar he heard a screaming sound.
>   (88–100)

As if to heighten the eerie atmosphere, Dryden briefly repeats the description, though in varied terms, on the second appearance of the horseman, as he repeats the description of the hunt.

All this is but a preparation for the depiction of the terror that seizes Theodore's friends. They are aghast, and the shrieks of the women mingle with the hoarse baying of the hounds and the piercing laments of the lady they pursue.

> The Gallants to protect the Ladies right,
> Their Fauchions brandish'd at the grisly Spright;
> High on his Stirups, he provok'd the Fight.
> Then on the Crowd he cast a furious Look,
> And wither'd all their Strength before he strook:
>   (282–6)

They recoil in alarm, and their paralysing fear is most vividly portrayed:

> The pale Assistants on each other star'd,
> With gaping Mouths for issuing Words prepar'd;
> The still-born Sounds upon the Palate hung,
> And dy'd imperfect on the faltring Tongue.
>   (306–9)

[1] Cf. H. G. Wright, *The first English translation of the 'Decameron'*, pp. 155–6.

Thus by an act of poetic divination Dryden conjures up all that was latent in Boccaccio's tale and develops it into a study of the effects of fear on the human mind.

All the resources accumulated during a long experience of the literary art are employed in the *Fables*. In 'Sigismonda and Guiscardo' one cannot fail to notice the repeated use of the epic caesura,[1] and of the well-known formula containing 'thrice'. It has been pointed out that the lines

> Thrice he began, and thrice was forc'd to stay,
> Till Words with often trying found their Way
> (306–7)

are imitated from *Paradise Lost*.[2] The same device occurs when Guiscardo knocks on the door:

> Thrice with a doleful Sound the jarring Grate
> Rung deaf, and hollow, and presag'd their Fate.
> (227–8)

By these means Dryden imparted a loftiness which suited the tragic theme.

Antithesis lends point to many passages, as in these two from 'Theodore and Honoria':

> Renew'd to Life, that she might daily die,
> I daily doom'd to follow, she to fly.
> (176–7)
> But in the Dead they damn'd the living Dame.
> (358)

As in these instances, alliteration frequently plays an important part. It may be either simple as in 'Cymon and Iphigenia'

> To *r*est by cool Eu*r*otas they *r*esort
> (94)

or complex as in 'Theodore and Honoria'

> Two Mastiffs *g*aunt and *g*rim her *F*light pursu'd
> And oft their *F*asten'd *F*angs in *B*lood em*b*ru'd.
> (113–14)

The alliteration is sometimes combined with repetition as in this passage from the same poem, where 'feeds' and 'looking' are repeated.

> *L*ooking he *f*eeds a*l*one his *f*amish'd Eyes,
> *F*eeds *l*ingring *D*eath, but *l*ooking not he *d*ies.
> (39–40)

Again in the melodious verses that describe the sleeping Iphigenia

---

[1] ll. 582, 635, 681, 705.   [2] Book i, 619–21.

'the fanning wind' appears in three successive lines in an alliterative combination of 'b' and 'r'.

> The fanning Wind upon her *Bosom Blows*,
> To meet the fanning Wind the *Bosom rose*;
> The fanning Wind and purling Streams, continue her *Repose*.
> (104–6)

The qualities of the *Fables* lent to them a popularity which lasted until the middle of the nineteenth century,[1] and the example that Dryden had given of mingling descriptions and allusions to contemporary affairs with stories from Boccaccio inspired a long series of tales in verse.

In his preface to *Tales Tragical and Comical*[2] Durfey acknowledges his indebtedness to Dryden's *Fables*: 'It was by Reading the Inimitable Mr. Dryden's last Work, that Curiosity grew in me to attempt these following Tales'. He asserts that Dryden had previously commended his 'Lyrical Genius' and now he turns to writing tales in verse, confident that even if he cannot attain to Dryden's smoothness and elegance, the reader will find that he possesses the gift of narrative. He considered that one of the stories in which he had been most successful[3] was the fourth in his collection, this being derived from the *Decameron*[4] of 'the Ingenious Boccace'. Durfey took especial pride in the 'Large Additions and Embelishment' that he had made and claimed that the reader would appreciate his 'Fancy' and his 'Improving' of the original.

Among the embellishments are a number of descriptions such as that of the hurried dressing of Nicoletta and her parents when Adrian and Pannuchio arrive, the lighting of the brushwood fire and the preparations for supper. He conveys the excitement of Nicoletta and gives a spirited account of the subsequent quarrel between Pannuchio and his host. Again he relates how the angry father was appeased by Adrian's fantastic invention of his friend's nocturnal dreams and sleep-walking:

> A Week is yet scarce past, since I
> Reliev'd thee from the Jeopardy
> Of ending all Intrigues at once,
> By fairly breaking of thy Bones;
> When thou did'st up the Chimney climb,
> Led by thy Dream to things Sublime,

---

[1] See H. G. Wright, 'Some Sidelights on the Reputation and Influence of Dryden's 'Fables'' in *R.E.S.*, 1945, xxi, pp. 23–37. (A tribute was paid to Boccaccio by Thomas Russell in his *Sonnets and Miscellaneous Poems*. Vide ante, p. 58. The sixth sonnet, on Boccaccio, serves once more to illustrate the supreme importance of the *Decameron* for eighteenth-century writers. All his other works had been eclipsed by the hundred tales.)

[2] London, 1704.   [3] THE Night-Adventures: OR *A Country Intrigue*.

[4] ix, 6. Durfey used the English version of 1620, as numerous verbal parallels show.

> A Phoenix-Nest was in thy Brain,
> Till thou cam'st tumbling down again,
> Contus'd with many a Jolt and Rub,
> And smear'd as black as *Belzebub*;
> When, had not I, amidst the Soot
> Rose up, and pull'd thee by the Foot,
> Thou would'st no doubt have Scal'd the Top,
> And from the outside had a drop;
> And just as then thou didst devise
> Of Nests, and Birds of Paradise;
> Thou now art Dreaming of Amours,
> And making Plighted Virgins Whores,
> Prating as if thou had'st thy Sence
> Of Love-toys, and Incontinence;
> When, Heaven help thee, all the Bliss
> Thou hast, or art like to possess,
> Whene'er thy frantick Fit begins,
> Is in the Dark to break thy Shins;
> Climb Chimneys amongst Grease and Soot,
> And break thy Neck perhaps to boot.[1]

(pp. 208–9)

Durfey develops this theme when he lets Pannuchio dream aloud and finally, before his departure, explain to the credulous host how his habit could be traced back to the iron discipline of his tutor which roused him from sleep to pore over his book and thus laid the foundation of his irregularities.

Another adornment that Durfey introduces is the use of similes of epic dimensions. Thus the good wife, startled by the discovery that she has made an error about the bed, is compared to a fawn quietly browsing in a park, suddenly terrified by a peal of thunder. More original is the simile of the tempestuous joy of a spaniel at his master's return to express Nicoletta's emotion on the appearance of Pannuchio

> Who'er has seen, at least to mind,
> A Creature of the Spaniel kind,
> When his lov'd Master, who has been
> For some time absent, enters in,
> Leap, Skip, and Wriggle, - - - bound up high,
> Run, throw down all things in his way,
> And show such wild, unruly Joy,
> As if by some mad Fiend possess'd,
> Or Quicksilver had fill'd his Breast.
> So with our love-sick Girl it fares.

(p. 191)

Another simile which would appeal to many of Durfey's readers wa that in which he glanced satirically at a Puritanical preacher of th

---

[1] The page references appended to the quotations are to the first edition.

late seventeenth century.[1] It is brought in to portray the embarrassment of Pannuchio as he tries to bamboozle the host:

> Here for some time he Coughing stood,
> As one not at Invention good;
> Or like our dull Tub-canting Drones,
> Or bold *Welch* Stickler, *David J - - - s*,
> Who would Convert us Sinful Men
> With Hum and ha - - - and, for, to - - then,
> Tautologies of three Hours speaking,
> On dreadful Dooms for Sabbath-breaking,
> Till like him having clear'd his way
> From Rheum, that stop'd what he wou'd say,
> Renewing what he late begun,
> His new Discourse, he thus went on.
>   (pp. 212–13)

In various ways Durfey tries to find reasons for features of the
original tale. Thus he evidently asked himself how Pannuchio first
became acquainted with Nicoletta. He provided an answer which came
readily enough to any one living a generation after the great plague
of 1665. It was that when the Black Death descended on Florence,
Pannuchio was placed for safety in the cottage of a herdsman and
there fell in love with his daughter Nicoletta. This provides a glimpse
of a rural idyll. But Durfey had no sympathy for rustics, and this is
illustrated by his attitude to the host who is made a figure of fun from
start to finish. He is a 'Churl' and 'Clodpate' who swears by 'Crumple
Horn' his 'Dappl'd Heifer', dreams 'Of Cattle that in Thickets
Brows'd' and when wakened,

>   like a Hog
> That rouz'd from Fellows of the Stye,
> Yells out a furious grunting Cry,
> Soon as he could his Snowt uprear,
> Crys oh!
>   (p. 201)

He has difficulty in pronouncing 'Pannuchio':

>   the Gentleman,
> Your Modest Lodger, Seigniour *Pan.* - - -
> *Pan.* - - - *Pan.* - - - A Pox upon his Name
>   (p. 205)

and listens open-mouthed to a tall story:

[1] David Jones was notorious for the eccentric violence of his sermons. In 1700 he
quarrelled with a man for mowing hay on a Sunday, and when the matter came before
the court of the vice-chancellor of Oxford University, Jones's conduct was such that
he was sent to gaol for contempt of court (*D.N.B.*, xxx, p. 93). He is satirised in *Novus
Reformator Vapulans : or, The Welch Levite tossed in a Blanket. In a Dialogue between
Hick — of Colchester, David J-nes and the Ghost of Wil. Pryn*. Printed for the Assigns of
Wil. Pryn, next door to the Devil, 1691.

> he gaping stood,
> Just like an Image made in Wood,
> The upper Jaw stretch'd wide from Lower,
> As if he would the Tale Devour.
>
> (p. 216)

The truth is that Durfey wrote as a city-dweller, and, as his preface admits, this tale was chiefly meant to 'divert the Youthful and Gay part of the Town'. He was uneasily aware that it was 'of a light wanton kind' but trusted that it would be 'Guarded from Capricious Censure, by the Authority of that Antique Author', Boccaccio. However, he evidently felt that this authority would hardly suffice to protect him from the criticism of the more serious reader, and he was all the more conscious of his vulnerability, because Jeremy Collier had rebuked him personally in his *Short View of the Profaneness and Immorality of the English Stage*. Boccaccio's tale was characteristic of the author's delight in the outwitting of the simple-minded, and this pleasure was shared by the keen-witted young man of society, but Durfey attempted to make some concession to the reaction set up by Collier. Hence he depicts the relationship between Pannuchio and Nicoletta as a genuine love-affair thwarted by her father's resolve to marry her against her will to a stupid rustic. On these grounds the intrigue of Pannuchio and Adrian is defended. But such a justification of their conduct only serves to reveal the superficiality of Durfey's attitude. He pays lip-service to morality but the prevailing temper of the tale is that of the cynical gallant.

At the end of the preface to his *Tales Tragical and Comical* Durfey held out the prospect of another such volume, among its contents being a number of stories on antique themes. The new collection, *Stories, Moral and Comical* contained 'Titus and Gissippus . . . Done from a Hint out of the *Italian* Prose of the Famous *Boccace*. Concluding with a Supplement, alluding to the Queens late Gracious Speech, Exhorting all to Amity'. The tale, which was dedicated to Queen Anne, was probably published in 1706.[1]

Durfey devoted some care to the characters of the tale and to Titus in particular. The emotional conflict within him between love and

---

[1] The *D.N.B.* Art. 'Durfey' gives 1706 as the date, the *C.B.E.L.* 1707. There is some internal evidence to serve as a guide. Reference is made to the duke of Marlborough and the bestowal of Woodstock on him. The bill enabling Queen Anne to do this passed through Parliament in February and March 1705 (cf. *Journals of the House of Commons*, xiv, pp. 510, 515). There is also an allusion to the queen's patronage of the stage and to the erection of a new theatre. The Queen's Theatre in the Haymarket, which Durfey had in mind, was opened on 9 April 1705. Finally, the 'late gracious Speech' of the queen refers to her address to both Houses of Parliament on 12 November 1705, in which she had appealed for national union (cf. *Journals of the House of Commons*, xv, p. 7).

friendship is elaborated, for it involved honour as well, and the clash between love and honour was calculated to interest Durfey's contemporaries. The long speech in which Boccaccio's Titus harangues Sophronia's relatives contained certain elements which the English narrator felt obliged to modify. In the circumstances Titus had to make out a strong case for the recognition of his marriage by her kinsmen, but despite Boccaccio's efforts he left an impression of self-complacency. Durfey strengthens his apology for praising his own merits and reduces to a minimum his reference to the fame and antiquity of his family. Later he tones down Titus's arrogant insistence on his position as a Roman and his disparaging, not to say insulting remarks about the Greeks. After his return to Rome Durfey's Titus takes steps to find his friend and thus escapes the charge, from which Boccaccio's hero cannot be exonerated, that in his conjugal happiness he allows the friend to whom he owes so much to slide into oblivion. As for the faithful Gissippus,[1] his emotion is heightened, and his distress in misfortune leads him to rail at all mankind both before he has left Greece and during the trial scene in Rome. Nor does Durfey overlook Sophronia. Her prototype is a passive figure who has to be told of the stratagem practised against her; she remains in complete ignorance until Titus's departure for Rome when she has to be informed that he and not Gissippus is her husband. As Durfey presents the situation, she herself discovers the truth on the morning after her nuptials, and he takes some pains to portray her violent resentment and her gradual acquiescence.

Durfey accounts for Titus's failure to remain in contact with his friend by means of a change that he makes in the tale. After a series of misfortunes has overtaken him, Gissippus leaves Athens and retires to a gloomy wood where Plato and Socrates had been wont to meditate.

> 'Twas hither to a Grott, with Bryers o'regrown,
> *Gissippus*, sad, forsaken and alone,
> Fled one relentless night, and laid him down:
> Th'ungentle Winds bluster'd around his Head,
> The baleful place was dark and full of dread.
>
> (p. 138)

For three months he dwells there, living on roots and wild berries, haws and sloes, and Durfey invests his abode with an almost romantic horror that harmonises with the hero's melancholy despair:

> The Bird of *Pallas* pearching o're his Head,
> Ne'r fail'd to give him Midnight Serenade;
> And oft, when Bears and Tygers, wanting Food,
> His Neighbours were, by scent of humane Blood,

---

[1] Durfey's spelling of the name is followed.

> A double Terror seiz'd his anxious Mind,
> To be surpriz'd, if these his Cave should find;
> Or by his Foes, the Brutes of humane kind.
>
> (p. 140)

In keeping with this exaggeration we observe that when Gissippus sets out for Rome, even though he is worn and emaciated by grief and hardship, he completes the journey in three days! A minor change now becomes necessary, because the cave where, in the original, Gissippus witnessed the nocturnal murder at Rome has already been introduced, and so in Durfey's version he has to lie on the cold floor of a ruined house. The name of the criminal is altered from Publius Ambustus to Brunivolgo, probably for metrical reasons.

Such a name has a theatrical ring, and the same effect is produced when Titus brooding over his love for his friend's betrothed, compares himself to the 'wild Banditti'. Durfey's grasp on the setting of the ancient world is precarious, and he thinks no more of the associations evoked by 'Banditti' than he does of the balls and plays at which Titus seeks to drown his cares. It is indeed his own environment that colours his portrayal of Titus and Gissippus, as may be seen clearly enough if we recall that he had in 1686 published a play called *The Banditti*. The theatre is never long absent from his mind, and in 'A Supplement, Parallel to the Story, and Address'd to my Countrymen of England' he combines a tribute to Queen Anne's patronage of the theatre with a fling at his old enemy, Jeremy Collier:

> But *Anna*'s gracious Beams, that Influence
> Declining Wit, and give new Life to Sense.
> (That when th'Immoral Moralist his Rage
> Thunder'd, in Exclamation on the Stage;
> Veyling with Robe Divine the Hypocrite,
> And pressing Truth beneath fallacious Wit;
> Which to the Sons of Blinded Zeal gave Laws,
> And made them preach down the Poetick Cause;
> False Reason against Charming Numbers bring,
> Mistaking oft Description for the thing.)
> With Rays indulgent to the Poets Art,
> Shed kindly Warmth, and cherishing Desert,
> Now make New Theatres more high aspire,[1]
> As once did *Thebes*, by fam'd *Amphion*'s Lyre.
>
> (p. 160)

It is, however, with the political aspect of his own world that Durfey is chiefly concerned. Bearing in mind the friendship of Titus and Gisippus, Boccaccio had eulogised amity at large. Durfey modifies this somewhat:

---

[1] The Queen's Theatre in the Haymarket (vide ante, p. 280, n. 1).

Discording *Romans*, touch'd with what they heard
No longer Jar, but Unity preferr'd,

(p. 156)

and it is this example which spreads far and wide. In the 'Supplement'
Durfey steps forward in person to emphasise the parallel:

> Shall gracious *Anna* then no period reach;
> *Exhorting ye to Union in each Speech*:
> Confirm'd in Sacred Sense, you ne're can be
> Securely happy, wanting Amity.
> Must She each *Session* waste her Heavenly Voice
> Commending precious Union to your Choice
> Yet no *Gissippus* of the Commons hears,
> Nor any Noble *Titus* 'mongst the Peers,
> Possest with her Angelick Inspiration,
> Will dole the Cordial to the Sickly Nation;
> Such Lunacy th'Infected Land does feel,
> Ill to take Counsel, and much worse to heal.

(p. 158)

To make his point still clearer he addresses

> to every one whom Faction sways,
> Whose byass'd Heart is not entirely bent
> To Union

(p. 163)

a fable about two pots, filled respectively with mice and frogs which,
as they floated down a river, longed for the food aboard a bark, while
on the bark 'A Ravenous Crane, of *Gallick* kind' planned to sink them
both. The whole ends with the moral,

> This is your case, ye Britains all,
>   By Feuds you still your selves undo;
> And like Old Rome, make Albion fall;
>   Which nought besides could overthrow.[1]

Thus Boccaccio's old tale is pressed into the service of political
propaganda which Durfey unites with his eulogy of the queen, and

---

[1] In her speech to Parliament on 1 November (o.s.) 1705 Anne touched on the
negotiations proceeding for union with Scotland: 'I am persuaded, that an Union
of the two Kingdoms will not only prevent many Inconveniences, which may otherwise happen, but must conduce to the Peace and Happiness of both Nations'. She
continued: 'There is another Union I think myself obliged to recommend to you in
the most earnest and affectionate Manner, I mean an Union of Minds and Affections
amongst ourselves: It is that, which would, above all Things, disappoint and defeat
the Hopes and Designs of our Enemies'. After dwelling on the machinations of those
who cast doubt on her devotion to the Church of England, she ended: 'I must be so
plain as to tell you, the best Proofs we can all give, at present, of our Zeal for the
Preservation of the Church, will be, to join heartily in prosecuting the War against
an Enemy, who is certainly engaged to extirpate our Religion, as well as to reduce
this Kingdom to Slavery' (cf. *Journals of the House of Commons*, xv, p. 7).

there is reason to believe that by the adroitness of this appeal to his contemporaries he contrived to gain a notable success.[1]

Mary Pix, who was to some extent under the influence of Congreve, resembled Durfey in that she wrote plays as well as trying her hand at a tale in verse. Her comedies were not without a strain of coarseness but evidently, like so many of her contemporaries, she was affected by the hostility of Jeremy Collier towards the drama of the time, and so her adaptation of a story from the *Decameron* reflects the changed atmosphere. She adjusted herself all the more readily because she had Dryden's example in the *Fables* before her eyes and also because she was a clergyman's daughter. Her father, the Rev. Roger Griffith, was apparently of Welsh descent, and the fact that Wales was the scene of one episode of the tale that she selected[2] may in some degree have governed her choice. She certainly speaks with pride of the martial deeds of the ancient Britons and with interest of Merlin's prophecies. But her chief motive is revealed by the title of her poem—*Violenta, or the rewards of virtue*, which appeared in 1704.

The didactic interpretation of the tale was not entirely without foundation in Boccaccio, who makes several allusions to the divine care that watched over the hero and his children. However, his main purpose was to relate a romantic narrative which should conform to the theme laid down by Filomena, 'the fortune of such as after divers adventures have at last attained a goal of unexpected felicity'. The French princess, who in the absence of her husband the dauphin at the wars, becomes enamoured of the regent, is characteristic of a group of passionate women in the *Decameron* who permit no obstacle to the realisation of their desires. So unscrupulous is she that when from a sense of loyalty, he repels her approaches, she accuses him of dishonourable conduct and compels him to flee to England. After the lapse of many years the princess, now queen of France, confesses the truth and dies penitent, and the count is reinstated. The largest part of the tale is taken up with the varying fortunes of the count and his children in England, Wales and Ireland.

Mrs. Pix looked upon this plot with the eye of a dramatist and modified it accordingly. Thus at the close the queen instead of confessing her offence to the archbishop of Rouen and to other men of note, herself discloses to the king the great wrong inflicted on Angiers. It

---

[1] I have in my possession a copy of the tale which is printed separately from the volume in which it originally appeared. The pagination at first differs from that of *Stories, Moral and Comical*. But after p. 48 there is a sudden leap forward to p. 153, and the pagination down to p. 167 follows that of the complete work. It would seem therefore that the tale was reprinted to meet a popular demand, and that the printer by an oversight, when following the original version, omitted to make the pagination consistent.   [2] ii, 8

was perhaps the same fondness for theatrical effect which induced her to let Angiers in person reveal his identity to the king rather than through the medium of his son. Again it is the dramatist who adds characters to account for the actions of Angiers. The first of these is a faithful old servant, Ernesto. It would seem as if Mrs. Pix had felt it unworthy of so outstanding a figure as Angiers that, when unjustly accused, he should flee in a fit of panic. In her version he therefore lingers in his palace, deliberating what to do. As in a play, some one is required to rouse him to immediate action, if his children are not to be sacrificed to the fury of the slighted princess. Ernesto performs this function and is then conveniently removed when he dies of the combined effects of old age and a storm in the Channel. On his arrival in England the bewildered Angiers is at a loss, but another character is brought forward by Mrs. Pix to aid him. Haunted by ancestral reminiscences of Britain, she makes this aged man a bard. He counsels Angiers to proceed to London and prophesies that there he will find a benefactor for his son and daughter. The latter, having assumed the name Florella instead of Violenta, receives help and then the bard appears once more to direct Angiers. He is to go to Wales where, it is foretold, his son Perrot will be equally fortunate. The words of the venerable sage on this occasion disclose that he feels death near at hand, and when he appears for the last time, it is in a vision. The spirit of the bard commands Angiers to return to England. His last prophecy is that before long Angiers shall see his native land.

Other substantial changes were made in the part of the plot relating to Mandevil and Florella. Whereas it had formed less than a third of Boccaccio's tale, Mrs. Pix increased the proportion to over one half.[1] This was done by adding various episodes. First Mandevil meets Florella and declares his love, and when she misunderstands and declares that she is resolved to maintain her honour and virtue, he explains that he wants a wife, not a mistress. In the next new scene Florella is moved to tears at the sight of her sick lover. Another episode shows Mandevil's mother pleading with her husband. He yields only to the extent that his son is to be soothed with promises which will not be kept. Then the exceeding happiness of the lovers is depicted. But a swift transformation is wrought by the father's revelation that his consent was merely a device to restore his son to health. Mandevil, now aware that his position is hopeless, shuns Florella, who in turn fears that her lover is a dissembler. However, when he comes to bid her farewell, he discloses the marshal's evil design. Then he leaves home, intending to go abroad. But his absence is discovered and the marshal relents. Mandevil is prevented from embarking, and letters

---

[1] Out of a total of 128 pages it takes up pp. 36 to 100.

from his parents and Florella induce him to return for the marriage. Undeniably Mrs. Pix, the dramatist, heightens the tension by these numerous fluctuations and by the clash of personalities, but Boccaccio's tale as a whole is dislocated.

Some of the characters in the original are likewise developed or transformed. Among these is Angiers. In Mrs. Pix's hands he acquires a pious air. For a moment at the outset he is overtaken by despair, but as a rule he bears adversity nobly, and however painful the contrast between his former state and his present lot,

> Piety forbids that he should Heav'n arraign,
> He knows the only Way to vanquish there,
> Is Patience, Faith unmov'd, and fervent Pray'r . . .[1]
>
> (p. 24)

Hence in London he prostrates himself on the pavement of St. Paul's,[2] while his children, 'early taught to pray', kneel beside him. For the same reason he shrinks from ending his suffering by suicide, since

> Our Priests pronounce eternal Pains
> To those who wearied out with Life's Disease,
> Shall dare to cure themselves e'er Nature please.
>
> (p. 34)

And he meekly bears all the calamities which Mrs. Pix heaps up as if to prove that

> Not *Hebrew Job* at length to Ills inur'd
> So much, or half so patiently indur'd.
>
> (p. 35)

One of the sources of these woes is the lord whom Angiers serves in Ireland. Boccaccio had related that the count had entered the household of a knight and that he found the menial tasks of a groom or lackey irksome. But for Mrs. Pix this is not enough. The count's master is a 'haughty Lord', 'fierce and severe', whom no service, however diligent, can please, and so Angiers

> Faultless is chid, nor dares he to complain . . .
>
> (p. 35)

Another haughty figure whom Mrs. Pix creates is the marshal into whose family Florella is received. He is depicted as proud and avaricious,

---

[1] Page references appended to the quotations are to the original edition.

[2] This reference to St. Paul's shows that Mrs. Pix did not read the tale in Italian. Boccaccio speaks of a church but does not name it. The English translation of 1620, which was evidently the version known to Mrs. Pix, tells how Angiers and his children stood 'at the Cathedrall Church doore'. Another feature that points to the English translation of 1620 is the name of the heroine Violenta who in the *Decameron* is called Violante. Similarly, the name Mandevil comes from the English version, for Boccaccio styles him Giachetto Lamiens. Cf. H. G. Wright, *The first English translation of the 'Decameron'*, p. 94.

valuing his wealth and possessions more than the happiness of his son. Again and again he exhibits a furious rage and, when thwarted,

> From his fierce Eyes the fiery Tempest came,
> Tumultuous Passion set him in a Flame . . .
>   (p. 61)

This cruel, crafty and worldly parent is utterly unlike the gentle father in Boccaccio who acquiesces in the proposal of his wife. But Mrs. Pix was determined that Mandevil's father should bear the responsibility for thwarting the marriage, and so his place is in the category of villains. Her male characters are either entirely bad like the Irish knight and the marshal or unbelievably good like Angiers. The latter's son is rendered even more laudable than in the original. Boccaccio had described how the plague had carried off all but a few servants, and so Perotto, famed for his prowess, was chosen as the husband of the Lord President's daughter. Mrs. Pix, however, establishes a personal relationship between them, for Perrot, hearing of the outbreak of the plague, hastens back from the wars in France to face all the horrors of the pestilence by her side. As for Mandevil, he is as perfect a hero as Sir Charles Grandison, faultless in word and deed. His native merit has been enhanced by the Grand Tour which Mrs. Pix, looking at the world with the eyes of the eighteenth century, assumes to have been part of a mediæval nobleman's education! At any rate, he is in one respect an improvement on his counterpart in the *Decameron*. Instead of pining and languishing passively, on occasion he can act. His calm reply to his infuriated father is not unimpressive; it certainly disconcerts the marshal:

> With Looks compos'd, he left the hateful Room;
> Nor cou'd his Father guess the Fate to come.
>   (p. 71)

It is significant that Mrs. Pix should exhibit Mandevil's mother in a favourable light. Boccaccio depicted her as one whose love would stick at nothing to promote her son's welfare. She discreetly puts the heroine to the test and only when her astuteness has been baffled by the firmness of virtue does she begin to entertain the possibility of a marriage. Perhaps Mrs. Pix felt that this unscrupulous attempt to exploit the situation of a defenceless girl was incompatible with the kindness that the marshal's wife had previously shown her. Possibly her womanly instinct rebelled against it. At any rate, she puts the blame on the marshal and presents Lady Mandevil as a submissive wife who, only when driven to despair, ventures to confront and even to rebuke him. One notices another shift of emphasis in the character of the dauphin's wife. Though the latter was not likely to command the respect of Mrs. Pix, she was not denied all sympathy. Her defence of her passion is not the individualistic argument of a frank voluptuary; on the contrary, she claims to be the victim of the social system. Like all her sex, she was allowed no say in the choice of a husband, and now the public interest which compelled her to marry the dauphin has summoned him to the wars and left her in solitude. Even in this form the character of the princess can have no personal connexion with Mrs. Pix, but one suspects that Florella is to some extent a projection of the narrator's own personality. She is something of a scholar, composes poetry, takes her Horace with her on an evening walk and finds consolation for the apparent unfaithfulness of Mandevil by reading the story of Theseus and Ariadne.

Florella's delight in solitude is not unique. Thus Mandevil, when stricken by love, retires to a 'Melancholy Grove', there to vent his grief and carve the signs of his passion on the trees. Later, on learning that he is not to be allowed to marry, he resolves to enter a monastery, just as Florella is bent on secluding herself in a nunnery. Nor is it only the young lovers who are ready to shut themselves off from the world. On the death of his wife Angiers seeks consolation in retirement and obeys with great reluctance the summons to act as regent during the absence of the king and dauphin. He flees to the dark groves and silent caves, for

> The World to him had now no pleasing Charms,
> Nor wak'd he with the once lov'd Sound of Arms:
> Thus liv'd the Count to eating Grief a Prey . . .
>
> (p. 3)

This sensibility of Angiers assumes a more active and extravagant form when the princess is incensed against him and he considers the plight of his children:

> But oh! when he beheld his little Pair,
> The Mothers Darlings, and the Fathers Care,
> In vain upon their Nurse and Servants call,
> The Floods so long restrain'd, in Torrents fall;
> At their sad Wants he cou'd no more forbear,
> Indulg'd his Grief with many a pitying Fear . . .
>
> (p. 18)

In a frenzy of despair he casts himself on the ground and curses the malignant star that ruled his birth. So intensely does Mrs. Pix feel for him that she interrupts the tale to appeal to the reader's emotions:

> I'd sing, my Muse, his Woes in such a Strain,
> That no sad reader might from Tears refrain:
> Sure all the generous World must weep to see
> Exalted Virtue in such Misery.
>
> (p. 24)

Her tender womanly heart certainly makes the tears flow copiously on many occasions. The reader will think it natural enough that Florella and Cammilla should pour forth their sorrow when their husbands depart for the wars, but he may be forgiven if he finds the sentiment of Mandevil and Florella excessive. The hero sighs and blushes with the same frequency as his beloved. Sometimes he is seized with 'Convulsive Transports' at her approach and tells her:

> All Night, on Beds of Down, I restless rave,
> On this cold Earth, I measure out my Grave . . .
>
> (p. 44)

He is prone to faint in her presence, his lips tremble as he raises her hand to kiss it, and one feels that his misery must end in death. Indeed, the crisis when his mother comes with the news that his father has relented appears to be leading to the same conclusion as Mackenzie's *Man of Feeling*:

> Too much transported at this Change of Fate,
> He cry'd, Your proffer'd Kindness is too late.
> The mighty Tides of Joy come on too fast,
> And weaken'd Life is gone too far to last;
> A dreadful Sound adds Terrour to their Fears,
> And fills the Room with piercing Shrieks and Tears;
> The Mother from the Pillow snatch'd her Son,
> And cry'd, Help all, or I am lost, undone.
>
> (pp. 65–6)

However, at the touch of Florella's hand Mandevil revives with astonishing celerity, and nowadays these scenes awaken not pity but laughter.

It is obvious that this display of sentiment unconsciously illuminates one facet of the era that was opening when *Violenta* was written. Elsewhere Mrs. Pix of set purpose tries to throw light on the manners of her own by idealising those of bygone generations:

> Few Wanton Dames, no broken Nuptial Bed.
>
> (p. 28)

The contrast is plain, though implicit. Other passages reflect the age more directly. In particular, the striking description of the plague in the episode of Perrot and Cammilla was calculated to appeal to a generation which knew either at first hand or from eye-witnesses the horrors of the great outbreak in 1665. Mrs. Pix herself was born the following year and in her childhood must have heard of the grim scenes enacted in England. As Defoe's *Journal of the Plague* indicates, there was a keen interest in the subject, and the following description of the sights witnessed by Perrot proves that Mrs. Pix also appreciated the macabre fascination of the deadly epidemic:

U

> Thro' all the Avenues, eagerly he flies,
> Still complicated Horrour meets his Eyes,
> And noysome Steams, from the unburied Dead arise.
> Here, lifted hands, in vain, for help do call,
> The Servant at his Master's Feet does fall.
> In one promiscuous Heap, lay Old and Young,
> The Rich, the Fair, the Healthful and the Strong;
> Then angry Heav'n sends the Destroyer forth,
> Who can express the Terrours of his Wrath!
> The Plague, with rapid Force, devouring Rage,
> Seems as 'twou'd clear this crowded busie Stage
> Of all that thinking Stock of humane Kind,
> Infects the Body, sinks the forming Mind;
> Dispair, and Black Idea's fill the Soul,
> Such Thoughts as all Religion wou'd controul.
>
> (pp. 103–4)

Afterwards the account portrays the psychological phenomenon noted long before by Thucydides and in the introduction to the *Decameron*:

> All ties are broke, the Fathers flies the Sons,
> The Mother from her bosom'd Infant runs;
> Dire Hate, in each infected Breast presides,
> And new made Bridegrooms shun their charming Brides:
> Death's grown so common, none will shed a Tear,
> Nature and Love are both o'ercome by Fear.
>
> (p. 104)

Then the birth of new hope is depicted, as the plague wanes with the passing of summer, and men resume their wonted lives:

> Bleak Winter, now, with nipping Frost draws near,
> Courted, desir'd, and hollow Winds that clear
> The hot, unwholsome, and polluted Air:
> Thinly the peopl'd Towns appear agen,
> The ruin'd Clime begins to look Serene;
> The untill'd Land's, again the Labourers Care,
> And Temples now, resound with Praise and Pray'r.
>
> (p. 106)

In a tale of adventure there was little scope for the satirical bent of the early eighteenth century, but Mrs. Pix cannot refrain from a gibe at those physicians who

> unmov'd, can see the Parents Cry,
> Lamenting Wife, or Friend stand sighing by,
> And gravely Answer, *Man was born to dye,*
> When they, perhaps, have hasten'd Natures Date,
> And lay their own Mistake, on guiltless Fate.
>
> (p. 54)

By contrast she holds up for praise the doctor attending Mandevil Incidentally, she eulogises Sir Samuel Garth, while at the same tim

renewing the attack on less competent practitioners. The physician in
the tale, she says,

>   with utmost care, consulted Health,
> Like generous *Garth* aim'd not alone at wealth;
> The Mean, the Great, his equal influence find,
> As sent by Heav'n, to heal and bless Mankind.
> In him the Graces with the Arts combin'd,
> Like Poetry and Wealth, but seldom Joyn'd,
> Yet here they Triumph all, while he with Ease,
> Can Charm, Relieve, and Conquer a Disease;
> A Stranger to the New Phantastick way,
> Which dresses first, and bids the Dying stay,
> He weigh'd each Circumstance e'er gave his Vote,
> Took not the common way, and kill'd by Rote;
> And by his nice Observances, could find
> The Body strugling with a tortur'd Mind.
>
>   (pp. 54–5)

The satire on doctors is not universal, but the condemnation of the
profligacy of the time is unqualified. For this purpose Mrs. Pix uses
Mandevil, and she is harsh in her condemnation:

> Scarce will this wanton Age my Tale Believe;
> A Constant Youth their Vice wou'd ne'er forgive.
> Now Love is grown the Universal Sport,
> The Men design to leave, e'er they begin to Court;
> Fickle their Nature's; roving their Desire,
> In various Heats, there is no real Fire.
> Of old, to one the Passion was Confin'd,
> They'd wait an Age to make the Fair one Kind;
> Changing's the Mode; a Lover is a Fool,
> And to be very Faithful's, to be very Dull.
>
>   (p. 49)

This attack on dissolute living is the essential truth of Mrs. Pix's
poem. The virtue of constancy in love is lauded time and again.
Mandevil himself aspires only to be known to posterity as a paragon
of constancy; Angiers admires him on this score, and the authoress
herself declares that Mandevil's example shall atone for the falseness
of the sex as a whole. Allied to this didacticism is the moralising tone of
various passages. Mrs. Pix meditates on the instability of fortune and
the certitude of death. True happiness, she therefore contends, can be
found only in pious faith and the upright life. She takes a glance at
such a problem as the freedom of the human will. But it is only a
glance, for she fears to ponder deeply. In fact, she deprecates too
searching a scrutiny and regards as truly blest the man

>   whose calm Breast,
> No deep Inquiry makes, to break his Rest.
>
>   (p. 108)

Her meditations are therefore narrow and superficial; she lacks the philosophic mind.

The slightness of her thought is matched by the feebleness of her lines in a crisis. The dauphin's farewell to Angiers as he sets out for the wars is ludicrous:

> Oh! thou my Dear and long try'd Friend he said!
> And on his Bosom kindly lean'd his Head.
>
> (p. 4)

And the plight of the unfortunate Angiers, hard pressed by the princess, all aflame with sexual passion, is related in terms not less absurd:

> Amaz'd, he spoke in th' mildest Phrase he cou'd,
> Instructs the Charming Princess to be good.
>
> (p. 12)

Yet nowhere is there such inadequacy as in Angiers' remark on the death of the faithful Ernesto: 'There was no need of this'.

It would, however, be unjust not to recognise that much of the verse is on a higher level. Like so many of her contemporaries Mrs. Pix had the gift of the telling phrase, and some of her lines are keen and pointed. For example, the portrait of Mandevil's mother, anxiously awaiting the opinion of the physician about her son, is not without effect:

> Longing the truth to know, yet truth she fears,
> Her trembling Voice is choak'd with rising Tears.
>
> (p. 57)

Thus in Mrs. Pix's hand, Boccaccio's romantic tale is transformed into a sentimental story which inculcates virtuous and constant love as a lesson to a dissolute society, and, like Durfey, she takes Dryden as her model in combining the narrative with a commentary on her age.

Though the heroic couplet under Dryden's powerful influence was used as the medium for many verse tales derived from Boccaccio, Matthew Prior went his own way. Among some fragments that he left behind is 'A Tale from Boccace'[1] which, as it pays a tribute to Queen Anne as the sovereign still reigning, must have been written before her death in 1714. Prior's intention to follow Milton rather than Dryden, for whom he cherished an imperfect sympathy that is notorious, manifests itself in the opening lines of the 'Prelude' that he addressed to the Duchess of Shrewsbury:

---

[1] See *Dialogues of the Dead and other Works in Prose and Verse*, ed. A. R. Waller, Cambridge, 1907, pp. 339–44. The tale is v, 9. This volume is often referred to as volume ii, *The Writings of Matthew Prior*, ed. A. R. Waller, 1905–7, Cambridge. The page references appended to the quotations are to this edition.

What Bocace with superior Genius Cloath'd
In Tuscan dress, and ludicrous Fontaine
(Modern Anacreon) well has imitated
In Gallic Style, Himself inimitable:
How e'er unequal to the glorious Task,
Yet of the noblest Heights and best Examples,
Ambitious, I in English Verse attempt.
But not as heretofore, the line prescrib'd
To equal cadence, and with semblant Sounds
Pointed, (so Modern Harmony advises)
But in the Ancient Guise, free, uncontroll'd,
The Verse, compress'd the Period, or dilated,
As close discourse requires, or fine description.
(p. 339)

It is evident also from the 'Prelude' that he was conscious of the exquisite harmonies of Boccaccio's prose and so felt constrained to defend an attempt to render it into English. He does so by claiming that English, far from being harsh, is

semblant to our Native Streams,
O'er little Flints and scatter'd Pebbles rolling
Its curled Wave, unequal not unpleasing
The Surface
(p. 341)

and that on occasion, when sensitively handled,

Softer than Down from Venus fav'rite birds,
Or flakes of feather'd Snow, the Accents fall!
(p. 341)

It could hardly escape a poet with such aesthetic sensibilities that if he were to write in the grand epic manner he would have to make some changes in the tale. Hence his preference for Clitia rather than Giovanna as the name of the heroine, though by contrast his retention of 'Frederic'[1] seems inconsistent. He also introduced Thestylis, who appears to be the nurse of Frederic, upholding his procedure by Virgil's mention of Caieta, the nurse of Æneas.[2] In view of the fragmentary nature of Prior's tale, one can only surmise what her part was to be. Most likely she was to tend Frederic in his cottage, when his fortunes had declined.

The scope for 'fine description' which Prior had associated with blank verse is exemplified by his picture of Frederic watering the rose and jessamine, propping the fig-tree and gazing at the clusters of half-purple grapes around the green elm. Such a scene blended well enough with the classical tradition and so did the account of the tournament and the revels on which Frederic squandered his money in the hope of winning his mistress's affection.

---

[1] Boccaccio's 'Federigo'.   [2] *Aeneid*, vii, ll. 1–2.

Clitia Seated
Sublime, commands the sports. Clitia's Device
Portray'd on Frederics Shield declares her Champion.
Music the splendid Ball and costly banquet
First fruits to hopeful Love by all his Zealots
Offer'd employ the softer Hours of Night,
Queen of the Feast reigns Clitia, Clitia's Name,
Adorns the Song, and at her Health alone
Breathes the shrill Hautboy, and the Clarion sounds.

(pp. 342–3)

Though all Frederic's lavish devotion was unrewarded at the time, it was not forgotten, and later she relented. The passage in which the transformation is described illustrates almost better than any other Prior's approximation to the grand style of epic imagery:

Not Snow melts faster on the craggy mount
The Alp, or Appen[n]ine, when Sol in Spring
Arising cheers the World, not Waves and winds
Subside more sudden, when great Neptune rears
His awful Trident, and commands a Calm
Then in one moment fell from Clitia's breast
The coldness of Disdain, the Widows Pride
And Prudery of the Sex.

(p. 343)

Prior's experiment is not without interest,[1] but any attempt to apply this method to the translation of Boccaccio's tales as a whole would have been misguided. Admirable in itself, the epic manner would have clashed with the subject-matter of the numerous tales which move on a homely plane. The spurious exaltation could only have produced a sense of burlesque and even of bathos.

Classical influence, though of a different order, is again perceptible in *The Nightingale* (1721), an anonymous version of the fourth tale of the fifth day. A story of passionate love, it recalled Catullus to the translator's mind, and on the title-page he quotes

---

[1] The theme found many admirers. It gave rise to a verse-tale by Hans Sachs and to a comedy by Lope de Vega. After the appearance of La Fontaine's version there followed a whole series of comedies and comic operas on the subject in eighteenth-century France. In Germany, under the influence of La Fontaine, Hagedorn turned the story into verse, and his rendering was used for a comedy, first acted at Vienna in 1776. In this year, as Goethe's letters to Frau von Stein indicate, he was pre-occupied with Boccaccio's tale. It would seem that his work was meant to be in dramatic form, and that the love of Federigo for Giovanna was to reflect Goethe's devotion to his correspondent (cf. R. Anschütz, *Boccaccios Novelle vom Falken und ihre Verbreitung in der Litteratur*, Erlangen, 1892, pp. 1–23). In England the great age for the popularity of the falcon story was the nineteenth century (vide post). However, inspired by La Fontaine's 'Le Faucon' in his *Contes et nouvelles*, as is shown by his tribute to his predecessor and by his borrowing of the name 'Clitia', Prior was well ahead of his countrymen.

Passer, Deliciæ Puellæ meæ
Quem, illa plus Oculis suis, amabat.[1]

However, the motto is only superficially apposite, for the preceding
line[2] in Catullus speaks of the death of the sparrow, which is irrelevant
to the tale of the nightingale. Nor is there any essential similarity
between the adolescent passion of Ricciardo and Caterina and the
unhealthy eroticism of Catullus and Lesbia.

Catullus was recalled to the English poet by an allusion to him in 'Le
Rossignol'. His tale is in fact derived, not from the Italian original, but
from this French source. The generalising introduction is omitted, but
in other respects La Fontaine is followed closely. Thus 'Lizio da Val-
bona' is replaced by 'Verambon', and both in the French and English
versions 'Giacomina' is declared to have been left nameless by Boccaccio,
no doubt because the Italian name was too stubborn for metre. In
accordance with La Fontaine also, the heroine is sometimes called
'Catherine' and sometimes 'Kitty', the latter corresponding to 'Cataut'.

The familiar form agrees with the conversational manner of the
poem which is modelled on the style of La Fontaine. Thus Catherine's
complaint about the heat of the bedchamber in the warm season is
framed as follows:

> When Morning came - - - - *Mamma*, she cry'd,
> Last Night, I thought I should have dy'd;
> This Room more stifling grows than ever,
> I certainly shall have a Fever,[3]
>
> (p. 8)

and her father's testiness, when she has begged her mother to let her
move into the gallery, is expressed in these simple words:

> The Gallery! what idle Tale!
> Your Daughter! and a Nightingale!
> Last Night, 'tis true, was hot; what then?
> The next it may be cool again.
> I sleep there well enough, is she
> More delicate and nice than We.
>
> (p. 9)

There is practically no embellishment in the form of description,
but when Catherine is pleading with her mother for permission to
sleep in the gallery, we have a glimpse of a southern background:

> In this most sultry Season there
> Comes from the Citron Grove, an Air
> That will refresh me, with its Breese;
> The Nightingale among the Trees,
> There chaunts its Love-song too . . .
>
> (p. 9)

---

[1] iii, ll. 4–5.   [2] Passer mortuus est meæ puellæ.
[3] The page references appended to the quotations are to the 1721 edition.

Similar qualities are displayed in *The Crane* which is derived from the fourth tale of the sixth day of the *Decameron*. It was written in 1730 but did not appear until 1787, when it was published in the March number of *The Gentleman's Magazine*.[1] The name of the author is not given, but it is stated that he had been a student of Merton College, Oxford. Verbal parallels show that the English translation of 1620 was his immediate source.

The scene is transferred from Florence to Venice, for no other reason than that Chichibio is a Venetian, but the alteration does involve an allusion to the clock of St. Mark's striking eight. The names of Chichibio and his love Brunetta are anglicised as 'John' and 'Sukey', which lends a more homely atmosphere to the tale. In keeping with this is the simplicity of the household in which John serves. It is impossible to think of Boccaccio's Currado Gianfigliazzi in person handing over the crane to his cook or of his summoning him to rise next morning, as John's master does.

The conflict in John's mind, torn as he is between his duty to the knight and his affection for Sukey, is developed, and a preamble is added which lays emphasis on this love theme:

> THE power of love, to guard the heart
> Against all dread of future smart,
> How bold the veriest coward proves,
> By one poor kiss from her he loves;
> How wit from danger sets us free,—
> Madam, lay down your work, and see.
>
> (1–6)

In fact, this theme becomes a central feature, whereas in Boccaccio's tale, in accordance with the conditions for all stories of the sixth day, the stress is laid on the ready answer with which an astute person extricates himself from a dilemma.

The poem is written in octosyllabic couplets which, despite an occasional faulty rhyme, are well managed. The verse flows agreeably, and the dialogue, which is freely used, moves with ease. The colloquial tone accords with the domestic setting in which the hero is a cook. Here is a passage which may serve as an illustration and which at the same time is interesting because of its allusion to Thomas Hearne, the great scholar, who was still living in Oxford when the 'Student of Merton College' composed his version:

> At Venice liv'd, in days of yore
> (The time let studious Hearne explore)
> A Knight, full hospitably bent,
> To give all hungry jaws content:

[1] pp. 256–7.

Redundant plenty deck'd his board,
With liquids fit for any lord:
No matter *whence* you came, or *when*,
Welcome to cut and come again.
His cook was John, a waggish blade,
As ever pie or pudding made;
With quibbles at his finger ends,
To nonplus foes, or tickle friends:
Nor scratch'd his head for Aye or No,
But answer'd smart, and *à-propos*:
Such witty answers would he give,
That folks would cry, 'John conno' live'.

(7–22)

One year after *The Crane* was composed, there appeared *A Collection of Poems* which contained two tales inspired by the *Decameron*. Despite the innocent-looking title-page, one of these tales was a contribution to contemporary politics. For some time past a violent feud had been raging between Robert Walpole and William Pulteney, the leader of the opposition. Lord Hervey was drawn in, and on 25 January 1731 he fought a duel with Pulteney. But the controversy with Walpole was of greater moment, for as the result of a rejoinder to an attack made on him in print by Walpole, Pulteney was struck off the roll of privy councillors. Amid the excitement generated by this antagonism an anonymous supporter of Pulteney joined in the fray. He had read the English translation of 1702[1] which had 'an ARGUMENT and MORAL added to each NOVEL'. The argument for the seventh tale of the first day ran 'The Covetousness of Great Men genteelly Banter'd' and the moral, 'Covetousness, above all other Vices, is most blameable in a Great Man, who ought to be good and generous to All'. This gave the English poet an idea for a means to censure Walpole.

In his dedication he speaks of the corruption that had overspread the age and was visible also in transactions of state, and he sought to criticise Walpole's acquisition of wealth, his lavish expenditure and his lack of generosity towards men of letters. The times were changing, and the aid of writers was less eagerly desired by a minister who believed that every man had his price and therefore preferred more direct methods of winning partisans.

The early part of the original story is considerably altered. Indeed, in the English version it becomes the chief feature. Boccaccio had told how Bergamino, by relating to Cane della Scala the generosity of the abbot of Cligni to Primasso, induced him to exercise a like munificence. In the preamble to the tale it is made clear that the meanness of Cane della Scala to Bergamino was nothing but a momentary deviation from

[1] Vide ante, pp. 261–2.

his normal custom. However, this passage was omitted in the translation of 1702, and so there was no obstacle here to an attack on Walpole. The poet settles down to his task at once, though he mentions neither person nor country:

> In days of Old, no matter where,
> There dwelt at Court a *Minister*;
> In highest State by Fortune plac'd,
> With Riches blest, with Titles grac'd;
> In Pomp, in Plenty so excelling,
> That Kings might envy well his dwelling:
> His real Merit would ye know,
> My Author says, 'twas but so, so:
> Of middling Parts, immensely vain,
> Lavish, yet greedy still of Gain.
> In fine, impartially to speak it,
> Was very Great,—and very Wicked.
>   To give of's Bounty an Example,
> Or rather, of his Wealth a Sample,
> He chose to live at Country Seat,
> And all in splendid Form to treat,
> At vast Expence,—some Authors speak
> Of fifteen hundred Pounds a Week.[1]
>
> (pp. 32–3)

If it had not been patent against whom this was directed, the last line would reveal who was aimed at, for Pulteney's organ, *The Craftsman*, on 7 November 1730 had affirmed that the housekeeping bills at Houghton, Walpole's huge mansion in Norfolk which was erected between 1722 and 1735, amounted to £1500 weekly.[2] Moreover, in ballads and broadsides he was represented as plundering the Treasury,[3] and there is an echo of these accusations in the question

> where's the Wonder?
> That he who robs, should waste the Plunder.
>
> (p. 33)

However, to make the meaning plain beyond all doubt, the English counterpart of Cane della Scala is now mentioned by name. He is 'Polmurus' which any reader with the slightest tinge of Latin could recognise as a disguise for 'Walpole'. 'Florio', who corresponds to Bergamino in the original, resolves to see what he can get by literary adulation.

> Much of POLMURUS he had heard,
> How he rewarded every Bard,
> For ODE, or SONG, or such-like Matter,
> That did but cry him up, and flatter.
>
> (p. 33)

---

[1] Page references are to the 1731 edition.
[2] *D.N.B.*, Art. 'Sir Robert Walpole'.   [3] Ibid.

But his expectations come to nothing:

> He wrote,—*Polmurus* read and smil'd
> While Time's in Rural Sports beguil'd.
> Good *Florio*, (quoth the courteous Lord)
> You're always welcome at my Board.
> Sir WITLING bow'd, thought he in time,
> Something more weighty'll pay my Rhime.
> Well on he writes—'tis still the same,
> Invited still,—still *Florio* came;
> Where in the Parlour or in Hall
> He din'd and supp'd,—and that was all.
>
> (p. 34)

However, when the tale of the abbot's liberality to Guido, as Primasso is here called, is over, Polmurus is stirred to generosity and bestows an annual pension on Florio. Such an ending was in accordance with Boccaccio but inconsistent with the unfavourable portrait of Walpole already drawn. Realising this, the English narrator smiles sceptically and hints how improbable it was that Walpole could be moved to act in this fashion:

> Some Reader, now methinks I hear,
> What Title does your Story wear?
> *The Miracle*,—my Muse replies,
> Or, *Statesman by Reproof made Wise*.
>
> (p. 38)

The dedication to Pulteney, to which allusion has already been made, maintained that none of the tales in the collection could offend the strictest virtue. Possibly the writer was uneasily aware that he might be criticised for translating his other tale from 'gay *Boccace*'. His treatment of the tale[1] itself is light-hearted enough, and his sympathy is on the side of the young gallant who triumphed over all obstacles to win the love of Isabell. He compares it to the passion of Hero and Leander. To enlist the support of the reader he also emphasises the malevolence of the old nun who discovers the secret of Isabell and hurries away to fetch a guard of female spies:

> as Carrion-Crows they watch,
> Or Bloodhound-Bayliffs on the Catch.
>
> (p. 27)

At the scene in the chapter-house these envious onlookers 'twitter with a malicious Joy' which clearly does not spring from virtue, and the writer spares no pains to make them unpleasing. He also heightens the outward austerity of the abbess and presents her as harsh and forbidding. When her sanctity is proved to be no more than superficial, the way is open for him to elaborate the moral of his source,[2] that 'No

---

[1] ix, 2.   [2] The translation of 1702.

body ought to accuse another of Crimes they are guilty of themselves',
and with an air of gravity to denounce vice and cant:

> Prepost'rous then it is to preach
> Of Faults in Others, when we know
> That We the same things daily do.
> For tho' Hypocrisy a while
> May screen us, and the World beguile,
> A Shame where e'er the Devil's in debt,
> 'Tis ten to one but he cries quit,
> And by some Accident reveals,
> All that the would-be Saint conceals;
> Whips off the Vizard in a trice,
> And shews the naked Face of Vice.
>
> (pp. 23–4)

The octosyllabic couplets flow smoothly, and the story gains in its easy
style by the colloquial reporting of speeches which find no place in
Boccaccio's rigidly condensed narrative. The writer uses the tale to
satirise hypocrisy. However, there was a marked anti-clerical leaning
in the English translation of 1702, and despite the general terms used
in this passage, the poem as a whole bears clear traces of this bias.[1]

Akin to this poem in some ways is *The Saint*, a translation by William
Ayre from the original Italian of the first tale in the *Decameron*. It was
published in 1734 and is on the whole a faithful, though not literal
version. The part of Musciatto is somewhat reduced, and his instructions to his rascally agent Ciapperello are omitted in order to focus
attention on the kernel of the story, Ciapperello's illness, confession
and death. A similar concentration can be traced in the list of sins
regarding which he is questioned before receiving absolution. A
number are transposed and grouped together. Through this economy
it is possible to lend more prominence in the confession to a few sins
without impeding the narrative. In particular, more space is given to
Ciapperello's admission that as a child he once swore at his mother.
The nature of the offence is not revealed at once, and the feigned
penitent's horror at its heinousness leads the reader to wonder what it
can be. Through the expansion of this passage Ayre ingeniously pro-
longs the suspense until at last the disclosure is made:

> He fetch'd up Sighs, as from a broken Heart;
> He wept aloud, he shudder'd with his Tears,
> He groan'd, Contrition at its Height appears.
> Son, said the pious Priest, thy lab'ring Mind,
> Has doubtless to some fav'rite Sin been blind;
> Thy Sorrow shews it; What can this have been?
> What Snare has thy poor Soul been taken in?

[1] It may be noted that the last line of the poem is an almost literal transcript of
the opening words of the tale in the version of 1702.

Worse than before he wept: The honest Priest
Stood mute, expecting Blasphemy at least;
Both trembled, CHIAPPERELLO shook the Bed,
And fault'ring in his Speech, he, sighing, said:
"This Sin has lain a Canker in my Breast,
"It never in my Life has been confess'd;
"Shame has prevented: Oh! that I should do
"This Thing, which Pardon won't be granted to:
"No; it's too heinous, that I always thought,
"Except almost a Miracle were wrought.
"Ah! cross my Bosom; Oh! I quite despair,
"My Soul is lost, unless redeem'd by Prayer.

        "Lost! said the Friar, put all such Fears away,
"A Soul so pure, may bear a small Allay:
"I'll answer to much more, for could it be,
"That ev'ry mortal Sin had liv'd in thee;
"All which the World has acted hitherto,
"All that 'till Doomsday it shall ever do:
"Hadst thou (knowing him Christ) without Remorse
"Been one, who lifted, nail'd him on the Cross,
"To thy Contrition he would lend an Ear,
"And cancel thee a Sin for ev'ry Tear:
"Fear not, confess it, keep thy *Faith* alive,
"Believe that I my Power from Heav'n derive;
"Absolv'd by me, thy Sins are blotted out,
"Bliss is thy Portion, Son, beyond a Doubt.

        "My Soul's Physician, I am much more calm,
"Methinks, in ev'ry Word you speak, there's Balm;
"My Case requires it much:—I was but young,
"Yet old enough to gain an evil Tongue;
"*I curs'd my Mother* . . .[1]

                        (pp. 15–16)

Ayre's sense of design is again displayed at the close of the poem which ends with the same line as it began. This device gives a feeling of completeness and unity.[2]

In detail as in the general outline of the poem Ayre produces artistic effects. The addition of a cross of massive gold, placed on the body of Chiapperello,[3] heightens the pomp of the interment, and the picture of the crowd cowering under the rebuke of the priest as he contrasts their sinfulness with the virtues of the dead man is most effective. Ayre's dialogue is simple and natural, and he employs antithesis with skill.

---

[1] Page references appended to the quotations are to the first edition.
[2] There is a similar effect, for example, in Coleridge's 'Frost at Midnight' and Keats' 'La Belle Dame sans Merci'.
[3] The anglicised form used by Ayre.

Incidentally the original tale had criticised the friars; Ayre redoubles the attack on their incontinence. Boccaccio's main object, however, was to turn a sceptical eye on the miraculous works ascribed to some holy men. But he did not call in question the intercession of saints. On the contrary, he is careful both at the opening and the close not to expose himself to a charge of unorthodoxy. It is here that Ayre differs most notably. In the preamble he says that prayers addressed to the saints 'on whom fond Men rely' may miss their goal because of the frailties of some reputed saints, though God in his mercy may nevertheless hear them. And in the conclusion he elaborates his opinion:

> I undertook, at first, to prove,
> That Pray'rs were safest made to God above:
> Saints made by Men, some Veneration claim,
> If such in Life preserv'd an honest Name.
> But for our Pray'rs, those to the Dead address'd,
> May chance to miss the Number of the Blest.
> Would you be taught of *God*? to him apply,
> His Ear is open to the Sinner's Cry:
> He to himself first learnt you how to pray,
> Distinguish'd Praises mark that gracious Day.
>
> (p. 20)

The point of view is that of a Protestant, but Ayre maintains a dignified restraint and will not stoop to vituperative propaganda.

Three years after Ayre's translation there appeared an anonymous version of another tale of roguery, *Fra Cipolla*, the last in the sixth day of the *Decameron*. The sub-title, 'Translated from the Original Manuscript, with Notes Historical, Critical and Moral', draws attention to a prominent feature. In an age remarkable for editorial work the writer claims to have in preparation an edition of Boccaccio which will make all others out of date. 'Tonson, in all his Pride, will be turn'd out of the most elegant Libraries to illustrate the Rails of Moorfields, and the Giunti themselves, the admir'd 1527,[1] . . . for which some Gentlemen, of my Acquaintance, have paid Twenty Pistoles, will then hardly be worth Twenty Pence'. He expresses his regret that he should be about to lower the value of such ornaments in the library of the bibliophile, but the public interest demands it, for his edition is based on a manuscript 'found in the Ruins of a Villa of Queen Joan's, near Capoua'.

The tale of *Fra Cipolla* is supposed to be a specimen, issued in advance, to satisfy a clamorous demand from the connoisseurs, and the pretence is maintained in the text by the insertion of 'Ingens Hiatus in M.S.' and 'Alter Hiatus in M.S. etiam valdè deflendus'. A critical

---

[1] A famous edition of the *Decameron*. Vide ante, p. 263.

apparatus is provided in the notes on particular lines or words. The nominal editor defends his refusal to observe heroic style and invoke a pagan muse by quoting Sir Richard Blackmore.

The good Man, from his Soul, abominated the Heathen Mithology, as appears from his excellent Prefaces to his Works; and as he says very well, *What have we to do with* Apollo, *is there not the good King* David *always ready to tune our Harps for us.*[1]

(p. 6)

Writing in the same vein, when he is in trouble over a rhyme, he cites the authority of Boileau's second satire and of *Hudibras*, 'who play'd the Game of Crambo better than most of us', to prove how grievous is the task of rhyming. In his concluding note he expresses confidence that the reader whom he has thus taken into his confidence will approve his work: 'How many curious Readings restor'd! What a number of beautiful Passages brought to light that were lost!' There is certainly one such curious reading, a passage in Italian which purports to come from the manuscript.[2] Actually, it is the writer's invention, though with his tongue in his cheek he claims that it possesses a 'curiosa Felicitas', which 'few, if any, of our modern Wits can attain to'. Here and elsewhere he reveals his knowledge of Italian and also of editions of Boccaccio such as that of Salviati.

Behind the façade of learning a lively mind can be perceived and a keen sense of form. No wonder then that a footnote indulges in some criticism of Boccaccio's tale, which is not without its weaknesses. When Fra Cipolla comes to Certaldo with his supposed feather from the wing of the Angel Gabriel, he leaves it in the care of his servant Guccio at the inn while he eats a meal before the service. Guccio, however, becoming enamoured of the kitchen-wench, Nuta, devotes all his attention to her and fails to keep a watchful eye on his master's precious relic. Owing to his negligence two practical jokers are able to remove the feather and substitute for it a coal from the fire. It is incontestable that the episode of the amour between Guccio and the hideous Nuta is both dull and repellent, and though it serves to account for the theft of the relic, many of the details could well have been dispensed with in the interests of the main theme. The translator therefore omitted it as tedious and disagreeable, and he declares that here Boccaccio 'nodded a little'. In order to concentrate upon Fra Cipolla's own adventure he also leaves out the names of the two jesters and suppresses all mention of Guccio in the later phase of the story. Evidently he felt that Boccaccio's remark concerning the ignorance of the people of Certaldo about the world overseas was superfluous and also that many of the fantastic names of places recorded by Cipolla

---

[1] Page references to first edition.   [2] p. 9, note.

in his account of his travels would be unintelligible to the English reader. He therefore limits the places visited by the friar to Jerusalem and the realm of Prester John. As the latter indicates, he took certain liberties in adding to the wonders related by Cipolla, others being '*Cath'rine* of *Sienna*'s Bib',

'The genuine Manuscripts of *Jude*,
And of the Song of *Solomon*'.

(p. 16)

and

'one of the Dice
Which did decide the great Contest,
Who was to have our Saviour's Vest'.

(p. 16)

But as a rule such changes are made only as a substitute for the rig-marole with which the ready-witted friar gulls the peasants of Certaldo and baffles the men who had played the trick on him. The translator does, however, expand the central scene which he assimilated to an English environment. Instead of addressing the crowd at the church door, the friar mounts the pulpit, and light is required as if for an evening service. The situation, as he opens the box, is well described:

... in this Box I have a Feather,
Pull'd from one Wing of his, but whether
From Right or Left, I am not sure,
And lying I cou'd ne'er endure.
Here we'll admire his steady Face;
The Box he opens with a Grace.
No Feather . . . only Coals he sees;
Bless me! (he mutters) how come these!
However, without Blush or Pause,
The ready Trickster boldly draws
Himself out of a Scrape that might
Confound an over-modest Wight,
The Box he shuts, and with a Mien
So sanctify'd and so serene,
Says he, The Ways of Providence
Are not perceiv'd by Human Sense,
They often are perplex'd in Mazes,
Which Man, no more than Beasts that grazes,
Can e'er find out, tho' I can prove,
That Things are wisely rul'd above.

(pp. 12–13)

The claim of Cipolla to truthfulness in the very midst of his men-dacity is a trait added by the English translator. He again goes out of his way to stress the mendacity of ecclesiastics when he elaborates a hint by Boccaccio in a passage about Cipolla's journey in foreign lands:

> I pass'd a Country, wide indeed!
> It makes my very Heart to bleed,
> To think the People are all Lyars,
> And in great Numbers Priests and Fryars.
>   (p. 13)

But his attitude is dictated not so much by doctrinal animosity as by intellectual scepticism. We are conscious of this once more when he refuses to believe in a vial containing the sweat of the Archangel Michael which, as he had read, was preserved at the Vatican and was reputed to be a wonderful sudorific. Always, however, it is the man of the world rather than the religious zealot who speaks. He condemns the clergy for their excessive preoccupation with politics and secular affairs and admires Boccaccio as

> the Scourge of wicked Monk,
> Intriguing Priest, and wanton Punk.
>   (p. 5)

Yet in all this he appears to be the detached observer who sees through the knavery of his fellow-men and, far from overflowing with indignation, laughs at the stupidity of those who allow themselves to be duped. Thus he ridicules the simple-witted Certaldesi,

> Who only Melons knew from Pumkins,
>   (p. 10)

and at the close scoffs at their gullibility:

> Who cou'd contain from laughing loud,
> To see the ign'rant silly Croud,
> So eager to be cross'd, that they,
> 'Till he came down, wou'd hardly stay.
> There was not any one Curmudgeon
> Who did not now become a Gudgeon.
>   (p. 18)

The moral with which his poem ends is that in all ages there have been knaves and fools, and there always will.

> In Christian, as in Pagan, Times we find
> Some Priests are cunning, and some Laymen blind;
> And that the Pleasure, often, is as great
> Of being gravely cheated as to cheat.
>   (p. 19)

In 1748 *Fra Cipolla* was published in a revised form as *The Popish Impostor*. There were some verbal alterations, a few omissions, and an indirect tribute to Pope is added, when the name of Cipolla is first mentioned:

> Not *Pope* himself cou'd make it chime.
> CIPOLLA wou'd elude the Skill
> Of the late Sov'reign of the Quill.
>   (p. 9)

X

The main change, however, lies elsewhere. All the scholarly apparatus is discarded with the sole exception of the reference to the gaps in the manuscript. The appeal to the bibliophile and the fashionable young man about town vanishes, and instead of the discreet ridicule of the intellectual we find the grave warning of the Protestant pamphleteer. There is no means of deciding whether the original author carried out the transformation, but the altered purpose is unmistakable. The title itself gives the first indication and the sub-title, 'A NARRATIVE VERY PROPER To be Read in Protestant Families of all Denominations', bears it out. The motto 'Tantum Hæc Religio[1] potuit suadere Malorum' again emphasises the intention, and the preface drives home the lesson with emphasis: 'Beware of the Jesuits'. It is true that the writer exonerates them from certain charges which he examines one by one. In his opinion they have no share in the pamphlets of political scribblers 'who would by malicious Insinuations alienate our Affections from the best of *Princes*, and misrepresent the Efforts of the greatest of *Ministers*'. Nor does he accuse them of causing mischief as financiers, for if

by *Brokers* are meant *Transactors* in *Stocks*, who may hurt the *Publick Credit* by spreading *false News*, this Imputation will also appear groundless to whoever reflects that the most considerable are *Israelites* firmly attached to the Government; and indeed (to do 'em Justice) the *Jews* in general behave like good Subjects, they promote Trade at Home, and are instrumental in improving it Abroad.

(Preface, v)

Lastly, he rejects the view of a dissenting preacher that the Jesuits were responsible for the South-Sea Bubble, a scheme more pernicious than the Gunpowder Plot. 'The good Man', he continues,

bitterly bewails the Vicissitudes in 1720, and wishes for his Soul that a Year of such infamous Changes cou'd be expung'd out of our Annals; *Footmen* skipp'd into their Masters Chariots, *Brokers* were transform'd into *Senators*, and *Matrons* . . . sacrific'd themselves and their Daughters to *Moloch*, a leading Director having debauched almost as many Women as *Muly Abdallah* the Emperor of *Morocco*.

(Preface, vi–vii)

The refutation of these charges appears sensible enough, but the writer maintains accusations equally fantastic. The Jesuits 'lurk about in Town and in Country, seeking whom they may seduce' and he 'that can enumerate the Dresses at a Masquerade, may tell the various Disguises of these wily Missionaries'. They are, he asserts, even to be found raving among the Methodists or teaching young girls to sing and dance, so that 'where they don't recommend their Idolatrous

---

[1] The text reads 'Relligio'.

Worship, they corrupt our Morals'. And the preface ends with an admonition to every father of a family to pay good heed to his wife and children. Assuredly in this poem we have travelled a long way from the author of *Fra Cipolla* and from Boccaccio himself. For however much Boccaccio may criticise ecclesiastical abuses and direct his satire against rogues and hypocrites, such blood-curdling propaganda was altogether alien to his genial tolerance.

There is a trace of anti-Catholicism even in George Ogle's *Gualtherus and Griselda*, which appeared in 1739, for in the letter to a friend by which it is prefaced he comments unfavourably on the preponderance of the clergy in Chaucer's day, talks of 'the Yoke of *Rome*', and rejoices that in his time circumstances are changed for the better, so that the clergy devote themselves to their spiritual call and leave temporal affairs to the laity. However, this is but a passing outburst. Ogle's chief design in his preface, which is more interesting than his translation, was to give an account of the story of Griselda, as it had been treated by Boccaccio, Petrarch and Chaucer. He corrects Dryden's statement in the *Fables* which ascribed the authorship to Petrarch, pointing out simultaneously that Boccaccio 'was rarely the Inventor, tho' always the Improver, of the Stories He relates'. But the correction is made in no carping spirit, for Ogle thought of Dryden with veneration and alludes to him more than once as a great man.

What he himself set out to do is explained in the following passage which also displays his appreciation of the work of his predecessors:

By What has been said, it is evident, that this Tale . . . has already pass'd thro' the Hands of BOCCACE, PETRARCH, and CHAUCER; that is, thro' the Hands of three Men of as great Genius as ever appear'd in one Age. BOCCACE may be suppos'd to have improv'd on Those He follow'd; PETRARCH most certainly improv'd on Him; and our Countryman undeniably improv'd on them Both. At the same Time that I say This, I must ingenuously confess, that tho' upon the Whole, I give the Preference to CHAUCER's Manner of treating this Story, yet, here and there, I thought He had omitted some Beauties discernible in PETRARCH; and still think, there are Others remaining in BOCCACE, which PETRARCH has omitted. I have compared them One with the Other; and have endeavoured to glean after Them, and found Occasion rather to add than to diminish'.[1]

As a critic Ogle is mainly concerned to expound Chaucer's qualities, as they had already been indicated by Dryden. However, he does incidentally praise Boccaccio's skill in linking one story with another, ranking him above Ovid in this respect, though he places Chaucer still higher. On the whole Boccaccio is considered only in a general fashion, but Ogle's letter is nevertheless valuable as an early attempt at the comparative study of literature.

[1] *Gualtherus and Griselda*, 1739, p. vii.

The same story was again turned into verse by Miss Sotheby, whose *Patient Griselda. A Tale From the Italian of Bocaccio* was published at Bristol in 1798. It is a straightforward version which in itself calls for no comment. However, the opening is worth a glance because Miss Sotheby, writing at the end of a period which had seen a progressive extension of women's cultural interests and only six years after the appearance of Mary Wollstonecraft's *Vindication of the rights of Woman*, makes an entirely new approach to the age-old theme. She sees in it a record of 'mad brutish deeds, and folly wild' and frowns upon the hero:

> great his guilt, whose tyrant acts I tell,
> Tho' fortune favour'd, and he prosper'd well.[1]
>
> (p. 1)

At the close this sentiment is blended with the contemporary belief in the worth of the humble man:

> And now, since hard Gualterio's future life
> Past undisturb'd by jealousy and strife,
> Crown'd by each bliss he thus unjustly sought
> And by Griselda's pangs so dearly bought,
> What shall we say?—But that all pow'rful heav'n
> Imperial souls in lowly huts has giv'n,
> While some, o'er nations born to rule and reign,
> Are fitter far to till the rural plain—
> For who like Gualterio, had assign'd
> Such unheard trials to a gentle mind?
>
> (p. 32)[2]

2. Tales in Prose

Just as Dryden had mingled grave and gay in his *Fables* and had been imitated by Durfey, so the same technique is applied in prose by the anonymous author of *A Banquet for Gentlemen and Ladies, Consisting of Nine Comick and Tragick Novels* which appeared in 1703. The preface displays the concern for morality which is typical of the age. It declares, 'there's no Room for Obscenity; therefore let not the Letcher expect to put his Bawdy Fist in our Dishes'. On the contrary, the reader will find everything 'very Pleasant, Harmless, and Innocent; no ways tending to Debauch your Manners, nor Corrupt your Reason'.

---

[1] Page references appended to the quotations are to the 1798 edition.
[2] A. C. Lee, *The Decameron, its sources and analogues*, London, 1909, p. 141, mentions a verse tale, 'The unfortunate lovers, or the history of Girolamo and Sylvestra' dated 1706, but says that he has no further particulars. I have not been able to trace this. It must have dealt with *Dec.* iv, 8, and is distinct from 'The Unfortunate Lovers' referred to below.

Three tales are borrowed from the *Decameron*, the translation of 1620 being followed, at times very closely. The fifth is 'The Cuckold turn'd Confessor',[1] though the scene is transferred from Rimini to Paris. The seventh, 'The Unfortunate Lovers', weaves together two stories. The characters of the seventh tale of the fourth day assemble in a garden, not in Florence, but in Paris, and there Diana, Cleomenes, Ariana and Fremont, as they are named here, while away the time in story-telling. Diana relates the mirthful tale of Ferondo[2] in a condensed form which calls the abbot Bernardo and the lady Dona Maria Esperansa, and has Bologna as its background. Cleomenes is the next narrator, and after he has concluded, the author intervenes. He says that the four friends little imagined 'what sudden Scene would disturb them in a few Minutes: But alas, the Vicissitude of Fortune is so uncertain, that when we imagine Danger afar off, or think not at all of it, then is it most near'. This is intended to prepare us for the death of the unfortunate lovers who, after Ariana has concluded her tale, die suddenly by the agency of the poisonous sage, on a bank of which they are sitting.[3] This work seems to have been widely read, for a fifth edition was printed in 1718.

The transfer of Boccaccio's tales to another setting, sometimes France, but more usually England, is found also in Alexander Smith's *History of the most Noted Highway-Men, Foot-Pads, House-Breakers, Shop-lifts and Cheats*. Here too there is an outward preoccupation with morality, though, like much other picaresque literature of the seventeenth and eighteenth centuries, it attempted to satisfy the love of adventures in low life, combining glimpses of the underworld with admonitions to follow good and shun evil. In the preface to the first volume the author claims that his book will deter from vice and promote virtue, and he repeats his assertion in the second:

I believe no Body of common Sense, who sees how miserable these Wretches have made themselves by their evil Courses, will be tempted to tread in the same Steps, which lead so directly to the *Gallows*; therefore I only shew which Way they took, how they stumbled, and hope that no Man in his Wits will be incited to follow them.[4]

On occasion he interweaves a denunciation of drunkenness:

Thus we may evidently see the fatal Consequences of *Drunkenness*; which odious Vice is now become so fashionable, that we may too often behold Sots contending for Victory over a Pot, and taking the measure of their Bravery by the Strength of their Brains, or Capacity of their Bellies. Taverns and

[1] *Dec.* vii, 5. [2] *Dec.* iii, 8.

[3] *Dec.* iv, 7. This tale became very popular in the nineteenth century. Vide post, pp. 348, 395-7, 417-21, 435.

[4] Quoted from the fifth edition, London, 1719-20, ii, Preface, p. ii.

Alehouses are the common Academies of Sin, where Drunkards make themselves expert in all those Arts whereby they gratify *Satan*, and, as it were, in
so many open Bravadoes, challenge the *Almighty* into the Field, and dare him
to do the worst he can.[1]

At the close of his work he paints a terrifying picture of the end of
these 'most wicked Wretches' and, far from seeking to glorify their
deeds or awaken sympathy for them, declares:

The miserable Fate which they suffer'd was but their deserved Due, since all
the Royal Indulgence which some of 'em have receiv'd, was only an Inlet to
the Perpetrating more and greater Villanies, even to a Defiance of Justice
drawing her Sword; wherefore as their Unparalleled[2] Insolence insulted over
the Laws of God and Man, by taking an Unaccountable Pride and Ambition
in breaking both, we ought not to be sorry at the Hang-man's Meritorious
Act of sending such case-harden'd Villains out of the Land of the Living.[3]

Such an edifying outlook seems to have little in common with that
of the *Decameron*. It must, however, be remembered that in the
English translation of 1620 every tale is provided with a moral.[4]
Consequently, the English reader would interpret many stories in a
way never intended by Boccaccio. Thus the adventures of Andreuccio
da Perugia are taken to prove 'how needfull a thing it is, for a man
that trauelleth in affaires of the World, to be prouident and well
aduised, and carefully to keepe himselfe from the crafty and deceitfull
allurements of Strumpets'.[5] It cannot be ascertained whether Smith
used this translation or not, but he borrowed this very tale and relates
it as an episode in the life of Will Bew. The latter, after committing
'a very great Robbery and Rape on the Road'[6] is compelled to flee to
France, where he meets with a series of adventures, which are merely
those of Andreuccio. Apart from a slight abridgement here and there
the transference of the story from Naples to Paris, and the ultimate
return of Will Bew to England, the original is imitated almost without
disguise.

Evidently Smith felt that he had discovered[7] a source which ough
to be exploited more thoroughly, and he afterwards drew again upon
the *Decameron*. Thus in the fifth edition we find a condensed version
of the eighth tale of the eighth day. The treatment is considerably
freer than in the story of Will Bew. The leading figure is Jonathan
Sympson, and the intrigue of his wife with a gallant is explained by

---

[1] Second edition, 1714, i, p. 102.   [2] The text has a misprint 'Unparalled
[3] Ed. 1714, ii, pp. 287–8.   [4] Vide ante, p. 19.
[5] *Dec.* ii, 5 (cf. *The Decameron*, London, 1620, f. 38 verso). See H. G. Wrigh
The first English translation of the 'Decameron', pp. 185–8.
[6] Ed. 1714, i, p. 134.
[7] There is a parallel to a tale in the *Decameron* in Richard Head's *The Englis
Rogue*, but the resemblance is too vague for one to feel confident that it is derive
from Boccaccio.

the fact that she was the daughter of a wealthy merchant who, solely on financial grounds, had prevented her from marrying the man whom she loved. Thus a certain justification is provided for the intrigue. Another striking change is Smith's rejection of Boccaccio's facile reconciliation of the two pairs of husbands and wives. In his version the aggrieved Sympson, in spite of the rich dowry that he has received with his wife, discards her and sends her home to her relatives.[1] Another tale that is given a somewhat different turn is associated with Thomas Rumbold, who, at the request of an innkeeper, agrees to transform his wife into a mare for a sum of fifty guineas. Unlike her prototype she is a shrew, and the landlord's object is to silence her scolding tongue. But, like his forerunner, the worthy Pietro da Tresanti, he interrupts the proceedings, and in doing so forfeits his money.[2] Strangely enough, in view of the fact that he had so much to choose from, Smith reintroduced the story of Andreuccio da Perugia, this time connecting it with a female rogue, Joan Bracey.[3] The scene is now transferred to Bristol, and Mr. Day, her dupe, is an eminent merchant of that city. As he had previously used the tale,[4] Smith is obliged to hide the traces of the original more thoroughly, and so after the episode in the house of Joan Bracey he omits all other incidents and imposes a rapid conclusion. Day, finding himself stripped naked, decides to feign madness,

and passing through the Streets, he did sing a Thousand Songs and Catches. Men, Women and Children in Amazement began to flock in great Crouds about him, hollowing and whooping after him till he arrived at a Friend's House, where being put to Bed, the Mob began to disperse; and afterwards sending for Cloaths, he went home in the Evening with a great deal of Ridicule and Shame.[5]

This humiliation of a respectable citizen for his deviation from the path of moral rectitude again betrays a temper quite foreign to that of Boccaccio.

In 1734 Smith's collection inspired Charles Johnson to publish *A General History Of The Lives and Adventures Of the Most Famous Highwaymen, Murderers, Street-Robbers, &c.* Here too there is occasional moralising, as when Johnson maintains that a young man ought to take care in choosing his associates, lest he should find himself entering on an evil life, even though he might before have had no vicious inclinations. He once more emphasises the fatal consequences of the first wrong step in his account of Jonathan Simpson,[6] and the experience of Jack Withrington is made to prove that not even a

---

[1] ii, pp. 163–4.   [2] iii, pp. 36–8. Cf. *Dec.* ix, 10.
[3] Vide ante. In the fifth ed., see iii, pp. 178–81.
[4] Fifth ed., i, pp. 103–7.   [5] iii, p. 181.   [6] He spells the name thus.

genuine, idealistic love can rescue the delinquent from his evil ways, strive as he will.[1]

Despite the gravity of his manner, however, Johnson's pose as a reformer does not carry conviction. He had a strong picaresque vein, and some of his tales are bloody, cruel and savage. It is significant that the title of his book refers not only to the lives but also to the adventures of his characters, and when he describes the doings of Isaac Atkinson, the pretence to veracity barely conceals their fictitious nature. The reader, he observes, may think the incident in question 'very odd, and perhaps a little improbable'. 'However', he goes on:

if he considers the Characters of the Persons concern'd in the Adventure, he will find nothing related but what may be supposed to have been really acted. *Boccace, La Fontaine*, and other celebrated Writers have met with universal Applause for Histories less reconcileable to Truth than this. But, be that as it will, no reasonable Man can be angry with an Author for giving what he has received. The Writers of the Lives of Highwaymen who have gone before, are a sufficient Apology for this and many other unaccountable Relations, which must of necessity be interspersed in this Work. A Reader that cannot relish these Passages, will find enough for his Diversion without them, and those who have a pretty deal of Faith may easily stretch it to our Standard. At least what will not pass for real Truth, may please by the same Rules as many of our modern Novels, which are so much admired'.[2]

As the above passage suggests, Johnson was more sophisticated than Smith. Not only did he know Boccaccio but also the numerous *Contes et nouvelles* of La Fontaine that were derived from the *Decameron*.[3] He was likewise familiar with those *Fables* of Dryden that were taken from Boccaccio.[4] And among the celebrated contemporary writers of whom he speaks Defoe can safely be reckoned as one with whose work he was acquainted. Certainly, Johnson displays an ingenuity worthy of Defoe, when he casts doubt on the reliability of Smith, even though he borrows much of his matter from his predecessor and often follows him word for word:

Captain *Smith* indeed . . . has generally found something to relate of every one he mentions, but then most of his Stories are such barefac'd Inventions, that we are confident those who have ever seen his Books will pardon us for omitting them.[5]

This criticism served another purpose: it skilfully explained why Johnson had no detailed account to give of Will Bew. Perceiving that Smith had used the tale of Andreuccio da Perugia twice, he determined

---

[1] p. 340.   [2] p. 114.

[3] The title of the 1705 translation from La Fontaine is typical in its appeal: *Miscellaneous Poetical Novels or Tales, Relating Many pleasing and instructive Instances of Wit and Gallantry In Both Sexes : Suited to the Belle-Humeur of the Present Age.*

[4] See p. 340, when he quotes from Dryden's *Cymon and Iphigenia*.   [5] p. 322.

to suppress one of the variations on this theme. Hence, with his keener sense of technique, he omitted the adventure ascribed to Will Bew, since it too obviously resembled Boccaccio's version. He embodied in his work Smith's tales of Thomas Rumbold and Jonathan Sympson. But he modified the ending of the second, carrying a stage further Sympson's hostility to his wife:

for when she came back from the Place he had sent her to, he refused her Admittance; and the next Day sold off his Stock, shut up Shop, and went off with all the Money he could raise, resolved never more to live in *Bristol*',[1]

and this crisis is the beginning of Sympson's downfall. Similarly, Johnson alters somewhat the conclusion of the tale about Day and Joan Bracey.[2] Day is able to return home without exposure to a jeering crowd. He himself tells of his mishap to some of his friends, who, while diverting themselves with him for the rest of his life, loyally keep the secret. From this it would seem that Johnson was less concerned than Smith to point the moral, an impression which is confirmed by certain additions that he made, all of them derived from the *Decameron*. Thus he ascribes to Claude Duvall and a companion the adventure of Pinuccio and Adriano, the young gallants of Florence,[3] without any disapproval of their conduct.[4] He also relates three escapades of Phillip Stafford, the highwayman, and each time the unscrupulous ingenuity of a man who lives by his wits is allowed to pass unchallenged. The first is in all essentials the account of how Gulfardo overreached Madonna Ambruogia, who nevertheless was unable to utter any complaint.[5] However, the fact that whereas Guasparruolo readily lends Gulfardo the sum for which he asks, it is taken for granted that Stafford must provide security, indicates clearly enough that the Englishman belongs to a world where men habitually prey on their fellows. Another striking difference may be traced in the contrasting attitudes of Gulfardo and Stafford towards the women they have outwitted. It is true that Gulfardo rejoices in the success of his stratagem, but he does not mock Ambruogia by spreading the news of her discomfiture. Stafford, on the other hand, 'took Care to get this Adventure whispered all over the Neighbourhood'.[6]

The same change of tone may be detected in the second exploit attributed to him.[7] This occurred when he had ridden across country into Buckinghamshire after a robbery on the high road. His adventure in the house of the lady who gave him hospitality is obviously based on that of Rinaldo at Castel Guiglielmo.[8] The song by which Stafford

---

[1] p. 343.
[2] See the lives of Edward and Joan Bracey, p. 321.
[3] *Dec.* ix, 6.
[4] p. 94.
[5] *Dec.* viii, 1.
[6] p. 79.
[7] pp. 81–2.
[8] *Dec.* ii, 2.

wins over his hostess is certainly quite in keeping with his character, as may be seen from the first stanza, which is typical of the whole:

> When first Procreation began,
>   Ere Forms interrupted the Bliss,
> Each Woman might love any Man;
>   Each Man any Woman might kiss.
>
> (p. 81)

And the rest of Stafford's behaviour is no more than might be expected after his conduct in the first tale. Having carried out this design, he suddenly bound her in bed and threatened her with death, if she did not give him her keys and direct him to the place where the valuables of the house were kept. She began to exclaim at such ingratitude but had to submit. Stafford secured the valuables, tied up the maid, lest she should give the alarm, and rode off to London. Such callous and ruffianly duplicity is, of course, consistent with Stafford's mode of living, but it would have seemed revolting to Rinaldo and his creator Boccaccio.

Just as the Restoration mood lingers in Stafford's song, so in his third adventure we are carried back to a time when the Cavaliers were tempted to employ almost any device against the hated and despised Roundheads. The victim of Stafford's wiles on this occasion is 'An antient rich Republican, who was pretty deep in the Iniquity of the Times'. Having married the daughter of a relative, a worthy cavalier, the republican is depicted as profaning 'the sacred Ordinance of *Wedlock*, purely to keep the Substance of his deceased Kinsman to himself, and to gratify the lecherous Remains of his carnal Appetite'. Johnson's point of view is revealed by his question: 'Who could blame a Woman of Taste for being dissatisfy'd in such Circumstances?' To achieve his ends Stafford dons the garb of a Puritan and obtains a post as the lady's servant. So well does he succeed in winning his master's confidence that any conversation which he may have with her is interpreted as the discussion of spiritual themes for their mutual edification. The culmination is reached in the incident of the pear-tree,[1] which ultimately goes back to the third episode in the tale of Pirro and Lidia in the *Decameron*.[2] The immediate source, however, is Thomas Durfey's play, *The Royalist*,[3] where Camilla, the wife of Sir Oliver Oldcut, chairman to the committee of sequestrations, is secretly loyal to Sir Charles Kinglove, the 'Royalist, one of the King's Colonels at *Worcester*-Fight, a Lover of Monarchy and Prerogative'. The comedy used three episodes as in Boccaccio's story of Pirro and Lidia, and Johnson detached the last from Act V, Sc. i and substituted the disreputable Phillip Stafford for the dashing cavalier.

---

[1] See pp. 77–8.   [2] *Dec.* vii, 9.   [3] Published 1682. Vide ante, pp. 248–9.

Nothing could better illustrate how well Boccaccio was acclimatised and how successfully he was adapted to an English environment. Yet in no tale was the assimilation complete. The narrative material might be skilfully adjusted to the English cities and countryside, but the mentality that shaped it was very different. The hard, cynical tone of the Restoration, echoing on into the early eighteenth century, and the didactic, edifying strain were alike incapable of blending with the worldly, yet in the main genial temper of Boccaccio. Occasionally his figures and those of Smith and Johnson have something in common, because they are types found in every land and every age. But more often than not the scheming of keen minds which Boccaccio loves is confined to an amorous adventure, and his adepts in the art of out-witting others in this sphere are worlds apart from the rogues of the seventeenth and eighteenth centuries.[1]

Boccaccio is again represented in *The Agreeable Companion*, printed in 1745. It contained one hundred and sixty polite tales and fables, 'In which are display'd The most material Incidents in Human Life. The whole collected for the Entertainment and Improvement of young GENTLEMEN and LADIES'. The second volume contains the additional information that the compilation was done 'By a Lady'. All that she derived directly from the *Decameron* was a condensed account of the fifth tale of the first day,[2] based upon the English trans-lation of 1702. However, there is another story which, although it differs widely from the ninth tale of the second day, may be connected remotely with the latter part, which relates the penalty inflicted on Ambruogiuolo. It describes how, while a Malaban prince was paying a courtesy visit to the commander of a Dutch fort, his men killed the sentinel. The prince sentenced the ringleader 'to be smeared over with Honey, and made fast to a Cocoa-nut Tree in the Sun till he died'. The tale then pictures what happened:

Those Cocoa-nut Trees producing a sweet Liquor called *Toddy*, bring vast Numbers of Wasps and large red Ants to drink the Liquor. Those Ants bite as painfully as the Stinging of Wasps. When the Sun begins to be hot, they leave the Top of the Tree, and burrow in Holes about the Root. In their Passage downward they fixed on the Carcass besmeared with the Honey, and soon burrowed in the Flesh. The poor Miscreant was three Days in that sensible Torment before he expired. The *Dutch* Captain begged every Day for a Pardon, or at least for a milder or quicker Death; but the Prince was inexorable.[3]

---

[1] The connexion between the *Decameron* and stories of English low life is glanced at by F. W. Chandler, *The Literature of Roguery* (London, 1907). The idea of investigating the subject in greater detail was suggested by this work. Cf. H. G. Wright, 'Boccaccio and English Highwaymen', *R.E.S.*, New Series, 1950, i, pp. 17–22.

[2] Cf. i, pp. 239–40. Tale lxxi.   [3] Cf. i, p. 386. Tale cxxv.

It is not clear what improvement the young gentlemen and ladies of the mid-eighteenth century were expected to derive from this polite tale. But there could be no doubt regarding the story of Alcander and Septimius, which Goldsmith included in *The Bee* for 6 October 1759 and again in the *Essays* of 1765. Ostensibly taken from a Byzantine historian, it is none other than the tale of Titus and Gisippus. It is a lucid and concise version; Goldsmith was clearly anxious not to lose time over details, as may be seen from this passage:

It would but delay the narrative to describe the conflict between love and friendship in the breast of Alcander on this occasion; it is enough to say, that the Athenians were at that time arrived at such refinement in morals, that every virtue was carried to excess. In short, forgetful of his own felicity, he gave up his intended bride, in all her charms, to the young Roman. They were married privately by his connivance, and this unlooked-for change of fortune wrought as unexpected a change in the constitution of the now happy Septimius. In a few days he was perfectly recovered, and set out with his fair partner for Rome.

The lengthy and eloquent apologia of Titus, on which Boccaccio had bestowed so much labour, is therefore eliminated, in order that the miseries of his Athenian hero Alcander may be more fully traced. Accused of having yielded Hypatia (the counterpart of Sophronia) to Septimius for money, he is heavily fined and, being unable to pay the sum within the required time, is stripped of his possessions and sold as a slave. He is carried off to Thrace and compelled to live in bondage and toil and hunger until he manages to escape to Rome.

There the hardships that he has undergone make him unrecognisable to Septimius, who has in the meantime become prætor. The situation is described by Goldsmith with a pathos that is not free from a touch of sentimentality:

in the evening, when he was going up to the prætor's chair, he was brutally repulsed by the attending lictors. The attention of the poor is generally driven from one ungrateful object to another; for night coming on, he now found himself under a necessity of seeking a place to lie in, and yet knew not where to apply. All emaciated, and in rags as he was, none of the citizens would harbour so much wretchedness; and sleeping in the streets might be attended with interruption or danger: in short, he was obliged to take up his lodging in one of the tombs without the city, the usual retreat of guilt, poverty, and despair. In this mansion of horror, laying his head upon an inverted urn, he forgot his miseries for a while in sleep; and found, on his flinty couch, more ease than beds of down can supply to the guilty.

When the true criminal confesses, Alcander is declared innocent, Septimius, who as prætor was his judge, descends dramatically from his tribunal, and all ends in 'tears and joy'. Hypatia, whose role is of the slightest, is not even mentioned at the close, and the whole tale is given a new bias. The emphasis is not on liberality or magnificence, which was the theme for the tenth day of the *Decameron*, but on suffering and distress overcome at last. It is therefore fitting that the inscription engraved on Alcander's tomb after his final years of happiness and ease should be: 'no circumstances are so desperate, which Providence may not relieve'.

It may have been the example of *The Agreeable Companion* that inspired the compilation of *A Companion for the Fire-Side*; *or*, *Winter Evening's Amusement*, which appeared in 1772. The editor claims for his work 'the laudable design of conveying instruction under the delightful dress of entertainments'. 'Here', he continues, 'the giddy youth may be taught to avoid snares of the most pernicious nature, whilst their minds may enjoy a relaxation from the incumbent duties of their station'.

The connexion between this aim and the story of 'Friar Philip's Geese'[1] is rather obscure. The tale is derived from the *Decameron*, though it is not one of the hundred but is inserted in the preamble to the fourth day. One is at first tempted to think that the editor borrowed it, not from the original, but from the English translation of 1702, where it was removed from its place and substituted for the indecent tale of Alibech and Rustico, the last of the third day. The argument in the 1702 version tells how 'Philipello renounces the World, and brings up his Son in a Wood, from his tender infancy . . . where he had no Companions but Birds and Beasts'. The picture thus presented, which differs somewhat from that of Boccaccio, is reflected in 'Friar Philip's Geese'. However, it acquires dimensions far beyond anything in the translation and, on further investigation, one can see that the story is derived through the medium of La Fontaine's 'Les oies de Frère Philippe'. The English prose adaptation omits the opening, in which the French poet defends himself against his critics, and concentrates on the tale itself. The youthful solitary, who grows up surrounded by birds and wolves, is suggested by the reference to

> Point d'autres que les habitants
> De cette forêt, c'est-à-dire
Que des loups, des oiseaux,

and it is the lines

> On l'avoit dès l'enfance élevé dans un bois.
> Là son unique compagnie
Consistoit aux oiseaux; leur aimable harmonie
> Le désennuyoit quelquefois.
Tout son plaisir étoit cet innocent ramage;
Encor ne pouvoit-il entendre leur langage

that inspire this passage:

[1] pp. 107–10.

This youth had from his infancy inhabited the woods and groves, where the winged choristers were his companions, whose delightful harmony used sometimes to cheer his lonely hours; their innocent melody was his sole delight, notwithstanding he was wholly unacquainted with the meaning of their tuneful language.

Thus under the influence of La Fontaine the son of Boccaccio's Filippo Balducci, a substantial citizen of Florence who withdraws to the neighbouring Monte Asinaio,[1] is depicted as spending his early years in a sequestered glade without name or location, a natural man who is in keeping with the age of Rousseau.

3. The Drama

The story of Guiscardo and Ghismonda again aroused interest because of its dramatic potentialities. However, the original tale undergoes considerable modification. In Mrs. Susannah Centlivre's *The Cruel Gift*, first published in 1717, it is assumed that Leonora is not a widow when she falls in love with Lorenzo; her affection for him is legalised by a secret marriage, and there is nothing unduly sensuous in their relationship. Lorenzo, as the reputed son of Lord Alcanor, is always understood to be of noble rank, and at the close it is revealed that he is actually the son of the duke of Milan, uncle to the king of Lombardy. Lorenzo has further claims to distinction, because he is an eminent general who has successfully defeated Lombardy and merited the gratitude of his king and his country. Thus Boccaccio's story of the passionate amour of an obscure page and a princess is elevated into a decorous love in the highest circles, with a background of international politics.

At the same time Mrs. Centlivre transforms the original simple plot into one far more intricate. She adds another pair of lovers. Learchus, the rival of Lorenzo at court and on the battlefield, wishes to marry his sister Antimora. Quite apart from this rivalry, obstacles stand in the way of their union. Lorenzo's friend Cardono is also devoted to Antimora, and there is bitter hostility between the family of Lorenzo and that of Learchus's father Antenor, which has become still more intense since Antenor tried to win the hand of Leonora for his son, with the result that both he and Learchus fell into disgrace. At the moment he again stands high in the king's favour and is bent on the ruin of Lorenzo. Spying on his movements, he learns of his secret visits to Leonora through the cave. At his suggestion the duke of Tuscany sends ambassadors to negotiate a marriage. Leonora having

---

[1] It stands between the Sieve and the Mugnone (cf. Emanuele Repetti, *Dizionario geografico fisico storico della Toscana*, Florence, 1833, i, p. 157).

rejected the proposal, Antenor awakens the king's suspicions, arranges
for him to witness a meeting between her and Lorenzo, and supervises
the arrest of the offender. After an abortive attempt by Lorenzo's
friends to set him free, Antenor incites the king to severe measures.
He agrees to the summary execution of Lorenzo and Cardono, and
when he defers the punishment of Antimora, Antenor commands that
she shall be put to death. However, he is thwarted by his own son, who
as governor of the citadel holds a key position. He refuses to yield to
Antimora's entreaties to let her brother escape, but he does spare
Lorenzo and conveys to Leonora the heart of one who has been slain
during the struggle to release the general. A *deus ex machina* in the
guise of a hermit now appears, to announce that he is the duke of
Milan who had been driven from his land by the Tuscans, and that
Lorenzo is his son. The king is in despair at what he has done, where-
upon Learchus brings forth Lorenzo, who is restored to his wife.
Cardono dies of his wounds, thus opening the way for the union of
Learchus and Antimora, while the sinister Antenor falls in quelling
a rising of the people on behalf of Lorenzo.

The hero is almost in every respect a noble and lofty character. His
love for Leonora is sincere and disinterested; he thinks more of safe-
guarding her reputation than of what he stands to gain from her royal
rank. The saviour of his country, he is the idol of the people and the
soldiers. On occasion, as when Antenor's machinations seem to have
triumphed, his wonted restraint can be shaken; but his quiet strength
asserts itself in these lines:

> No, thou'rt not worth my Breath; and I disdain thee:
>
> Tho' none can guard against a Villain's Arts,
> Fortune can ne'er subdue a brave Man's Soul:
> In Love and War, I've reach'd the top-most Summit,
> And Ages hence I shall be read with Wonder;
> Whilst thou, the most detested of thy Kind,
> Shalt be with Horror mention'd—Lead on.
>
> (III. ii)

Every inch a soldier, he prepares for death with calm dignity and in
this last great crisis even forgives Antenor:

> Fain I in Peace wou'd Life's Remains employ,
> And as I bravely liv'd, wou'd bravely die.
> Beyond the Grave no Enemy can come,
> And I shall rest at Quiet in my Tomb.
> Death is a Debt we all to Nature owe,
> No matter then how soon or late we go:
> But dying well, is what we should propose,
> And leave to Heaven the Vengeance on our Foes.
>
> (IV. ii)

Leonora is a more emotional character. On the one hand, she is less stubborn in her attitude towards her father and with tears in her eyes asks his forgiveness for marrying without his consent; on the other, this gentleness can be transformed into violent denunciation of Antenor for his intrigues or into raving grief when the supposed heart of Lorenzo is brought to her. Yet if on this occasion she wildly calls on Heaven for vengeance and attempts suicide, she is capable of self-control, boldness and resourcefulness in most of her trials. Like Boccaccio's heroine, she displays great constancy and resolution, but it is all the stronger in her because it is based not only on depth of passion but also on the consciousness of her virtue.

Like his daughter, the king is human enough. His chief defects are not pride and ferocity, but credulity and irascibility. He is far too easily convinced of the guilt of the lovers, and the fact that they are married seems almost to add to their offence in his eyes and stir him to frenzy. Yet when his resentment has abated, he recalls his duty as a king to act like a judge and not a ruthless avenger. He has fallen a victim to Antenor's wiles, but he refuses to do more than send Lorenzo into exile. Not until the rising of the people appears to threaten the state does he agree to more serious penalties. Even then he keeps his head. He deals with Lorenzo, the immediate source of danger, and defers action against Antimora. It is only in this alarming situation that he commands that the heart of Lorenzo shall be torn from his breast and presented to Leonora. His later remorse, when Lorenzo's identity is disclosed, and his joy on finding that the prisoner is still alive, round off a character who after all is not unattractive, because the dramatist has loaded much of the responsibility for the sufferings of Lorenzo and Leonora on the unscrupulous minister, Antenor.

Of the figures who have no counterpart in Boccaccio, one of the most important is Learchus. He is almost flawless and even his opponent Lorenzo admits that by general consent 'his Mind is rich in ev'ry Virtue'. He earnestly seeks reconciliation with the house of his rival and, when torn between love and duty, maintains his loyalty to the king. Far from rejoicing over the plight of Lorenzo, he dislikes the task of informing Lorenzo of his approaching death, especially when he has learnt that the doomed man is Leonora's husband. So too he performs with gentleness and tact the mission of conveying the heart to Leonora, afterwards bidding her attendants to watch over her with every solicitude. Strongly conscious that he has resisted all temptation to yield to love and turn against the king, he feels entitled to admonish him for the misery that he has created. Learchus's goddess is 'Superior Virtue', and he prefers to be known as good rather than great. One feels that in his position Sir Charles Grandison himself could hardly have done better.

The cult of virtue, so typical of the age when the play was written, inspires Learchus to reject fame, honour and wealth, if divorced from moral rectitude. Above all he sets the welfare of his country:

> He who for Interest, or for base Revenge,
> Should in a private Quarrel fell his Foe,
> Deserves the Scorn of every good man for't;
> But he who would enslave his native Land,
> Give up the reverend Rights of Law and Justice,
> To the detested Lust of boundless Tyranny,
> Pollute our Altars, change our holy Worship,
> Deserves the Curses both of Heaven and Earth,
> And, from Society of human Kind,
> To be cast forth among the Beasts of Prey,
> A monster far more savage . . .
> I know no Glory, but my Country's Good,
> Nor Anger bear 'gainst any, but her Foes;
> But all her Enemies are mine; for her
> I'd make this Body one entire Scar,
> Ere I would see my Country made a Prey,
> Or know the King, to whom I've sworn, distress'd;
> And this I hold to be all brave Men's Duty.
>
> (I. i)

Some parts of this speech are hardly relevant to the plot. In particular, the allusion to a possible change of religion by a despotic ruler is superimposed upon the dramatic material. Of this there is not the slightest hint in Boccaccio's tale.

Mrs. Centlivre again stresses the value of upright and disinterested patriotism in her portrait of Lorenzo, the ideal leader:

> The Man, tho' ne'er so meanly born in Blood,
> That, next his Soul, prefers his Country's Good;
> Who more than Interest, does his Honour prize,
> And scorns by secret Treachery to rise;
> That can the base and gilded Bribe disdain,
> Prevent Reflections on his Prince's Fame,
> And point out glorious Virtues for his Reign:
> That Man should be a Monarch's chiefest Care,
> And none but such should Royal Favours wear.
>
> (III. iv)

This repetition is deliberate, for Mrs. Centlivre intended Learchus and Lorenzo to stand out in contrast to Antenor, the scheming politician who is without conscience and without ideals. He knows nothing of pity, love or friendship. For him men and women are so many pawns in a game. He is a past master in dissimulation and uses affairs of state for his personal aims; he dupes the king as Iago did Othello, first

Y

dropping hints and then offering proof. His mind moves swiftly, and even though his plans may sometimes receive a check, he is never disconcerted. Intellectually he surpasses all the rest and as he gloats over the defeat of his enemies, unswerving in the pursuit of his revenge and ambition, he is a dark and menacing figure whom no one can ignore. It is with his exposition of his philosophy of life that the play opens, and it ends with the king's comments on his counsellor's doom:

> But oh! be warn'd by his unhappy Fate,
> What Dangers on the doubling Statesman wait!
> Had he prefer'd his King's and Country's Good,
> This public Vengeance had not sought his Blood;
> But while the secret Paths of Guilt he treads,
> Where Lust of Power, Revenge, or Envy leads,
> While to Ambition's lawless Height he flies,
> Hated he lives, and unlamented dies.
>
> (v. i)

The prominence thus given to Antenor makes it obvious that Mrs. Centlivre intended the part to be a leading one, and this is confirmed by the fact that when *The Cruel Gift* was first produced in 1716, the role was given to no less an actor than Quin. At times one has the feeling that the dramatist has envisaged Boccaccio's tale against the background of contemporary England. Only in this way can one account for the intrusion of the reference to the possible overthrow of the established religion by a tyrannical sovereign. Another remarkable feature is the insistence on the hostility between the prime minister and Lorenzo, and on the efforts of the politician to oust the famous general from the royal favour. Inevitably one recalls the intrigues of Harley against Marlborough, which had been terminated by the death of Queen Anne only two years before the play was first acted. There is indeed much in common between Harley and Antenor. Like the latter, Harley was a shrewd and unscrupulous manipulator of public affairs, notorious for his indifference to truth, his constant scheming for the advancement of himself and his family, and his skill in swaying his monarch with an eye to his own advantage. For the same purpose he entertained secret relations with foreign courts, and though outwardly well-disposed towards his rivals, he was an unreliable friend. It is obvious that Antenor is no mere replica of Harley, any more than Lorenzo can be equated with Marlborough. But the parallel was sufficiently close for it to interest the audience in 1716, and it is likely that one of the features that appealed to the prince of Wales at the first performance was the resemblance of Antenor to the politician whom George I had so steadfastly distrusted. There is all the more reason for believing this, because the Epilogue, written by Nicholas Rowe and spoken by Mrs. Oldfield, who took the part of Leonora, after a spirited denunciation of duplicity and intriguing with the court of Avignon, singled out the prince as the embodiment of the contrasting virtues:

> See how his *Looks* his *honest Heart* explain,
> And speak the Blessings of his *future Reign*!
> In his each Feature, Truth and Candour trace,
> And read *Plain Dealing* written in his *Face*.

It is possible that Mrs. Centlivre's play was inspired in some measure by Dryden's 'Sigismonda and Guiscardo', which contained the motive of the secret marriage of the lovers and a hint for the introduction of the politics of the day into a tale from the *Decameron*. This can only be a surmise, but Frederick Howard, earl of Carlisle, openly avows the indebtedness of *The Father's Revenge* to Dryden, whom, unlike Mrs. Centlivre, he follows in retaining the tragic close. In the Prologue to his play, which was first published in 1783,[1] Howard says:

> He from Italia's fount, would frequent bring
> The dismal tale, the tender heart to wring;
> Each stormy passion of the breast to move,
> By Guiscard's fate, and Sigismonda's love;
> If, following him, a Bard should dare explore,
> And search that mine which had been pierced before:
> If, on the Stage, he now presumes to shew,
> By such great masters touch'd, dark crimes and woe;
> The bold attempt forgive, the Poet spare,
> Nor, though you wept before, deny the tear.
> And if, in varied form, and order new,
> He brings again the wretched to your view,
> 'Tis to those masters but fresh worship paid,
> And added incense on their altars laid.

However, the liberties taken by Howard in manipulating Boccaccio's tale are more extensive than those of Dryden. Like Mrs. Centlivre's heroine, Segismonda is not a widow, and her relationship to Guiscard is a normal one. The sole purpose of the secret meeting between them is to consider the possibility of marriage, which is later performed by a friar. But Howard lends a romantic colour to their love. Guiscard is

---

[1] It was privately printed and did not contain the Prologue. The latter was added in 1800, when the tragedy appeared with Carlisle's poems in an edition with plates from designs by R. Westall, limited to twenty-five copies. Other editions followed (cf. Lowndes, ii, p. 374, and Dibdin, ii, p. 388). No doubt the author was encouraged to print the play so often by the fact that while criticising it in some respects, the aged Johnson had praised it in others (cf. Boswell's *Life of Johnson*, ed. G. B. Hill and L. F. Powell, Oxford, 1934–50, iv, pp. 247–8). Horace Walpole also thought well of it. He remarked that certain situations were like what had been seen on the stage and in saying this he was no doubt thinking of Mrs. Centlivre's *The Cruel Gift*; but he considered the language and imagery beautiful and the two chief scenes very fine (cf. *Letters*, ed. Mrs. P. Toynbee, Oxford, 1903–5, xiii, pp. 38 and 70).

a foundling, discovered by Tancred on the sea-shore, and, growing up side by side with Segismonda, has been her constant companion. During his absence on a crusade he has been spurred on to great deeds by his devotion to her. One difficulty confronts him. His commander Manfred also wishes to marry Segismonda but generously withdraws because Guiscard had saved his life in battle. One obstacle still remains in the person of Monforti, Tancred's minister, who also aspires to win Segismonda. He exploits the dissatisfaction of the people with their ruler by stirring up a conspiracy. Tancred is enraged by this plot and by the secret marriage of Guiscard, a mere foundling, to his daughter. Surprise follows surprise. Guiscard ascertains that his father is a noble Turk, named Hassan, but when Hassan proves to be Conrad, the hated enemy of Tancred, the ruler's fury knows no bounds. He orders the execution of Guiscard and himself hands the vase to Segismonda. On finding that it contains her husband's heart she dies of shock, and the remorseful Tancred falls in despair upon her body, resigning the throne to Manfred.

The latter is brave and magnanimous, but he is outshone by Guiscard. A model warrior, he is the essence of modesty, gentleness, chivalry and loyalty. His only fault lies in loving too well, and his last thoughts are of Segismonda. The princess too is notable for her gentleness. A delicate, shrinking creature, poles apart from her prototype in the *Decameron*, she is a prey to fear and forebodings of evil. Her timidity joins with her sense of propriety to make her hesitate before she consents to Guiscard's plan for marriage and flight. When her husband is carried off by the guards, she leans half-swooning on her uncle's arm, so that we are prepared for the end when her frail nature gives way under the strain and she dies, breathing forgiveness.

There is a similar lessening of rigorous passion in the character of Tancred. He is not devoid of nobility and tenderness. But his violent temper and his readiness to take the advice of evil counsellors lead him to hasty acts of tyranny which anger the people and bring sorrow upon his own family. He is even more unbalanced than his prototype in *The Cruel Gift* and indulges in wild accusations of libidinousness and bestial sensuality, for which there is no warrant in the relations of Guiscard and Segismonda as they are depicted by Howard. Yet at times he is a pathetic figure as when he declares to his daughter:

> O my child,
> Long as these eyes, unveil'd with clouds, may gaze
> Upon thee, long as my dull'd hearing wakes
> To that enchanting voice, a little sun-shine
> Still faintly trembles on my evening landscape.
>
> (II. ii)

When his wrath has abated, his natural goodness asserts itself, and he is filled with regret, which is all the more poignant, because it comes too late.

Tancred's errors are due in large measure to the baneful influence of Monforti. He is his master's evil genius. He is not so outstanding or so powerful a figure as Antenor, but they are alike in manipulating their monarch to suit their purposes and in their subordination of the public interest to their own designs. The people loom far larger in importance than in *The Cruel Gift*, and Monforti feigns sympathy with them, but at heart disdains them. They are 'gull'd fools' whose favour must be courted so long as it is needed, but afterwards can be cast aside.

In contrast to Monforti, the king's brother, the aged archbishop of Salerno, seeks to guide Tancred in the right direction, and he speaks of the people with genuine feeling:

> O that proud-hearted men but once could know
> The penetrating throb, one generous pang
> Of the breast heaving at the poor man's blessing,
> Or at the ill-articulated thanks
> Of modest worth reliev'd!
>
> (I. i)

He sees only too clearly that Tancred is ignorant of his subjects' lives and recognises the perils that lurk in such aloofness. Hence his plea that Tancred shall base his throne, not on fear and violence, but on esteem and devotion, for the prince is secure whose power is established in the people's love:

> That is the citadel for kings: 'tis there,
> Safe as our Alpine eagle who looks down
> On storms that combat in the aetherial plain,
> May'st thou look down upon all worldly mischief;
> 'Tis from that height thou'lt see the storms of envy,
> The plots of desperate guilt, th'assassin scheme
> Of disappointed pride, and all the rage
> Of frustrated ambition break beneath thee.
>
> (III. ii)

He couples this admonition with a warning of the fate that lies in store for monarchs who overtax the patience of those committed to their care:

> There's a judgement-seat
> Where purple kings, high as their full-blown pride
> Or flattery can set them, will be summon'd:
> 'Tis in their subjects' rigorous inquisition
> They must forestall the more tremendous process
> That waits beyond the grave—Think'st thou thy people,

Because they bear, don't feel their injuries?
The time may come when wrongs like these may teach them
To wreak just vengeance on their hard oppressor.[1]

(III. ii)

These words have a peculiar significance if we recall that *The Father's Revenge* was published two years before Cowper's denunciation of despotism in France and six years before the outbreak of the French Revolution. The archbishop embodies the growing awareness of that mounting sense of injustice which, as all those who had any political intuition could divine, must soon find an outlet in elemental violence.

Not less closely connected with the spirit of the age is Howard's use of the argument advanced by Ghismonda in favour of merit rather than hereditary rank. It is true that he conforms to the usual practice of the dramatists who have treated the theme by revealing at the close that Guiscard is of distinguished ancestry. But when Segismonda first falls in love with him, she knows nothing of this. What is still more remarkable, when Guiscard discovers his origin just before the marriage ceremony and informs Segismonda, she forgets all about the letter containing the news, which does not affect her decision to accept him as her husband. So little does Guiscard's rank weigh with her that she brushes it aside, saying:

> But what has birth, or titled parentage,
> A long-drawn lineage, or a proud descent,
> With real love? Disclaim thy noble birth,
> For that methinks deprives me of a proof
> Of what I dare do for thee.

(IV. ii)

Such sentiments, expressed by the earl of Carlisle, indicate how strong was the equalitarian current of the period, and illustrate his power of interpreting Boccaccio's tale in accordance with the political pressure of his time.

David Garrick's *Cymon*, though its connexion with Boccaccio's tale is but tenuous, is another play in all likelihood inspired by Dryden. It was printed again and again. After it first appeared in 1766, there followed editions in 1767, 1768, 1770, 1778, (1784) and (1786),[2] as well as a Dublin edition in 1771. The title-page styles the play ' dramatic romance', and the story is certainly given a romantic turn by the introduction of Merlin and Urganda, with whom the enchanter is in love. She too has magic powers and uses them in an effort to win

---

[1] The last two lines of this quotation are to be found in the 1783 edition but not in that of 1800. The omission is significant.

[2] Cf. Allardyce Nicoll, *A History of Late Eighteenth Century Drama*, Cambridge 1927, pp. 202, 263. The edition of 1766, not recorded by Nicoll, was probably pirated. Cf. Pickering and Chatto's catalogue 333, item 216.

Cymon. But the idiot Cymon falls in love with Sylvia, an Arcadian figure who is envied by all the shepherdesses. They intrigue against her, and Urganda employs all her arts to remove her from Cymon's presence. All is ended by the intervention of Merlin, who reveals that Sylvia is not a shepherdess but a princess, and the lovers gain the throne of Arcadia, so that there is fitness in the dance of shepherds and shepherdesses at the close.

A certain amount of comedy is provided by Dorus, the governor of Arcadia, and his mirthful deputy Linco. But the emphasis throughout is on spectacle. The Prologue states this frankly enough:

> As for the plot, wit, humour, language—I
> Beg you such trifles kindly to pass by;
> The most essential part, which something means,
> As dresses, dances, sinkings, flyings, scenes!—
> They'll make you stare!

With a wave of her wand Urganda transforms the stage into a magnificent garden and in Act IV causes an old castle to vanish and the demons of revenge to appear and perform their rites. In the fifth act she turns a grotto into black rocks and conjures up the Black Tower where she plans to hold Sylvia prisoner. But to the accompaniment of thunder the tower and rocks give place to a magnificent amphitheatre, and Merlin emerges where the tower had sunk. Round this amphitheatre are grouped all the characters at the close, including the knights of the different orders of chivalry who are sent to protect the marriage of the lovers. Cymon, Sylvia and Merlin 'are brought in triumph drawn by *Loves*, preceded by *Cupid* and *Hymen* arm in arm'.

There is also a strong musical element in the play, solos, duets and choruses being freely interspersed. The music, composed by Michael Arne, is so prominent that, as the printed text indicates, certain omissions had to be made in the stage version.

The Epilogue tries to ward off criticism of this type of entertainment:

> I see some malecontents their fingers biting,
> Snarling, "The ancients never knew such writing—
> "This drama's lost!—the managers exhaust us
> "With *opera's, monkies, mab* and *Dr. Faustus*"

and expresses the hope that the variety it provides will 'keep the critics under'.

As the numerous editions of the play show, despite its dramatic weakness it enjoyed great popularity. In 1792 another version appeared in which the operatic effect was heightened by the insertion of new airs and choruses. At the same time the procession at the close was made more elaborate. In addition to all conceivable sorts of knights and squires, a motley crowd of figures took part—an Indian chief and

Indians, a huntress with greyhounds, Turkish soldiers, a Scythian warrior, an Amazon with her attendants, Arcadian shepherds, a Cupid leading a knight, covered with a silver net, a fairy and a troop of Fairies, six virgins chained, piping fauns, Hymen, a band of Cupids drawing an altar, more Cupids hovering over it and others feeding doves below. The procession was followed by a tournament, first between two Moors, then between the Giant of the Burning Mountain and a dwarfish knight, and finally between a Spanish and an English Knight, the latter remaining victorious! It would be absurd to judge this Christmas pantomime too seriously, for its dramatic value is but slight—as Horace Walpole says, 'only Garrick's ginger-bread double-gilt'.[1]

The musical appeal is also strong in *The Cooper*, which was published in 1772. It is in fact described as a musical entertainment, the airs being composed by Dr. Thomas Arne. The ultimate source is the second tale of the seventh day of the *Decameron*, but it is derived immediately from *Le Tonnellier, Opéra-Comique, mêlé d'ariettes*, which was acted and printed in Paris in 1765.[2] It is obvious that Boccaccio's tale is completely unsuitable for the stage, and *The Cooper* is a free adaptation of the situation that it describes.

The scene is laid in the shop of a cooper, old Martin. With him lives Fanny, a young country girl, whom he has brought up since the death of her parents. Martin talks of marrying her, but her affection is set on Colin. After a number of incidents, including the entry of a drunken farmer called Twig and the flight of Colin from the irate Martin, the old cooper enters the tub and begins to work on it. Colin returns and stands laughing with Fanny, especially when Martin says that he does not think that Colin will have much desire to come there again. Martin asks Fanny to tell him a comical story to pass the time more merrily. She sings him a song which is nominally a gibe at another old cooper called Jacques who had wooed a young girl but was ousted by a youth named Cymon who kissed her while Jacques stood in a tub, cleaning it from inside. Unaware of the irony of the situation, Martin laughs uproariously. However, raising his head over the edge, he sees Colin kissing Fanny. At first he is enraged, but when Colin offers to take over a debt of £50 that Martin owes, agreement is reached on the marriage of Colin and Fanny, and all drink and sing together. In a modified form Boccaccio's tale is thus inserted into a dramatic framework.

The process of adaptation was applied also to older English plays,

---

[1] *Letters*, ed. Mrs. P. Toynbee, Oxford, 1903–5, xv, p. 102.

[2] According to the British Museum Catalogue the authors were N. M. Audinot and F. A. Quétant.

and so in 1790 Mrs. Aphra Behn's *The Rover*[1] was revised by J. P. Kemble and acted at Drury Lane. He altered the part in which Blunt, the Essex squire, figures. On more than one occasion allusions to sexual passion are eliminated, and words like 'whore' and 'pimp' are avoided. In the third act the scene where Blunt is decoyed by Lucetta is changed and instead of falling into the noisome 'Common Shoar' he descends into a 'passage'. The subsequent episode in which Blunt emerges to curse himself for his simplicity in being thus beguiled, is omitted. It would seem as if Kemble aimed at greater refinement and as if the jovial but coarse Blunt was no longer considered likely to please the audience. But the modification did involve the rejection of one essential feature of the tale in the *Decameron*.

The role of Blunt was a mere incident, touched with farce, but Mrs. Centlivre's play *The Busie Body*, which was first published in 1709 and reached its seventh edition in 1787,[2] based its structure to a much larger extent on the *Decameron*, Act II being derived from the fifth tale, and Act III from the third tale, of the third day. There is a notable difference, however. Instead of Francesco Vergellesi and his wife and her lover Ricciardo, we have Miranda, Sir Francis Gripe,[3] her aged guardian, and Sir George Airy who seeks to marry her, a relationship which makes the story more probable. In Act I Gripe agrees to let Sir George see Miranda for ten minutes in return for a hundred guineas, provided that Gripe remains in the same room. At the beginning of Act II Sir George is expected. In contrast to Boccaccio's tale, where the husband imposes silence on his wife, Miranda in an attempt to convince Gripe that she prefers him suggests that she shall remain silent. Sir George soon understands that she is dumb by arrangement and manages to converse with her by the same kind of device as in the tale. However, variety is lent to the old theme in a number of ways. Thus Sir George first kisses and then embraces Miranda, Sir Francis rushing forward angrily, each time to be repelled by Sir George with his sword. Again, at the end of the interview Sir George pretends to read a letter from her which he makes up on the spot. Further, whereas Ricciardo contrives to indicate to Vergellesi's wife how they are to meet, in the play it is Miranda who formulates the plan. In Act III in the very presence of Gripe she sends a message to

---

[1] Vide ante, pp. 246–7.

[2] Cf. Allardyce Nicoll, *A History of Early Eighteenth Century Drama*, Cambridge, 1925, p. 304.

[3] The name makes it likely that Mrs. Centlivre used the 1620 version of the *Decameron*. 'Francis' corresponds to 'Francesco', and 'Gripe' is suggested by the adjective 'gripple' applied to him for his avarice. The title of the play may also have been derived from the use of the word early in the English translation of the story of Vergellesi.

Sir George which, under cover of a warning not to molest her, notifies him of an assignation, which is the same technique as that employed by the lady of Florence in the third tale of the third day.

It is interesting to observe that Mrs. Centlivre, not unnaturally, has attached far greater importance to Miranda, who repeatedly takes the initiative. In keeping with this is the speech in Act IV when she justifies her conduct as she awaits Sir George. She weighs her 'rigid knavish Guardian', who would have married her 'to his nauseous self, or no body', against the young and generous Sir George, and she concludes that her action is not so rash as it may seem. Thus a tale of amorous intrigue is transformed into a battle of wits, in which the sympathy of the spectator is enlisted on behalf of youth triumphing over grasping old age. Incidentally, at the same time the play conforms to the demand for greater morality in the theatre.

VI

THE DECAMERON
IN THE NINETEENTH CENTURY

THE works of Boccaccio, the *Decameron* in particular, had long been an object of interest for bibliophiles, but on 17 June 1812 an event occurred which not only made a stir among collectors but also created a sensation in the general public. On that day the edition of the *Decameron* printed by Christopher Valdarfer in 1471 was offered at auction as part of the duke of Roxburghe's library. It is a remarkable fact that although one week later Napoleon was to open his ill-fated Russian campaign by crossing the Niemen with half a million men, he took care to send his representative to the sale. However, it was knocked down to the marquis of Blandford, after a long struggle with Earl Spencer and his son Lord Althorp, for £2,260. 'The echo of that fallen hammer', says Dibdin, 'was heard in the libraries of Rome, of Milan, and St. Mark. Boccaccio himself startled from his slumber of some five hundred years'.[1]

In England the effect was seen in press reports and in such a periodical as *The Gentleman's Magazine*,[2] and in a series of works, one of the most notable being *The Bibliographical Decameron*. As the title indicates, it is concerned with rare books, and Dibdin's account is cast in a form suggested by Boccaccio. The conversations take place at the country house of Lorenzo who has just returned with Philemon from a continental tour. They have bought precious books which they show to Lisardo and Lysander, accompanied by their wives, Almansa and Belinda. The visitors, not to be outdone, also bring their treasures. A monarch, provided with a sceptre and wreath, is elected for each of the ten days. As the season is autumn, when 'the leaves of the forest had put on their marygold tints', and 'the tranquillity of the air was only broken by the melancholy note of the robin', the discussions take place indoors, but they alternate, much in the manner of the *Decameron*

---

[1] Cf. Dibdin, iii, pp. 64–5. Only four copies are now extant. Those in the British Museum and the Bibliothèque Nationale are imperfect. The two perfect copies are in the Biblioteca Ambrosiana in Milan and the John Rylands Library, Manchester. (Cf. *Gesamtkatalog*, vol. iv, item 4441.) The Rylands copy is the one sold in 1812 to the marquis of Blandford, later duke of Marlborough, from whom it was acquired by Earl Spencer in 1819 for £918 15s. [2] August 1812.

with outdoor scenes, walks in the garden at sunset or in the moonlight, and a ride to the abbey of St. Alban's. References to Nature lend relief, and in general there is a similarity to the framework of the *Decameron*. In passing, a tribute is paid to Boccaccio's narrative powers[1] and to his humour, wit and invention.[2]

In 1820 J. Payne Collier followed with *The Poetical Decameron; or, Ten Conversations on English Poets and Poetry, particularly of the Reigns of Elizabeth and James I.* He claimed that the general scheme of the work was formed long before *The Bibliographical Decameron* appeared. It opens with a description of a journey of three friends by boat on a serene August evening from Westminster Bridge to Mortlake. After their arrival at the house of one of the party it was agreed that, as the weather was intolerably hot, they should spend the middle of each day in the library, while the mornings and evenings were devoted to other occupations and amusements such as sailing. After this, however, nothing more is heard of the setting, and there is a mere sequence of ten days' heterogeneous talk on old books, until at the close Collier adds that because of the beautiful weather and the lovely surroundings the guests were 'prevailed upon to prolong their stay, and to continue their enquiries'. The book, which ends thus lamely, has nothing to do with the *Decameron*, though there is a faint reflection of Collier's familiarity with it in the induction.

A similar work was planned by the antiquary Joseph Hunter, writing under the name of Martin Field in 1829. The fragment of *A Shakespear Decameron*[3] begins with a dialogue between 'A' and 'B' in the 'Alpine cell' of the latter who lives in retirement, cut off from the world and 'communing with it only through books'. He has been joined by 'A' who has come to the mountains for sport but has developed a sudden enthusiasm for Shakespeare. They are to be joined by another enthusiast, and a plan is drawn up to devote ten days to the discussion of various aspects of Shakespeare's work. It is likely that Hunter was inspired by Collier. His scheme has but a vague association with the *Decameron*, but at least something is there, whereas Joseph Lunn's *Horae Jocosae; or the Doggerel Decameron*[4] is simply a collection of ten facetious tales in verse and nothing more. On the other hand, Joseph Downes's *The Mountain Decameron*, which appeared in 1836, has a connexion with Boccaccio, though it is but loose. The work is divided into ten days. The author writes in the character of a Quaker whose physician has advised him to make a tour in Wales. He addresses this doctor and describes some of the landscapes that he sees, in the company of a major, a clergyman and a physician. He also

---

[1] ii, p. 457.   [2] iii, p. 469.
[3] Add. MS. 24,884 in the British Museum.   [4] London, 1823.

relates the tales that are told. On some days, however, none are told. Occasionally a tale is spread over two days and sometimes, even within the day, the flow of the narrative is interrupted, so that the author may intersperse his opinions on politics, poetry, society, solitude—in short anything that 'mountain-air or mountain-quiet may set us thinking about'. Nevertheless, eccentric and shapeless though this book may be, it bears clear marks of the work from which it originated.

Another sign of the interest in Boccaccio at the beginning of the nineteenth century is the publication of the *Decameron* in Italian in 1802 and again in 1825. Each edition bears the London imprint, and the second[1] has an introduction by the famous Italian poet Ugo Foscolo.[2] In addition, there appeared in 1802 *Novelle scelte del Boccaccio*[3] and in 1806 *Italian Extracts*[4] which also contained some of Boccaccio's tales. There was likewise great activity in publishing translations of the *Decameron*. The version of 1741, still further expurgated, was reissued with a valuable introduction by E. Dubois in 1804,[5] and this edition was reprinted in one volume in 1820. Two years later followed an edition[6] which restored the tales omitted by Dubois, giving certain passages in French and Italian. A substantial part of the introduction is stolen from Dubois. The year 1822 saw the publication of another edition with coloured aquatint plates by J. Findlay.[7] There is a textual connexion with the edition of Sharp, but the introduction differs, though it too draws on Dubois.

In the latter part of the nineteenth century there was a revival of the old translation of 1620, when Henry Morley edited a selection of forty stories. He retains the whole framework, and it makes a curious impression when one reads the connecting matter that leads on to a tale, only to find 'OMITTED' on page after page and now and then several times on one page. However, the edition of Dubois was the dominant influence, as may be seen from the text employed by W. K. Kelly in 1861, though he approximates to the Sharp edition of 1822 with regard to expurgation. In 1872[8] the last-mentioned edition was taken over in unscrupulous fashion by Thomas Wright without any acknowledgement. The only point of interest is the insertion of the

---

[1] Published by William Pickering. Some copies contain ten plates after T. Stothard.

[2] Then a refugee in England.

[3] Edited by Leonardo Nardini. Cf. Marshall, p. 357.

[4] Edited by Antonio Montucci. Cf. Marshall, p. 357.   [5] In two volumes.

[6] Published by William Sharp in four volumes.

[7] Published in two volumes by James Griffin. This edition is very rare. My copy contains eleven plates, six in vol. i, five in vol. ii. One of the plates illustrates the tale of Lorenzo and Isabella.

[8] The title-page gives no year of publication, but the preface is dated 2 December 1872.

ten designs by Stothard.[1] Dubois is again the ultimate source of an edition of twenty-one tales, of which twenty are from the *Decameron*, published in 1887. The group is divided into ten days which have nothing to do with the original. The introduction, which, incidentally, appropriates a good deal from Dubois, explains that the conversations which precede the narratives have been discarded as irrelevant. Despite his pose as a liberator from 'the ignorant and bigoted Puritans' the editor is chiefly concerned with erotic stimulus, as his additions to the tales clearly prove.

Of a very different order is the translation of the *Decameron* by John Payne in 1886. The introduction owes nothing to Dubois and though it is perhaps too speculative, it shows personal acquaintance with such a work as *Fiammetta*, which enables Payne to write in a fresh and agreeable fashion. His translation also is original, and he set himself to do what his predecessor of 1620, with whom he was familiar,[2] had done—to render Boccaccio into a highly-wrought literary style which would attract the connoisseur. Payne's Pre-Raphaelite idiom, archaic to the point of affectation though it may seem to us nowadays, is comparable to the elaborate alliterative manner of the Jacobean translator.

Quite apart from the accounts of Boccaccio and his writings given in various translations of the *Decameron*, there were appreciations of his work by the critics. Eminent among these was an anonymous writer in *The London Magazine*,[3] He alludes indirectly to the sale of the Valdarfer *Decameron* in 1812 and remarks that 'a single copy of some of the earlier editions has sometimes fetched a price which would purchase a useful collection of books sufficient for the purposes of a man of letters'.[4] While resisting the fanatical admiration of some devotees, the author of the review concedes the merits of Boccaccio as a stylist and his contribution to humanism. Another important essay was that which discussed Thomas Roscoe's *Italian Novelists* in *The Edinburgh Review*.[5] After a valuable general survey the critic examines in detail some of the tales selected from the *Decameron*.

[1] Vide post, p. 341. Wright's edition met with some success. Thus it was published again at Derby in 1894.

[2] In his Biographical Note he refers to Boccaccio, ' "that first refiner of Italian prose", as one of his old English translators quaintly styles him'. The phrase is found on the title-page of the first five days in the 1625 edition of the 1620 version.

[3] 1 June 1826, pp. 145–57. He was probably Ugo Foscolo. At any rate, the article was chiefly based on his earlier work and contains a review of his preface to his edition of the *Decameron*, which would explain why he here remained anonymous. Cf. E. R. Vincent, *Ugo Foscolo An Italian in Regency England*, Cambridge, 1953, p. 200.

[4] p. 145.

[5] Vol. xlii, no. lxxxiii, April 1825, pp. 174–206.

Up to a point he disagrees with Roscoe's choice, his own preference being for certain of those[1] which Hazlitt had praised so highly.[2]

In pictorial art themes derived from the *Decameron* were also popular. More than anyone else Stothard found delight in the rural background rather than in the stories. In 1811 he exhibited at the Royal Academy 'The Scene of Boccaccio's Tales' and in 1818 'Fête Champêtre'. These were followed in 1819 by 'The First Part of the Decameron' and 'The Second Part of the Decameron'. In 1820 came 'The Mill', 'The Garden', 'The Supper by the Fountain', 'Pampinea elected Queen, and receiving the Crown of Laurel from Philomena' and 'The Meadow'. Finally, in 1826 he exhibited a new composition with the title 'Fête Champêtre'.[3]

But the tales themselves, especially those in Dryden's *Fables*, proved a source of inspiration to artists. The Swiss painter, Johann Heinrich Fuessli, who settled in England and went by the name of Fuseli, found the story of 'Theodore and Honoria' entirely congenial to his romantic taste, and in 1817 his work on this subject appeared at the Royal Academy.[4] The Pre-Raphaelites also found pleasure in these themes. About the middle of the century G. F. Watts was attracted to the tale of the avenging spectral huntsman, and his enormous painting remained on the walls of his studio after it had been taken over by the Cosmopolitan Club.[5] Millais turned to 'Cymon and Iphigenia', painting a first study in 1847 and completing it in 1851.[6] Leighton too, fascinated by the legend of the transforming and ennobling power of beauty, depicted 'Cymon and Iphigenia' in 1884.[7] The poetry of Keats inspired paintings, based on the tale of 'Isabella', by Millais,[8] Holman Hunt[9] and Watts, and W. B. Johnstone likewise treated the subject in a work shown at the Royal Scottish Academy in 1854. The fresco of C. W. Cope for the House of Lords in 1848 and his painting 'The Marriage of Griselda' indicate the interest still taken by the Victorians in the mediæval tale of self-sacrificing womanhood. In conclusion, mention should be made of Rossetti, in whom

---

[1] See pp. 183–4.   [2] Vide post, pp. 344–8.

[3] Mrs. Bray, *The Life of Thomas Stothard*, London, 1851, pp. 240–2. Among the pictures still in Stothard's possession at his decease and sold at Christie's in June, 1834, were a number suggested by the *Decameron* (cf. Mrs. Bray, op. cit., pp. 242–3) Samuel Rogers acquired some of Stothard's work, including a 'Fête Champêtre' (cf. Mrs. Bray, op. cit., p. 235). Vide post, p. 344.

[4] John Knowles, *The Life and Writings of Henry Fuseli*, London, 1831, i, pp. 416–17.

[5] Sir Mountstuart E. Grant Duff, *Notes from a Diary*, 1851–72, London, 1817, , p. 100.

[6] M. H. Spielmann, *Millais and his Works*, London, 1898, p. 167.

[7] Mrs. Russell Barrington, *The Life, Letters and Work of Frederic Leighton*, London, 906, ii, pp. 258, n. 1, and 389.

[8] 1849. In the Walker Art Gallery, Liverpool.

[9] 1868. In the Walker Art Gallery, Liverpool.

poetry and painting unite with peculiar intimacy to convey the impressions left on his sensitive mind by Boccaccio.[1]

1. Comments on Boccaccio, more particularly on the *Decameron*

In one way or another the knowledge of the *Decameron* became widespread among men of culture in the nineteenth century. It is therefore not surprising to find an entry in Thomas Moore's *Diary*[2] which describes how at Lord Lansdowne's country house the conversation after dinner included a discussion of the merits of Dryden's 'Cymon and Iphigenia'. Other writers like Wordsworth read the *Decameron*, for this is probably the work that he meant, when he said that 'Boccaccio' figured in his library at Racedown in 1797.[3] With Sir Walter Scott he shared an admiration for Dryden's *Fables*.[4] Shelley too was a reader of Boccaccio, but not through any intermediary. In a letter to Leigh Hunt on 27 September 1819 he praises him and quotes:[5] 'Bocca bacciata non perde ventura, anzi rinnuova, come fa la luna'.[6] He introduces these words when Nature addresses Peter Bell and observes:

> So thought Boccaccio, whose sweet works might cure a
> Male prude, like you, from what you now endure, a
> Low-tide in soul, like a stagnant laguna.[7]

Shelley's sensitive ear had caught the music of Boccaccio, and 'ventura' and 'luna' echo in 'cure a', 'endure, a' and 'laguna', though with deliberately burlesque effect. His friend Byron, after he had removed from Venice to Ravenna, was continually reminded of Boccaccio's tale of Nastagio degli Onesti as he rode daily in the neighbouring forest, and when, as a sympathiser with Italian aspirations for liberty, he was invited to a dinner in the Pineta by a local patriotic society, he half-expected to hear the sound of the ghostly rider hunting his prey.[8] Every time that Byron mentions this tale, he couples with it a reference to Dryden's 'Theodore and Honoria' which had clearly left a deep impression upon him.[9] This is the only tale from the *Decameron* that Byron touches on, and it is possible that when reading

---

[1] Vide post, pp. 363–5.   [2] 30 December 1818

[3] *Letters*, 1841–50, p. 1335.

[4] *Early Letters*, 1797–1805, pp. 540–1; *Letters*, 1806–11, p. 458c.

[5] From the end of *Dec.* ii, 7. Vide post, pp. 350, 363.

[6] Cf. Shelley's *Works*, Julian Edition, London and New York, 1926–30, iii, p. 272.

[7] *Peter Bell the Third*, book iv, st. xiv.

[8] Cf. *Letters and Journals*, ed. R. E. Prothero, London, iv, p. 320 and v, pp. 140 and 206.

[9] He notes that Dryden had substituted Guido Cavalcanti for Boccaccio's hero. Writing from memory, he wrongly calls him 'Ostasio degli Onesti'.

of the harshness of a woman and her punishment, he was not unaffected
by his unhappy marital relations. However, his interest in Boccaccio
was not narrowly limited. His protest at the violation of his tomb in
the church of St. Michael and St. James in 1783, when religious bigots
took advantage of a recent edict prohibiting burial in churches to
break the stone that covered the sepulchre and cast it out into the
adjoining cloisters, is filled with genuine indignation at this insult to
a dead genius:

> Boccaccio to his parent earth bequeath'd
> His dust,—and lies it not her Great among,
> With many a sweet and solemn requiem breathed
> O'er him who form'd the Tuscan's siren tongue?
> That music in itself, whose sounds are song,
> The poetry of speech? No;—even his tomb
> Uptorn must bear the hyæna bigot's wrong,
> No more amidst the meaner dead find room,
> Nor claim a passing sigh, because it told for *whom*.[1]

The condemnation of this act, combined with the eulogy of Boccaccio
as the shaper of the melodious Italian tongue, is followed by a tribute
to the three great writers Dante, Petrarch and Boccaccio in which
Byron ranks him almost as high as the others:

> But where repose the all Etruscan three—
> Dante, and Petrarch, and, scarce less than they,
> The Bard of Prose, creative Spirit, he
> Of the Hundred Tales of Love—where did they lay
> Their bones, distinguished from our common clay
> In death as life?[2]

Coleridge's approach to Boccaccio differs completely from that of
Byron. It is characteristic of his far-reaching mind that in his reading
of Boccaccio he should penetrate into regions unknown to most of his
English contemporaries. Few indeed were those who had turned the
pages of *De genealogia deorum*, a work which even in the Middle
Ages was not the most popular of Boccaccio's writings. Yet a casual
reference in one of his note-books shows that Coleridge was acquainted
with the strange figure of Demogorgon.[3] Watching the cloud effects
on a dim November night in 1803, he speaks of

white vapour that, entirely shapeless, gave a whiteness to the circle of the sky,
but stained with exceedingly thin and subtle flakes of black vapour, might be
happily said in language of Boccace (describing Demogorgon, in his *Genealogia De Gli Dei*) to be vestito d'una pallidezza *affumicata*.[4]

Evidently it was Betussi's Italian translation[5] that Coleridge used,

---

[1] *Childe Harold*, Canto iv, st. lviii.   [2] Ibid., st. lvi.   [3] Vide ante, pp. 37–41.
[4] Cf. *Anima Poetae*, ed. E. H. Coleridge, London, 1895, p. 46.
[5] The words occur in the opening lines of Book i.

Z

but nothing seems to be ascertainable about the edition. On the other hand, it is known that he possessed four volumes of the *Opere* published at Florence in 1723-4, among the contents of which was the life of Dante. Attracted to this by his admiration for the great epic poet, Coleridge was struck by a passage which in his opinion could only have sprung from the violent prejudice of a woman-hater. The animosity which is openly displayed in the *Corbaccio* does in fact peep through in the lines where Boccaccio comments on the error of Dante's relatives in persuading him to marry after the death of Beatrice, with the result that the genius who had been wont to move among emperors and princes, to converse with poets and philosophers, to devote himself to his studies and to brood over the mysteries of the universe in solitude, was now limited to the society of a jealous woman with whom he had to live, grow old and die. A thousand and one petty, material preoccupations absorbed his energies till he rebelled against this domination. Boccaccio therefore maintained that since a husband is thus fettered to a being who is not what he would like to have, but what Fortune grants, marriage should be left to rich fools, lords and labourers. Those of philosophical mind should give themselves up to philosophy, a better spouse than any other. In spite of his own unfortunate experiences of married life, Coleridge rejected this counsel and in the *Biographia Literaria*, mingling his criticism with practical advice to young authors, he warns them not to isolate themselves from the rest of the human species but to be men first, and writers only in the second place:

Instead of the vehement and almost slanderous dehortation from marriage which the *Misogyne*, Boccaccio, addresses to literary men, I would substitute the simple advice: be not *merely* a man of letters! Let literature be an honourable *augmentation* to your arms; but not constitute the coat, or fill the escutcheon![1]

It was presumably Coleridge's interest in the less known writings of Boccaccio that led him in 1815 to plan a translation. In May of that year he told Samuel Rogers that if a publisher could be induced to buy the manuscript when it was ready for the press, he would embark on the enterprise. However, in spite of Rogers' good offices the project fell through, and by 7 October Coleridge had abandoned his intention. It is significant that from the outset he had excluded the *Decameron* for, unlike most contemporary critics, he viewed this work with disapprobation. As his comments on English writers in various places indicate, he strongly disliked anything that savoured of coarseness or impurity. Consequently, it is not surprising to find that in his lecture

[1] *Biographia Literaria*, Ch. xi. Cf. 2-volume edition by J. Shawcross, Oxford, 1907, i, p. 158.

on 3 February 1818 he censured the *Decameron* in no measured terms for the same defect as 'poisons Ariosto', 'interposes a painful mixture in the humour of Chaucer' and 'once or twice seduced even our pure-minded Spenser'. With a complete lack of discrimination he ignored the tales of an idealistic bent and rejected the book as a whole. He made no allowance for a difference of manners in earlier stages of society and condemned 'the gross and disgusting licentiousness, the daring pro-faneness, which rendered the *Decameron* of Boccaccio the parent of a hundred worse children, fit to be classed among the enemies of the human race'. Possibly it was the distaste with which he regarded these tales that caused him to pass over Boccaccio in discussing such plays of Shakespeare as are derived from this source. It was highly inconvenient to recognise any obligation on his part, and Coleridge preferred the distorting silence of the partisan to the unflinching truthfulness of the critic. Yet he is known to have been deeply moved by the story of Lorenzo and Isabella. In his essay 'On consistency of Opinion' Hazlitt records:

I have heard him talk divinely (like one inspired) of Boccaccio, and the story of the Pot of Basil, describing 'how it grew, and it grew, and it grew,' till you saw it spread its tender leaves in the light of his eye, and wave in the tremulous sound of his voice.[1]

Moreover, when in a reasonable frame of mind, he was willing to concede that

we owe to him (Boccaccio) the subjects of numerous poems taken from his famous tales, the happy art of narration, and the still greater merit of a depth and fineness in the workings of the passions.[2]

And despite his hostility to the *Decameron*, he must have read it attentively, for he singles out the fantastic name 'Schinchimurra' from the long ninth tale of the eighth day as being appropriate for a fool.[3]

Towards Boccaccio's style, however, which had always been highly praised, Coleridge was not favourably disposed. He took exception to it on the ground that it was too much influenced by classical models and had a cramping effect on later writers; the fact that it had found imitators all over Europe only intensified his disapproval. To Boccaccio he says,

we owe the doubtful merit of having introduced into the Italian prose, and by the authority of his name and the influence of his example, more or less throughout Europe, the long interwoven periods, and architectural structure

[1] *London Magazine*, 1821. Cf. Waller and Glover, xi, 517.
[2] 1811 Lectures, no. 3. Cf. Shedd, iv, 241.
[3] See his Notebook xviii, p. 2, to which my attention has been directed by Miss Kathleen Coburn.

which arose from the very nature of their language in the Greek writers, but which already, in the Latin orators and historians, had betrayed a species of effort, a foreign something which had been superinduced on the language, instead of growing out of it; and which was far too alien from that individualizing and confederating, yet not blending, character of the North, to become permanent, although its magnificence and stateliness were objects of admiration and occasional imitation. This style diminished the control of the writer over the inner feelings of men, and created too great a chasm between the body and the life.[1]

To the 'hyperlatinization' which Coleridge found uncongenial in Sir Thomas Browne no less than in Boccaccio, there was a further objection —the barrier that it raised between the author and the ordinary man. If, as Coleridge admitted, the *Decameron* enjoyed a wide circle of readers, he considered that its popularity was due to the fascination of the subject-matter triumphing over the obstacle of the style.

About Boccaccio's poetry Coleridge had little to say, for he thought it of slight interest, apart from the possibility that the eight-line stanza used in the *Teseida* was the invention of the author. But the romances did appeal to him powerfully, partly because of their skill in exhibiting the human passions, partly for 'the wild and imaginative character of the situations'. The selection of the last reason, which is as typical of the romantic critic as his dislike of too rigid a style because of the restraints thus imposed on the overflow of the inmost feelings, suggests that it was probably the *Filocolo* which Coleridge had in view and which he would have wished to rescue from an undeserved neglect. It was comprised in the edition of the *Opere* that he possessed, and by no mere coincidence the only comments in the four volumes relate to this romance.

In a note on the last leaf of the first volume he remarks:

Boccaccio from a sense possibly of poetic justice; herein followed by a goodly company of poetic sons—Ariosto, Camoens etc.—reversed the scheme of the early Church and the Fathers of the First Century—they, namely transferred the functions and attributes of the Pagan Godlings & Goddesses & Nymphs to deified Bishops, Monks & Nuns. Boccaccio the functions and histories of Hebrew Prophets & Prophetesses and of Christian Saints and Apostles—nay the highest mysteries and most aweful objects of Christian Faith to the names & drapery of Greek & Roman Mythology.

In support of his statement he refers to a passage early in the *Filocolo*, where mention is made of the struggle waged by Jove, the ruler of the heavens, with Pluto, who, aspiring to greater power than was fitting, was exiled for ever with his companions in the gloomy realms of Dis. Furthermore, Boccaccio continues, Jove created Prometheus, to whom he gave dear and noble company. This was obviously what Coleridge

[1] 1811 Lectures, no. iii. Cf. Shedd, iv, 241.

was envisaging when in his lecture on 3 February 1818 he assigned to Boccaccio the responsibility for 'a large portion of the mythological pedantry and incongruous paganism which for so long a period deformed the poetry, even of the truest poets'. 'To such an extravagance did Boccaccio himself carry this folly', he adds, 'that in a romance of chivalry he has uniformly styled God the Father Jupiter, our Saviour Apollo, and the Evil Being Pluto'. It was again the pagan element in Boccaccio's work, so characteristic of Renaissance Italy, that inspired Coleridge to enter a note on the fly-leaf of Volume I of the *Opere*. It refers to the scene in the *Filocolo* where the wise instructor Racheo, as soon as the young prince and the fair Biancafiore have learnt to read, puts before them Ovid's *Ars amandi*—'il santo libro'. And Coleridge exclaims: 'The Holy Book Ovid's Art of Love!! This is not the result of mere immorality. Multum multum hic jacet sepultum'. What lay buried there Coleridge defined in a footnote to 'The Garden of Boccaccio'. Alluding to the above scene, he observes:

I know few more striking or more interesting proofs of the overwhelming influence which the study of the Greek and Roman classics exercised on the judgments, feelings, and imaginations of the literati of Europe at the commencement of the restoration of literature.[1]

The poem to which these words are appended was meant to illustrate a design by Stothard. It formed part of the series which the artist had exhibited at the Royal Academy. Attention was thus drawn to them, and when Ugo Foscolo edited *Il Decamerone*, to make the edition more valuable, ten plates engraved by Augusto Fox from Stothard's designs were included in some copies.[2] It was probably these illustrations that gave an idea to Frederick Mansel Reynolds, the editor of *The Keepsake*, who, like other editors of annuals about this time, scoured the studios for pictorial material. A letter by Coleridge[3] speaks of 'a few epigrams which Mr. Reynolds selected from an old memorandum book of mine, and a poem written for one of the engravings—"Boccaccio's Garden"'. From this it is clear that Reynolds must have approached Coleridge and asked him to write a poem to go with the engraving by F. Englehart after Stothard's drawing which appeared in *The Keepsake* in 1829. However, as the poet reveals, the illustration was not handed to him by Reynolds, but by a friend, who, as E. H. Coleridge informs us, was Mrs. Gillman. Entering the room and seeing Coleridge in one of those moods of dejected reverie with which she was only too familiar, she placed the design quietly on his desk. At first he but half saw:

[1] Cf. Shedd, vii, p. 320. [2] Vide ante, p. 334.
[3] Cf. *Unpublished Letters of Samuel Taylor Coleridge*, ed. E. L. Griggs, London, 1932, ii, p. 421.

Boccaccio's Garden and its faery,
The love, the joyaunce, and the gallantry!
An Idyll, with Boccaccio's spirit warm,
Framed in the silent poesy of form.[1]
(15–18)

Roused from his despondency by the stimulus thus received, Coleridge
depicts the scene in lines that answer well to the details of the design,
though 'the high tower' with its 'tinkling bells' can hardly be discerned in *The Keepsake*. Then, inspired by 'old Boccaccio's soul', and
breathing 'an air like life', the poet escapes from the garden to the
surrounding countryside of Tuscany. And now, freed from the dreary
numbness of the present, he no longer calls in vain upon the past for
relief, but blends his own memories of the Tuscan landscape in the
spring of 1806 with his impressions drawn from Boccaccio, in a delicate
evocation of the urbane charm and cultured grace of Italy:

The brightness of the world, O thou once free,
And always fair, rare land of courtesy!
O Florence! with the Tuscan fields and hills,
And famous Arno fed with all their rills;
Thou brightest star of star-bright Italy!
Rich, ornate, populous, all treasures thine,
The golden corn, the olive, and the vine.
Fair cities, gallant mansions, castles old,
And forests, where beside his leafy hold
The sullen boar hath heard the distant horn,
And whets his tusk against the gnarlèd thorn;
Palladian palace with its storied halls;
Fountains, where Love lies listening to their falls;
Gardens, where flings the bridge its airy span,
And Nature makes her happy home with man;
Where many a gorgeous flower is duly fed
With its own rill, on its own spangled bed,
And wreathes the marble urn, or leans its head,
A mimic mourner, that with veil withdrawn
Weeps liquid gems, the presents of the dawn;—
Thine all delights, and every muse is thine;
And more than all, the embrace and intertwine
Of all with all in gay and twinkling dance!
(73–95)

Finally, against this background with its long tradition of civilisation
he conjures up Boccaccio himself, seated with a manuscript of Homer
on his knees and in the folds of his mantle, near the heart, 'Ovid's
Holy Book of Love's sweet smart'. And in this happy mood he recap-
tures something of Boccaccio's half-pagan gaiety:

[1] 'The Garden of Boccaccio'. Cf. Shedd, vol. vii.

> O all-enjoying and all-blending sage,
> Long be it mine to con thy mazy page,
> Where, half concealed, the eye of fancy views
> Fauns, nymphs, and winged saints, all gracious to thy muse!
>
> (101–4.)

This is Coleridge's last word about Boccaccio. Earlier he had declared that Italy for him meant Dante, Ariosto and Giordano Bruno. Yet in the twilight of his life the earnest Christian thinker and subtle metaphysician, to whom Boccaccio had seemed a stranger, yielded to the joyous vitality of this incarnation of the Renaissance spirit.

Though he was not unfamiliar with the life of Boccaccio and singles out his falling in love with Fiammetta in the church of St. Lorenzo and his dedication of his life to the Muses,[1] Samuel Rogers was like Coleridge in that he was specially interested in the setting of the *Decameron*. In his *Italy*[2] he speaks of Florence where the graceful spire of Santa Maria Novella catches his eye. It carries his mind back to the company of ladies and gentlemen who assembled there during the plague and

> Who, when Vice revelled and along the street
> Tables were set, what time the bearer's bell
> Rang to demand the dead at every door,
> Came out into the meadows; and, awhile
> Wandering in idleness, but not in folly,
> Sat down in the high grass and in the shade
> Of many a tree sun-proof—day after day,
> When all was still and nothing to be heard
> But the cicala's voice among the olives,
> Relating in a ring, to banish care,
> Their hundred tales.[3]

Of these tales Rogers mentions only one—that of Frate Cipolla. But the places where they were supposed to have been told excited his curiosity, and one bright November morning he set out and followed the movements of the narrators, beginning and ending in Santa Maria Novella. He saw the Villa Gherardi with its painted rooms, open galleries and middle court, fragrant and gay with flowers; then the Villa Palmieri,

> Where Art with Nature vied—a Paradise
> With verdurous walls, and many a trellissed walk
> All rose and jasmine, many a twilight-glade
> Crossed by the deer.[4]

[1] See 'The Pleasures of Memory' in *Poems*, 1834, pp. 51 and 106.
[2] He visited Italy in 1815. The first part of the poem was published anonymously in 1822. The second part appeared in 1828, but as it did not sell well, Rogers issued it in a revised form, with illustrations by Turner and Stothard in 1830.
[3] Not in 1822 section. Quotations from 1840 ed., p. 22.   [4] Ibid.

and so on to the Valle delle donne with its clear lake. The designs by Stothard in his possession[1] helped Rogers to visualise the scene, and his own description pictures not less gracefully the mode of life of the narrators:

> The morning-banquet by the fountain-side,
> While the small birds rejoiced on every bough;
> The dance that followed, and the noon-tide slumber;
> Then the tales told in turn, as round they lay
> On carpets, the fresh waters murmuring;
> And the short interval of pleasant talk
> Till supper-time, when many a siren-voice
> Sung down the stars; and, as they left the sky,
> The torches, planted in the sparkling grass,
> And every where among the glowing flowers,
> Burnt bright and brighter.[2]

Even more than Rogers, Hazlitt was a great lover of Boccaccio and on his visit to Italy in 1825 was continually haunted by his shade. At Maiano he felt enriched by the view of his house and the Valley of Ladies, and at Turin he thought that in the graceful, downcast looks of the young women he could read the very soul of the *Decameron*. But long before this date he had declared repeatedly his passionate admiration for Boccaccio. The earliest reference occurs in a letter to Miss Stoddart at the beginning of 1808. In his use of the characters of the *Decameron* to further his love-making he is unique among English writers. Being impatient to have news of her, he asks:

Are you gone into a nunnery? Or are you fallen in love with some of the amorous heroes of Boccaccio? Which of them is it? Is it with Chynon, who was transformed from a clown into a lover, and learned to spell by the force of beauty? Or with Lorenzo, the lover of Isabella, whom her three brethren hated (as your brother does me), who was a merchant's clerk? or with Federigo Alberigi, an honest gentleman, who ran through his fortune, and won his mistress by cooking a fair falcon for her dinner, though it was the only means he had left of getting a dinner for himself? This last is the man; and I am the more persuaded of it, because I think I won your good liking myself by giving you an entertainment—of sausages, when I had no money to buy them with. Nay now, never deny it! Did not I ask your consent that very night after, and did you not give it? Well, I should be confoundedly jealous of those fine gallants, if I did not know that a living dog is better than a dead lion: though, now I think of it, Boccaccio does not in general make much of his lovers: it is his women who are so delicious.[3]

As time passed, Hazlitt revised this opinion and came to like Boccaccio's lovers, as he did those of Shakespeare, for their tenderness and manly spirit and their freedom from insipidity and cant. In other respects, however, his attitude to Boccaccio underwent no change. On the

---

[1] Vide, ante, p. 335.   [2] Ibid.
[3] Cf. P. P. Howe, *The Life of William Hazlitt*, London, 1922, p. 106.

contrary, with characteristic tenacity he clung to his old favourite. In his essay 'On Novelty and Familiarity' he tells of the sheer happiness, the heart's ease with which he used to read the *Decameron*. The tale of Federigo Alberighi in particular moved him as if it had been his own experience. Treating a similar theme in the essay 'On Reading Old Books' he says:

The only writer among the Italians I can pretend to any knowledge of, is Boccacio, and of him I cannot express half my admiration. His story of the Hawk I could read and think of from day to day, just as I would look at a picture of Titian's![1]

Boccaccio's characters became part and parcel of him, so that in order to convey his thoughts in a totally different sphere from that of literature, their figures came to him unsought. Thus when he heard that Kellerman had left his heart to be buried on the battlefield of Valmy, where the invading Allies had been repulsed in the early days of the French Revolution, he exclaimed:

Oh! might that heart prove the root from which the tree of Liberty may spring up and flourish once more, as the basil-tree grew and grew from the cherished head of Isabella's lover![2]

For him Boccaccio was truly more than a name. He tried to summon up a picture of the old narrator and thought that one who was not only a great reviver of learning but also a man of the world must have had something in his features to distinguish him from the moderns. This personal interest in Boccaccio made the account of his interview with Petrarch doubly attractive to Hazlitt, but he would have been still better pleased if he could have seen Chaucer in company with the author of the *Decameron* and heard them exchange their best stories, the Squire's Tale against the story of the falcon, and, in a very different vein, the Wife of Bath's Prologue against the adventures of Friar Albert. In his old age, when life had little more to offer him, Hazlitt found solace for his cares by recalling former pleasant memories. On his walks he would imagine the ground covered with primroses and purple hyacinths, and the air full of singing-birds as many summers before, and even the wind sighing through the tall wood had its associations. In fancy, he says,

I distinguish the cry of hounds, and the fatal group issuing from it, as in the tale of Theodore and Honoria. A moaning gust of wind aids the belief; I look once more to see whether the trees before me answer to the idea of the horror-stricken grove, as an air-built city towers over their grey tops.

[1] *The Plain Speaker*, 1826, Essay xx. Cf. Waller and Glover, vii, p. 227. This story was popular with many nineteenth-century writers (vide post). Nor was it forgotten in the twentieth (cf. Angela Thirkell, *The Brandons*, 1939, p. 273).
[2] *Table-Talk*. Cf. Waller and Glover, vi, p. 121.

> 'Of all the cities in Romanian lands,
>   The chief and most renown'd Ravenna stands.'

I return home resolved to read the entire poem through, and, after dinner, drawing my chair to the fire, and holding a small print close to my eyes, launch into the full tide of Dryden's couplets (a stream of sound), comparing his descriptive and didactic pomp with the simple pathos and picturesque of Boccaccio's story.[1]

Still more pathetic in tone is 'The Sick Chamber', in which, in the very presence of death, with a strong consciousness of his precarious tenure of existence and the rapidity with which his vitality was ebbing away, he evokes the past and longs once more to turn the pages of the *Decameron.*

Often as Hazlitt speaks of Boccaccio in his personal essays, the allusions to him in the formally critical writings are still more numerous. Indeed, from the beginning of his literary activity hardly a year passes without some reference to the *Decameron*. As early as January 1814, in an article for *The Morning Chronicle* on 'Why the Arts are not Progressive?' he claims Boccaccio as one of the great artists who tower above their successors and who, relying entirely on nature, possess a strength of imagination which enables them, unlike the scientist, to reach the utmost summit of perfection in one stride. In the same year he twice protested against the estimate of Boccaccio as a mere purveyor of lewd tales. The vulgar ear, he felt, had been caught by these critics, while it remained deaf to so delicate a portrayal of sentiment as the story of the falcon. Such gross-minded readers in his opinion simply revealed their own mentality and travestied the *Decameron*. With passionate conviction he asserted that only the unclean of heart or the ignorant, commonplace critic who accepted his ideas ready-made, could possibly maintain an unfavourable attitude towards Boccaccio. He would have wished to see Byron trying to rescue him from this undeserved obloquy rather than eulogising the poetic genius of Pope. For his own part, he did not shrink from proclaiming the view that English literature had profited far more from contact with Italian literature as a whole and from Boccaccio in particular, than by what it had learnt from French literature, the one borrowing being successfully grafted on the national genius and lending it new strength and vitality, while the other enfeebled and impoverished it.

There was one period of English literature in which Hazlitt discerned a special affinity with the world of Boccaccio. In the Elizabethan age, no less than in that of Boccaccio, men lived dangerously; adventure was ever present, and catastrophe lurked round the corner. Marlowe, the lover of beauty, was stabbed in a tavern brawl, and the richness

---

[1] *London Weekly Review*, 1828. Cf. Waller and Glover, xii, pp. 322–3.

and animation of the hundred tales stand out against the grim scenes of the pestilence at Florence. And when Hazlitt came to individual authors, he found in Heywood's Pardoner a kinsman of Fra Cipolla, while Dekker's command of simple pathos seemed comparable to that of the *Decameron*. It was Boccaccio's mastery of pathos and of sentiment that Hazlitt especially admired, and he held that from this point of view Chaucer was his inferior. On the same ground the episodes in *Don Quixote*, in spite of the praise bestowed on them, appeared to him trifling beside the serious tales of Boccaccio. Similarly, he declared that his own contemporaries might learn the meaning of true sentiment from such a story as that of the falcon, and he recommended it to Byron, so that he might 'get rid of his hard *bravura* taste, and swashbuckler conclusions'. 'Had Frederigo Alberigi had an aviary of Hawks, and preserves of pheasants without end', Hazlitt adds,

he and his poor bird would never have been heard of. It is not the expence and ostentation of the entertainment he set before his mistress, but the prodigality of affection, squandering away the last remains of his once proud fortunes, that stamps this beautiful incident on the remembrance of all who have ever read it.[1]

There are many such tributes scattered among Hazlitt's writings, but for the fullest and most coherent exposition of his opinions about Boccaccio we must turn to his review of Sismondi's *Literature of the South of Europe* in 1815. He begins by criticising the author on the ground that he seems to be more devoted to the modern writers of Italy than to 'those who appear to us objects of greater curiosity and admiration', namely, Dante, Petrarch and Boccaccio. Then he proceeds to blame Sismondi for losing so fine an opportunity of doing Boccaccio the justice which the world had till then denied him.

He has in general passed for a mere narrator of lascivious tales or idle jests. This character probably originated in the early popularity of his attacks on the monks, and has been kept up by the grossness of mankind, who revenged their own want of refinement on Boccacio, and only saw in his writings what suited the coarseness of their own tastes. But the truth is, that he has carried sentiment of every kind to its very highest purity and perfection. By sentiment we would here understand the habitual workings of some one powerful feeling, where the heart reposes almost entirely upon itself, without the violent excitement of opposing duties or untoward circumstances.[2]

After this definition Hazlitt indicates those tales which best seem to illustrate his opinion:

In this way, nothing ever came up to the story of Frederigo Alberigi and his falcon. The perseverance in attachment, the spirit of gallantry and generosity displayed in it, has no parallel in the history of heroical sacrifices. The feeling

---

[1] *London Magazine*, 1821. Cf. Waller and Glover, xi, 501–2.
[2] *Edinburgh Review*, 1815. Cf. Waller and Glover, x, p. 68.

is so unconscious too, and involuntary, is brought out in such small, unlooked-for, and unostentatious circumstances, as to show it to have been woven into the very nature and soul of the author. The story of Isabella is scarcely less fine, and is more affecting in the circumstances and the catastrophe. Dryden has done justice to the impassioned eloquence of the Tancred and Sigismunda; but has not given an adequate idea of the wild preternatural interest of the story of Honoria. Cimon and Iphigene is by no means one of the best, notwithstanding the popularity of the subject. The proof of unalterable affection given in the story of Jeronymo, and the simple touches of nature and picturesque beauty in the story of the two holiday lovers, who were poisoned by tasting of a leaf in the garden at Florence, are perfect masterpieces. The epithet of Divine was well bestowed on this great painter of the human heart.[1]

Even if by any chance Hazlitt's previous championing of Boccaccio had passed unnoticed, so stirring a plea could hardly escape the attention of men of letters. But, as if to make doubly certain, two years later Hazlitt transferred these remarks bodily to his *Characters of Shakespeare*, where, in spite of the effort to relate them to *All's Well That Ends Well*, they form an obvious digression.[2]

On consideration of what he had already said of Boccaccio, it seems to have occurred to Hazlitt that there was one trait in the tales which had been neglected, and that was their poetic quality. He hastened to make good the omission in his *Lectures on the English Poets* which he delivered in the first two months of 1818. Speaking of poetry in general, he asserted that metre does not constitute the whole difference between verse and prose, and as instances of prose works which bordered on poetry he quoted *The Pilgrim's Progress, Robinson Crusoe* and the tales of Boccaccio. 'Chaucer and Dryden', he goes on,

have translated some of the last into English rhyme, but the essence and the power of poetry was there before. That which lifts the spirit above the earth, which draws the soul out of itself with indescribable longings, is poetry in kind, and generally fit to become so in name, by being 'married to immortal verse'.[3]

Since the poetic spirit was thus inherent in Boccaccio's stories, it was but natural that an attempt should be made to lend them poetic form, and Hazlitt recommended that the example set by Chaucer and Dryden should be followed in his own day:

I should think that a translation of some of the other serious tales in Boccaccio and Chaucer, as that of Isabella, the Falcon, of Constance, the Prioress's Tale, and others, if executed with taste and spirit, could not fail to succeed.[4]

As a critic of Boccaccio, Hazlitt has limitations which are readily perceived. Of his works other than the *Decameron* he knew little or

---

[1] *Edinburgh Review*, 1815.   [2] Cf. Waller and Glover, i, pp. 331–2.
[3] Ibid. v, pp. 13–14.   [4] Ibid., v, p. 82.

nothing, and on the one occasion when he alluded to them, he dismissed them airily as 'epic poems and theology'. Even in dealing with the *Decameron* his range is narrow. He confines himself to some ten out of the hundred tales. Most of these have romantic love as their theme, and it is upon this slender basis that he builds up his generalisations. It has also to be remembered that for the most part Hazlitt founded his opinions, as is shown by the forms of the names that he uses, on the English translation which was first published in 1620. As a result he sees this work only through the veil cast over it by the translator. To some extent this explains the notable difference between his estimate and that of Coleridge. Yet even if allowance be made for the distorting effect of the English intermediary, Hazlitt's picture is obviously one-sided, the conception of an advocate and not of a judge. But so doughty a champion could not fail to leave a mark. The reiteration of his personal impressions exercised a potent influence on the choice of themes by various nineteenth-century poets in making their adaptations from Boccaccio, and helped to shape the opinions of a critic like Leigh Hunt.

It is uncertain when Hunt first began to read Boccaccio, but he had learnt Italian before he was arrested for his attack on the Prince Regent, and the pages of the *Parnaso Italiano* helped to while away the term of his imprisonment. By 1818 his knowledge was sufficient for him to pick and choose among Italian writers. He preferred Boiardo and Pulci to Ariosto, but it seemed to him that Petrarch, Boccaccio and Dante were the greatest of them all. In his enthusiasm he urged Shelley to become familiar with the author of the *Decameron*. Hence his request to Mary Shelley that she should make her husband carry out his promise. In particular Shelley was to read

the tales of the Falcon: of the Pot of Basil, of the king who came to kiss the young girl that was sick for love of him; and of the lover who returned and found his mistress married on account of false reports of him, and who coming in upon her at night-time, and begging her to let him lie down a little by her side, without disturbing her husband, quietly broke his heart there.[1]

This admonition bore fruit, and a letter from Shelley in 1819 shows that the *Decameron* was known to him in the original. He was about to set out for Florence and wished that Hunt would join him there. They would try, he says,

to muster up a 'lièta briganta',[2] which, leaving behind them the pestilence of remembered misfortunes, might act over again the pleasures of the Interlocutors in Boccaccio.[3]

After telling Hunt that he has of late been reading 'this most divine

---

[1] Cf. *The Correspondence of Leigh Hunt*, ed. by his Eldest Son, London, 1862, 2 vols., i, 150. [2] i.e. 'brigata'. [3] *The Correspondence of Leigh Hunt*, i, 150.

writer', he announces that Boccaccio's 'serious theories of love' agree with his own.[1] Hunt may well have felt some astonishment at Shelley's discovery of this community of ideas, but, on the birth of his son Percy, made a jesting allusion to the matter, saying, 'kiss my new friend for me twenty times, and its mother (Boccaccione volente) twenty more'.

In the spring of 1820 someone lent to Hunt Count Baldelli's *Vita di Boccaccio*. The views which this little volume contained of places described in the poet's works, doubtless contributed to Hunt's decision in the autumn of the following year to escape from his troubles at home to the land of such pleasing memories. At Pisa he saw the Arno, 'the river of Dante, Petrarch and Boccaccio', and although it was shrunken in the summer drought and sandy-coloured, it was 'the river of the great Tuscan writers, the visible possessor of the name we have all heard a thousand times'. The name of Byron's house in which Hunt stayed at Genoa set him wondering whether this Casa Saluzzi had any connexion with the 'Markis of Saluces' who married Griselda, for 'classical and romantic associations abound so at every turn in Italy that upon the least hint a book speaketh'. Hunt was conscious of this when he lodged at Florence in the Via delle Belle Donne, hard by the church of Santa Croce; he was aware of it again as he walked outside the city, when 'Fiesole and Boccaccio burst upon me from the hills', and he was doubly aware of it once he had settled at Maiano. Such was his veneration for Boccaccio that he regretted the changes which the landscape had undergone since his time and would gladly have sacrificed some of the vines and olives for the restoration of the woodland and the lake in the Valley of Ladies. Speaking of the intimate relation between Boccaccio's works and Maiano, he says:

That many-hearted writer . . . was so fond of the place, that he has not only laid the two scenes of the *Decameron* on each side of it, with the valley which his company resorted to in the middle, but has made the two little streams that embrace Maiano, the Affrico and the Mensola, the hero and heroine of his *Nimphale Fiesolano*. A lover and his mistress are changed into them, after the fashion of Ovid. The scene of another of his works [the *Ameto*] is on the banks of the Mugnone, a river a little distant; and the *Decameron* is full of the neighbouring villages.[2]

Out of the windows of one side of Hunt's home he saw the turret of the Villa Gherardi, to which, according to Boccaccio's biographers, his 'joyous company' retired in the first instance from plague-stricken Florence. From the other side he could see Fiesole, where Boccaccio's father had owned a house; at his feet lay the Valley of Ladies, and

[1] He then quotes from the end of *Dec.* ii, 7, the words already mentioned. Vide ante, p. 336.

[2] *Autobiography*, Ch. 21. A useful modern edition of Hunt's *Autobiography* is that edited by J. E. Morpurgo, London, 1949.

farther away the Mugnone and the mountains of Pistoia. From his study, where Baldelli's *Life* lay on the table, he looked over the castellated top of Boccaccio's house to vineyards and olive groves, with the valley of the Arno and the Apennines in the distance. The view of Florence from the terrace, 'clear and cathedralled', was declared by Hazlitt 'a sight to enrich the eyes', but Hunt for his part clung to his Boccaccian haunts as to an old home.

I lived with the true human being, with his friends of the *Falcon* and the *Basil*, and my own not unworthy melancholy; and went about the flowering lanes and hills, solitary indeed, and sick to the heart, but not unsustained . . . My almost daily walk was to Fiesole, through a path skirted with wild myrtle and cyclamen; and I stopped at the cloister of the Doccia, and sat on the pretty melancholy platform behind it, reading or looking through the pines down to Florence.[1]

Owing to illness and anxiety, Hunt was plunged at times into dejection. He forgot his early conception of Italy as an earthly Paradise, 'the land of perpetual sunshine, and fruits, and flowers, and mountain walks, and Petrarch, and Ariosto, and Boccaccio, 'for he had seen lemon and orange groves languishing in a bitter wind and olives yearning this way and that, and bristling with cold. Even in Tuscany clouds veiled the skies in June, and heavy showers were not the less drenching, nor the gusts less boisterous, because they sped from behind Boccaccio's house. On other occasions he grew weary of the long summer and would gladly have exchanged the dusty vineyards for leafy lanes and green meadows. He missed the towering oak and elm, and longed for a stroll through hayfields in June, to revel in woods and grass and wild flowers. In such a mood he would exclaim:

We have the best part of Italy in books; and this we can enjoy in England. Give me Tuscany in Middlesex or Berkshire, and the Valley of Ladies between Harrow and Jack Straw's Castle. The proud names and flinty ruins above the Mensola may keep their distance. Boccaccio shall build a bower for us out of his books, of all that we choose to import; and we will have daisies and fresh meadows besides.[2]

However, Hunt was not always thus engaged in translating himself from his exile back to England. The discovery of some English trees and even a meadow in the Valley of Ladies enabled him to effect a compromise, for these,

while I made them furnish me with a bit of my old home in the north, did no injury to the memory of Boccaccio, who is of all countries, and who finds his home wherever we do ourselves, in love, in the grave, in a desert island.[3]

Another sight which gave Hunt a singular pleasure was that of a flock of pigeons careering about the hamlet of Fiesole and flashing

---

[1] *Autobiography*, Ch. 21.   [2] Ibid.   [3] Ibid.

white in and out of the green trees. As he watched, he could not help
fancying that they were the souls of the gentle company in the
Decameron, come to enjoy their old haunts in peace. It seemed to
him that no falcon would attack them, because of the beautiful story
which they had told of him. Yet even with these graceful literary
associations Hunt could not repress a longing now and then for a walk
over the fields at Hampstead, and when the time of his departure came,
he left Maiano without regret. But he was steeped in Boccaccio, and
the scenes about him on the homeward journey were coloured by his
reminiscences. Thus at Poirino he saw issuing from two coaches a
group of Dominican friars, each holding a bottle of wine in his hand,
while the abbot at their head held two, and the spectacle recalled some
of the jovial figures in the *Decameron*.

There were, however, other works of Boccaccio with which Hunt was
acquainted, and in this respect he occupies a remarkable position among
English writers after the Jacobean age, for since that period attention
had for the most part been directed to the hundred tales. In addition
to the *Ninfale Fiesolano*, to which he refers in connexion with his
account of Maiano, he had read Boccaccio's life of Dante. He likewise
knew the *Ameto*, which he had before him as he wrote to Shelley in
the spring of 1820. In his 'Criticism of Female Beauty' he afterwards
drew from it illustrations of the mediæval ideal of womanly beauty.
He had also read *De genealogia deorum*, and one is led to surmise
whether it was not through him that Shelley heard about the figure
of Demogorgon.[1] Hunt describes the book as 'a work of prodigious
erudition for that age, and full of the gusto of a man of genius', and
while he points out that Boccaccio could not help laughing at the
credulity of the ancients in making a god of so squalid a creature as
Demogorgon, he thinks that he must have had a lurking respect for
him, 'inasmuch as mud and dirt are among the elements of things
material, and therefore partake of a certain mystery and divineness'.
The *Teseida* was yet another work that came to Hunt's notice. In 1820
he had not seen it, and in speaking of Chaucer's *Knight's Tale* he
mentions how greatly neglected the Italian source had been, so that
the Italians, according to his belief, were as unfamiliar with it as
foreigners. His ignorance at this stage, however, did not deter Hunt
from the following comment:

Chaucer thought it worth his while to be both acquainted with it, and to
make others so: and we may venture to say, that we know of no Italian after
Boccaccio's age who was so likely to understand him to the core, as his English
admirer, Ariosto not excepted. Still, from what we have seen of Boccaccio's
poetry, we can imagine the Theseide to have been too lax and long. If Chaucer's

---

[1] Vide ante, pp. 37–41.

Palamon and Arcite be all that he thought proper to distil from it, it must have been greatly so; for it was a large epic. But at all events the essence is an exquisite one. The tree must have been a fine old enormity, from which such a honey could be drawn.[1]

When Hunt had actually seen the *Teseida*, its prolixity merely served to heighten his admiration of Chaucer's skill as a narrator and to establish the conclusion which before he had arrived at mainly by guesswork. It was now clear to him that Boccaccio was not a great poet, though he was great and of a poetical nature, for his 'heart and nature were poems; but he could not develop them well in verse'.[2]

For Boccaccio as a writer of prose and for the personality that lay behind it, Hunt nevertheless felt the highest respect. He was attracted to this tender genius, the 'lover of books and gardens', whose 'sweetness of nature' was everywhere manifest. At the sight of roses covering the front of a cottage in winter his thoughts would wander to Boccaccio's tale of the magician who conjured up a fragrant garden in January, and when imagining a heaven for himself, he desired to hear another *Decameron*, told by the master of simple pathos. It was his great pleasure to recall these tales, whether in the original or in the adaptations of Dryden, Keats or Barry Cornwall, while Landor's *Pentameron*, 'a book of the profoundest humanity', with its portrayal of Dante, Petrarch and Boccaccio, was for him an unfailing source of delight.

In his insistence on 'the nobler character of Boccaccio' Hunt openly acknowledged himself a follower of Hazlitt, whom he regarded as a torch-bearer who had dispelled the darkness in which the true spirit of the great writer had long been enshrouded. This achievement was all the more remarkable, because in his opinion the modern Italians had shown no understanding of Boccaccio's real merits:

His greatest admirers talk of little but his mirth, his knowledge of the knavish part of the world, and his style. If an ecclesiastic defends him, it is upon the ground of his affording warnings to young men, and of his not meaning any thing against the church. Eulogiums on his style always follow as a matter of course. Nothing is said, or said with any real conviction, of all those delightful pictures of innocent love, tenderness, and generosity, which are enough to keep some of the finest parts of our nature young and healthy.[3]

Like most of his English contemporaries, Hunt was above all drawn to Boccaccio's tales of high sentiment, and he believed that in this respect he was recapturing what had appealed to Petrarch and Chaucer but what had eluded Dryden with all his brilliance. In his praise of Boccaccio, Hunt at times appears faintly cloying, and one misses the

---

[1] Cf. 'May-Day' in *The Indicator*, xxix, 26 April 1820.

[2] Cf. *Essays by Leigh Hunt*, ed. A. Symons, London, 1887, p. 81.

[3] *Bacchus in Tuscany, A Dithyrambic Poem, from the Italian of Francesco Redi, with notes original and select. By Leigh Hunt.* See the 'Notes', pp. 135–6.

2A

definite critical principles of Coleridge and the virile appreciation of Hazlitt. Nevertheless, he wrote with considerable knowledge of Boccaccio's works as a whole and with intimacy and charm of their Tuscan setting.

It was in 1823 that Bryan Waller Procter, a friend of Leigh Hunt, published 'The Letter of Boccaccio',[1] using, as was his practice, the pen-name 'Barry Cornwall'. The letter is supposed to be addressed to Fiammetta from Florence in the latter part of Boccaccio's life. It has very little relation to reality and gives a romantic interpretation of his life and mind. It may be granted that far less was known about him at the beginning of the nineteenth century than at present, but Cornwall did not exert himself in the least to provide a solid foundation of such information as was then available.

In this epistle, which reflects the personality of Procter far more than his own, Boccaccio recalls his last meeting at Naples with Fiammetta and his promise to tell her the story of his life. This is merely an awkward device to introduce the survey which Boccaccio proceeds to make. After a vague account of his childhood he tells of his studies with Cino, of his becoming a monk and his abandonment of the monastic calling to lead a dissolute life in Florence. He rejected the Carthusian's counsel and would hear nothing of faith or true love:

> So, misted by a strange voluptuous air,
> I travelled on in intellectual gloom.[2]
>
> (p. 137)

A transformation was wrought by his genuine love for Olympia who lived not far from Florence. The simplicity of her cottage and the beauty of her silvan environment were in keeping with the purity of her character. The personality of Olympia is invested with the fragrance of

> citron woods that shook out vast perfume,
> And myrtles dowried with their richest bloom.
>
> (p. 139)

Her premature death left Boccaccio a sad and serious man.

His visit to Naples served to distract his mind from its grief, and Procter describes vividly what a revelation it was for this native of northern Italy to see

> Its blue skies and Palladian palaces,
> (Like Eastern dreams,)—statues and terraces,
> And columns lustrous with poetic thought;
> All filled with groups arrayed in antique dress,
> (Nymphs and Arcadian shapes, gods, goddesses)

---

[1] In *The Flood of Thessaly, The Girl of Provence, and other Poems*.
[2] Quotations from the first edition.

From base to palmy capital marble-wrought,
And colonnades of marble, fountain-cool,
Amongst whose labyrinthine aisles the breeze
Roamed at its will, and gardens green, and trees
Fruited with gold, and walks of cypresses,
Where Revel held her reign (a gay misrule)
Nightly beneath the stars. And there the seas
Which wander in and out thy sunny bay,
Soothe Ischia and the crowned Procida,
Bright islands, with a thousand harmonies . . .

(p. 141)

Finally, Boccaccio traces his development after leaving Naples and indulges in a prophetic vision of the future.

Incidentally, Procter analyses Boccaccio's relations with Fiammetta who is exhibited in a light alien to the author of *Amorosa Fiammetta*. Though her beauty is extolled, it is above all her spiritual qualities that are emphasised. The church where Boccaccio first saw her affects the whole conception of her nature. With the solemn sound of the pealing organ is blended a song that appears to come from the lips of a priestess, lost in holy aspiration. Her gaze is turned skywards, and Boccaccio is spellbound until

At last, a fine and undulating motion,
Like that of some sea-bloom which with the ocean
Moveth, surprized thee in thy holy lair,
And stole thee out of silence, lady fair!
I saw thee go,—scarce touching the cold earth,
As beautiful as Beauty at her birth,
Sea-goddess, when from out the foam she sprung
Full deity, and all the wide world hung
Mute and in marvel at perfection born.

(p. 145)

The acquaintance that followed ripened into love, but not sensuous passion. Rather Boccaccio figures as a grave humanist who, with Fiammetta as his disciple, reads Petrarch as well as Homer and other great writers of Greece. He develops her intellect and guides her to truth. She stands forth to all time, not as a notable example of fierce sexual desire, but as one whose function it was

To lift low passion from its brute despair,
And save the poetry of love from dying.

(p. 150)

Consequently, when Boccaccio departed from Naples, though the separation from Fiammetta cost him many a pang, he mastered his pain and found that his mind was free and that he could scan life with piercing sight. The humanist becomes the philosopher. He has forgotten the past, but now and then the old memories return, and he is filled with longing for bygone, happy days.

It is significant that when Boccaccio recalls Fiammetta it is against a background of natural beauty, even as he had done with Olympia, and the time when these memories steal upon him is usually the hour of sunset. Then he conjures up the bay of Naples and its islands, washed by a sunlit, glassy sea, or Fiammetta in the palace garden culling flowers for a garland, the rising moon seen through the cedar-tree at twilight, riding among stars and clouds. More than once Boccaccio contrasts the scenery of Florence with that of Naples, always to the advantage of the latter, because he prefers the sea to an inland landscape of wood and hill, meadow and river. In all these passages Procter is obviously injecting his own feelings into the soul of Boccaccio. More directly he ascribes to the mediæval writer the sensibility of the nineteenth century when he explains his flight from monastic life as the longing of a nature-lover to escape into the open:

> I was forest-bred,
> And loved to wander in my infancy,
> And made a young acquaintance with the sky,
> With rocks and streams, rich fruits and blushing flowers,
> And fed upon the looks of Morning, when
> She parteth with the beauty of the Hours.
>
> (pp. 135–6)

Attractive as some of these episodes are, they tend to disturb the balance of the poem. In other respects the discursive tendency is still more evident. The homage to Petrarch in connexion with the account of Fiammetta's reading is disproportionate. The praise of the *Decameron* is also too long, though Boccaccio may be forgiven for his confident declaration that it will prove an inspiration to future generations. He maintains that great men will treasure it and that their fame will mingle with his for all time. He predicts that his renown

> shall be seen from shore to shore,
> And heralded by spirits who shall soar
> On their own wings and mine unto the sky,
> Supremest poets, who can never die.
>
> (p. 135)

Though one may feel that such passages could profitably have been curtailed, they are not altogether irrelevant. However, there are parts of the poem which destroy the artistic unity of the whole. Thus on the pretext that Florence in comparison with Naples was a bellicose state, Procter indulges in a long tirade against war. Here and again at the close, when Boccaccio looks forward to an age of universal peace and social equality, it is manifest that he is simply the mouthpiece for

Procter's opinions and aspirations. There is indeed some affinity between Procter and Shelley, but the honest sentiment of the one is of very different potency from the fervent idealism of the other, and the prophecies attributed to Boccaccio are trivial compared with the visions of Shelley in *Hellas* and *Prometheus Unbound*.

Landor resembles Procter in the adoption of a fictional device to present his interpretation of Boccaccio, but he had the advantage of knowing more about him and the scene of his activities, for circumstances had cast his own lot in the surroundings which were closely associated with Boccaccio's name and work. When Hunt was living at Maiano, Landor occupied the Palazzo Medici at Florence, and in 1829 he bought the Villa Gherardescha at Fiesole 'upon the spot where Boccaccio led his women to bathe when they had left the first scene of their story-telling'. Above stood the convent of the Doccia, overshadowed with cypress, the Valley of the Ladies formed part of his estate, and in his grounds, luxuriant in vine, fig and olive, ran the Affrico and Mensola. He describes the spot thus:

> Where the hewn rocks of Fiesole impend
> O'er Doccia's dell, and fig and olive blend.
> There the twin streams in Affrico unite,
> One dimly seen, the other out of sight,
> But ever playing in his smoothen'd bed
> Of polisht stone, and willing to be led
> Where clustering vines protect him from the sun,
> Never too grave to smile, too tired to run.
> Here, by the lake, Boccaccio's *Fair Brigade*
> Beguiled the hours, and tale for tale repaid.[1]

This spot, so rich in memories, was to Landor an inestimable treasure, and he prized its possession greatly. He speaks of the splendour of Italian skies that

> o'er Boccaccio's happy valley shone,
> Valley which I, as happy, call'd my own,[2]

and would fain have remained there with friends and children. But

> Its quiet was not destined to be mine;
> 'Twas hard to keep, 'twas harder to resign.[3]

Before he took a final leave of this tranquil scene, he wrote these lines:

> Run glibly on, my little Affrico,
> Content to cool the feet of weary hind
> On thy smooth pavement, strown for him with moss;
> Regretting not thy vanisht lake, and maids
> Aside its bank, each telling tale for tale;
> Revert thee rather, and with pride record
> Here blythe Boccaccio led his *Fair Brigade*.[4]

[1] Cf. Welby, xvi, p. 36.
[3] Ibid., xvi, p. 36.
[2] Ibid., xv, p. 297.
[4] Ibid., xv, p. 236.

To have lived long years in this environment engendered in Landor a peculiar sense of intimacy with the author of the *Decameron*. The fact that Boccaccio had criticised the conduct of the monks and had been criticised in return also helped to win the sympathy of one who was even more consistently anti-clerical. How highly Landor esteemed Boccaccio may be gathered from his praise of the *Decameron* as an immortal work, next in rank to *The Divine Comedy*, and although in power of uttering his thoughts in metrical form, Boccaccio seemed inferior to Petrarch, Landor maintained that he was more liberally endowed with fancy and imagination. 'There are stories in the *Decameron*', he says,

which require more genius to conceive and execute than all the poetry of Petrarca, and indeed there is in Boccaccio more variety of the mental powers than in any of his countrymen, greatly more deep feeling, greatly more mastery over the human heart, than in any other but Dante.[1]

Landor does not hesitate to condemn some of the tales which appeared to him so coarse that modesty must cast them aside and only the depraved can receive any amusement from them. But 'in the greater part' he exclaims,

what truthfulness, what tenderness, what joyousness, what purity! Their levities and gaieties are like the harmless lightnings of a summer sky in the delightful regions they were written in.[2]

Other impressions of Boccaccio are conveyed indirectly in the imaginary conversations between Boccaccio and Petrarca and between these two and Chaucer. In the first the humanity of Boccaccio is emphasised, when he tolerantly declares that a man without vices and infirmities would not be worth knowing, for he would be void of tenderness and compassion, and so his friends could expect no allowance to be made for their own frailties, nor sympathy in their misfortunes. In the second Landor brings out the preoccupation of Boccaccio with the world about him rather than with the supernatural. Doubtless he felt that in this respect there was an affinity between him and Chaucer, and he would have understood Keats's confession 'Wonders are no wonders to me. I am more at home amongst men and women. I would rather read Chaucer than Ariosto'. In view of Boccaccio's lively interest in his fellows it is only natural that Landor should make him dismiss the marvellous as 'the commonest pedlary of the markets, and the joint patrimony of the tapsters', whereas he admits his preference for such events as will admit us into the recesse of the human mind. Landor also seeks to indicate what early English

[1] *The Foreign Quarterly Review*, 1843, 'Francesco Petrarca'. Cf. Welby, xii, p. 42
[2] 'Francesco Petrarca'. Cf. Welby, xii, p. 46.

literature had to learn from Boccaccio, when he places these words in Chaucer's mouth:

I will attempt to show Englishmen what Italians are; how much deeper in thought, intenser in feeling, and richer in imagination, than ever formerly: and I will try whether we can not raise poetry under our fogs, and merriment among our marshes.[1]

The most elaborate presentation of Boccaccio, however, is in the *Pentameron* which had been begun in Fiesole, though by the time of its publication in 1837 Landor had returned to England. With memories of Boccaccio crowding so thickly upon him he conceived the work which served to distract his thoughts from the cares that weighed upon him. He depicts Boccaccio as vowing during an illness that, if he recovers, he will acknowledge God's mercy by burning the *Decameron*. Having learnt of this, Petrarch comes to dissuade him from so immense a sacrifice. During his five days' visit they discuss many topics, in the course of which Landor's conception of Boccaccio is fully revealed through Petrarch. Boccaccio is extolled as the most creative and imaginative genius that Italy has produced, one who has displayed in his writings more character, more nature, more invention than either Greece or Italy had ever seen. In spite of the *Decameron*'s faults, 'Would you consume a beautiful meadow because there are reptiles in it; or because a few grubs hereafter may be generated by the succulence of the grass?'[2] Petrarch recognises that some of the tales are too licentious but refuses to agree with the severe moralist in claiming that they lead to excesses. He goes so far as to contend that some ardent spirits will be content with reading Boccaccio when they would otherwise appease their excitement by action. Nevertheless, he wishes that the indecorous element could be eliminated. Nor would this entail a drastic alteration, for only some twelve or thirteen tales would be affected. Criticism of Boccaccio's style is also implied when Petrarca advises him not to be too ceremonious in the structure of his sentences; the modulations of voice and language being infinite, a writer should adapt himself to them with equal flexibility. He rejects Boccaccio's plea for the imitation of such authors as Cicero, declaring that to copy him would not enable a man to attain consummate mastery. Rather he should enter into the mind and heart of his own creatures and, thinking of them alone, pay no heed to style in itself.

In his strictures on the lack of decorum in the *Decameron* Landor is at one with Coleridge, though his condemnation is less sweeping and more reasonable. His comments on Boccaccio's style likewise have

[1] *Imaginary Conversations*, 1829, i, 214. Cf. Welby, ii, p. 247.
[2] Cf. Welby, ix, p. 152.

much in common with those of Coleridge. On the other hand, he agrees with Hazlitt in regarding him as a supreme artist in portraying the emotions and above all in conveying a sense of pathos. In his treatment of the horrible, Landor holds that in some ways he is to be preferred to Dante, for Ugolino affects us like a skeleton, by dry, bony verity, and if the reception of Guiscardo's heart by Ghismonda or of Lorenzo's head by Lisabetta had been so nakedly described, it would have been unbearable. But the eulogy is not undiscriminating:

Lisabetta should by no means have been represented cutting off the head of her lover, '*as well as she could*' with a clasp-knife.[1] This is shocking and improbable. She might have found it already cut off by her brothers, in order to bury the corpse more commodiously and expeditiously. Nor indeed is it likely that she should have intrusted it to her waiting-maid, who carried home in her bosom a treasure so dear to her, and found so unexpectedly and so lately.[2]

However, the criticism of such details does not blind Landor to the skill of Boccaccio in general. He finds a conspicuous example of his art in the tale which follows that of Lorenzo and Lisabetta. In the story of Andrevuola and Gabriotto the narrator contrives to work upon the reader's feelings by merely suggesting the horrible, as in a dream, when 'le pareva veder del corpo di lui uscire una cosa oscura e terribile', while he afterwards casts a spell upon him by introducing palpable forms and pleasing colours to relieve and soothe: 'E avendo molte rose bianche e vermiglie colte, perciocchè la stagione era'.

Landor does well to insist on this point, and his remarks show much insight. But above all it is Boccaccio's power of drawing every kind and condition of men that appeals to him. His range is astonishing; none but a genius could have exhibited the wise, the witty and the simple as he has done. Though Dante may have more fire and energy, Boccaccio has an equal command over the depths of thought and the treasure of fancy and surpasses him in variety and animation, and in naturalness and veracity of characterisation. Landor goes still farther and asserts that in vivacity and versatility of imagination, in the narrative and the descriptive, in the playful and the pathetic, the world never saw his equal before Shakespeare.

Ariosto and Spenser may stand at no great distance from him in the shadowy and unsubstantial; but multiform Man was utterly unknown to them. The human heart, through all its foldings, vibrates to Boccaccio.[3]

It was chiefly these immortal creations of the *Decameron* that won Landor's devotion. To Boccaccio's other work he paid but little heed.

---

[1] Boccaccio, of course, does not speak of a 'clasp-knife' but 'un coltello'.
[2] Cf. Welby, ix, p. 166.   [3] Ibid., p. 288.

No doubt the love of Fiammetta and Boccaccio[1] inspired some of Landor's finest prose when he described the poet's dream of her, but the figures that hovered in his memory were those of the hundred tales:

we can scarcely walk in any quarter from the gates of Florence, without the recollection of some witty or affecting story related by you. Every street, every farm, is peopled by your genius: and this population can not change with seasons or with ages, with factions or with incursions. Ghibellines and Guelphs will have been contested for only by the worms, long before the *Decameron* has ceased to be recited on our banks of blue lilies and under our arching vines. Another plague may come amidst us: and something of a solace in so terrible a visitation would be found in your pages, by those to whom letters are a refuge and relief.[2]

If there were English exiles in Italy who admired Boccaccio, they had their Italian counterparts in England. One of the best known was Gabriele Rossetti. Under the sway of his experiences in the insurrectionary agitations that broke out in the kingdom of Naples in 1820 and 1821, he persuaded himself that during the Middle Ages there existed a secret movement,[3] with ramifications in many countries, among them Italy, France and England. He believed that it had an anti-papal bias, and so its adherents, the Knights Templar, were severely handled with the approval of Rome. Dante, Petrarch and Boccaccio were among the initiated, and Petrarch in particular, having relations with so many writers at home and abroad, occupied a central position. According to Rossetti, it was to him that Chaucer fled from the wrath of the Catholic clergy in England. Like the great Italian writers, Chaucer was a cryptic poet whose words conveyed to those who had the clue far more than appeared on the surface.

Rossetti claims that Boccaccio was well aware of the profound secret and justifies his opinion by the sympathetic attitude shown towards the Knights Templar in *De casibus virorum illustrium*. They were 'la nostra schiera', 'i nostri',[4] which Rossetti takes as meaning members of the same party. He also lends a new aspect to Boccaccio's conversion by the Carthusian monk, Beato Petronio, when he ascribes it,

[1] It plays a part in Landor's drama, *Andrea of Hungary and Giovanna of Naples*, first published in 1839 (cf. Welby, xiii, pp. 279–341), where Boccaccio and Fiammetta lend a lyrical quality to scenes with a background of gardens. They appear again in *Giovanna of Naples*, also first published in 1839 (Welby, xiv, pp. 1–44), but the love theme is here quite subordinate. The poem 'Departure from Fiammetta' (Welby, xvi, p. 181) illustrates once more Landor's interest in this episode of Boccaccio's career. [2] Welby, ix, p. 251.

[3] *Sullo Spirito Antipapale che produsse la Riforma, e sulla segreta influenza ch' esercitò nella letteratura d'Europa, e specialmente d'Italia come risulta da molti suoi classici, massime da Dante, Petrarca, Boccaccio*, London, 1832.

[4] Rossetti is here quoting from the chapter 'Lodi della patientia' in Book ix of Giuseppe Betussi's translation.

not to remorse for the occasional indecency and the attacks on the Church in the *Decameron* but to the discovery of the organisation which he and Petrarch had joined.

Guided by these fantastic theories, Rossetti proceeded to examine the works of Boccaccio. Everywhere, even in the *Amorosa Visione* and the *Ninfale d'Ameto*, he finds support for his views. He maintains that the *Urbano* is intended to relate how Frederick I, the bitter opponent of the Papacy, was the first emperor to embrace the secret society. *Fiammetta* consists of 'seven mystic books'; the *Vita di Dante* is entirely in secret language and contains Dante's hidden life; the *Filocolo* is not a romance but a hieroglyphic commentary on the *Divine Comedy*, in which everything, however small, holds a secret. Even more important for Rossetti, however, was *De genealogia deorum*.[1] Here he found a happy hunting-ground, and he has recourse to it again and again, returning triumphant with some new booty. The fourteenth chapter was above all the one that attracted him because of its exposition of the allegorical interpretation of poetry.

To what strange conclusions Rossetti was led may be seen from a consideration of his remarks on the *Decameron*. He saw a mystical import in the numbers seven and ten, this being the number of the women narrators and that of the days on which tales were told. He dwelt at length on the seventh tale of the third day which he insisted on regarding as an episode in the life of Dante. Nor was he in the least perturbed by the fact that the learned Manni, who had ransacked every conceivable source for Boccaccio's tales, had failed to observe any such origin. Rossetti remarks that as a result his attribution might be thought fantastic, but he replies confidently: 'By no means; this, more than any other, has an historical foundation, since it is the life of the Florentine poet Dante as a member of the sect'. As one might expect, the three tales that mention Paradise, Purgatory and Hell,[2] are also seized on by Rossetti, though most readers will have difficulty in seeing any mystical intention in them, and the same is true of his attempt to twist the story of Guido Cavalcanti in the same direction.[3] Still more extraordinary is Rossetti's discussion of the tales of Rinaldo d'Asti[4] and Rinieri and Elena.[5] In each of these the hero is exposed to the bitter cold of a snowy night, and in the second he takes his revenge by exposing the lady that had caused his suffering to the heat of a summer sun. Rossetti will have it that the falling of snow is a symbol for papal persecution, and of the second tale he writes: 'A more bold and bitter satire was never written against the Roman Church and never will be'. Following this train of thought, he presents Griselda

---

[1] Vide ante, p. 43.   [2] iii, 4; iii, 8; iii, 10.
[3] vi, 9.   [4] ii, 2.   [5] viii, 7.

as another mystical figure, the aim of the story in which she appears being to recall the cruelty of Charles IV to the secret society. All writers who handled the tale of the long-suffering Griselda, and Rossetti evidently linked Chaucer with Petrarch and Boccaccio, were seeking to recommend to their persecuted sect patience for the present and hope for the future. Literary criticism practised in the manner of Rossetti can only lead to strange vagaries, and the interpretation of the *Decameron* on these lines would, as he says, 'produce the most curious book in the world'!

It may be doubted whether Rossetti's allegorical exposition ever was widely accepted. Nevertheless, he did find one follower in the anonymous author[1] of *Tales from Boccaccio* (1846), whose anti-Catholic prejudice was reinforced by Rossetti's bias. To most people, however, there can be little attraction in fantasies so ill-founded. But at least Gabriele Rossetti's studies did mean that his family grew up in an environment where Boccaccio was as familiar as Dante.

Like his father, Dante Gabriel Rossetti was interested in Boccaccio, partly because of the great mediæval writer's devotion to Dante. In his translation of the *Vita Nuova* and in *Dante and his Circle* Rossetti alludes to Boccaccio's *Life* and to his commentary on Dante. He is evidently attracted to him because he was 'so reverent a biographer' and dwelt on the *Divine Comedy* with an awe-filled admiration. It was this association with Dante that led Rossetti to translate two sonnets by Boccaccio, 'To one who had censured his public Exposition of Dante'[2] and 'Inscription for a Portrait of Dante,[3] both of which bear witness to Dante's greatness. In the *Decameron* too there was material that caught Rossetti's attention, because it threw light on Dante's contemporaries, Guido Cavalcanti and Cecco Angiolieri.[4]

However, he also appreciated the *Decameron* for its own sake and drew upon it for his pictures. The lines at the close of the seventh tale of the second day, 'Bocca baciata non perde ventura, anzi rinnuova come fa la luna',[5] gave him the idea for his oil-painting 'Bocca Baciata' in 1859. Nine years later he made an enlarged replica in water-colour, 'Bionda del Balcone'.[6] Undoubtedly Rossetti read his Boccaccio with the eye of a painter, and the rural scenes interspersed between the tales must have given him aesthetic satisfaction. In a sonnet by Boccaccio with a setting akin to these scenes he found a 'beauty of colour' that might recall the painted pastorals of Giorgione and 'a playful charm very characteristic of the author of the *Decameron*':

[1] Possibly J. C. Hobhouse. Vide post, p. 367.
[2] 'Se Dante piange, dove ch'el si sia.'
[3] 'Dante Alighieri son, Minerva oscura.' Vide ante, p. 33.
[4] *Dec.* vi, 9 and ix, 4. See *The Early Italian Poets.*
[5] Vide ante, pp. 336, 350. [6] Cf. Marillier, pp. 76–7; 154; 159.

By a clear well, within a little field
Full of green grass and flowers of every hue,
Sat three young girls, relating (as I knew)
Their loves. And each had twined a bough to shield
Her lovely face; and the green leaves did yield
The golden hair their shadow; while the two
Sweet colours mingled, both blown lightly through
With a soft wind for ever stirred and still'd.
After a little while one of them said,
(I heard her) 'Think! If, ere the next hour struck,
Each of our lovers should come here to-day,
Think you that we should fly or feel afraid?'
To whom the others answered, 'From such luck
A girl would be a fool to run away.'[1]

Another sonnet, translated by Rossetti, depicts a similar group in a typical Italian scene. The sun is high, the sea motionless, only a light breeze occasionally stirs the tree-tops, and as the poet takes refuge from the heat in a grove, he hears a voice so sweet that it sounds like a nymph, a goddess or an angel singing to herself.

And there my lady, 'mid the shadowings
Of myrtle-trees, 'mid flowers and grassy space,
Singing I saw, with others who sat around.[2]

This was the Fiammetta who kindled Rossetti's imagination. There can be no doubt that the love of Boccaccio for Fiammetta, like that of Dante for Beatrice, touched the poet who himself loved with an ardent devotion. He could therefore enter into the feelings of Boccaccio in his sonnet addressed to Dante in Paradise after Fiammetta's death, when he begs, through the great master, that she will pray for their speedy reunion.[3] Even more, however, Rossetti was impressed by the sonnet describing Boccaccio's last glimpse of Fiammetta:[4]

Round her red garland and her golden hair
I saw a fire about Fiammetta's head;
Thence to a little cloud I watched it fade,
Than silver or than gold more brightly fair;
And like a pearl that a gold ring doth bear,
Even so an angel sat therein, who sped
Alone and glorious throughout heaven, array'd
In sapphires and in gold that lit the air.
Then I rejoiced in hoping happy things,
Who rather should have then discerned how God
Had haste to make my lady all His own,

---

[1] 'Intorn' ad una fonte, in un pratello'. Cf. *The Works of Dante Gabriel Rossetti*, ed. W. M. Rossetti, London, 1911, p. 414.

[2] 'Guidommi Amor, ardendo ancora il sole.' Cf. *Works*, p. 413.

[3] 'Dante, se tu nell' amorosa spera.' Cf. *Works*, pp. 412–13.

[4] 'Sovra li fior vermigli e' capei d'oro.' Cf. *Works*, p. 413.

Even as it came to pass. And with these stings
Of sorrow, and with life's most weary load
I dwell, who fain would be where she is gone.

The surpassing loveliness and the resplendent colours of the vision, the buoyant hope too swiftly changed into bitter grief, the weary longing for reunion in Paradise—all this is faithfully conveyed by Rossetti.

Some little time after the tragic death of his wife in 1862 he painted a head of Fiammetta,[1] and in 1878 this was followed by an oil-painting called 'A Vision of Fiammetta'.[2] The picture sprang from the above sonnet of Boccaccio, but Rossetti treated the theme freely. The red garland and the cloud disappeared; instead we see Fiammetta standing under an apple-tree, holding in one hand a heavily-laden branch of blossom. Against the grey trunk her dull-red robe and reddish-brown hair stand out in relief, while her bright blue eyes contrast with the pink-white apple blossoms that surround her. Two bright blue butterflies and an aureole round her head add still more colour, while a bird hovers over her.[3] To accompany his picture Rossetti wrote a sonnet:

Behold Fiammetta, shown in Vision here.
    Gloom-girt 'mid Spring-flushed apple-growth she stands;
    And as she sways the branches with her hands,
Along her arm the sundered bloom falls sheer,
In separate petals shed, each like a tear;
    While from the quivering bough the bird expands
    His wings. And lo! thy spirit understands
Life shaken and shower'd and flown, and Death drawn near.

All stirs with change. Her garments beat the air:
    The angel circling round her aureole
    Shimmers in flight against the tree's grey bole.

The introduction of the tree shading the figure of Fiammetta is a deviation from Boccaccio and recalls a similar setting in other sonnets of his translated by Rossetti. By comparison with the original poem this version seems to have lost in glowing splendour, but to have acquired in exchange freshness and delicacy of colour. The spirit too is altered, for the simple mediæval faith embodied in the flight of the angel is obscured and replaced by the symbolism of the falling blossom, even as the poignant sorrow of Boccaccio is transmuted into hope and confidence:

While she, with reassuring eyes most fair,
A presage and a promise stands; as 'twere
    On Death's dark storm the rainbow of the Soul.[4]

[1] Marillier, p. 158.   [2] Ibid., p. 164.
[3] Ibid., p. 137 and the illustration facing p. 138. Also *Works*, p. 229.
[4] 'Fiammetta (For a Picture)'. See *Ballads and Sonnets*, London, 1881, p. 329, and *Works*, p. 229.

2. Tales in Verse

In 1805, while still an undergraduate at Cambridge, John Cam Hob-house adapted the tale of Masetto[1] and four years later he published it in *Imitations and Translations from the Ancient and Modern Classics*. He treats the story with some freedom, placing the convent in Genoa and eliminating the steward. In some places he is more discreet, but elsewhere he introduces such terms as 'punk' and 'whore' which are at variance in their coarseness with the graceful language of the original. What is more important, however, is the liberty that Hobhouse takes in introducing matter not found in his source. A quotation from Chaucer, a contemporary of Boccaccio, caused him no qualms, but the invocation of Pope's opinion on women he thought more daring.

> Chaucer, to female frailties blind,
> And much a friend to all the kind,
> A certain strange opinion hath,
> (You read it in the wife of Bath:)
> 'In every station, every hour,
> Woman is fondest still of power.'
> But Pope, a mighty master too,
> Opines their ruling passions two;
> And says, that all the sex obey
> The love of pleasure or of sway:
> That is, the sex (to say no more)
> Must play the tyrant or the whore.
> What moralist shall dare decide
> Between the powers of lust and pride?
> The men whose wanton wives elope,
> Agree, no doubt, with Mr. Pope.
> Whose mates are chaster much and crosser,
> Will give the preference to Dan Chaucer.[2]

Such an anachronism seemed to Hobhouse to call for an apology, and he defends it on the ground that 'only the outlines of the story in the original Italian are here imitated and preserved'. The same conten-tion would, of course, justify his allusion to the entanglement of Frederick, duke of York, with the adventuress Mary Anne Clarke, a public scandal at the time when the translation was made.

There is in fact a notable satirical bent in Hobhouse's version, and it is not for nothing that he cites among his authorities Chaucer and Pope. It is true that Boccaccio's tale has also an undercurrent of satire but it lies in a genial recognition that the weakness of the flesh is not confined to the laity. Hobhouse, on the other hand, writes as a Protes-tant and an apostle of enlightenment. In his hands the tale is given an anti-Catholic direction and at the close is turned into a burlesque:

---

[1] *Dec.* iii, 1.   [2] *Imitations and Translations etc.*, 1809, pp. 117–18.

> A mighty miracle behold,
> As great as those perform'd of old;
> By Mary's hairs, or Peter's toe,
> St. Bridget or Barromeo (sic!),
> To us the heavenly mercies reach,
> And give the dumb the power of speech.
>
> (p. 127)

Moreover, the faithful, who believe in a miracle which is no miracle but a conspicuous example of human frailty, are made the object of derisive laughter:

> And thus since then the deaf and dumb
> In crowds before the convent come;
> In pious hopes to gain their shares
> Of comfort by the vestals prayers:
> And like the blest Massetto prove
> The mighty power of heavenly love.
>
> (p. 128)

Some of the characteristics displayed in this adaptation are exhibited in *Tales from the Decameron*, which appeared in 1846. It contains 'The Abbot of Florence' and 'Salvestra'.[1] Although the volume is anonymous, there is good reason to believe that the author was Hobhouse.[2] His method is similar to that employed in 'The Miracle', but the practice of grafting contemporary allusions and a personal point of view on the old story is developed in a high degree. Nor does Hobhouse now feel constrained to offer any defence, perhaps because in the meantime Byron's *Don Juan* had provided a notable illustration of the brilliant success that might attend such a procedure.

The choice of 'The Abbot of Florence' was governed by the same considerations as had led Hobhouse to 'The Miracle'. The tale of the pious and naïve Ferando, duped by a cunning abbot who takes advantage of his supposed death and punishment in Purgatory to further his designs against Ferando's wife provided similar material. And at the close, as in the earlier poem, there was a miracle calculated to amuse the somewhat cynical translator. In the *Tales from Boccaccio*, however, the Protestant bias has become more sharply defined, and the bogey of Roman Catholicism haunts Hobhouse with such persistence that even in 'Salvestra' a wily and worldly priest, Père Lebrun, is allowed to intrude and seek to divert the thoughts of the faithful Girolamo from his love in Florence to the fair women of Paris. Both here and in the first tale the ecclesiastic is depicted as abusing his power of absolution with complete lack of scruple. In his introduction,

---

[1] *Dec.* iii, 8 and iv, 8.

[2] In what follows it is assumed that this is so. Cf. H. G. Wright, 'John Cam Hobhouse as the author of *Tales from Boccaccio with modern illustrations*', *M.L.R.*, 1948, xliii, pp. 84–8.

even more than in the text of the poem, Hobhouse reveals his animosity, the flames of which had been fanned by the Tractarian movement. He speaks bitterly of Pusey and Sewell, and although he does not mention Newman by name, it is evident that he regarded his conversion in 1845 as a betrayal. In these circumstances he thought the time ripe 'to review the testimony of a Boccaccio to the corruptions of the Church of Rome' and consequently he makes the extravagant assertion that 'The Abbot of Florence' is essentially a religious poem. In his eyes Boccaccio was 'proleptically a Protestant',[1] an enlightened thinker struggling against the forces of reaction and obscurantism. He presents the author of the *Decameron* as a liberator whose efforts to remedy the abuses of his age bring upon him the hatred of the religious. In short, he paints the same picture as Byron had done in *Childe Harold*[2] and as he himself was again to paint thirteen years later in *Italy*.[3]

As was only to be expected of so strong a Whig, Hobhouse imports not only his religious views but also his social and political sympathies into his versions. On occasion, with an amazing anachronism, he displays Ferando as an exponent of Tory morals and adds the comment:

> We now hear more than fifteen out of twenty gents,
>   Think duelling the Christian end of quarrels;
> And that by our prosperity is meant high rents:
>   In short, that all mankind are stupid squirrels,
> Who rush for ever round an iron cage
> Instead of going farther every age.
>
> (Canto II, st. xlvii)

And when Hobhouse crosses the Channel, despite the splendour of French society and its intellectual brilliance, this English Whig finds a sad falling off from the heroic courage of the Revolution. Once he had praised Napoleon at the expense of the Bourbons,[4] but now he condemns all Frenchmen for having abandoned the ideal of liberty and surrendered to him.

Hobhouse's dislike of absolute monarchy was strong, and when such a system in the reign of Nicholas I quelled the Polish rebellion with blood and terror, it intensified his opposition, as may be judged from these lines:

> They say, that Nicholas, the Russian czar
>   Flogged Polish ladies at the Insurrection
> When Warsaw threw his impious chains afar,
>   (A weak rehearsal of the resurrection),

---

[1] See the 'Sketch of the Life and Writings of Giovanni Boccaccio', p. xli, in *Tales from Boccaccio.*   [2] Canto IV, st. lviii. Vide ante, p. 337
[3] *Italy: Remarks made in several visits from the year 1816 to 1854*, pp. 241–9.
[4] Cf. *D.N.B.*, Art. 'John Cam Hobhouse'.

And tho' unarmed was maddened into war!
　　But fate and doctors like a large dissection,
So thousands died because a villain ruled:
While Saints maintained the human blood was cooled!
　　　　　　　　　　(Canto II, st. xlv)

But though he had little good to say of kings, Hobhouse was animated by very different feelings towards Queen Victoria. He could never forget that first council at Kensington Palace on 30 June 1837, of which he has left so excellent a description. It coloured his outlook in later years and created in him a genuine devotion:

Nations are often kept without their dinner—
　　(I wish they'd try this method on their kings),
But not upon our Queen; I would not thin her
　　Most gracious face for twenty sovereigns,
For, let me whisper (this ourselves between),
Like Melbourn I am too fond of the Queen!
　　　　　　　　　　(Canto II, st. xxxviii)

Of women in general Hobhouse had little good to say. It is significant that in 'Salvestra' Girolamo's mother is portrayed as hard and ambitious, with her thoughts on rank and money rather than on the happiness of her son. The Florentine merchant's widow is transformed into 'Lady Sighieri', and Hobhouse unkindly ascribes the death of Lionardo to the nightly curtain-lectures that she inflicted upon him. Gertrude, the wife of Ferando, is no less unpleasant. Her assertion that

　　　　　　　　if wedded peace were mine,
　　I should all wives in piety eclipse,
And nought save Watts' hymns should pass my lips
　　　　　　　　　　(Canto I, st. xxxvi)

is hardly borne out by her later conduct, and at the close there is a touch of malice in Hobhouse's account of the 'great resignation' with which she bore Ferando's return from his reputed sojourn in Purgatory. Ferando too, he hints, has suffered from the loquacity of his wife, which in fact is the fate of all married men:

We left our hero in a purgatory
　　Where every husband is, or else will be;—
Should any Caudle contradict my story,[1]
　　(And make an oath to his felicity—)
Adding, he's married been (memento mori!)
　　Of mortal years the space of twenty-three:
It proves he is accustomed to his Bedlam,
And feels the butcher's knife no more than dead lamb.
　　　　　　　　　　(Canto III, st. i)

---

[1] An allusion to Douglas Jerrold's *Mrs. Caudle's Curtain Lectures*, published like the *Tales from Boccaccio* in 1846.

2B

In another passage he describes the awakening of the poet from a mood of imaginative ecstasy and exaltation 'to critics, taxes, wives and kings', and in an outburst of high-spirited gaiety he tells how this knowledge of the disadvantages of wedlock enabled him to resist the allurements of women:

> once I felt to polygamy inclined,
> And thought of taking one or two wives more,
> But very fortunately changed my mind,
>   When just about to enter the Church door,
> By thinking if I had of wives a cart full,
> It would be rather more than even *my* heart full.
>
> (Canto II, st. xii)

It is unusual for him to speak of individual women among his contemporaries, but he does make an exception in favour of Lady Hester Stanhope, whose conversational power he eulogises, though sarcasm is mingled with admiration.[1]

However, his satirical power is directed more forcibly against men of letters. Powell's tragedies are ridiculed as a patchwork of scraps from Browning and Horne, and Horne himself is dismissed as 'dismal'. The poetry of Rogers is summed up as 'water-gruel', and on his return from Purgatory Ferando relates that the

> unpoetical old fellow,
> Beat off the Muses with his silk umbrella!
>
> (Canto III, st. xxxiv)

He had news too of an even more prominent figure and said

> that Wordsworth was made beadle
> And Poet Laureate to the spinster Nine;
> Moreover, that he still would spout, and read all
>   His ponderous verses to those nymphs divine!
> Apollo told his sisters they would need all
>   Their patience for his "Volume on the Rhine;"
> For having there to praise Victoria's cousins,
> He'd multiplied *his* dulness by *their* dozens!
>
> Whereat the bard waxed furious, and swore
>   That future ages should read every word,—
> In fact, he meant to write seven volumes more!
>   'Tis said, when poor posterity had heard
> The precious legacy they had in store,
>   They forthwith to Olympian Jove preferred
> Their prayer, that if events were thus to fall,
> They'd really rather not be born at all!
>
> (Canto III, st. xxxv, xxxvi)

---

[1] Possibly he had in mind the interview between her and Byron in which 'she regularly attacked him on the low opinion he professed of female intellect. B. . . . had no chance with her, but took refuge in gentlemanlike assent and silence' (cf. T. Moore, *Memoirs, Journal and Correspondence*, v, p. 270).

Wordsworth's earlier poems are also glanced at, and the love-affairs of Peter Bell excite the critic's laughter. But what irks him almost more than anything else is that the man whom the Queen had chosen as Poet Laureate in 1843, should have written the series of sonnets 'praising hanging'.

There are, however, other English writers such as Browning and Blake whom Hobhouse introduces into his adaptations, to praise and not to condemn. In his opinion Browning far outshone Wordsworth by reason of his tragic power. 'I once met him in the flesh', he says,

and was much pleased with his fine, earnest, manly conversation. As to his works they decidedly stamp him as the greatest Poet of the day . . . A critic has denominated him the Son of Minerva, and the Euclid of the Poets: whatever may be said of his being an "*obscure poet*," he is certainly the finest Tragic Author of the day. There are no dramas of modern times equal to the "Return of the Druses," and "Colombe's Birthday." Mr. Horne, in his "lively" book called the "Spirits of the Age," has hit the nail upon the head in his estimate of the genius of Robt. Browning![1]

Not less interesting than this illustration of Browning's reputation in 1846 is a tribute, equally appreciative, to Blake. Hobhouse considers his *Songs of Innocence* and *Songs of Experience* incomparable in their 'touching simplicity and brilliant word-tinting'. 'The most finished poet might learn something from these unelaborate effusions', he goes on, 'were it not that the production of such pieces at all is little short of miraculous. It is not Art, but Inspiration'.[2] Hobhouse was moved not only by the quality of the poems but also by the compassion which they revealed for the poor and the outcasts of society. It appealed to the humanitarian element in him which was revolted by Wordsworth's sonnets on capital punishment. No doubt it was this trait in his character which made him responsive to *The Purgatory of Suicides*, a poem written by Thomas Cooper, the Chartist Poet, while in Stafford Gaol.[3] And the combination of sentiment with gaiety in Barham evoked the following lines:

> Ingoldsby, whose spirit ne'er was cold,
>   When want and suffering urged its story true:
> Methinks I now thy jocund face behold,
>   Thou best and wittiest of the mirthful crew.[4]

Despite his hard-headed rationalism there was a powerful sensibility in Hobhouse. This comes to the surface in his idealistic conception of love in the poem 'Salvestra'. The romantic tale of Boccaccio in some ways becomes even more romantic. In his despair the faithful lover Girolamo carries his devotion to the length of suicide, an act

---

[1] pp. 190–1, note to 'The Abbot of Florence'.   [2] p. 199, note.
[3] Published in 1845. Cf. *Tales from Boccaccio*, pp. 158 and 203, note.
[4] p. 95, 'The Abbot of Florence', Canto III, st. xxxvii.

which Boccaccio as a good Catholic could not have condoned, and at the same time the story takes on a social value, for the lovers are pitted against the forces of an established order, and even as in Keats's 'Isabella' love is thwarted by the mercenary hostility of ambitious relatives.

Allied to this sensibility is Hobhouse's love of retirement. As old age drew on, he longed for nothing more than the tranquillity of private life. He had had his fill of politics and when Lord Melbourne resigned in 1841, Hobhouse also gave up his office. Although he was induced to resume his post in Lord John Russell's cabinet in 1846, six years later he practically withdrew from public affairs. It is not fanciful to see in some passages of the *Tales from Boccaccio*[1] a reflection of his unwillingness to abandon the peace of the countryside. In the Prologue he longs for a hermit's cell in a sequestered wood where he could meditate. Again in 'The Abbot of Florence' he exclaims:

> By Heavens! it must be a pleasant thing
> To live and die within a garden land,—
> To see the bursting herbage in the spring,
> And watch as day by day the buds expand!
> To hear the sweet birds in the morning sing,
> Those songs which the pure heart can understand!
> To sit at noon beneath the leafy tree,
> Whose rustling makes a music like the sea.
>
> And then to watch the twilight shadows creep
> Over the mighty heavens, like a thought
> Glooming the mind; to know the world asleep
> And nature to the breast of midnight caught!
> To feel the silence passionately deep,
> 'Till every sense is to its climax wrought!—
> For one sweet year of life like this, I'd give
> In glad exchange the years I have to live.
>
> (Canto I, st. xxx, xxxi)

Hobhouse's love of Nature is not limited to the English countryside. It appears also in his picture of the valley of the Arno covered at dawn and eve with mist, in 'Salvestra',

> nor grey nor sad—
> But bathing all in gold.
>
> (Canto I, st. vi)

In Florence at sunset man's handiwork combines with Nature to create a scene of memorable beauty:

> There, behold,
> Gorgeously tinted, the Duomo loom;
> The Campanile, in a mist of gold,
> And the tall tower of Vecchio, in soft gloom,
>
> (Canto II, st. xxiii)

[1] It was probably written in the latter part of 1846. Cf. H. G. Wright, *M.L.R.*, xliii, pp. 84–8.

while palaces and churches glitter under a cloudless sky. And at dawn
the silver, misty veil is raised,

> While burst the soaring vapours, and dissolve
> Upon the pine-clad mountain-sides away,
>
> (Canto III, st. x)

until the music of the deep bell wakens the city from her slumbers
amid her orange groves.

For Florence Hobhouse had a peculiar affection. He made it the
setting of his first tale,[1] even as he had made Genoa the scene of 'The
Miracle'. By comparison, Paris seems sophisticated, though he is blind
neither to its charm as a focus of culture nor to the fascination of its
women. Not only the artistic beauty but also the literary associations
of Florence hold sway over him, and when he maintains in 'Salvestra'

> Who knows not Florence, knows not Italy;
> Not Italy, the world,
>
> (Canto I, st. iv)

he is thinking of the great writers whose fame is indissolubly linked
with Florence. Byron too was sensitive to these memories,[2] but it is
significant that, unlike his friend, Hobhouse gives pride of place to
'our own Boccaccio' and unites himself to the author of the *Decameron*
in the phrase 'Ego et Rex meus'. In the survey of the life and work of
Boccaccio prefixed to the *Tales from Boccaccio*[3] he attempts an estimate
of his achievements. While he admits the historical interest of some of
his writings, only the *Filostrato* and in a lesser degree *Fiammetta*
appeal to him among the minor works. Without hesitation he regards
the *Decameron* as Boccaccio's masterpiece. Despite the coarseness of
certain tales which, as he points out, reflect the taste of mediæval
Italy, even as Chaucer mirrors the similar taste of mediæval England,
he is an enthusiastic admirer of 'the clearness, precision, the pleasing
simplicity, and the rhythmical flow' of Boccaccio's style.[4] And so he
terms him, in Byron's phrase, 'the Bard of Prose'.

Much as he esteemed the *Decameron*, Hobhouse did not scruple to
employ its tales for his own purpose, and there can be no doubt that
Byron's *Don Juan* showed him the way. He holds up the narrative at
will to discourse on contemporary men, women and manners, from

[1] 'The Abbot of Florence'. Boccaccio speaks vaguely of the abbey as being in
Tuscany.   [2] Cf. *Childe Harold*, iv, st. lvii and lviii.
[3] He shows himself familiar with such Italian scholars and commentators as
Manni, Manetti, Baldelli and Tiraboschi, and as his 'Introduction Supplementary'
proves, he had read the characterisation of the Middle Ages in Gabriele Rossetti's
Comento Analitico della Divina Commedia and *Lo spirito antipapale di Dante*. His *Italy*
reveals his acquaintance with Ugo Foscolo's 'Discorso storico' in his 1825 edition of
the *Decameron*, Panizzi's *Essay on the Romantic Narrative Poetry of the Italians* and
Muratori's *Dissertazioni sopra le antichità italiane*.
[4] *Tales from Boccaccio*, p. xxxviii.

Jullien, the French conductor, to Hullah, the 'dancing-master', and fashionable ladies' low-necked dresses. He satirises the up-to-date doctor arguing about the desirability of vaccinating children, while the resurrected Ferando patiently waits for attention, and he mingles his own emotions with meditations on death and the strange medley of good and evil in the world. He passes swiftly from grave to gay, but on the whole it is the lighter vein that predominates. He surprises by his juxtapositions—' 'Tis either . . . the devil or my master' and 'Which would ashame a Bishop or a Bandit', and by his puns:

> And thus the vulgar thought him quite angelic,
>   And deemed him less of Tellus than of Heaven,
> Hoping to get a *toe* some day as relic,
>   And all their sins "in toto" then forgiven.
>   ('The Abbot of Florence', Canto I, st. v)

As might be expected of the robust rationalist who declared that 'piety proceeds from looking sallow', Hobhouse exerted all his satiric humour to depict the punishment of Ferando in Purgatory:

> Thereon he lashed him with most famous spite,
>   And as he lashed he sung a funeral hymn,
> Pausing at times to say it served him right,
>   Declaring he'd excoriate every limb,
> And that he must endure this every night
>   Till e'en the stars of Heaven grew old and dim!
> At this Ferando took to raving madly,
> And swore the Saints were acting very badly.
>
> "Where's Saint Ignatius? Where's Saint Jeremy?
>   And where my patron Saint old Gregory?
> How could he ever let the villains bury me?
>   Oh! may the Saints all come to beggary,
> If they don't send old Charon's boat to ferry me
>   From this vile place;—you've got my leg awry
> You'll break the bone, you villanous old goblin,
> And I thro' all Eternity go hobbling."
>   (Canto II, st. xxxv, xxxvi)

The same burlesque tone and the same ingenious rhymes occur in the account of the terror that seizes the monks when Ferando re-emerges into daylight:

> The jolly monks were going to their breakfast,
>   When suddenly they heard Ferando call:
> Their first attempt was fright—a kind of make fast
>   To any thing, even a play-house wall:
> Then they began to pray aloud, and shake fast,
>   As tho' they never meant to rest at all;
> And then they got into a kind of frantic
>   Hopping and jumping, like the Polka antic.

Then they subsided to an adjuration
    Of sin and Satan, ghosts and heretics,
Calling on Heaven to extirpate a nation,
    Because a deadish man was playing merry tricks;
One gourmand monk began a long oration
    On ill results, when men their sherry mix
With ale, port, rum, and stout, in stomach vault;
But, they all said, the salmon was in fault.
(Canto III, st. xvi, xvii)

But the laity come in for their share of mocking laughter when the
varying rumours among the people are described after the death of
Ferando:

Some swore they heard the clanking of his chains;
    And some swore that he had no chains at all:
Some that he roared aloud with hellish pains,
    While others said he let no murmur fall:
One lady, blest with rare poetic brains,
    Distinctly swore, that coming from a ball
She saw the goblin, miserable croaker,
Dance in his fetters Jullien's last new Polka.
(Canto II, st. xxi)

Similarly, when Ferando has been restored to life, his neighbours as
in Boccaccio regard him with some alarm at first, but it is Hobhouse
who adds with sarcastic humour:

One woman did not stay to pay her rent,
    She'd been the day before her chattels selling:
Sometimes therefore a ghost may seem to play
His tricks suspiciously near quarter-day.
(Canto III, st. xxviii)

Ferando's reception by his own servants is portrayed with a rollicking
verve comparable to that of Cowper's *John Gilpin*, an additional zest
being lent to the comic effect by the anachronistic presentation of the
house as a nineteenth-century English mansion:

Ferando reached at last his lawful door,
    Then rang the bell and gave his usual knock:
The housemaid came, but fell upon the floor
    In strong hysterics at the sudden shock:
The footman sprung up stairs and gave a roar,
    Which made the house like any cradle rock:
The cook rushed up to see what was the matter,
And screamed "a ghost," then dropped her pudding batter.
(Canto III, st. xxix)

Tales from Boccaccio is a strange medley, as typical a product of
the English mind as any modern pantomime. The author of the
Decameron might well be astonished to see his tales diverted to the

service of Protestant propaganda, utilised for a running commentary on nineteenth-century England and pressed into the tradition of English humour. But whatever liberties Hobhouse might take, he was serious enough in his enthusiasm for Boccaccio as a literary creator and as an apostle of enlightenment. The two tales that he adapted seemed to him characteristic of one who not only sought to entertain but also to sweep away barriers to social progress and free men from bondage. Boccaccio was 'a great soul', a 'deathless Mind', and because he came as an emancipating force to the mediæval world, his English admirer bade him look down with disdain

> On all who deem thy impulses unsound,
> And strive to fetter Thought, which never can be bound![1]

Another anonymous work was *Spirit of Boccaccio's Decameron* which was published in 1812, the year of the Roxburghe sale. But here again it is possible to identify the author. He was almost certainly Thomas Moore[2] who had a good knowledge of Italian. In the main his claim on the title-page to have gone back to the original, is justified, but it is possible that he was in some little measure guided by the translation of 1620.[3]

His version is divided into three days, on each of which ten tales are related, but in two of these he weaves together two stories, so that the total is thirty-two.[4] Every day of the *Decameron* is represented, though only one tale is taken from the first day and from the sixth. Moore allowed himself complete freedom, assigning the stories to whatever speaker he thought fit and employing the links between the tales only if they happened to suit his grouping. Similarly, he did as he pleased about the election of a king or queen for each day and about the choice of a theme. Songs are used even more extensively than in the *Decameron* but always the contents are independent of Boccaccio. The descriptions of the natural background are more faithful, but here too Moore goes his own way, mingling with Italian scenes English or Irish landscapes that lingered in his memory.

Another new feature is the introduction at the beginning of the

---

[1] Cf. 'The Abbot of Florence'. Dedication 'To the Spirit of Boccacio'.

[2] Cf. H. G. Wright, 'Thomas Moore as the Author of *Spirit of Boccaccio's Decameron*', *R.E.S.*, 1947, xxiii, pp. 337–48. In what follows Moore will be alluded to as the author.

[3] Certain changes for decency in *Dec.* i, 4, iii, 1 and v, 10 point to this. In addition, the word 'nona' at the end of the 'Introduzione' is wrongly interpreted as in the translation of 1620. Moore takes it to be 9 a.m. instead of 3 p.m. Consequently, the characters are made to retire for sleep and rise early next morning, instead of withdrawing for the siesta. As a result the reference to the great heat loses its significance.

[4] They are in this order: Day I: v, 3; v, 6; iv, 2; v, 4; ii, 3; i, 4; v, 2; viii, 4; vi, 4; x, 6. Day II: ii, 2; x, 5; iv, 5; iii, 6, iii, 8; viii, 10; iii, 1; x, 2 + ii, 4; ii, 10; ix, 9. Day III: vii, 1; v, 10; ix, 6; viii, 2 + vii, 3; vii, 6; iv, 10; vii, 7; iii, 3; vii, 9; ii, 9.

third day of an episode in which the ladies and gentlemen array themselves in rich and brilliant costumes,

> Which they'd exhibited at balls,
> At masquerades, or carnivals.[1]
>
> (ii, p. 226)

Moore clearly found pleasure in these glowing colours and did not perceive how improbable it was that the fugitives from the plague in Florence would send there for fancy dress. But this gay attire was more to his taste than the grim scenes so vividly depicted by Boccaccio, over which he hurries as quickly as may be:

> Weary am I of this sad theme,
> No more on wretchedness I'll dwell.
>
> (i, p. 23)

Quite apart from his manipulation of the general design, Moore had to consider what his attitude should be to the less seemly tales in the *Decameron*. In doing so, he did not forget the defence of Boccaccio in the 'Conclusione dell' autore' which he translated for the benefit of the English reader. Nevertheless, he felt that some concession must be made to contemporary taste which differed from that of the Middle Ages. His scheme, as he states in his 'Explanation to the Ladies', was to avoid anything objectionable, while at the same time he would not yield to false delicacy. It is true that Moore eliminated certain features from a number of tales,[2] but far from being a rigorous censor, he allowed himself considerable latitude in working out his policy. Indeed, it may be said that what he took away with one hand, he restored with another, for in his descriptions of the charms of Belcolore and Niccolosa[3] there is a voluptuousness which is due solely to his fancy.

Many details are modified, sometimes it may seem capriciously. Names of persons are often substituted for those in Boccaccio's tales; others are transferred. Occasionally an alteration in the name of a place gives rise to difficulties. Thus in one story the husband, who, in the original, sets out from Florence for Genoa, is made to *sail* from Padua to Ancona.[4] Equally odd is the fact that the abbot of 'Cligni'[5] is supposed to own a palace at Venice.[6] This strange development is due to the combination of two tales, that of Ghino di Tacco and that of Landolfo Ruffolo. These characters are fused into one, and the hostility of the hero towards the Abbot arises from the opposition of the latter to his marriage with the Abbot's niece Ermilina (a figure unknown to

---

[1] All quotations are from the edition of 1812.
[2] *Dec.* i, 4; iii, 1 and 3; iv, 10; v, 4 and 10; vii, 7 and 9; viii, 10; and ix, 6.
[3] Day ii, 6; and iii, 3.   [4] Day iii, 8.
[5] That is, Cluny in France.   [6] Day ii, 8.

Boccaccio) who connects the two stories. Another such fusion[1] brings together the priest of Varlungo and Madonna Agnesa's admirer, Fra Rinaldo, under the name of Garbino. Such a procedure Moore thought legitimate, even as he omitted and condensed whenever he held it advisable.

Now and then he also varied the plot by introducing an entirely new feature. This is seen most conspicuously in the beast-fable with which he adorned the story of the travellers who visit Solomon at Jerusalem. As Boccaccio tells the tale, the second of them, Melisso, was puzzled to know why in spite of his lavish hospitality he was loved by none. The wise king gave the laconic advice: 'Love', and the story ends with a brief statement that he acted on this counsel with happy results. Evidently Moore thought this too tame. So in his version Solomon advises Melisso, whose trouble lies not in himself but in his extravagant wife who is too fond of the company of male advisers, to go to 'Pieria's mount, and view what's there'. This gives Moore an opportunity to let his poetic fancy play freely. What Melisso finds belongs to the realm of Mandeville rather than of Buffon—a cerulean-blue antelope, with horns transparent and clear as crystal. The Syrian who watches over this beautiful creature explains that formerly she was able to range freely through lands rich in fountains, flowers and aromatic plants, but that as she neglected her mate and went gadding with antelopes of a common breed, he penned her in and shut out all others. From this Melisso learnt how to cure his flighty wife.[2] In another story, that which contains the wager theme used by Shakespeare in *Cymbeline*,[3] a change is made that is interesting, though less substantial. The intriguer of Boccaccio bribes a poor woman to convey him into the heroine's bedchamber, but Moore, perhaps thinking of the weight of the chest, presents matters differently. His villain buys a chest wrought with Chinese characters and, dispatching a note to Zineura which purports to come from a foreign friend of her husband Bernard at Macao, says that he is sending him a chest of very precious teas. Then, concealing himself in it, he lets his slave have it carried to Zineura's house by a porter.

The presence of Bernard's friend at Macao is curious, and if we enquire further, we discover other facts about him which are more curious still. His letter ends thus:

> Allah preserve thee, and thy race.
> May'st thou the prophet's first heav'n deck,
> Prays at Macao Osebeck.

> (iii, p. 213)

The juxtaposition of these two names was probably inspired by the

---

[1] Day iii, 4.   [2] Day ii, 10.   [3] Day iii, 10 = *Dec.* ii, 9.

Voyage to China and the East Indies of Peter Osbeck, a Swedish scholar, who incidentally mentions the port of Macao.[1] But why then should 'Osebeck' be a Mohammedan? This was due to association with the Turkish name Osbech which occurs in one of Boccaccio's tales.[2] Moore employs it again in the story of the two travellers already mentioned and transforms the Giosefo of the original into 'Osbeck Goseffo', who is described as 'a mounted Mussulman'. Another such example of the introduction of Mahommedans into Boccaccio's tales is found when Paganino[3] is referred to as a Moorish corsair, and when Chinzico tries to recover his wife whom Paganino has abducted, she quotes the prophet:

> Mahomed says, 'cursed are those,
> Who unto Christians eyes expose'.
>
> (ii, p. 181)

The Sultan who punishes the villain in the tale of Zineura performs the same office, of course, in the *Decameron*. But the name Selim which Moore bestows on him is significant because it appears again in the last part of *Lalla Rookh*. The hero of this episode is the future emperor of India, and the poem ends with the union of Selim and Nourmahal. In the same way Zineura is married to the Sultan, instead of being restored to her husband Bernard who, in Moore's version, by divine retribution has conveniently 'clos'd a life of pain'.

The interest in the Levant and the Orient thus revealed in *Spirit of Boccaccio's Decameron*, a tradition inherited from the eighteenth century, reveals itself in many other ways. Hence Moore's attempt to depict the Sultan's court.

> Rich sherbet golden goblets crown'd;
> On Turkey cushions Selim sate,
> Surrounded by his lords of state,
> Who, while they hear the jester joke,
> Chew opium, and through rose-pipes smoke . . .
>
> (iii, p. 232)

Some features of this mode of life could be gleaned from many works, but in the main this picture is derived from P. Russell's *Natural History of Aleppo*,[4] though Moore sets aside Russell's assertion that the Turks do not chew opium but swallow it. The oriental background is again conjured up, this time more vaguely, by a simile in the tale of Rinaldo[5] when a bath and supper are prepared for him

> With so much elegance of taste,
> A Queen might lave, and Sultan feast.
>
> (ii, p. 14)

---

[1] London, 1771, i, p. 178. [2] *Dec.* ii, 7.
[3] *Dec.* ii, 10. [4] Edition of 1794, Ch. i. [5] *Dec.* ii, 2.

And the lady's bedchamber is enveloped in an atmosphere of sensuous ease and heavy oriental perfume:

> mattresses of camel's hair,
> Were laid on down of cygnets fair;
> O'er these were thrown fine India sheets,
> Perfum'd by all Arabia's sweets.
>
> .   .   .   .   .
>
> A Grecian lustre all illumes,
> And urns Egyptian burn perfumes.
>
> (ii, pp. 21–2)

Oriental cosmetics are likewise glanced at in the story of Constantia and Martuccio.[1] The old Saracen woman to whom the heroine is taken at Susa is depicted as having 'eyelids limn'd with blackest lead', and her attendants also have 'blacken'd eyes'.[2] The practice is described in detail by Russell[3] and Thomas Shaw,[4] from whom Moore had culled his information.

In other tales there are allusions to houris;[5] the magician consulted by Ansaldo in order to obtain a garden full of flowers in midwinter[6] proves to be a genie.[7] Similarly Pietro Canigiano, who helps Sala-baetto to outwit Madonna Iancofiore,[8] is presented as the man

> Who humbled so Tartaria's Khan.
>
> (ii, p. 106)

And Moore, who had read *Accounts of Independent Tatary*,[9] once again mentions the Tartars in the tale[10] where Neri degli Uberti buys an estate near Castello da Mare,

> From that town so far,
> As could a Tartar's gut-strung bow,
> A well-tipped feather'd arrow throw.
>
> (i, p. 180)

These echoes of Moore's reading of books of oriental travel for *Lalla Rookh* are heard more audibly in the tale of Melisso and Goseffo who, having received wise counsel from Solomon, set out together from Jerusalem for their homes in Laiazzo and Antioch. They take 'a circuitous route' and

> travel unfrequented roads,
> Tow'rds Bofra's mountainous abodes;
> A desert to the eastward stretch'd,
> By which these mountains must be reach'd.
> The second day its verge they gain,
> And as they cross the parching plain;

---

[1] *Dec.* v, 2.   [2] i, p. 146.

[3] *The Natural History of Aleppo*, 1794 ed., i, p. 111.

[4] *Travels or Observations relating to Barbary*. Cf. Pinkerton, xv, pp. 660–1.

[5] ii, pp. 37, 96; iii, p. 232.   [6] *Dec.* x, 5.   [7] ii, pp. 38–40.

[8] *Dec.* viii, 10.   [9] Pinkerton, ix, pp. 320–85.   [10] *Dec.* ix, 6.

Perceiving some wild Arab bands,
They swiftly race o'er arid sands,
Their sobbing horses forward press;
And gain a shrubby wilderness.
From whence through thirst each panting steed
Is hardly able to proceed.
They mounted a steep rugged ridge,
And saw with joy below a bridge,
Through which a rapid river ran,
And by its side a caravan.
Hence anxiously our trav'llers speed,
Here mules and camels drink and feed;
And drivers their Borroccias fill,
Afresh with water from this rill;
And here the friends in palm-tree shade,
Their own and horses thirst allay'd.

(ii, pp. 196–7)

The bridge is the Ponte all' Oca of Boccaccio, and here as in the *Decameron* Goseffo finds the explanation of Solomon's enigmatic advice. But the 'buono uomo' sleeping by the bridge who helps him with the interpretation here appears as a 'dervise'. The explanation is to be found in Richard Pococke's *Description of the East*.[1] Near Aleppo, which he had reached in a caravan, Pococke noted 'a convent of dervises', and it may be surmised that it is one of these who has strayed into Boccaccio's tale. There is all the more reason to think so, because there are many features of his account of his journey which answer to those in the above description. He tells how the caravan crossed the desert and how glad he was on occasion to take shelter from the intense heat under shady trees by a rivulet. He relates also most vividly with what apprehension they journeyed because of bands of Arab marauders and how the appearance of strange horsemen made the travellers halt, in order to proceed in close formation or take up their arms against attack. It is Pococke also who enables us to understand the allusion in Moore's version to Bofra, a place that seems to be otherwise unknown. Pococke observes that Aleppo is a trading-centre visited by a caravan from 'Balsora or Bosra, on the Euphrates'. Moore probably misread 'Bofra' as Bofra'[2] and with poetic licence located it among the mountains of Syria.[3]

To another traveller in this region, Henry Maundrell, the author of *A Journey from Aleppo to Jerusalem*,[4] Moore was indebted to some extent for his account of the route taken by Melisso and Goseffo.

[1] Moore probably read it in Pinkerton, x, p. 527.
[2] In Pinkerton, x, p. 527, it is printed 'Bofra'.
[3] Pococke discusses at length the situation of Mount Pieria, which was one of the goals of the travellers. Cf. Pinkerton, x, notes on 547 and 551.
[4] Moore used it for *Lalla Rookh*. Cf. his *Poetical Works*, vi, p. 310. It is printed in Pinkerton, x, pp. 305–79.

> For fifteen days they journey'd on,
> Through Balbeck to mount Lebanon:
> Sometime for rest they there delay'd,
> Amid stupendous cedars' shade,
> From thence through olive mounts they roam,
> Wash'd by the fierce Orontes foam;
>
> .   .   .   .   .
>
> They wind along its mazy course
> Through meadows sweet, and caverns hoarse,
>
> (ii, pp. 200–1)

amid slopes covered with myrtles and oleanders. The impression of the Orontes was possibly derived from Bruce's description of how, in trying to ford the river swollen with rain, he and his horse were swept away by the violent current.[1] Finally, it was Russell's *Natural History of Aleppo* that inspired the lines:

> Along this river's bank they view
> The Ornithoga lily blue,
> With azure petals spreading far,
> And there entitled Bethlem's star.[2]
>
> (ii, pp. 200–1)

Moore knew full well that there was no blue variety of ornithogalum, even as he was aware that the Syrian antelope was not sky-blue and that the Turks did not chew opium. He was neither botanist, zoologist nor anthropologist but a poet, and his aim was not scientific accuracy but artistic effect. For him this eastern world was one of wealth, magic and mystery, of peril and hardship, of rich colour and languorous perfume. Though less fabulous, it had something of the fascination of Mandeville's wondrous lands. Sensing this exotic attraction hidden beneath the narrative of prosaic travellers, Moore used it to heighten the potency of Boccaccio's tales, realising as he did so, that the author of the *Decameron* himself had not been indifferent to the appeal of this oriental world.

Even in realms less remote he found material suitable for a romance. Hence in the story of Salabaetto he makes the wily Belcolore[3] attempt

---

[1] *Travels to discover the Source of the Nile.* This work was known to Moore who in a note to *Lalla Rookh* (cf. *Poetical Works*, vi, p. 176) quotes him on the subject of Balbec. He cites him again in *Lalla Rookh* on the subject of the 'Mountains of the Moon' (cf. *Poetical Works*, vi, p. 165, note). An allusion to this is likewise made in *S.O.B.D.* i, p. 161, in connexion with the hideous Ciutazza (cf. *Dec.* viii, 3).

[2] It is possible that Moore when speaking of 'Ornithoga lily blue' remembered that the blue lotos grew not far away in Persia (cf. *Lalla Rookh* in *Poetical Works*, vi, p. 81 and note). But he did not need any such prompting, as may be seen from the fact that he knew from Russell (*The Natural History of Aleppo*, 1794, ii, p. 152) that the Syrian antelope was either light or dark brown, and yet portrayed it as 'cerulean blue'. He worried as little about such matters as he did about turning 'ornithogalum' into 'ornithoga' or 'cereus' into 'cerea'.

[3] In *Dec.* viii, 10, she is Iancofiore.

to lure him on by an account of her royal birth, for she would have him believe that she is a Spanish princess, destined to marry the king of Sicily, and doomed to instant death if any report of intimacy with a lover should be spread abroad. Her brother, according to her account, is forced by circumstances to live incognito, but when restored to power, he will shower princely riches and titles upon her friends. The whole incident is like a fairy-tale but it serves to dupe the gullible young Florentine merchant. Still more remarkable is the transformation that the episode of the magician undergoes in the tale of Ansaldo and Dianora. Far from being humane and generous, the Armenian genie of Moore's version is selfish and evil. Without warning he discloses that he himself loves Dianora, reduces his rival to statuesque immobility and offers all his powers to win her. There is one limit to his magic—he cannot create a bird, as she asks. But at her request he turns himself into a linnet, when she promptly wrings his neck. The result is an upheaval in Nature which is strongly reminiscent of the phenomena described by Dryden in 'Theodore and Honoria':[1]

> The day assumes a pitchy gloom,
> Fork'd lightning, the wild clouds illume;
> Loud thunder rolls, the garden quakes,
> Hoarse torrents roar, the arbour shakes,
> Entranc'd pale Dianora lies . . .
>
> (ii, p. 39)

and after these convulsions in Nature have died away, she awakens in sunlight to find her husband before her and Ansaldo on his knees, giving thanks for his deliverance from the spell. A combination of love and terror, though in a less awe-inspiring form, occurs in the tale of Ghino and Ermilina.[2] Once the outlaw has the abbot of Cligni in his grip, he discloses that he is Landolpho whom the ecclesiastic had caused to be thrust into a dungeon. On learning that he was to be broken on the wheel, he had slain the gaoler and escaped, and, after suffering shipwreck, assembled a mighty band of followers. But he is no common outlaw and no conventional lover. His arrest is due, not to base conduct, but to his defiance of corruption and tyranny:

> I only view'd with jealousy,
> The pomp, the ignorance and pride,
> The wealth and domineering stride,
> Of churchmen, who would trample down,
> The true supporters of the crown;
> The people, and their gains devour,
> Then with the mighty rod of pow'r,
> Cast shackles on that impious tongue,
> That durst proclaim the glaring wrong.
>
> (ii, p. 155)

---

[1] Cf. ll. 264–6 and 336–7.   [2] Vide ante, p. 377.

Thus the Ghino of Boccaccio, 'a man redoubtable by reason of his truculence and his high-handed deeds',[1] is metamorphosed into the faithful lover and reforming hero, the saviour of the people. Nor does he bear any lasting rancour against the abbot but repays evil with good. At the close his merits in true romantic fashion are rewarded by the Pope, who restores his estates and makes him captain of the guard.

In some of the passages just discussed there is a certain theatrical quality. This is especially pronounced in a number of recognition scenes. Conspicuous among these is the reunion of the long-parted Ghino and Ermilina. Wrapped in cloak and hood, he moves slowly before her, casts off his mantle and reveals 'his dazzling vest, and sword-belt bright'. Ermilina raises her eyes and

> 'Landolpho lives!' she cries, 'all's well!'
> And fainting on his bosom fell.
>
> (ii, p. 153)

There is the same surprise in the tale of Salbetto,[2] when two curtains suddenly fly apart and disclose Belcolore.[3] A similar mechanical contrivance lets in the moonlight at the bagnio and reveals the identity of Lorenzo to Catella.[4] Another dramatic device is used in the story of Constantia[5], who is recognised by her foster-mother through a birthmark like a strawberry on her shoulder. Finally, to induce a villain to confess his crime, a ghostly apparition at midnight is employed in the tale of Zineura. Ambrose is boasting about the stratagem with which he won the wager, when

> a lamentable cry
> Sigh'd through the pictur'd tapestry;
> A female death-like form appear'd,
> Wrapp'd in a shroud, with blood besmear'd;
> Advancing, her left side unbound,
> Reveal'd a deep and deadly wound,
>
> .   .   .   .   .
>
> Approaching Ambrose stern it stood,
> While horror stagnated his blood;
> Then sadly shook its ghastly head . . .
>
> (iii, p. 233)

Shrinking before its glassy eye, the terrified culprit falters his confession and is carried off to a gloomy cell, where he dies of a guilty conscience. The spectre is, of course, Zineura who casts off the winding sheet and stands forth, her innocence established and her honour regained.

In lighter vein disguise figures in the story of Ferondo and the abbot[6] who, when the time for the supposed resurrection of Ferondo has

---

[1] J. M. Rigg's translation.   [2] The form used in *S.O.B.D.*
[3] Ibid., ii, p. 97.   [4] Ibid., ii, p. 65.   [5] *Dec.* v, 2.   [6] *Dec.* iii, 8.

come, equips himself with Aaron's beard and rod and in this array goes to summon his dupe. The spectacular is also introduced into another tale of dupery when Fra Alberto d'Imola,[1] enraged at the betrayal of his secret relations with Lisetta, confronts her, a dagger in one hand and a vial of poison in the other, when his threats are cut short by a knocking at the door, and an ominous situation dissolves into comedy as the friar plunges from the balcony into the water below. Moore again satisfies his taste for spectacle when he presents the narrators of the tales in their gay fancy dress at the beginning of the third day— a scene which he himself describes as 'a rainbow troop of figurantes'[2] or ballet-dancers.

Even the landscape may acquire a theatrical air as if to harmonise with the sensational nature of the tales as related by Moore. This is seen very clearly in the tale of Zineura when she draws near to the dark hollow where she is to be murdered:

> Through dells and craggy paths they ride,
> With shrubby clifts on either side,
> From whose high summits pines arise,
> Displaying to the trav'llers eyes,
> Tall spiry heads of verdant hue,
> Stretching to heaven's celestial blue;
> Their gloomy shade, and tow'ring height,
> Repel now the last ray of light.
>
> (iii, pp. 219–20)

Equally wild is the setting of the ambuscade in which Ghino overpowers the abbot of Cligni and his escort. The setting sun gleams on the mountains and dances on the halberts of the cavalcade. Marble rocks and pine-covered slopes rise above the unsuspecting train. Then all at once Ghino appears, wearing black armour and a helmet adorned with blood-red hair. Like Byron's *Giaour* who was to win fame in 1813, one year after the publication of Moore's translation, he rides a sable steed at a furious pace, and standing with drawn sword on the highest peak, is as memorable as the Giaour halting with uplifted arm on the sea-shore:

> His sabre from the scabbard flew,
> And soon a herald rose to view,
> With brazen trump, and banner bright,
> Mounted upon a courser white.
> From his shrill trumpet burst a clang,
> Which through the hollow caverns rang.
>
> (ii, p. 143)

The creator of such a romantically dramatic episode is also quite capable of turning his hand to satire. Naturally, Moore is limited by

---

[1] *Dec.* iv, 2.   [2] i, p. 10.

2C

the material that the *Decameron* affords. But in one tale at least he jests at the doctor's love of money, though his laughter is genial like that of Chaucer when writing on the same theme. The physician in question, appropriately enough, is a practitioner at Salerno, and it is his opiate which accidentally causes the mishap to Rugiero Jeroli.[1] He is about to operate on a patient with a carious bone in his leg, when he is summoned to attend to a number of men who have been injured in a fray. In an amusing way Moore shows how he is torn between the dictates of his professional conscience and the desire for gain, and how in the end he solves the dilemma to his own profit.

> The shrewd physician, on this warning,
> Consider'd how he might till morning,
> Defer his operation on,
> The man who had the rotten bone.
> As of this patient he was sure;
> The others were not so secure.
> Thinks he, to leave this friend I'm loth,
> The merits let me weigh of both;
> My patient *here*, can't well be worse,
> My patients *there*, will serve my purse.
> Old Bruno *here*, may mortify.
> Ten times as many *there* may die.
> Fool should I be to reason more,
> What's *one* man's life to half a score?
> His conscience lighten'd of its load,
> To Malfi rapidly he row'd.
>
> (iii, pp. 102–3)

Despite the restrictions inherent in a translation, Moore's personality emerges in various ways. The scenery of Italy, as might be expected of one who in 1812 had not yet visited that country, is not portrayed with convincing intimacy. In fact, the most striking picture is that of the journey of Alessandro through the vineyards of France, up through larch-woods to the heights where Mont Blanc towers aloft in the sunshine and avalanches burst around.[2] It is clear that Alpine scenery must have fascinated Moore long before he saw it with the bodily eye. When he did behold Mont Blanc with Russell, we know that 'he was speechless and in tears', overcome by its sublimity.[3] His ignorance of Italy curbed his fondness for description, though here and there a glimpse is given. But one suspects that for want of familiarity with the natural setting of the tales in the *Decameron* he was forced to rely on his own experience at home. Hence the river along which Chinzica and his wife drift while angling for bream[4] and the trout stream which

---

[1] *S.O.B.D.*, Day iii, 6. Cf. *Dec.* iv, 10.   [2] i, p. 118.
[3] *Memoirs, Journal and Correspondence*, 1853–4, ed. Lord John Russell, p. xv.
[4] *S.O.B.D.*, ii, p. 172.

takes the place of Boccaccio's fish pond in the tale of Neri degli Uberti[1]
are probably an evocation of some scene in Ireland. The same is true
of his picture of the lake at twilight towards the end of his book.
The glowing splendour of the setting sun has yielded to the silver light
of the moon; willows and aspens are mirrored in the water lying at the
foot of wooded hills with groups of trees on the slope, and cereus and
nyctanthes,[2] night-flowering shrubs, pour forth their fragrance,

> While nought disturbs the sheet serene,
> Save now and then a cygnet's flash;
> Or dash of fishes as they rise,
> At evening's glowing mothy flies.
> As these breaks undulating flow,
> The liquid landscape waves below;
> And as the watery ruffles cease,
> The scene resumes its wonted peace.
> (iii, pp. 243-4)

One may be sure too that something of Moore's own enjoyment of
choice food and drink has found its way into his translation. It is a
connoisseur who speaks of wines like Tokay, Lunelle and Christi
Lachrymæ, such cordials or liqueurs as Persico and Noyau. Oysters,
quail pies, and, supreme delight of the epicure, ortolans with toasted
cheese, enhance the festivities of Boccaccio's characters, and Moore is
as little perturbed by such anachronisms as ices and pineapples as by
a tea-party.[3] Again it is the sympathetic translator who speculates
humorously on the cause of Rugiero's thirst:

> Whether from some fatigue he'd taken,
> Or whether he had eaten bacon;
> Or rather, I'm inclined to think,
> From innate love he bore for drink,
> He never could a bottle spy,
> Without his lips becoming dry.
> (iii, p. 104)

Similarly, it is not a severe teetotaller, but the translator of Anacreon,
who reports Rugiero's decision after his misadventure with the doctor's
opiate:

> From this time forth Jeroli's brain,
> At sight of vials whirl'd in pain,
> And when in future love he sought,
> He always his own liquor brought.
> (iii, p. 122)

It would, however, be wrong to interpret Moore's love of con-
viviality as an expression of sensuous materialism. In fact, he was an

[1] Ibid., i, pp. 185-6.
[2] Cf. H. G. Wright, R.E.S., xxiii, p. 347.
[3] S.O.B.D., iii, p. 118.

idealist whose outlook manifests itself even in the uncongenial setting
of Boccaccio's tales of amorous intrigue. It is because he holds women
in high esteem that he provides justification for the conduct of
Beatrice in the infidelity of her husband Egano,[1] and his conception
of love emerges clearly from his attitude to the swashbuckling Lam-
bertino whose overbearing manner so terrifies Helena that she

> Had no alternative to chuse,
> So gave the brute a rendezvous.

To which Moore adds the revealing comment:

> In truth had he not been a brute,
> Forc'd charms he'd scorn, as acid fruit;
> What, but a sottish tasteless beast,
> Could on reluctant beauty feast?
>
> (iii, p. 85)

At its height Moore's idealism shines forth, not in his versions of the
tales, but in the matter which he places before and after them. In the
dialogue between *Book and Reviewers* at the beginning of the book,
the critics declare:

> Strong evidence attends thy blundering tongue,
> That thou to rude Hibernia dost belong;
> From whence we scarce can entertain a hope,
> A thing can spring that don't deserve the rope.
> The Scotch at present are, beyond all doubt,
> A nation moral, orderly, and stout.
> To prove what nature civiliz'd may do,
> Now Caledonia ventures to review;
> And Scotland's Poets, when matur'd in age,
> May by their works enrich Apollo's page;
> Tho' they were but two centuries ago,
> A turbulent ferocious brutal foe—
> Blood-thirsty, fierce, inflexible to bow,
> As the wild Irish savages are now.
>
> (i, pp. 12–13)

A footnote makes it clear that the satirical tone of these lines was
inspired by a remark in the *Quarterly Review*.[2] Moore contrasts the
law-abiding character of the Irish in 1600, for which Sir John Davis
vouches, with their reputed 'turbulence, ferocity and brutality' in
1810 and exclaims ironically 'Mirabile Dictu. What gigantic strides to
civilized perfection'.[3] If he was goaded on to refute the opinions of the
Tory reviewer, it was because he resented the aspersion on his country
and not because he failed to recognise the merits of Jeffrey and his
fellows. This is made evident by a passage in the 'Conclusion' where
his heart warms at the thought of the sympathy shown to his country

---

[1] iii, pp. 129, 132.   [2] November 1810, p. 342.   [3] *S.O.B.D.*, i, p. 13.

by Scottish critics, and his gratitude is so profound that he can even
bear their condemnation of his work:

> Hail! Caledonia—learn'd Edina hail!
>   Hail! Scotch reviewers, tho' you damn these sheets,
> Hibernia stands not lightly in your scale,
>   For which my heart your minds enlighten'd greets.
>
> (iii, p. 248)

The emotion that had found vent in the laughter of satire, at the close
of the book gushes forth in the eloquence of sentiment. One cannot help
recalling the passion of the *Irish Melodies* on which Moore was still
engaged when *Spirit of Boccaccio's Decameron* was being composed.
The immediate occasion of this overflow of feeling is the scene when
the story-tellers have retired to rest at the end of the third day.
Addressing his readers, Moore bids them also slumber calmly, and
then the unhappy state of Ireland comes surging into his mind:

> When shall poor Erin so repose in peace,
>   When from her couch may be expell'd the thorn,
> When shall blood-reeking ghastly visions cease,
>   To let her rise refresh'd on breezy morn?
> When persecution, ignorance, and pride,
>   From ruling councils banish'd shall go forth,
> She then may be by her own merits try'd,
>   And valued in proportion to her worth.
> When matricides corruption's bribes shall spurn,
>   And patriotic principles assume,
> Again Ierne to *those* sons will turn,
>   Tho' Nero-like they've rip'd her teeming womb.
> When proud Britannia may in wisdom deign,
>   Her goading rods for silken reins to change,
> Then Erin's genius and her rosy train,
>   O'er her green bosom joyfully shall range.
>
> (iii, pp. 247–8)

Acutely as he feels the miseries of his country, Moore nevertheless
remains an optimist, for he refuses to believe that reason, tolerance
and enlightenment will not one day gain the victory:

> The time will come when prejudice's clouds,
>   Dispell'd shall be by reason's cheering ray,
> And the dark mist which confidence enshrouds,
>   Will fly before her as night flies from day.
>
> (iii, p. 248)

The fear that the book might meet with an unfavourable reception
at the hands of the reviewers was not an expression of mock modesty.
Moore was well aware of its imperfections, as is proved by his dedication
to the earl of Llandaff, no less than by the motto from Voltaire on the
title-page:

Censeurs malins, je vous méprise tous,
Car je connais mes défauts mieux que vous.

In the dialogue between *Book and Reviewers* he analyses them without mercy. There is some warrant for the objection to 'clanking repetition' and 'faulty rhymes'. Both originate in the choice of the octosyllabic couplet as the metre for the tales. The strain on the ingenuity of the translator in finding rhymes is obviously greater in an extensive work than if a longer line had been employed. The result is that Moore in spite of his dexterity is often compelled to resort to a Hibernian pronunciation to secure variety.

These weaknesses are offset by the merits of his verse. It is smooth and fluent and excels in familiar speech. The ease of such a passage as the following could only be attained by a master of conversation:

'You seem beyond all bounds distress'd;
Consider not your horse and purse,
But thank St. Julian 'tis no worse.
Take comfort, Sir, within this house,
For, dress'd as my departed spouse,
To him you such resemblance bear,
I can't but fondly on you stare.
In short, I know not what I do,
And nearly had saluted you'.[1]

(ii, pp. 20–1)

And in the tale of Lydia and Nicostratus there is a lively dialogue when, in the pursuit of her intrigue, she induces him to part with a sound tooth:

She soon to Nicostratus said,
'A truth to tell I'm half afraid,
You cannot surely but observe,
Your pages' conduct while they serve'.
'Yes, that I have most certainly,
And often thought to ask them why.'
'My love, the youths would deem it treason,
To let you know the real reason;
But my regard surmounts all fear,
So plainly I must tell you, dear,
What ever lately has befel,
Your breath exhales a carious smell;
A grievous circumstance to me,
As well as to your company.'
Exclaim'd he, 'What! my breath impure,
No tooth have I unsound I'm sure.'
'Perhaps you may, love, open wide,
Your mouth and let me look inside.'
She then examin'd every part,
And soon exclaim'd, 'My precious heart!

[1] Cf. *Dec.* ii, 2.

So long how could you with it bear,
Here's one as rotten as [a] pear;
If its extraction you delay,
'Twill all your sounder ones decay.
So I advise, beyond a doubt,
Immediately you get it out.[1]

(iii, pp. 188–9)

It is true that Boccaccio did not emerge unchanged from the process
of translation. However, Moore was better qualified than most English
writers for the task by his interest in the amatory writers.[2] He could
enter with light-hearted zest into the gallant adventures of the
Decameron. At the same time his own happy marriage enabled him to
value those stories of true love in which it also abounds. The result
was that his work on the whole might justly claim to represent the
Spirit of Boccaccio's Decameron.

The comic element in the *Decameron* was adequately represented
in the translations of Hobhouse and Moore but as a rule it is passed
over in favour of tales of romantic love. However, isolated stories of
an amusing or satirical kind are rendered by James Payn,[3] Sir John
Hanmer, J. R. Planché and R. B. Brough. Hanmer[4] takes up the
theme to which Rogers had alluded in *Italy*, the story of Frate Cipolla.
However, he approached the subject, not in a mood of dogmatic
acerbity, but with an air of detached amusement. This is evident from
the motto, taken from Molière,[5] which he prefixes to his tale:

A lui non plus qu'à son Laurent
Je ne me fierai, moi, que sur un bon garant.

The quotation is all the more apt, since the friar, on addressing the
crowd outside the church of Certaldo, finding that a burning coal has
been substituted for the feather of the angel Gabriel's wing that he
had promised to show, promptly asserts that it is from the fire in which
St. Laurence was roasted to death. But Hanmer is not concerned to
attack the friars as a whole and so he suppresses the fantastic list of
bogus relics that Frate Cipolla claimed to have brought back with him
from Jerusalem and confines himself to the one episode in the career
of the friar. Of course, he leaves no doubt that Cipolla is a rogue. But
he is a lovable rogue, a sort of clerical Autolycus. Perhaps Boccaccio's

---

[1] Cf. *Dec.* vii, 9.
[2] This is true in particular of *The Poetical Works of the Late Thomas Little, Esq.*
Moore later pleaded for charity towards this early volume of his, because the poems
that it contains 'were . . . the productions of an age when the passions very often give
a colouring too warm to the imagination'. Cf. the article cited above, *R.E.S.*, xxiii,
p. 344.   [3] Vide post, pp. 436–7.
[4] *Fra Cipolla, and other poems*, London, 1839. Page references appended to quotations
are to this edition.   [5] *Tartuffe*, I. i. 71–2.

description of his merry face combined with his stay in the village inn
to carry Hanmer's thoughts back to Chaucer's friar Hubert. In temper
he and Hanmer's Cipolla were somewhat alike. Cipolla's very name
was

> redolent of cheer,
> Nor he belied it with a mien severe,
> Nor took his gettings churlishly for right,
> If priest by day, he gossip was by night;
> And all the women loved the tales he told,
> And children laughed his antics to behold.
>
> (p. 10)

Again, like Hubert he devoted his attention to those who could afford
to reward him well.

> He would that all knew how the Scriptures teach
> 'Tis not the poor want saving, but the rich.
>
> (p. 10)

However, he avoided extremes, not frequenting the very opulent but
paying his calls in 'snug streets', where people know the value of
money:

> He came, and preached how wealth abideth not;
> And oft a portion to his convent drew,
> And proved, at least, his saying might be true,
> Shriving for profit penitents like these.
>
> (p. 11)

As Hanmer was chiefly interested in Cipolla, he discarded the scene
in which Boccaccio had described how the friar's servant Guccio became enamoured of Nuta and through his neglect of his master's
belongings gave the waggish Giovanni del Bragoniera and Biagio
Pizzini a chance to substitute the coal for the feather. He therefore
replaces this complicated apparatus by a single agent whom he portrays
thus:

> a boorish churl and rude
> With leathern looks that changed not with his mood,
> Dull from his birth, no faith inspired his brain,
> E'en superstition strove for him in vain,
> Dark is her night, but still with stars supplied—
> His darkness was a chaos or a void.
> Nor signs, nor power of holy church he knew,
> That changes hardest things, with heavenly dew,
> E'en hearts of men, and what can harder be,
> Or change more great than sin to sanctity,
> At things beyond him like an ape he mowed,
> And oft it passed for reverence with the crowd.
>
> (pp. 16–17)

It is this dull-witted fellow who fills the place of Boccaccio's two
sportive companions. At the close, with a sense of humour, Hanmer

depicts him as believing Cipolla's tale and kissing the coal that he himself had left in the friar's possession.

It is possible that in his condensation of this part of the tale Hanmer was actuated not merely by a desire to concentrate on Cipolla but also by a longing to escape from the sweat-laden atmosphere of the inn-kitchen in August, which Boccaccio describes with such merciless realism, out into the open air. For the English writer the setting was almost as important as the story itself, and, perhaps following Chaucer's example at the opening of the *Canterbury Tales*, he alters the season of the year from the height of summer to late spring with all its fresh and verdurous beauty:

> 'Twas the soft season when the sycamore
> Bursts in full foliage, and its pensile flower
> Doth all the bees with its sweet breath invite,
> And fairy bells, so tremulous and light,
> Till twilight ushers in the summer night.
>
> (pp. 11–12)

Hanmer, who was a great lover of Italy,[1] sees in a wide survey, not only the landscape but also the human activities of village and countryside:

> stars were rising o'er
> The inn's long gallery and its open door—
> And horseman, pacing through the archway near,
> Who back to Florence turned from country cheer;
> Far swelled the horn along the mountain side,
> And goats came bounding to their gentle guide,
> The peasant girl, with distaff in her hand,
> And her young sisters rolling in the sand;
> And faintly rose the evening wind along
> The brushwood paths, and murmured with her song.
>
> (p. 12)

Then came night, when

> the cypress shadows fell
> Calm in the moonlight over wall and well;
> Few sounds along the scattered street were heard,
> Some wandering steps, some lattice faintly stirred;
> Tall seemed each figure lingering in the shade,
> And o'er their heads the light bat flickering played.
>
> (pp. 17–18)

Finally, at break of day vine-dressers sally forth, hook in hand, from the village, where all is silent except for the old crones who ply their household tasks, while the mules await the bells that summon them on their way. These sketches have an undeniable charm, and they can

---

[1] Cf. his 'Sonnets', published in 1840, which deal chiefly with Italian subjects and scenes.

at least be justified as an indication of the background against which
we can see Cipolla himself. On the other hand, it would seem as if
one vignette had been introduced merely to express Hanmer's delight
in the scene, as is proved by its general character:

> 'Tis sweet to wander and at eve behold
> Some sunlit city, loved and famed of old,
> And all its towers in purple light arrayed,
> And darker now, and reddening into shade.
> And sweet the rest at noontide, by the well
> For pilgrims hewn, where some old citadel
> Throws its long shadows o'er the road, and fills
> The winding passes of the hoary hills;
> Those heaped up hills, with many a deep ravine,
> And half hid village and its towers between,
> And white rock jutting from the shadows dun,
> Of rifted marble, glittering in the sun,
> Seen leagues around, the mountain Gonfalon.
>
> (p. 20)

Apart from some careless rhymes, Hanmer uses the heroic couplet
effectively, and as the last three lines just quoted indicate, he varies
his metre by means of triplets. In all probability, like other writers of
the age, he learnt the device from Dryden. It may well be that he
also was affected by him as a satirist, for despite Hanmer's customary
genial humour, there are now and then some piercing thrusts as in
the lines when he relates how it was in vain for any one to plead for
alms when Cipolla was about:

> And graver matrons the procession joined,
> And beldams old, that lagging limped behind;
> A shadowy fatal sisterhood they came,
> And greeted none but beggars, and the lame;
> Halting, with these they ran an envious race,
> And gathered round the church, and filled the place;
> And alms they begged, but age hath little need,
> And saints come first in charitable creed.
>
> (p. 20)

The second humorous tale belongs to the same day as that of Frate
Cipolla. It is the story of Chichibio,[1] and this version has been ascribed
to J. R. Planché.[2] The process of anglicisation which had been begun
in the sixteenth century and continued in the eighteenth,[3] is carried
still further in 'The One-Legged Goose'. The scene is transferred from
Venice to Hertfordshire. The cook is not a man but a woman, and it is

---

[1] *Dec.* vi, 4.

[2] Cf. *Notes and Queries*, 15 May 1909, p. 388. It is to be found in *Routledge's Temperance Reciter*, pp. 182–4. The B.M. Catalogue gives the date of publication as [1874].   [3] Vide ante, pp. 163, 296–7.

Peggy's lover John who begs for a leg of the bird that she is cooking.
The bird in question is not a crane, but a goose, and when Peggy's
master is to be convinced that it had, while still alive, only one leg, they
sally forth, not to the bank of a river, but to the neighbouring house
of Farmer Grains. In keeping with this background the dialogue
attempts to represent the rustic speech, not only of John and Peggy
but also of the squire himself. He is portrayed as the simple-witted
country gentleman, and the emphasis here is far more on his stupidity
than on the astuteness of his cook. The opening lines of the poem
depict him thus:

> He loved to smoke his pipe with jovial souls,
> Prided himself upon his skill at bowls,
> At which he left his neighbours in the lurch;
> On Sundays, too, he always went to church—
> Took, during sermon time, his usual snore,
> And gave his sixpence at the door.
>
> (p. 182)

The transformation is complete, and Boccaccio might well be excused
if in this homely figure he failed to recognise the noble citizen of
Florence whom he had introduced into the *Decameron*.

There was a good deal in common between Planché and R. B.
Brough, as is shown by their production of extravaganzas and burlesques for the stage.[1] This spirit animates 'A Story from Boccaccio',
published in the first number of *The Train*.[2] The tale of Pasquino and
Simona[3] was in itself serious enough, but in Brough's hands it undergoes a transformation, as we perceive from the tone of the opening
stanzas, in which he explains that he cannot refrain from communica-
ting his pleasures, whatever they be, to others, such as his neighbour
Mr. Jones:

> So, in Literature's garden, when I've met a song or story
>   That has raised a pleasant smile, or caused a pleasant tear descend;
> Should you chance to call upon me, be admonish'd I should bore ye
>   With the whole of the transaction from beginning to the end.
>
> I've been reading in Boccaccio, where I've stumbled o'er a treasure
>   That I'd somehow overlooked, although I've loved the book[4] for years;
> It's a quarter after midnight, and I can't expect the pleasure
>   Of a visitor to favour me with sympathy and ears.

---

[1] Vide post, pp. 456–7 and cf. *C.B.E.L.* iii, p. 601.
[2] January 1856, pp. 36–40. I am indebted to Geoffrey Tillotson for pointing this
out to me.
[3] Vide ante, pp. 309, 348; post, pp. 417–21, 435.
[4] This reference to the *Decameron*, as though it were the only work of Boccaccio,
provides another illustration of the pre-eminence that it had acquired in the nineteenth century.

> So I'll put the tale on paper, just as well as I can do it
> (For I can't wait till the morning for a call from Mr. Jones);
> And I fancy, e'en in my hands, you'll be able to get through it,
> As, in any clumsy setting, we can value precious stones.

Brough confesses that he has never been in Italy and renounces any attempt at local colour. He therefore transfers the scene from Florence to the Adriatic, possibly under the influence of Ruskin's *The Stones of Venice* which had appeared from 1851 to 1853:

> a Roman villa there had stood;
> And with moss and vines half hidden, broken columns lay a-crumbling,
> Which I won't attempt to paint, as only Mr. Ruskin could.
>
> And, were I to try, the beauties of the sky, and sea, and ocean
> To depict, our travell'd critics would be quickly down on me;
> All I want is to convey a golden, dreamy kind of notion
> Of a garden, in the sunset, by the Adriatic Sea.

The tale does not even mention the names of the chief figures. They are simply two lovers, and the garden with its crocuses and daisies is unconvincing, as Brough himself appears to feel. However, he tries to account for the poisonous plant by attributing the former ownership of the garden to a wizard. The hero's sudden death is described in a stanza which brings the situation vividly before the reader's eyes:

> Scarce within his reach of arm, he spied a plant of curious prickle;
> It was tempting from its distance (still one hand about her head)—
> Could he reach it? lo, a triumph! it is plucked, its fibres tickle;
> He must chew it—he has done so—in a moment he IS DEAD!

It is difficult to believe that Brough was very much in earnest here, and the flippancy of the next stanza heightens this doubt. Yet perhaps he was not altogether without sympathy for the lovers, as the two following stanzas indicate, in spite of their melodramatic air:

> He was dead, and she was living! Earth and sea, and sky, and ocean,
> All were changed—the light of life was gone, rekindled ne'er to be;
> In the dark she stood alone; the sun had sunk with plummet motion;
> Not a star shone o'er the blackness of the Adriatic Sea!
>
> It was black, and cold, and sudden—she was hopeless, calm, and frigid;
> Ne'er a moan escaped her bosom, on her brow was ne'er a frown;
> She was broken, she was frozen, she was pulseless, she was rigid;
> Can the Lily wave its petals when the North has blown it down?

At any rate, the artist who provided illustrations at the beginning and the end of the poem accepted these lines in good faith and seized on the metaphor of the lily for his own purpose. There was little in Brough's vague description of the garden which he could utilise:

Boccaccio's sage-bush is not even mentioned. In the first engraving he therefore depicts the sun setting over the sea and in the foreground two lilies growing out of an urn. The tailpiece shows an inky sky swept by a furious storm and, as a symbol of the fate of the lovers, two lilies broken and bent to the earth.

The latter part of Boccaccio's story—the charge of murder brought against the heroine, and her sudden death as she demonstrates to her accusers how the chewing of the leaf had brought such unexpected disaster—is related by Brough in a greatly condensed and simplified form. Then, as if he feared to be thought sentimental, he adds a postscript:

> There's my story—do you like it? from Boccaccio I've departed
>   In the features; but I've given you, at all events, the bones.
> It's a first attempt: if bullied, or but met with praise faint-hearted,
>   Why, in future, I shall go to bed, or knock up Mr. Jones.

Such light-hearted and even facetious treatment of one of Boccaccio's serious tales by an English writer is unusual.

Far more numerous and more notable, however, is the group of tales in verse that portray love—passionate and noble. To them might be applied the motto adopted by B. W. Procter for *A Sicilian Story*:[1] 'Nunc scio quid sit amor'. Certainly it would have been appropriate for Keats's 'Isabella', which he mentions on 27 April 1818 in writing to John Hamilton Reynolds. It was then just completed as a compliment 'to Boccace'. As has been recognised,[2] the choice of the theme was no doubt inspired by Hazlitt's lectures three months earlier. At first sight it may appear strange that on this occasion Keats should employ the French form of the Italian writer's name, since Hazlitt invariably alludes to Boccaccio, and the translation of the *Decameron* used by Keats refers to it as the work of 'John Boccacio'. The explanation probably lies in Keats's diligent study of Dryden's *Fables*, where 'Boccace' is always found. Keats read the fifth edition, published by Awnsham Churchill in 1684, of the English translation of 1620.[3] The name 'Isabella' is derived from this source, which substituted it for the Italian 'Lisabetta'. More important, however, are other changes in the Jacobean version. The love-affair, as related by Boccaccio, was frankly sensual, and it was the discovery of Lisabetta's nocturnal visits to Lorenzo that enraged her brothers. The English translator, on the other hand, describes the matter thus:

---

[1] Vide post, pp. 414–17.

[2] First by D. Nichol Smith who pointed it out to H. W. Garrod. See the latter's communication to *T.L.S.*, 19 March 1925, p. 199.

[3] An account of Keats's indebtedness to the English translation of 1620 was given by H. G. Wright, *T.L.S.*, 17 April 1943.

Long time continued this Amorous League of Love, yet not so cunninly (sic!) concealed, but at length the secret meeting of *Lorenzo* and *Isabella*, to ease their poor Souls of Loves oppressions, was discovered by the Eldest of the Brethren.[1]

This is not very precise, but the drift is clear when we hear later that the brothers were all the more inclined to delay the revenge, 'no evil Act being (as yet) committed'. In yet another respect the translator exhibited the conduct of Lorenzo and Isabella in a more favourable light. In the *Decameron*, after she has seen the murdered Lorenzo in a vision, she is afraid to say anything about it to her brothers and so schemes how to test the truth or falsehood of her dream. She therefore asks their leave to go a little way out of the city for recreation, and by means of this subterfuge is able to carry out her plan. By contrast, the wording of the translation—'Having obtained favour of her Brethren, to ride a days journey from the City'—is studiously vague and avoids any conscious deception on Isabella's part.

Various other features are peculiar to the English translation. Thus the attendant who accompanies Isabella is referred to in general terms by Boccaccio as one who had formerly been with them (that is, the family), which in le Maçon's rendering becomes 'vne qui auoit seruy autresfois en leur maison'. The English translator is more definite about the nature of her service, speaking of Isabella's 'trusty Nurse, who long time had attended on her in the house'. Again, the circumstances in which Lorenzo's body is disinterred are somewhat different. In Boccaccio it is Isabella alone who performs this gruesome task, but in the English version she is aided by her nurse, and they dig up the body together. By a miracle of the kind in which mediæval writers delighted, the corpse is described by Boccaccio as being in no wise decayed.[2] The English rendering on the other hand introduces an important modification—the body is 'as yet very little corrupted or impaired'. Evidently the translator was too much of a rationalist to accept the tale as he found it. The same tendency, aided no doubt by his fondness for alliteration, explains another change that he made. In Boccaccio the heroine uses a knife to sever Lorenzo's head from the body and carries out the operation by herself. The practical English translator, however, insists that she had brought 'a keen Razor with her'[3] and was enabled to cut off the head 'by help of the Nurse'.

When Isabella has returned home, it is to be remarked that in Boccaccio, before putting the head in the pot of basil, she wraps it in

---

[1] *Dec.* iv, 5. Ed. of 1684, p. 183.

[2] He does not state how long the interval is between the murder and the vision, but he gives the impression that some time passes.

[3] 'Razor' alliterates with 'regard' and 'wrapped'. Cf. H. G. Wright, *The first English translation of the 'Decameron'*, pp. 105–6.

a piece of fine cloth, which in le Maçon appears as 'vn beau drap de soye'. The English version, with its love of alliteration, makes of this 'a Silken Scarf'. Subsequently, as Boccaccio's heroine sits weeping over the pot, she is observed by prying neighbours, and when her brothers note her fading beauty, these gossips inform them of what they have seen. Consequently, there is a definite connexion between the tittle-tattle of the neighbours and the brothers' resolve to take away the pot of basil. The same account is given by le Maçon; however, his text in certain editions translates 'disser loro' not by 'leur dirent' but by 'luy dirent'.[1] The English translator, who here seems to have been following le Maçon, found this puzzling and rendered the passage freely:

> The Neighbours noting this behaviour in her, observing the long continu-ance thereof, how much her bright Beauty was defaced, and the Eyes sunk into her Head by incessant weeping, made many kind and friendly motions, to understand the reason of her so violent oppressions; but could not by any means prevail with her, or win any discovery by her Nurse, so faithful was she in secresie to her. Her Brethren also waxed weary of this cariage in her. . .[2]

In this version therefore the actions of the neighbours and the brothers are dissociated. One last feature of the English translation may be mentioned—the folk-song at the close, the 'canzone' of Boccaccio, is rendered by 'an excellent Ditty'.

How was Keats affected by the form in which the story reached him? The most striking characteristic of 'Isabella' is the idealisation of the heroine's love for Lorenzo. The poem knows nothing of the incidents which gave the brothers some justification for their murder-ous attack on Lorenzo, an attack as stealthy as his liaison with their sister had been. All hint of sensuality is banished from the lines:

> These brethren having found by many signs
> What love Lorenzo for their sister had,
> And how she lov'd him too.
>
> (st. xxi)

Having deprived them of their reasonable grievance—the seduction of their sister by an employee—Keats was compelled to provide another motive for their machinations, which he found in the mercenary souls of these 'Baälites of pelf', and in the frustration of their ambi-tious design to marry Isabella

> To some high noble and his olive-trees.
>
> (st. xxi)

This in its turn led him to conceive of their business operations, extend-ing as they do from the Arctic to Ceylon and Malaya, as on a scale

---

[1] Cf. H. G. Wright, *The first English translation of the 'Decameron'*, pp. 268–9.
[2] 1684 ed., p. 184.

better suited to an English capitalist of the nineteenth century than to a Florentine trader of the fourteenth.

Keats went still further. Since he was to portray an ideal passion, he made the lovers as free from blemish as possible. He was evidently perturbed by the reference to the fact that Lorenzo had at one time cast his eyes upon other 'Beauties in the City', even though he renounced all thought of them for the sake of Isabella, and so the poet suppresses all mention of these earlier episodes as incompatible with a love unique, all-absorbing and self-sufficient. Keats's Isabella also moves on a lofty plane, untouched by human frailties, and so quite consistently, he follows the English translator in avoiding any suggestion of cunning or deceit in her. Hence, instead of hoodwinking her brothers in order to gain their consent to her departure from Florence,

> she had devised
> How she might secret to the forest hie.
>
> (st. xliii)

The fact that Keats passes over some of the grim details of the disinterment of Lorenzo is also related to this tendency towards idealization. In particular, he abstains from mentioning the razor which Isabella, in the version of 1620, takes with her. There was about the provision of such an instrument an air of practical calculation, as one trained in medicine like Keats must have perceived. But he doubtless felt that what was well enough in a surgeon was altogether inappropriate in a heroine distraught with love and grief.

In other respects, however, he agrees closely with the English translation. His shrinking from 'wormy circumstance' in st. xlix has nothing to justify it in the miraculous preservation related by Boccaccio and can only be accounted for by the presentation of the incident in Keats's source. Again, he depicts Isabella as receiving the aid of her nurse in disinterring the body and in severing the head:

> With duller steel than the Perséan sword
> They cut away no formless monster's head,
> But one, whose gentleness did well accord
> With death, as life.
>
> (st. l)

In this fashion Keats reinforces the impression of Isabella's delicate womanliness conveyed by the poem as a whole.

Similarly, he follows the version of 1620 in making the brothers' decision to remove the basil-pot independent of any comment by outsiders. Indeed, he takes yet another step, and, still bent on idealising this love-affair, dismisses the prying neighbours who keep daily watch over Isabella's every movement. Some curiosity remains, but at least it is the interest of relatives and not the idle and malicious talk of unsympathetic strangers. Moreover, the very words in which this part of the poem is framed seem to elevate it above a mean and petty world:

> and many a curious elf,
> Among her kindred, wonder'd that such dower
> Of youth and beauty should be thrown aside
> By one mark'd out to be a Noble's bride.
>
> And, furthermore, her brethren wonder'd much
> Why she sat drooping by the basil green . . .
>
> (st. lvii, lviii)

Like the English translator, too, Keats speaks of 'the silken scarf' in which Lorenzo's head was wrapped and of the 'ditty' sung throughout the countryside about the fate of Isabella. Her attendant too is her nurse, whom Keats pictures as an 'aged Dame' with lean hands and 'locks all hoar', so that, by this embodiment of ancient devotion, he may add pathos and indirectly enhance the attractiveness of the heroine, just as the relationship of Angela to Madeline does in the 'The Eve of St. Agnes'.

It is also possible that 'Isabella' was affected by other parts of the *Decameron* as well as by the tale itself in the English version.[1] In particular, this applies to the scene of Lorenzo's murder. The story in the original Italian has little to say about it, for Boccaccio was above all concerned with swift narration. The event, not the place, was for him the main thing. Evidently the crime was committed somewhere near Messina, the town where Lorenzo had fallen in love with Lisabetta, but the route taken by Lorenzo and her brothers is extremely vague. They went outside the city, and in 'a very solitary and remote place' Lorenzo was slain and buried. When his ghost appears to Lisabetta, it makes no precise statement about the spot where the body lies, but merely indicates 'where they had interred him'. Lisabetta obtains permission to go 'a little way out of the city', and when she and her attendant arrive at the scene of the murder, all we hear is that she cleared away the leaves and dug where the ground seemed less hard. On the whole, the version of 1620 follows all this faithfully enough, except that the translator, with his usual partiality to alliteration, introduces a slight modification for the sake of this literary device:

Having obtained favour of her Brethren, to ride a *d*ays journey from the *C*ity . . . they rode *d*irectly to the *d*esigned place, which being covered with some store of *d*ryed leaves, and more *d*eeply sunk than any other part of the

---

[1] Cf. H. G. Wright, 'Possible Indebtedness of Keats's "Isabella" to the *Decameron*', *R.E.S.*, New Series, 1951, ii, pp. 248–54.

Ground thereabout, they *d*igged not far, but they found the body of the murthered Lorenzo.[1]

Even with this change the only impression that Keats could glean from the tale itself was that the murder occurred in a hollow in a lonely wood at no great distance from Messina.

The poem, on the other hand, transfers the scene to the vicinity of Florence. In considering why Keats did this, we cannot afford to overlook the variant 'Boccace of green Arno' (l. 145)[2] which by associating the two names suggests that it was perhaps Boccaccio who inspired the removal of the tale from Messina to Florence. In that case we are led to ask whether some hints may not be derived from parts of the *Decameron* outside the tale. In the Induction Boccaccio does tell us something of the neighbourhood of Florence when he relates how the narrators, leaving the city behind them, arrived at their destination, 'which was seated on a little Hill, distant (on all sides) from any High-way, plentifully stored with fair spreading Trees', and this isolated dwelling, chosen because it decreased the risk of infection by the plague, was 'due piccole miglia' or, as the version of 1620 says, 'about a Leagues distance' from Florence. Again in the links that unite the ten days of the *Decameron* and provide an artistic relief from each series of tales, Boccaccio is glad to linger a while in the pleasant garden of the palace where the narrators are assembled, or amid its sylvan surroundings.

In one such passage at the end of the sixth day he depicts at length the Valle delle donne. Here

was a small running Brook, descending from one of the Valleys, that divided two of the little Hills, and fell directly through a Vein of the intire Rock it self, that the fall and murmur thereof was most delightful to hear . . . and arriving in the Plain beneath, it was there received into a small Channel, swiftly running through the midst of the Plain, to a place where it stayed, and shaped it self into a Lake or Pond . . . This Pond was no deeper, than to reach the breast of a man, and having no mud or soil in it, the bottom thereof shewed like small beaten gravel . . . And not only was the bottom thus apparently seen, but also such plenty of Fishes swimming every way, as the mind was never to be wearied in looking on them. Nor was this water bounded in with any banks, but only the sides of the Meadow, which made it appear more sightly as it arose in swelling plenty. And always as it superabounded in this course, lest it should overflow disorderly: it fell into another Channel, which conveying it along the lower Valley, ran forth to water other needful places.[3]

[1] 1684 ed., p. 184. In this passage 'alquanto fuor della terra' has been inaccurately rendered by 'a days journey' for the alliteration in 'd'. For the same reason 'dove men dura le parve la terra' is incorrectly translated by 'more deeply sunk than any other part of the Ground thereabout'.

[2] Cf. Keats, *Poetical Works*, ed. H. W. Garrod, Oxford, 1939, p. 221.

[3] 1684 ed., pp. 291–2.

Apart from the reference to the pool with its fish darting about, the most striking feature is the picture of a stream liable to grow turbulent in flood, but making its way through narrow channels which prevent the inundation of the surrounding plain.

In 'Isabella' the journey is in the reverse direction. Attended by Lorenzo, the brothers first ride to the Arno. What information Keats had about the river we do not know. But it is conceivable that Cary's somewhat inaccurate translation of Dante's 'fiumicel' by 'brooklet'[1] induced him to believe that the Arno was much smaller than in reality. It would therefore be easy for Keats to identify the river with the brook that issued from the Valle delle donne. Bearing this possibility in mind, we can follow the course of the riders to

> where Arno's stream
> Gurgles through straiten'd banks, and still doth fan
> Itself with dancing bulrush, and the bream
> Keeps head against the freshets.
>
> (st. xxvii)

This makes us wonder whether the 'straiten'd banks' were not suggested by the lower channel of Boccaccio in the above description and the 'freshets' by the mention of the 'swelling plenty' of the brook. The 'bream', which perhaps is introduced for the sake of the rhyme, is not without a counterpart in Boccaccio's narrative, though he is content not to define the species of fish visible to the characters of the *Decameron*.

Mounting still higher up the Arno, Lorenzo and the brothers 'pass'd the water' and entered a lonely forest. This is precisely what we should expect, for the Valle delle donne, to which the ladies among the narrators withdraw in order to bathe, is appropriately secluded. Hills surround it, 'covered with small Thickets, or Woods of Oaks, Ashes, and other Trees', and in the valley is a copse,

planted with Trees of Firr, Cipress, Laurel, and Pines, so singularly growing in formal order, as if some artificial or cunning hand had planted them, the Sun hardly piercing through their Branches from the top to the bottom, even at the highest, or any part of his course.[2]

The emphasis in Boccaccio is all on the privacy that the wood affords, and there is no hint of gloom or terror. But by the alchemy of Keats's imagination this sombre, sunless grove, 'the dark pine roof', ominous in its brooding silence, the abode of Fear and Death like Wordsworth's grove of yews, becomes 'a forest quiet for the slaughter' of Lorenzo, which is committed in 'the sodden turfed dell', conjured up by the

---

[1] *Purgatory*, xiv, 18. This was accessible to Keats, as the whole of the *Divine Comedy* in Cary's translation had been published in 1814.
[2] 1684 ed., p. 291.

words 'more deeply sunk than any other part of the Ground' in the English version of the story. At the same time Keats does not forget 'other trees', and through the agency of Lorenzo's ghost he intersperses beeches and chestnuts. He also covers the ground with heather and 'red whortleberries', just as he had lined the banks of the Arno with 'dancing bulrush'. From the ghost we learn too that

> a sheep-fold bleat
> Comes from beyond the river
> (st. xxxviii)

to his grave. This may be linked with his words in the next stanza:

> I am a shadow now, alas! alas!
>   Upon the skirts of human nature dwelling
> Alone: I chant alone the holy mass,
>   While little sounds of life are round me knelling,
> And glossy bees at noon do fieldward pass,
>   And many a chapel bell the hour is telling.
> (st. xxxix)

The two passages, taken together, indicate that the spot where he was slain, though solitary, is not too far removed from the haunts of men, and Lorenzo's words imply that it is within reach of fields and a chapel. The essence of this passage is found in the Induction to the eighth day, where Boccaccio relates how

The Queen and her Company, being all come forth of their Chambers, and having walked a while abroad, in the goodly Green Meadows, to taste the sweetness of the fresh and wholesom air, they returned back again into the Palace, because it was their duty so to do. Afterward, between the hours of seven and eight they went to hear Mass, in a fair Chappel near at hand, and thence returned to their Lodgings.[1]

Here again Keats adds details in the form of the sheep and the bees, evoked by the reference to the 'Green Meadows', but one can perceive that he drew his first sketch from the *Decameron*, amplifying what he found wherever he thought fit and blending the scattered details into an artistic whole in the finished picture.

The removal of the tale from Messina to Florence also helped Keats to find a reason for the brothers' hatred of Lorenzo. As Florence had so long been renowned for trade and finance, Keats sought the motive in the ambitious minds of the Florentine merchants who were anxious to make a good match for their sister. Such a marriage is, of course, a common theme, but one cannot help noticing that shortly after the tale of Lorenzo and Isabella[2] comes that of Jeronimo and Silvestra[3], which has as its subject the parting of these Florentine lovers by an

---

[1] 1684 ed., p. 335.   [2] *Dec.* iv, 5.   [3] *Dec.* iv, 8.

ambitious relative on the ground of a disparity in rank and fortune. By the machinations of his mother, Jeronimo, the son of a wealthy merchant, is sent on a journey from Florence to Paris, 'to gain experience in Traffick and Merchandize', and though the offence is less grave than the crime of Isabella's brothers, it leads to the same fatal result, the death of the two lovers. One is all the more inclined to think that Keats's 'Isabella' may have been influenced by this story, because John Hamilton Reynolds, who urged him to write the poem, was especially interested in the tales of the fourth day and himself wrote a metrical version of the seventh and the ninth.[1]

Another possible affinity, this time of a minor order, is to be observed in the phrase that describes the plan of the brothers to marry Isabella

> To some high noble and his olive-trees.
>
> (st. xxi)

The association of high rank and olive-trees may be a reminiscence of the sixth tale of the tenth day where it is related how 'an ancient Knight named Signior *Neri degli Vberti*, forsaking then the City with all his Family and great store of Wealth' bought some land covered with olives and other trees and laid out a garden where he later entertained the king.

Once more our eye is caught when we read of 'the break-covert blood-hounds' (l. 221). It is remarkable, for whereas it alludes metaphorically to the chase, the bloodhound is not ordinarily used for hunting. The hypothesis may be put forward that we have here a vivid impression retained by Keats from the eighth tale of the fifth day.[2] The vision seen by Anastasio of Guido's vengeful ghost, pursuing with his hounds the woman who had been so obdurate in her lifetime, is thus depicted in the version that Keats read:

he looked amazedly round about him, and out of a little Thicket of Bushes and Briars round ingirt with spreading Trees, he espied a young Damosel come running towards him, Naked from the middle upward, her Hair lying on her Shoulders, and her fair Skin rent and torn with the Briars and Brambles, so that the blood ran trickling down mainly, she weeping, wringing her Hands, and crying out for mercy so loud as she could. Two fierce Blood-Hounds also followed swiftly after, and where their Teeth took hold, did most cruelly bite her.[3]

Not less memorable is line 288, where the voice of Lorenzo's ghost is compared to 'hoarse night-gusts sepulchral briars among'. The simile is as striking as it is unusual. We are perhaps at first disposed to interpret 'sepulchral briars' as referring to some neglected church-

---

[1] Vide post, pp. 417–26.

[2] Vide ante, pp. 275–6, 336. It may be noted that Dryden, when dealing with the same incident in 'Theodore and Honoria', speaks of 'Mastiffs' and 'Hell-hounds'.

[3] 1684 ed., p. 251.

yard. However, there are two of Boccaccio's tales which may have been
the starting-point. One is the story of Gisippus, in which the English
version of 1620 describes the nocturnal wanderings of the despairing
Gisippus in Rome and his ultimate arrival in 'an old ruinous part of
the City, over-spread with Briers and Bushes, and seldom resorted unto
by any; where finding a hollow Cave or Vault, he entred into it' and
later witnessed a quarrel between two robbers, of whom one was slain.
The other tale is the first of the fourth day and so in close proximity
to that of Lorenzo and Isabella. Here we read how Guiscardo makes his
way by night through a 'vent-light . . . overgrown with briars and
bushes' to the cave which gives him access to Ghismonda. It is on
emerging from this desolate spot on the hill-side that he is seized and
led away to a cruel death. In each case we have the association of a
cave with briars, night, and death. The sound of the wind that Keats
calls to his aid, in either the one setting or the other, would complete
the powerful simile.

In contrast to this eerie, nocturnal music is that evoked by the
allusion to the tune of Boccaccio's ghittern.[1] The word is rare in the
Decameron. In fact, it occurs only in the fifth tale of the ninth day.
Hence it would appear that this story must have contained some
feature to hold Keats's attention. It tells of the love of Calandrino for
Nicholetta and how he tried to woo her:

On the morrow carrying his Gittern thither with him, to no little delight of
his Companions, he both played and sung a whole Bed-role of Songs, not
addicting himself to any work all the day; but loytering fantastickly, one while
he gazed out of the window, then ran to the gate, and oftentimes down into
the Court, only to have a sight of his Mistress.[2]

Calandrino is a burlesque figure, the butt of his friends, and Boccaccio's
treatment is farcical. Nevertheless, one wonders whether this scene,
transmuted so as to blend with the ardent devotion of Lorenzo, did
not inspire the Pre-Raphaelite picture of stanza xxv:

> And as he to the court-yard pass'd along,
>   Each third step did he pause, and listen'd oft
> If he could hear his lady's matin-song,
>   Or the light whisper of her footstep soft.

As an example of narrative 'Isabella' is not outstanding. At the
beginning it moves too slowly, though later, under the guidance of
Boccaccio, there is a notable improvement. What is most remarkable,
however, is the enrichment of the tale with matter drawn from other
parts of the *Decameron* and with Keats's poetic imagination. Nature is

[1] l. 150. The variant spelling 'guittern', recorded in Garrod's edition of Keats's
Poetical Works, closely resembles that of the *Decameron* known to Keats.
[2] 1684 ed., p. 408.

used to lend beauty, but it is always well controlled and subordinated to the general design. It is no ornamental excrescence but an integral part of the poem, closely linked to the emotions of the heroine. As the title of the poem indicates, it is she who is the central figure, and the melancholy that is never far away in Keats finds expression as she sits lamenting her loss in a bleak setting that harmonises with her grief, even as it does with that of Wordsworth's heroine in *The Thorn*.[1]

> And she forgot the stars, the moon, and sun,
> And she forgot the blue above the trees,
> And she forgot the dells where waters run,
> And she forgot the chilly autumn breeze.
> (st. liii)

Thus if Keats lacks the terse mastery of Boccaccio, his poetic vision bestows on the old tale a new and poignant significance by presenting human sorrow against the background of the universe.[2]

Although the influence of Dryden in turning to Boccaccio in the *Fables* may have had its effect on Keats, that influence operates only in a general way in 'Isabella'. On the other hand, it is most palpable in William Wilmot's poem, *The Tale of Gismunda & Guiscardo*, published in 1819.[3] For the most part it is written in the heroic couplet, interspersed with triplets and alexandrines. In details we find many similarities to Dryden's 'Sigismonda and Guiscardo'. In Wilmot the heroine is Tancred's 'idol'; in Dryden, 'The worship'd idol of her father's eyes'. In each version Tancred is wont to visit his daughter in quest of relaxation from affairs of state; in each, on the fateful day, he goes to her apartment about noon and, finding her absent, as he thinks, with her train of maidens, falls asleep in a chair either behind, or at the head of her bed. Although Wilmot reverts to Boccaccio and departs from Dryden in making Tancred escape through the window, he returns to him again in the picture of his sullen gloom as he schemes revenge. He also borrows from Dryden the secret marriage by a priest, and it is evident that he has been affected by Dryden's line:

> The conscious priest, who was suborn'd before.
> (151)

---

[1] And she is known to every star,
   And every wind that blows;
   And there, beside the Thorn, she sits
   When the blue daylight's in the skies
   And when the whirlwind's on the hill,
   Or frosty air is keen and still.

[2] Matthew Arnold touches on the Isabella Story in his 1853 *Preface*, para. 22. Arnold prefers Boccaccio's treatment.
[3] Page references are to this edition.

Whereas Dryden probably meant only 'procured', Wilmot interprets 'suborn'd' unfavourably. Hence

> by mammon led
> A priest his orison had o'er them read,   (p. 21)

and hence also Gismunda's declaration to her father:

> An hireling priest has ratified my vow:
> The man I spurn, but to the altar bow.   (p. 32)

Gismunda's sternness to the bearer of the goblet is explained by what Wilmot had read in the *Fables*, and his simile for her tears, 'silent as vernal shower', was probably suggested by 'a sober show'r of rain'. The closest verbal parallels occur in these passages:

> (a)   And grant thy youth was exercis'd in arms,
>   When love no leisure found for softer charms . . .
>   ('Sigismonda and Guiscardo' ll. 434–5)
>
>   And if thy youth—'twas exercised in arms,
>   Ne'er left thee leisure for love's softer charms . . .
>   (*Gismunda & Guiscardo*, p. 32)
>
> (b)   her hands yet hold
>   Close to her heart the monumental gold
>   ('Sigismonda and Guiscardo', ll. 713–4)
>
>   She instant clasped the monumental gold,
>   And till her struggling spirit sunk to rest,
>   Held it all fondly pressed against her breast.
>   (*Gismunda & Guiscardo*, p. 68)

   The characters are essentially the same in both writers. Like Dryden, Wilmot emphasises the heroic mind of Gismunda, investing her at the same time with something of the temper of Cleopatra. Thus when the heart was disclosed in the goblet,

> Around she turned, nor shudder'd at the sight,
> But with a marble look, unmoved, severe,
> Without another groan, a sigh, a tear,
> Majestic rose, the golden goblet took,
> Raised it aloft, and thus collected spoke.   (p. 63)

Having drunk the deadly potion, she

> with the air, the dignity of Queen,
> Her canopy ascended, calm, serene:
> There laid her down, and decently to die
> Drew down her robe, and pulled the curtains nigh,
> Placed on her heart the cup, wherein his clay
> So dear was lodged, and held it as she lay
> With eyes upraised—and thus composed and mute
> Awaited death—determined—resolute.   (p. 66)

Wilmot modifies slightly the death-scene in that Gismunda, on hearing the wailing of her women, turns slowly towards them and as if asking for silence gently lays her finger on her lips before she expires.

More important is Wilmot's insistence on her virtue. Though he does not reject the youthful passion of Boccaccio's tale, he tones down the amorous ardour that Dryden had introduced. It cannot be said that Gismunda's attitude to the priest conveys an impression that there was any great depth in her morality, but Wilmot does assert that she was resolved never to cast away 'sacred modesty', despite the voluptuous environment in which she lived.

It was evidently this aspect of her character that led him to abandon the device of the message in the cane. How was Gismunda to inform Guiscardo of her love without appearing forward? The disclosure is arranged in this fashion. There is a report that she is to marry the prince of Pisa, and when Guiscardo observes her looking at a pocket-mirror cased in gold that Tancred had given her, he thinks it to be a portrait of the prince. She hands the mirror to him and says that if he looks, he will see the man whom she loves. He confesses his love and at once regretting his audacity, is about to kill himself; but she restrains him and then, seized with confusion, flees.

An entirely new trait in Gismunda is her love of pensive communion with Nature. At the beginning of the tale she is seated on a cliff gazing over the sea and musing on her love. Again in the third canto she sits in the shade of a cypress, thinking of Guiscardo who is imprisoned in a tower, to which she proceeds in order to sing of her devotion. When he has given a sign of recognition, she takes her lute and sings again.

Equally romantic is the history of Guiscardo himself. A foundling, brought up by Tancred, he was left at Salerno by crusaders returning from the wars, and when he grew up, displayed courage in repelling corsairs who had landed. With his

> hyacinthine curls,
> Youth-blooming cheeks, two strings of orient pearls
> Peeping through lips of coral,
>
> (p. 33)

he possesses godlike beauty and moves with the grace of the palm-tree waving on the mountain-top. This paragon is of English descent, and all women are pleased to behold

> Fair Albion's lily, rose, and tress of gold,
> Her noble frankness, that ne'er frankness shocks,
> Ingenuous front, bold port, and eye, that mocks
> Th'insulting Gaul, and braves him to the field,
> Except to beauty's eye unknown to yield.
>
> (p. 10)

This strange intrusion into Boccaccio's tale only becomes intelligible if we recall that the poem was written four years after the battle of Waterloo. But leaving aside Wilmot's strutting patriotism, we can still find Guiscardo interesting as an example of romantic idealisation, since he combines every quality of body and mind. Yet in a spiritual crisis this intrepid figure is overcome by his feelings. Thus when he learns that Gismunda loves him, if he does not grow faint like Keats's Porphyro, his agitation is equally violent:

> from his palsied hand the mirror dropped.
> At each attempt to speak his efforts vain,
> He pressed the throbbing arteries of his brain,
> Till slowly raising his love-streaming eyes,
> On her's he fixed them.
>
> (p. 15)

The sentimentality of the last two lines of this passage, which brings to mind the second stanza of Keats's 'Ode on Melancholy', recurs in a somewhat different form in connexion with Tancred. His emotion in the death scene, indicated by Boccaccio, is intensified to the point of ludicrous exaggeration:

> Tears, which the world he would have given to shed,
> Stopped short, and refluent sought their fountain-head.
> His pulse scarce beat: gazing he torpid stood,
> As through its channels crept his curdled blood.
>
> (p. 67)

When Gismunda dies, her maidens lament till one of them imposes silence by pointing to the motionless Tancred. Then suddenly

> woe, like hurricane, was heard again.
> Hark! hark! whose cry is that of maddening grief
> Calling on God for mercy—for relief?
> Again it calls, and to those accents wild
> Responsive echo cries, 'my child! my child!'
> Poor Tancred!—oh, lament no more the dead!
> She's gone! lament that now devoted head.
>
> Long had he sat, 'ere tears began to flow,
> A living corpse—sad spectacle of woe!
> His chin reclining on his breast: his eye
> Fixt on the ground in dumb despondency.
> At length one trickling tear was seen: 'he lives,'
> They cried: another and another: 'he revives.'
>
> (pp. 69–70)

Then at last his grief finds full vent:

> He felt the tempest, that within had brewed,
> Burst forth, and with it life itself renewed:
> Roared out his woe, and frantic with despair,
> Plucked at his beard, and tore his hoary hair,

Upon her lifeless corpse his body flung,
Embraced it, kissed it, hugged it, to it clung,
Implored them both in mercy to forgive,
Howled out for death—and yet was doomed to live!

(p. 70)

Uncontrolled violence of passion is united with a mood of sentimental forgiveness at the close of Wilmot's version, as if remorse could atone so soon for Tancred's savage crime. His appearance at the exequies of Guiscardo and Gismunda, barefoot, his head shaven, wearing a hair shirt and carrying a crucifix, draws a tear from every eye. Afterwards he turns friar and retires to a convent, where he passes away calmly on a still autumn evening.

Like some of his contemporaries, Wilmot was fond of descriptions of scenery, and even in the opening lines of the poem Nature is praised as a source of inspiration to those who love her. As he had travelled in Italy when a young man, Wilmot makes the most of his familiarity with the background of the tale. In an autobiographical digression he describes a journey that he made from Salerno to Paestum.[1]

we at eve's cool hour
Salerno quit to shun day's scorching power.
The moon was up: but, oh, how wond'rous fair!
Far brighter there than here, so pure the air;
While reigned a genial warmth, that breathed within
Love, but such love as only fools deem sin,
And gave as[2] through that Eden we were driven
An infelt bliss, a foretaste, sure, of heaven.
Sometimes we passed beneath th'o'erarching vine
Drawn 'cross the road . . .

.   .   .   .

Sometimes we saw on mountain's pine-clad brow
A lonely convent frown on us below.
Sometimes would lie through orange groves our way,
Where we heard thrill the night-bird's amorous lay,
While oft beneath the vine-leaf's darkened shade
We marked the fluttering moth so rich arrayed,
We stopped t'admire the hues its Argus-wings displayed.
But for what charmed afar: woods, vallies, glades,
The distant Apennines' broad lights, dark shades,
In which their Alpine scenery was dressed—
These I'll pass o'er: they cannot be expressed.
Yet would I tell thee, as adown the steep
We heard far off the mountain's torrent leap,

[1] The discovery of ancient Greek temples at Paestum about the middle of the eighteenth century, stimulated the interest of English travellers. Cf. T. Spencer, *Fair Greece Sad Relic*, London, 1954, pp. 157, 195.

[2] The printed text reads 'us'.

How midst the stillness of that heavenly night
Its plaintive echo filled us with delight.
And I would tell thee how, when in the grove
Was hushed awhile the bulbul's tale of love,
We heard the grasshoppers o'er meads embrowned
Chirp ever and anon, while all was lulled around.
And fain of villas would I tell thee too,
Seated, like those, sweet Claude enchanted drew:
Of ruin'd aqueducts, whose arches still
Mark, where once journied many a mountain-rill:[1]
Of temples lovely, though to time a prey,
Hanging where then the wild-goat sleeping lay:
Of leafy cots, at whose green porches hung
The pond'rous pumpkin, where its foliage clung:
Of bubbling fountains, heard midst clumps of pine:
Of grots, like those, delightful Mantuan, thine,
Where the lone goatherd at the noon-tide heat,
Sat gazing round from out his cool retreat,
And saw his flock, where cowering kites repair,
Securely climb, and seem to hang in air.

(pp. 57-9)

Conscious though he was of his inability to convey the magic of the scene, Wilmot was clearly aware of its beauty. So completely had it taken possession of him that, when he tried to depict Gismunda's vision of a Celestial Paradise where lovers would be reunited, it was tinged with the colouring of the Italian landscape. For him the view from the hill overlooking the bay of Salerno was a veritable fairyland; and he tells with infectious delight of the gardens surrounding Tancred's castle—the waterfall flowing down the rock in the background, the meandering stream, the silver cascades, the marble fountains spreading coolness in the heat of summer, the citrons, pomegranates, acacias, myrtles and cypresses, and the fragrance of the flowers wafted by the soft air after sunset. One walk is described with aloes basking in the sun in long vistas of China vases and here, if Haroun Alrashid had strayed and heard the fountain playing, he might have thought that he had gone to take the air in his own gardens. This veil of oriental mystery is cast over the Italian scene once more when Ghismunda's maidens are seen wandering at nightfall through the gardens and relating Arabian tales, or dancing on the lawn to the sound of the clashing cymbal. The gaiety combines with the beauty of the setting to emphasise the misery of Gismunda who, meditating on death, sits in the gloom of the cypress like a wounded hart that has sought out a refuge:

---

[1] In the B.M. copy of the first edition of this work, this line and the preceding one are added in autograph, with a note to the effect that they were omitted by an oversight of the corrector of the press.

The silver moon, the stillness of the night,
That would 'ere this have filled her with delight,
Soon as the nightingale's first thrill she heard,
Left but a blank, now hearing the sweet bird.
The lilies gleaming through the twilight shade,
The statues seen at distance through the glade,
Grew pale and paler, as she looked around,
And all seemed changed in her loved pleasure-ground.
                              (pp. 42–3)

It was chiefly owing to Wilmot's sensitiveness to the beauty of Nature that he was able to swell Boccaccio's tale to a poem of four cantos, occupying eighty pages. But this means a certain disproportion. Nor is this excessive preoccupation with Nature his only weakness. His narrative technique is faulty too. Thus, when he explains how Guiscardo was impelled to confess his love because fear of overstepping his rank was overcome by the thought of Gismunda married to a rival, Wilmot says:

Thou guest'st already, surely, what I mean,
How jealousy . . . but stop, I'll paint the scene.
                              (p. 11)

He again intervenes in person to introduce the account of his journey to Paestum. In doing so he draws the reader's attention to the fact that he is abandoning the story of Gismunda:

And here I'll leave her too, awhile to string
Anew my lyre, and for a moment sing
Those summer-nights, which in that softer clime,
I've found so heavenly.
                              (p. 57)

And the heroine is left to brood over the approaching death of her lover while Wilmot sets out on the road to Paestum. In the end, half-reluctantly, he breaks off the reminiscences of this happy episode and returns to his story:

Of these, and of a hundred beauties more
Fain would I tell thee, I've such ample store,
But that I must such pleasing themes forego
To sing Gismunda's fate, and end my tale of woe.
                              (p. 59)

The person whom he addresses at intervals in the course of his poem is 'Emma'. Presumably she was his wife, but after a sudden and unexplained emergence early in the poem, she returns from time to time with a disconcerting effect. One such occasion is shortly before the Salerno-Paestum digression when, by way of comment on Gismunda's reverie, Wilmot tells how he once dreamt that he and Emma

were seated on a stile looking at their 'old associates', the lambs, the
sheep and a goat, when all at once these tame creatures began to gaze
upon him fiercely until he woke with a start. The episode is trivial and
out of harmony with the heroine's grief, and its introduction as forced
as the dream is irrelevant. But even more conspicuously Wilmot's
inadequacy is revealed at the end of the poem when 'Emma' makes
a last disastrous appearance. Like Guiscardo and Gismunda, Tancred
now is dead,

> And of them all that rests to keep
> Their memories from eternal sleep,
> Is, Emma, the sad tale I've told
> That only shows, they lived of old.
>
> (p. 80)

How vastly superior is Dryden's ending! But even if Wilmot falls
short of the great master in so many ways, his version is interesting
as a re-presentation of 'Sigismonda and Guiscardo' in terms of the
romantic period, with all the warmth of colour derived from personal
memories of the Italian scene.

Some of Wilmot's defects are visible in B. W. Procter's[1] version of
the tale of Lorenzo and Isabetta which was written under the inspiration of Leigh Hunt and first appeared in 1820 as *A Sicilian Story*. As
the title indicates, this version keeps close to Boccaccio, to the extent
that the scene is laid in Sicily. On the other hand, Procter makes his
hero Guido a native of Milan, not Pisa. In accordance with the author's
bent, Guido develops into a romantic figure. His social status is raised,
and he is depicted as the last member of a famous house, driven into
exile at Genoa. His appearance is as distinguished as his lineage, and
he casts a spell on all whom he encounters. It is likely that Procter
transferred Guido's home to Genoa because he wished to display him
as a great seafarer. If Guido has not known such strange adventures as
Othello, he has at least travelled far and wide, and Isabel loves to hear
how he entered the Pacific,

> rolling thro' the billows green,
> And shook that ocean's dead tranquillity.
>
> (st. ix)

Moreover, he has visited lands unknown to Boccaccio; he has mounted
the St. Lawrence and stood by Niagara, and he has watched the Indians
at their sun-worship and gazed on wild deer roaming amid intermin-
able forests, the lair of the serpent and the savage.

Isabel too is of high rank and is first seen in her palace, where a
masque is in progress. In its way the scene is as romantic as those
associated with Guido, and something of its beauty clings to the heroine:

[1] Vide ante, p. 354.

fresh waterfalls
That rose half hidden by sweet lemon bowers
A low and silver-voiced music made.

(st. iv)

In the distance the flame of Etna mounted skywards and overhead the stars shone through the midnight darkness.

One of the most effective passages is that which describes the affliction of the heroine after she has been deprived of the heart:

And then into the dreary wilderness
She went alone, a craz'd, heart-broken thing;
And in the solitude she found a cave
Half hidden by the wild-brier blossoming,
Whereby a black and solitary pine,
Struck by the fiery thunder, stood, and gave
Of pow'r and death a token and a sign:
And there she lived for months: She did not heed
The seasons or their change, and she would feed
On roots and berries, as the creatures fed
Which had in woods been born and nourished.

(st. xviii)

Once, and once only was she seen, and then
The chamois hunter started from his chace,
And stopped to look a moment on her face,
And could not turn him to his sports again.
Thin Famine sate upon her hollow cheek,
And settled Madness in her glazed eye
Told of a young heart wrong'd and nigh to break,
And, as the spent winds waver ere they die,
She to herself a few wild words did speak,
And sung a strange and broken melody;
And ever as she sung she strew'd the ground
With yellow leaves that perished 'ere their time,
And well their fluttering fall did seem to chime
With the low music of her song.

(st. xix)

Here an intimate bond between man and Nature is implicit, and elsewhere in *A Sicilian Story* the same is true. Thus Guido's account of America pictures man, untouched by civilisation, in harmony with the primæval forest:

Nature there in wildest guise
Stands undebased and nearer to the skies;
And 'midst her giant trees and waters wide
The bones of things forgotten, buried deep,
Give glimpses of an elder world.

(st. ix)

Both Guido and Isabel live close to Nature, and their love unfolds against a background of running streams and waves quivering under the breeze at sunset. Similarly, after Guido's death, it is as if it were his spirit in the basil-tree which

> Tow'red in unnatural beauty, waving there
> And whispering to the moon and midnight air.
>
> (st. xv)

No doubt it is an instinctive awareness of the mystic union of man and Nature that urges Isabel in her grief to seek refuge in mountain woods and caves. But Procter gives no palpable form to this cloudy consciousness. Once, after the scene describing the ravine where Guido's body lies, he appears to be on the verge of doing so. He certainly maintains that Nature speaks to man, but the message is indefinite. The description is as follows:

> It was a spot like those romancers paint,
> Or painted when of dusky knights they told
> Wandering about in forests old,
> When the last purple colour was waxing faint
> And day was dying in the west: the trees
> (Dark pine and chesnut, and the dwarfed oak
> And cedar) shook their branches 'till the shade
> Look'd like a living spirit, and as it played
> Seem'd holding dim communion with the breeze:
> Below, a tumbling river rolled along,
> (Its course by lava rocks and branches broke)
> Singing for aye its fierce and noisy song;
> And there on shattered trunks the lichens grew
> And covered, with their golden garments, death;
> And when the tempest of November blew
> The Winter trumpet, 'till its failing breath
> Went moaning into silence, every green
> And loose leaf of the piny boughs did tell
> Some trembling story of that mountain dell.
>
> (st. xi)

One perceives that something is missing. Fluently though Procter writes, the passage lacks a sense of direction. Too often he allows himself to ramble on or to stray aside, and the poem is weakened by prolixity or digression. He has no unifying philosophy and too little artistic discipline. That is why *A Sicilian Story* suffers from a comparison with Keats's 'Isabella'. In places, as Shelley said, it is 'pretty enough',[1] but it has no clear design, and the style is unequal. The song of Isabel is dull indeed by the side of the snatches of artless music sung by the heroine of Keats's poem, and the ending, which aims at the simplicity of the ballad, comes near to bathos:

[1] *Letters*, ed. R. Ingpen, 1914, ii, p. 839.

This is the tale of "Isabel,"
And of her love the young Italian.

(st. xxi)

Nevertheless, the poem appealed to the taste of romantic readers, and in two years three editions were published.

A Sicilian Story was quickly followed[1] by *The Garden of Florence: and other poems* in which John Hamilton Reynolds published two tales in verse, 'The Garden of Florence' and 'The Ladye of Provence', based respectively on the seventh and ninth in the fourth day of the *Decameron*. The Advertisement recalls that they 'were to have been associated with tales from the same source, intended to have been written by a friend', but Keats completed only one story, 'and that is to me now the most pathetic poem in existence!'

For the first poem Reynolds uses the heroic couplet in stanzas of varying length, sometimes ending the stanza with a triplet and occasionally completing it with an Alexandrine. To some extent he condenses the original, omitting the second pair of lovers, Lagina and Stramba and also the two men, Atticciato and Malagevole, who unite with Stramba to accuse the heroine of murdering Pasquino when he has been poisoned by the leaf of the sage in the garden. They become merged in the Florentine populace in the background. On the other hand, the character of the Potestate who has to question the supposed culprit is developed. As one interested in the law Reynolds draws a full-length portrait of this judge, who embodies all the great traditions of English justice and only in his tearfulness departs somewhat from the customary reserve of a high legal authority.

> The Judge, a passionless and aged man,
> Look'd mildly on the creature, young and wan,
> That stood in unmoved gloom,—as forest pines
> When winds are still,—before the Florentines,—
> While turbulent thoughts, clothed in tumultuous breath,
> Clamour'd of cruel hate and desperate death.
> He heeded not each fierce report,—but turn'd,
> And with a voice that seem'd like sound inurn'd,
> Commanded silence:—silent were the crowd
> Before his tone austere and visage proud!
> Potent in length of days and might of mind,
> His very look could sway the people-kind!
> Then looking on Simonida,—some tears
> Ran down his lined cheek, his cheek of years,—
> And pity on his awful brow just brake,
> As morn first tinges night—and forth he spake.
>
> 'We must cast rashness by:—this mute young thing
> Claims in her anguish, patient questioning.

[1] In 1821.

2E

> She looketh not of guilt,—and therefore ruth
> Should shield her sorrow, till the utter truth
> Appears by more than seeming circumstance.—
>
> .   .   .   .
>
> The truth alone I seek,—till that be known
> (And may it still claim pity's gentlest tone!)
> I do vouchsafe thee the respect of all . . .
>
> (st. xxiv, xxv)

However, Reynolds was most concerned with the lovers, and he amplifies and transforms what Boccaccio had related about them. In the original the tale of Pasquino and Simona was expressly meant to show that love is found even in the humblest walks of life. Boccaccio's hero is clearly an apprentice to a wool-dealer, but in Reynolds's version his social status is raised, and he becomes

> a young merchant—fair as young—
> Of noble courage, eloquent of tongue . . .
>
> (st. v)

When he lies dead, the tone is pitched still higher, and the poet asks:

> Where is his gallant lip, his falcon eye—
> His fair and thoughtful forehead—calm and high!—
> His handsome gloomy locks of curled hair,
> His warm embrowned cheek—his noble air
> And deep melodious voice—so manly sweet!
>
> (st. xix)

Though Simonida, as Reynolds, following the English translation of 1620, calls Simona, still gains her living as a spinner, she too is seen with the eyes of a romantic poet. With her dark tresses, 'pearled ear', 'pearl-fair hands', rosy cheeks and lily-white brow she seems a counterpart of Pasquino. She is all youthful innocence and gaiety, and her cheerfulness, as she sings all day, makes the work fly from her hands. In order to display her in a pleasing domestic interior Reynolds invents a scene in which she prepares an evening meal for her father when he returns home from labouring in the woods.[1] This dutiful affection is a trait which distinguishes her from her predecessor in the *Decameron*. Simona consents to Pasquino's request that she shall contrive to come with him to the garden for their greater ease and security, and for this purpose she hoodwinks her father by feigning to go to San Gallo for the pardoning and then betaking herself straight to the place agreed

---

[1] It is possible that the idea of making him a woodcutter was suggested to Reynolds by the word 'timber' in the following passage from the translation of 1620 which describes the dawning love of Simonida for Pasquino: 'As natural instinct was her Tutor thereto, so wanted she not a second main and urging motion, a chip hewed out of the like timber, one no better in birth than her self' (cf. the edition of 1684, p. 190, which was the one that Reynolds, like Keats, no doubt used).

on with her lover. The English translation of 1620, though less definite about the heroine's stratagem, also seems to take her duplicity for granted. Reynolds's Simonida is far different. Like Keats, he idealises the lovers and insists throughout on Simonida's piety and sincerity. Every morning she says 'her young orisons with bowed heart' and on the tragic Sunday which was to witness her death

> After prayer
> She veil'd her forehead, and adown the stair
> Went, by her father's leave, for she had said
> The story of her love unvarnished:
> First to Saint Gallo, for his pardon pure,
> The damsel pass'd; and then, serenely sure,
> She met Pasquino . . .
>
> (st. xi)

Here is no concealment, for there is nothing to conceal. Indeed, the love of Pasquino and Simonida is beyond reproach:

> They met all innocence—and hope—and youth;
> And all their words were thoughts—their thoughts, pure truth.
>
> (st. vi)

This carries one stage further the declaration of the translation of 1620 that no immodesty passed between the lovers, whereas in the *Decameron* their relationship is yet one more example of burning passion. Again, Reynolds's tale follows the Jacobean version in representing the visit to the garden as a sedate stroll. However, Reynolds is independent in letting it occur on the first day after the engagement of Pasquino and Simonida, and he conveys admirably the luminous joy that they feel:

> Their eyes in married lustre could not part,
> But, lighted by the radiance of the heart,
> Shone on each other.
>
> (st. xii)

Their devotion is whole-hearted like that of Lorenzo and Isabella, and no thought of others enters their minds. The numerous Florentine youths who pine for Simonida make no impression upon her, and because her love is all-absorbing, she is stunned by the death of Pasquino. Boccaccio's heroine was not slow to shriek for aid, but Simonida behaves in accordance with the account in the translation of 1620, where she is seen 'in a gastly amazement, all her senses meerly confounded'.[1] She gazes at the body as if it were strange to her, as if she had ceased to exist; her voice fails and she is reduced to 'statue-like despair'. Before the Potestate she stands mute and motionless, and later when she does speak, it is with convulsive gasps. Her misery is

[1] 1684 ed., p. 191.

as overwhelming as that of Keats's Isabella. She dies with Pasquino's name on her lips, even as he had died with his eyes fixed on her.

Reynolds intensifies the pathetic effect when he limits the interval between the flowering of their love and their death to less than twenty-four hours, in much the same way as Shakespeare compressed events in *Romeo and Juliet.* He also seeks to heighten the tragedy by letting Pasquino, when about to taste the deadly leaf, deride the supposed valuable properties of sage as an old crone's superstition. Indeed, he jests only a moment before he falls dead. A sense of impending disaster has already been aroused by the poet's warnings that the lovers' happiness will be short-lived. Sadness creeps over his tale like

> a slow cloud, and forms
> A gloom like that which prophesies of storms!
> (st. viii)

It is probable that Reynolds had the same intention when he related the fortunes of the lovers against an autumnal background of yellowing leaves. His purpose is certainly clear when he describes the shadows of Pasquino and Simonida on the laurels as they walk to and fro in the garden, and tells afterwards how

> Her solitary shape return'd, and gave
> A shade like something wandering from the grave.
> (st. xx)

As might be expected from the title of the poem, the garden occupies an important position. With its fragrant flowers and trees and singing-birds it lends beauty to the tale. At the same time Reynolds creates a solemn atmosphere which harmonises with the Sabbath day and the piety of Simonida:

> The lofty foliage lent a tender gloom,
> Like that which doth through holy buildings come,—
> Where, as adown the shafted aisles you stray,
> The very silence seems to feel and pray.
>
> .   .   .   .   .   .
>
> The paths were still—save when the small bird threw
> His morning notes around, like sprinkled dew,—
> And even the bird's light voice but seemd' to wake
> A hymn to silence, even for silence' sake!
> (st. xiii, xiv)

The air of sabbatical calm on this autumn morning is akin to that in Keats's 'Eve of St. Mark'. Very striking too is the way in which the birds' joyous song and the roses filled with bright dew are used to suggest the mood of the lovers before the disaster and then the contrasting mood of Simonida after Pasquino's death:

The dew was on the leaf, it look'd chill tears,—
Not pearls, as to the lovers it appears!
The hanging white rose shudder'd in the air,
As it were sick with grief, and pale with care;—
The birds were painfully alive with song:—
She heard,—and, drown'd in grief, went silently along.
(st. xxi)

So intimately is this romantic garden associated with the lovers that Reynolds, departing from Boccaccio and his Jacobean authority, has them buried there and not in the church of San Gallo.

The lonely nightingale and watching star
At eve for ever their companions are!
(st. xxxiii)

From other poems in the volume it is evident that Reynolds, whose marriage took place about 1821, was at the time of their composition much concerned with love, and one has a strong impression that his own experience sharpened his sympathies for Pasquino and Simonida. There is, for example, a personal note in a digression on the lover, watching the moon and the stars as he lies vainly trying to sleep. And his attitude towards the dead hero and heroine is significant. Boccaccio had not disguised his tender feelings for them, but in view of the nature of their love he leaves their fate in the next world obscure:

Oh! happy souls for whom one and the same day was the term of ardent love and earthly life! Happier still, if to the same bourn ye fared! Ay, and even yet more happy, if love there be in the other world, and there, even as here, ye love![1]

The English translator of 1620 regards them as 'poore infortunate Louers, whose Starres were . . . inauspicious', but despite his compassion he will not go further than to say:

How to censure of your deaths, and happines to ensue thereon by an accident so straunge and ineuitable: it is not within the compasse of my power, but to hope the best.

Reynolds, keenly alive to the tragedy of so premature an end to the happiness of Pasquino and Simonida, also regards them as unfortunate lovers. Nevertheless, he confidently maintains:

auspicious were your stars
To end your mortal lives and fervent love
In one day's space! Heaven hath ye both above![2]
(st. xxx)

[1] J. M. Rigg's translation.
[2] These lines are important because they show that Reynolds was following the 1684 edition which had altered the 1620 edition and read: 'Oh poor unfortunate Lovers, whose Stars were so auspicious to you, as to finish both your mortal lives, and fervent love, in less limitation than a days space.'

The theme of tragic love, this time in the highest ranks of mediæval society, again attracted Reynolds in 'The Ladye of Provence'. Boccaccio's tale of the friendship between two knights and of how Messer Guiglielmo Rossiglione revenges himself on Messer Guiglielmo Guardastagno, when the latter falls in love with Rossiglione's wife, by murdering him and serving his heart as a dish for the lady, is one of the grimmest in the *Decameron*. Indeed, it is remarkable that a story which offered a parallel to some of the bloody revenge plots of Seneca should have been almost entirely neglected by the Elizabethan playwrights.[1] Perhaps it was an instinctive awareness of its dramatic possibilities that led Reynolds to hark back to the dominant sixteenth-century tradition and choose blank verse as his medium.

Rossiglione's wife, nameless in the original, he calls Indreana, this being probably suggested by Andreana, which he found in the English version of 1620, in the sixth tale of the fourth day, instead of Boccaccio's Andrevuola. Another change that he made was to bestow a new name on Rossiglione, as he claimed that Rossiglione 'would not accommodate itself to metre'. He replaced it by Francesco Virgillisi, who figures in the fifth tale of the third day. The spelling of this name indicates that Reynolds had read one of the later editions of the Jacobean translation.[2] Certainly, 'The Ladye of Provence' contains many verbal similarities to this version, far more indeed than 'The Garden of Florence'. They are especially numerous in the latter part of the story after Virgillisi and Indreana have seated themselves to supper.[3] Reynolds adds a character, Gardastagno's[4] wife, whose devotion to her husband is intended as a contrast to the conduct of Indreana. She is a gentle, timid creature, and when for a reason which she cannot divine an estrangement springs up between her and her friend, when Indreana makes excuses and absents herself, she shuts herself up in her chamber. Though Gardastagno has wronged her, after his death she mourns him and enters a convent.

Reynolds was not without a sense of the mediæval setting. He depicts the two ladies sitting over their broidery and talking of their ornaments

---

[1] Vide ante, p. 197.

[2] The form in the original was 'Vergellisi' which was followed in the English translation of 1620 and in the text of the tale in the second edition of 1625, though here the preamble has 'Vergillisi'. The editions of 1634, 1657 and 1684 read 'Virgillisi'. As Keats used the fifth edition of 1684, it may well be that Reynolds had recourse to the same copy.

[3] After the murder Virgillisi wraps his enemy's heart in his lance's 'bandelot'. During and after the supper scene the following are derived wholly or in part from the Jacobean translation: 'Many fair speeches', 'Trust me, madam', 'I pray you, sir', 'I will resolve thee quickly', 'Sighs vehement brake forth', 'Nor house with one, who fills my thoughts with blood', 'a great gazing window', 'Like a body without its soul, stood Virgillisi Confounded'.

[4] 'Gardastagno' is the form used by Reynolds.

and rich apparel, their hawks, palfreys and hounds, their pages and their lords. Similarly, to emphasise the intimate friendship of the knights, he portrays them as hunting the boar together:

> They were as brothers in their sports,—their joys,
> Their wonted occupations,—and there never
> Went by the day, but the wild forest boar
> Burst from its lair, before two gallant Hunters,
> Mounted alike,—and habited alike,
> With spears of the self-same fashion. Side by side
> They rode, like the godlike brothers of old,—and never
> Fail'd in the sharing of the chase's dangers.
> There you should see them skirting the deep wood,
> In mantles greener than the sombre pine,—
> And cheering on the hounds with voices, tuned
> By long society to sound as one.[1]
>
> (p. 158–9)

Perhaps it was Reynolds's fondness for the world of chivalry that caused him to alter the circumstances of the murder. In the *Decameron* Rossiglione lies in wait for his foe, and when he arrives with two servants, pierces him with his lance. Reynolds portrays Gardastagno as wandering alone in the woods musing about Indreana, as he awaits the arrival of Virgillisi according to their agreement. Consequently, he avoids the treacherous ambush, unworthy of a knight, and produces a dramatic scene. Gardastagno decides to seek Virgillisi's castle and ask for news of him:

> He turn'd his steed.—Hark! o'er the quiet grass
> Came the sound and ring of steeled trappings,—loud,
> And louder,—and anon a knight was seen,
> With two attendants,—armed from the crown
> Down to the heel complete;—their faces hid
> By the closed beaver;—and their steeled garments
> Sheening and sounding in the golden sun.
>
> .   .   .   .   .   .
>
> And with no curbed pace the knight came on.
> He flash'd his sword in the startled light—and spurr'd
> His black and rushing barb
>
> (pp. 165–6)

and cut the hated Gardastagno down.

The woods, especially at sunset, appear to have fascinated Reynolds and from time to time he gives us glimpses of them as the background to the doings of his characters. At the very beginning he describes the two castles, lit up by the glow in the western sky and embedded in the surrounding trees. Here the woodland seems to offer peace and security, but when Virgillisi withdraws thither to brood over his wrongs on long

---

[1] Quotations from the edition of 1821.

and silent walks, it takes on a sombre air. Quite different again is the
mood when Gardastagno rode abroad, thinking of Indreana,

> into a cool wood,—
> A cool enchanting wood,—where the grass spread
> Its gentlest verdure under arched trees,
> And the yellow lustre of the evening sun
> Flooded the topmost branches—and stream'd through
> The broken foliage, down to the green grass.
> He rode unarm'd and tenderly along,
> And slowly, for a lustrous sunset gave
> Its poesy to the heart—and they who love,
> Cannot but idle when the eve is fair.
>
> (pp. 163–4)

The murder of Gardastagno coincides with the setting of the sun:

> the deep wood-shadows fell
> Heavily down to earth—and the night gusts
> Of the chilling wind ruffled the lofty trees,
> Making a dismal moaning, as for death.
>
> (p. 167)

But it is not only the death of Gardastagno that the poet has in mind.
The eerie moaning forebodes the suicide of Indreana, which is again
closely associated with the giant trees and the western sky. From this
moment no light shines on the forest. All we see is the figure of Virgillisi, a prey to remorse, prowling and shuddering in the woods.

The circumstances leading to the suicide of Indreana and the suicide
itself are described with touches of vivid detail. The heroine, dreaming
in the twilight at the lattice with her lute by her side, the revelation
of Virgillisi's hideous revenge, her plunge through the open window,
the sound of the crashing branches, and then the sickening silence,
while her scarf, caught by the casement, streams into the night. The
subsequent emotions of Virgillisi are also well portrayed, though the
picture of his remorse is somewhat exaggerated:

> through the night
> Strange phantoms trampled o'er his heart, and died
> Fiercely before his eyes.—His menials heard
> Pitiful screams at midnight in his room,
> But never might they break his solitude.
> At last, grief-madden'd,—from Provence he fled,—
> No one knew whither: He return'd no more!
>
> (p. 174)

One of the motives for his flight, the fear of the vengeance of the
country-folk, which is mentioned by Boccaccio and the English translator of 1620, is omitted by Reynolds. In this way the action of Virgillisi is due entirely to his guilt-haunted mind. What cause then had

he to feel the pangs of conscience? Boccaccio leaves no doubt that
Guardastagno and Rossiglione's wife were lovers; their relations illustrate his belief in the invisible power of love, regardless of law or moral
code and regardless of consequence. Hence the husband's anger was
fully justified, and only the means employed to wreak his vengeance
could be condemned. The Jacobean translator is somewhat ambiguous.
He asserts that Guardastagno 'became over fondly enamoured' but adds
that he cannot say whether 'this idle love . . . sorted to effect, or no'.
Later, however, he makes the heroine declare that she has not been
unchaste, and this statement is accepted when Rossiglione laments the
'loss of a chast and honourable Wife, and through his own over-
credulous conceit'.[1] Reynolds conforms in a general way to this interpretation, and Indreana rebuts all charges of unchastity. But he
emphasises more strongly than the English translator the offence of
the lovers. He chides Indreana for not repelling Gardastagno's advances
and points out that 'this lawless passion', thus unchecked, 'grew on
to dangerous strength'. Similarly, he is careful to express his disapprobation of Gardastagno's longing for Indreana as he wanders in the
wood:

> Thus did he shame, with an unworthy love
> And erring speech, the ear of hallow'd eve!
>
> (p. 165)

And when Gardastagno sees Virgillisi rushing upon him, conscious of
his guilt, he awaits his doom steadfastly:

> He knew the voice of his wrong'd friend—and sought
> No safety—death was near—and he could die.
>
> (p. 166)

As is shown by the last words of this passage, Reynolds was not
entirely hostile to Gardastagno. In fact, the lawyer and the lover were
at variance within him. On legal and ethical grounds he had to
recognise that Indreana and Gardastagno were at fault. Yet he himself
was young, and despite his occasional asperity, at other times he abates
his rigour. In this mood he sees those whom he had elsewhere condemned, as a 'wretched pair of frail fond lovers' who

> walk'd, and read,
> And gazed upon each other, even as two
> Guiltless adorers in the heart of youth.
>
> (p. 163)

And at the close his instinctive sympathy breaks forth in favour of
'the Unfortunates'.

As this analysis shows, Reynolds's two verse tales possess a certain
imaginative quality and a sense of unity and artistic design, but his

---

[1] Quotations are from the 1684 edition.

poetic expression does not achieve the inspired perfection and intensity of his friend Keats. If 'The Garden of Florence' and 'The Ladye of Provence' had appeared in the same volume as 'Isabella', the disparity would have been only too manifest.

Unlike Reynolds, it was to the Italian text[1] of the *Decameron*, the 'celebrated store-house of matter for tales, novels, and plays'[2] that Charles Lloyd turned in 1821 for his rhymed version of the story of Titus and Gisippus. However, he modified it so extensively that it has little in common with Boccaccio's work. Titus never leaves Athens for Rome; nor does he make the famous speech to the Athenians. Gisippus is not sent into exile and never visits Rome. Consequently, he is not tried for murder, and the scene where Titus attempts to save him by asserting that he is the criminal, is eliminated. In fact, everything is focused on events in Athens. But here again the situation is different. Far from being surrounded by a circle of influential relatives, Sophronia is the daughter of a poor widow upon whom, without Sophronia's knowledge, the benevolent Gisippus has bestowed a stipend. Moreover, the marriage is not a family arrangement, for Sophronia has her say in the matter. Titus falls in love with her, as in Boccaccio, on the occasion of a visit to her home with Gisippus. But Lloyd introduces an episode to explain the later violence of Titus's passion. Near Piræus, Titus one day catches sight of Sophronia returning from Salamis in a boat which strikes a rock. He rescues her from the rough sea, and from that moment she loves him as ardently as he loves her. Yet both are conscious of their obligation to Gisippus. Another factor that weighs with Titus is the memory of the kindness that he received from Chræmes, to whom on his death-bed he had given a solemn promise ever to remain the friend of Gisippus. He has therefore refrained from trying to see Sophronia again.

However, as the story opens, Gisippus announces in dramatic fashion that he must leave Athens that same evening, even though the nuptial feast is fixed for the very next day. Without explaining his mysterious departure he bids Titus convey the message to Sophronia. Torn between friendship for Gisippus and his secret love for Sophronia, Titus collapses on her threshold. After a painful scene, in which both Titus and Sophronia endure great mental anguish, he rushes out into the night. Next morning Gisippus on his way encounters his friend in a state of delirium and learns the reason for his suffering. His own secret is then disclosed. Some months after he had become plighted to Sophronia, he chanced to make a voyage to Salamis where he fell in love with an orphan called Lesbia who returned his affection. It was

[1] See the Advertisement to 'Titus and Gisippus' in *Desultory Thoughts on London, Titus and Gisippus, with other poems*, p. 159.   [2] Ibid., p. 159.

to see Lesbia who lay sick unto death as the result of her hopeless longing that he had left Athens in such haste. Now all ends happily with the union of Gisippus and Lesbia, and Titus and Sophronia.

It is above all in the psychology of the characters that Lloyd is interested. In keeping with the condition imposed at the end of the ninth day of the *Decameron*, the tale of Titus and Gisippus, like all those of the tenth day, dealt with the theme of generosity. Lloyd was an essentially serious writer, and all the characters in his story, men and women alike, are distinguished by their high-mindedness. He maintains that

> Only minds noble thus can nobly love;—
>   And noble minds are to themselves a law;—
> None ever such an ecstasy could prove
>   Who knew not virtue's consecrating awe.
>
> (st. 77)

On the other hand, he denies

> That ever true love did a comfort know,
>   Where lawless bliss by lawless means was gain'd.
>
> (st. 87)

It is the clash between passion and principles that he seeks to depict, and he explores at length the eddies and currents of emotion that sway all his figures, but especially Titus and Sophronia. A tale of friendship becomes a study of feeling struggling with conscience, and the development is made especially clear if we compare Sophronia with her passive counterpart in Boccaccio.

However, the whole poem is pitched in too high a key. The outward effects of sentiment are exaggerated. It is true that Boccaccio had described how Titus languished for unrequited love. But Lloyd introduces a Lesbia who pines and wastes away until her limbs are shrunk and feeble, and his Titus behaves in an incredible fashion. Illness follows illness. He faints at Sophronia's door, and when she has restored him to consciousness, he stands like a statue, his glazed eyes emitting an unnatural glare until he dissolves into floods of tears. Having said farewell, he foams at the mouth and in delirium races wildly through the streets, clenching his hands and tearing his hair, until an artery bursts. Even the stout-hearted Sophronia suffers from 'faultering knees', and only Gisippus appears to face his troubles with relative equanimity.

This heightening of emotion is accompanied by a corresponding manifestation of natural phenomena. Gisippus leaves Sophronia's dwelling amid the growl of thunder and the lurid glare of lightning, and next morning the sunrise is an equally lurid red. The mood of misery and ill-omen is intensified in the stanzas that follow:

Towards winter autumn then was verging:—then,
    For the first season, with unmuffled face,
Had winter dar'd to stalk thro' ev'ry scene,
    And rob the pale earth of that lingering grace
Of tints, of flowers, of leaves, which seem'd to lean,
    With a meek trust, in the prolong'd embrace
Of nature: for the first time, then arose
The distant mountains clad with morning snows.

Upon the half-stripp'd branches, which did bend
    To the wild blast, here droop'd a yellow leaf,
And there a brown one. With day's light did blend
    A sombre shade which spoke of nature's grief.—
To the eager air the season seem'd to lend
    A piercing shrewdness; and if still a sheaf
Broke the long furrows' level, soddening rains
Had smear'd its golden hue with dingy stains.

The leaves whirl'd eddying towards the plashy ground;
    Their lustre gone, the shrivell'd flow'rets droop'd;
And, from afar, on every side around,
    Were heard deep bodings, as if tempests, coop'd
In viewless caves, thence issued with profound
    And gusty menaces: the night-wolf whoop'd
A dismal requiem to the waning year:—
All sights look'd sorrow, and all sounds breath'd fear.

Th'autumnal moon with pale and watery face
    Westward was verging, and her shadowy rim
Thin, floating, mist-like clouds, seem'd to embrace;
    Hovering about her, as if they would dim
Her silver light; so shorn her golden grace,
    So like a spectre did her glances swim
On that cold morning's brow, that she might well
The demon seem that wove its blighting spell.
                              (st. 107–10)

The passage is effective in its way, but in the meantime the narrative
waits, and when Lloyd resumes, one is conscious of the delay. The
author himself is sometimes uncomfortably aware of such weaknesses.
He indicates this uneasiness by some such phrase as 'But to return to
Titus',[1] 'Return we now to Titus',[2] or 'I have long digress'd'.[3] Even
more marked is the awkwardness of this stanza:

Such Titus was. Such had his intercourse
    Been with Sophronia! I will not detain
My patient hearers with a long discourse
    Touching the *cause* Gisippus did sustain
From his troth'd bride that night such strange divorce:
    If ye consent to listen to my strain,

[1] st. 53.   [2] st. 125.   [3] st. 88.

> *That will*, like many other things, in time,
> Be in the record of this simple rhyme.
>
> (st. 52)

When the moment for revelation of this secret comes, Gisippus is so
overcome with embarrassment that he has to hand over the task to
the poet:

> He spake of this, but so mysteriously,
> That his defects the bard must need supply.—
> Thus somewhat still is left for me to say . . .
>
> (st. 150–1)

Again the reader is pulled up with a jerk, and this halting technique
makes it evident that despite his poetic qualities and his apt quotations
from Tasso and Ariosto, Lloyd had not mastered the art of the tale in
verse.[1]

The note of hysteria, rising at times to frenzy, which is audible in
Lloyd's 'Titus and Gisippus', is entirely lacking in Coventry Patmore's
poem, 'The Falcon',[2] which also has noble love as its theme. It was
written in haste at the publisher's request, in order to lend more

---

[1] A comparison of the first tale in *Stories after Nature* by Keats's friend Charles
Wells exhibits a similar defect. The volume was first published anonymously in 1822,
and the story in question, which is in prose, is a free adaptation of the Titus and
Gisippus theme. The scene is laid in Ravenna. Julia, the only daughter of a judge,
falls in love with his secretary, Lysius. When her affection is not reciprocated, her
health begins to fail. The judge approaches Lysius and he consents to marry her, but
on hearing that a large estate in Athens has come unexpectedly into his possession,
he breaks off the match and departs for Athens.

Three years pass, and to prevent Julia from brooding over her sorrow, the judge has
a cell built behind a buttress near his seat in the court of justice and provides it with
curtains. One morning a man in tattered apparel is brought in and charged with
murder. Julia recognises him and leaves the court. Though Lysius protests his
innocence, he is sentenced to death, but Julia, having dyed her face and neck and
hands and tied her hair in knots, and dressed in ragged clothes, returns to declare
herself the murderer. Next morning she is condemned to death. However, the man
who is supposed to have been killed recovers his senses and accuses the murderers.
Nothing is said of what happens to them! Then Julia

> took Lysius's hand and kissed it, and a tear fell on it; so she departed. When she
> touched him he trembled like a child (for he knew her), but was dumb with
> remorse and wonder. After this time Julia became more peaceful, seeing she had
> saved her lover's life.

Lysius is touched by her magnanimity and, having retrieved his fortunes in Athens,
comes back to Julia's house at Ravenna:

> When she came into the hall she wondered who this stranger might be; but when
> he fell at her feet, thanking her for his life, asked pardon for the past, and besought
> her hand, she shouted, and fainted in his arms.

Thus Boccaccio's tale of friendship is made one of romantic and sentimental love.
As an example of narrative, it warrants the opinion of Swinburne in the prefatory
note to Wells's *Joseph and his Brethren* in 1876 that his work lacks 'the direct aim
and clear comprehension of story which are never wanting in Boccaccio'.

[2] In the original edition of 1844 the poem was called 'Sir Hubert'.

ample proportions to the volume in which it was to appear in 1844.[1]
Patmore was therefore far from content with this tale,[2] but in contrast
to the figures in Lloyd's story those of Patmore are marked by poise
and restraint. The theme was well suited to his outlook on life. His
comment when he intervenes in person is characteristic:

> in noble bosoms, love once lit can never cease.
>
> (p. 405)

He amplifies this in the next few lines:

> Who say, when somewhat distanced from the heat and fiercer might,
> 'Love's brand burns us no longer; it is out,' use not their sight:
> For ever and for ever we are lighted by the light:
>
> And ere there be extinguish'd one minutest flame, love-fann'd,
> The Pyramids of Egypt shall have no place in the land,
> But as a nameless portion of its ever-shifting sand.
>
> (p. 405)

This ideal love then is the central theme, and the unswerving devotion
of Federigo to Giovanna, here called Sir Hubert and Lady Mabel, lends
itself admirably to Patmore's interpretation. Nevertheless, it may be
objected that his vision is now and then too romantic. He heightens
the attraction of the hero by declaring that women forswore marriage,
since they could not wed him. Again, if Hubert retains his falcon when
all his wealth has gone, it is solely because its eyes remind him of
Mabel's, and in poverty he finds, not only peace and freedom of the
mind but plenty as well. Such improbabilities do not carry conviction.
In other directions, however, there is much to praise. One of the most
striking features of the story is its condensation. Because he wishes to
concentrate attention on the relationship of Hubert and Mabel, Patmore eliminates his servant and her brothers. Even the son, who is in
the end the means of uniting the hero and heroine, barely appears.
Boccaccio had much to say of the boy's acquaintance with Federigo
and his consequent love of the falcon; at even greater length he records
the conversation between child and mother, Giovanna's reluctance to
ask Federigo for the bird, and her ultimate yielding to the entreaties
of her sick boy. Patmore keeps his eyes fixed all the time on the theme
of faithful love. Anything else—maternal affection, the devotion of the
servant, the worldly wisdom of the brothers dissuading from marriage
with a penniless man—he thrust aside. Details which in Boccaccio's
eyes were essential for verisimilitude are omitted. Patmore does not
bother about the laying of the table for the meal and even leaves

---

[1] Cf. F. Page, *Patmore A Study in Poetry*, Oxford, 1933, p. 34.

[2] In view of the circumstances in which the poem was written and of Patmore's
dissatisfaction with it, the text of the later version given by Basil Champneys in the
edition of 1928 has been preferred. Quotations are from the 1928 ed.

Mabel, while Hubert cooks the falcon, to look after herself, without any indication of where she is or what she is doing.

This terseness is reminiscent of the traditional ballad which again comes to one's mind because of the opening stanzas in which the story is rapidly set in motion. But an even more notable example of this technique is to be observed when we examine the lengthy explanation by Giovanna of her errand and the equally lengthy apology of Federigo for his inability to comply with her request. All this is compressed by Patmore into a few words:

> In midst of this her dinner, Mabel gave her wish its word:
> 'My wilful child, Sir Hubert, pines from fancy long deferr'd;
> And now he raves in fever to possess your famous bird.'
>
> 'Alas!' he said, 'behold it there.'
>
> (p. 408)

Having made his narrative so economical in many respects, Patmore feels himself at liberty to expand it in others. This applies especially to the ending which he invents. On leaving his house, Mabel invites Hubert to visit her, so that they may meet as friends. After the lapse of some months she sends her page to beg him again to come. As he is ignorant of her son's death, he fails at first to understand her hint that things are changed. Then his eyes chance to fall on her black dress, and all suddenly becomes clear,

> as when the moon,
> Long labouring to the margin of a cloud, still seeming soon
> About to swim beyond it, bursts at last as bare as noon.
>
> (p. 410)

Such passages as that just quoted are also characteristic of Patmore's occasional relaxation of his severe discipline in order to satisfy his love of natural beauty. The longest occurs just before Mabel arrives at his house in quest of the falcon. It is a spring morning, and the joy that is abroad harmonises with the spontaneous happiness of Hubert at the unexpected approach of the woman for whom he has sacrificed all his fortune.

> The wind was nearly risen; and the airy skies were rife
> With fleets of sailing cloudlets, and the trees were all in strife,
> Extravagantly triumphant at their newly gotten life.
>
> Birds wrangled in the branches, with a trouble of sweet noise;
> Even the conscious cuckoo, judging wisest to rejoice,
> Shook around his 'cuckoo, cuckoo', as if careless of his voice.
>
> (p. 406)

Then the clouds disappear and now in its zenith the sun shines forth in all its brilliance. The hour of dazzling splendour is well chosen to symbolise the relationship of Mabel to Hubert. To kindle the sympathy of the reader to a still greater intensity Patmore describes the throbbing ecstasy of the nightingale's song, until it is interrupted when Mabel approaches through the myrtles. One may criticise the improbability of the nightingale's lyric rapture at high noon, but at least one can appreciate the poet's desire for a dramatic entry and his sense of unity. Another sign of his power of construction is the return, at the close, of the first stanza in a slightly varied form which imparts an impression of completeness.

In spite of the English names of the characters, the poem has an air of strange romance. This land has valleys that flow with oil and wine, and we breathe this vaguely exotic atmosphere again in the lines:

> her mouth
> Was sweet beyond new honey, or the bean-perfumed South,
> And better than pomegranates to a pilgrim dumb for drouth!
>
> (p. 407)

These Biblical and Swinburnian overtones help to carry the reader on the wings of fancy to the realm of perfect, faithful love.

It seems highly probable that when Patmore at the age of twenty-one turned to Boccaccio, it was indirectly under the influence of Hazlitt[1] of whom his father was the disciple.[2] We cannot say whether or not Emma Martin's *Frederic and the Falcon*, published in 1847, was also inspired by him. In her short prologue, however, she makes it clear that she is writing in the tradition of Dryden's *Fables*. 'Mr. Dryden', she says, 'translated

three of Boccaccio's romances, but left untouched that of Frederic and the Falcon. Without possessing the dignity of Cymon and Iphigenia, the strong personal interest of Sigismonda and Guiscardo, or the wild dramatic grandeur of Theodore and Honoria, in tenderness and chivalrous feeling it is the highest. The temptation was great, though recalling Dryden to the reader's memory, to translate this beautiful Italian romance into English verse.'

Her tale is a straightforward rendering of no particular interest, and the authoress was right in alluding to her 'simple strain'.

Further proof of the popularity of this story is afforded by its inclusion in James Payn's volume, *Stories from Boccaccio*, which appeared in 1852, along with five other tales. 'Federigo and Giovanna' is quite successful. In the original there are few figures, and the background is but lightly sketched, which enables Payn without too much effort to concentrate attention on the two central figures. However, certain features of Boccaccio's story are omitted, such as the discussion between the brothers about a second husband for the widowed Giovanna and the presence of her attendant when she visits Federigo, the second

---

[1] Vide ante.   [2] Cf. F. Page, op. cit., p. 21.

omission in its turn necessitating the introduction of a moment of hesitancy on her part:

> And came unto the door of him she spurned
> And lifted the mean latch, and blushed, and turn'd,
> But thought of her pale boy and entered in.
>
> (p. 20)

On the other hand, certain descriptions are added. In particular, there is an account of Federigo's love of hawking and his affection for his falcon. Payn pictures his feelings when he has to kill the bird and is not altogether free from sentimentality when relating its death:

> his brave bird he caught,
> (If that be caught which comes unto the breast
> With outspread trustful wings as to its nest,)
> And slew; its large grey eyes with wonder ta'en
> As were his own with tears.
>
> (pp. 20–1)

But the most notable addition is the autumnal background that serves as a prelude to the tale with its initial narrative of Federigo's misfortunes. The landscape blends with his mood of bleak dejection:

> A light wind goeth through the trees,
> And stirreth up along the leas
> A single dead leaf here and there,
> For the lofty heads are bare
> And the gnarled arms on high
> Outstretch them, naked, to the sky;
> A strange and faintly solemn sound
> Circleth all the landscape round,
> As if the yet green fields foreknow
> Of blighting frost and drifting snow,
> And have their grateful grief to pour
> For sunlit Summer, now no more.
> A time for pale cheeks, and dim eyes,
> Despairs, and bitter memories.
>
> (p. 17)

There is a fundamental affinity between Payn's use of nature here and in 'Guiscard and Ghismond'. The love of these two famous characters flowers with the wild rose in summer; it withers when the snows of winter fall. The footprints of Guiscard, plain for all to see, betray him, and he is slain by the waiting Tancred and his men. The discovery and the murder therefore take place in a way quite different from that in the original. Equally free is Payn's account of the dawning love of Ghismond. As Tancred's falconer the hero rides out with him and Ghismond who, while stroking the hawk in Guiscard's hand, whispers her directions, unnoticed by her father. The situation is all

2F

the more incredible, because the opening lines of the tale describe the courtly isolation of Ghismond and the haughty vigilance of Tancred:

> Well is Salerno's palace fenced by many a nightly guard,
> High are the walls its sentries pace, strict in their watch and ward
> And o'er its fosse so broad and deep, light as his free foot springs,
> Never may Guiscard hope to cross . . .
>
> (p. 12)

The truth is that Payn has set out to emphasise the disparity in rank between the lovers and to make them even more remote than in Boccaccio's tale. His version is a romantic illustration of the triumph of love over all barriers.

Apart from the glimpse of a mediæval castle with its armed warriors, we are in a vague world. Payn has removed the messenger who brings Tancred's gift of her lover's heart to Ghismond, the message being conveyed by a silver scroll round the cup of gold. He also deprives Ghismond of her attendants, so that the scene which presents their distress after their lady has poisoned herself vanishes, and with it the picture of the penitent king. There is no moving farewell between father and daughter, and the clash of personalities is to a large extent lost. The old humanistic plea for merit in preference to 'gentle blood' is also sacrificed for the sake of romantic love, and the marshalled eloquence of Boccaccio's heroine degenerates into the incoherence of mere hysteria:

> Ghismond thus, with eyes of fire, broke forth in accents wild;
> I need not, Hypocrite, thy words to tell my love is dead,
> Look on thy hand, thou murderer, whence comes that curséd red;
> Talk not to me of *blood*; Great God! how *gentle* was the pack
> That slew my noble Guiscard? Did they stab him in the back?
> How many were ye? Was it dark? Ay! I'm a woman; kill,
> Save *me* the blow, thrice valiant prince, I'll thank you an you will.
>
> (p. 14)

In 'Girolamo and Salvestra' the omissions affect the plot in an equally vital way. The part of Girolamo's mother in frustrating his love of Salvestra is ignored, and his guardians are replaced by shadowy personages referred to as 'they'. Much is lost also in the latter part of the tale with its vivid picture of the dilemma of Salvestra and her husband when Girolamo is found dead in their bed-chamber, the sudden death of Salvestra over the body of Girolamo in the crowded church and the interment of the lovers in a common grave. For this terse and moving sequence Payn substitutes the somewhat stagey death of Salvestra immediately after she has discovered that Girolamo is no more.

A quest for romantic effect is observed also in the changed surroundings of Girolamo. The well-to-do Florentine merchant of Boccaccio is

dissociated from his mercantile setting, and we read of his marble
halls, his gold and gems, his gilded domes and groves and princely
wares, and of the merry minstrels in his service. His passion is as
exaggerated as his wealth, for whereas Boccaccio had written soberly:
'Girolamo non sentiva ben, se non tanto, quanto costei vedeva',[1]
Payn draws a wilting Keatsian figure:

> Then day by day his eye grew dim and the red left his cheek,
> From his sunk heart scarce gathered he the failing breath to speak.[2]
>
> (p. 9)

The solid Florentine background evaporates once more in 'Pasquino
and Simona'.[3] Except these two all persons vanish; time and place are
vague, and the characteristic Italian garden is replaced by a scene,

> Where the green moss a swelling bosom heaved,
> That had no memory of the lightest tread,
> And the wild eglantine was interleaved
> With the sweet suckle, which had overspread
> With honeyed breath a streamlet bordered bower.
>
> (p. 4)

Payn cares little for the realistic detail of Boccaccio. So careless is he
in his conjuring up of a land that never was, that he calls Simona in
one line a cotton spinner and in the next shows Pasquino bringing her
wool! They seem to live in isolation, and the sense of a social environment is lacking. Gone is the judge summoned to investigate the crime
with which Simona is charged; gone too is the penitence of her accusers
and their remorseful burial of the lovers, and with all this Payn
sacrifices the dramatic tension, even as he does in 'Girolamo and
Salvestra'. Instead of poignancy he gives the reader pathos and sentiment. Simona is transformed into an orphan, and when Pasquino is
overtaken by death, she goes mad and with a vacant smile she croons
a 'low sad soothing song'. As a narrator Payn cannot compare with
Boccaccio. In the very first stanza he discloses that Simona is to die
young and already in the twelfth he tells the secret of the poisoned
sage-leaf, which Boccaccio had carefully kept back till the end. His
technique is also unsatisfactory in other respects. His lines limp, and
at times he unintentionally produces a comic effect in what aims at
being a tale of high romance, as when he addresses Love:

> How wilful of thee thus to enter in her
> Who was but a poor orphan cotton spinner!
>
> (p. 1)

---

[1] 'Girolamo was not at ease except when he saw her.'
[2] A. de Musset wrote a tale in verse, entitled 'Silvia', on this theme. Cf. H. Hauvette, 'Musset et Boccace', *Bulletin italien*, xi, 1911.
[3] The theme is treated in de Musset's verse-tale, 'Simone'. Cf. Hauvette, loc. cit.

'Gomito and Constance' is still more loosely connected with Boccaccio. The part of the tale which deals with the fate of the lovers after she puts out to sea is eliminated. Consequently, there is the vagueness of attachment which we have seen to be typical of Payn; the only place mentioned is Lipari; the only persons, Gomito and Constance. The story is changed from one that culminates in a happy reunion into a narrative of misfortune. Constance sets out on her voyage, not to seek the missing Gomito, but to seek death in her despair at his failure to return; and when he does return, only to find her gone, he commits suicide by plunging into the sea.

The tone is forced and unnatural as when Gomito, seized by the 'madly dear conviction' that Constance had died for him, shrieks wildly. There is also an intrusion of sentimentality in the passage where Gomito thinks of the shallop which he had made for Constance and which was to prove her doom. He recalls:

> How she did thank me kindly
>   ('Twas on her birth-day too)
> And how we softly glided
>   Over the calm clear blue.

(p. 29)

However, the weakest part of the poem is the description of the rejoicing at Lipari when Gomito's ship after a prolonged absence unexpectedly reaches port:

> Oh and to see the landing!
>   God, it was good and grand,
> The knees that bowed before thee,
>   There on that very strand,
>
> And the sweet lips that gave thee
>   Thanks with a heart-sprung prayer
> 'Ere with a joyous throbbing
>   Glued to a kindred pair!

(p. 27)

It is evident from such bathos that Payn was bound to fail as a writer of serious poetry. But in 'Isabel', the sixth of the tales from Boccaccio,[1] he found himself. He follows his usual practice of merging the specific in the general, with the exception, however, that instead of a whole group of strict nuns he depicts only one, the rigorous Clara. As she pries on Isabel and then denounces her to the abbess, her personality emerges clearly like that of the monk watching Brother Lawrence in Browning's 'Soliloquy of the Spanish Cloister'. Her austerity is carried to such a pitch that she demands the burial alive of

---

[1] *Dec.* ix, 2.

the culprit. But despite some minor alterations the ending of the tale resembles that of Boccaccio:

> For e'en the Abbess' self soon took preferment,
> And Clara, of the Nuns, alone ne'er earn'd interment.
>
> (p. 36)

The dialogue is lively, easy and natural. All scathing satire on monastic abuses is avoided, and the whole is animated by a lightly ironical humour which conforms to the atmosphere of Boccaccio's story.

It was a tale of generosity, the fourth of the tenth day, that gripped Tennyson. It is embodied in 'The Golden Supper' which has a curious history. This poem was published at the end of 1869, though the collection in which it appeared bore the date 1870.[1] Later it was attached as a sequel to 'The Lover's Tale', which Tennyson after some hesitation had excluded from his *Poems* of 1833 and which did not appear till 1879.[2] The hero is Julian, who has grown up in the same house as his cousin Camilla. The childhood friendship ripens into love on his part, but not on hers, for her choice falls on Lionel. When Julian discovers this, he sets forth to dwell in solitude. There he is haunted by strange visions, accompanied now by the mournful sound of a tolling bell, now that of joyous wedding-bells. All this is related by Julian, but the later development, the incidents of 'The Golden Supper' are told by another speaker. This sequel is introduced somewhat awkwardly by the line

> He flies the event; he leaves the event to me.[3]
>
> (p. 72)

The narrator tells how Camilla marries Lionel and how Julian then returns home. He contemplates going abroad in order to forget but lingers on until one day the tolling bell announces that she is dead. Now the tale is launched. Tennyson thinks it necessary to explain one feature on which Boccaccio had not commented. That is, the fact that according to the custom of the land the body was not placed in a coffin but left in the vault with the face exposed. Again, he accounts for Julian's ability to see where Camilla lies. The moon, shining through a grating, lights up her face. Another feature that he comments on is the reverence with which Julian kisses her, only to find that she is still alive. In his counterpart there is more of passion than reverence, and in this alteration Tennyson shows a finer sensitiveness than Boccaccio. The rest of the tale unfolds in much the same way as in the *Decameron*. However, Tennyson has lavished all his resources on the description

---

[1] C. Tennyson, *Alfred Tennyson*, London, 1949, p. 383.
[2] Ibid., pp. 129, 375, 383, 447.   [3] Quotations from the 1879 edition.

of the banquet and of Camilla's attire which enhances her beauty and
her grace,

> Slow-moving as a wave against the wind,
> That flings a mist behind it in the sun.
>
> (p. 89)

Still more important is the transformation in the atmosphere. We are
no longer in Bologna but in a land which is waste and solitary, and
when the narrator encounters Julian, it is in

> A dismal hostel in a dismal land,
> A flat malarian world of reed and rush!
>
> (p. 80)

This sense of abnormality pervades the poem. It affects the guests, one
of whom seeing the beautiful lady's likeness to Camilla, shudders as
if she were a spectre. But that is not altogether surprising, for at one
end of the hall Julian has draped two great funereal curtains round a
picture of Camilla. No wonder that, despite the richness of the feast,
those present refrain from jesting, partly because of Julian's eyes,
partly because of 'something weird and wild about it all'. If there is
an eerie air about the banquet, the ending is no less strange. It is clear
that a figure like Julian, hypersensitive to the point of morbidity,
could never settle down to live happily with the reunited husband and
wife as Messer Gentil Carisendi does in close friendship with Nicco-
luccio Caccianimico and Madonna Catalina in Bologna. Instead, he
recoils from the display of love and gratitude, and abruptly exclaiming
'It is over', mounts his horse and rides away for ever from his native
land.

   While Tennyson was composing 'The Golden Supper', George Eliot
was at work on another tale of generosity, *How Lisa Loved the King*,
which appeared at Boston in the same year as Tennyson's poem. As
the envoy states, she had read the story long before and, finding
pleasure in it, resolved, like Keats in 'Isabella', to translate it as a
tribute to Boccaccio. Having visited Italy in 1860 and again in 1861
to study the background of *Romola*, in 1867 she went to Spain and
steeped herself in its history with an eye to the composition of *The
Spanish Gypsy*. After its publication she turned to the tale in the
Decameron (X, vii) which appealed to her because it combined both
of her interests—Spain and Italy. The time when the events of
the story occur is after Sicily has been freed from French domination
and come under the rule of the king of Aragon. The very first line

> Six hundred years ago, in Dante's time

has a precision which can be ascribed to George Eliot's reading for the
other two works, and she makes a good deal more than Boccaccio had

done of King Pedro as the heroic liberator, even returning to him and
the rising of the Sicilians in the last stanza. He unites in his person the
finest qualities of Spanish chivalry. It is the nobility of this 'king of
cavaliers' that accounts for his generosity and compassion towards
Lisa, the young daughter of a Florentine apothecary who had settled
in Palermo, when she falls in love with him. There was one feature
of the original that George Eliot found unsatisfactory. That was the
conclusion. In the Italian tale the king declares that he will always be
Lisa's knight, but for her husband he chooses a poor nobleman,
Perdicone, and lavishes precious gifts and domains[1] upon him. Nothing
has been heard of him before, and as a mediæval vassal he must submit
to the king's will. It is indeed a situation comparable in some ways to
that of Bertram and Helena in *All's Well that Ends Well*, with the
difference that Perdicone accepts readily enough, whereas Bertram is
resentful at having a wife imposed upon him. To overcome the feeling
that Perdicone may be keener on the possessions than on Lisa herself,
George Eliot describes at the outset how he made overtures to her
father Bernardo who approved of the match. To this extent the way is
prepared for the union of Lisa and Perdicone.

However, it is above all to Lisa herself that George Eliot devotes her
attention. The young maiden of fifteen is pictured in these terms:

> Her body was so slight,
> It seemed she could have floated in the sky,
> And with the angelic choir made symphony;
> But in her cheek's rich tinge, and in the dark
> Of darkest hair and eyes, she bore a mark
> Of kinship to her generous mother earth,
> The fervid land that gives the plumy palm-trees birth.[2]
>
> (pp. 12–13)

Her emotions are skilfully analysed. Still half a child, she does not
imagine that any man has ever pined for one so simple as herself, and
so she dreams of loving some great hero whose achievements would
compare with those of the warriors of Troy, Roland, the Cid or Amadis.
She finds her romantic ideal in King Pedro. She realises, of course,
that he will pay no more heed to her as he rides by than to a pigeon
sitting on a wall or balcony—just a spot of colour and no more. Yet she
feels herself to be as queenly as any queen:

> For they the royal-hearted women are
> Who nobly love the noblest, yet have grace;
> For needy suffering lives in lowliest place,
> Carrying a choicer sunlight in their smile,
> The heavenliest ray that pitieth the vile.

---

[1] One of these, Calatabellotta, is changed into Cataletta, for the sake of the metre.
[2] *How Lisa loved the King*, Boston, 1869.

> My love is such, it cannot choose but soar
> Up to the highest; yet forevermore,
> Though I were happy, throned beside the king,
> I should be tender to each little thing
> With hurt warm breast, that had no speech to tell
> Its inward pang; and I would soothe it well
> With tender touch and with a low soft moan
> For company.
>
> (pp. 18–19)

Her childlike tenderness and innocence, traits created by the poet, are intensified by the imagery with its references to small birds and, above all, allusions to flowers such as wood-lilies and roses. When her frail body is wasting away for love, the watchers see how, as she sleeps,

> her drooping head
> Turned gently, as the thirsty flowers that feel
> Some moist revival through their petals steal.
>
> (p. 21)

She has thought of asking Minuccio to plead for her to King Pedro, and in her dream she sees him

> Touching his viola, a chanting low
> A strain that, falling on her brokenly,
> Seemed blossoms lightly blown from off a tree;
> Each burthened with a word that was a scent.
>
> (p. 22)

Indirectly the fresh fragrance of the blossom becomes associated with the sleeper, and in another passage her youthful beauty is mingled with that of the flowers at dawn, when, on the occasion of the king's visit to her, joy returns and

> a smile
> As placid as a ray of early morn
> On opening flower-cups o'er her lips was borne.
>
> (p. 38)

Thus George Eliot bestows grace and charm on Lisa, and the harmony of her flowing couplets blends with it to create a poem of no mean artistry.

It is not surprising that Swinburne, who, like George Eliot, had come under the influence of Italy, should have been led to Boccaccio. His first attempt to turn a story from the *Decameron* into English verse appears to have been made about 1859.[1] The tale that he chose

---

[1] Cf. the catalogue of *The Ashley Library*, vol. vi, p. 42. Of the thirteen leaves mentioned by T. J. Wise as being in his collection, the first seven correspond roughly to the first 101 lines of *The Two Dreams*, and pp. 11, 12 and 13 seem to belong to the death scene, though they do not follow closely that in the later poem. On the other hand, pp. 8, 9 and 10, which have been bound with the rest, appear to have no connexion with this tale.

was the sixth of the fourth day which had as its theme those whose
loves had a disastrous close. Swinburne called it 'The White Hind' but
later he revised it and published it in *Poems and Ballads* in 1866 as
'The Two Dreams'.

As the title of the earlier version indicates, Swinburne intended to
retain the essential features of Boccaccio's narrative. There Gabriotto
dreams that while hunting he caught a she-goat whiter than snow,
which he tamed, and then, as he lay with her head in his lap, a black
greyhound bit him to the heart. It is impossible to say what was the
nature of Andrevuola's dream in Swinburne's first draft, but in the
later version it is a striking development of the original. Boccaccio
contented himself with saying that the heroine saw something 'dark
and frightful' issue from Gabriotto's body and carry him underground.
In Swinburne this vague description becomes more concrete and
detailed. Out of Gabriotto's throat Andrevuola saw crawl

> a live thing flaked with black
> Specks of brute slime and leper-coloured scale,
> A devil's hide with foul flame-written grail
> Fashioned where hell's heat festers loathsomest.[1]
> (p. 300)

What is more, this monster devours him before her eyes. Similarly,
in picturing the after-effect of this vision Boccaccio tells simply of the
haunting dread that entered her soul, whereas Swinburne enhances
the feeling of horror by depicting an abnormal, menacing dawn:

> My waked eyes felt the new day shuddering
> On their low lids, felt the whole east so beat,
> Pant with close pulse of such a plague-struck heat,
> As if the palpitating dawn drew breath
> For horror, breathing between life and death,
> Till the sun sprang blood-bright and violent.
> (p. 300)

If there is merely a development here, the dream of Gabriotto is
entirely changed and has no relationship to that in the *Decameron*.
Swinburne employs all his resources to create a vision of overmastering
sensuous beauty. First Gabriotto relates how he perceived a smell of
pounded spice and fragrance, the whole as potent as amber and rose;
then a cool, naked sense of bud and blossom beneath his feet, while his
veins beat like a lute and feelings ran through every limb. Rich in
colour, perfume and sweetness and sensation, in music and flowers,
this is but a prelude to the vision of women bathing, all aglow with
warm light.

[1] *Poems and Ballads*, 1866.

> . . . even from wall to bed,
> I tell you, was my room transfigured so.
> Sweet, green and warm it was, nor could one know
> If there were walls or leaves, or if there was
> No bed's green curtain, but mere gentle grass.
> There were set also hard against the feet
> Gold plates with honey and green grapes to eat,
> With the cool water's noise to hear in rhymes:
> And a wind warmed me full of furze and limes
> And all hot sweets the heavy summer fills,
> To the round brim of smooth cup-shapen hills.
>
> (pp. 303–4)

This atmosphere, heavily charged and exquisitely voluptuous, prepares the approach of a woman. As she stoops low, her mouth catches him like that of a snake, but all he feels is a faint and tender sting, though the fang leaves a great wound. Truly, this vision is utterly unlike that of Boccaccio's Gabriotto who suffers acute pain, as his breast is gnawed through and his heart torn away by the fierce coal-black greyhound.

Nor is this the only liberty that Swinburne takes. He condenses the tale in various ways. The prefatory discussion on the trustworthiness of dreams, a subject dear to the mediæval mind, is cast aside. The part of Andrevuola's maid is restricted to a minimum. In Boccaccio she has a large share in the action. She is instrumental in bringing the lovers together secretly and joins her mistress in weeping over the dead man. She advises Andrevuola what to do, though the latter rejects her counsel, and helps to wrap Gabriotto in a silken cloth and carry him towards his home. Faithful to the end, she retires with Andrevuola to a nunnery. Swinburne mentions her but once and then briefly, when she is told by her mistress, without consultation, how to come to her aid in the interment of the body. If the maid is thus reduced to insignificance, another figure, that of the Podestà, is removed completely. Boccaccio relates that as Andrevuola and her maid are carrying Gabriotto through the street, they are met by the guards and placed under arrest. The Podestà, who like others holding this office in the *Decameron*, abuses his powers, offers to release her if she will comply with his desires. When she indignantly rejects his infamous proposal, he is about to use force, and only the arrival of her father, Ser Averardo, saves Andrevuola. There is nothing of all this unsavoury episode in Swinburne, who limits the appearance of Ser Averardo to three lines at the beginning of the poem. He is of importance only as the heroine's father and not in himself. Swinburne eliminates the meeting between him and Andrevuola, her prayer that he will pardon her for loving Gabriotto without his knowledge, his ready consent and his provision for the public funeral of the dead lover with all pomp and ceremony.

The omission of the major part of the tale after Gabriotto's death is made possible because in Swinburne's version he is buried in the garden, and then the poem hastens to the close:

> And afterward she came back without word
> To her own house; two days went, and the third
> Went, and she showed her father of this thing.
> And for great grief of her soul's travailing
> He gave consent she should endure in peace
> Till her life's end; yea, till her time should cease,
> She should abide in fellowship of pain.
> And having lived a holy year or twain
> She died of pure waste heart and weariness.
>
> (p. 307–8)

Swinburne was perhaps all the more anxious to move swiftly here, because the pace in the earlier part of 'The Two Dreams' had been slowed down. He had spent some time over a description of the rose-garden and the coming of spring and lingered over a picture of Andrevuola and her home. The dawn of love in Gabriotto and the wooing were also described. But Swinburne dwelt longest on the evolution of the relationship between the lovers. Even in the opening lines of the poem he had made it clear that sorrow would be their portion:

> And though the rain fall often, and with rain
> Late autumn falls on the old red leaves like pain,
> I deem that God is not disquieted.
> Also while men are fed with wine and bread,
> They shall be fed with sorrow at his hand.
>
> (p. 292)

Such a beginning is ominous and the course of the love of Gabriotto and Andrevuola is in keeping. Even before the tragic death of the hero it had undergone a change; joy had given place to disillusionment. As Swinburne conceives of it, there is fever and thirst and pain in love; something of its first rapture evaporates and no devotion can recapture it.

> They were too near love's secret to be glad;
> As whoso deems the core will surely melt
> From the warm fruit his lips caress, hath felt
> Some bitter kernel where the teeth shut hard:
> Or as sweet music sharpens afterward,
> Being half disrelished both for sharp and sweet;
> As sea-water, having killed over-heat
> In a man's body, chills it with faint ache;
> So their sense, burdened only for love's sake,
> Failed for pure love.
>
> (pp. 295–6)

The lovers reach a stage when exhilaration has given place to weariness. There follow

> Passionless months and undelighted weeks,
>
>   (p. 297)

and

> pleasure has for kinsfolk sleep and death.
>
>   (p. 296)

Swinburne makes the impression infinitely more potent by means of the setting in which this love waxes and wanes. The garden too undergoes a gradual transformation. The early freshness fades as March merges into April and April into May. It

> Seemed half deflowered and sick with beaten leaves

and

> The flowers had lost their summer-scented cheeks,
> Their lips were no more sweet than daily breath:
> The year was plagued with instances of death.
>
>   (pp. 297–8)

The interlude of Gabriotto's dream adds to the tension which mounts steadily until the death-scene. The air becomes more and more sultry and oppressive. The leaves are 'heated', noon weighs on the hot, heavy-headed flowers, the heart of the rose aches, and it seems

> to breathe hard with heat as a man doth
> Who feels his temples newly feverous.
>
>   (p. 306)

A moment later Gabriotto is dead, even in the midst of his burning love.

After that the passion ebbs away and the air seems to clear. In harmony the diction, strained and even precious at times in the quest for potency, becomes simple and unadorned. So when Gabriotto is interred beneath the rose-bush and the overhanging boughs of the apple-trees:

> There under all the little branches sweet
> The place was shapen of his burial;
> They shed thereon no thing funereal,
> But coloured leaves of latter rose-blossom,
> Stems of soft grass, some withered red and some
> Fair and fresh-blooded; and spoil splendider
> Of marigold and great spent sunflower.
>
>   (p. 307)

The ending is equally simple and more austere. Andrevuola in her convent does not linger for many a year as in Boccaccio but dies soon after, and Swinburne for once imparts to the couplet something of that monumental terseness which it so often has in earlier writers:

> This word was written over her tomb's head;
> 'Here dead she lieth, for whose sake Love is dead.'
>
>   (p. 308)

'The Two Dreams' is carefully designed and executed—a highly-wrought, sophisticated work of art. On it Swinburne has lavished, sometimes almost to excess, the splendour of his imagery. It is steeped in light and rich in colour and fragrance, embellished with flowers and music. From Boccaccio's tale the sensuous element is isolated and heightened till it becomes well-nigh unendurable. At the same time Swinburne discards the sensuousness, joyous and unquestioning, of Boccaccio and invests the love of Gabriotto and Andrevuola with a disenchantment which turns its fire to ashes. Upon a totally different interpretation of life he imposes his own conception as it is expressed in 'The Year of the Rose':

> The time of lovers is brief;
> From the fair first joy to the grief
>   That tells when love is grown old,
>   From the warm wild kiss to the cold,
> From the red to the white-rose leaf,
>   They have but a season to seem
>   As roseleaves lost on a stream
> That part not and pass not apart
>   As a spirit from dream to dream,
> As a sorrow from heart to heart.[1]
>
> (p. 53)

Even without the intervention of Fate all love is fore-doomed to speedy death.

This inherent pessimism and this process of choosing only one aspect of Boccaccio's tale are again discernible in 'The Complaint of Lisa' which was published in 1878. In dealing with the theme that had already been treated by George Eliot, Swinburne makes a different approach. He cares nothing for the historical setting, his prime concern being with Lisa's despair. In the original tale[2] this had been conveyed by Minuccio to the king. Swinburne lets the young girl utter her own lament, as she grieves, almost to the point of death, for unavowed and unrequited love. To this end he uses imagery which contrasts sharply with that of Boccaccio. The latter had spoken of pain and smart, burning heat and flame; Swinburne, on the other hand, uses flower imagery. This is more restricted and more definitely symbolical than the corresponding imagery of George Eliot. Like Blake, Swinburne employs the sunflower as a symbol of love, but his treatment is quite original. In Blake it stands for frustration and barrenness, in Swinburne for the triumphant consummation which brings to fruition. With him King Pedro is the sun-flower,

---

[1] *Poems and Ballads Second Series*, 1878.   [2] Vide ante, p. 438.

> With golden eye following the golden sun
> From rose-coloured to purple-pillowed bed,
> From birthplace to the flame-lit place of death.
>
> (p. 66)

In one passage the new image blends with the old image of fire:

> A kingly flower of knights, a sunflower,
> That shone against the sunlight like the sun,
> And like a fire, O heart, consuming thee,
> The fire of love that lights the pyre of death.
>
> (p. 64)

Lisa, who speaks these lines, has her own symbol. She too is a flower, but the flower of a weed, so utterly insignificant and so completely hidden that it passes unheeded. In vain it gazes the livelong summer day at the sunflower.

> . . . the white star-flower turns and yearns to thee,
> The sick weak weed, not well alive or dead,
> Trod underfoot if any pass by her,
> Pale, without colour of summer or summer breath
> In the shrunk shuddering petals, that have done
> No work but love, and die before the day.
>
> (p. 67)

To suggest this humility in another way Swinburne once changes his image, and Lisa is compared to 'a worm in my lord's kingly way'. This evokes another train of thought, and the worm becomes a symbol of death. In its turn this bends Lisa's thoughts to burial and so to the underworld of the *Divine Comedy*, where Paolo and Francesca come to her mind:

> I read long since the bitter tale of her
> Who read the tale of Launcelot on a day,
> And died, and had no quiet after death,
> But was moved ever along a weary way,
> Lost with her love in the underworld.
>
> (p. 63)

'Dead' and 'Death' echo like a funeral knell in every stanza, and beat out a melancholy admonition—love must die. Like 'The Two Dreams', Lisa's plaintive song reflects Swinburne's philosophy which would not admit the facile, worldly conclusion of the tale in the *Decameron* and therefore rejected all else but her lament.

The poem is a lyric, not a narrative, and the double sestina replaces the heroic couplet. The imagery is far less complex than in 'The Two Dreams', and in some ways the greater simplicity is more effective. But the style is still that of a conscious artist, as may be seen from the opening lines:

> There is no woman living that draws breath
> So sad as I, though all things sadden her.
> There is not one upon life's weariest way
> Who is weary as I am weary of all but death.
> Toward whom I look as looks the sunflower
> All day with all his whole soul toward the sun;
> While in the sun's sight I make moan all day . . .
>
> (p. 60)

And in the last stanza the devices of alliteration and repetition, linking word to word and line to line, are even more potent:

> Song, speak for me who am dumb as are the dead;
> From my sad bed of tears I send forth thee,
> To fly all day from sun's birth to sun's death
> Down the sun's way after the flying sun,
> For love of her that gave thee wings and breath
> Ere day be done, to seek the sunflower.
>
> (p. 68)

Like Swinburne, John Payne was attracted by the Middle Ages and loved the spirit of the period as it was embodied in Dante and as it lingered, though transformed, in Spenser. He translated Villon and the *Decameron*. Six years before his version of the latter work was published in 1886, he included in his *New Poems* 'Salvestra' from the eighth tale of the fourth day. Its history is curious. Evidently it was in existence as early as 1871 and contained seven stanzas, written just before the capitulation of Paris, which denounced the Prussian invasion. These lines were detached from their context and published under the title of 'France' in *Songs of Life and Death*, 1872. They did not figure in the 1880 version of the, tale which was therefore not completed until the *Poetical Works* were issued in 1902.[1] Carried away by his friendship for contemporary French writers, artists and musicians, Payne did not pause to reflect what an anachronism they were in a story from the *Decameron*. This is all the more singular because he had a keen sense of form and admired the craftsmanship of Boccaccio. For him the latter was

> that enchanter of the past, who filled
> The ears of men with music sweet and wild,
> When in the world he breathed strange scents upon
> That sheaf of flowers men called Decameron.[2]
>
> (p. 199)

[1] Cf. vol. ii, p. 387.

[2] John Payne, *New Poems*, 1880. Addressing Boccaccio, Payne declares that he seeks to echo the magical sweet tune

> Thou sangest in the garden's golden noon,
> With youths and maidens lying, myrtle-crowned,
> Upon the flower-glad carpet of the ground.
>
> (p. 200)

Payne esteemed the lightness of his touch in dealing with a merry tale or an amorous adventure and the dignity, pathos and poignancy with which he handled the tragic and sentimental. His well-controlled satire and his skill in narrative and the description of natural beauty also called forth eulogies from Payne. But most of all he praises Boccaccio's power of inspiring terror in the tale of Nastagio degli Onesti and his unsurpassed command of pathos in the stories of Ghismonda, Lorenzo and Lisabetta, Gabriotto and Andrevuola, Pasquino and Simona, and Girolamo and Salvestra.[1]

However greatly Payne valued the last of these, certain features in his opinion called for change, if the impression of an overwhelming romantic passion was to prevail throughout. Taking Florence as the setting, Boccaccio had seen no reason why he should not fit the story into a mercantile community. His Salvestra is the daughter of a tailor and Girolamo the son of a wealthy merchant. It is about the business of the shop and in the shop itself that Girolamo's guardians converse with him. So far as he can, Payne removes these unabashed allusions to trade. Girolamo's mother is a countess; his father had been three times 'prior' of Florence, and

> His argosies
> Had swept for treasure all the Indian seas,
> Heaping his hands with gorgeous pearl and gold
> And ingots cast in many an Orient mould.
>
> (p. 210)

In short, like the brothers in Keats's 'Isabella', he is elevated to a plane remote from the world of ordinary commerce. And although the story made it essential for Payne to maintain a disparity in rank between the lovers, he avoids everyday associations by speaking of Salvestra's father as a clothworker, just as Keats had avoided any reference to Lorenzo as an employee in a shop. Needless to say, Payne's hero has no connexion with a shop but lives in a palace, and if he goes to Paris, it is to gain a knowledge of 'all things liberal'.[2]

The guardians disappear, and the responsibility for sending Girolamo to Paris falls exclusively on his mother. Every suggestion of unpleasantness about her in Boccaccio is magnified and others are added. She is hard and stern, haughty and domineering; she discovers the lovers together and, crouching under the thick foliage of the wood, spies upon them. In her guile she is resourceful and persuasive,

> That treacherous mother with the red bane-mouth.
>
> (p. 227)

---

[1] Cf. T. Wright, *The Life of John Payne*, London, 1919, p. 90. The MS. there quoted is not in T. Wright's collection preserved at Olney, as his widow kindly informs me.

[2] Even Payne's translation of the *Decameron* seems to shrink from the word 'shop' and in both iv, 5 and iv, 8 'fondaco' is rendered by 'warehouse'.

Thus a shrewd and unscrupulous woman of the world, sticking at nothing to secure what she considers the best interests of her son, becomes a cruel and malicious enemy to love, whom Payne curses. Another character for whom he did not care was Salvestra's husband Paolo. Boccaccio depicts him as a considerate husband and a thoroughly good fellow. Payne found him inconvenient in the world of romance and, although he could not get rid of him, he kept Paolo in the background and took good care that after Salvestra's death he did not appear to vent his grief and relate to his friends all that had happened.

In Payne's version all sympathy is focused on the lovers, and he elaborates everything that Boccaccio had written about them. He dwells on their beauty and explains their dispositions—the one sensitive and affectionate in the highest degree, the other cold as marble. The account of their relationship as children is greatly expanded, and he adds a description of their dawning love against the idyllic background of a wood near Girolamo's home. After the hero's return to Florence from Paris Boccaccio's account of his feelings, a masterpiece of succinctness, is developed into a lengthy analysis. Girolamo wanders aimlessly, dazed and with vacant eyes, through the halls of his palace and from there to the wood, reviving old memories. He is attacked by a fever, and it seems as if he would succumb, but the desire to see Salvestra restores him. It occurs to him that perhaps he has been slandered and that if he could but see her, the old love and joy would return. He therefore haunts all the places where she was wont to pass. At last he meets her at the church-door, leaning on her husband's arm. She looks at him as a stranger and he is filled with sorrow. Then a new idea presents itself. Possibly she has failed to recognise him, wasted as he is by illness, and hope is born again. There is yet another possibility, viz. that she has been bewitched, and so he prays with intense fervour to the Holy Virgin and the saints, and not content with that, has recourse to the occult,

> Culling night-herbs, and on a scroll blood-writ
> Burning strange cipherings beyond man's wit.
>
> (p. 238)

These fluctuating emotions, these alternations between hope and despair, culminate in Girolamo's resolve to see Salvestra and find out the truth. Payne describes how he waits from afternoon till nightfall to enter unnoticed the house so rich in potent association with her, and on the bedchamber scene the poet employs all his skill. Salvestra's beauty as she lies sleeping, Girolamo's entreaties, and her emotion at the memory of the past are all related with great effect. So is the death of Girolamo—not in a convulsion of agony as in Boccaccio, but in peace after

2G

one last prayer to Mary full of grace
And one last Ave intermixed with sighs.
(p. 257)

The death of Salvestra herself, as she falls prone over the body of Girolamo in the church, follows Boccaccio's account closely. But Payne enhances the impression of sorrow when he tells how, as she lies in silence, there comes the melancholy sound of the bell tolling for her faithful lover.

To heighten the poetic quality of this tragic tale Payne introduces many references to flowers. In fact, he is so fond of them that he occasionally gives them a space out of all proportion, as when he devotes no less than seven stanzas to flowers which are emblems of the lovers' fate. However, as a rule he uses them with artistic discretion, and nowhere more so than in the woodland scene:

Full of bird-song and scent of forest-flowers
    The coppice was, and very sweet and cool
In the hot noontide were its trellised bowers,
    Set by the glass of some dream-haunted pool,
    Whereon the sleepy sweetness of the lull
Of silence brooded; and its every glen
Was set with purple of the cyclamen

Or starred with white of amaryllis blooms,
    Pale flower-dreams of the virginal green sward,
That made faint sweetness in the emerald glooms.
(p. 219)

Not only the surroundings possess this natural beauty, but Florence itself is rich in its association with flowers, and blending with them, it has created the flowers of painting. It is the

Fair flower city, peerless in the world,
    Germ-garden of the golden blooms of Art.
(p. 202)

It is therefore in keeping that Salvestra's house should be redolent of lilies and jasmines, and that flowers should lend charm to the imagery of the bedchamber scene. Girolamo kisses the sleeping Salvestra

As softly as a fallen flower, that lies
And floats upon a river, lily-wise.
(p. 248)

Similarly, after the first grey gleam of dawn has revealed the pallid face of the dead hero, the introduction of a flower-image relieves the grimness of the sight:

the day began to put forth flowers,
Pale buds of morning opening from the husk
Of the small hours.
(p. 258)

Girolamo is again associated with the scent of flowers and myrtles when he conceals himself in the garden near Salvestra's home and awaits the approach of evening. He finds the time long until the glittering light fades on the Arno and the nightingales begin to sing. At the same time the fragrance of the flowers, the sunset and the waning light are made to suggest momentarily the death-scene which is soon to follow:

> Full wearily the unwilling day wore on:
>   It seemed to him the light would never die:
> Across the west like blood the sunset shone;
>   And to his sense, as sadly he did lie,
>   The wafts of air seemed laden heavily
> With incense for the dying, and the surge
> Of ripples sounded like a funeral dirge.
>
> At length the lagging daylight made an end
>   Of gradual death; and to the grateful night
> He heard the sweet sound of the bells ascend
>   From many a convent-steeple in his sight;
>   The dusky town put forth pale buds of light;
> He heard the throb of lute-strings, and afar
> The silver chirp of some soft-swept guitar.
>
>   (p. 241)

At the close it is appropriate that Girolamo and Salvestra, whose love had wakened to the ripple of a brook in the greenwood, should be laid to rest, not in a tomb like Boccaccio's lovers, but under the trees beside the running waters of the Arno.

The world that Payne conjures up is one of brave knights, fair ladies, and white-walled cities rich in fragrant pleasances. Of course, he is aware that this is an incomplete picture of the Middle Ages; he had not read Villon for nothing. Yet even if Payne was in some degree acquainted with the graver traits of mediæval life, it was on the whole a romantic age that his imagination called forth, and he loved to take refuge in it from nineteenth-century England where he felt singularly out of place. Three poems in the same collection as 'Salvestra', 'Of the Singers of the Time', 'Aspect and Prospect', and 'Tournesol', illuminate his attitude and incidentally enable us to understand why he chose the tale of Girolamo and Salvestra. Like William Morris, he revolted against a period from which beauty seemed to have vanished. He was repelled by the squalor of modern towns, and so he wrote:

> What have we done with meadow and lane?
>   Where are the flowers and the hawthorn-snow?
> Acres of brick in the pitiless rain,—
>   These are our gardens for thorpe and stow![1]
>
>   (p. 128)

[1] 'Of the Singers of the Time'.

In his eyes wealth and luxury, gold and gems were no compensation for hungry bodies and starving souls. He was painfully aware of 'the sordid strife for gain' and the suffering and hatred begotten of social injustice. Yet the spectacle did not provide him with a theme for poetry; it merely rendered him unhappy. He was saddened by the stress of the time, filled with hopeless yearning and numbed as if by icy winter. Nor was there any faith to buoy him up, for the old beliefs had fallen. In such an age, he felt, 'Songs and singers are out of date', for no one could sing with all the sadness of the world clinging to his heart-strings. In the following passage from 'Tournesol' something of the dissatisfaction and unrest of Matthew Arnold and William Morris is heard:

> . . . the folk through the fretful hours are hurled
> On the ruthless rush of the wondrous world,
> And none has leisure to lie and cull
> The blossoms that made life beautiful,
> In that old season when men could sing
> For dear delight in the risen Spring
> And Summer ripening fruit and flower.
> Now carefulness cankers every hour;
> We are too weary and sad to sing;
> Our pastime's poisoned with thought-taking.
> The bloom is faded from all that's fair,
> And grey with smoke is the grievous air.
> None lifts to luting his hand and voice
> Nor smites the strings with a joyful noise;
> For all that sing in the land are pale;
> Their voice is the voice of those that wail
> For beauty buried, and hang the head
> For the dream of a day evanishèd.
>
> (pp. 3–4)

Such a cheerless time, it seemed to Payne, was attuned neither to love nor poetry, and so he turned to the past.

In doing so he came to Boccaccio and in 'Salvestra' once more he inveighs against his own age with its 'hard swift life' and 'unblissful toil'. As in 'Tournesol' he contrasts the past with the present and laments that love has fled:

> Time was, fair God, when thou heldst fuller sway,
> And all folk were thy thralls in gentilesse:
> Time was when men were simpler than to-day,
> And life was not one fierce and loveless stress
> Of unrelenting labours in the press
> Of joyless souls, when men had time to rest
> And toy with grace and beauty, unreprest.
>
> (p. 197)

In the Middle Ages men prized chivalrous deeds, and love held universal sway. It was not a matter for calculation, but

> A natural impulse of untainted souls,
> That had no thought of praise or recompense
>   For what was but an instinct—and the goals,
>   Towards which our life's sore-troubled current rolls,
> Had not yet darkened all the innocent air
> With lurid lights of greed and lust and care.
>
> (p. 207)

The mediæval spirit, Payne maintains, was embodied in Girolamo who believed in love, pursuing it with single purpose, and was prepared to give up his life in the quest. Hence the story of 'Salvestra' appealed to him as one 'of perfect love in death fulfilled'.

However, the total impression left on the reader by the poem is very different from that created by Boccaccio's tale, where, despite the tragic close, one feels that the beauty of life has been triumphantly vindicated. Not so with Payne, who is always haunted by the idea of death. In 'Aspect and Prospect' he sees it looking from the lover's eyes and declares

> We may not hope for peace at last
> Save where the shade of Sleep is cast,
>   And from our eyes Death's soft hand clears
>   The thought alike of smiles and tears.
>
> (p. 290)

Such is his obsession that in his version of the old tale weariness clings to him, and he can but long for quiet and dreamless sleep when life is done. In him there is no stoic endurance, no passion for reform. Nor has he the consolation of faith in immortality:

> I look but for the end of wearying,
> For pain to cease and sorrow to be dumb.
>
> (p. 272)

Far from drawing any assurance from the devotion of Girolamo that love at least is durable, he cries:

> only this we know,—
> Afar Death comes with silent steps and slow.
>
> (p. 270)

But this certitude does not fill him with dismay, for he has long loved death. Therefore,

> I praise thee, seeing thou alone,
> Of all things underneath the heavens born,
>   Art all assured. For is it not unknown
> Whether the gold sun on another morn
> Shall glitter, or the Spring come to adorn
>   Once more the woods and fields with winter pale?
>   This but we know, Thou Death shalt never fail!
>
> (p. 275)

Thus Boccaccio's tale of love ends as a pæan to Death.

For once Payne escaped from the mood of 'ces fleurs de tristesse', as he termed his collected poems in the dedication to Stéphane Mallarmé, when he translated Boccaccio's charming 'Intorn' ad una fonte, in un pratello' which had appealed to Rossetti before him.[1] But the grave mood is the more characteristic, and the other poems by Boccaccio that caught his eye are all in serious vein. 'To his own soul, exhorting it to repentance'[2] envisages the prospect of death but finds reassurance in the thought that penitence will win pardon even at the eleventh hour. 'To Petrarch Dead' also attracted Payne. No doubt this was partly because it touched on Boccaccio's devotion to Fiammetta, the far-reaching effect of which Payne emphasises in the introduction to his translation of the *Decameron*.[3] However, its main interest was the theme of death and the reunion of Petrarch with Laura, and Boccaccio with Fiammetta:

> Now, dear my lord, unto those realms of light
>   Thou'rt mounted, whither looketh still to fare
>   Each soul of God elect unto that share,
> On its departure from this world of spite;
> Now art thou where full oft the longing spright
>   Drew thee, with Laura to commune whilere:
>   Now art thou come whereas my lovely fair
> Fiammetta sitteth with her in God's sight.
> Yea, with Sennuccio, Cino, Dante, thou
> Assured of ease eternal dwellest now,
> Things seeing our intelligence above.
>   Oh, in this world if I was dear to thee,
>   Draw thou me straight to thee, where I may see,
> Joyful, her face who fired me first with love.[4]

The same archaism of style, which also marked Payne's version of the *Decameron*, may be observed in his rendering of 'Ballata',[5] a lament for lost youth so piercing in its melancholy, that it must have stirred the translator's heart:

> The flower, that's lost its sheen,
> Once faded, nevermore becometh green.
>
> My sheen I've lost; again
> My beauty will not be as 'twas whilere,
> Since their desire is vain
> Who waste the time and think it to repair:
> I am no Spring, fore'er
> Each year renewing and becoming green.

[1] *Poetical Works*, ii, p. 186. For D. G. Rossetti's version vide ante, p. 364.
[2] 'Volgiti, spirto affaticato, omai.' Cf. *Poetical Works*, ii, pp. 185–6.
[3] Edition of 1893, pp. xv–xvi.
[4] 'Or sei salito, caro signor mio.' Cf. *Poetical Works*, ii, p. 185.
[5] 'Il fior, che'l valor perde'. Cf. *Poetical Works*, ii, p. 381. Other examples of archaism are 'whilere' in 'To Petrarch Dead' and 'will and gree' in 'To his own Soul'.

I curse the evil time
When I the days of youth let lapse away:
Maid being in my prime,
Methought not yet to have been cast astray.
They waxen no more gay
Who lose the first flower of Love's primal sheen.

    Ballad, it grieveth me
That I to music may not set thee. Lo!
Well is it known to thee
That my heart dwells with sighs and tears and woe
And shall be ever so
Till my life's candle cometh to the green.[1]

In dealing with Boccaccio, Payne is preoccupied with death, even as
Swinburne was, but in comparison he lacks energy, and in his melancholy becomes a languid, low-pulsed kinsman of Matthew Arnold.

3. The Drama

Garrick's *Cymon*, with or without change, was still popular in the nineteenth century.[2] It was acted with additions by H. R. Bishop at Covent
Garden on 20 November 1815.[3] The essential part of the action was
abridged in a 'Comic Pantomime Call'd the Enchanter or Harliquin
(sic!) Cymon' which was submitted to the Lord Chamberlain by J.
Holt, the proprietor of the Olympick Theatre, on 19 December 1828.[4]
As the title indicates, Cymon is transformed into Harlequin. This occurs
when the enamoured Urganda finds that he resists her advances. In her
rage she also turns Sylvia into Columbine. Another striking feature is
the introduction of a sphinx and a 'massive Griffin', both of whom
speak in oracular fashion. But it is on the pantomime figures that the
author spends most of his energy. They are a strange medley—Bohemian
minstrels, a pedlar, beggars, a ballad-singer, a blind fiddler, a hatter,
a fat cook, a Jew, a lobster-woman, a chimney-sweep, a fine lady, a
milliner, a dancing-master, a flash coachman, a peace-officer, a
gardener, an artist, a butcher, a clown, a mandarin, Chinese ladies
and Eskimos, together with such classical figures as Furies, Spirits and
Arcadians. A number of these sing irrelevant songs, and after the
pantomime, which has no relation to the Cymon story, is ended, the

---

[1] 'i.e. be burned out, come to extremity, a metaphor taken from the old usance
(still prevalent in some parts of Scotland and England) of auction by inch of candle,
it being the custom in some places to colour the lower end of the candle used for the
purpose green' (*Poetical Works*, ii, p. 381, note 2).
[2] *Cymon*, probably an adaptation of the old play, was performed on 1 February 1813
(cf. A. Nicoll, *A History of Early Nineteenth Century Drama, 1800–1850*, Cambridge,
1930, ii, p. 437).   [3] *D.N.B.*, Art. 'H. R. Bishop'.
[4] Formerly in the Lord Chamberlain's archives; now in the British Museum.

final scene shows the defeat of Urganda by Merlin and the union of Cymon and Sylvia as the rulers of Arcadia.

Yet another revision was undertaken by J. R. Planché,[1] for a performance at the Lyceum on Easter Monday, 1 April 1850. The date suggested to him a light-hearted treatment of Garrick's romantic adaptation. In Scene 1, after an air sung by Spring, April the First appears and with an easy touch alludes to those who had previously written on the theme:

> On the Stage it's been put too, by Garrick, Arne, Bishop,
> And now, in my own way, I've ventured to dish up—
> The young gudgeon, Cymon, in hope that he will
> Prove, as the French say, a fine "Poisson d'Avril."[2]

Then April sings an air and presents the main characters one by one:

> First, Merlin, the Wizard of Wales, behold,
> To bring him to Greece, Mr. Garrick made bold;
> With the story, he'd nothing on earth to do,
> But the greater the nonsense, the better for you.
>
> The next is Urganda, a fairy high-flown,
> By neither Boccaccio, nor Dryden known;
> Her charms are so potent, that none can withstand her—
> But love, you will find, makes a goose of Urganda.
>
> Here's Cymon, who, 'till he by love was taught,
> Knew nothing, and "whistled for want of thought;"[3]
> If all were to whistle, who think they think,
> What a saving there would be in Printer's Ink.
>
> There's Iphigenia, called Sylvia—why?
> 'Twould puzzle a conjuror to reply;
> For whichever you please, you may give your voice,
> For "you pays your money, and takes your choice."[4]

Planché alters the form of the play considerably. Much of the singing is eliminated, and different songs are inserted. The ending is also modified. When Urganda is conjuring up the Black Tower,[5] April appears and calls her an April fool. Thereupon the scene changes to the Bower of Paphos, the Abode of Love among the Roses. Cymon is discovered in the centre. Merlin enters with the shepherds and shepherdesses, and April concludes with a song.

This way of rounding off the play is less fantastic than what had

---

[1] The text is most readily accessible in *Extravaganzas*, London, 1879, iv, 47–86.

[2] Cf. *Extravaganzas*, iv, p. 54.

[3] Dryden, 'Cymon and Iphigenia', l. 85, 'And whistled as he went, for want of thought'.

[4] Cf. *Extravaganzas*, iv, pp. 54–5.   [5] Vide ante, p. 327.

been handed down to Planché, and it has some relevance to the original story, since Paphos is in Cyprus, the background of the love-theme. But Planché was a hard-headed writer, and he finds the whole tale absurd. Thus when in his English dramatic model he reads how the love of Cymon and Sylvia is sealed by an exchange of bouquets, he cannot refrain from this satirical comment through the agency of April:

> Now, this is what Bards have thought worthy their strains.
> And how Cymon's supposed to have come by his brains;
> When, really, I think that one needn't be clever,
> To prove he's a much greater fool, now, than ever.
> Here's a wench, till this morning, a sight he ne'er got of,
> That he'd rush into church with, not knowing a jot of
> Her family tree, or her family acres,
> Or, who is to pay even butchers and bakers![1]

The tone is antithetic to the extravagant romance of Garrick's play, especially as it had been developed by later writers. It may be that Dryden would have approved of this ridicule. At any rate, Planché cannot have been unfamiliar with the element of satire in the *Fables*, for he had studied 'Cymon and Iphigenia'. Incidentally, when speaking of the heroine, he introduces a passage which throws some light on the reputation of this work in 1850:

> By-the-bye—you mayn't know much about her yourselves,
> Unless you have lately been dusting your shelves;
> For who, upon earth, into Dryden now looks?
> Or any such old musty poetry books.[2]

In Planché's version of the play manner and comment blend admirably. The jocular tone, the colloquial style, the occasional burlesque rhymes, are the very antithesis of high-flown romance.

This tradition is continued by Edward John Smyth Lee, though he turns his back on Garrick's time-honoured *Cymon*. Lee's *Cymon and Iphigenia*[3] was licensed on 9 August 1864 for performance at the New Bower Operetta House. The burlesque intention is disclosed in the opening scene where a wood with gigantic ferns and a moonlit stream appears as the curtain rises. Queen Mab converses with her fairies about the sleeping Iphigenia:

---

[1] Cf. *Extravaganzas*, iv, p. 61. With this tone one may compare that of a few lines in Planché's tale, 'The One-Legged Goose'. The squire was a butcher,

> but whether that
> Argues in favour of his understanding,
> Or militates against it, is a question
> That I would wish to have no hand in,
> But leave it to your cool digestion.

[2] Cf. *Extravaganzas*, iv, p. 61.
[3] At present in the archives of the Lord Chamberlain at St. James's Palace.

Queen   A pretty maiden by our royal word,
        To bring her here I wonder what's occur'd?
Sunshine Strange to find a lady sleeping in a wood,
        A little tired perhaps—
Brightbeam   or a little screwed.
Sunshine (*picking up a book*)
        See, I've found the cause of all this stupor,
        'Proverbial Philosophy' by Tupper.

On the entry of Cymon, the comments of the fairies explain that, though he is handsome,

        His mind is dark, he hasn't any sense.

The queen continues:

        Ah, young ladies, with that we can dispense.
        Sense departs as soon as woman doth rule
        And every lover makes himself a fool.

Then, looking at Cymon,

        How he gapes about; he's far gone indeed
        And of prompt assistance stands much in need.
        Sweet youth, what's up? you really look quite pale.

Cymon   Have I been taking too much bitter ale?
        What pretty girls, and what a lovely valley!
        I'm at the play, and that's the *corps de ballet*.

The fairies wave their wands to the sound of music. Cymon, now in love with Iphigenia, kneels before her. His wooing is a parody of that of Richard III:

        Here's my sword, it's sharp and its point is hard,
        Take me up or plunge it in my gizzard.

Iph.   Like lady *Anne*, what's in another play.

Queen Mab bids them farewell; there is dew on the grass, and she suffers from rheumatism. There follows a duet after Cymon has decided to communicate with his father:

Iph.   Don't give way, sweet youth, I pray,
        To sad procrastination,
        Or like the man asleep in the train
        You'll miss your destination.

Cymon   I'll go at once and ring him up,
        Not waiting invitation,
        The language I will pour out then
        Will produce strong perspiration.

In Scene 2 Cymon is grief-stricken on learning that Cypseus has

betrothed his daughter Iphigenia to Pasimond and resolves to ask
Queen Mab's advice. No sooner has he gone than Bullbracken, Tipple,
and others enter with a letter from Pasimond, and the swooning
Iphigenia is carried away to the ship to the sound of the sailors' chorus.
Queen Mab promises her aid to Cymon in Scene 3 and urges him to
set forth in one of the ships lying in the harbour. Scene 4 shows Cymon
intercepting Bullbracken's ship when Iphigenia has barely awakened
from her stupor. The fierce struggle of Boccaccio's tale is reduced to a
farce. Cymon cuts Bullbracken's coat to pieces, in order to satisfy
Pasimond that a desperate struggle took place, and the whole ends with
dancing to a lively polka. Scene 5 takes place in the hall of Pasimond's
house. The militia are mustered in ludicrous array. The men are of
different sizes; the tall men are dressed in very tight clothes, the small
men in clothes much too large for them. A cry is heard: 'A sail!', and
the militia hastens away. Ormisda then enters and tells his brother of
his despair, because Cassandra, whom he loves, is plighted to Lysimachus. Pasimond makes light of his troubles and bids him go to her
parents and ask for the money lent them some time before. They
will not be able to pay, and then Ormisda can offer to cancel the debt
in return for Cassandra. After Ormisda's departure, the captain of the
militia returns to announce that the *Salt Sarah* is about to reach port.
Thereupon Bullbracken and his crew enter with large pieces of plaster
on their faces, and using crutches, slings, bandages and sticks. The
enraged Pasimond threatens to have them all hanged but a moment
later his attention is diverted by the news that Cymon's ship has been
wrecked. In Scene 6 Cymon, Iphigenia and their crew are discovered
sitting on the rocks. When a march is heard in the distance, Cymon
vows to 'die game', but lets himself be arrested by a policeman.

Policeman   I appeal to your sense; best keep quiet.
Cym.   A *peeler* turned *appealer*.

After this incident Ormisda tries to win Cassandra by using the argument of the bill, and she reluctantly consents. Pasimond and Ormisda
decide that they shall be married next day, but Cymon and Lysimachus agree to carry off the brides, gaining access to the palace with
the connivance of a policeman. Scene 7 presents the banquet in
Pasimond's palace with the militia in attendance. A ballet is performed
and Cymon and Lysimachus enter in the disguise of street-acrobats.
Cymon seizes Iphigenia, and the soldiers run away in terror. In the
general fight that ensues Pasimond and Ormisda, who have been
drinking heavily, are knocked down, and Cymon and Lysimachus
carry off the brides. In Scene 8 all four appear in a cave, with their
escort of police! Then Pasimond and Ormisda arrive with their followers, and a struggle seems imminent. But Queen Mab appears and

pleads for peace and friendship. The characters fall into a mock-sentimental group, and Cypseus and his friend Tickletoes come in at different entrances. They are in travelling costume and announce that they have arrived by telegram. Finally, the scene changes to Queen Mab's abode in fairyland.

Thus, as in some earlier versions, the English fairy tradition is mingled with Boccaccio's tale. But the heroic element in the original is reduced to farce, and the transforming power of love and beauty is obscured in this uncongenial atmosphere. Nevertheless, taken for what it is meant to be, this lively burlesque has many qualities. Above all it is amusing.

However modest the dramatic merits of Planché and Lee may be, their work was at least seen on the stage. That is not true of certain sketches or scenes by B. W. Procter, all written in blank verse. These are 'The Two Dreams',[1] 'The Broken Heart',[2] 'The Falcon',[3] 'Love Cured by Kindness',[4] and 'The Florentine Party'.[5] They received high praise from Charles Lamb, but their dramatic value is negligible.

In 'The Two Dreams' Andreana and Gabriello successively relate their dreams, and then the hero dies. That is all. There is no conflict, the dialogue is perfunctory, and as drama the sketch is worthless. Procter tried to eke out his material by amplifying Andreana's dream. She describes how on a sultry night she saw the stars on their course make a noise like a hissing serpent and how each in turn came and stood over Gabriello's head and then sank in darkness, the last being Saturn, his natal star. The strange creature that carries off the hero is well portrayed, 'a shadowy thing' that rose from his body and stood in silence by him:

> It was not
> Flesh, no nor vapour; but it seemed to be
> A dismal compound of the elements,
> Huddled by chance together ere the form
> Of man was fixed and fashioned into beauty,
> Then like a loathsome and unfinished thing,
> Flung aside for ever.[6]

The feeling of horror is intensified by attendant phenomena. As Saturn's light is extinguished, there is a hideous noise as though a globe were cracking, the sound of

> horrid laughs,
> And shrieks and syllables—in an unknown tongue[7]

---

[1] *Dec.* iv, 6. Cf. *Dramatic Scenes*, London, 1819, p. 1.
[2] *Dec.* iv, 8. Cf. *Dramatic Scenes*, p. 114.
[3] *Dec.* v, 9. Cf. *Dramatic Scenes*, 1857 ed. (not in 1819 ed.).
[4] *Dec.* x, 7. Cf. *Dramatic Scenes*, p. 57.
[5] *Dec.* iii, 2; v, 5. Cf. *Essays and Tales in Prose*, Boston, 1835, ii, pp. 233–51.
[6] *Dramatic Scenes*, 1819 ed., p. 6.   [7] Ibid., p. 6.

is heard, and vast wings beat overhead. Again, when Andreana dreams
that Gabriello is snatched away into the yawning earth,

> there came out blue fires, and sounds of torture,
> Curses and shrieks—then solitary laughs.[1]

Gabriello ridicules these fantasies, as he does his own dream. But he
grows increasingly serious and begins to ponder on life and to wonder
whether life itself is not a dream. Of one thing he is sure—the spirit is
immortal:

>   How fine
> And marvellous the subtile intellect is.
> Beauty's creator! it adorns the body
> And lights it like a star. It shines for ever;
> And like a watch-tower, to the infidel
> Shows there's a land to come.[2]

This passage is, of course, alien to the original story, but its insertion
as an immediate prelude to Gabriello's death shows that Procter was
not entirely without dramatic sense, though as a whole the sketch is
too slight.

There is more substance in 'Love Cured by Kindness'. Boccaccio's
tale of Lisana's love for the king of Sicily[3] was calculated to appeal to
Procter. However, he evidently thought that in such a romantic story
the figure of the apothecary was out of place, and he transforms
Lisana's father into an artist, just as in 'The Two Dreams' he had
given the events a setting in high society by an allusion to Count
Strozzi as a visitor to Andreana's house. Another change was to remove
the queen, no doubt because Procter thought it unseemly that Lisana
should bestow her love on a married man.

The sketch contains two scenes. The first shows Don Pedro with
his courtiers in the banquet-room. The king toasts the queen of Naples,
Julio drinks to Lisana and in reply to Don Pedro's enquiry praises her
beauty. Ippolito tells his master of Lisana's illness and its cause. At
once the king sets out to visit her, taking Ippolito with him, and on the
way ascertains that the young courtier has loved her all his life. The
second scene is in Lisana's bedchamber. Don Pedro graciously acknowledges the devotion of Lisana and tactfully, while expressing his
willingness to be her friend, pleads for Ippolito who has generously
sacrificed himself by telling his lord the story of her love. Lisana is
won over and agrees to marry Ippolito, who is called in to receive Don
Pedro's wishes for her happiness.

There is here some attempt at dramatic tension. In particular, the
creation of Ippolito is important. He takes over the functions of
Minuccio and Mico da Siena. Moreover, his marriage to Lisana has a

---

[1] Ibid., p. 7.   [2] Ibid., p. 11.   [3] Vide ante, pp. 349, 438–40, 445–7.

firm foundation in his well-tried affection, whereas at the end of Boccaccio's tale, Perdicone, of whom nothing has been heard before, is married to the heroine, 'he not gainsaying'.[1] Even so, Procter's version has something of the atmosphere of a fairy-tale.[2]

On the other hand, there is more of the stuff of drama in 'The Broken Heart', though it is allowed to transpire far too soon that the hero will die. The first scene shows a violent clash of wills between Jeronymo and his mother. The hero has returned to Florence from Paris and with bitter jests upbraids her. She is reduced to tears, as he declares that he will die, now that he knows of Sylvestra's marriage. There is an energy in his character that Boccaccio's Girolamo lacks, and some of his chiding vaguely recalls Hamlet's rebuke of Queen Gertrude. He completely dominates his mother. Yet despite his resentment of her actions, his parting word is to bless her. The second scene, laid in Sylvestra's bedchamber, enhances the impression of Jeronymo's nobility. After they have indulged in reminiscences of childhood, they discover the cause of their estrangement. Nevertheless, when Jeronymo lies dying, he begs Sylvestra to forgive those who have wronged them:

> One's a mother, and may feel,
> When that she knows me dead.[3]

As in 'The Two Dreams' there is a sensational strain. Quite without need, Jeronymo talks to Sylvestra of ghosts in a way that fills her with terror:

> spirits quit their leaden urns, to tempt
> Wretches from sin. Some have been seen o'nights
> To stand and point their rattling fingers at
> The red moon as it rose; (perhaps to turn
> Man's thoughts on high). Some their lean arms have stretch'd
> 'Tween murderers and their victims: Some have laugh'd
> Ghastly, upon—the bed of wantonness,
> And touch'd the limbs with death.[4]

Contrasting with this macabre element, Nature is used in a passage where Sylvestra reminds her lover:

> How we were wont, on Autumn nights, to stray,
> Counting the clouds that pass'd across the moon
>
> .   .   .   .   .
>
> And figuring many a shape grotesque:
> Camels and caravans, and mighty beasts,
> Hot prancing steeds, and warriors plum'd and helm'd,
> All in the blue sky floating.[5]

---

[1] 'non recusante'.

[2] It is interesting to compare this with de Musset's comedy, *Carmosine*, on the same theme. Cf. H. Hauvette in *Bulletin italien*, xi, 1911 and L. Lafoscade, *Le Théâtre d'Alfred de Musset*, Paris, 1901, pp. 157–67.

[3] 1819 ed., p. 124.   [4] Ibid., p. 119.   [5] Ibid., p. 120.

Such lines are by no means isolated in Procter's plays. In fact, his love of Nature is still more obvious in the opening scene of 'The Falcon'. Frederigo is sitting outside his cottage brooding over his poverty but finds consolation for his wretchedness in the golden silence of the sunset. The entry of Giana and her maid sets the plot moving. The women withdraw to an arbour in the orchard after Giana has learnt casually that Frederigo was disinherited by Count Filippo because he would not marry according to his wishes. Left alone, Frederigo summons Bianca and asks what they can offer the guests. He suggests, by a singular anachronism, that he should shoot something with his gun. But Bianca replies that this would take too long, as the birds are too shy because of his falcon Mars. This gives him an idea. He kills Mars, and the scene ends with Frederigo's lament over the falcon:

> Mars! my brave bird, and have I killed thee, then,
> Who was the truest servant—fed me, loved me so,
> When all the world had left me? Never more
> Shall thou and I in mimic battle play,
> Nor thou pretend to die, (to die, alas!)
> And with thy quaint and frolic tricks delight
> Thy master in his solitude.[1]

Then, after picturing the courage with which Mars would attack the fiercest birds of prey, Frederigo concludes:

> for me
> Who kill'd thee—*murdered* thee, poor bird; for thou
> Wast worthy of humanity, and I
> Feel with these shaking hands, as I had done
> A crime against my race.

In the second scene Giana explains her errand, her sick boy's desire for the falcon. The suspense is well maintained until in the end Frederigo has to relate what he has done and why. She is already predisposed in his favour by his former devotion and by what she has heard of his being disinherited. Now in her gratitude she declares that she will marry him forthwith. This leads to long, ecstatic speeches by Frederigo, punctuated only by Giana's remark 'Oh! you rave' or 'Why, now thou'rt mad indeed'. He can hardly bear to let her go, and his feelings culminate in another lyrical outburst. To stress the mounting emotion the last sixteen lines abandon blank verse for the heroic couplet.

As in all his dramatic sketches Procter selects carefully from Boccaccio's tale and eliminates some events and characters. Nothing is heard of the boy's death, nor of the initial opposition of Giana's brothers to her marriage with Frederigo. Thus everything is directed towards

[1] For 'The Falcon' see 1857 ed.

the portrayal of Frederigo's relationship to Giana, but opportunities for dramatic conflict are thrown away.

The last of the sketches, 'The Florentine Party', takes its name from the scene—a meadow, near Florence, sloping down to a river, with Fiesole visible in the distance. From a wood there enter the narrators of the *Decameron*. The opening words, spoken by Neiphila, show that Procter was not insensitive to the graceful description at the beginning of the third day. When the company is seated, Philostratus tells the second story of that day. It is treated with some freedom but the situation remains essentially the same. At the close the feast is served, Philostratus sings a song, and then Emilia tells another story, which is a free adaptation of that related by Neifile about Giannole and Minghino on the fifth day of the *Decameron*. The dialogue that precedes and accompanies the tales is brisker than usual in Procter's work, and the narrative portion is condensed, so that the whole displays a sense of proportion. However, it is evident here as elsewhere in these 'dramatic scenes' that he had no idea of practical stagecraft. They provide yet one more illustration of the unfamiliarity of many writers at this time with the needs of the theatre.

How difficult it was for serious drama to make itself heard is illustrated by Gerald Griffin's *Gisippus*. He finished it before his twentieth year was completed and hoped to see it performed at one of the best-known theatres when he arrived in London in 1823. But as the preface to the play[1] states,

at that time, the public taste was vitiated by managers who yielded to the depraved appetites of the multitude, instead of endeavouring to correct them. Mechanical wonders, cataracts of real water, brilliant scenic representations and sights of an amphitheatrical and popular character usurped the place of the legitimate drama, and after many distressing difficulties, and much valuable time sacrificed in the attempt, he gave it up as hopeless.

After Griffin's death his friends approached Charles Kean unsuccessfully, and they again failed when they submitted the play to the manager of one of the smaller theatres who based his rejection on a cursory reading of *Gisippus* on the outside of an omnibus. However, in the end Macready accepted it, and it was produced at Drury Lane on 23 February 1842, with Macready as Gisippus and Helen Faucit as Sophronia.

Like Charles Lloyd in his verse tale,[2] Griffin felt that the manner in which Boccaccio had allowed Gisippus to substitute his friend in the nuptial union, without the knowledge or consent of Sophronia, was intolerable. Some justification had to be found, and she had to approve. The early part of the play is devoted to this problem. It emerges

---

[1] London, 1842.   [2] Vide ante, pp. 426–9.

gradually that Titus Quintus Fulvius, known in the play as Fulvius, has for some time past been absorbed in his love for a girl of Corinth, but thanks to the scoffing advice of Chremes he resolves to forget her. As for Gisippus, he has been patiently wooing Sophronia for three years, and now after much hesitation she has agreed to marry him, though he is conscious that he has still not won her confidence. In the second scene of Act I Sophronia confesses to her friend Hero that she already repents her promise:

> What an inconstant thing is woman's will,
> On what a trifle may the happiness
> Of a whole existence hang. A summer wind
> That is but air—nothing—may turn an argosy.
> And the poor word in weary weakness uttered,
> Hath power to bind beyond release or hope
> A life's whole destiny.

Then comes the news that Fulvius has been called to Rome, not because his father has died, as in the *Decameron*, but by order of the Emperor. He catches sight of Sophronia who is veiled. She exercises a strange attraction, and he sets forth the doctrine of the elective affinities which Goethe had made familiar:

> I know not why,
> But though we sure have never met before,
> That form already grows upon my soul
> Familiar as a memory of its childhood.
> Our sages teach, (and now I find them reasonable.)
> There is between the destinies of mortals
> A secret and mysterious coincidence
> Drawn from one mighty principle of Nature;
> A fixed necessity—a potent "must"
> That sways mortality through all its harmonies!
> That souls are mingled and hearts wedded, ere
> Those souls have felt the dawning of a thought;
> Before those hearts have formed a pulse, or yet
> Begun to beat with consciousness of being!
> My heart is governed by a fate like this,
> And drawn to thee, unknown—unseen.
>
> (I. ii)

The conversation turns to the lady of Corinth whom Fulvius had known, and it is disclosed that their estrangement was due to a misunderstanding. Sophronia throws back her veil, and Fulvius recognises her as the woman whom he still loves. The knowledge that she is betrothed to his friend Gisippus and regards herself as bound to obedience reduces him to despair. Despite Fulvius's resolve to control himself, he interrupts the wedding festivities and quarrels with Gisippus, only to repent and declare that the latter shall yet think

2H

nobly of him. By this time the unhappy Sophronia wishes to defer the
marriage, and Gisippus promises to release her from all obligations if
he can make her happy. But she knows herself committed and is not
unmindful of duty and honour. Nevertheless, she feels that they are
both victims and are going to a sacrifice, though he is unaware how
profound is her misery.

When Fulvius comes to see her once more, it is Sophronia who
exhibits the greater strength of mind. She points out that if they
were to forget their obligations to Gisippus, they would forfeit their
self-respect. Fulvius's sense of honour reawakens and, saying that
Gisippus must never learn of their affection, he bids her farewell.
Unknown to them, Gisippus has overheard all, and though he is overcome with distress and foreboding of trouble to come, hurries them
away to a temple where the nuptial rite is performed.

The third act deals with the reasons for the disaster that now overtakes Gisippus. As in Boccaccio the relatives of Sophronia are incensed
against him. They even accuse him of accepting a bribe from Fulvius.
But Griffin provides another explanation. Gisippus is sued by a money-
lender who is vividly described by Pheax:

> But now I met old Davus, the rich usurer,
> Taxing his withered limbs, to seek his pleader,
> One shrivelled arm close pinioned to his side,
> The hand fast clenched upon a musty parchment,
> Which, next his skin, looked fair; the other wandering,
> With bony fingers stretched, in the act to grasp,
> (Fit emblems of the miser's double craft,
> *Getting and keeping*[1])—his small weasel eyes
> Glanced every way at once—his countenance
> Looked like a mask made out of an old drum-head,
> In which the bones at every motion rattled
> From mere starvation. Flesh is a garment, Sir,
> Far too expensive for his use.
>
> (III. i)

Another new feature is Gisippus's intended appeal to Fulvius. A
meeting is arranged before Gisippus has time to convey even a hint
of his troubles, but a new messenger from Rome calls Fulvius away
immediately. He writes to Gisippus but the latter feels that he has
been deceived. Forthwith he is arrested and sold to a Sicilian merchant.
In anger Gisippus sends the parchment declaring him a slave to
Fulvius.

In the last two acts the scene is transferred from Athens to Rome.
In spite of his success and his election to the office of praetor, Fulvius

---

[1] The fact that this phrase is italicised is clearly meant to acknowledge the
borrowing from Wordsworth's sonnet 'The world is too much with us'.

is cold in his manner to Sophronia, because he holds her family responsible for the misfortunes of Gisippus whom he has been unable to trace. In contrast to the splendour in which Fulvius lives is the poverty of Gisippus, who stands outside the praetor's mansion. Fulvius does not recognise the haggard and unkempt Gisippus, though the latter is convinced that his former friend has ignored him deliberately. His grief is turned to indignation when he is struck by the lictors and thrust aside. Chremes, who is the living friend of Fulvius and not, as in Boccaccio, the dead father of Gisippus, also fails at first to recognise him; he afterwards tries to console him and ponders how the two can be reconciled.

If Griffin has made a minor change by substituting Fulvius as praetor for Boccaccio's Varro, his alteration of the episode of the two robbers in the cave is more substantial. It is, of course, a mere coincidence that Gisippus should take refuge in this spot and witness the quarrel in which the one robber slays the other; equally it is by chance that Titus comes to the trial when Gisippus is charged with the murder and then, recognising his friend, attempts to take the guilt upon himself. Evidently Griffin felt that in the tale this sequence of coincidence demanded too much of the reader. He therefore eliminates the cave and the robbers, and brings about the recognition in a different way. Gisippus wanders away from Fulvius's house in utter dejection until he reaches a burying-ground at nightfall, where, as he leans on a tomb, he soliloquises on death:

> This is his court,
> Here does he hold his reign of stirless fear,
> Silence his throne—his robe of majesty,
> The hue of gathering darkness. Here, his minister—
> The night-bird screams, and the hoarse raven iterates
> His warning from the left. Diseases flit
> Like spectres through the gloom, clothed in damp mist
> And tainted night-air—yet the grim slayer
> Will send no kindly shaft to me.
>
> (IV. iii)

The macabre element has dramatic point, for Gisippus has barely ended his speech and descended into the tomb, when he witnesses a murder. Chremes, who is on an errand for Fulvius, is dogged by Lycias, a servant in the praetor's household. There is a long-standing feud between Chremes and Lycias which has culminated that day in the dismissal of the latter, who left the house of Fulvius muttering threats against Chremes. Now he takes his revenge, and Chremes has only time to hand to Gisippus certain scrolls before he dies. It might be objected that Griffin has merely replaced one coincidence by another. But he prepares the way for this incident by the offer made by Fulvius in the preceding scene of a guard to protect Chremes as he passed the burying-ground. A similar attempt at verisimilitude occurs in connexion with the recognition. The scrolls left by Chremes are taken to Fulvius in his capacity as praetor, who learns from them that Gisippus is in Rome, and when he is given the bloody sword of the supposed murderer, he perceives it to be that of his old friend.

In the final scene at the place of execution Gisippus speaks bitterly against the injustice and inequality of the world and is bent on death, when Fulvius rushes in to save him. Gisippus, his soul overflowing with all his long pent-up grievances, rebuffs him angrily. It is only with the approach of Sophronia that he grows calmer and allows himself to be reconciled to Fulvius, exclaiming, as he fixes his eye on Sophronia, 'All for thee!'

The ending is too hasty to be quite convincing, and occasionally the dramatic machinery creaks loudly. But there are some powerful moments in the play. The sources of conflict are varied, and Griffin shows a command of tension and surprise. The play is well linked together, and although it is obviously a product of the age, it is free from the more extreme manifestations of romantic extravagance. Nevertheless, the theme was unable to hold the audience for any length of time.

The story of Griselda did not afford very promising material to a nineteenth-century dramatist, but an effort to cast it into the form of a play was made by Sir Edwin Arnold in 1856.[1] Strangely enough, in spite of the happy ending he styled it 'a tragedy', which suggests some confusion of purpose. In order to spin out the plot for five acts numerous characters are introduced. Griselda has a village friend, Lenette, who accompanies her to court, and Jacinta, a waiting-woman. In addition to a councillor, Pietro Mala, Antonio, a lord in waiting, and Martino, the sergeant of the guard, we find Bertolo, the head-falconer and Bertram, a troubadour. Martino is, of course, the agent for carrying out Walter's orders for the removal of the children to Padua, while conveying the impression to Griselda that they are to be put to death. Most of the others have little to do, beyond bringing messages, except to comment unfavourably on the actions of the marquis and to eulogise the conduct of Griselda. An attempt to provide some relief by a clash among these minor figures is hardly successful, for most of them remain colourless. The sergeant, who under the gruff exterior that he has been commanded to display to Griselda hates the

---

[1] An adaptation of a German play on the subject by 'F. Halm', i.e. E. F. J., Freiherr von Münch-Bellinghausen, had been made by Sir R. A. Anstruther. It was first printed in 1840 and performed at Edinburgh on 26 January 1841 (cf. A. Nicoll, *A History of Early Nineteenth Century Drama*, 1800–1850, Cambridge, 1930, ii, p. 244).

task imposed upon him, has some vitality, but he has too slight a part for more careful delineation. Only Janicola, Griselda's aged father, has much individuality. He is attractive in his robust independence and his shrewd peasant distrust of the marquis's desire to marry his daughter.

Arnold follows Boccaccio in presenting Griselda's unbreakable love and wifely patience. Only once does it show signs of giving way, and that is when she is summoned to return from her cottage to get the palace ready for the supposed new bride. The dramatist does his best to depict Walter's anguish of mind, as he piles up one sorrow after the other on the meek Griselda's head. But his whole scheme is a mystery, and not even Arnold's suggestion that the plan emanated from Walter's sister can justify his action or render it palatable to the modern reader.

In order to enhance the value of his play Arnold introduces a number of lyrics. Most of these are placed in the mouth of Bertram, the troubadour, but a stanza like the following gives little confidence in his craft:

> All the woes the morrows make us
> 　Never spoiled a present bliss;
> Feres that take us may forsake us,
> 　Dio!—dearer is the kiss;
> Better then to love and rue it
> Than to never love.
>
> (II. iii)

Though he is called Bertram di Bocca d'Oro,[1] he hardly lives up to his name. In fact, Griselda is quite his equal in song. She sings one stanza in Act I, Sc. ii, just before the first appearance[2] of the marquis at her home, and the full lyric, of which this stanza is a part, immediately before the death of her father.

Griselda has the power of poetic speech on many occasions and, even when she is pleading with Bertram for a simple song, her choice of words is out of keeping with her humble origin:

> 　　　　　　　　　　　　I have thought,
> Listening to many a modern line and lay
> Of minstrelsy excelling, that their strings
> Strove for too great an utterance, and so missed
> The ready road that quiet music finds
> Right to the heart; like as an o'erstrained bow
> Shoots past the butt. Dame Nature doth not thus,
> And minstrels are her children, and should stand
> Close at their mother's knee to learn of her.
> Look! when she will be beautiful or great,
> She strains not for her rainbow or her stars,

---

[1] Bertram of the Mouth of Gold.
[2] He comes disguised as a trader, an incident unknown to Boccaccio.

But with deft finger works her wonders in
With an unruffled quiet, a soul-felt
And unregardful strength,—so that her storms,
Her calms, night, day, moon-risings and sunsets,
Wood-songs and river-songs, and waves and winds,
Come without noise of coming. Ah! I love,
When 'tis voiced tenderly—a simple song,—
A song whereto the caught ear listens close,
To hear a heart, and not a chord speak out
Musical truthfulness.

(II. iii)

The voice is the voice of Griselda, but the words are those of Arnold who is satisfying his lyric instinct at the expense of his dramatic purpose. For him the mediæval period was an age of high romance, and the trials of Griselda, like the troubadours, tournaments and merchants in disguise in the background of the play, belong to a pale land of wonder which is remote from the traffic of the stage.

A far better play is Mary Elizabeth Braddon's *Griselda*, which was licensed for performance at the Princess Theatre on 8 November 1873.[1] From the beginning it has a firmer foothold on reality. In the opening scene in the homely surroundings of Griselda's cottage home, her father Paolo is shown in conversation with her mother Anna. He has just returned from Saluzzo. Fatigued by the journey, he is in an irritable mood, for he has learnt that the handsome young cavalier, who since the spring has been paying attentions to Griselda, is none other than the marquis himself. His wife, who bustles about her preparations for their meal, agrees with him, though reluctantly, that the visits must cease. But their anxiety about Griselda's virtue is momentarily forgotten when Anna exclaims:

Saints I smell
A smell of burning—Tis the macaroni.

This exposition is followed by the entrance of the villain, Cosmo, the cousin of the marquis. He has heard of Gualtiero's love-affair and assumes that it is a low amour. An ambitious aristocrat, he feels only contempt for any one who can

stoop
To breathe love whispers in the willing ear
Of some rude shepherds wench, with blowzy cheeks,
A flat face tanned by summers fiercest suns
And roughened by east winds.

For his part, he will soar as high as the stars; and a king's daughter is a fitting spouse for him. At this moment Gualtiero enters and asks whether Cosmo knows the inmates of the cottage. He rejects with

---

[1] At present in the Lord Chamberlain's archives at St. James's Palace.

disdain the suggestion that he could be acquainted with uncouth peasants:

> The male a clod,
> His female like him—and their spawn, young clods,
> Shaped the paternal image—huge rough hands—
> Splay feet—flat noses—swart and freckled skins,
> Thick waists—coarse hair—in brief a kind of delf
> Made for the common uses of this life
> And of no account when broken.

Gualtiero, on the other hand, maintains that God in his justice counterbalances the hardship of poverty by compensating bounties:

> and among them
> You may count beauty—on Giottos canvas
> The peasant girl with lifted dovelike eyes
> Becomes the ideal Madonna—Your true painter
> Asks not the lineage of the beautiful.

With characteristic cynicism Cosmo proposes that Gualtiero should enjoy Griselda's love without marriage, but the marquis will not listen. He has long been urged to marry, but though he has sought far and wide and encountered many who were fair, and some of rank and wealth that would have doubled his own, he has found none after his own heart except Griselda. His courtiers, who have arrived, appear to agree with his romantic design, but among themselves declare him mad. He bids the ladies of the court enter the cottage and array Griselda, and when she comes out in her bridal attire, even Cosmo is impressed:

> If beauty could destroy a plain man's peace
> Her's is the face to do it.

The second act presents Gualtiero and Griselda in a terraced garden of the palace at Saluzzo. Their happiness is complete. He has lavished robes, gems and money upon her, and she in her turn has used this wealth to relieve the wants of the poor:

> I scarce could bear the burden of my gladness
> Wer't not that I can share it with the humble.

However, news comes that this joyful idyll will have to be interrupted, for the Genoese are preparing an army against the infidel pirates of Barbary, and Gualtiero's support is expected. Griselda instinctively rebels, but on reflection she feels it right that he should play his part. He contemplates entrusting her to the care of Cosmo in his absence. Griselda has misgivings about him, but acquiesces in the end.

When Griselda has gone out, Cosmo brings in Lelio, the steward of Gualtiero. Lelio produces his accounts and proves that the revenues have been squandered since the marriage. He complains of Griselda's extravagance:

> she gives right and left—noon and night—
> In kind and money—the gown off her back—
> The pasty from the larder. She has made
> Your villa on the hill an hospital—
> Adopts stray children—shelters aged beggars.
> I saw three in the kitchen as I passed,
> Disputing for a roast kid stuffed with chesnuts.
> The palace is demoralised.

Quick to seize an opportunity, Cosmo declares that Griselda loves her husband only because he tolerates her lavish expenditure and insinuates that her love would not stand a serious test. Gualtiero proclaims his faith in her, but doubt has been sown in his mind, and after some hesitation he is won over by Cosmo's proposal that he should be allowed to try her constancy. His attitude to Griselda changes abruptly, and when she returns, holding her gown full of bread which she distributes to the children and beggars that follow her, he rebukes her. Griselda is nonplussed and can only ask 'am I dreaming?' However, Gualtiero continues to speak harshly and even hints that she may help him by killing herself. Rejecting her entreaties, he tells her that he means to marry again, this time a lady of noble birth which wrings from Griselda a cry of anguish:

>   No, not that
> I could not suffer that.

He then says that out of compassion, so that she may not witness this, he will send her to an ancient hunting lodge. In a moving speech Griselda replies:

> Let it be where thou wilt. Showed it more fair
> Than these thy gardens, running o'er with flowers
> And musical with nightingales, it were
> A living grave to me without thy presence:
> But I will not complain—thou hast been pleased
> To mock me with a dream of happiness;
> So swift awaking dazes me;
> I have not all my sense left—But I know
> That thou canst change my fate, but not my love.
> That lives above thy power to wound or slay
> And will live on, though thou shouldst neer be moved
> From this strange cruelty. I've been thy wife
> Just three short months, and I shall be thy slave
> To the end of life.

Gualtiero is swayed by her gentle submission and relents:

> My love, awake; sweet, it was but a jest.
> Shame on my folly! I have been too hard.
> Look up, Griselda; *I do* love thee more
> For thy divinest patience—if a love
> So full could know increase.

Cosmo calls him a consummate fool and bids him complete the work by sending her to the lodge in the gloomy mountains.

It is here that Act III takes place. Griselda's attendant, Anita, describes the noble spirit of her mistress who, in spite of Gualtiero's strange behaviour, will hear nothing against him. She displays the courage of a Roman wife and spends her time in prayer and in caring for her son to whom she has given birth. On the arrival of Lelio, Griselda is eager for news of Gualtiero. But Lelio can only bring rumours of his wild revelry in the Genoese camp and of an attempt to obtain a dispensation from the Pope, so that he may marry the daughter of Duke Malatesta. To which Griselda replies indignantly:

> Little know I
> The laws of church or state—but this I know—
> Heaven made us one, and *if* the Pope can part us,
> *God* and the Pope must be antagonists.

Once more her anger bursts forth when Lelio points out that if Gualtiero marries again, her son will become illegitimate. Like Hermione in *The Winter's Tale* she is less concerned about herself than about the slur on her child. Her inclination is to speak out boldly and denounce Cosmo to his face for his share in her grief. But for her son's sake she resolves to control her feelings. The entry of Cosmo leads to a scene of mounting tension. He tries to kindle her jealousy by talking of the daughter of Malatesta, but she remains meekly silent. Then he harps on the supposed desire of Gualtiero for a son of great lineage on both sides. This elicits only a calm reply:

> I have read history, Signor, in my prison
> And there I find the greatest men have owed
> Fame to their deeds, and not their ancestors.

However, when he declares his passionate love for her, she can restrain herself no more and condemns his duplicity. The arrival of Gualtiero puts an end to the wooing which Griselda now interprets as a device to test her fidelity. The two go out to see their child, but Cosmo has had him and Anita removed, in the hope that, the child once gone, he will prevail the more easily in his designs on Griselda. A moment later Gualtiero returns with the news that the child is missing. He is followed by Griselda who refuses to look at Gualtiero, lest she should curse him, and wanders away distraught to seek her son among the mountains.

In Act IV, which opens in Paolo's cottage, Gualtiero is stricken with remorse. He has come to kneel at the feet of Griselda and to ask for pity. Gradually she regains consciousness and a reconciliation takes place. In the second scene Lelio grumbles to Anita about the banquet that has been ordered, though no one knows what it is for. It offends his sense of economy. In the final scene Cosmo reveals that he is equally puzzled, but he has determined that if Gualtiero is to marry again, then he will take Griselda, for his evil passion has been transformed into genuine love. This is part of the dramatist's preparation for a happy ending. Gualtiero has breathed threats of bloody vengeance to be inflicted on Cosmo, but in the end the punishment is psychological. Cosmo has been sent to bring in the new marchioness. He raises her veil to present the lady to the citizens, only to find that it is Griselda. Though Gualtiero calls him a double traitor, he is content with having baffled him, and when Cosmo kneels to Griselda, she bids him rise, and the play ends on a note of forgiveness and rejoicing.

By the introduction of Cosmo, Miss Braddon places the chief responsibility for Griselda's trials on his shoulders. Gualtiero may seem too credulous and pliant, but he is no sadist. The reduction of the number of children to one son involves a limitation of the period of Griselda's suffering and a corresponding diminution of the strain on the spectator's sense of probability. In every way the test is made more tolerable. However, the outstanding feature of the play is the greater importance attached to the heroine. She has a richer personality than her counterpart in Boccaccio. If she is submissive, it is either because of her love of her husband or of her affection for her child. She is certainly not an automaton and has plenty of spirit beneath her self-control. In the hour of trial her dignity and restraint are faintly reminiscent of Shakespeare's Hermione. Her care for the poor from whom she had sprung is another sympathetic trait, and her conduct justifies her claim that nobility is to be gauged not by titles, but by actions. By contrast, Lelio serves in part a comic purpose. His prosaic concern with expenditure, his complaint of waste, even while he feathers his nest by exacting five per cent from all tradesmen, lets in the air of everyday life. Thus he acts as a counterpoise to the lofty emotion of the lovers, and even if the play as a whole is one of idealistic and romantic devotion, it is not detached from reality. Though Miss Braddon modifies Boccaccio's tale considerably, her adaptation has a sound basis in the need for adjustment in the process of transferring the story into a play. She displays some grasp of the stage, and in particular uses suspense and surprise effectively. Only the ending is somewhat tame and unconvincing.

In April 1882, nine years after the production of *Griselda*, R. Reece and H. B. Farnie wrote *Boccaccio*, which they described as an 'Opera Comique' in three acts, with music by F. von Suppé.[1] It is a fantasy, which has but the slenderest connexion with Boccaccio's life, though it does draw upon some tales of the *Decameron*. Boccaccio, who is

[1] At present in the Lord Chamberlain's archives at St. James's Palace.

referred to as a 'Student, Romancer and Satirist', is the central figure. He revels in disguise and is here, there and everywhere, animating all and directing the action. He is in love with Fiametta who has been brought up as the adopted daughter of Lambertuccio, an olive-grower. Disguised as a yokel, he persuades Lambertuccio that a tree in his garden is haunted and induces him to climb it. In the interval he kisses Fiametta. Like his prototype Nicostratus,[1] Lambertuccio resolves to have the tree felled. The original tale has obviously been toned down, and so has another,[2] which is used in Act II. In this episode of the opera, Pietro, prince of Palermo, woos Isabella, the wife of a cooper named Lotteringhi.[3] When the cooper returns home, the prince is forced to hide in a barrel. Isabella explains to her husband that she has sold the barrel to a contractor. Pietro emerges and says: 'For six crowns I expect a *sound* cask. Do you call this watertight, sir?' To which the intoxicated Lotteringhi replies: 'Ash watertight ash I am!' The grand duke of Florence had wished the prince of Palermo to marry his niece, and it now turns out that this is none other than Fiametta. But at the close the match is broken off, and the grand duke, anxious to make amends to his niece for her forced betrothal, gives his consent to her marriage with the man of her choice. She chooses Boccaccio. The prince is resigned to his lot, and all ends in general rejoicing.

It would seem that the opera is a free adaptation of a comedy in five acts by Bayard.[4] This, however, is much closer in spirit to the tales of amorous adventure in the *Decameron*, whereas the English version conforms to the pattern of romance and culminates in the marriage of the poor man of genius to the lady of high degree.

Though there was no such disparity of rank, it was a disparity of fortune in two lovers that formed the basis of Tennyson's one-act play, *The Falcon*. This was accepted by the Kendals and performed for the first time at the St. James's Theatre on 18 December 1879. It was well received and ran for sixty-seven nights.[5] As the dramatist was able to read Italian, it is possible that he knew the tale in its original form. However, it is certain that he also relied on the text of the translation of 1741, as it was to be found in numerous editions. There he could find the names 'Giovanna' and 'Federigo degli Alberighi'.[6] There is a

---

[1] *Dec.* vii, 9.　　　　　　　　　　　　　　　　　　　　[2] *Dec.* vii, 2.

[3] The name is borrowed from *Dec.* vii, 1.

[4] *Boccace, ou le Décaméron*, acted for the first time in Paris on 23 February 1853. Cf. *Bibliothèque Dramatique*, vol. 49.

[5] C. Tennyson, *Alfred Tennyson*, London, 1949, p. 447; A. Nicoll, *A History of Late Nineteenth Century Drama*, Cambridge, 1946, ii, p. 594.

[6] The edition of 1741 reads 'Frederigo', but from 1804 onwards the name was replaced in this version by 'Federigo'.

textual parallel when Giovanna, in reply to Federigo's remark, ' 'Tis long since we have met!', says:

> To make amends
> I come this day to break my fast with you.[1]

Again, there is an echo of the translation when Giovanna, commenting on her brother's desire to marry her to a rich man, observes:

> I think you know the saying—
> 'Better a man without riches, than riches without a man'.[2]

It has been suggested[3] that Tennyson was acquainted with Longfellow's rhymed version 'The Falcon of Ser Federigo' in *Tales of a Wayside Inn*, but the evidence given is not convincing.[4] In fact, the impression left by a comparison of the play with earlier interpretations of the story is not of Tennyson's indebtedness, but of his independence.

The woman that Federigo had to attend him in his poverty is of so little importance in Boccaccio that she is nameless and is mentioned only in a few words. Tennyson developed her into a character that is anything but shadowy. As Federigo's old nurse she is devoted to him but she takes advantage of her privileged position to criticise his extravagance. The most conspicuous instance of his folly is the purchase of a diamond necklace that Giovanna admires and his gift of it anonymously to her. Point is lent to Elisabetta's scathing comment by the sight of her as she sits darning in the opening scene. She is equally caustic in her comments on Giovanna, though she has a weakness for her and still hopes that she will relent and marry Federigo. How lifelike this minor figure is may be seen from the following passage:

I knew it would come to this. She has beggared him. I always knew it would come to this! (*Goes up to table as if to resume darning, and looks out of window.*) Why, as I live, there is Monna Giovanna coming down the hill from the castle. Stops and stares at our cottage. Ay, ay! stare at it; it's all you have left us. Shame on you! *She* beautiful! sleek as a miller's mouse! Meal enough, meat enough, well fed; but beautiful—bah! Nay, see, why she turns down the path through our little vineyard, and I sneezed three times this morning. Coming

---

[1] *The Falcon*, 1884 ed., p. 105. Cf. 1741 translation: 'I am come to make you some amends . . .'

[2] Ibid., p. 137. Cf. 1741 translation: 'I would sooner have a man that stands in need of riches, than riches without a man'.

[3] Rudolf Anschütz, *Boccaccios Novelle vom Falken und ihre Verbreitung in der Litteratur*, Erlangen, 1892, p. 34.

[4] Some of Anschütz's arguments fail because he omitted to take into account the English translation of 1741. As for his contention that the friendship of Giovanna's little son with Federigo, and his consequent desire for the falcon that he had come to know well, were inspired by Longfellow, the similarity is to be explained as arising from the original tale. The other parallels that Anschütz traces between Tennyson and La Fontaine, Dauvilliers, Sedaine, J. Barbier and M. Carré do not prove that he had even heard of them.

to visit my lord, for the first time in her life too! Why, bless the saints! I'll be bound to confess her love to him at last. I forgive her, I forgive her! I knew it would come to this—I always knew it must come to this![1]

Another person that Elisabetta rebukes is Filippo. He is Federigo's foster-brother, and when his tongue wags too freely, she disciplines him as if he were still a boy, though he is a soldier who has served in the wars. He is ever full of light-hearted jests, and despite Federigo's extreme poverty, Filippo takes it all with ironic laughter. Thus he informs Federigo that they have no silver spoons left:

Sold! but shall I not mount with your lordship's leave to her ladyship's castle, in your lordship's and her ladyship's name, and confer with her ladyship's seneschal, and so descend again with some of her ladyship's own appurtenances.[2]

Again, as he waits on Giovanna at table, with the same mock-exaggeration of respect he says:

Here's a fine salad for my lady, for tho' we have been a soldier, and ridden by his lordship's side, and seen the red of the battle-field, yet are we now drill-sergeant to his lordship's lettuces, and profess to be great in green things and in garden-stuff.[3]

With his outward air of nonchalance and capacity for a humorous attitude in a desperate situation he is an original creation.

Like the subordinate figures in the under-plots of Shakespeare's comedies, Elisabetta and Filippo give us the sense of reality in contrast to the romance of the main characters' actions. In various ways Tennyson has enriched this romantic colour. An important device, invented by him, is a withered wreath that hangs on the wall when the curtain rises. We begin to perceive its significance about half-way through the play. Federigo, taking it down, tells Giovanna:

> That wither'd wreath is of more worth to me
> Than all the blossom, all the leaf of this
> New-wakening year.[4]

Tennyson, aware of the undesirability of delaying the action, resists the temptation to insert a long description which would have given him pleasure, and the material that he introduces is linked to the plot. Federigo recalls briefly how he obtained the wreath:

> A lady that was beautiful as day
> Sat by me at a rustic festival
> With other beauties on a mountain meadow,
> And she was the most beautiful of all;
> Then but fifteen, and still as beautiful.
> The mountain flowers grew thickly round about.

[1] 1884. ed., pp. 99–100. [2] Ibid., p. 115.
[3] Ibid., pp. 123–4. [4] Ibid., pp. 109–10.

> I made a wreath with some of these; I ask'd
> A ribbon from her hair to bind it with;
> I whisper'd, Let me crown you Queen of Beauty,
> And softly placed the chaplet on her head.[1]

The young lady was Giovanna, and it is disclosed that when she rose and the wreath fell on the ground, she was too shy to return for it, and Federigo, thinking himself scorned, went off to the wars. In a romantic fashion that Bernard Shaw's Bluntschli would not have commended, he wore the wreath like a rosary round his neck when he went into battle and, stained with his blood, it accompanied him as a prisoner. The gradual revelation of these facts moves Giovanna profoundly, but though she is now a widow and free to marry again, there is a serious obstacle. Her brother is opposed to the match for a reason unknown to Boccaccio. There is a long-standing hostility between their families, like that which separates Romeo from Juliet. As Giovanna explains,

> His grandsire struck my grandsire in a brawl
> At Florence, and my grandsire stabb'd him there.
> The feud between our houses is the bar
> I cannot cross.[2]

Nevertheless, her emotion grows slowly more intense, and when she learns that Federigo has sacrificed his beloved falcon to provide her with a meal, her love triumphs.

Tennyson gives the play a happy ending, for he refuses to let Giovanna's son die, Federigo declaring:

> We two together
> Will help to heal your son—your son and mine—
> We shall do it—we shall do it![3]

These words show how far apart are Tennyson and Boccaccio, for even in his tales of romance the latter did not shrink from grief and pain. Yet even if this Tennysonian romance does not ring quite true, and even if there is substance in Fanny Kemble's criticism that it is 'an exquisite little poem in action',[4] at least he has succeeded in imparting to it by means of his humorous and lifelike characters an air of greater reality than we can find in many of the nineteenth-century plays on themes taken from the *Decameron*.

[1] 1884 ed., pp. 110–11.   [2] Ibid., p. 104.   [3] Ibid., p. 145.
[4] *Alfred Lord Tennyson a Memoir by his Son*, London, 1897, ii, p. 242.

CONCLUSION

As a result of our investigation it is clear that Boccaccio's influence extended in many directions and penetrated into the most remote nooks and crannies. It affected the ruler and his courtiers as well as the humble listeners to the ballad; it absorbed the scholar in his study no less than the crowd in the theatre. At the same time we observe how the interest in his writings shifts from period to period, focusing now on one form, now on another, so that as we proceed from the Middle Ages to the end of the nineteenth century, the pageant of literary modes unfolds before us in response to the subtle variations of taste and the cultural forces of successive eras.

At the beginning, as in France and Spain, it was the Latin works that predominated. They brought the mythology of the ancient world within the scope of a wider circle of readers and helped to lay the foundations of literary criticism. Still more important in some respects, they presented a gallery of portraits of the great figures of classical antiquity;[1] the vicissitudes in their careers were traced, and they became living models of vices to be shunned and virtues to be extolled. Through the agency of Lydgate working on the authors of *The Mirror for Magistrates* other exemplars were found in the annals of Britain, which prepared the way for the history play and, when the mechanical conception of Fortune's wheel had yielded place to the mysteries of Fate and human character, opened up the possibilities of Elizabethan tragedy. The illustrious figures of *De casibus* and *De claris mulieribus* provided material for the great controversy on the merits and de-merits of women, and the disputants found ample support for their opposing points of view in Boccaccio. However, the power of his learned compilations had begun to wane by the end of the sixteenth century and was soon to be exhausted, though the awe-inspiring figure of Demogorgon was to emerge once more at the command of Shelley.

It was but natural that the Latin writings should at first be those most commonly read, since their language was the international medium of communication. The knowledge of Italian, on the other hand, was a much rarer accomplishment. Hence the wonderful good fortune for English literature that its first great poet was sent on

[1] On the importance of this see F. Brie, 'Mittelalter und Antike bei Lydgate', *Englische Studien*, 1929, lxiv, pp. 261–301.

missions in the course of which he could hear the tongue of Boccaccio and obtain the manuscripts of the *Teseida* and the *Filostrato* which inspired the *Knightes Tale* and *Troilus and Criseyde*. But it was not until the sixteenth century was well advanced that a greater proficiency in Italian became more usual, though even then French often served as an intermediary. Still, before 1600 *Fiammetta*, the *Ninfale Fiesolano* and a part of the *Filocolo* had been given to the English public.

On the other hand, the *Decameron* was relatively slow in making itself felt, and in this respect sixteenth-century England offers a striking contrast to Italy[1] and Germany. There is no English writer who has recourse to the hundred tales so frequently as Hans Sachs, and the impact on the period as a whole is less massive[2] than in these two countries. This phenomenon can be explained to some extent by the lack of a translation of the whole work till 1620. Nevertheless, stimulated by Chaucer's example as a narrator of tales in verse, three stories had found their way into English through French or Latin versions in the fifteenth century; others followed in the sixteenth, again through the old channels, but also, in the latter part of the age, direct from the Italian. Many of them were regarded as examples of the caprices of Fortune, and therefore in keeping with those afforded by *De casibus* and *A Mirror for Magistrates*. The writers who retold Boccaccio's tales were also familiar with this English continuation, and one of them found nothing incongruous in the embodiment of a stanza from it in a story from the *Decameron*. Serious tales such as those of Grisild, Titus and Gisippus, and Guiscardo and Ghismonda were used for early experiments in drama. Towards the end of the period, however, signs of an interest in more light-hearted themes were evident in prose versions and in plays. But it remained for the seventeenth century, especially after the translation of 1620 had appeared, to exploit the tales of amorous intrigue in numerous comedies. Some of them, which introduced low life, were utilised for under-plots that served as a counterpart to the subject-matter of the main action.

In the eighteenth century, as Italian literary influence declined while that of France grew in importance, Boccaccio lost something of his popularity. The more serious tone in the drama militated against the choice of themes from the *Decameron*. In spite of this, a few playwrights maintained the tradition, and Garrick struck out a new path with his *Cymon*, from which, even if its æsthetic value is slight, sprang a long succession of farces and pantomimes extending well into the

---

[1] For an account of the influence of the *Decameron* in Italy, vide post, p. 482.

[2] Cf. Julius Hartman, *Das Verhältnis von Hans Sachs zur sogenannten Steinhöwelschen Decameronübersetzung* (*Acta Germanica*, ed. R. Henning, Neue Reihe, Heft 2), Berlin, 1912, and in particular the 'Übersicht über die auf die Decameron-Übersetzung zurückgehende deutsche Literatur des XVI. Jahrhunderts' (pp. 3–18).

nineteenth century. The falling off in eighteenth-century drama was accompanied by vigorous development elsewhere, and the preoccupation with low life expanded from comedy to prose narrative, when Smith and Johnson pilfered the *Decameron* for adventures which they ascribed to English highwaymen. The tale in verse, aided by La Fontaine, received a powerful stimulus from Dryden's *Fables*, and the example set by him of introducing allusions to contemporary affairs reinforced the well-established tendency to assimilate Boccaccio's stories to English surroundings. When joined with more personal comment in the manner of Byron, this practice later created a medley as strange as anything in an English pantomime. In the *Fables* too the eighteenth-century bent for satire found expression through the medium of the *Decameron*, and in other hands than those of Dryden it became yet more active. An anti-clerical bias which had peeped through in the sixteenth century now at times came into the open and lingered there into the Victorian era.

The sentimental love-story did not thrive in the eighteenth century, though 'The Unfortunate Lovers' combined an emotional appeal with the age-old lament over the fickleness of Fortune.[1] However, it was in the nineteenth century that the romantic tales in the *Decameron* flourished most freely, ranging from gentle idealism and unswerving devotion to fierce passion and the bitter-sweet of love, and in this sphere Hazlitt's advocacy moved both poets and dramatists. The story of the falcon in particular enjoyed a popularity which had a parallel on the Continent and in America. A new impetus was derived from a group of writers who were familiar with Italy, some of them with Boccaccio's native haunts. But whether the poets themselves had visited Florence, Naples and Fiesole or not, as was to be expected of an age that delighted in Nature, they adorned their verse with landscape descriptions. Occasionally these are employed with great effect as in Keats's 'Isabella', but more often they are developed to excess, and the narrators are as uncontrolled in their design as in their display of sentiment. Not unconnected with this phenomenon is the new interest in the background of Boccaccio's masterpiece. To this earlier writers had apparently remained insensitive, though Henry Tilney is a notable exception. For the most part they regarded the *Decameron* merely as a treasury of good tales. Coleridge, however, was quick to realise the delicate charm of the rural setting, and engravers like Stothard and Turner were soon invited to embellish the Italian scene by their art. It is likely that the idea of such book-illustration was suggested by the work of some of the most famous French engravers in eighteenth-century editions of the *Decameron*. It is also conceivable that Hogarth

---

[1] Vide ante, p. 309.

and Fuseli were inspired in the same way to portray on canvas striking figures or episodes in the tales, this tradition being sustained and reanimated by the Pre-Raphaelites. What with one cause and another, the *Decameron* had by now ousted all the other works from the mind of the public at large, so that Hobhouse could write 'It is almost forgotten that Boccaccio was a poet'.[1]

Yet as we look back, we perceive that in England there is no such array of prose imitators as in Italy.[2] It was above all the poets and dramatists who entered into contact with the complex series of Boccaccio's works. To mention only Chaucer, Spenser, Shakespeare, Jonson, Dryden, Coleridge, Keats and Shelley is a roll-call of most of the illustrious names in English literature. If we add to these Lyly and Sidney, Hazlitt, Landor, Rossetti, Tennyson and Swinburne, the assembly is still more dazzling. Even the grave Bacon and Wordsworth, and perhaps Marlowe and Milton, were aware of Boccaccio from afar, and the quicksilver of his mind ran towards a host of minor figures. It may be conceded that much of what he inspired is neither sublime nor profound, for he was neither mystic nor philosopher. Moreover, in passing beyond the Alps and the Rhine to the

horribilem insulam ultimosque Britannos,

his work underwent a sea-change. Nevertheless, he had a rare narrative power, great love of beauty, a keen sense of form and an intimate knowledge of the human heart, all of which survived the long journey and remained to speak from mediæval Italy in accents audible across the centuries to many generations of Englishmen, from Chaucer to Tennyson.[3]

[1] *Italy*, 1859, p. 242.
[2] Cf. A. Chiari, 'La fortuna del Boccaccio', in *Questioni e correnti di storia letteraria*, ed. A. Momigliano, Milan, 1949, pp. 275–348. This study also records plays and tales in verse inspired by Boccaccio. See further V. Branca, *Linee di una storia della critica al 'Decameron'*, Milan, 1939.
[3] A sketchy account of the European indebtedness to Boccaccio is given by F. N. Jones, *Boccaccio and his Imitators* . . . Chicago, 1910. For references to studies dealing with various aspects of the subject see G. Traversari, *Bibliografia boccaccesca*, Città di Castello, 1907, and the *Appendice Bibliografica* to V. Branca's work mentioned above.

INDEX

1. General

Abbot, George, archbishop of Canterbury, 191
Academy, the Royal, 335, 341
Academy, the Royal Scottish, 335
Academy della Crusca, 190
Academy of the Intronati, 196
Acciaiuoli, Andreina, Countess degli, 33
Accolti, Bernardo, *Virginia*, 213, 215, 216
Accounts of Independent Tatary, 380
Æneas Sylvius, *see* Pius II
Agincourt, 4
Agreeable Companion, The, 315
Agrippa, Henricus Cornelius, *De nobilitate et præcellentia foeminei sexus*, 35; *Of the vanitie and vncertaintie of Arts and Sciences*, 116
Alcibiades, 15–16
Alexandria, 6
Alighieri, Dante, *see* Dante
Alonso of Cartagena, 4
Alphonsus, Petrus, *Disciplina Clericalis*, 134
Althaea, 9, 37
Althorp, Lord, 331
Amadis, 115, 439
America, 415
Amsterdam, 113, 261, 263
Anacreon, 387
Ancona, 377
Angiolieri, Cecco, 363
Anne, Queen, 280, 282, 283, 322
Anne, queen of France, 28
Apennines, the, 351, 411
Aragon, 22, 438
Aretino, Pietro, 194
Arezzo, Antonio d', 113
'Arigo', 113
Ariosto, Lodovico, 38, 339, 340, 343, 349, 351, 352, 358, 360, 429
Aristotle, 250; *Politics*, 115
Arne, Thomas, Dr., 328, 456
Arno, 350, 351, 372, 402, 403, 404, 451
Arnold, Sir Edwin, *Griselda*, 468–70
Arnold, Matthew, 407, 452, 455

Artegall, 34
Arthur, King, 11, 12, 19, 21
Ascham, Roger, 115
Asinari, Federico, 184
Athens, 6
[Audinot, N. M., and Quétant, F. A.], *Le Tonnellier*, 328
Augsburg, 113, 213
Ayala, Pedro Lopez de, 3
Aylmer, John, bishop of London, 115
Ayre, William, *The Saint*, 300–2

Babington Plot, 150
Bacchus, 37
Bacon, Francis, *De sapientia veterum*, 43
Baldelli, Giovanni Battista, Count, *Vita di Boccaccio*, 350, 351, 373
Baldwin, archbishop of Canterbury, 212
Baldwin, William, 23, 25
Balguy, Charles, 262
Ballads, 170–3
Banester, Gilbert, 122–6, 128, 130, 131
Banquet for Gentlemen and Ladies, A, 308–9
Barham, Richard Harris, *The Ingoldsby Legends*, 371
Barnfield, Richard, 37, 40
Barry, Mrs., 205
Bangor, 199
Basle, 83, 115, 211, 213
Bayard, Jean F. A., *Boccace*, 475
Beaton, David, archbishop of St. Andrews, 25
Beauclerk, Topham, 263
Beaumont, Francis, 'The Triumph of Honor', 'The Triumph of Love', 229–30
Beauvau, Louis de, 59
Beccaria, Antonio, 44
Bee, The, 316
Behn, Aphra, *The Rover*, 246, 329
Benoît de Ste. More, 61, 74, 83–7
Bercher, William, *The Nobility of Women*, 35
Bernard de Ventadour, 73

Beroaldo (Beroaldus), 115, 133, 134, 194, 264

Berry, John, duke of, 4, 113

Betussi, Giuseppe, 33, 36, 37, 41, 42, 263, 337, 361

Bevis of Southampton, 115

Beza (Théodore de Bèze), 183

Biblioteca Ambrosiana, 331

Bibliothèque Nationale, 114, 331

Birck, Sixt, 213

Bishop, Sir Henry Rowley, 455

Blackman, William, 108

Blackmore, Sir Richard, 303

Blake, William, 371, 445

Blanca, queen of Aragon, 22

Blanchefleur, 1, 115

Blandford, marquis of, 331

Blennerhassett, Thomas, 24

Blount, Sir Thomas Pope, *De Re Poetica*, 189, 190

Blurt Master-Constable, 217–18, 246, 247

Boccaccio (Boccacio, Boccace, Bocace, Boccas, Bocase, Bocasse, Bocas, Bochas, Bokase, Boocas), Giovanni,

De casibus virorum illustrium, 2, 3, 4, 5–28, 33, 103, 156, 263

De claris mulieribus, 2, 3, 4, 5, 28–36, 81, 103, 263

De genealogia deorum, 2, 3, 33, 34, 36–43, 103, 337–8, 352, 362

De montibus, 2, 3, 36

Ameto, 1, 44, 352, 362

Amorosa visione, 1, 44, 362

Corbaccio, 2, 9, 35, 44, 99, 338

Decameron, 1, 2, 17, 33, 81, 103, 104, 110, 112, 113–478; *see also* Part 2 of Index

'Translation of 1620', 114, 185, 191, 199, 200, 244, 253–4, 265, 270, 275, 277, 286, 309, 310, 329, 333, 334, 349, 376, 397–9, 400, 401, 402, 403, 404, 405, 406, 418, 419, 421, 422, 424, 425

'Translation of 1702', 261–2, 315, 317

'Translation of 1741', 262, 333, 475–6

'Translation of Antoine le Maçon', 113, 157, 160, 191, 213, 398, 399

'Translation of John Payne', 334

Pictorial representations of the *Decameron* (wood-cuts, engravings, paintings, designs, fresco), 191, 261, 263, 264, 265, 333–4, 335, 341, 343, 344, 363–5

Minor poems of Boccaccio, 33, 363, 364–5, 454–5

Bodleian Library, 3, 125, 142, 170, 253

Boiardo, Matteo Maria, 58, 349

Braddon, Mary Elizabeth, *Griselda*, 470–4

Breugel, Gerrit Hendricx, van, 114

British Museum, 21, 28, 123, 162, 194, 195, 262, 328, 331, 332, 394, 412, 455

Browne, Sir Thomas, *Religio Medici*, 190–1

Browning, Robert, 370, 371, 436

Bruce, James, *Travels to discover the Source of the Nile*, 382

Bruni, Leonardo, 115, 123, 131, 172

Bruno, Giordano, 194, 343

Buchanan, George, 183

Buckingham, George Villiers, duke of, 26

Buckingham, Henry Stafford, duke of, 23

Buckingham Palace, 265

Burdet, Sir Nicholas, 23

Burgh, Benedict, 22

Burgundy, 3, 4

Burlei, Sir Simon, 25

Burns, Robert, 173

Burton, Robert, *The Anatomy of Melancholy*, 190, 194

Byron, Lord, 336, 346, 350, 373; *Don Juan*, 367; *Childe Harold*, 368, 373

C., H. [? Care, Henry], *Female Preeminence*, 35

C., H., *The Forrest of Fancy*, 156–7

C., H. [? Crompton, Hugh], *The Glory of Women*, 35

C., I. [? Cumber, John], *The Two Merry Milke-Maids*, 236–8, 254

C., T., *Galesus Cymon and Iphigenia*, 142–6, 147, 149

Cambridge, 184, 185, 187

Camiola, 34

Cammelli, Antonio, 184

Camoens, Luiz de, 340

Canterbury, 7

Carew, Thomas, 40

Cartwright, William, *The Siedge*, 241–4

Cary, Henry Francis, 403

Castiglione, Baldassare, *The Courtier*, 104

Castille, 3

Catanensi, Philippa, 12, 17, 26

Catherine, Queen, 125

Catullus, 294–5

Cavalcanti, Guido, 336, 362, 363

Caxton, William, prologue to *King Arthur*, 21; *Historie of Jason*, 37; *Recuyell of the Historyes of Troye*, 37

Cecil, Sir William, 108

Celestina, 4

Centlivre, Susannah, *The Cruel Gift*, 318–23; *The Busie Body*, 329–30

Certaine Worthye Manuscript Poems, 126

Certaldo, 33, 37, 189

Chappuys, Gabriel, 105, 107

Charles of Orleans, 4

Charles II, 266

Charles V, king of France, 113

Chastellain, Georges, 3, 4

Chaucer, Geoffrey, 9, 44, 114, 165, 211, 264, 345, 347, 353, 358, 361, 363, 366, 373, 392
  Anelida and Arcite, 45
  The Booke of the Duchesse, 123
  Canterbury Tales, 45, 114, 393
    Clerk's Tale, 116–22, 138, 142, 171, 307
    Franklin's Tale, 229, 236
    Knight's Tale, 45–58, 89, 100, 352, 353
    Merchant's Tale, 122
    Monk's Tale, 5, 21
    Squire's Tale, 345
    Wife of Bath's Tale, 117, 345
  The House of Fame, 45
  Parlement of Foules, 45
  Troilus and Criseyde, 19, 56, 59–101, 103, 121, 170

Chettle, Henry, *see* Dekker, Thomas, *Patient Grissell*

Chloris, 34

Churchill, Charles, 264–5

Churchyard, Thomas, *Churchyards Challenge*, 25, 26

Cicero, 6, 11, 359; *Orations*, 115; *De Officiis*, 159

Cid, the, 439

Clapam, David, *A Treatise of the Nobilitie of Woman Kynde*, 35

Clarke, Mary Anne, 366

Clim of the Clough, 165

Cobler of Caunterburie, The, 164–5, 192

Coleridge, Ernest Hartley, 341

Coleridge, Samuel Taylor, 337–43, 360; *Biographia Literaria*, 338; 'The Garden of Boccaccio', 342–3

Collection of Poems, A, 297–300

Collier, Jeremy, 266, 267, 280, 282

Collier, John Payne, 108; *The Poetical Decameron*, 332

Cologne, 131

Colonne, Guido delle, 36, 74, 83–4

Companion for the Fire-Side, A, 317–18

Concini, Concino, 25

Constantine, the Emperor, 10

Cooper, The, 328

Cooper, Thomas, *The Purgatory of Suicides*, 371

Cope, Charles West, 335

Coplande, Robert, 132

Coriolanus, 12

Cornhert, Dirck, 114

Cornwall, Barry, *see* Procter, B. W.

Cotswolds, 7

Cox, Captain, 161

Craftsman, The, 298

Crane, The, 296–7

Cristine de Pisan, *The boke of the Cyte of Ladyes*, 35

Cromwell, Henry, *alias* Williams, 212

Da Montemagno, Bonaccorso, *Controversia de Nobilitate*, 212, 213

Dante, 1, 7, 33, 115, 116, 117, 189, 211, 337, 338, 343, 347, 349, 350, 358, 360, 361, 362, 363, 364, 4̇0̇5̇, 438; *The Divine Comedy*, 4̇4̇0̇, the episode of Paolo and Francesca, 446

Davenport, Robert, *The City-Night-Cap*, 170, 238–40

Davis, Sir John, 388

D'Estrées, Gabrielle, 198

De Hooge, Romain, 261

De Musset, Alfred, 'Silvia', 435; 'Simone', 435; *Carmosine*, 462

De Vega, Lope, 294

Decameron, The Spanish, 190

Defoe, Daniel, *Journal of the Plague*, 289

Dekker, Thomas, *The Roaring Girle*, 27; *Patient Grissell*, 207–11

De la Pole, William, 212

Delilah, 18

Deloney, Thomas, *The Garland of Good Will*, 170

Demogorgon, 37–41, 337, 352

Devonshire, the duke of, 131, 133

Dibdin, Thomas Frognall, *The Bibliographical Decameron*, 330

Dolben, David, bishop of Bangor, 199

Dolce, Lodovico, *Didone*, 179, 184

Domenichi, Lodovico, *La nobiltà delle donne*, 35

Donne, John, 107

Douglas, Gavin, 42

Downes, Joseph, *The Mountain Decameron*, 332

Dryden, John,
  Æneis, dedication of the, 265
  Albion and Albanius, preface to, 189
  All for Love, 254, 259
  Fables, 57, 264, 265, 277, 292, 307, 312, 335, 336, 353, 397, 432
    'Cymon and Iphigenia', 264–77, 336, 348, 456, 457
    'Sigismonda and Guiscardo', 204, 218, 264–77, 323, 348, 407–9, 414

'Theodore and Honoria', 264–77, 336, 345–6, 348, 383, 405
'The Flower and the Leaf', 40
The Pilgrim, Epilogue to, 266
'Threnodia Augustalis', 266
Troilus and Cressida, 101
Du Bartas, Guillaume de Saluste, seigneur, 190
Dubois, Edward, 333, 334
Dürer, Albrecht, 32
Durfey, Thomas, *Squire Oldsapp*, 247–8; *The Royalist*, 248–9, 314; *Tales Tragical and Comical*, 277–84

Edinburgh Review, The, 334, 347
Edward III, 7
Edward IV, 4
Edward, the Black Prince, prince of Wales, 6
Edwardes, Richard, *Damon and Pithias*, 178
Eleanor, duchess of Austria, 28
Elector Palatine, the, 237
Eliot, George, *How Lisa Loved the King*, 438–40
Elizabeth, Princess, 237
Elizabeth, Queen, 167, 178, 183
Elyot, Sir Thomas, 133–6, 137, 138, 139, 140, 141, 142, 170, 195
Erasmus, Desiderius, 104; *Epistolae*, 192; *De Ratione Studii*, 37
Essex, Robert Devereux, earl of, 212
Estienne, Henri, *see* Stephen, Henrie
Eurydice, 9
Evelyn, John, 189
Eyb, Albrecht von, *Clarissimarum feminarum laudatio*, 35

Fabyan, Robert, 23
Faivre, Pierre, 3, 4
Fancies ague-fittes, or beauties nettle-bed, 115
Fane, Sir Francis, *Love in the Dark*, 245–6
Farmer, John, *An Essay on the Learning of Shakespeare*, 58
Farnese, Alessandro, Pope Paul III, 166
Farnie, Henry Brougham, 474–5
Faucit, Helen, 464
Ferdinand, archduke of Austria, 32
Ferrers, George, 23
Field, Martin, *see* Hunter, Joseph
Fiesole, 2, 111, 350, 351, 357, 359, 464
Findlay, J., 333
Flemyng, Robert, dean of Lincoln, 5
Fletcher, John, *The Two Noble Kinsmen*, 57; *Monsieur Thomas*, 230–1; *Women Pleas'd*, 231–3, 240, 241; *The Knight of*

Malta, 233–4, 236; *The Widdow*, *see* Jonson, B., and Middleton, T., 234–6
Flora, 34
Florence, 1, 2, 111, 211, 263, 296, 318, 343, 349, 350, 351, 356, 357, 361, 372–3, 377, 396, 402, 404, 417, 448, 449, 450, 462, 464
Florio, John, 191
Floris, 1, 115
Fluellen, 211
Foreign Quarterly Review, The, 358
Foscolo, Ugo, 333, 334, 341, 373
France, 7, 12, 35, 36, 44, 105, 113
Francis I, king of France, 113
Fraunce, Abraham, 37; *Victoria*, 184, 187–8
Frederick, duke of York, 366
Frederyke of Jennen, 221, 223
French Revolution, the, 326, 345, 368
Fuessli, Johann Heinrich [Fuseli, Henry], 335

Galigai, Leonora, 25
Galileo, Galilei, 114
Garrick, David, 206; *Cymon*, 326–8, 455–7
Garth, Sir Samuel, 290–1
Gellius, Aulus, 6
Genoa, 350, 373, 377, 414
Gentili, Alberico, 184
Gentleman's Magazine, The, 296, 331
Gentleness and Nobility, 213
George I, 322
George, prince of Wales, 322–3
Germany, 35, 36, 113, 116, 212
Giannini, Giuseppe, 263
Gibbon, Edward, 263
Gifford, Humphrey, 102
Gillman, Mrs., 341
Giolito, Gabriele, 106
Giunti, the, 263, 302
Godly Queene Hester, 213
Goethe, Johann Wolfgang von, 294, 465
Goldsmith, Oliver, 316–17
Goubourne, Jo., 108–112
Graie, Lady Anne, 183
Grantham, Henry, 102, 103
Gray, Thomas, 263
Greathead, Robert, *The Testament of the Twelve Patriarchs the Sons of Jacob*, 191
Greene, Robert, *Alcida*, 105; *Ciceronis Amor*, 168; *Frier Bacon and Frier Bongay*, 37, 38, 207; *Morando, The Tritameron of Loue*, 168; *Perimedes the Blacke-Smith*, 168; *Philomela*, 169, 170; *The Spanish Masquerado*, 167

Greig, Gavin, 173
Greneacres, 22
Grieg, Edvard, 173
Griffin, Gerald, *Gisippus*, 464–8
Griffin, James, 333
Griffith, Rev. Roger, 284
Grosseteste, Robert, bishop of Lincoln, 212
Guarini, Baptista, 184
Guercin, Antoine, 108–11

Hagedorn, Friedrich von, 294
Hall, Edward, 23
Hall, Joseph, 107
Hanmer, Sir John, *Fra Cipolla, and other poems*, 391–4
Harley, Robert, earl of Oxford, 322
Harvey, Gabriel, 114–15
Hastings, William, lord, 143, 147
Hatton, Sir Christopher, 106, 178
Hatton, Sir William, 106
Haughton, William, *see* Dekker, Thomas, *Patient Grissell*
Hauvette, Henri, 110
Hawes, Stephen, 42, 44
Hawkins, Sir Thomas, *Vnhappy Prosperitie*, 26
Hazlitt, William, 335, 344–9, 360, 397, 432
Head, Richard, *The English Rogue*, 310
Hearne, Thomas, 296
Hebræus, Leo, 38
Heerstraten, Egidius, van der, 33
Henry IV, king of France, 198
Henry V, 7, 11
Henry VI, 23
Henry VII, 4, 42
Henry VIII, 32, 33
Henryson, Robert, 100
Hercules, 34
Hervey, John, lord, 297
Heywood, Thomas, *Gunaikeion*, 35, 37
Higgins, John, 23, 24
Hobbes, Thomas, *Decameron Physiologicum*, 190
Hobhouse, John Cam, 58, 363, 482; in *Imitations and Translations*, 366–7; *Italy*, 373; [*Tales from Boccaccio*], 367–76
Hoby, Sir Thomas, 33, 34, 37
Hogarth, William, 264–5
Holland, 113
Homer, 57, 342, 355
Hood, Robin, 162, 165
Horne, Richard Henry, 370
Hortis, Attilio, 26
Howard, Frederick, earl of Carlisle, 323–6

Howard, Sir George, 157
Hullah, (?) John Pyke, 374
Humphrey, duke of Gloucester, 3, 4, 5, 6, 7, 11, 22, 29, 36, 44, 114
Hunt, William Holman, 335
Hunt, Leigh, 58, 336, 349–54, 414
Hunter, Joseph, *A Shakespear Decameron*, 332
Huntington Library, 196
Hymenæus, 184–7

Idley, Peter, *Instructions to his Son*, 22
Iole, 34
Ireland, 387, 388–9
Italy, 35, 36, 109, 116, 209, 210, 211, 224, 343, 386, 393–4, 438, 440

Jacob, Sir Hildebrand, 263
James I, 236
James I of Scotland, 28
Jeffrey, Francis, lord, 388
Jenynges, Edward, *Alfagus and Archelaus*, 137–42
Jerrold, Douglas, *Mrs. Caudle's Curtain Lectures*, 369
Joan of Arc, 7
Joan, Pope, 35
Job, 119
Johanna, queen of Sicily, 33
John XII, Pope, 10
John the Fearless, duke of Burgundy, 4
John the Good, king of France, 6, 7, 113
John Rylands Library, 331
Johnson, Charles, *A General History Of The Lives and Adventures Of the Most Famous Highwaymen*, 311–15
Johnson, Samuel, 263, 264, 323
Johnstone, William Borthwick, 335
Jones, David, 278–9
Jones, John, *Adrasta*, 240–1
Jones, William, 212
Jonson, Ben, *The Alchemist*, 37, 38; *The Devil is an Ass*, 227–8; *Time Vindicated*, 199; *The Widdow, see* Fletcher, J., and Middleton, T., 234–6
Joseph of Exeter, 83
Jovius, Paulus, 105
Julian, the Emperor, 11
Julius Cæsar, 7, 23, 24

K., E., 34, 37, 44
Kean, Charles, 464
Keats, John, 353, 358, 429; 'The Eve of St. Agnes', 105; 'Isabella', 397–407, 416, 417, 419, 420, 448; 'Ode on Melancholy', 410; 'The Eve of St. Mark', 420
Keepsake, The, 341, 342

Kellerman, François Christophe, Marshal, 345
Kelly, W. K., 333
Kemble, Fanny, 478
Kemble, John Philip, 329
Kendals, the, 475
King, John, bishop of London, 191
Kirkcaldy, 173
Knights Templar, 11–12

La Fontaine, Jean de, 263, 294, 295, 312, 317–18, 476
Lamb, Charles, 460
Lancilot du Lake (Launcelote), 115, 116
Landor, Walter Savage, *The Pentameron*, 353, 359; *Andrea of Hungary and Giovanna of Naples*, 361; *Giovanna of Naples*, 361
Laneham, Robert, 161
Langbaine, Gerard, 240, 241
Lansdowne, Henry Petty-Fitzmaurice, lord, 336
Lazarillo de Tormes, 217
Le Maçon, Antoine, *see* Boccaccio, *Decameron*
Lee, Alfred Collingwood, 308
Legenda Sismond, 122
Leghorn, 263
Leicester, Robert Dudley, earl of, 3
Leighton, Frederic, lord, 335
Leonora, queen of Aragon, 22
Lessing, Gotthold Ephraim, *Nathan der Weise*, 194
Leubing, Heinrich, 113
Lewicke, Edward, *Titus and Gisippus*, 136–7
Lewis, Clive Staples, 91, 94
Lignano (Linian), Giovanni di, 122
Llandaff (Landaff), Francis James Mathew, earl of, 389
Lodge, Thomas, 190
Lollards, the, 11
London Gazette, The, 254
London Magazine, The, 334, 339, 347
London Weekly Review, The, 346
Longfellow, Henry Wadsworth, *Tales of a Wayside Inn*, 476
Louis XIII, 25
Louvain, 28, 33
Lover's Stratagem, The, 253–60
Lucan, 37, 39
Lunn, Joseph, *Horae Jocosae; or the Doggerel Decameron*, 332
Lycurgus, king of Thrace, 37
Lydgate, John, *The Fall of Princes*, 5–22, 23, 24, 26, 29, 36, 129, 156; *The Siege of Thebes*, 33, 36–7, 98

Lyly, John, *Loves Metamorphosis*, 104–5; *Euphues*, 134
Lyndesay, Sir David, 25
Lynn, 143
Lyons, 34, 105, 108, 109, 113, 191

Mab, Queen, 457, 459, 460
Macao, 378–9
Mace, René, *Les Trois Anneaux*, 194
Machiavelli, Niccolò, 194, 224
Mackenzie, Henry, *The Man of Feeling*, 289
Macready, William Charles, 464
Maiano, 344, 350–2
Mallarmé, Stéphane, 454
Manetti, Giannozzo, 373
Manlius, Marcus, 21
Manni, Domenico Maria, 362, 373
Mannyng, Robert, of Brunne, *Handlyng Synne*, 21
Margaret of Anjou, 23
Margaret, queen of Navarre, 113
Maria d'Aquino, 1
Maria, queen of Navarre, 22
Marie de' Medici, queen-regent, 25
Marlborough, John Churchill, duke of, 280
Marlowe, Christopher, *Dr. Faustus*, 39, 237
Marney, Sir Henry, 131
Marshe, Thomas, 143
Marston, John, *Parasitaster*, 218–19
Martin, Emma, *Frederic and the Falcon*, 432
Martinelli, Vincenzio, 263
Mary, queen of Scots, 150
Massinger, Philip, *The Maid of Honour*, 34; *The Guardian*, 240
Matthieu, Pierre, *Aelius Sejanus* and *Histoire des Prosperitez Malheureuses*, 25–6
Maundrell, Henry, *A Journey from Aleppo to Jerusalem*, 381–2
Mead, Richard, 263
Medwall, Henry, *Fulgens and Lucres*, 213
Melbancke, Brian, *Philotimus*, 104
Melbourne, William Lamb, lord, 369, 372
Meleager, 9, 37
Merlin (Merlyn), 256–7, 284, 326–7, 456
Merton College, Oxford, 296
Messina, 7, 402, 404
Metz, 101
Mexia, Fernan, *Libro yntitulado nobillario*, 3
Middleton, Thomas, *The Widdow*, *see* Fletcher, J., and Jonson, B., 234–6
Mielot, Jean, 212

Milan, 414

Millais, Sir John Everett, 335

Milton, John, 114, 292; *Paradise Lost*, 40, 41, 276

Mirror for Magistrates, A, 22, 23, 24, 25, 26, 27, 143, 146, 147

Modred, 11, 12

Molière, Jean Baptiste Poquelin, *Tartuffe*, 391

Mont Blanc, 386

Monte Asinaio, 318

Monthly Review, The, 264

Montjoy, Christopher, 213

Montucci, Antonio, 58, 108, 333

Moore, Thomas, 336; *Lalla Rookh,* 379, 380, 381, 382; *Poetical Works of the Late Thomas Little,* 391; [*Spirit of Boccaccio's Decameron*], 376–91

More, John, 114

More, Sir Thomas, 114

Morley, Henry, 333

Morning Chronicle, The, 346

Morris, William, 451, 452

Morte Arthure, 81, 115, 116

Morton, James Douglas, earl of Morton, 26

Mount Etna, 415

Mugnone, 2, 318, 350, 351

Muratori, Ludovico Antonio, 373

Murmurers, The, 191

Naples, 1, 111, 354–5, 356

Napoleon I, 331

Nardini, Leonardo, 333

Nelson, Horatio, lord, 80

Nenna, Giovanni Battista, *Il Nennio,* 212

Newman, Thomas, 106, 107

Niagara, 414

Niccols, Richard, 24, 27

Nicholas I, tsar of Russia, 368–9

Nightingale, The, 294–5

Nürnberg, 32

Oedipus, 8, 15, 17

Ogle, George, *Gualtherus and Griselda,* 307

Oldfield, Mrs., 323

Orpheus, 9

Osbeck, Peter, *Voyage to China and the East Indies,* 378–9

Ovid, 30, 105; *Ars amandi,* 341, 342

Oxford, 114, 184

Padua, 115, 187, 377

Paestum, 411, 413

Painter, William, *The Palace of Pleasure,* 34, 147, 157–61, 213, 221

Panizzi, Antonio, 58, 373

Paolo and Francesca, *see* Dante

Paris, 7, 28, 105, 113, 263, 373, 448, 449, 462

Parker, Henry, lord Morley, 32–3

Parnaso Italiano, 349

Patmore, Coventry, 'The Falcon', 429–432

Payn, James, *Stories from Boccaccio,* 391, 432–7

Payne, John, 'Salvestra', 447–53; translation of *Decameron,* 334, 454; translation of poems by Boccaccio, 454–5

Peacham, Henry, *The Compleat Gentleman,* 194

Pearl, 43

Pedro, Don, constable of Portugal, *Tragedia de la insigne Reyna Isabel,* 23

Peend, Thomas, 172

Pembroke, Mary Herbert, countess of, 37

Pepys, Samuel, 244

Percy, William, *A Forrest Tragaedye in Vacunium,* 196–9

Peter, Lady Marie, 183

Petrarch (Petrak, Petrarca), Francesco, 5, 33, 37, 106, 107, 115, 116–22, 196, 264, 307, 337, 347, 350, 351, 353, 355, 356, 358, 359, 361, 363

Philip II, king of Spain, 3

Phillip, John, *Patient Grissell,* 173–8

Phillips, Edward, *Theatrum Poetarum,* 189

Pickering, William, 333

Pierce the Ploughman's Crede, 212

Pinkerton, John, *A General Collection of Voyages and Travels,* 380, 381

Pisa, 350, 414

Pistoia, 351

Pius II, Pope, 59, 115, 116; *Euryalus,* 115

Pius V, Pope, 167

Pix, Mary, *Violenta,* 284–92

Plague of 1665, the, 279, 289–90

Planché, James Robinson, 'The One-Legged Goose', 394–5, 457; revision of Garrick's *Cymon,* 456–7

Plato, 115

Pleasaunt disport of diuers noble personages, A, 102

Pliny, 191

Plutarch, 36

Pocke, Richard, *A Description of the East,* 381

Poggio, Bracciolini, *Facetiæ,* 115

Pope, Alexander, 263, 305, 346

Pope, Walter, *Select Novels,* 196

Portugal, 4, 23

Powell, Thomas, 370

Premierfait, Laurent de, 4, 6, 7, 10, 11, 13, 14, 17, 20, 113, 114

Prior, Matthew, 'A Tale from Boccace', 292–4

Procter, Bryan Waller, 353, 354–7; 'The Letter of Boccaccio', 354; *A Sicilian Story*, 397, 414–17; 'The Two Dreams', 'The Broken Heart', 'The Falcon', 'Love cured by Kindness', 'The Florentine Party', 460–4

Ptolemy II, 6

Pulci, Luigi, 349

Pulteney, William, earl of Bath, 297–9

Pusey, Edward Bouverie, 368

Pynson, Richard, 22

Pyramus, 115, 172

Quarterly Review, The, 388

Queen's College, Oxford, 184

Quin, James, 322

Radcliffe, Ralph, *De patientia Griselidis*, 173; *De Titi et Gisippi amicitia*, 178

Radigund, 34

Raleigh, Sir Walter, 40

Ravenna, 146, 336

Ravenscroft, Edward, *The London Cuckolds*, 249–50

Redi, Francesco, 353

Reece, Robert, 474–5

Regimen Sanitatis Salerni, 187

René, king of Sicily, 59

Reynolds, Frederick Mansel, 341

Reynolds, John Hamilton, 397; *The Garden of Florence and other poems*, 405, 417–26

Rhodes, Richard, *Flora's Vagaries*, 244–5

Rich, Barnaby, 172

Richard I, 7

Richard II, 54

Richard III, 129

Richardson, Samuel, 94, 107; *Clarissa Harlowe*, 57

Robert, king of Anjou, 1

Roberto, king of Sicily, 34

Rogers, Samuel, 335, 338, 343–4, 370; *Italy*, 343–4, 391

Roland, 439

Roman de la Rose, 7

Rome, 20–1, 166, 168

Romeo, 130, 172

Roscoe, Thomas, *Italian Novelists*, 334

Rossetti, Dante Gabriel, 335–6, 363–5, 454

Rossetti, Gabriele, 43, 361–3, 373

Rotterdam, 113

Rowe, Nicholas, 322

Rowland, David, 217

Rowlands, Samuel, 38; *The Knave of Clubbes*, 195

Ruscelli, Girolamo, 157

Ruskin, John, *The Stones of Venice*, 396

Russell, John, bishop of Lincoln, 5

Russell, lord John, 372, 386

Russell, Patrick, *The Natural History of Aleppo*, 379, 380, 382

Russell, Thomas, 58, 277

Sachs, Hans, 113, 294

Sack-Full of Newes, The, 161, 163

Sackville, Thomas, earl of Dorset, 23, 24

Sacrificio, Il, 196

St. Alban's, 3

Saint Augustine, 4

St. James's Palace, 457, 470, 474

St. John's College, Cambridge, 184

St. Lawrence, River, 414

Salamanca, 105

Salerno, 187, 411, 412, 413

Sallust, 30

Salter, Thomas, *A Mirrhor made for all Mothers*, 36

Salutati, Coluccio, 5

Salviati, Lionardo, 184, 191, 275, 303

Sandford, James, 116

Santillana, marquis of, *Comedieta de Ponça*, 22–3

Saragossa, 28

Schlegel, Friedrich von, 58

Scole House of Women, The, 35

Scotland, Royal Library of, 36, 114

Scotland, Union with, 283

Selimus, 37, 39

Seneca, 3; *Thyestes*, 197, 422

Seville, 105

Sevin, Adrien, 101

Sewell, William, 368

Shakespeare, William, 360
  The Two Gentlemen of Verona, 66
  A Midsummer Night's Dream, 34, 57
  The Merry Wives of Windsor, 233
  Romeo and Juliet, 420
  Richard III, 458
  Henry V, 210, 211
  All's Well that Ends Well, 211–16, 348, 439
  Troilus and Cressida, 101, 192
  Measure for Measure, 217, 238–9
  Hamlet, 237
  Othello, 224
  Cymbeline, 193, 220–6, 250–3, 378
  The Winter's Tale, 220, 473

Sharp, William, 333

Sharpham, Edward, *Cupid's Whirligig*, 219

Shaw, Thomas, *Travels or Observations relating to Barbary*, 380

Shelley, Mary Wollstonecraft, 349

Shelley, Percy Bysshe, 336, 349, 350, 416; *Peter Bell the Third*, 336; *Hellas*, 357; *Prometheus Unbound*, 40, 41, 357

Shirley, James, 27

Shore, Jane, 25

Shrewsbury, Adelhida Talbot, duchess of, 292

Sicily, 33, 34, 59, 438

Sidney, Sir Philip, 184; *An Apologye for Poetrye*, 43

Siena, 196

Sir Gawain and the Green Knight, 54

Sismondi, Jean Charles Léonard Simonde de, *Literature of the South of Europe*, 347

Smith, Alexander, *A History of the most Noted Highway-Men*, 309–11

Smith, Joseph, 263

Smyth, Walter, 114

Sotheby, Miss, *Patient Griselda*, 308

Southerne, Thomas, *The Fatall Marriage*, 205–6

South-Sea Bubble, the, 306

Spain, 35, 44, 101, 102, 105, 113, 172, 438

Spanish Armada, the, 34, 167

Spartacus, 12

Spectacle of Louers, The, 132

Spencer, Earl, 331

Spenser, Edmund, 126, 360; *The Shepheardes Calender*, 34, 37, 44; *The Faerie Queene*, 34, 38, 39, 41, 108

Spirit of Boccaccio's Decameron, see Moore, Thomas

Stanhope, Lady Hester, 370

Stein, Charlotte, Frau von, 294

Steinhöwel (Steinhövel), Heinrich, 28, 113, 116

Stephen, Henrie, *A World of Wonders*, 193, 194

Sterne, Laurence, 263

Steward, Mrs., 265

Stothard, Thomas, 333, 341, 343, 344

Strassburg, 28

Strode, Ralph, 60

Summonte, Giovanni Antonio, *Istoria della città e regno di Napoli*, 26

Suppé, Franz von, 474

Swift (Swif), Jonathan, *A Tale of a Tub*, 194

Swinburne, Algernon Charles, 432, 455; prefatory note to Charles Wells's *Joseph and his Brethren*, 429; 'The Two Dreams' ('The White Hind'), 440–5; 'The Complaint of Lisa', 445–7

Sylvester, Joshua, 190

T., C., *Nastagio and Trauersari*, 146–9

Tales from the Decameron, see Hobhouse, J. C.

Tarltons newes out of Purgatorie, 162–4

Tasso, Torquato, 34, 429

Tate Gallery, the, 264

Temple, Sir William, 189

Tennyson, Alfred, lord, 'The Golden Supper', 437–8

Themistocles, 12

Theodosius, the Emperor, 11

Thirkell, Angela, *The Brandons*, 345

Thisbe, 115, 172

Thomas, William, 115

Thucydides, 290

Tilney, Edmund, *The Flower of Friendship*, 103–4, 481

Tincker of Turvey, The, 193

Tiptoft, John, earl of Worcester, 23, 212

Tiraboschi, Girolamo, 373

Titus and Gisippus, 178

Tivoli (Tiuoly), 166

Toledo, 3

Tonson, Jacob, 302

Tottel, Richard, 22

Tourneur, Cyril, *The Atheist's Tragedie*, 204–5

Tractarian movement, the, 368

Trece questiones muy graciosas, 102

Treize elegantes demandes damours, 102

Trinity College, Cambridge, 126, 127, 192

Tristan (Tristram), 115, 116

Troy, 439

Tupper, Martin Farquhar, *Proverbial Philosophy*, 458

Turbervile, George, *Tragical Tales*, 149–56

Turner, Sir James, 28, 37, 189

Twyne, Thomas, *The Schoolmaster*, 162

Tyrwhitt, Thomas, 58

Ulm, 28, 113

Valdarfer, Christopher, 331, 334

Valle delle donne, 112, 344, 350, 351, 357, 402

Vallensis, Robert, 38

Vallon, Annette, 101

Valmy, 345

Venice, 34, 37, 108, 263, 296, 336, 377, 394

Vérard, Antoine, 28, 113

Verseline, Frauncis, 108–9
Verzellini, James (Jakob), 108–9
Victoria, Queen, 369, 370, 371
Villon, François, 451
Virgil, *Æneid*, 30, 32, 42, 57, 293
Vives, Juan Luis, 104, 115
Voltaire, François Arouet de, 389–90

Wales, 210, 211, 226, 284, 332, 456
Walker Art Gallery, Liverpool, 335
Walpole, Horace, 323, 328
Walpole, Sir Robert, 297–9
Walter, William, *Guystarde and Sygys-monde*, 131–3; *Tytus and Gesyppus*, 133, 134
Walton, Izaak, 184
Warner, William, *Albions England*, 162
Warton, Thomas, 58
Warwick, Guy of, 115
Warwick, Richard de Beauchamp, earl of, 114
Warwick, Ambrose Dudley, earl of, 147, 158
Waterloo, 410
Watts, George Frederic, 335
Watts, Isaac, *Hymns*, 369
Wayland, John, 22
Wells, Charles, *Joseph and his Brethren*, 429; *Stories after Nature*, 429
West, Richard, 263
Westward for Smelts, 192–3, 221
Whethamstede, John, abbot of St. Alban's, 3
Whetstone, George, *Heptameron of Ciuill Discourses*, 165–7

Whitgift, John, archbishop of Canterbury, 115
Williams, Hugh, 199
Wilmot, Robert, 178, 181–3, 196, 199
Wilmot, William, *The Tale of Gismunda & Guiscardo*, 407–14
Winstanley, William, 195–6
Wise, Thomas James, *The Ashley Library*, 440
Witart, Claude, 4–5
Wither, George, *Britain's Remembrancer*, 199
Wolfe, John, 115
Wollstonecraft, Mary, *A Vindication of the rights of Woman*, 308
Women, attacks on, and sympathy with, 9–10, 21–2, 29, 35–6
Worcester College, Oxford, 108
Wordsworth, William, 336, 370–1, 403, 466; *Lyrical Ballads*, 101; 'The Thorn', 407; 'Troilus and Cresida', 101
Wotton, Sir Henry, *Tancredo*, 184, 196
Wotton, William, 189
Wright, Thomas, 333, 334
Wright, Thomas (of Olney), 448
Wyer, Nicolas, 142
Wyle, Nicolaus von, 35
Wynkyn de Worde, 131, 133

Xerxes, 15

York, 7
Young, Bartholomew, *Amorous Fiammetta*, 105–8, 115

Zenobia, 5
Zieriksee, Kornelius von, 131

2. Borrowings from and allusions to particular tales in the *Decameron*

Day I, i, Ayre, W., *The Saint*, 300–2
Day I, iii, Painter, W., *The Palace of Pleasure*, 157–61; Burton, Robert, *The Anatomy of Melancholy*, 194
Day I, iv, [Moore, T.], *S.O.B.D.*, 376
Day I, v, Painter, W., *The Palace of Pleasure*, 157–61; *The Agreeable Companion*, 315
Day I, vii, *A Collection of Poems*, 297–9
Day I, viii, Painter, W., *The Palace of Pleasure*, 157–61
Day I, x, Painter, W., *The Palace of Pleasure*, 157–61

Day II, ii, Painter, W., *The Palace of Pleasure*, 157–61; Fletcher, J., with Jonson, B., and Middleton, T., *The Widdow*, 234–6; Johnson, C., *A General History . . . Of the Most Famous Highwaymen*, 313–14; Rossetti, G., 362; [Moore, T.], *S.O.B.D.*, 376
Day II, iii, Painter, W., *The Palace of Pleasure*, 157–61; [Moore, T.], *S.O.B.D.*, 376
Day II, iv, Painter, W., *The Palace of Pleasure*, 157–61; [Moore, T.], *S.O.B.D.*, 376
Day II, v, Painter, W., *The Palace of Pleasure*, 157–61; Fraunce, A., *Victoria*, 187–8; *Blurt Master-Constable*, 217–18; Behn, A., *The Rover*, 246–7; Smith, A., *History of the most Noted Highway-Men*, 310; Johnson, C., *A*

General History . . . Of the Most Famous Highwaymen, 310–11

Day II, vi, Greene, R., *Perimedes the Blacke-Smith*, 168

Day II, vii, Rossetti, D. G., 363

Day II, viii, Painter, W., *The Palace of Pleasure*, 157–61; *The Forrest of Fancy* 157; Pix, M., *Violenta*, 284–92

Day II, ix, *Westward for Smelts*, 192; Stephen, H., *A World of Wonders*, 194; Shakespeare, *The Winter's Tale*, 220, *Cymbeline*, 220–6; Durfey, T., *The Injured Princess*, 250–3; *The Agreeable Companion*, 315; [Moore, T.], *S.O.B.D.*, 376

Day II, x, [Moore, T.], *S.O.B.D.*, 376

Day III, i, Hobhouse, J. C., in *Imitations and Translations*, 366–7; [Moore, T.], *S.O.B.D.*, 376.

Day III, ii, Procter, B. W., 'The Florentine Party', 464

Day III, iii, Stephen, H., *A World of Wonders*, 193; Marston, J., *Parasitaster*, 218–19; Jonson, B., *The Devil is an Ass*, 227–8; Fletcher, J., with Jonson, B., and Middleton, T., *The Widdow*, 234–6; Rhodes, R., *Flora's Vagaries*, 244–5; Fane, Sir F., *Love in the Dark*, 245–6; Centlivre, S., *The Busie Body*, 329–30; [Moore, T.], *S.O.B.D.*, 376

Day III, iv, Rossetti, G., 362

Day III, v, *The Forrest of Fancy*, 157; Jonson, B., *The Devil is an Ass*, 227–8; Rhodes, R., *Flora's Vagaries*, 244–5; Centlivre, S., *The Busie Body*, 329

Day III, vi, [Moore, T.], *S.O.B.D.*, 376

Day III, vii, Rossetti, G., 362

Day III, viii, *The Cobler of Caunterburie*, 165; Southerne, T., *The Fatall Marriage*, 206; *A Banquet for Gentlemen and Ladies*, 309; Rossetti, G., 362; [Moore, T.], *S.O.B.D.*, 376; [Hobhouse, J. C.], *Tales from the Decameron*, 367–76

Day III, ix, Painter, W., *The Palace of Pleasure*, 157–61; Shakespeare, *All's Well*, 211–17

Day III, x, Rossetti, G., 362

Day IV, Preamble, *A Companion for the Fire-Side*, 317–18

Day IV, i, Banester, G., *Legenda Sismond*, 122–6; *Certaine Worthye Manuscript Poems*, 126–31; Walter, W., *Guystarde and Sygysmonde*, 131–2;

Painter, W., *The Palace of Pleasure*, 157–61; Deloney, T., *The Garland of Good Will*, 171–3; Wilmot, R., Hatton, C., and others, *Gismond of Salern*, 178–81; *The Tragedie of Tancred and Gismund*, 181–4; Wotton, H., *Tancredo*, 184; Percy, W., *A Forrest Tragaedye*, 196–9; *Ghismonda*, 199–204; Dryden, *Fables*, 'Sigismonda and Guiscardo', 265–77; Centlivre, S., *The Cruel Gift*, 318–23; Howard, F., *The Father's Revenge*, 323–6; Hazlitt, W., 348; Landor, W. S., 360; Wilmot, W., *The Tale of Gismunda & Guiscardo*, 407–14; Payn, J., *Stories from Boccaccio*, 433–4

Day IV, ii, *Tarltons newes out of Purgatorie*, 162; Whetstone, G., *Heptameron of Ciuill Discourses*, 166; Greene, R., *The Spanish Masquerado*, 167; Hazlitt, W., 345; [Moore, T.], *S.O.B.D.*, 376

Day IV, iv, Turbervile, G., *Tragical Tales*, 150–1

Day IV, v, Turbervile, G., *Tragical Tales*, 153; Hazlitt, W., 344, 345, 348; Hunt, Leigh, 349, 351; Landor, W. S., 360; [Moore, T.], *S.O.B.D.*, 376; Keats, J., 'Isabella', 397–407; Arnold, M., 407; Procter, B. W., *A Sicilian Story*, 414–17

Day IV, vi, Landor, W. S., 360; Swinburne, A. C., 'The Two Dreams' ('The White Hind'), 440–5; Procter, B. W., *Dramatic Scenes*, 460–1

Day IV, vii, Turbervile, G., *Tragical Tales*, 153–4; *A Banquet for Gentlemen and Ladies*, 309; Hazlitt, W., 348; Brough, R. B., 'A Story from Boccaccio', 395–7; Reynolds, J. H., *The Garden of Florence and other poems*, 417–21; Payn, J., *Stories from Boccaccio*, 435

Day IV, viii, Turbervile, G., *Tragical Tales*, 152–3; Hazlitt, W., 348; Hunt, Leigh, 349; [Hobhouse, J. C.], *Tales from the Decameron*, 367–76; Payn, J., *Stories from Boccaccio*, 434–5; Payne, J., 'Salvestra', 447–53; Procter, B. W., *Dramatic Scenes*, 462

Day IV, ix, Turbervile, G., *Tragical Tales*, 151–2; Percy, W., *A Forrest Tragaedye*, 196–9; Reynolds, J. H., *The Garden of Florence and other poems*, 422–5

Day IV, x, *Hymenæus*, 185; [Moore, T.], *S.O.B.D.*, 376

Day V, i, C., T., *Galesus Cymon and Iphigenia*, 142–6; Greene, R., *Morando*, 168; *Ciceronis Amor*, 168; Burton, R., *The Anatomy of Melancholy*, 194; Dryden, *Fables*, 'Cymon and Iphigenia', 265–77; Garrick, D., *Cymon*, 326–8, 455–7; Hazlitt, W., 344, 348; Planché, J. R., 456–7; Lee, E. J. S., *Cymon and Iphigenia*, 457–60

Day V, ii, *The Cobler of Caunterburie*, 164; Greene, R., *Perimedes the Blacke-Smith*, 168; [Moore, T.], *S.O.B.D.*, 376; Payn, J., *Stories from Boccaccio*, 436

Day V, iii, [Moore, T.], *S.O.B.D.*, 376

Day V, iv, *The Nightingale*, 294; [Moore, T.], *S.O.B.D.*, 376

Day V, v, Procter, B. W., 'The Florentine Party', 464

Day V, vi, *The Cobler of Caunterburie*, 164; [Moore, T.], *S.O.B.D.*, 376

Day V, vii, *The Forrest of Fancy*, 157; Beaumont, F., 'The Triumph of Love', 229–30

Day V, viii, T., C., *Nastagio and Trauersari*, 146–9; Turbervile, G., *Tragical Tales*, 154–5; *The Forrest of Fancy*, 157; Dryden, *Fables*, 'Theodore and Honoria', 265–77; Byron, Lord, 336; Hazlitt, W., 345, 348

Day V, ix, Prior, Matthew, 'A Tale from Boccace', 292–4; Hazlitt, W., 344, 345, 347, 348; Hunt, Leigh, 349, 351; Patmore, C., 'The Falcon', 429–32; Martin, E., *Frederic and the Falcon*, 432; Payn, J., *Stories from Boccaccio*, 432–3; Procter, B. W., *Dramatic Scenes*, 463–4; Tennyson, *The Falcon*, 475–8

Day V, x, [Moore, T.], *S.O.B.D.*, 376

Day VI, iv, *Tarltons newes out of Purgatorie*, 163; *The Crane*, 296–7; [Moore, T.], *S.O.B.D.*, 376; [Planché, J. R.], 'The One-Legged Goose', 394–5

Day VI, ix, Rossetti, G., 362; Rossetti, D. G., 363

Day VI, x, *Tarltons newes out of Purgatorie*, 162–3; Greene, R., *The Spanish Masquerado*, 167; Stephen, H., *A World of Wonders*, 193; *Fra Cipolla*, 302–5; *The Popish Impostor*, 305–7; Rogers, S., 343; Hazlitt, W., 347; Hanmer, Sir J., *Fra Cipolla, and other poems*, 391–4

Day VII, i, *The Cobler of Caunterburie*, 165; [Moore, T.], *S.O.B.D.*, 376

Day VII, ii, *The Cooper*, 328; Reece, R. and Farnie, H. B., *Boccaccio*, 475

Day VII, iii, Stephen, H., *A World of Wonders*, 193; [Moore, T.], *S.O.B.D.*, 376

Day VII, iv, Fletcher, J., *Monsieur Thomas*, 231

Day VII, v, Rhodes, R., *Flora's Vagaries*, 244–5; *A Banquet for Gentlemen and Ladies*, 309

Day VII, vi, Twyne, T., *The Schoolemaster*, 162; *Tarltons newes out of Purgatorie*, 163; Stephen, H., *A World of Wonders*, 193; Rowlands, S., *The Knave of Clubbes*, 195; Tourneur, C., *The Atheist's Tragedie*, 204–5; Fletcher, J., *Women Pleas'd*, 232; Ravenscroft, E., *The London Cuckolds*, 249–50; [Moore, T.], *S.O.B.D.*, 376

Day VII, vii, *The Sack-Full of Newes*, 161; Davenport, R., *The City-Night-Cap*, 239–40; Fane, Sir F., *Love in the Dark*, 245–6; Durfey, T., *Squire Oldsapp*, 247–8; Ravenscroft, E., *The London Cuckolds*, 249–50; [Moore, T.], *S.O.B.D.*, 376

Day VII, viii, *The Cobler of Caunterburie*, 165; Fletcher, J., *Women Pleas'd*, 232; Massinger, P., *The Guardian*, 240; Durfey, T., *Squire Oldsapp*, 247–8

Day VII, ix, Durfey, T., *The Royalist*, 248–9; Johnson, C., *A General History . . . Of the Most Famous Highwaymen*, 314; [Moore, T.], *S.O.B.D.*, 376; Reece, R. and Farnie, H. B., *Boccaccio*, 475

Day VIII, i, Johnson, C., *A General History . . . Of the Most Famous Highwaymen*, 313

Day VIII, ii, [Moore, T.], *S.O.B.D.*, 376

Day VIII, iii, Peacham, H., *The Compleat Gentleman*, 194

Day VIII, iv, Whetstone, G., *Heptameron of Ciuill Discourses*, 167; Fletcher, J., *Monsieur Thomas*, 231; [Moore, T.], *S.O.B.D.*, 376

Day VIII, vi, Peacham, H., *The Compleat Gentleman*, 194

Day VIII, vii, Painter, W., *The Palace of Pleasure*, 157–61; *The Cobler of Caunterburie*, 164; Rossetti, G., 362

Day VIII, viii, Fletcher, J., *Women Pleas'd*, 232; Jones, J., *Adrasta*, 241;

Smith, A., *History of the most Noted Highway-Men*, 310–11; Johnson, C., *A General History . . . Of the Most Famous Highwaymen*, 313

Day VIII, ix, Peacham, H., *The Compleat Gentleman*, 194; Coleridge, S. T., 339

Day VIII, x, [Moore, T.], *S.O.B.D.*, 376

Day IX, i, Cartwright, W., *The Siedge*, 242–4

Day IX, ii, Twyne, T., *The Schoolemaster*, 162; Warner, W., *Albions England*, 162; Stephen, H., *A World of Wonders*, 193; Burton, R., *The Anatomy of Melancholy*, 194; Fletcher, J., *Monsieur Thomas*, 231; *A Collection of Poems*, 299–300; Payn, J., *Stories from Boccaccio*, 436–7

Day IX, iii, Peacham, H., *The Compleat Gentleman*, 194

Day IX, iv, Rossetti, D. G., 363

Day IX, v, Peacham, H., *The Compleat Gentleman*, 194

Day IX, vi, Durfey, T., *Tales Tragical and Comical*, 277–80; Johnson, C., *A General History . . . Of the Most Famous Highwaymen*, 313; [Moore, T.], *S.O.B.D.*, 376

Day IX, ix, [Moore, T.], *S.O.B.D.*, 376

Day IX, x, Smith, A., *History of the most Noted Highway-Men*, 311; Johnson, C., *A General History . . . Of the Most Famous Highwaymen*, 313

Day X, ii, [Moore, T.], *S.O.B.D.*, 376

Day X, iii, Painter, W., *The Palace of Pleasure*, 157–61

Day X, iv, Turbervile, G., *Tragical Tales*, 151; Painter, W., *The Palace of Pleasure*, 157–61; Fletcher, J., *The Knight of Malta*, 233–4; Tennyson, 'The Golden Supper', 437–8

Day X, v, Painter, W., *The Palace of Pleasure*, 157–61; C., I., [? Cumber,

John], *The Two Merry Milke-Maids*, 236–8; *The Lover's Stratagem*, 253–60; [Moore, T.], *S.O.B.D.*, 376

Day X, vi, [Moore, T.], *S.O.B.D.*, 376

Day X, vii, Hunt, Leigh, 349; Eliot, George, *How Lisa Loved the King*, 438–40; Swinburne, A. C., 'The Complaint of Lisa', 445–7; Procter, B. W., *Dramatic Scenes*, 461–2

Day X, viii, Walter, W., *Tytus and Gesyppus*, 133; Elyot, Sir T., *The Gouernour*, 133–6; Lewicke, E., *Titus and Gisippus*, 136–7; Jenynges, E., *Alfagus and Archelaus*, 137–42; Greene, R., *Philomela*, 169; Deloney, T., *The Garland of Good Will*, 170; Radcliffe, R., *De Titi et Gisippi amicitia*, 178; *Titus and Gisippus*, 178; Winstanley, W., 195–6; Davenport, R., *The City-Night-Cap*, 238; Durfey, T., *Stories, Moral and Comical*, 280–4; Goldsmith, O., in *The Bee*, 316–17; Lloyd, C., *Desultory Thoughts on London, Titus and Gisippus, with other poems*, 426–9; Wells, C., *Stories after Nature*, 429; Griffin, G., *Gisippus*, 464–8

Day X, ix, Painter, W., *The Palace of Pleasure*, 157–61

Day X, x, Chaucer, *The Clerk's Tale*, 116–22; Deloney, T., *The Garland of Good Will*, 171; Radcliffe, R., *De patientia Griselidis*, 173; Phillip, J., *Patient Grissell*, 173–8; Pope, W., *Select Novels*, 196; Chettle, H., Haughton, W., and Dekker, T., *Patient Grissell*, 207–11; 216; *Patient Grissel* (a puppet-play), 244; Ogle, G., *Gualtherus and Griselda*, 307; Sotheby, Miss, *Patient Griselda*, 308; Hunt, Leigh, 350; Rossetti, G., 363; Arnold, Sir E., *Griselda*, 468–70; [Anstruther, Sir R. A.], 468; Braddon, M. E., *Griselda*, 470–4